# Concerning Consequences

# Concerning Consequences

STUDIES IN ART, DESTRUCTION, AND TRAUMA

Kristine Stiles

The University of Chicago Press *Chicago and London*

KRISTINE STILES is the France Family Professor of Art, Art History, and Visual Studies at Duke University.

The University of Chicago Press, Chicago 60637
The University of Chicago Press, Ltd., London

Printed in the United States of America

24 23 22 21 20 19 18 17 16 15    1 2 3 4 5

ISBN-13: 978-0-226-77451-0 (cloth)
ISBN-13: 978-0-226-77453-4 (paper)
ISBN-13: 978-0-226-30440-3 (e-book)

DOI: 10.7208/chicago/9780226304403.001.0001

Library of Congress Cataloguing-in-Publication Data
Stiles, Kristine, author.
Concerning consequences : studies in art, destruction, and trauma / Kristine Stiles.
pages cm
Includes bibliographical references and index.
ISBN 978-0-226-77451-0 (cloth : alkaline paper) — ISBN 978-0-226-77453-4 (paperback : alkaline paper) — ISBN 978-0-226-30440-3 (e-book) 1. Art, Modern—20th century. 2. Psychic trauma in art. 3. Violence in art. I. Title.
N6490.S767 2016
709.04′075—dc23
2015025618

⊗ This paper meets the requirements of ANSI/NISO Z39.48–1992 (Permanence of Paper).

In conversation with Susan Swenson, Kim Jones explained that the drawing on the cover of this book depicts directional forces in "an X-man, dot-man war game." The rectangles represent tanks and fortresses, and the lines are for tank movement, combat, and containment: "They're symbols. They're erased to show movement. I'll draw a tank, or I'll draw an X, and erase it, then re-draw it in a different position. . . . But when they're killed they're erased and that leaves a ghost image. So the erasing is a very important element of the war drawings. . . . The important thing is that it's always changing" (Susan Swenson, "Conversation with Kim Jones: April 25, 2005. New York City," in *Kim Jones: War Paint* [Brooklyn, NY: Pierogi, 2005], 4). Two years earlier, Jones described his "war drawings" as images of "a war that never ends" in *Teaching a Dead Hand to Draw: A Studio Visit with Kim Jones*, a fifteen-minute video codirected by David Schmidlapp and Steve Staso (2003).

FOR KITTY (1921–2001)

# Contents

# Acknowledgments

*Concerning Consequences* is dedicated to the memory of my mother, Katherine Haller Rogers Dolan, known as Kitty. She understood better than anyone the double meaning of the phrase "concerning consequences," with its attention to the inevitability of cause and effect, and the challenges of taking responsibility for one's actions. My guide and source of courage, Kitty taught her five children to work and play hard, and to endure. At her own risk, she rescued me in my late teens from a disastrous future, ensuring that I got a university education. Kitty thrived under the big sky of the American Southwest, where four of us five were born. True to the vistas of the high plateau, she insisted that her children "think big!" I have tried to honor her directives, and I hope that this book contains some of her vigor, for better or worse. Ours is a close family, although we all live at a distance from each other. I cannot imagine a world without my sisters and brothers and their families, from youngest to oldest: Victoria Dolan Tierney, Stephen Rogers Dolan, Constance Sue Dolan Lyons, and Paul Gregory Dolan Jr. My step-grandmother Marion Lane Rogers Sr. (ninety-six years old at the time of this writing) and my aunt Marion Lane Rogers Jr. have both been sources of wisdom, inspiration, moderation, and great joy all of my life. My father, Paul Gregory Dolan Sr., gave me the bedrock experiences necessary to fathom the subjects of this book.

This book is immensely enriched by daily conversations with my close friend, the art historian Kathy O'Dell, who since graduate school has read and commented on nearly all of my work. My scholarship would not be what it is without the companionship of and dialogues with my colleagues and friends at Duke University: Julie Tetel Andresen, Bruce Lawrence, miriam cooke, Claudia Koonz, Rick Powell, C. T. Woods-Powell, Neil McWilliams, and Olga Grlic. I also want to acknowledge Graham Auman, Eugenie Candau, Bruce Conner, Susan Roth, Ronald M. Batson, Mark D. Hasencamp, Lynn Hershman Leeson, Jean-Jacques Lebel, Carolee Schneemann, Joan Rothfuss, Edward A. Shanken, Peter d'Agostino, Sherman Fleming, Dan and Lia Perjovschi, and Paul Schimmel. Finally, Pushkin, Pasha, Bo, Eryk, and Faynce, each in their own way over the years, have sustained me with unconditional love; and Eryk and Faynce have taught me the meaning of boundaries.

Many of my former students, some now professors of art history themselves, and many of my current ones have worked on various iterations of this book over many years. I thank them all for their dedication, abiding friendship, thoughtful intelligence, and laughter: Kathryn Andrews, Liberty Berkey, Jay Bloom, Kaira Cabañas, Jay Curley, Katherine de Vos Devine, Laurel Fredrickson, Valerie Hillings, Susan Jarosi, Rebecca Katz, Jane McFadden, Tamara Mann, Lauren Reuter, Adam Starr, Amy Vickers, and Gabrielle Weiss. Nicole Hess Kempton, Mitali Routh, and Jasmina Tumbas contributed to more aspects of this book than I even want to remember. I am especially indebted to Erin Hanas, who saved me from my dyslexic, impatient self with her calm, thoughtful professionalism and wicked sense of humor, all of which helped to bring this book to press.

How does one thank the indomitable Susan Bielstein, executive editor at the University of Chicago Press? Susan has always believed in my work, and must take full responsibility for these essays finding their way out of exhibition catalogues and obscure journals. Anthony Burton and James Whitman Toftness attended to all my questions and helped to prepare the manuscript for publication. I particularly want to acknowledge Renaldo Migaldi for his virtuoso precision, expertise, and care in editing this book, and for heavy lifting of many dangling modifiers. I would also like to thank June Sawyers for an ideal index.

Research for this book dates to 1978 and includes fellowships from the University of California, Berkeley; the American Association of University Women; and Duke University's Arts and Sciences Research Council, Women's Studies, Center for International Studies, and Center for Soviet and East European Studies. The US Department of Education, through its Global Course Development Program, awarded me a grant in 1994 for developing the first course on the subject of documentary photography of the nuclear age, and for the exhibition *James Lerager: Tales from the Nuclear Age*, which I curated at the former City Gallery (now CAM) in Raleigh, North Carolina. A National Endowment for the Humanities Fellowship (2000) and a John Simon Guggenheim Foundation Fellowship (2001) also supported my work and teaching on documentary photography of the nuclear age. I received the United States Information Agency Grant for "American Studies and the Romanian Transition to Democracy" in 1994 for research in Romania and in art and trauma. KulturKontact Austria, in Vienna, and the Soros Foundation, in Bucharest, also supported research in Romania and contributed to the seminar I have taught at Duke University since 1995, Trauma in Art, Literature, and Film. Duke University's Provost's Common Fund made possible the exhibition I curated at the Nasher Museum of Art at Duke, *States of Mind: Dan & Lia Perjovschi* (2007). An invitation from Robert Sikorski, coordinator of international programming at Duke University, to curate the exhibition *Jean Toche: Impressions from the Rogue Bush Imperial Presidency* (2009) at Duke's John Hope Franklin Center for Interdisciplinary Studies was made possible by that center, and the catalog was funded by Duke University's Center for International Studies. The immense generosity of the Robert Rauschenberg Foundation in New York supported my exhibition *Rauschenberg: Connecting and Collecting* (2014) and its online catalog, which can be accessed at http://shuffle.rauschenbergfoundation.org/exhibitions/nasher/.

# Introduction

"If sacrifice is necessary, it must be accompanied by the appropriate ceremonies, [as] an unceremonious sacrifice is a crime against the natural world,"[1] With this comment, the Chinese artist Ai Weiwei closed his reflections on the torture of the Moon Bear, the Asian black bear with a white crescent on its chest that is strikingly similar to some genera of prehistoric bears. After the animal is captured, and before it is confined to a "crush cage" too small for it to stand up or turn around in, tubes are inserted painfully into its gall bladder to extract bile, a valuable commodity in traditional Chinese medicine. The Moon Bear is often caged from ten to twelve years; its muscles atrophy, and even if it is rescued, Ai explains, it remains "wrecked in spirit" and displays "characteristics common to manic depressives," or psychological trauma.[2] In protest, the artist declares: "The world belongs to animals . . . willing to live with us," but only in "trust. . . . When trust disintegrates, the world will crumble, and nothing can thrive."[3] Ai continues with a reference to social responsibility: "Any animal that considers itself of a higher order," as humans presumably do, "should, by duty, protect weaker animals." The result of failing this trust is "terror," "cruelty," and a "helpless world."[4]

The human animal can also become "wrecked in spirit," a common condition of post-traumatic stress disorder (PTSD), the etiology of which the American Psychiatric Association identified in 1980.[5] PTSD may include many, and sometimes all, of the following alterations in somatic and psychological functioning: impaired affect and difficulty interpreting, expressing, or acknowledging internal emotional states; intrusive thoughts, flashbacks, and nightmares; numbing and dissociation; and the psychic intrusion of the death imprint. The more specific term, "complex post-traumatic stress disorder" (C-PTSD), has been used to describe prolonged exposure to physical, psychological, and/or sexual abuse; captivity and the inability to flee a situation; being forced to succumb to the restraint and abuse of a perpetrator; the continuous impact of racism, homophobia, and other disruptions of identity; extended exposure to war, dictatorial regimes, cults, and terrorism; and the impact of natural disasters.[6]

Extreme, prolonged circumstances in which one is forced to lose complete control may lead to the loss of a sense of a unified self, a condition often diagnosed as dissociative identity disorder (DID), previously known as multiple personality disorder (MPD). Symptoms include involuntary disconnection from reality, compartmentalization, and splitting of identity, a process that entails walling off of memories, thoughts, and actions, which may lead to the development of two or more alternate personalities. In addition, studies have shown that the DNA of children exposed to extraordinary and protracted psychological, physical, and/or sexual abuse shows "wear and tear normally associated with aging."[7] Neuroscience confirms the biological basis of trauma, and the fact that pain can "force an indelible impression on the brain . . . be it mammalian, reptile, or even invertebrate," affecting the hippocampal formation which is critical to declarative memory.[8] Despite scientific evidence and growing public awareness of the impact of trauma on humans and animals, an urgent need continues worldwide for much deeper understanding of the complexities of trauma and its dire consequences.

Since the mid-1980s, when trauma studies began to emerge, humanists have located the concept of trauma as a category of knowledge in modernist psychoanalytic and psychiatric discourses,[9] genealogies,[10] the Holocaust,[11] war, genocide, the nuclear age, terrorism,[12] sexual violence and cults,[13] race, sex, and gender discrimination,[14] animals,[15] environmental disaster,[16] colonialism, migration, and diaspora.[17] Michel Foucault's groundbreaking *Madness and Civilization: A History of Insanity in the Age of Reason* (1961) is considered foundational to critical theories of trauma, for its scrutiny of madness in formations of history and memory. Beyond examining the epistemological adjudication of reason and madness in the institutions of the Western Enlightenment, Foucault did not discuss trauma directly. Nevertheless, at the end of *Madness and Civilization*, he summoned Goya's *Disparates* (ca. 1815–23) to describe the "man cast into darkness."[18] Such psychic despair leaves one numb, with the sense of being dead while still living: experience akin to what Foucault described as "screams from black holes."[19] Foucault's description anticipated by nearly twenty years the dissociated sense of inner nothingness that would be diagnosed as a primary condition of PTSD.[20] From the perspective of critical theory grounded in Foucault's work, it is reasonable to frame the emergence of trauma studies within psychoanalysis and corresponding modernist fields, especially considering that the French psychoanalyst Pierre Janet identified and named "dissociation" in 1889 as a foundational condition of trauma.[21]

Modernist histories, theories, and practices, however, are inadequate to account for trauma in the visual arts, where its representation could be said to have appeared for millennia, albeit under changing terminologies. To depart from modernism as the originating locus of the concept of trauma, this introduction turns to the Upper Paleolithic paintings in what is known as the *Shaft of the Dead Man*, a shaft located in the extensive underground cave at Lascaux in southwestern France. Parietal images with similar stylistic imagery were executed throughout the region's caves for a period of some twenty-four thou-

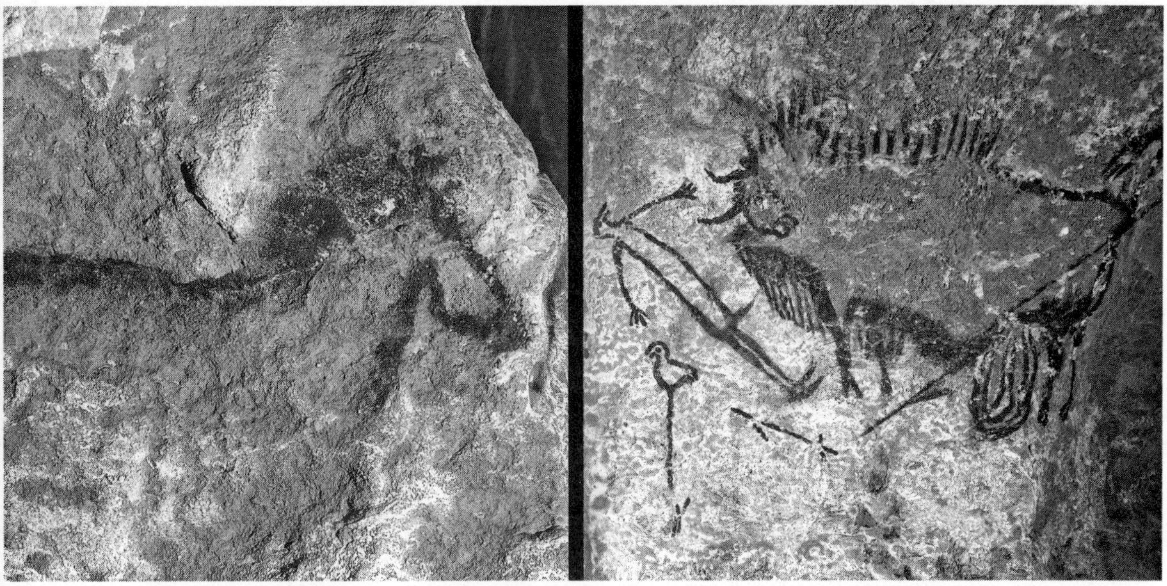

FIGURE 1. *Scene of the Dead Man* in the "Shaft of the Dead Man," ca. 16,800 BCE, Lascaux caves near the village of Montignac in the Vezère Valley, Dordogne, France. Iron oxide and manganese, mixed with water and animal fat, and charcoal.

sand years, from approximately 34,000 to 10,000 BCE.[22] The images in the shaft at Lascaux carbon date to about 16,800 BCE, and belong to what is known as the "shaft scene" (figure 1). I approach the "shaft scene" with the view that it is the earliest known representation of trauma, and I focus on what I describe as "the Bison's gaze" to introduce the supposition that the Paleolithic artist or group of artists (hereafter described as artist[s]) who depicted its primary narrative image—a ferocious encounter between a man and a bison—crafted a unique, multifaceted pictorial schemata for the purpose of communicating the worldly affect of violence and its traumatic circumstance.[23] My aim is to situate the shaft scene's imagery as a cornerstone of visual representations of trauma that belong not to modernism but to deep time, and most likely with unknown antecedents tens of thousands of years earlier. I will further suggest that the shaft scene may be understood as a visual corollary to Ai's twenty-first-century discussion of the Moon Bear's trauma, and that the pictorial and imaginal metaphors in the shaft scene bespeak the conscious effort of the Lascaux artist(s) to respond to the trust placed in them to reveal and transmit the exigencies of their time.

I am fully aware of the numerous obstacles to proposing a prehistoric lineage for images of trauma, risks that the anthropologist Margaret W. Conkey has systematically enumerated. Her warnings include that attempting to read images without words, from the standpoint of photographs and drawings rather than from direct access to the works themselves, may be suspect;[24] that the interpretive field within which such paintings have been approached "is as tectonic, varied, and even as ironic as can be imagined";[25] and that while it is "likely" that such images "have something to do with symbolic and spiritual worlds," these worlds "lie outside the scope of what are considered plausible inferences in an archaeological time period for which even ethnographic analogies or the direct historical method are weak or lacking."[26] Whether or not these ancient paintings can be examined as historical evidence remains in question, according to Harvard anthropologist Ofer Bar-Yosef, who observes that such theories remain "suppositions."[27]

Despite these steep obstacles, Bar-Yosef also notes, "there is no way to satisfy the entire community of investigators because interpretations of the same evidence vary."[28] In a related comment, Conkey avows, "If there ever were a corpus of imagery that *should* be taken as historical evidence, it is . . . the thousands of images made in caves and rock shelters over at least a thousand generations [my emphasis]."[29] Taking Conkey's and Bar-Yosef's admonitions under advisement, I proceed with their cautionary encouragements. For, as Jean-Luc Nancy writes, it remains incumbent to make an effort to understand "the creation of the world and curiosity, [as] however far humanity is from being the end of nature or nature the end of humanity . . . the end is always being-in-the-world and the being-world of all being."[30] This book is a record of being-in-the-world for other beings.

## THE BISON'S GAZE

The *Shaft of the Dead Man* is located in a fissure of the Lascaux cave with a drop of six meters (nearly twenty feet) into a pitch-black space where carbon dioxide can reach high levels of toxicity. The artist(s) executed the scene on the wall that faces the descent into the shaft's small space, which was accessible to only a few who would have shimmied by rope into the darkness, illuminating their way with small lamps flaming with deer fat ignited by juniper wicks. An elegant, highly polished, rose-colored sandstone lamp with two enigmatic signs incised on the upper face of its handle was found on the floor of the shaft among other lamps and cultural artifacts, offering evidence of how the artists lit their way.[31] On one wall of the looming rock face, the artist(s) depicted a brutal scene of mortal combat with no equal in Paleolithic art, in which less than 10 percent of animals depicted "appear to have been wounded or killed."[32] If the shaft scene eventually proves not to have been the first visual discourse on trauma, then it will certainly remain one of the most sophisticated compositional depictions on trauma in the history of art.

The shaft scene is constituted in two parts: a narrative scene on one wall and a solitary horse on a facing wall. Although the narrative scene has been widely interpreted, the single horse is uniformly disregarded in efforts to decipher the entire conceptual scheme of the ensemble of paintings in the shaft. The primary narrative, to which most attention has been focused, includes a bison with lashing tail, flying mane, gleaming humanlike eyes, and exposed entrails hanging in loops from its belly. The woolly beast's head faces an ithyphallic man who is either in the midst of falling backward or already lying on the ground, but the bison's gaze is directed toward the viewer and at its own entrails, which are disemboweled by the javelin that pierces its body. The position of the figure on the ground is ambiguous, suggesting that the bison may have killed the man; but there is no evidence of goring, unless it is his penile erection, which may also be a consequence of death.

A staff with a bird's head standing upright in the ground near the man's body has prompted scholars to consider the figure a shaman disguised as a "bird-man."[33] A lance-throwing tool with a hook at its end that enables a hunter to propel a spear more effectively lies near the feet of the prone figure. This innovation in Upper Paleolithic weaponry has led some scholars to identify the man as the "spear thrower." What has been overlooked in discussions of this scene is the fact that the spear thrower itself lies nowhere near the site from which the spear apparently was hurled—namely, from behind the bison, as its point of entry and exit attest. Positioning the spear in the animal's body in this way and turning the bison's head toward its hindquarters, the Lascaux artist(s) seem to have sought a visual means to recognize the existence of viewers outside the immediate frame of representation, be they a hunter, who continues to be incriminated by the bison's gaze over millennia, or other witnesses called to attest to these events.

On an opposite wall of the shaft is the lone horse. This equine is a crucial figure in my interpretation of the shaft scene, for how it provides access to the broader social message regarding trauma that I think the Lascaux artist(s) aimed to convey. Though it is an animal of flight, the legs of the horse are not depicted, as are the full bodies of many of the other similar standing, grazing, and galloping horses in the main hall of the Lascaux cave. Rather, by attending only to the horse's upper torso—its head, neck, shoulder, withers, loin, croup, and haunch—the shaft scene artist(s) sharply focused on its attention to the scene, demonstrated by its pricked ears, poll held high, and keen, raised, and tense expressive posture. All of these physiological elements emphasize the equine's acute senses of sight, hearing, and smell, which for millennia have made horses sentinels, entrusted to watch over herds and nearby animals and to warn of impending danger.

By placing the horse at a safe distance from the main scene, and by separating it from the herd—an act that inculcates a state of alarm in an isolated horse—the artist(s) may have introduced it as a visual device to also alert viewers to a threat in the environment that its vigilance would register long before humans could perceive it. Such compositional devices suggest that the artist(s) meant to convey something of the dependence of Paleolithic society on the physiological aptitude and mental attitude of the horse as a guardian against imminent peril. In this context, it is significant that the bestiary in Lascaux is principally of herds of horses, whereas, here in the shaft, the introduction of the hypervigilant lone horse reinforces the distress implied by the traumatic content that is registered in the shaft's main scene and beyond.

Finally, a rhinoceros stands to the left of the prone man, with its back turned to the drama. I do not consider the rhinoceros in the following discussion of the shaft scene narrative, because radiocarbon dating confirms that it was painted at a much later date.[34] Furthermore, as Norbert Aujoulat, head of the Department of Parietal Art in France for thirty years, points out, the main scene, including the observing horse, was painted in one graphic style while the rhinoceros was painted in an entirely different style, leading "very early on" to it being "interpreted as an unrelated element" in the scene. A series of pigment analyses confirmed Aujoulat's argument, and revealed "appreciable differences of composition and texture [and] the colouring agent" for the rhinoceros.[35] Six pairs of black dots in three vertically paired regular intervals appear just under the rhino's tail and extend in a line beyond it. The symbolic purpose of such dots is yet to be deciphered, but according to André Leroi-Gourhan, they appear to "mark the beginning and end of [a] whole decoration or of different parts of it."[36] If Leroi-Gourhan is correct, then the presence of the black dots might serve to confirm for viewers encountering the painting at a later period that the rhinoceros was added after the completion of the primary narrative scene. For these reasons I turn my back to the rhinoceros, which turns its back to the scene, in order to discuss the remarkable narrative event more carefully.

"Despite the numerous possibilities offered by the vast wall surfaces," Aujoula astutely observes, "only a very localized fraction of the space [of the shaft] was exploited."[37] Unlike the majority of images in the cave, where continuous friezes of animals appear, the shaft scene has a narrative that the artist(s) self-consciously contained in order to maximize its explicit message of a traumatic human/animal encounter. The point is that the artist(s) invented new compositional devices to communicate the social and ethical affect of this savage event, and organized their composition to both acknowledge the presence of viewers and converse visually with them. The goal of this protracted visual program was carefully realized in what might be identified as four innovative stylistic techniques: (1) the bison's gaze as a sign of the animal's recognition of its own wounded hindquarter, spilling entrails, and imminent death; (2) the bison's all-too-human gaze at a viewer standing in the space of the shaft; (3) the bison's gaze at the horse as a witness, another animal that is able to attest to the lethal events while standing at a distance across the narrow shaft; and, most astonishing, (4) the bison's gaze at something or someone outside of the frame of representation, even perhaps outside the shaft and the cave as a whole. Of greatest import, the bison's gaze serves as a narrative device calling into question as much of what is marked as of what is unmarked in its spatial field: the mores of Paleolithic viewers.

Let us review. First, the component parts of the shaft scene include a narrative visualization of suffering, dismemberment, and certain death, as well as a prone ithyphallic man, possibly dead or in a trancelike dissociated state. Second, let me emphasize that in addition to being the first known work of art to visualize trauma directly, the shaft scene may also be the first known composition to tell a story in the round. Therefore, because the narrative content and storyline depend not only upon the central scene but also on the horse as witness at a distance, the work might be considered a panorama. Third, the visual story unfolds in triplicates, including three distinct characters (man, bison, and horse), three symbolic objects (bird-headed staff, spear-throwing tool, and lance), and three positions for spectators (viewers in the space of the shaft; implied hunter[s] outside the scene but in the shaft space; and hunter[s]/viewers beyond the walls of the shaft).

All of these viewing positions convert seeing into the act of witnessing the social and cultural impact of trauma in the human-animal-technological world in which a spear-throwing tool has amplified the lethal impact of the lance. The shaft scene narrative presents a complicated, nuanced composition of traumatic witnessing and testifying, conveyed through sophisticated composition, conceptual complexity, and composite narrative—all formal innovations that expand its descriptive features into scenes within scenes: (1) the bison witnesses an attacker and the horse; (2) the horse witnesses both the prone man and the disemboweled bison from beyond the frame of the primary scene but within the pictorial context of the shaft enclosure, and also sees and/or senses the danger of hunter(s)/viewer(s) outside the visual evidence of the shaft scene; (3) a viewer within the shaft witnesses the primary scene and the horse that watches; and (4) someone unseen—hunter(s)/viewer(s)—witnesses being witnessed by the bison and the horse.

Finally, an even more distant scene that simultaneously comprises memory and continuous enactment is implied. For the bison's imperturbable stare over eighteen thousand millennia suggests a refined self-consciousness on the part of the artist(s), who sought to convey the psychological effect of the animal's appeal to viewers not only to witness and remember, but also to testify in the present and in the future to the tragic and traumatic content of the event. This appeal extends the interior space into the exterior world, carrying the encrypted content forward in time. It must be said, too, that as an index of Paleolithic cultural respect for and dependence upon both bovine and equine warnings of physical and psychical emergency, the presence of the bison and the horse anticipate the historical role these two animals have played as both metaphors for and metonymies of the gods in world myth and religion.[38] The bison's gaze is a reminder of atrocity, as much as the horse's alert attention confirms the will and instinct to preserve life. The artist(s) of the shaft scene acknowledge the rage and the stoic suffering of the bison, and certify the deadly power of technology (the lance and spear-throwing tool). They also honor the wisdom, vigilance, and passivity of the horse, presenting it as the embodiment of moral conscience deployed to awaken the viewer-as-witness to the unfolding devastation.

My reading of the shaft scene contributes to wide-ranging scholarly debates about and interpretations of the *Shaft of the Dead Man*, which include the contention that it resembles celestial temporal constellations;[39] that it is connected to hunting magic and perhaps is the reenactment of a hunting accident;[40] that it pictures a shaman in a trance induced by the high levels of carbon dioxide in the cave, especially in the shaft; that it expresses neurological visual phenomena and mental imagery related to dreams, altered states of consciousness, and hallucinations;[41] and that the shaft is a sacred place with occult power at "the heart of the sanctuary" (a name sometimes given to Lascaux as a whole).[42] This last allusion to a spiritual place in the bowels of the cave refers as much to the confines of the shaft as a sacred place as it does to the fact that the composite human-animal bird figure may be what archaeologists have identified as a type of sorcerer figure found in other Paleolithic parietal art from remote areas in the region.[43] The archaeologist and historian Nancy K. Sandars also considers the shaft scene to depict possibly a "natural or supernatural crisis [that] may have driven the artist . . . to make up a scene," and she argues that the inaccessibility of the shaft "adds much to the . . . atmosphere of something secret and deeply significant."[44]

For his part, upon first viewing the paintings in the upper hall at Lascaux, Georges Bataille suggested that they provide evidence of the "extreme self-effacement of man before the animal—and of man just turning into a human."[45] In this comment, Bataille seems only to denote the animal world depicted throughout Lascaux, but not the content of the shaft scene, dominated as it is by the altercation between man and beast in which the human is anything but self-effacing. In a later text, he suggests that the shaft scene could be interpreted as "the alteration of taboo and transgression [and] the religious aura that surrounded the animals as they were done to death."[46] In this scenario, either a predator human has disemboweled an animal, inflicting certain death, or a shaman is dissembling as an animal (bird).

While Bataille did not mention trauma as the result of the breach of taboo and transgression, he did identify "man [as] the being who has lost, and even rejected, that which he obscurely is, a vague intimacy."[47] Bataille also held that paintings like the shaft scene were evidence that the Lascaux artist(s) understood human separation from animality and sought "a reunion with nature through the operation of sacrifice in the realm of the sacred."[48] For Bataille, this reality proved that "to subordinate is not only to alter the subordinated element *but to be altered oneself* [my emphasis]."[49] According to Angus McDonald, in searching for redemption Bataille read intimacy with nature through what he called the "birth of art." Art constituted "an excess not a utilitarian activity," and was a vehicle for "a celebration of the ability to represent the animal life surrounding the painter with an intimacy thought irrecoverable," but was also a loss that could be retrieved through an understanding of "the essential ideas of taboo, transgression, law, the sacred and evil."[50]

When Bataille surmised that the shaft scene represented human "separation from animality," he could not have known that the image belonged to the epochs-long parting of humans and animals, which later archaeological evidence and scholarship has proved. Neither could he have known that the Lascaux artist(s) depended upon a much older tradition, identifiable in the paintings discovered in 1994 at Chauvet-Pont-d'Arc in the Dordogne region of France. The Chauvet paintings have been repeatedly radiocarbon dated from between 32,410 to 30,340 BCE, and are currently among the oldest known Paleolithic paintings in the region, if not the world.[51] Two Chauvet paintings are pertinent to and perhaps antecedents for the Lascaux shaft scene: a composite human-animal figure, the *Venus and the Sorcerer*, which appears on an outcropping of stone hanging one meter above the floor in the Salle du Fond, or End Chamber, the deepest alcove of the Chauvet cave; and the representation of a solitary horse in a recessed niche also in the Salle du Fond. Carbon dating suggests that the different parts of the hybrid *Venus and the Sorcerer* were painted within an interval of more than one thousand years. The pubic triangle and vulva were incised first in the stone, followed by the painting of a horned bison (*The Sorcerer*) with a penetrating gaze that is integrated into the composition, its legs doubling as the legs of the Venus and its body pressed against her with its head curled onto her belly. The upper part of the belly of the Venus is integrated into the belly and shoulders of a lion with a formidable head. Finally, a magnificently painted horse, auguring the lone horse of the shaft scene, is painted in a separate niche in the rock of the Salle du Fond.[52] Worth remarking upon is the fact that the artist(s) of both Chauvet and Lascaux reserved an inner chamber for a unique narrative representation and a sole horse.

In pointing to this similarity, let me emphasize that while the iconography and narrative skills displayed by the Lascaux artist(s) may belong to aesthetic canons in operation at least fifteen thousand years earlier, their skill in visual narration is much advanced from that of the Chauvet painters. The composite figure of *Venus and the Sorcerer* has nothing to do with the traumatic realism of the Lascaux scene; and there seems to be little narrative link, as there is in Lascaux, between the beautiful horse in Chauvet and the semiotic fusion of woman, bison, and lion, even though its proximity is significant. In Lascaux this juxtaposition contributes to a distinct narrative in the round that offers a story freighted with penetrating psychological and social commentary. Such works prove that the skills displayed by the Lascaux artist(s) belong to aesthetic canons at least twenty-four thousand years older, themselves indebted to millennia of artistic invention and mastery of both representation and narrative. These representational traditions include the accurate artistic observation, nuanced rendering, use of diverse materials, technical application, realism, plot complexity, and exquisite insight into human and animal emotion, all of which the Lascaux shaft scene exhibits.

More specific to the context of trauma is the Lascaux artists' commentary on the human capacity to inflict pain, suffering, and death, and the animal's concomitant agency to react with emotion and its own deadly force. Could the shaft scene be an ancient form of social engineering by artist(s) entrusted to appeal to the moral conscience of Upper Paleolithic viewers by representing the consequences of brute force, augmented by technological means? As Maurice Blanchot would put it, remarking on Bataille's observations, the Lascaux painters "make us enter into an intimate space of knowledge."[53] There, in subordinating another, as Bataille perceptively insisted, one is "*altered oneself*." However imprecise our understanding of the conditions of Paleolithic knowledge and mores may be, the deeper significance of what these artists conveyed about the human-animal nexus remains insistent. The Lascaux artists initiated viewers into the surfeit of violence of their period in terms of the interrelation between humans and their technologies and animals and their emotions, and they provided visual access to the volatile conditions that the historic record supports.

The shaft scene was painted during great cultural and environmental change. *Homo sapiens* began to emerge as the dominant species in the midst of the demise of *Homo neanderthalensis*, who mysteriously disappeared around 10,000 BCE. Increasingly, archaeologists are dating the painted caves of southwestern France and northeastern Spain to thousands of years earlier, and hypothesizing that Neanderthals were the artists who may have painted them.[54] This is also the period of the recession of the Ice Age and of the global warming that permitted northern migration. A veritable population explosion took place within villages, which grew from as few as four hundred to as many as a thousand inhabitants.[55] This period of rapidly changing climate also witnessed increased hunting in which more effective weapons accompanied the extinction of some fifty species of large animals. It may be that the shaft scene provides insight into a momentous period when the disappearance of large game had already begun to be perceived in a manner akin to what Ai Weiwei labeled "a crime against the natural world"—a traumatic act worthy of representation and recognition.

This altered environmental and cultural crisis requires a brief detour into what Michael Winkelman calls "the shamanic paradigm in cave art" in his study *Shamanism: A Biopsychosocial Paradigm of Consciousness and Healing* (2010). Drawing on numerous fields including neuroscience, evolutionary psychology, art, archaeology, and anthropology, Winkelman discusses the origins of modern human cognition as demonstrated in art, and as it relates to shamanistic practices. He argues that the shaman's "healing rituals played an essential role in the defense of the psychic integrity of the community," which was accomplished by various "ecstatic state[s]," such as "trance," "the language of the animals," "inhabiting animal spirits," and "acts central to shamanistic practice" of shamans who were healing those believed to have "lost their souls."[56] Winkelman continues:

> Selection for the role of the shaman was often derived from a prolonged period of illness or insanity that was caused by the spirits who chose the individual for the shamanic role. The worsening of the individual's circumstances often then led to experiences interpreted as death, . . . [during which] the spirits healed the initiates by giving new rules of life that made the person a "wounded healer."[57]

The experience of a psychic death and quest for spiritual power was a solitary vigil, Winkelman adds, involving the appearance of "savage beasts that attacked and killed the initiate, but then reassembled the person with new capacities and powers, a death-and-rebirth experience that empowered the shaman."[58]

Winkelman and, increasingly, other scholars link this shamanic activity to the "new mentality" evinced in cave art, namely the mental capacity "to produce . . . the dramatic evolution of material culture" which took place sixty to thirty thousand years before the present.[59] Such social advances included "cognitive fluidity for integrating technical intelligence and social intelligence in the production of artifacts that were *designed to send social messages* regarding status group affiliation, and relationships through personal decoration and adornment [my emphasis]."[60] While some scholars attribute the capacity for symbolic processes to the impact of language on consciousness, Winkelman observes that "art involved an imagetic, presentational, analogical modality that necessarily predated spoken language," and that, as a result, "language, spoken or otherwise, cannot explain the evolution of artistic representations."[61]

For Winkelman, the emergence of art and religion began around 100,000 BCE and reflects meta-representation that is dependent upon imagery and mimesis.[62] He also notes that the combination of animal and human figures resulted from a growing ability "to integrate the social intelligence and natural history intelligence with personal and social identity," and that it produced "cross-modular integrations" related to various types of cognitive abilities, from religious, animistic, and anthropomorphic thought to "the interpretation of self, others . . . found in totemism."[63] Such integrative cognition led to the capacity for symbolic representation and collective expression and "shared group consciousness and culture."[64] The shaman served to expand animal ritual conduct, or "isopraxis," wherein "animals automatically imitate each other's behavior as a means of identifying other members of one's own species."[65] Such mimetic behavior enabled shamans to provide psychologically and socially adaptive advantages that were necessary to the development of more complex human systems, and which may have led to "the extensive focus on the animal 'other,'" producing an emotionally charged identification that resulted from the act of killing and of witnessing pain and death.[66]

Certainly such a view is in keeping with interpretations of the man in the shaft scene as a shaman/birdman in a trance with his bird staff nearby. It would also support the interpretation of the death of the ithyphallic man, as the act of killing and the fear of death led to compensatory strategies which included ritual dancing and singing, trance, and artistic representation.[67] Trance actions also mimicked the adaptive animal behavior of "freezing" that is typical of mammals and primates when faced with predators. Through these adaptations the limbic system developed, controlling emotional and behavior functions and long-term memory, among other things. Most importantly, Winkelman adds, "Hunting must be seen as a central feature enhancing consciousness and awareness of death, as hunting produced death in animals and exposed the hunter to risk of the same," and rituals prepared hunters for such "life-threatening activities."[68]

This chain of developments over millennia can be said to have culminated in the shaft scene and other yet unknown works which offer legible access to Upper Paleolithic artists' visualizations of a traumatic episteme that served the purpose of "healing and enhanced survival" for a "hominid population in which the capacity for ritual enhancement of well-being was a common feature of humanity."[69] The "psychodramatic struggles" that produced the "wounded healer" seem also to be at work in the shaft scene's unprecedented formal innovation.[70]

Armed with the visual episteme of the Paleolithic artist(s), we may now return to Ai Weiwei, with whom this meditation began. Ai writes:

> If we say that artists must interpret their existence, and interpret their physical and spiritual state, this interpretation would unavoidably touch upon the era in which they exist, and upon the political and ideological state of that era and, naturally, the artist's worldview. This worldview is presented through artistic languages and ambiguity, and just like all the other things that we call "facts," it has clear-cut characteristics and is immiscible. Even so, art's transparency is then possibly "multiple" or "indistinct." Here, ambiguity and suggestion create a substantial spiritual orientation, like an outstretched hand pointing to an indecipherable and unexplainable space, a forward direction where nothing and everything, can happen.[71]

Similarly, the painter(s) of the shaft scene could be said to have appealed with an outstretched hand (in the form of the bison's gaze and the attuned ears of the alert horse) to the political and ideological state of things in the era, and that this metaphorical hand, through the import of visual narrative, pointed forward over millennia to the present day wherein nothing and everything can happen, just as the immiscible flows into culture as the solubility of one liquid into another.

Faced with nothing and everything, Ai posed two questions: "Who can clearly explain that utter lack of substance that is left after a fixed gaze? Contrarily, who can clearly understand the profound deceit that remains after careless and inattentive eyes?"[72] In these questions he seems to ventriloquize the unspoken quest in the bison's steady gaze, which bespeaks a helpless world that advances the threat of those wrecked in spirit along with their multigenerational legacies. Ai's questions refer to sight not for its own sake, but as an instrument of action, and as a fundamental imperative to deploy the fixed gaze in careful, attentive, and thoughtful ways that are vital to the humanity of humanity. The utter lack of substance and the deceit he identifies are what enable the destruction, violence, and trauma visible in the betrayal of careless eyes.

As is well known, the gaze concerned Jacques Lacan. In 1964 he noted that "the eye is only the metaphor of . . . the pre-existence of a gaze" that ameliorates the eye's ability to see "only from one point," when the truth of sight is that one is "looked at from all sides."[73] The basis of this confusion between a focused and an all-encompassing gaze, Lacan explained, exposes "the split between the eye and the gaze . . . manifest at the level of the scopic field," which he believed was "no doubt to be found in a more primitive institution of form."[74] Lacan identified that primitive state as "a real *specific prematurity of birth* in man," an "organic insufficiency" in the split between one's *Innenwelt* (inner world) and the *Umwelt* (outer world), which "effects one's sense of reality [emphasis in original]."[75] In specifying what he meant by the prematurity of birth, Lacan explained that "primordial Discord" is found in humans, who as a species are "impaired by a kind of dehiscence of the organism in the womb," dehiscence being the wound of being born too soon and gestation that is incomplete.[76] Lacan felt that not only is maturation in the womb not long enough to form a fully developed human psyche, but also that a "primordial" prematurity itself exists in evolution in the transformation from animal to *Homo sapiens*.

Lacan's intuition is not far from recent anthropological research on the emergence of cognitive modernity (or behavioral modernity) in Paleolithic symbolic thought.[77] Could it be that the artist(s) who executed the bison's gaze already grasped, on both a cognitive and intuitive level, the implications of the split in the human *Innenwelt* and *Umwelt*, picturing it in a narrative painting with multiple viewing positions? What of their understanding of the intelligence of animals as visualized in the bison's gaze? Given the growing scholarship in ethology and animal studies on animal behavior and animals' remarkable capacity for understanding and empathy, the question is not frivolous.[78] The prescient responsiveness of the Paleolithic artist(s), so vivid in the shaft scene, would appear to posit an ethics of human/animal interaction along a continuum of life and death, which indicated mutual understanding exemplified in the representation of one in each other's terms: the reversal of human/animal identification, from the bird-staff-become-man to the bison's human look, and from the isolated *Innenwelt* of the bison (with a wrecked-in-spirit mortal gaze) to the *Umwelt* of the bird-man (with the public erection common to an animal).

I am contending that like an outstretched hand, this painting implores a substantial engagement from the witness, asking beholders to enunciate the traumatic implications of the scene, to arrive at a moral judgment about the past in relation to the present, and to address what Didier Fassin and Richard Rechtman call, in another context, "the moral responsibility of society in relation to the distress of the world."[79] The shaft scene affirms the self/other awareness of the Paleolithic artist(s), and the consciousness of the ceremonial role of art in expressing the concerning consequences of traumatic events some eighteen thousand years before Susan Sontag, in *Regarding the Pain of Others*, wrote:

> It seems a good in itself to acknowledge, to have enlarged, one's sense of how much suffering caused by human wickedness there is in the world we share with others. Someone who is perennially surprised that depravity exits, who continues to feel disillusioned (even incredulous) when confronted with evidence of what humans are capable of inflicting in the way of gruesome hands-on cruelties upon other humans, has not reached moral or psychological adult-

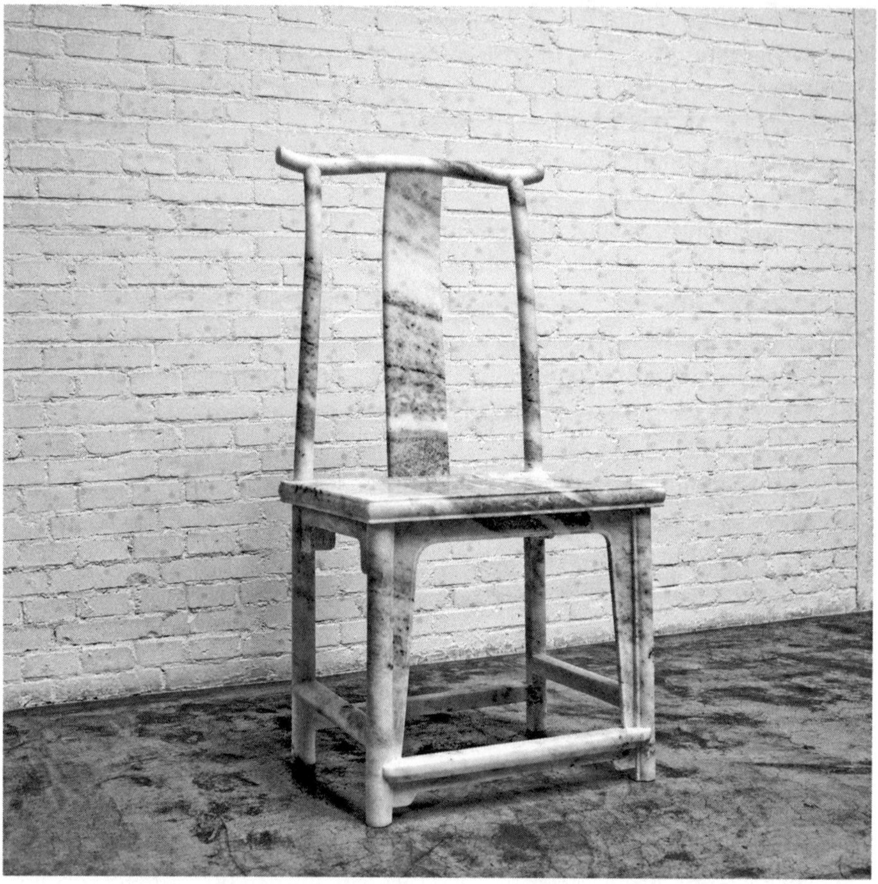

FIGURE 2. Ai Weiwei, *Marble Chair*, 2008. Marble, 120 × 56 × 46 cm. Photography by Ai Weiwei. Courtesy of the artist.

> hood. No one after a certain age has the right to this kind of innocence, of superficiality, to this degree of ignorance, or amnesia. . . . Let the atrocious images haunt us . . . The images say: This is what human beings are capable of doing . . . Don't forget.[80]

Ai Weiwei never forgot. Rather, he confirmed his preparedness in a blog on May 28, 2009. Pretending to caution himself, Ai advised: "Be careful! Are you ready?" Then, responding to his own warning, he answered:

> I'm ready. Or, rather, there's nothing to get ready for. One person. That is everything that I have, it is all that someone might possibly gain and everything that I can devote. I will not hesitate in the time of need, and I won't be vague.[81]

This striking declaration represents Ai's stance, a commanding affirmation that this "one person" will sacrifice himself for his principles with unambiguous clarity and decisiveness. Ai's *Marble Chair* (2008), in its solitary dignity, exemplifies his readiness, political resolve, and spiritual orientation (figure 2).[82]

*Marble Chair* is a metaphor of the artist-as-witness, whose life and art are evidence of his commitment to the social body, and who stands ready to fill the void left after the gaze departs and refusing to allow the careless eye its negative authority.

*Marble Chair* might also be understood to sit in for the unidentified Chinese man, standing in for the collective will, who stopped the column of fifty-nine tanks on June 5, 1989, during the protests in Beijing's Tiananmen Square. Unlike that man's spontaneous response to the threat of tanks, Ai's continued confrontations with the Chinese government represent a battle that honors the memory of his father, the renowned poet Ai Qing, denounced under Mao by an anti-rightist movement as an enemy by the state. Sent in 1958 with his wife and baby (Ai Weiwei having been born in 1957) first to a labor camp in Beidahuang, Heilongjiang, Ai Qing was then exiled to Shihezi, Xinjiang, where he was consigned to clean public toilets until Mao's death in 1976. Having lived through and witnessed his father's humiliation, Ai Weiwei never ceases to confront and resist the Chinese state. In his opposition, the artist joins the history of charismatic, traumatized leaders.[83]

Exposure to risk is the story of Ai's life, and the reason he can write: "In a great majority of circumstances, it was difficulty that helped me. I'm a despicable thing, because I have hope for people."[84] In the next breath, he states:

> I've never seen "the People." What is the People? The People is the sum total of many persons, and the summation of people is imperceptible and intangible. Mao said: 'Only the People have the power to create history.' One person is a person; a multitude of people is the People. One ambling person is a vagrant, a pariah; a throng of people cramming into train cars to go on holiday, tens of thousands of people flooding into the same location--this is the People. . . . Who helps the people-something that never existed—is a fool.[85]

As a vagrant pariah, Ai maintains hope, courage derived from what he associates with the act of discernment. Stating that while he did not receive a proper education, he became "like a traveler at dusk [trying to] discern which direction I was headed."[86] His optimism is also a form of poetry that reflects his ambition to become "that rare kind of negative example, [who] endow[s] my existence with a certain kind of necessity."[87] Such an individual provides the outstretched hand to the world.

## BIOGRAPHY AND TRAUMA STUDIES

"The problem with your scholarship is that it is not easy to find and not readily accessible," commented Ivana Bago, a Zagreb-based curator and doctoral student, whom I mentor in art history at Duke University. Pausing, she added, "No, the real problem is that you have been *held captive by artists* and your writing is hidden in artists' exhibition catalogs and monographs." With her usual precision and lightning-quick insight, Ivana introduced the dilemma of writing monographic essays about artists rather than, in her words, "writing something abstract that other scholars can pick up and make their own." Yet Marina Abramović dubbed me the "atom bomb"; Carolee Schneemann accused me of "pinning artists to the wall like butterflies"; and Joseph Kosuth described me as "a taxonomic terrorist." These are hardly descriptions of someone "held captive by artists." Still, Ivana is partially correct about the fate of these essays becoming invisible in the kinds of publications that a diminishing number of people read. Still, I remain unapologetic for being an artist-centered art historian. Artists' work, ideas, and biographies are the very material of art, and the ephemeral aspects of those lives and their production of objects intertwine with history, society, and culture. Probing the entanglements of biography yields insight into objects, texts, and/or actions and their functions as intermediaries between the individual and culture.

Jacques Derrida cogently argued for the necessity of biography shortly before his death, when he told an interviewer:

> I am among those few people who have constantly drawn attention to this: you must (and you must do it *well*) put philosophers' biographies back in the picture, and the commitments, particularly political commitments, that they sign in their own names, whether in relation to Heidegger or equally to Hegel, Freud, Nietzsche, Sartre, or Blanchot, and so on.[88]

Derrida's position stands in stark contrast to that of the art historian Rosalind Krauss, who opined in 2007 that the culprit responsible for the current resurrection of the biographical subject for contemporary scholarship "is the 'twisted dialectic' called trauma."[89]

> Trauma befalls a subject who was unfortunately absent—too distracted or decentered to defend him- or herself properly at the time of the attack. The life story of the traumatic subject is thus the account of a fundamental absence and lack of preparation. Because of this, trauma studies is addicted to biography, which is to say, to the reconstruction of decentering and the shattering that is its result.[90]

The contrast between these two points of view regarding the necessity or ruination of biography proves that recourse to biography remains contentious, even while being a critical portal through which comprehension of culture and history must pass.

Scholarship on trauma in art history developed in the 1990s, a somewhat tardy entrance to the field, due in no small measure to the methodological suppression and substitution of biography with a poststructuralist emphasis on the construction of gender, sexuality, identity, class, and other burgeoning social theories. These topics and their theoretical analysis have proved invaluable over the years, even if only slightly altering the angle of attention to the role of biography in an artist's life and production.[91] In some ways art history has moved back to biography for its access to the otherwise unknown "commitments," as Derrida remarked, and for insight into the unarticulated thoughts, passions, and behaviors of artists in all their irrational and simultaneously reasoned logic. Most of all, biography is essential when it comes to writing about trauma, especially in performance art where the artist's body/psyche is the material of the work of art.

Art historians began to resist biography in the 1980s, partly on the basis of such failures of psychobiography as Freud's analyses of Leonardo da Vinci and Michelangelo.[92] In a groundbreaking 1988 article on the state of psychoanalytic research in art history, art historian Jack Spector opened with an account of the methodological questions facing the discipline, and he cited Arthur Danto's insistence that art history must arrive at a "totally different structure." Danto's "The End of Art," written four years earlier, had been the lead essay in a volume edited by Berel Lang devoted to the "death of art." Addressing this article, Spector observed: "Danto . . . sees the replacement of artists by philosophers in his Hegelian version of the future."[93] Danto's prediction, like that of Hegel before him, has not come to pass. Quite on the contrary, with the arrival of the "pictorial turn," heralded in 1992 by W. J. T. Mitchell, artists are once again celebrated, but with greater recognition of their intellectual and philosophical contributions.[94]

Neglecting trauma as an appropriate field for art historical research, mainstream art history by and large also ignored the history of performance art well into the 1990s.[95] But trauma studies and performance art converged in the Italian sociologist Lea Vergine's 1974 publication *Il corpo come linguaggio (La "Body-art" e storie simili)*. While Vergine raised the question of trauma in the context of the development of body art, she proceeded to dismiss it in her conclusion as representing "dissociation, melancholy, delirium, depression, and [the representation of] persecution manias."[96] In 1987, Donald Kuspit applied his interest in British psychiatrist Donald W. Winnicott's theories of transference to Adrian Piper's work.[97] Kathy O'Dell wrote about masochism in 1988,[98] the same year in which I completed a monograph on destruction in the performances of Raphael Montañez Ortiz.[99] Leo Bersani's *Culture of Redemption* (1990) had an immediate impact in art history, and my essay "Shaved Heads and Marked Bodies: Representations from Cultures of Trauma" (1993) had been reprinted in French, German, and Romanian by 1995. Peggy Phelan's *Unmarked* (1993) and *Mourning Sex* (1997)[100] and Hal Foster's *The Return of the Real: The Avant-Garde at the End of the Century* (1996) received widespread attention in both art history and cultural studies.[101] Griselda Pollock's first essay on the art and theory of Bracha Ettinger came out in 1996,[102] followed by Ernst van Alphen's *Caught by History: Holocaust Effects in Contemporary Art, Literature, and Theory* in 1997,[103] with O'Dell's *Contract with the Skin: Masochism, Performance Art and the 1970s* appearing in 1998.[104] By the late 1990s, trauma had become a legitimate subject in art history.

The advent of trauma studies in the United States is also indebted to the civil rights movement, the women's movement, gay liberation, and now LGBT activism. Trauma studies also owe a debt to the impact of the personal testimonies, teaching, and consciousness-raising practices of feminist artists.[105] Trauma began to appear in mainstream culture in such works as Art Spiegelman's *Maus: A Survivor's Tale* (1991) and Andrew Jarecki's documentary *Capturing the Friedmans* (2003), which chronicles the domestic environment, familial relations, and biography of a father (Arnold) and one of his three sons (Jesse), who are both accused and convicted of sexually molesting Arnold's students in a computer class he has taught in their home. Monographic exhibition catalogues on artists whose work has dealt with aspects of traumatic circumstance have increased exponentially since the late 1980s. A few examples are *In Context: Yayoi Kusama, Soul-Burning Flashes* (1989),[106] Mike Kelley's *Educational Complex* (1995),[107] *Doris Salcedo* (1998),[108] and *Louise Bourgeois: Memory and Architecture* (1999).[109] Group exhibitions on trauma, and the use of the term to describe an artist's work, gained increasing legitimacy from the end of the twentieth century into the twenty-first, as in *Telling Tales* (1998),[110] *Trauma* (1999),[111] *In the Aftermath of Trauma: Contemporary Video Installations* (2014),[112] and *Alberto Burri: The Trauma of Painting* (2015).[113]

In the early 2000s, an explosion of publications would appear that contextualized trauma in diverse subjects: widowhood in India;[114] Iron Age archaeology;[115] early modernity;[116] long-term unemployment;[117] lesbian experiences;[118] war and combat;[119] the "disappeared" people of Chile and Argentina;[120] the terrorist attacks of 9/11;[121] rape;[122] domestic violence;[123] television hospital dramas;[124] a variety of subjects in photography, theater, and art;[125] the odd pairing of incest and the Holocaust in film;[126] and, for its traumatic dimension, the interconnection between Eros and Thanatos.[127] A host of publications by younger scholars appeared in the mid-2000s, like Jill Bennett's *Empathic Vision: Affect, Trauma, and Contemporary Art* (2005) and Lisa Saltzman and Eric Rosenberg's edited anthology *Trauma and Visuality in Modernity* (2006), a book curiously and erroneously marketed as being "among the first in the field of art history to explore the relation between the traumatic and the visual field in the modern period."[128] In 2004 the Tate Modern in London would advertise talks on trauma by such eminent scholars as W. J. T. Mitchell, who would publish *Cloning Terror: The War of Images, 9/11 to the Present* in 2011, and Griselda Pollock, who would publish *After-Effects/After-Images: Trauma and Aesthetic Transformation in the Virtual Feminist Museum* in 2013.[129]

As this brief overview of trauma studies in art history suggests, scholarship in the 1990s opened the way for widespread application of trauma theory in the humanities and beyond. The explosion of trauma scholarship also brought trauma fatigue, which, in his response to a graduate student's doctoral defense of a dissertation on trauma, a Duke colleague sighed: "Haven't we had enough trauma?" Clinical psychologists have long been familiar with the negative reception of trauma as a subject, and they caution about the stigma that attaches to work on trauma and with traumatized individuals.[130] Trauma fatigue became more prevalent with the increase in genocide worldwide, the bombing of the World Trade Center and the Pentagon on 9/11, the emergence of world terrorism and multiple conflicts in the Middle East, the upsurge of the terrorist Islamic State in Iraq and Syria (ISIS), and the impact of global migration and diaspora, environmental disasters, sex trafficking and sexual and physical violence,[131] satanic cults,[132] international gangs like MS13,[133] drug cartels,[134] trafficking in organs,[135] and the veritable epidemic of PTSD suffered by veterans and child soldiers. There is also mounting evidence of, and scholarship on, the effects of multigenerational trauma.

Regardless of the ever more urgent need to address trauma worldwide, artists and critics are justified in also expressing concern about the proliferation of discourses on trauma. Hakim Bey, for example, worried about fetishizing the traumatized artist, and cautioned that especially those who produce sexually explicit work like that of Sue Williams, Kiki Smith, Jake and Dinos Chapman, and Tracey Emin, to name only a handful, may become victims of "systematic/economic disempowerment."[136] Mike Kelley, who tragically committed suicide in 2012, was impatient with "living in a period in which victim culture and trauma are the rationale for everything."[137] He turned his disdain into the sardonic and brilliant biographical sculptural installation *Educational Complex* (1995). He based this sixteen-foot-long tabletop of interconnected model buildings on his memory of every educational institution he had ever attended, and included spaces for the rooms, corridors, and other architectural features that he could not remember. These blank spaces represent Kelley's satire of the widespread occurrence of and emotional debate over "recovered memory syndrome," the phenomenon in which repressed memories of traumatic events, especially incest and sexual abuse, resurface years after the initiating events. *Educational Complex* also recalls the detractors of this movement, those associated with "false memory syndrome," who argue that such memories are inaccurate, compromised, and sometimes invented under the guidance or pressure of unprofessional or untrained therapists.[138]

Richard J. McNally, a Harvard clinical research psychologist, considered the "politics of trauma" in *Remembering Trauma* (2003).[139] He argued that the definition of PTSD had been too broadly applied, and suggested narrowing it to include "only those stressors associated with serious injury or threat to life"—a suggestion that would drastically alter the public discussion of rape, incest, abuse by clergy, and the traumatic affect of racism and homophobia, to name just a few potentially trauma-inducing contexts and actions.[140] McNally presents his conclusion that most traumatic experience is remembered soon after the event, as if his view represents objective scientific research, when much evidence suggests that memories of traumatic events reoccur over time unpredictably. McNally's bias is apparent in his strong support of Ian Hacking's curiously fervent effort to discredit the diagnosis of multiple personality (dissociative identity disorder) and Hacking's effort to blame clinicians attached to recovered memory therapy of the spurious "rewriting" of patients' "souls."[141] While McNally accounts for those who *do* recall their traumas, he does not equally offer an explanation for those who *do not* remember them, and his extensive bibliography and research do not cite key publications that would challenge his results.[142]

As significant as this debate is in clinical psychology and society, it has not been widely addressed in trauma studies on art. On the contrary, monikers proliferate that turn trauma in art into an art historical movement. Some of these include "confessional art,"[143] "abject art,"[144] "trauma art,"[145] "wound culture,"[146] and "victim art."[147] All these terms risk subsuming traumatic imagery in overarching aesthetic frames that remove art from the events to which artists have attested, sequestering and trivializing their work in the art industry as a trauma commodity.[148] What is more, in the continuing pursuit of what Harold Rosenberg identified nearly fifty years ago as "the tradition of the new," some appear to want to move beyond one "ism" to the next, as the title of the afterword of Jill Bennett's *Empathic Vision*, "Beyond Trauma Culture," seems to recommend.[149]

## CONCERNING CONSEQUENCES

It stands to reason that, having introduced the phrase "cultures of trauma" in 1993 to describe the situation in Romania and other Eastern European countries following the Velvet Revolutions in 1989, I must answer to having initiated perhaps the first trauma "ism" in the arts. It may be difficult to believe in today's climate, drenched with the awareness of PTSD, that the explosion in trauma studies was unimaginable in 1992 when I first presented this phrase at a conference entitled "War and Feminism" at the Rockefeller Foundation's Bellagio Center. Even then I noted that contemporary Romanian artists were engulfed in trauma, and I identified the exponential advance of trauma as a worldwide phenomenon. Therefore, I stand by the phrase "cultures of trauma" as prescient of what has indeed become a global epidemic.

Accordingly, *Concerning Consequences* is divided into five parts. Part 1, "Cultures of Trauma," contains four essays that were foundational in my thinking and theorizing about trauma. Part 2, "Doubles," refers to traumatic dissociation, doubling, and metaphors for dissociated personality in the work of five artists: Istvan Kantor, Franz West, Lynn Hershman Leeson, Larry Miller, and Yoko Ono (the last of whom adopted the imagery of doubling when fusing with John Lennon as the double entity "LENONO"). Part 3, "Shooting Range," includes an essay on Chris Burden that addresses his notorious performance *Shoot* (1971) in the context of his meditation on and response to the many political assassinations in the United States in the 1960s, including the killing of Black Panthers and the 1970 National Guard shooting of students protesting the Vietnam War at Kent State University. Part 3 also includes artist Kim Jones, who served in the Vietnam War but never shot anyone, and Jean Toche, who uses a Polaroid camera to shoot mocking self-portraits that express his resistance to every aspect of culture, politics, religions, and much more. Part 4, "Corpora Vilia," is a term I introduced in 2000 in an essay on the Austrian artist Valie Export.

The phrase is derived from the plural of "*corpus vile*," something felt to be of so little value that it could be experimented upon without concern for loss or damage.[150] In this section I use the term to signal the extremes represented in the art of Marina Abramović, William Pope.L, Barbara Turner Smith, Henry Flynt, and Rudolf Schwarzkogler. Part 5, entitled "Terminal Culture," reintroduces a concept I first suggested in a talk at Ars Electronica in 1992.[151] "Terminal culture" applies to Robert Rauschenberg's insistent effort "to act" in "that gap" between art and life in his effort to avoid the incommensurability of what he called the "blinding fact" of both art and life"; Andy Warhol's foresight regarding the demise of cultural conventions, augmented by the ubiquity of capitalism, advertising, and technology; Maurice Benayoun's futurological imaging of trauma in virtual reality; and the hybrid, cyborgian identity that Wangechi Mutu constantly reinvents in her art.

The essays in *Concerning Consequences* do not appear in chronological order. The most recent date from 2014: "Rauschenberg's 'Gap'" originally appeared under another title in the online exhibition catalog *Rauschenberg: Collecting & Connecting*,[152] and "Warhol's 'What'?" appears here for the first time, having been given as a talk in 1993 and then revised and expanded specifically for this book. I wrote the oldest essay in this book in 1978, during my graduate student days at the University of California at Berkeley. Entitled "1978: 1.1.78–2.2.78," the essay was intended to mime the two voices in Lynn Hershman Leeson's doubling as the persona "Roberta Breitmore," and to represent the odd double exigencies of someone who functioned, as I did at the time, in the role of both a scholar and an artist. Each voice is not quite what it wants to be: one has a scholarly tone, the other a not quite street slang.[153] The year 1978 was also when I began working on the subject of destruction in art, the topic that inevitably led me to consider trauma as an underlying condition in almost every artist who used destruction and violence in his or her art, and to recognize trauma in the preponderance of the biographies of artists working in performance art.

In those years, destruction *in* art was so unfamiliar that it was inevitably understood as destruction *of* art, or iconoclasm, and I clearly remember a talk on "violence" that the renowned psychoanalyst Bruno Bettelheim gave in 1980, at the Museum of Modern Art in San Francisco, in which he opened by explaining that the category of violence did not exist in most reference books. Nearly two decades later, Alain Badiou could address the violence of the twentieth century in a series of lectures at the College International de Philosophie given between 1998 and 2001. These formative talks resulted in his book *Le Siècle* (The Century; 2005). Badiou grounded his analysis in the metaphor of the "beast," drawing on Osip Mandelstam's poem "The Age" (1923).[154] Following Badiou and Mandelstam, Giorgio Agamben issued the following injunction in his 2011 essay "What Is the Contemporary?": "The poet—the contemporary—must firmly hold his gaze on his own time, so as to perceive not its light but rather its darkness."[155] An individual who dedicates "his" life to the "darkness," however, must pay for "his" contemporariness with that life by becoming one "who must firmly lock his gaze onto the eyes of his century-beast, [and] who must weld with his own blood the shattered backbone of time."[156] Having locked onto the beasts of contemporary violence, destruction, and trauma for nearly four decades, I confirm Agamben's view: she pays with her life if she marries (for better and worse) the beasts of her time.

I came to the subject of violence and destruction in art while leafing through old art magazines in 1978, and was suddenly riveted by a photograph of the Holocaust survivor Gustav Metzger, who was using acid to spray paint on and destroy a series of three consecutive canvases, each installed on a large metal frame, in a public performance entitled *South Bank Demonstration* (1961). The photograph brought to mind a 1939 comment by Georges Bataille on the eve of World War II, when the philosopher acknowledged the great effort of art to proceed "from itself, its own reality," and urged that art "must dominate the struggle of good against evil, in the same way that a violent earth tremor dominates and paralyzes the most catastrophic of battles."[157] Eight years later, in 1947, confronted with the future of humanity after the use of the atomic bomb, Bataille urged: "It is better to live up to Hiroshima than to lament it."[158] Contrary to Theodor Adorno's view that "writing poetry after Auschwitz is barbaric," Bataille insisted: "In truth, man is equal to all possibilities, or rather, the impossible is his only measure."[159]

Such texts as these by Bataille and such images as those by Metzger brought me in 1980 to search out Metzger in Frankfurt, Germany, and conduct a series of long, still unpublished interviews with him. The now famous artist was then completely obscure and had forgotten many of the details of the Destruction in Art Symposium (DIAS), which he had launched and presided over: a rambling month-long event in September 1966 that included a three-day symposium and many performances by some fifty artists from fifteen countries around the world. These interviews with Metzger, along with the dozens of other interviews I conducted with DIAS participants—artists, poets, and psychiatrists—helped me bring the reconstruction of DIAS into focus as the subject of the dissertation I was writing, and they remain foundational in my concern for the worldly consequences of destruction, violence, and trauma.

To a person, the artists discussed in this book have lived up to the beasts of our time. This is true for those who pioneered "destruction in art," and for the documentary photographers who recorded the invisibility of the nuclear age; for those who exposed the imprint of the beast on their bodies and psyches, and for those who fought in the century's wars; for those who rejected the virulent racism and sexism of our time, and for those who also fought back in art and life against sexism and homophobia; for those who pictured the darkness of life, and for those who have shown its light. All of the art discussed here, in one way or another, is the expression of a visual language wrought by destruction, violence, and trauma. Collectively, these essays argue that such art has a constructive social function, linking the consequences of aesthetic form to a set of specific aesthetic, cultural, political, and personal histories, conditions, and relations. Each essay in this book concerns something that has happened to someone in life, from whose consequences a sequence of events and questions of value have unfolded, and through which an artist translated pain into art. Thinking about such consequences, in my 1993 essay "Shaved Heads and Marked Bodies" (included in this volume), I called for an empathic understanding of trauma and its manifestations in art.

The French artist known as ORLAN has grappled with the beasts of our time: sexism, ageism, and the conditions of the postbiological cybernetic body. She could be said to be one of the few artists whom Agamben could have named but did not, and one of the few who literally "weld with her own blood the shattered backbone of time" that he described. Repeatedly undergoing cosmetic surgery, ORLAN has suffered in an effort to recreate herself first as a sardonic composite of Western art historical beauty, following that with disfigurement (by having forms normally used to enhance cheekbones in cosmetic surgery inserted over her eyebrows), and then altering her image digitally into hybrid constructions that draw on paradigms of pre-Columbian and African physiognomy and concepts of beauty. Eventually, the result has become what she considers a new social entity who celebrates her effort to determine her own identity beyond the controls of heredity, family, and state. In the poster *I Have Given My Body to Art* (1995), ORLAN is pictured after a 1993 operation (figure 3). The essence of the image of trauma, the photograph is a picture of abjection in which the otherwise beautiful ORLAN appears with heavily bruised eyes, distorted nose, swollen lips, and disheveled hair. In "Carnal Art," she writes that her work swings between "defiguration and refiguration [as an] inscription in the flesh [that] is a function of our age [in which] the body has become a 'modified ready-made,' no longer seen as the ideal it once represented."[160]

In such thinking, ORLAN boldly rejects what Badiou calls "the revenge of the scientific problem over the political project," and refers to genetic engineering as a feminist political project that uses scientific means.[161] "What is to be done about this fact," Badiou asks, "that science knows how to make a new man?" ORLAN answers: a new woman. Badiou rejoins with an epic silence, adding only that "inane ethical committees will never provide us with an answer."[162] What this situation promises, he opines, "will come to pass precisely because . . . it will happen in accordance with the automatism of things."[163] ORLAN disproves automatism (as a theory of the machine body uncontrolled by consciousness) by giving her body to art, in the name of art, and by audaciously confronting the century-beasts.[164] In her acceptance of the postbiological revolution, she dares to gaze at trauma in order "to perceive *in* this darkness a light [Agamben's emphasis]."[165] Of artists who confront trauma this boldly, it could be said that they resemble the horse in the *Shaft of the Dead Man*: they face a mounting emergency and function as sentinels for the helpless world.

Neither Ai Weiwei, ORLAN, nor John Duncan are the focus of essays in this book, even as they haunt this introduction. Duncan is the artist who in 1980 performed *Blind Date*. In this action, he purchased a female corpse in Tijuana for

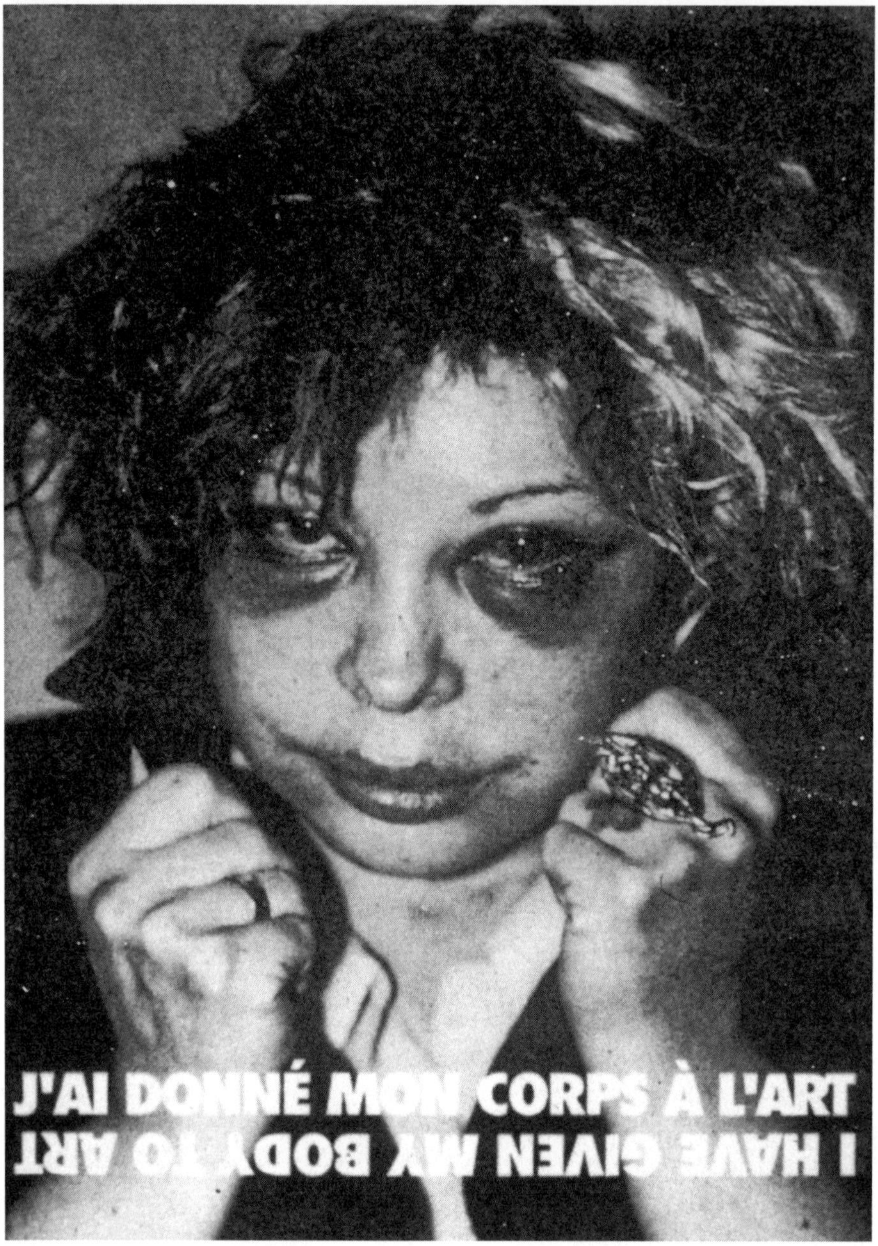


FIGURE 3. ORLAN, *I Have Given My Body to Art*, 1995. Poster produced by the Sandra Gering Gallery, New York. This image is a reverse print of the photograph ORLAN produced on November 25, 1993, entitled *Portrait Produced by the Body-Machine Four Days after the Surgery-Performance*. It is $86\frac{2}{3} \times 65$ in. in two sections of $43\frac{1}{2} \times 65$ in., and each Cibachrome print is mounted in Diasec. Photography by Vladimir Sichov for Sipa-Press. Courtesy of the artist and Sandra Gering Gallery. © 2011 Artists Rights Society (ARS), New York/ADAGP, Paris.

the purpose of sexual intercourse and audiotaped his sex act with the dead body. He then returned to the United States to have a vasectomy in order "to make sure that the last potent seed I had was spent in a cadaver."[166] Duncan's violating act resulted in intense self-disgust, which is why he planned "to torture" himself "physically and psychically" before committing it.[167] This tragic event entailed all the subjects considered in this book: biography, politics, ethics, and the potential of trauma to overwhelm morality.

*Blind Date* is one of the most controversial actions in the history of art. I have argued that it represents Duncan's attempt to assert his life *in art* against his experience of death *in life*—a traumatized psychic death symbolized in violent self-debasement, self-loathing, and heartrending pathos.[168] His very real, contemptible, and desperate act conveyed the palpable signature of his pain and excruciating numbness unto psychic death. As Duncan himself attested, his act unfolded within the epistemological spaces ensured by male hegemony and phallic rule, which seek to guarantee virility and power by any means. In *Blind Date*, Duncan carried the patriarchal ideal to a grotesque extreme, unmasking its real impotence. His personal suffering derived from the conflict implicit in the fact that while he enjoyed all the privilege accreted to a white male, he psychologically cohabited the disempowered, lifeless condition of the woman whose corpse he violated. Emotionally frozen, John Duncan "risked the ability to accept myself. I risked the ability to have sex . . . and the ability to love."[169] In other words, as I wrote: He fucked himself to death.

Duncan's extreme self-loathing can be traced to experiences he recounted in an installation he created five months after *Blind Date*, entitled *If Only We Could Tell You* (1980). Installed in the American Hotel, a refurbished flophouse in the industrial section of downtown Los Angeles, Duncan painted a room in the building black, mounted an electric sander inside a closet in the room, and then locked the closet door. On the wall opposite the locked closet, Duncan hung a framed typed text that read, line after line:

> "We hate you little boy."
> "We hate you little boy."
> "We hate you little boy."
> "We hate you little boy."

Following those four lines, Duncan's "essay" continued:

> We saw you all covered with our blood. We saw you piss and shit all over yourself. We cleaned you up, put food in your fucked-up little mouth. We kept you alive, you ungrateful little bastard . . . We always knew you'd be half-human baggage. You're a blight on our lives . . . Ugly little body with the sex exposed . . . Just look at the mess you've made of everything . . . Every bit is your fault. A dog could have done a better job. We should have put a pillow over your face when we had the chance . . . Why don't you do everyone a favor and kill your-

self. We love a man in uniform. Die, you tit-sucking zombie. Wounded men are so romantic. Go out and blow your head off, prick. We are fed up. Just go out and die.
DIE DIE DIE DIE DIE DIE DIE DIE DIE DIE DIE DIE DIE DIE DIE
DIE DIE DIE DIE DIE DIE DIE DIE DIE DIE DIE DIE DIE DIE DIE
DIE DIE DIE DIE DIE DIE DIE DIE DIE DIE DIE DIE DIE DIE DIE
DIE DIE DIE DIE DIE DIE DIE DIE DIE DIE DIE DIE DIE DIE DIE[170]

While reading this wretched testimony of abuse, one could also listen to the whirring of the electric sander, a sound that reiterated the agony of a mind engulfed in the chaos of traumatic experience. *Blind Date* cannot be understood without also acknowledging how learned self-hatred shaped Duncan's consciousness and art. Such is the legacy and the image of trauma in art to which this book is dedicated. Such is the sacrifice and the ceremony some artists make to right the crimes of the world.

Art is a riddle. It is everything else but *what* it is, and also exists somewhere other than *where* it is, as Heidegger pointed out in "The Origin of the Work of Art" (1935–37). Paradoxically, art is what it is, and this accords also with Wittgenstein's observation that "the totality of facts determines what is the case, and also whatever is not the case" (proposition 1.12). Such a view, he held, is the basis for a "picture theory of language," and for how we "make to ourselves pictures of facts." Art is indeed one of an infinite variety of "pictures of facts." Yet because art is simultaneously personal, issuing from an artist's experience, the "facts" that art "pictures" approximate both personal and collective events and ideas. All the essays in this book explore this intersection, and specifically focus on how an artist's work concerns aspects of trauma in the life of the planet.

# I. Cultures of Trauma

# Survival Ethos and Destruction Art (1992)[1]

## I

*The genocidal mentality is neither biologically ordained nor intractable. It is part of a malignant historical direction that extends into general realms of technology, ultimate power, and finally illusion. But there are other ways of thinking and feeling, already well under way [which] propel us, in fits and starts, toward a change in consciousness, toward a new narrative. . . . At issue is an expansion of collective awareness, an altered sense of self that embraces our reality as members of a single species and thereby opens up new psychological, ethical, and political terrain.*

ROBERT JAY LIFTON AND ERIC MARKUSEN[2]

In their work on the Jewish Holocaust and the psychological effects of "nuclearism," or the world ethos of nuclear weapons, Robert Jay Lifton and Eric Markusen chart a "genocidal mentality." Their findings suggest the emergence of a "species mentality" that reflects a way of being and knowing in the world which is the result of the vast "genocidal systems . . . of deterrence," the ends of which mean only "omnicide," or the destruction of all life.[3] "Genocidal mentality" also manifests itself in massive "dissociative" behavior, the psychological term used to suggest "a broad category of psychological mechanisms, which include psychic numbing, doubling, disavowal, and denial."[4] The various psychological defense mechanisms belonging to dissociation also serve, Lifton and Markusen observe, "as psychological facilitator(s) for deterrence, helping to reduce the kind of psychic stress that would be morally useful and appropriate" to combat the pervasive threat to survival.[5] Such dissociative behavior also has been proven clinically to be a marked symptom of those who have been raised in an environment of alcoholism, or have suffered physical and sexual abuse, and dissociative behavior is, as well, a characteristic response to racism. Given the staggering numbers of individuals worldwide who experience some or all of these dissociative provoking experiences, "genocidal mentality" appears nearly ubiquitous and the conditions of survival ever more precarious.

Certain kinds of presentational art forms have demonstrated a predisposition for and an ability to convey the ontological effects of the technology, phenomenology, and epistemology of destruction and the ways in which individuals and the collective negotiate the resulting crisis of survival. These performances and/or public events often feature advanced technology and/or use the body or body surrogates. Robots and other mechanized body substitutes sometimes serve as the aesthetic site for the representation of the conjunction of social and political practices and in interrelationships that collude in destruction. The tacit agreement among certain artists to situate the body at the center of the discourse of destruction and survival cannot properly be called a "tendency," and it is certainly *not* an "art" movement, "ism," or aesthetic. Rather, it is a response to the "genocidal mentality," an answer or countercharge that is cross-cultural, postindustrial, interdisciplinary, and multinational, and which shares no unified aesthetic, method, or technique. Examples of this work are found in disparate performative practices throughout the twentieth century, but the subject of destruction and its relation to survival has been explored increasingly and systematically since World War II in Europe, the United States, Japan, and the industrialized countries of South America.

"Destruction art" is the term I have adapted to identify the presentational works that situate the body in the center of the question of destruction and survival. Indeed, such art might just as appropriately be called "survival art" if it did not originate in the terminology, aesthetic, and theoretical practices of Gustav Metzger and Rafael Montañez Ortiz, to whom I shall return. The term "destruction art," then, is merely an identificatory device, a concise index of a wide anthropological field. Destruction art, like such broad tendencies as Arte Povera, is inclusive rather than exclusive, defies narrow definitions, and is found at moments in the practices of diverse artists. Few artists have sustained a focus solely on destruction, with the exception of Metzger and Ortiz—and even they have altered the terms of their theoretical discourse over time. For destruction art is exhausting. It requires not only consideration of the most urgent and often overwhelming conditions of life, but also constant vigilance so that the dissociative desires to escape into numbed acquiescence do not prevail.

Because destruction art is not a movement, it has never been systematically organized or methodically publicized and thus resists categorization, for the lack of a manageable identity. The result is that in many ways it is culturally invisible. On the one hand, obscurity permits these artists' actions and survivalist messages to infiltrate social and political spheres without being co-opted into the market system. On the other hand, concealment within culture makes such art vulnerable to mystification, neglect, and disappearance. Often those who do work on questions of survival do not know of the intent of these artists. Thus, even Lifton, who has made unique contributions to these concerns, can state:

> In my work I take three dimensions that you can roughly connect with . . . our contemporary situation. The first is the breakdown of traditional symbols and of modern parallels or developments of those symbols; the second is the mass media revolution; and the third is imagery of extinction or threat of extinction. *This last is the most difficult for art to confront, and I don't know if it's really been represented yet* [my emphasis].[6]

In destruction art, artists present the "imagery of extinction" localized in the body, the object, which is offered as a destructible material and/or an agent of that destruction. In this sense, the performative practices, which I associate with destruction art, recapitulate the technological conditions, effects, processes, and epistemologies of terminal culture. But destruction art is not only about the presentation of the conditions of destruction. It is also one of the means by which a world consciousness is being formed that may contribute to the construction of an altered sense of self, which is necessary to insure human survival.

I want to propose that destruction art is the visual corollary to the discourse of the survivor: it bears witness to the tenuous conditionality of survival—survival itself being the fundamental challenge posed by humanity in the twentieth century and to humanity in the twenty-first century. Destruction art is the only attempt in the visual arts to grapple seriously with both the technology of actual annihilation and the psychodynamics of virtual extinction. It is one of the few cultural practices to redress the general absence of discussion about destruction in society in order to marshal human conscience into collective awareness and resistance. In this sense, the overriding values of the artists associated with destruction art are ethical. Their aesthetic presentations consider the state of social emergency, of culture crisis, as the ultimate moral dilemma; and yet these artists are not moralists. As Gottfried Hattinger wrote in the exhibition devoted to destruction and technology, entitled *Out of Control* (1991):

> Some years ago, Vilem Husser wrote that the telematic society is a structure for the adduction of catastrophes. With the highly developed industrial society, a multi-faced potential of destruction has grown, the effects of which have become obvious in the Gulf war and in the increase in violent conflict management all over the world. This is the background of *Out of Control*, a topic that well befits the present-day social scenario. Nevertheless, a festival like Ars Electronica is no moral instance and beyond any speculative ambition. We do not want to raise our index finger in admonition but rather lay it into the open wounds.[7]

Destruction art is about open wounds—those caused by the institutions and practices that develop and deploy the weapons of destruction, that engineer the reproductive technologies of gender and class domination, or that mastermind the artificial intelligence systems and their application to robotics. (See Hans Moravec's *Mind Children* for his chilling contribution to this "post-biological" world.)[8] Destruction art is about violations, those defilements continually perpetrated against the bodies and psyche of women and men. But destruction art is not a utopic project. Rather, it is a pragmatic one, enacted by artists who are profoundly skeptical but not cynical, and who commingle responsiveness with reaction, and fear and loathing with great trust in the aggregative potential of art. This potential to unite and heal is a project different from what formerly was considered the redemptive role of art in society and represents a structure of belief, stated quite simply by Günter Brus when he wrote: "To life I say yes!"[9]

## II

In his important early work on destruction and trauma, Lifton identified a survivor as "one who has encountered, been exposed to, or witnessed death and has himself or herself remained alive."[10] Death here may be literal as in the actual extinguishing of life, psychological as in the destruction of the sense of self, or ecological as in natural disaster. Whatever the text of survival, it must be read through the discourse of destruction, and Lifton asks the rhetorical question: "Is Hiroshima our text?"[11] Indeed, as representation, Hiroshima identifies destruction as both the extremity and the center of survival where the body figures as the text.

Survival, Lifton writes, leaves a "death imprint" that is accompanied by "death anxiety, death guilt, or survivor guilt," guilt that entails a "sense of debt and responsibility to the dead."[12] Survival also causes a "psychic numbing" that incapacitates the individual's ability to feel and to confront certain kinds of experiences, and impairs essential mental functions of symbolization.[13] The wholesale psychic numbing that is the foundation for a "genocidal mentality" exists internationally and increases as the death of the body is engineered in certain scientific practices identified above.

Omnicide obliges reflection on the nature of disappearance, a concept taken up by Jean-Francois Lyotard in his book *Heidegger and "the jews"*, where he coins a phrase, "the Forgotten," to signify a condition that is neither "a concept nor a representation but a 'fact' as factum (Kant)," which we are "obligated before the Law . . . to remember."[14] "The Forgotten" is "something that never ceases to be forgotten," a state that "one has tried to forget by killing it" but which advances, nevertheless, "in the direction of the immemorial through the destruction of its representations of its witnesses, 'the jews.'"[15] Here Lyotard indicates that "'the jews' are the object of a dismissal with which Jews, in particular, are afflicted in reality."[16] Lyotard's "the jews" is a refinement and historical specification of the "catastrophe" Nietzsche forewarned is the inevitability of the "failure to reflect."[17]

Destruction is the agent and process of disappearance in our time of "the Forgotten," "the jews." The interdependence of "the jews" and "the Jews" is relevant to destruction art and the materiality of survival. But by collapsing the forgotten content of experience, "the jews," into the historical expunging of Jews, Lyotard continues the sublimation of the discourse on the actual site of dismissal: the destruction of bodies. Although "the jews" may be a metaphor for historical bodies, nevertheless the formation of "the Forgotten" is a representation that continues to perpetuate the dismissal of destruction as the overarching condition of survival that, through the substitution, continues to be forgotten.

The terms of destruction art originate from a real Jew, a real survivor of destruction: Gustav Metzger. In five manifestos written between November 1959 and July 1964, Metzger laid out the basis for "auto-destructive art," which is also the foundation of destruction art. In his first manifesto (November 4, 1959), exactly contemporaneous with the first happenings, Metzger systematically formulated a theory and a practice concerned with destruction as a social and aesthetic phenomenon. He had his first tract distributed at 14 Monmouth Street, a London Gallery. It states:

> *Auto-Destructive Art*
> Auto-destructive art is primarily a form of public art for industrial societies.
> Self-destructive painting, sculpture and construction is a total
> unity of idea, site, form, color, method and timing of the disintegrative process.
> Auto-destructive art can be created with natural forces, traditional art techniques and technological techniques.
> The amplified sound of the auto-destructive process can be an element
> of the total conception.
> The artist may collaborate with scientists, engineers.
> Self-destructive art can be machine produced and factory assembled.
> Auto-destructive paintings, sculptures and constructions have a lifetime
> varying from a few moments to twenty years. When the disintegrative process is complete the work is to be removed from the site and scrapped.[18]

Metzger intended "auto-destructive art" to be realized principally in public monuments to be erected on civic sites. These structures would contain complex technological and electronic internal devices that would cause them to implode and self-destruct within a period of twenty seconds to twenty years. Site-sensitive and site-specific, interdisciplinary and requiring collaboration between scientists and artists, these works would be context-determined and therefore social, collective, and collaborative. Machine-made, the structures would also be technical representations of the intrinsic interdependence between the processes of natural decay and cultural (particularly urban) crisis. Most importantly, "auto-destructive art" would disappear.

"Auto-destructive art" condenses a vast experiential and technological territory of destruction (and its concomitant survivalist ethos) into a manageable representation. Its temporal duration operates both as a representation *and* a presentation, an image *and* an enactment of effacement that recalls but also gives substance to the forgotten, "the jews." As the rematerialization of memory in its original destructive form, the absent presence of the felt past returns as known experience, no longer "there" but transformed into a new state "here." Destruction art, in its first manifestation as "auto-destructive art," is the constant public and social reminder of destruction, its technological agents, its spatial and temporal processes, and its human results.

Metzger formulated his theory precisely twenty years after he was sent to England at the age of twelve in 1939, following his family's arrest by the Gestapo in Nuremberg. Twenty seconds, then, is a temporal analog for the time it took to destroy his personal world by killing his family; twenty years, the time of gestation in his own auto-transformation. Temporality in destruction art is the index of duration that confronts consciousness with the cycle of construction and destruction manifest in cultural artifacts and technological objects as well as in nature. This temporality reinscribes the psyche of the social body with a memory of the finite, which must function as an affective agent in the reaggregation of a survivalist consciousness.

Temporality in Metzger's art signifies not only in cultural terms, but in political terms as well. Metzger retained his Polish passport while living in Great Britain until 1948, when he decided to become stateless. This life experience reflects the geopolitics of the disappeared, which Paul Virilio has identified as one of the conditions of "pure war":

> Disappearance of place and individual, refusal of citizenship, of rights, of *habeas corpus*, etc., . . . is spreading all over the world. It's easier to make people disappear one by one, ten by ten or thousand by thousand than to shut millions up into camps, as they did in Nazi Germany. Even if Gulags and concentration camps still exist—and they do, alas—disappearance is our future.[19]

The concrete evidence of corporeal existence in the carnage of bombed cities and towns with dead bodies to be buried or burned that was the result of past wars no longer exists, since the crematoria and thermonuclear vaporization obliterate all reckoning with death and destruction. "Pure war," and destruction art in this sense, refer to the technical and psychological readiness, the ubiquity of war that currently shapes political as well as social relationships, and that contributes to the "epistemo-technical," a way of knowing and being-in-the-world based on the technology of war.[20]

A vivid example of Metzger's practice is his *South Bank Demonstration* of July 3, 1961. Wearing a gas mask as a protective device, Metzger sprayed hydrochloric acid on three nylon tarpaulins—white, black, and red, a reference to Kasimir Malevich and Russian Suprematism—stretched over an enormous series of three frames that measured seven feet high, twelve and one-half feet long, and six feet deep (figure 4). The nylon material dissolved within fifteen seconds after contact with the acid. Metzger positioned himself against a complex of urban office buildings and a crowd of men, many in business attire. Visually suggestive of the military-industrial complex, this image recalled the dire warning Dwight D. Eisenhower had issued only five months before Metzger's lecture-demonstration, in his farewell address from the White House Oval Office on January 17, 1961:

> This conjunction of an immense military establishment and a large arms industry is new in the American experience. The total influence—economic, political, even spiritual—is felt in every city, every state house, every office in the federal government. We recognize the imperative need for this development.

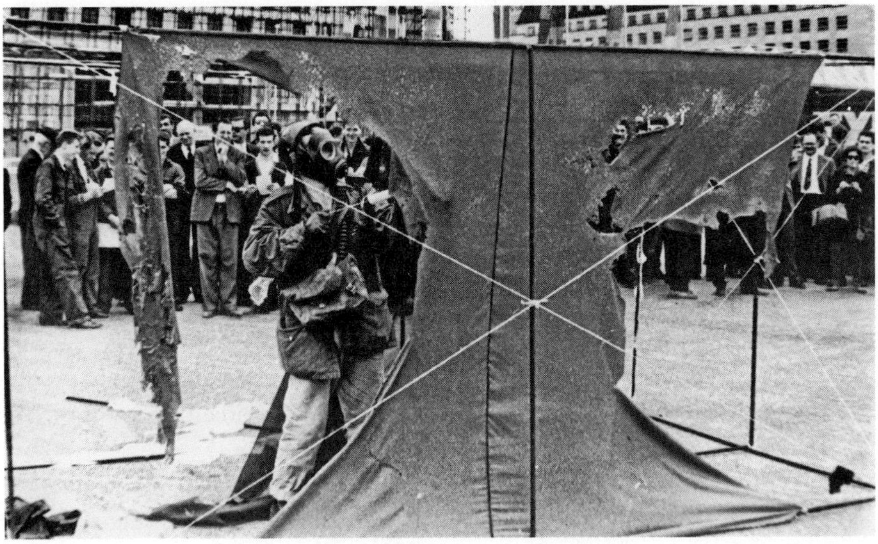

FIGURE 4. Gustav Metzger demonstrating his "auto-destructive art" in his *South Bank Demonstration*, July 3, 1961, London. Metzger paints using a spray gun and hydrochloric acid on three nylon sheets colored white, black, and red and each hung on a separate metal frame. The sheets begin to disintegrate after a few seconds and are completely dissolved after twenty minutes. Photograph by Keystone / Hulton Archive / Getty Images.

> Yet we must not fail to comprehend its grave implications. Our toil, resources and livelihood are all involved; so is the very structure of our society.

As the agent of destructive forces, Metzger displaced war from the actual field of militarized combat by utilizing the substances of destruction to dissolve materials and thus to reenact upon the "field" of the picture space the symbolic map of the conduct, process, content, and result of destruction. His action situated war as representation in the civic site of the production of destruction:

> The drop drop dropping of HH bombs . . . mirrors the compulsive perfectionism of arms manufacture—polishing to destruction point. Auto-destructive Art is the transformation of technology into public art. The immense productive capacity, the chaos of capitalism and of Soviet communism, the co-existence of surplus and starvation; the increasing stockpiling of nuclear weapons—more than enough to destroy technological societies; the disintegrative effects of machinery and the life in vast built-up areas on the person.[21]

The self-conscious sophistication of contemporary intellectual "discourse" stands in marked contrast to Metzger's loaded and subjective "words," emotional words that may embarrass but that are unmistakably *real*, the direct expression of an involved, impassioned, angry, and fearful victimized man.

Destruction art is oppositional in refusing the elisions of linguistic abstraction that unwittingly contribute to the perpetuation of the destructive epistemology of Western culture, an epistemology so thoroughly perfected by "defense intellectuals" in the policies and technology of extinction, and about which Carol Cohn has so insightfully written. She critiqued "the professional discourse" of the men whose minds are used "in the service of militarization" for its "extraordinary abstraction and removal"—smart bombs, friendly fire, clean bombs, countervalue attacks, and collateral damage—because of the ways in which such language denied what she "knew in reality."[22] Related, and deeply sobering, is Lifton's confirmation of her attack on such "professional discourse," when he observed:

> A certain amount of numbing is probably necessary in most professional situations—in the midst of an operation a surgeon cannot afford to experience fully the consequences of failure—but it is surely excessive in our society and in our century. So great is the diminished emotion in professionals that it well may be that becoming a professional is in itself part of still another devil's bargain in which one ceases to feel much about the central—the most threatening—questions of our time.[23]

The denaturing and abstraction of the actual experience of destruction is the triumph of the technology of that destruction. Great care must be exercised to prevent theoretical abstractions from becoming part of the suppression of actual experience that culminates in the denial of identity altogether. Such denials conspire in the destruction of bodies and are the unforgivable consequence of mistaking the map for the territory. They are the *decidable* danger that resides in Jacques Derrida's concepts of "difference" and "undecidability."[24] But at the same time, the task of destruction art includes the deconstruction of the double character and determinacy of Cartesian-inscribed binary divisions: body/mind, war/peace, destruction/creation. In this sense, the project of destruction art resembles the deconstructionist theory with which it simultaneously but independently emerged in the early 1960s. It is significant that Derrida's *De la grammatologie* was published a year after Metzger brought the various tendencies of destruction art together as a cohesive discourse and representation in the *Destruction in Art Symposium* (DIAS) in 1966. Metzger's stated aim in organizing DIAS was to create an interdisciplinary forum for an inquiry into the relationship of destruction in art and society. Derrida's parallel objective was to "seek a new investigation of responsibility, an investigation which questions the codes inherited from ethics and politics" in the "political and institutional structures that make possible and govern our practices."[25]

DIAS was the temporary organization for a multicultural and multidisciplinary international event that attracted nearly one hundred artists and poets (most of whom were the pioneers of happenings and concrete poetry) from fifteen countries in Eastern and Western Europe, the United States, South America, and Japan. Among them were the resonant core of artists associated with the subculture or avant-garde underground in the mid-1960s—John Latham, Wolf Vostell, Jean-Jacques Lebel, Al Hansen, Ortiz, Hermann Nitsch, Günter Brus, Otto Mühl, Kurt Kren, Peter Weibel, Yoko Ono, Henri Chopin, Bob Cobbing,

John Sharkey, Ivor Davies, and Dom Sylvester Houedard. Among those who sent works to DIAS but were unable to attend were Milan Knížák, Ad Reinhardt, Diter Rot, Enrico Baj, and many others. One of the most surprising contributions came from a group of Argentinean poets and painters (Luis Alberto Wells, Silvia Torras, Jorge Roiger, and Jorge López Anaya) who had been assembled by the painter Kenneth Kemble to exhibit under the title *Arte Destructivo* at the Galeria Lirolay in Buenos Aires, 1961. Kemble sent documentation to the DIAS organizers of the group's activities, photographs of altered and destroyed objects that they had exhibited as sculpture, and sound tapes of their destruction music and poetry. Shortly after this exhibition, the group dissolved, and not until DIAS did the material resurface. In addition to artists, two psychologists also participated in DIAS: Ehrling Eng, an American working with Vietnam veterans, and Joseph Berke, also an American and a psychiatrist (then collaborating with R. D. Laing) at Kingsley Hall, where he worked with the famous patient Mary Barnes.[26]

DIAS took place in London throughout September, and was widely publicized both in a special August edition of *Art and Artists* devoted to "auto-destructive art" and in numerous press conferences that included actions by such artists as Latham, Ortiz, Davies, and Bernard de Vries and Irene Donner van der Weetering of the countercultural, politically activist Provos, a Dutch group that derived its name from *provoceren*, Dutch for "to provoke." The three-day symposium at the Africa Centre was situated carefully in the middle of the month to balance art practice with theory, so that the theoretical papers presented by various artists would focus attention on their serious engagement with the problems raised by destruction in art and society and thereby contribute to a forum for public debate. Performances took place before and after the symposium in the Africa Centre, at the Jeannette Cochrane and Mercury Theatres, and at St. Brides Institute. Events also occurred at Better Books, the London bookshop that functioned in the mid-1960s as a gathering place for the international literary and artistic underground. The Free School Playground, located in a working-class district near Notting Hill Gate, a barren *terrain vague* that had not been cleared of World War II bombing debris, served as the unseemly but appropriate site for most of the actions that included fire and explosives.

The diverse collection of artists and poets who participated either directly or indirectly in DIAS were unified in their response to the theme of destruction in art. Yet, they never comprised a movement, nor as a group produced a manifesto or publication. They never established a meeting place to discuss and share ideas, nor did they exhibit as a group again after DIAS.[27] Apart from the month of events, DIAS represented a special moment in which a small body of international artists shared a discriminating attitude about the use of destruction as an element in the creation of art, as a conceptual frame, as an attitude to the world, and as a way of relating subject matter in art to events and conditions in society. But the very formation of DIAS facilitated the congregation and identification of artists who had been working on problems of destruction in art and life internationally. In this important function alone, DIAS remains the pivotal moment for the discussion of destruction art, like a crystal gathering and then refracting the many concerns of these artists. These concerns have been amplified internationally since the late 1970s in certain aspects of the punk scene, in the events staged by Survival Research Laboratories in San Francisco, in the work of the organization "V2" (Rik Delhaas, Alex Adreansens, and Joke Brouwer) in S'Hertogenbosch, Holland, in the sound actions by the Polish artist Zbigniew Karkowski, in the robots of Jim Whiting from Great Britain, and in the work of many artists who exhibited together in *Out of Control* in September, 1991.

DIAS was also the model for a number of subsequent exhibitions in which artists learned to expand the languages of destruction art. It was, for instance, the prototype for the conference entitled The Dialectics of Liberation, organized by R. D. Laing and David Cooper. Such prominent intellectuals and public figures as Paul Goodman, Stokely Carmichael, Erving Goffman, Herbert Marcuse, and Gregory Bateson lectured at this conference, which occurred in London in July 1967, ten months after DIAS. This event coincided precisely with the three-day trial of Metzger and the Irish poet and playwright John Sharkey, Metzger's principal assistant in the organization of DIAS. The pair were found guilty of having presented Hermann Nitsch's fifth action of the *Orgies Mysteries Theater*, a work the court described as "an indecent exhibition contrary to common law."[28]

The simultaneity of this conference with Metzger and Sharkey's trial is instructive in its juxtaposition of the divisions of power and authority that shape the systems, practices, institutions, and performances of Western culture. The textual and expository exegesis of those who participated in The Dialectics of Liberation presented no threat, framed as it was in the vaguely sentimental idealistic terms of liberation, terminology that conformed to the authoritative, abstract, restrained, measured, and ostensibly objective codes of academic discourse. By comparison, "destruction-in-art" represented a direct, contentious, strident, and unsentimental discourse, and its practices were raw, passionate, involved, impatient, skeptical, pessimistically critical, and sometimes dangerous and beyond control.

In his lecture "The Discourse of Language" (1971), Michel Foucault called for the restoration of discourse to "its character as an event."[29] Nitsch's work, and the juridical response to it visited upon Metzger and Sharkey, indeed returned the discourse of destruction to its character as an event. The punishment meted out to the artists—and, by extension, to DIAS itself—inscribed upon them the "guilt" of destruction that must be read as the single most important evidence of the affective power of DIAS and the events it sponsored in revealing the very systems, institutions, and epistemological foundations of destruction that it set out to criticize.

## III

The "guilt" laid on the organizers of DIAS is that of the survivor who bears witness for the collective. Thus do the individual body, the body of practices I want to call destruction art, and the social body have a symbiotic connection in that individual and collective bodies are also events in the history of society. In this sense, the interventions of destruction art are central to *any* discourse on survival within or outside of the disciplines of art and aesthetics.

Only Metzger and Ortiz ever specifically used the terminology of "destruction" and systematically explored it as the principal focus of their work. For example, in his "Destructivism: A Manifesto" (1962), Ortiz wrote: "[The] destroyers, materialists, and sensualists dealing with process directly . . . are destructivists and . . . understand the desperate need to retain unconscious integrity. . . . The artist's sense of destruction will no longer be turned inward in fear. The art that utilizes the destructive processes will purge, for as it gives death, so it will give to life."[30] Throughout the 1950s, Ortiz did extensive research on Freud's concepts of the unconscious and its effects on behavior, and he studied the metaphysical existentialism of Nietzsche, Kierkegaard, Heidegger, and Sartre. He was moved deeply by Norman O. Brown's *Life Against Death* (1959). A Puerto Rican-American of mixed European, North African, and Yaqui Indian heritage, Ortiz sought alternatives to Western cultural traditions and was particularly impressed by pre-Columbian art and ritual. By 1961 he had begun a series of destroyed furniture, especially mattresses and chairs, that he called *Archaeological Finds*. Four years later, he began *Destruction Realizations*, actions that included ritual sacrifices of chickens, the destruction of musical instruments, and other ceremonial practices.

While Wolf Vostell never used the term "destruction" as part of the theoretical description of his practice, his concept of *dé-coll/age* must be mentioned here. Vostell adopted the term in 1954 as a synthesis of destruction/creation (he found it in *Le Figaro*, where the word *décollage* was used to describe the simultaneous takeoff and crash of an airliner). His syllabic division of the word inverts the constructive process of collage and deconstructs the binary creation/destruction into semiotic units symbolic of temporal transformation: *"de"* and *"coll"* name oppositions while *"age"* refers to temporality. Vostell's sensitivity to the semiotic range of the French term owes something to the context in which such poet-painters as Raymond Hains, Jacques Villeglé, and Françoise Dufrêne in Paris and Mimmo Rotelia in Italy developed *l'affiche lacerée*. It was also in this context and at this time that such artists as Bernard Aubertain, Diter Rot, and later Arman, Knížák, and Jean Tinguely incorporated destructive elements in their work.

However similarly located in problems of destruction and creation, the formulations of Metzger, Ortiz, and Vostell were not only very different from each other but were even contentious, conditioned by their distinct cultural contexts of Europe (Metzger and Vostell) and the United States (Ortiz), each representing unique responses to and ideological strategies for coping with and affecting their individual situations. Yet for all their differences, these three men share the critical social experience of having existed at the margin of Western cultural hierarchies, in terms of the racial and religious discrimination and the actual or virtual annihilation they experienced: Metzger is the stateless victim of the Holocaust, Vostell was a German who spent his youth in fear,[31] and Ortiz is a dark-skinned Puerto-Rican American who spent part of his youth in south Harlem, the survivor of deadly adolescent gang warfare of the barrio and of the vicious, relentless racism of the United States.

Destruction art produces a response slightly different in men than in women. The body—actual, or extended in mechanical robots—is the principal territory for the demonstration of destruction and survival in both men's and women's productions. While male artists have explored the relationship of that body to the objects and technologies of destruction, as well as to the assertion and recuperation of identity, women artists have regularly confined their investigations to the reconstruction of the self.[32] Yoko Ono's destruction scores for performances, paintings, and sculptures onward from the late 1950s and Niki de Saint Phalle's paintings *Feu a volonté* (1961), plaster-surface constructions filled with bags of pigment which exploded with color when fired upon with a rifle, demonstrate that women have not been exempt from the destruction of materials—including the surfaces of their own bodies, as the performances of self-mutilation by Gina Pane have shown. But the vast majority of women's destruction art explores the problem of the obliteration of identity and the decentering of the self, so that while the Holocaust may be the representative text, a text that is in part read through the technologies of destruction, that text must return to the reading of the material universe of the body's pain.

In *The Divided Self*, R. D. Laing recalls "a little girl of seventeen in a mental hospital" who told him that "she was terrified because the Atom Bomb was inside her."[33] This metaphor for the annihilation of the self, which is bound to the destruction of self-esteem, intimacy, and the ability to love or be loved, is also part of the trust of destruction art. In her *Cut Piece* (1964–66), Ono sat motionless on a stage after inviting the audience to come up and cut away her clothing. This denouement anticipated the institutionalized objectification of women as cultural detritus so systematically presented by Karen Finley, who in an essay entitled "I Was Not Expected to Be Talented," wrote: "I'd like for you to feel pain, to feel my pain . . . I hate people who have a reason for everything. They can't just accept the fact that bad things happen to good people because if they did they'd be like me—out of control."[34] Ono stated: "People went on cutting the parts they do not like of me."[35] In numerous performance works, videos, and films, Valie Export has probed the lesions society leaves on the human body: "Man is rolling in broken glass without bleeding to death. He proves stronger than the ambient system by overcoming its point of impact, the body. The cuts in the skin are no longer lethal, they are openings giving access to the intima, to the innermost lining membrane of the vessels, to our selves."[36] As the survivor of sexual and physical abuse, Lynn Hershman whispers to the video witnesses: "Don't talk about it." In her autobiographical video trilogy *Electronic Diary* (1986–89), Hershman, also a Jew, recounts in an autoanalysis that the origins of her own eating disorders are in incest, violations whose origins and results she equates to the cosmology of Hitler, the vampire, and Holocaust survivors alike.[37]

Such works, on and in the actual body of the artist, intervene in the imagined neutrality *between* subject and object, where they insert the voice of survival that is the representation of the pain of destruction. Destruction art is the renegotiation of that pain. Elaine Scarry has argued that "the only state that is as anomalous as pain is the imagination," and that "while pain is a state remarkable for being wholly without objects, the imagination is remarkable for being the only state that is wholly its objects."[38] Destruction art represents and presents the relationship between pain and imagining. "Pain does not simply resist language," writes Scarry; it "actively destroys it, bringing about an immediate reversion to a state anterior to language, to the sounds and cries a human being makes before language is learned."[39] She continues, "Because the person in pain is ordinarily so bereft of the resources of speech, it is not surprising that the language of pain should sometimes be brought into being by those who are not themselves in pain but who speak on behalf of those who are . . . and thus there come to be avenues by which this most radically private of experiences begins to enter the realm of pubic discourse."[40]

In 1962, Ono wrote "Conversation Piece," a score for an action requiring the narration of pain. It reads:

> Bandage any part of your body.
> If people ask about it, make a story
> and tell.
> If people do not ask about it, draw
> their attention to it and tell.
> If people forget about it, remind them of it and keep telling.
> Do not talk about anything else.[41]

Invented and bandaged wounds articulate psychophysical pain. This impulse to narrate suffering, to describe the unspeakable conditions of interior life, is central to finding a voice through and by which to repossess and recover a sense of the concreteness of personal experience. More urgent is the need to communicate the auto-constructed reality *to someone else*—to materialize it. Western culture needs subjects to bear witness to the contents of survival and the historical bodies upon which the text of destruction has been inscribed. The body in destruction art bears such witness and thereby offers a paradigm for a "resisting body," that private, complex, signifying system of the self, a person who acts on behalf of both the individual and the social body.

## IV

Destruction art is this witness. When the content of human experience is conveyed through the potentially subversive presence of human sentience, the body becomes the vehicle for the realization of the essential intersubjectivity upon which survival depends. The body is the signifying vortex of the contingent relationship between nature (the body) and culture (social constructions). Performance art is the medium that conveys human sentience in the visual arts most directly. Destruction art is the kind of performance art where conditions of human emergency are most vividly displayed.

Because of the trust destruction art keeps with the preservation and survival of the body, it suggests antecedents in the visual arts outside of those conventionally ascribed to performance art. Art historical lineage traditionally traces performance from Futurism to Russian experimental art, Dada, Surrealism, and into action painting. But such a survey only links the incidence of live actions in one movement to the presentational events in another, differentiating merely between formal styles and historical periods. But because destruction art originates neither in a movement nor a style, its heritage includes aesthetic traditions from which it draws its survivalist codes. I want to suggest that the sources for destruction art include not only the performative practices of the modernist avant-garde but the humanist concerns traditionally linked to figuration. Especially since the 1950s, performance art has played a key role in recuperating the body as a medium from the various orthodoxies of nineteenth-century academic figuration and twentieth-century social realism. In this way, performance art has reconstituted and affirmed the human body as a significant form and subject matter. Not only has it deepened the disparate and undeveloped issues of embodiment present in its antecedent modernist moments, but also its unprecedented historical achievement is its transformation of figurative representation into embodied presentation.

Oskar Schlemmer is central to this history. Significantly, while serving on the battlefield in 1918, Schlemmer wrote, "The new artistic medium is a much more direct one: the human body."[42] Four years later, he designed the Bauhaus logo, situating a schematized head at the signifying center of modernism. He continued to explore the human body when he introduced his course titled "Man" (in the generic sense of human) at the Dessau Bauhaus. Schlemmer's figurative murals, paintings, reliefs, and sculpture together form a theoretical project continuous with the introduction of the body onto the Bauhaus stage. He set forth his theory in such texts as "Man and Art Figure" (1925), which proposed the expansion of visual knowledge beyond the inherited conventions of painting and sculpture into human action.[43] Schlemmer identified the fundamental nature of humanity in the "immediacy" and "independence" of "body, voice, gestures, and movements."[44] He considered sensory perception appropriate material for art: "psychical impulses," "the sensate, psycho-sexual mechanical" dimensions of body, or the "dematerialized aspects of human reality" and the "laws" of the human organism that "reside in the invisible workings of his inner self . . . the heartbeat, circulation, respiration, the activities of the brain and nervous system."[45] Decades before Hans Namuth's photographs of Jackson Pollock's painting process prompted Harold Rosenberg to describe action painting as an existential arena, Schlemmer wrote: "We shall observe the appearance of the human figure as an event. . . . With a certainty that is automatic, each gesture and each movement is drawn into the sphere of significance."[46]

War propelled Schlemmer to seek a radical aesthetic alternative capable of recovering not only an ethical standard of art but a form and representation powerful enough to confront social and political conditions that promised incomprehensible human suffering. Equally stunned by the atrocities of war, Yves Klein came to a similar conclusion. He observed after World War II that the body, whether in material presence or imprinted appearance, remained the core of human measure: "Hiroshima, the shadows of Hiroshima; in the desert of the atomic catastrophe they constituted evidence, terrible evidence beyond any doubt, but still evidence of hope for the permanence (though immaterial) of the flesh."[47] Klein's longing for affirmation of the permanence of human presence is mirrored in Michelangelo Pistoletto's profound anxiety about the figure in his paintings on Mylar that reflect the viewer while simultaneously representing his own body. Of these works, Pistoletto wrote in 1962:

> Born in 1933, I live in the heart of this century, in this gigantic century. . . . At ten years of age I find myself in the middle of the "World War," the last "Great War," terribly great, great as terror. The mountains are mountains of death, the factories are factories of death, the chimney's smoke bodies. . . . My problem is therefore great. What is God: Great problem. What is Art: An equally great problem. . . . Fontana's holes, Burri's sacks. Burri made his sacks in the concentration camp . . . Bravo Burri. My problem is so great that I look at myself in the mirror and search within myself, in my image, for the answer, the solution, in my own image. And I work on the mirror.[48]

Pistoletto's mute reflective figures testify to the environment of the human condition and recall kinetic landscapes such as Jean Tinguely's *Study for the End of the World, No. 2* (1962), constructed on the desert outside of Las Vegas, the militarized testing grounds for the atomic bomb. During this same period, Yoko Ono wrote her score for the performance of *Blood Piece* (1961): "Blood Piece: Use your blood to paint. Keep painting until you faint (A). Keep painting until you die (B)."[49]

For too long, artists, critics, and historians alike have been embarrassed by their inadequacy when confronted with questions of human survival. There are, fortunately, exceptions to the rule. This is director and theorist Herbert Blau's emotional statement in *The Impossible Theater* (1964):

> I saw the terrors of the present through the despair of the ages. I remember trying to write a poem about the cobalt bomb, which invariably turned facetious the more I saw it as the apocalyptic extension of Original Sin, which meant nothing to me as dogma but everything as metaphor. It wasn't that I was intellectually wrong, only the enormity of it all was such that when you did think about it you could only laugh or rage, or pick your liver in silence."[50]

While Blau openly acknowledges here his existential anguish and his sense of futility, his confession departs from the "manly" stoicism and brooding remove demanded of artists of his generation and perpetuated by critics of following generations.

For example, Serge Guilbaut devotes an entire chapter in *How New York Stole the Idea of Modern Art* to the creation of an American avant-garde, in which he defends the "abstract idiom" against the "bourgeoisified, clinical, and detached account of atomic horror" by such writers as John Hersey.[51] It is exceedingly difficult to account for Guilbaut's views, particularly his evaluation of Hersey's *Hiroshima*, 1946, as "bourgeoisified" and "clinical." Here is Hersey:

> Mr. Tanimoto found about twenty men and women on the sand spit. He drove the boat onto the bank and urged them to get aboard. They did not move and he realized that they were too weak to lift themselves. He reached down and took a woman by the hands, but her skin slipped off in huge, glove-like pieces. He was so sickened by this that he had to sit down for a moment. Then he got out into the water and, though a small man, lifted several of the men and women, who were naked, into his boat. Their backs and breasts were clammy, and he remembered uneasily what the great burns he had seen during the day had been like: yellow at first, then red and swollen, with the skin sloughed off, and finally, in the evening, suppurated and smelly. . . . He lifted the slimy living bodies out and carried them up the slope away from the tide. He had to keep consciously repeating to himself, "These are human beings."[52]

Guilbaut also quotes critic Dwight Macdonald, who rejected such work for its "naturalism [that] is no longer adequate, either esthetically or morally, to cope with the modern horrors"; but ironically, he cites Macdonald's 1946 article "The Root Is Man," a text that, at least in title alone, establishes the human figure at the center of all concerns.[53] Guilbaut also describes Barnett Newman's aesthetic position in terms that reveal the antipathy that artists of the New York School had for direct experience and for confrontation with the horror and fear of their own historical period, an antipathy that mainstream criticism perpetrates today—whether in terms of Greenbergian formalism or of Marxist orthodoxy such as Guilbaut's own: "As Dwight Macdonald had done in writing about the bomb, Newman here emphasized that the horror of modern conditions could not be represented or described. To do so was unworthy of the artist; it was to descend to the level of *Life* or *The New Yorker*, to wallow in the filth of everyday life. To depict the horror, to describe it, was tantamount to accepting it."[54]

But some artists were able to break through the dissociative behavior of both artists and critics, to release the numbing I described in the beginning of this paper that characterizes the emotions of the survivor, and, yes, to "wallow in the filth of everyday life" in which the construction of a genocidal mentality was and remains every person's responsibility. Such artists rejected the censorious superiority and conventions of art world dogma in order to press forward their humanist concerns, however unsavory, unsophisticated, unguarded, and unarmed. No wonder most of them are marginalized, ignored, and left out of art history.[55] These artists communicated their sense of urgency through the body.

I want to propose that the artists who shifted from figuration to the medium of the body itself not only appended the *re*presentational model of the visual arts to a presentational form, they also contributed to the revitalization of representational figuration that took place in the late 1970s and 1980s.[56]

While such shifts are enormous in formal terms alone, what interests me far more are the ways in which humanist questions were reconstituted. Performance art—and, more particularly, destruction art—repositioned the humanist content of art in the wider epistemological transformations taking place throughout world culture. Such a reconstitution of the humanist project reflects the shift from the transcendent subjectivity of holistic humanism to a polysemic humanism characterized by independent subject positions, the constituent elements of which reflect divergent social and political spheres. In this regard, I concur with Ernesto Laclau and Chantal Mouffe in their essay "Post-Marxism without Apologies": "We have rejected the idea that humanist values have the metaphysical status of an essence and that they are, therefore, prior to any concrete history and society. However, this is not to deny their validity; it only means that their validity is constructed by means of particular discursive and argumentative practices."[57] Artists concerned with destruction have focused this discourse most clearly. For their work implicitly insists that the human figure, above all others, is the privileged signifier of the social, material, and historical conditions of the body. They summon the actual body as the ultimate means by which to quicken and intensify the dialogue on survival on which all issues of humanism turn, if we are to reconstruct this concept as a value, as I believe we must.

## V

Western society and its most compelling aesthetic productions continue to perpetuate the epistemological ethos of destruction. But art that once reflected, mirrored, and passively represented the abstract conventions and patterns of knowledge now actively presents the literal embodiment of psychic wounds, urban bedlam, and militarized consciousness at the crisis core of terminal culture. But this epistemology also has healing roots, traditions that are intertwined in the very technology, languages, and practices of destruction.

Foucault recovered the Greek term *epimeleia heautou*, which stood for the psychological and intellectual condition of being interested in taking care of one's self, of work on the self.[58] The term equally described the responsibilities of power. *Epimeleia heautou* implied attention, knowledge, technique, a work of meditation that required understanding the necessities of the world, not imposed upon the individual by civil law or religious obligation, but rather as a choice about existence made by the individual who decided whether or not to care for the self, and thereby, to care for the world. Foucault pointed out that *epimeleia heautou* described a condition in which individuals "acted so as to give to their lives certain values [for] it was a question of making one's life into an object for a sort of knowledge, for a *techné*—for an art."[59]

Destruction art communicates the visual knowledge that may recuperate the materiality of life from the violent, discontinuous destructions that imperil survival. The body may be a tool in the *techné* of survival, and may function as a transit between agency and process, language, experience, and their objects to close the lesion between *techné* and *logia* (word, speech, or knowledge) that has inhered in the modern concept of technology.

I have proposed often that the primary communicating codes of the visual arts were transformed in the presentation of the body. The unprecedented achievement of the body as an active agent in art has been to visualize the perpetually shifting but mutually identifiable relations of power and need within the exchange of subject/object relations. When the body becomes the material support, subject, and content of art, it holds the possibility of shifting the determined and fixed relations demanded by the prior objective status of art into the interplay of subjectivities established and transmitted in body gestures, systems, and relations. The private body is used as formal material, subject matter, and content into which the experiences and institutions of the body politic are collapsed. In these terms, *the body holds the possibility for becoming both an aesthetic and a social sign that also commutes political power.* Lifton believes that the task of the artist is "to reveal the exquisite details of the experience of desymbolization" and "the breakdown of viable relationships with symbols and symbolic forms [that] is an impairment in the 'psychic action' of the 'formative process' . . . associated with severe manifestations of psychic numbing."[60] In destruction art, the body conveys the interdependent, interconnected, and contingent state of the individual and the collective in survival. That embodiment holds the potential to reconnect experience to the objects of that experience, and thereby to intervene in the destructive practices, institutions, and technologies that threaten extinction.

When faced with extinction, the artist must, if she or he takes responsibility for his or her trust, put art in the service of survival. This does not imply that all art must assume the task of destruction art, but it does mean that art has a particular social function that requires an ethical position on the question of survival, no matter what formal resolution that work finally assumes. I believe destruction art recovers the social force of art from instrumental reason and the economies of late capitalism, for it constantly reinscribes the profound significance of the survival of the body in the oppositions it deconstructs. Destruction art is a warning system, an aesthetic response to human emergency that occurs in the lapse between theory and practice in terminal culture; it presents the pain of bodies, the anxiety of minds, the epistemology of technology, the specious claims of ideology, the absence of ecological responsibility, the loss of human integrity and compassion, and the violence that structures both gender and sexual relations. Just as destruction art is the image of resistance in the form of an event, it is also an important means to survival that must be continuously explored.

# Shaved Heads and Marked Bodies: Representations from Cultures of Trauma (1993)[1]

## I

A multitude of representations and cultural productions emanate from social and political events located in, and imprinted with, trauma, the ancient Greek word for wound. These images and attendant behaviors constitute the aggregate visual evidence of the "cultures of trauma"—a phrase I want to introduce to denote traumatic circumstance manifest in culture—discernible at the intersection of aesthetic, political, and social experience.[2] While research in traumatogenesis has proliferated during the past two decades, few have examined the cultural formations that result from, and bear illustrative witness to, the impact on world societies of the ubiquitous wounds of trauma. Meditating on the history of trauma, British psychiatrist Michael R. Trimble observed that its "etiology and pathogenesis . . . remains *invisible*" [emphasis added].[3] Yet, however invisible its origin and development, the cultural signs of trauma are *highly visible* in images and actions that occur both within the conventional boundaries of visual art and in the practices and images of everyday life. This essay explores two of these sites: shaved heads and marked bodies.

Trauma may be defined concisely as "an emotional state of discomfort and stress resulting from (unconscious and conscious) memories of an extraordinary, catastrophic experience that shatter the survivor's sense of invulnerability to harm."[4] War, with its institutions and practices, is a ubiquitous source of trauma. But the genesis of trauma is not limited to the effects of war, since the abuse of bodies destroys identity and leaves results parallel to war and its consequences. For several centuries, trauma was diagnosed as neurosis.[5] But the term "post-traumatic neurosis," used to describe the symptoms of shell-shocked World War I veterans, was changed to "post-traumatic stress disorder" (PTSD) in 1980 when the symptoms of Korean and Vietnam war veterans began to be diagnosed as stress. This diagnosis refers to a heterogeneous group of causes with a homogeneous set of behaviors: disassociation; loss of memory coupled with repetitive, intrusive, and often disguised memories of the original trauma; rage; addictive disorders; somatic complaints; vulnerability; guilt; isolation; alienation; detachment; reduced responsiveness; inability to feel safe or to trust; and numbing.[6] Causes include war; shock; concentration camp experiences; rape, incest, and sexual abuse; racism; shocks related to natural disasters or accidents; prolonged periods of domination, as in hostage and prisoner-of-war situations; and the brutal psychological conditions perpetrated by some religious cults. I do not want to suggest that the omnipresence of trauma means that all traumatic experiences are the same. But if one considers the genocide of Armenians, Cambodians, Indians and Pakistanis, Bosnians, Rwandans, Kurds, Sudanese, or African Americans in the United States; or the cultural influence of the disappeared among Argentinians, Chileans, El Salvadorians, or Brazilians; or the boat people of Vietnam and Haiti; or multigenerational survivors of the Holocaust,[7] the Russian gulag, and the Chinese Cultural Revolution, then the occurrence and advance of trauma is staggering and global. Indeed, the world's approximately forty million refugees, most of whom are women and children, offer a material image of trauma. If the capitals of the cultures of trauma were identified, they would be the second largest city in Pakistan or the third largest city in Malawi, both of which are refugee camps![8]

At the nexus of the cultures of trauma is the highly celebrated new world order, which began not with the fall of the Berlin Wall in 1989, but with the ethos of the Holocaust and nuclear age. The epoch of the Cold War and its aftermath might be understood as an age of trauma in which threats increase exponentially, especially with the grim reality of the thriving global business in weapon-grade plutonium and enriched uranium contraband, and of such nuclear industry disasters as Three Mile Island (1975) and Chernobyl (1986) [and, since this essay first appeared in 1993, Fukushima Daiichi in 2011].[9] The US response to the so-called rape of Kuwait in the Gulf War (1990–91) was perhaps itself as much an excuse to dismantle Iraq's nuclear weapons capacity as to restore Kuwait's sovereignty [again, wars in Iraq (2003–10) and Afghanistan (2001–present) have been fought for similar justifications]. Where such continuous peril exists, trauma is constant. The task is to undermine its invisibility. For its concealed conditions and silence are the spaces in which the destructions of trauma multiply.

This essay considers two sites within the cultures of trauma. "Shaved heads" are a representation referring both to an image and to a style, resulting from a wide variety of social and political experiences outside of the context of the visual arts. "Marked bodies" are a representation pertaining to the performative paradigm that developed within society and the visual arts, an aesthetic practice that is rooted deeply in cultures of trauma in accordance with larger political frames of destruction and violence.

## II

*Image I*: The community gathered in French towns and villages to shear her head with animal clippers and then smear the sign of the swastika in soot on her bald forehead (figure 5). The citizens judged her a "horizontal collaborator" for having sex with German soldiers during World War II. Denigrated and

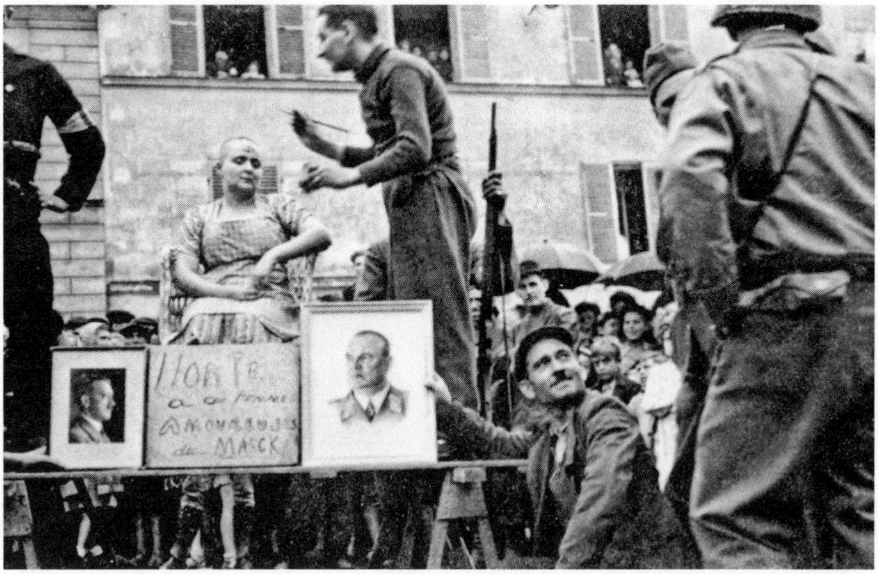

FIGURE 5. In the immediate aftermath of the liberation of Paris, a woman accused of some form of collaboration with the Germans, which may have ranged from political or financial to personal and sexual, is forcibly having her head shaved and a swastika painted on her forehead. In the foreground is a photograph of Hitler, a photograph of an unidentified man, and a poster declaring, "Shame on these women who love the Marck." ("Marck" was French slang for Germans, and a pun on the name of German currency.) Paris, France, 1944. © LAPI / Roger-Viollet / The Image Works.

denounced as a whore, she was even stripped naked, sometimes before being paraded through town, a token of the emblematic territories, defamations, and controls of war. She remained solitary amidst the molesting, persecuting assembly, exiled in a particularly sordid historical moment in a throng of her countrymen and women.

Horizontal collaborators served as metonymic signifiers for the "vertical collaborators" who, under the Vichy government, maintained an upright appearance while they capitulated to the Germans, raised their hands in the Nazi salute, and welcomed "the New Europe" into their beds. These women with shaved heads were used as communal purgatives, scapegoats for the French who themselves had whored for jobs in Germany, for extra food, and for peacetime amenities, especially during the years 1940 to 1943. In 1944 and 1945, photographers Robert Capa and Carl Mydans documented the terrible brutality to women accused of sexual collaborations with the Germans; Alain Renais referred to such incidents in *Hiroshima Mon Amour* (1959), and Marcel Ophüls included documents of one such incident in the town of Clermont-Ferrand in his film *The Sorrow and the Pity* (1969).[10] Female collaborators whose crimes were not sexual were not treated with the same kind of corporeal violations as were the horizontal collaborators whose primary sedition was to have slept with the enemy. The ritual scrutiny by French communities of the intimate affairs and bodies of "their" women suggest that these women's crime was vulvic, the vaginal betrayal of the patrimonial body of the state. The assault on, and psychological domination of, the female body and the photographic and filmic records "taken" or "shot" of her, on display on communal viewing stands, all typify physical and scopic aggression linked to sexuality, especially sanctioned in the "theater of war."[11] War condones and ritualizes the destruction and occupation of territories and bodies. Marked as properly owned by the community, the women whose heads were shaved confirm feminists' observations that wars are fought for, among other things, privileged use of the bodies of women.[12]

The visual discourse of the phallocratic order may be seen in the shaved female head, the site where rule by the phallus joins power to sexuality.[13] Phallic rule is fundamental in cultures of trauma and forms the nexus between war and sexual abuse, a site where assaults on the body and identity produce similar traumatic symptoms. In *Shattered Selves: Multiple Personality in a Postmodern World*, political theorist James M. Glass argues that the justification for taking women issues from the same "perversion of power and the arrogance of patriarchal assumptions over the possession of women." This is the same kind of "sadism and power, used to inflict harm," that results in incest and other kinds of sexual abuse. He concludes that "to the extent that power moves beyond its ordered field and beyond its respect for the lives and bodies of others . . . [it] is not much different from political forms of power which define sovereignty as the infliction of harm, the punishment of bodies, and the depletion of life."[14]

Nowhere is this conjunction more agonizing than in the testimony of Bok Dong Kim, a Korean military comfort woman (*jugun ianfu*), one of the many Asian women abducted for sexual service during World War II by the Imperial Army under the name of the Japanese emperor. Kim testified about war crimes against women on June 15, 1993, at the Center for Women's Global Leadership during the International Conference on Human Rights in Vienna. She explained that after her body was unable to continue to provide sexual services for as many as fifty soldiers a day, her blood was used in transfusions for the wounded. The comfort woman provided the furniture of sex, and her body, when broken, became a mere blood bag from whose veins the life of one woman was drained into the health of many men. The ferocity of her experience is unbearable and is related to the pornography made of the rapes of Bosnian women who were conquered as territory, possessed, and displayed.[15]

Hélène Cixous and Catherine Clement, French feminist theorists, identify the "intrinsic connection . . . between the philosophical, the literary . . . and the phallocentric," which, they argue, is a bond "constructed on the premise of woman's abasement [and] subordination of the feminine to the masculine order."[16] Shaved heads signify humiliation, a visual manifestation of a supralineal condition of domination and power that joins war and violence to the abuses of rule by the phallus. The doctrine of male hegemony is global and founded in the texts of organized world religions. In the Judeo-Christian tradition, this instrument is the Bible:

> I want you to know that the head of every man is Christ; the head of a woman is her husband; and the head of Christ is the Father. Any man who prays or prophesies with his head covered brings shame upon his head. Similarly, any woman who prays or prophesies with her head uncovered brings shame upon her head. It is as if she had had her head shaved. Indeed, if a woman will not wear a veil, she ought to cut her hair. If it is shameful for a woman to have her hair cut off or her head shaved, it is clear that she ought to wear a veil. A man, on the other hand, ought not to cover his head, because he is the image of God and the reflection of his glory. Woman, in turn, is the reflection of man's glory. Man was not made from woman but woman from man. Neither was man created for woman but woman for man. For this reason a woman ought to have a sign of submission on her head, because of the angels. (Corinthians I 11:1–16)

The above citation from the New Testament is anticipated in the Old Testament:

> The Lord said: Because the daughters of Zion are haughty, and walk with necks outstretched ogling and mincing as they go, their anklets tinkling with every step, the Lord shall cover the scalps of Zion's daughters with scabs, and the Lord shall bare their heads. On that day the Lord will do away with the finery of the anklets, sunbursts, and crescents; the pendants, bracelets, and veils; the headdresses, bangles, cinctures, perfume boxes, and amulets; the signet rings, and the nose rings; the court dresses, wraps, cloaks, and purses; the mirrors, linen tunics, turbans, and shawls. Instead of perfume there will be stench, instead of the girdle, a rope, and for the coiffure, baldness; for the rich gown, a sackcloth skirt. Then, instead of beauty: Your men will fall by the sword, and your champions, in war; her gates will lament and mourn, as the city sits desolate on the ground. (Isaiah 3:16–26)

This passage recasts the theme of women's culpability in the original fall from grace. Here the vanity and narcissism with which she is charged are cited as the source for the demise of men in war by the sword. He shall check her haughty and seductive ways, the Lord God, who shall mete punishment upon her body in the form of scabs, stench, and baldness.

The French were not alone in shaving the heads of women who slept with the enemy. Bertolt Brecht recorded similar proprietary national interests, rights, and rites regarding the sexuality of German women in his poem "Ballade von der 'Judenhure' Marie Sanders" (Ballad of Marie Sanders, the Jew's Whore; 1934–36). Brecht wrote that Marie Sanders, a woman from Nuremburg, was "driven through the town in her slip, round her neck a sign, her hair all shaven . . . ."[17] Her crime was to have slept with a Jew.

In yet another context, African-American novelist Ishmael Reed summons the specter of a shaved head in his book *Reckless Eyeballing*. This time, however, the image refers to the war between the races. Advocating shaving the heads of black feminist writers whom he accuses of collaborating with white feminists,

Reed growls, "They deserve what they get. Cut off their hair. . . ."[18] Reed charges black feminists with acting on behalf of white men in whose name white feminists serve to emasculate black men: "To turn the afro man into an international scapegoat . . . showing black dudes as animalistic sexual brutes." Reed's rage lives in the "colonialist program" identified by Frantz Fanon, in which "the woman [is given] the historic mission of shaking up the man"—a strategy described by Gayatri Spivak as "brown women saved by white men from brown men."[19] Reed detested any association with the architects of colonization, white men, whom he labeled "the biggest cannibals [who] have cannibalized whole civilizations[;] they've cannibalized nature, they'd even cannibalize their own mothers."[20]

Reed's diatribe, coupled with his misogynistic advice to shave black women's heads, offers a multifarious view of the convoluted manifestations of rule by the phallus. Kinship, race, or national identity, for Reed, resolves the question of sexual access to female bodies, and entry into them is determined by war, colonization, enslavement, incest, and rape. Here the Bible offers instruction, complete with shaved heads:

> *Marriage with a Female Captive.* When you go out to war against your enemies and the Lord, your God, delivers them into your hand, so that you take captives, if you see a comely woman among the captives and become so enamored of her that you wish to have her as wife, you may take her home to your house. But before she may live there, she must shave her head and pare her nails and lay aside her captive's garb. After she has mourned her father and mother for a full month, you may have relations with her, and you shall be her husband and she shall be your wife. However, if later on you lose your liking for her, you shall give her her freedom, if she wishes it; but you shall not sell her or enslave her, since she was married to you under compulsion. (Deuteronomy 21:10–14)

The doctrine of privileged right to women, especially "comely" women, mandated in Deuteronomy, has chilling social reverberations in Reed's text. But it also has demoralizing parallels in cultural practices. For example, the 1973 film *Soylent Green*, directed by Richard Fleischer, depicts a ravaged and famine-ridden chaotic New York in the year 2022, a warlike environment in which every luxury, from strawberry jam to "comely" women, is guarded jealously.[21] Beautiful women are assigned to apartments as furniture and are provided for only as long as the incoming male tenant agrees to continue to rent them—or, in the language of Deuteronomy: "if later on you lose your liking for her, you shall give her her freedom. . . ." Moreover, Thorn West (Carlton Heston) refers to Shirl (Leigh Taylor-Young) as a "hell of a piece of furniture" and as being "like a grapefruit," both metaphors interchangeable with the ways in which the actual bodies of the comfort women mentioned earlier were used as furniture and nutrient. But while women are without question the majority of those who suffer the rule of the phallus, this fact does not abrogate the reality that men, too, may be and are abased in phallocracy. Few more striking and unpredictable examples of such men exist in this constellation than the skinhead.

Skinheads derived their look in part from identification with "West Indian immigrants and the white working class," James Ridgeway explains in his horrifying history of the rise of a new white racist culture.[22] Dick Hebdige adds that it was "those values conventionally associated with white working-class culture which had been eroded by time that were rediscovered embedded in [the black musical culture of] ska, reggae, and rocksteady."[23] Prevented from participating in white male power and privilege because of their class and lack of education, skins adapted an appearance of marginality with respect to Western systems of power. They also condensed a stunning array of different cultural and political sites and meanings into an image. The result was a representation of absolute brute force, signified by the shaved head but also by such articles of clothing as black army-surplus combat boots and camouflage gear.

Skins visualized interconnected networks of brutality ordinarily categorized as different in culture. These include the hardened countenance of the military man under whose sign society contracts death; the veneer of the outlaw, or prisoner of ball, chain, and spiked collar, whose transgressions bar him from the privilege to kill; the demented, dangerous, unpredictable mental patient shaved and lobotomized; an image of ravaged and diseased bodies, radiated and suffering; and, finally, the debased aspect of the concentration camp Jew, the ultimate picture of oppression.[24] The image of the skinhead contains the powerful and the abject, the oppressor and the oppressed, the killer and the killed.[25]

Skins would seem to differ from the women with shaved heads cited above because they appear to be the agents in the reconstruction of their own identity. To a certain degree, they are. But agency depends upon a more complex set of relations that involve not only personal will but social forces. Thus, the constitution of an image like that of the skins that is aimed at vitiating the impression of helplessness and powerlessness succeeds better in betraying and reinforcing the locus of its identity in the trauma of that threat.

Toni Morrison addresses this seeming paradox when she points out how the United States is simultaneously a "nation of people who decided that their worldview would combine agendas for individual freedom," and the "mechanism for devastating racial oppression."[26] Morrison thus demonstrates how such apparent paradoxes are better understood as the reciprocal ways in which different languages, cultural representations, social and political institutions, and races and sexualities comprise identity. Morrison's deconstruction of this intertextuality offers further access to the links shared by the black Ishmael Reed and white skinheads. "The Africanist character," she writes, becomes a "surrogate [who] enables . . . whites to think about themselves . . . to know themselves as not enslaved, but free; not repulsive, but desirable; not helpless, but licensed and powerful; not history-less, but historical; not damned, but innocent; not a blind accident of evolution, but a progressive fulfillment of destiny."[27]

Skinheads live contradiction. Their social experience is to be enslaved, repulsive, helpless, and damned, and to belong to the very group that has a history and a promise of fulfillment in which they cannot share. This paradox is also the foundation for the anger that incited the dispossessed French in World War II, for Reed's rage, and for the skins' lethal frustration—a fury that takes its revenge upon the bodies of the women proclaimed their own. This delusion of possession helps to explain why the image of a happy coupling between a white woman and a black man is described in a 1981 Aryan Nation flyer as "the ultimate abomination." For if nothing else belongs to the British or American (French/German/Japanese/African/Serbian/Iraqi, etc.) skinhead, socially fucked by other men, he alone will fuck a woman's white/black/brown/yellow/red body.[28] The vicious retaliation of the skinhead unfolds within the epistemological spaces insured by white male hegemony, a phallic rule in which his virility becomes merely a caricature unmasking the reality of his impotence, a lack derived from the fact that he actually cohabitates the same disempowered spaces as do women and all other dominated peoples. His inadequacy sustains his obsession with white supremacy, in which, fortified by emblematic images of superiority and power, he attempts to exercise the authority of which he has been deprived.

All of these shaved heads inhabit the visual memory of culture, a memory of the history of war, domination, and colonization across whose pages bodies reach back to the Old and New Testaments and forward to the white power of skinheads, the youth para-military arm of ultraconservative groups whose theology is based on scripture and who act out of a belief in their divine right to be on top, where power and sexual abuse fire the cultures of trauma. "Organization by hierarchy makes all conceptual organization subject to man," Cixous and Clement write; and that organization "is located in the logocentric orders that guarantee the masculine order a rationale equal to history itself."[29]

## III

*Image II:* In the performance *Test of Sleep*, Amalia (Lia) Perjovschi, a Romanian artist, covers her body with white paint over which she inscribes a complex sequence of symbols resembling hieroglyphic marks, untranslatable signs, a visual language that she then animates with gestures deployed in silence; hand, arm, leg, and full-body signals enacted in her home before her husband, the only witness (figure 6). Perjovschi's principal means of communication, beyond the direct, but silent, intimate liaison with her husband, artist Dan Perjovschi, is through photographs, documents that he—as husband, collaborator, and beholder—recorded. Her action took place in 1988, one of the darkest years of Romanian captivity under the autocratic totalitarianism of Nicolae and Elena Ceauşescu, who were assassinated on December 25, 1989. In 1993, in Timisoara, site of the Romanian revolution, Eastern European artists gathered for the performance festival *Europe Zone East*. Dan Perjovschi's action was to sit silently while the word "Romania" was tattooed on his upper left forearm (figure 7).[30]

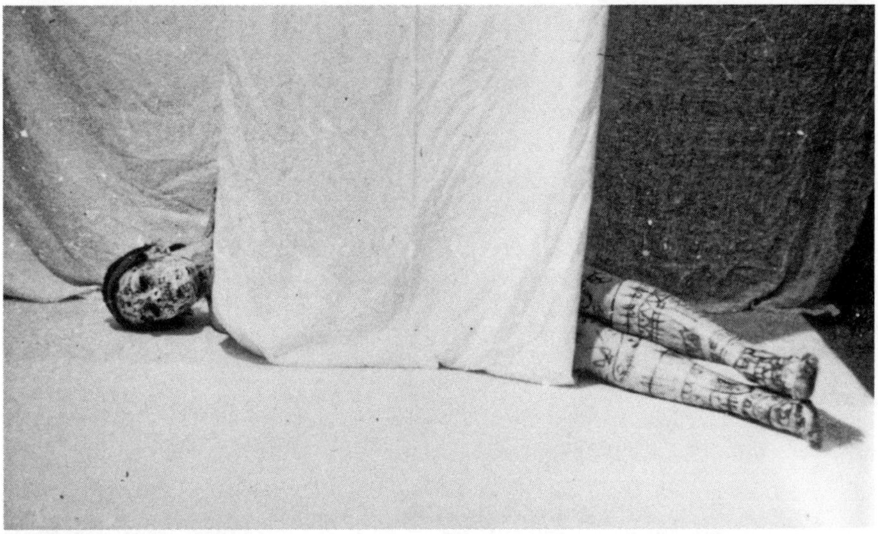

FIGURE 6. Lia Perjovschi, *Test of Sleep*, 1988. Body action in the artist's flat, apartment #53, Italiana Street 22, Block Y3, Oradea, Romania. Photograph by Dan Perjovschi. Courtesy of the artist.

While shaved heads provided visual access and insight into the linkage between power and sexuality that contributes to the construction of cultures of trauma, Lia and Dan Perjovschi's marked bodies enunciate the silence that is a rudiment of trauma and a source of the destruction of identity. Silence was maintained efficiently by the Romanian secret police, the Securitate, which enforced Nicolae Ceauşescu's crushing control. In large measure that organization was successful, through the sheer force of rumor and hearsay that numbered the Securitate, with its system of informers, at one in six Romanian citizens.[31] No one remained above suspicion. Fear and secrecy resulted in the effective supervision of all aspects of Romanian life. Stealth was augmented by reports of reprisals against challenges to authority, threats that were invigorated by actual punishments. Romanians endured their conditions, which were extreme even among nations of the former Soviet bloc, in isolation. Preventing its citizens from travel, the government retained Romanian passports and politically sequestered the nation from exchange with most of the world. Romania resembled a concentration camp especially in the 1980s, when Lia and Dan Perjovschi (both born in 1961) were in their twenties.[32]

While such coercion was the most obvious process by which Romanians were traumatized into obedience, a double bind, comprised of intense nationalism coupled with economic shortage, incapacitated the people into perceiving themselves absolutely dependent upon a government that they could not criticize without being labeled unpatriotic.[33] This paradoxical predicament reinforced what Katherine Verdery, a US anthropologist specializing in Romanian culture, calls the "symbolic-ideological" discourse in Romania, a discourse that utilizes "the Nation . . . as a master symbol."[34] Romanian debates over national

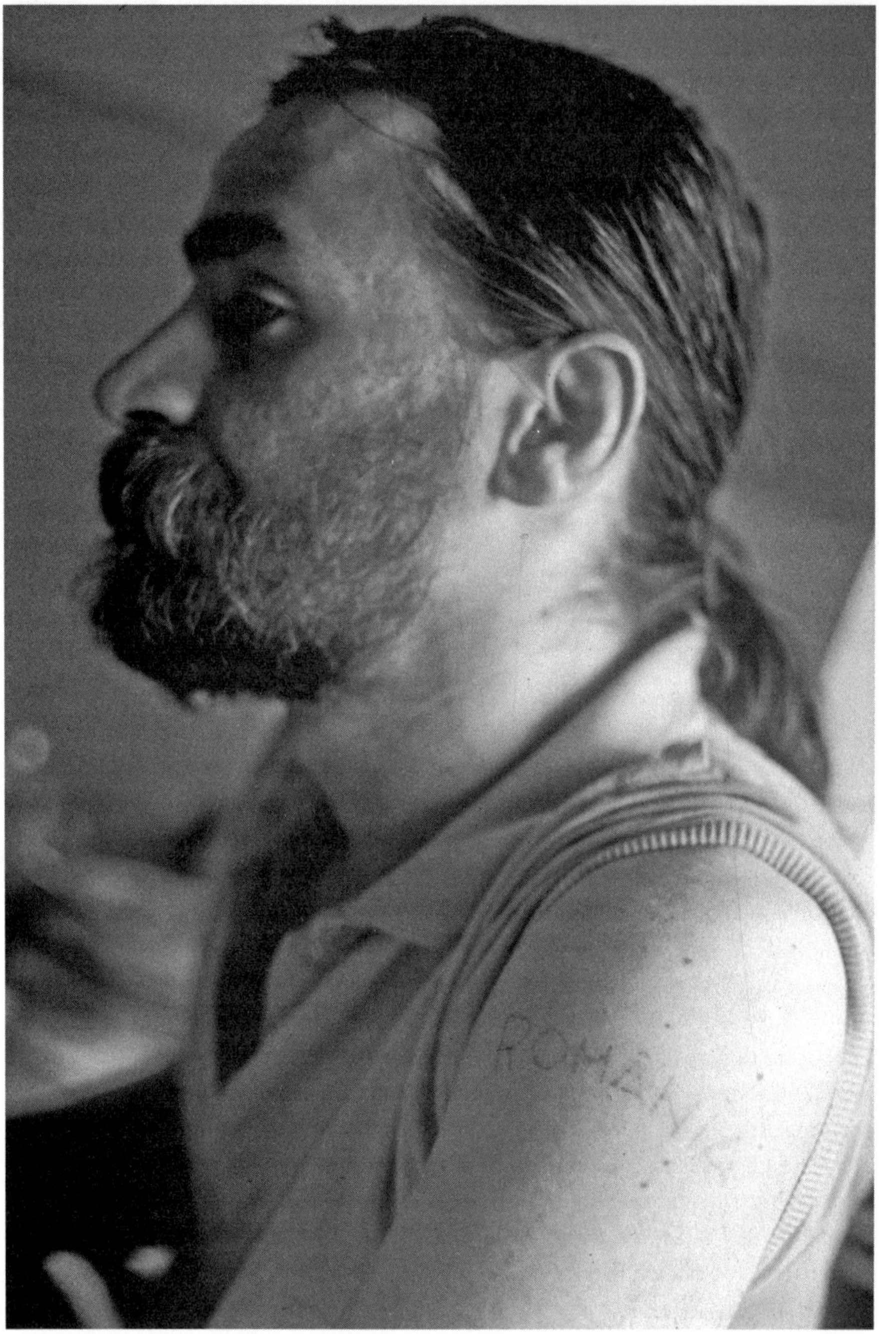

FIGURE 7. Dan Perjovschi, *Romania*, 1993. The artist is being tattooed during the performance festival "Zone 1: East Europe," curated by Ileana Pintilie at the Art Museum, Timisoara, Romania. In a performance in 2003, influenced in part by this essay, Perjovschi had the tattoo removed. Photograph by Lia Perjovschi. Courtesy of the artist.

identity rose to a fever pitch in the 1980s, especially with the programmatic decimation of Romanian traditional life, the destruction of villages, and the relocation of peasants and workers into bleak city block houses—all of which were part of a massive relocation and urbanization project that followed Ceauşescu's 1971 visit to North Korea, China, and North Vietnam during which he inaugurated a "'mini-cultural revolution' with renewed emphasis on socialist realism."[35]

The ambitious reconstruction of Romanian cities included the erection of high-rise apartment complexes in an idiosyncratic hybrid Korean-Chinese style imitative of the International style. In the redevelopment of Bucharest, especially between 1984 and 1989, some fifty thousand people lost their Beaux-Arts and Victorian homes to an unrivaled and infamous architectural complex that includes the vulgar Casa Poporului (House of the People), which was funded by Romanian taxes at the expense of all other civic, social, industrial, and agricultural projects. Like its historical antecedents, Ceauşescu's building campaign was aimed at a monolithic representation of power meant to arouse awe and complete compliance. An effective means of social control, the sterility of Casa Poporului and its surrounding buildings mirrored the repression of the Romanian's interior life.

But questions related to Romanian national identity did not originate in Ceauşescu's regime. They reside deep in Romanian history and consciousness, both of which have been split for centuries between the philosophical and teleological worldviews of the Occident and the Orient, as well as along the geographical political exigencies of North/South and East/West. Romanians trace their bipolarity to the occupation in 106–7 CE of the Roman Emperor Trajan, who invaded the ancient lands of the Carpatho-Danubian people, the Geto-Dacians. Since Neolithic times the Gateo of the lower Danube and the Dacians of the Carpathian mountains had inhabited what is now modern Romania. Such divisions make Romanians especially vulnerable to psychological fragmentation, and contribute to the renowned "distrust of all the cherished notions . . . of progress and history characteristic" of Balkan peoples, according to Andrei Codrescu, a Romanian expatriate poet living in the United States.[36] The historic rupture of Romanian national identity was reinforced in and is echoed by the shattering of personal identity under Ceauşescu. Verdery has recognized a "social schizophrenia" among Romanians that she has described as an ability to experience a "real meaningful and coherent self only in relation to the enemy party."[37]

The artist Ion Bitzan (1924–97), an admired professor of art at Nicolae Grigorescu Academia de Arta in Bucharest, provides a special example of this schism. Bitzan lived through the regimes of Stalin, Gheorghiu-Dej, and Ceauşescu. Under Stalin, Bitzan learned as a student that transgression was impossible. He remembered the painful "unmaskings" (his term) during which students denounced each other and their professors, denunciations accompanied by obligatory applause—the same obligatory applause required at the very mention of

Stalin's name.[38] Bitzan's terror was so deep, he remembered, that he felt "guilty for being human," and was afraid of "being an enemy of the party, an enemy of the State, an enemy of the Soviet Union."

In 1964 one of Bitzan's paintings was selected for inclusion in the Venice Biennale. A Socialist Realist work of "a lorie filled with wheat, a field worker, and a red flag in the corner," it had the socialist subject and style that, like the applause, was mandated. Bitzan felt his work was "perfect" because he had composed it precisely according to the rules for the Golden Section. When he traveled to Venice to attend the Biennale, however, he saw the assemblages and collages of Robert Rauschenberg, the American artist who received first prize there. Bitzan returned to Romania confused, disturbed, and embarrassed by his own art. He felt himself to be a provincial outsider, and was humiliated by the very painting of which he had been so proud.

Three years later, Bitzan began to make collages and constructions, and to fabricate exquisite handmade papers on which he wrote in a flowing and elegant, but secret and unreadable, personal language. He created these works, however, only in the privacy of his studio. In public, he continued to paint in a Socialist Realist style. Like many Romanian artists, he capitulated to Ceauşescu's frequent requests to paint "Him" or "Her"—the terms Romanians used for Nicolae and Elena. For his compliance, Bitzan earned money, prestige in the Art Academy, and the right to travel. He "sold" himself, "but only for an hour or so a day when I worked on their pictures," he later insisted. The rest of the time, he turned the canvases of Him or Her—emblems of his repression—to the wall and returned to his secret life. In telling this story for the first time, Bitzan became, in his own words, "ashamed," and left the room. I, too, felt shame, as my interview had taken the familiar form of an interrogation. Before contributing to and witnessing Bitzan's humiliation, I had been sheltered from understanding the interview form of discourse as a persecuting interrogative.

Bitzan's private collages, handmade papers, artist's books, and indecipherable texts are all a microcosm of the conflict that characterized Romanian artists' conduct, their need to invent alternative languages and to make hidden private works. Verdery's observation about Romanians' "social schizophrenia" is related to Bitzan's experience. Comments by a number of Romanians confirm her view. Alexandra Cornilescu, a linguist from Bucharest University, has noted that survival in Romania depends upon "hedging."[39] Hedging means that one cultivates the ability to live multiple lives. Romanians have learned to say one thing and mean something else, to speak in layered codes impenetrable to informers and often even confusing to friends, and to use their eyes and gestures as if they were words. (Or, as Andrei Codrescu confessed, "I lie in order to hide the truth from morons.")[40] "Repressive discourse," Cornilescu continued, "gradually developed towards a rigid inventory of permissible topics; religion, non-dogmatic philosophy or political theories, poverty, prisons, concentration camps, political dissidents, unemployment, sex, etc., were, as many taboo topics, unmentionable and, largely, unmentioned in repressive discourse."

Nothing is more pernicious in the "discourse of fear" than the problem identified by Cornilescu when she writes that in Romania, "if an object/person/phenomenon is not named, then it does not exist." With the word "Romania" emblazoned on the surface of his body, Dan Perjovschi staked the authenticity of his existence on a name. His tattoo divulges the dependence of his identity upon his country, a territory marked by centuries of uncertainty and the challenged, manipulated, and traumatized conditions in which he and his fellow Romanians lived. But his tattoo is also an indeterminate sign signifying the synchronicity of a visible wound and a mark of honor. A symbol of resistance and icon of marginality, it is a signature of capture, a mask that both designates and disguises identity. As a signifier for the charged complexity of Romanian national identity, the tattoo brands Dan Perjovschi's body with the arbitrary geographical identity agreed upon by governments, and it displays the ambiguous psychological allegiances such boundaries inevitably commit to the mind.

Dan Perjovschi's action-inscription also conveys some of the content of the accreted spaces of Romanian suffering and guilt—guilt he addressed when he explained that in Romania, where both prisoners and citizens habitually were transformed into perpetrators, guilt and innocence intermingle inseparably. And he asked, "Who may point a finger?" Similarly, Judith Lewis Herman describes the process by which incest victims are silenced and made to become complicit in their own abuse: "Terror, intermittent reward, isolation, and enforced dependency may succeed in creating a submissive and compliant prisoner. But the final step in the psychological control of the victim is not completed until she[/he] has been forced to violate her[/his] own moral principles and to betray her[/his] basic human attachments. Psychologically, this is the most destructive of all coercive techniques, for the victim who has succumbed loathes herself[/himself]. It is at this point, when the victim under duress participates in the sacrifice of others, that she[/he] is truly 'broken.'"[41] Only in the 1990s did such experiences begin to be verbalized in Romanian discourse. Cornilescu explains that in the media, terms such as "survival," "nightmares," and "shock therapy" appear increasingly as metaphors describing the past and referring to the current transitional period. Such words comprise the language of trauma and provide new textual evidence of the stress that punctuates the Romanian imagination.

But Romanian silences must be understood in the context of silences that result from terror threatened by the situation and its perpetrator(s), from the repressed silences shielding victims from the pain of memory, and from the "robotization" that results from chronic captivity.[42] These silences represent only some of a host of traumatic silences. All these conditions lead to what many researchers describe as the "conspiracy of silence," a complex environment that culminates in the silence remembered by Holocaust, incest, and rape survivors.[43] Herman proposes that the shame, fear, and horror that the traumatized experience is augmented by public denial of trauma; and even the behavior of mental health professionals, who "listen too long and too carefully to traumatized patients, often become suspect among their colleagues as though contaminated by contact."[44]

Romanians feel contaminated. This emotion is embedded in journalistic metaphors that refer to Romania as a "dead" or "diseased body, [an] organism . . . undergoing some form of therapy . . . severe pain . . . nightmares," and in need of "shock therapy." Such "therapy" is administered in a collage created by Romanian artist Ion Grigorescu. In a black-and-white photomontage, overpainted and decorated with collage elements in gold foil, Grigorescu depicted himself as Saint George slaying a dragon. Entitling the work *Bine si Rau* (Good and Evil; 1986), Grigorescu montaged two photographs of himself together to create a composite image of a conqueror and a vanquished figure. In the image, Grigorescu appears to leap over the figure, who bends over a large boulder. The vaulting Grigorescu plunges a huge wooden stake through the back of the bent figure, killing the dragon that turns out to be himself. Driving the stake into his own back, Grigorescu spills his own blood; it gushes from his self-inflicted wound and pours over the rock that breaks his fall.

Set against the backdrop of a landscape image around this striking scene, the murder takes place in what appears to be a room, an architectural space created when the artist drew faint lines of gold ink that traced the perspectival space of a box. On one of the room's transparent walls, Grigorescu reproduced an image he appropriated from a representation of the Last Judgment, in which "an angel steps on a dying rich miser," and above which the hand of the angel reaches down to pull the figure up by his hair, "seiz[ing] his soul."[45] Grigorescu interprets this moment as a representation of his own soul being rescued to heaven, and writes: "In visual art, I is representing We. I use it (I) to teach this. 'To love the other like yourself,' the corollary is to forgive the other, given (forgiven) my own ambivalence." Above these two images, a tiny collage in silver foil is of Saint George on his horse, with a spear topped by a cross. In the top left corner is a semicircle representing "an opening in the sky wherefrom a hand holds the balance of the judgment." In this work, Grigorescu collapses self-sacrifice into the martyrdom of Romania. Visually comparing his own suffering to that of a sacrificed Christian, driving the stake through his own heart, Grigorescu dashes the evil of the split self, and sheds his blood on the rock that suggests Saint Peter's church.

The recollection of the Roman Catholic faith draws the Occident into this dramatic scene of violence. Internal repression and external invasion commingle across the territories of power, faith, self-sacrifice, violence, guilt, and martyrdom. These complex threads weave through Grigorescu's image of pain as visual witness to a conflict in which all are implicated. Inside individual subjectivity, and outside the social and political world of competing ideologies and teleologies, Grigorescu confesses his own culpability. Such a representation gains even more force as an authentic image of Romanian social and psychological experience when it is considered in light of the observation that Romanians "resist anything that resembles the construction of state power [yet] simultaneously . . . live with internalized expectations of a state that is paternalistic, that frees them of the necessity to take initiative or worry about their pay checks, hospital bills, pensions, and the like. They simultaneously blame the state for everything and expect the state to resolve everything [in an] . . . amalgam of accusation and expectation."[46] Grigorescu's collage becomes even more compelling when one learns that he produced these photographic self-portraits in private, performing a ritual exorcism in secret, a furtiveness demanded by the political exigencies of the period.

Such hidden performances recall other actions Grigorescu did alone, before the gaze of his own camera. A self-portrait from 1975, for example, features another striking image of the martyred artist, this time with a crown of thorns encircling his neck. Another self-portrait shows him with an elongated neck, over which the image of the Egyptian King Tutankhamun's renowned coffin is superimposed. In another series of autoportraits, Grigorescu created body actions in his own living quarters. One series, entitled *The Tongue* (ca. 1973–75), pictures only a mouth, teeth, and a tongue, gaping wide in a clear invocation of a scream. The choking, silently screaming, entombed self-image offers another representation of Romanian self-recrimination, guilt, anger, futility, and suffering. "Sufferance" was a term Cornilescu also used in her discussion of textual practices in the contemporary Romanian press. Suffering cohabits the silences that, as literary theorist Elaine Scarry argues, "actively destroy" language in a process that brings about "an immediate reversion to a state anterior to language."[47]

In *Test of Sleep*, Lia Perjovschi conjures that anterior state. As the apparatus of the dream condenses and displaces meaning, so Romanian silence registered existence as somnambulant. "Everyone in Romania silently calls out loudly," Lia said. "I wanted to draw attention to that inner life, to make it possible for people to understand it without words." Even the title of her action *Test of Sleep* offers textual access to the blocked layers of the performative unconscious available in sleep. Sanda Agalidi, a Romanian artist and expatriate living in the United States, has also summoned the idea of sleep in relation to Romanian social reality. Agalidi writes about the "determined will" necessary to maintain aspects of the estranged self, to create an "alternative language": "as the words awaken, [the] bad world falls asleep."[48] In both artists' metaphors, the silence of sleep parallels repression but also approximates a space within which a different language may be formed, a language that Lia described as the "discrete communication" she enacted in *Test of Sleep*. Mikhail Bakhtin, a victim of Stalin's despotism, might have compared Lia Perjovschi's corporeal narrative to the heteroglossia of the oppressed who long to speak for themselves. Bakhtin observed that all social life is an ongoing struggle between the attempt of power to impose a uniform language and the attempt of those below to speak in their own dialects (heteroglossia).[49] The struggle between the multiplicity of internal voices and the monolithic voice of external authority breeds trauma.

## IV

Many theorists of postmodernism celebrate schizophrenia, or decentered fragmentation, as the cultural sign of postmodern political resistance to holistic models of self and society associated with the hegemony of the humanist paradigm.[50] My personal experience, knowledge of Romania, and scholarship all support different conclusions, for such theories fail as viable theoretical constructs when they are called upon to address the actual experiences of Romanians. James M. Glass, who believes that the textual critique of postmodern resistance to unicity is not only "naive but dangerous," has argued similar conclusions. Such theories collapse before the actual conditions that people with trauma suffer; postmodern interpretations of schizoanalysis cannot account for or move toward healing the terrible incapacitating fragmentation and the agonizing internal struggle for the unity without which it is impossible to survive trauma and function. Glass asks, "Is it not equally as important to understand and interpret the world from the point of view of the victims themselves?"[51] Scarry approaches this question from a slightly different position. She insists that trauma sometimes causes so much suffering that "the person in pain is . . . [so] bereft of the resources of speech . . . that the language for pain should sometimes be brought into being by those who are not themselves in pain but who speak on behalf of those who are."[52] Yet while trauma may be so severe that victims might require someone other than themselves to speak, recovery depends upon victims speaking for themselves.

Mute, but gesturing, Lia Perjovschi wrote the language of internal spaces on the surface of her own body—words that, although reversed and unreadable, narrated her private suffering. Speechless and immobile, his body imprinted with an inscription, Dan Perjovschi documented the interdependence of the psyche, identity, and ideology in history. The couple's art provides ocular witness to, and gestural voice for, the prolonged psychological, intellectual, and physical oppression that transformed Romania into a culture of trauma. Through their signifying bodies, they suggest means to express "the corporeal threat in social and political experience [and] the inexorable human link between subject and subject."[53] In performances such as theirs, the body and its languages may transform victimization into personal agency. "Write yourself," Helene Cixous declared. "Your body must make itself heard."[54]

"The systematic study of psychological trauma depends on the support of a political movement," Herman has argued—a movement "powerful enough to legitimate an alliance between investigators and patients to counteract the ordinary social processes of silencing and denial."[55] Lia and Dan Perjovschi contribute to such an alliance by producing cultural signs that convert invisible pain into images that can be shared with, and scrutinized by, the public. Such actions impart the visual language of survivors and, however specific to Romania, they remain paradigmatic of the kinds of representations that are found in cultures of trauma. Analysis of the regularization of trauma is of pressing importance and may advance understanding of its human consequences. Marked bodies and shaved heads visualize the aggregate forms of suffering. Should we learn to recognize them, we may reform. But I am not optimistic.

## AFTERWORD

Two years after this essay was first published, I lectured widely on its subject in the United States and abroad. Three questions were repeatedly asked after each lecture:

1. Why, if I choose to shave my own head or tattoo my own body, is this not an act of self-empowerment, a wresting of my own fate and identity from historical antecedents?
2. Can it be said that all historical examples of shaved heads and tattooed bodies conform to your paradigm and are "representations from cultures of trauma?"
3. Is there implicit in your argument a value judgment, moral or ethical, of people who elect to have their heads shaved or their bodies tattooed?

The frequency with which especially women (though not exclusively women) posed these questions necessitates a response.

With reference to the first question, my interlocutors' cross-examination was urgent. Women have insisted that by choosing to shave their own heads, they have refused to surrender to classical representations of female beauty and have "taken control" of their own representation and self-image. The shaved head, they insist, is a sign of personal agency, of resistance, of independence from the paradigm of the erotic woman. They have seized power from history; they persist. Women of all age groups, sexual preferences, class, race, and education have made this argument. The aggressiveness with which this view is avowed is typified by a remark made to me by three different women, on three different occasions, in three different US cities. Each one said she could "see me being shot" for my views. Obviously, something deeply critical to a woman's sense of self and personal agency is at stake.

Especially since the mid-1970s in Western culture, alternative groups have celebrated and practiced body modification. Tattooing, multiple piercing, scarification, and head shaving have been on the rise and have become fashionable—even perceived as de rigueur and obligatory by some marginalized or self-selected alternative groups. Writing on behalf of such body modification, V. Vale and Andrea Juno, editors and publishers of *RE/Search* magazine, a celebrated and internationally distributed art journal, situated these practices "amidst an almost universal feeling of powerlessness to 'change the world'"; they insisted that body modification permits "individuals [to] change what they do have power over: their own bodies." They continued:

> A tattoo is more than a painting on skin; its meaning and reverberations cannot be comprehended without a knowledge of the history and mythology of its

bearer. . . . These body modifications perform a vital function identical with art: they 'genuinely stimulate passion and spring directly from the original sources of emotion, and are not something tapped from the cultural reservoir.' (Roger Cardinal) Here that neglected function of art, to *stimulate the mind*, is unmistakably *alive*. And all of these modifications bear witness to personal pain endured, which cannot be simulated.[56]

These comments suggest that to mark the self is to make of oneself a work of art, to exact agency and self-representation from history, and to be "alive," not "simulated"—in other words, to be not a product of what Vale and Juno characterize as "civilization" with its "stifling and life-thwarting logic." But the equation of primitivism with agency is, as Marianna Torgovnick correctly observes in *Gone Primitive*, "a modern and post-modern . . . version of the idyllic, utopian . . . wish for 'being physical' to be coextensive with 'being spiritual'; the wish for physical, psychological, and social integrity as a birthright, within familial and cultural traditions that both connect to the past and allow for a changing future."[57] Neither an individual nor individuated groups of self-selected people can escape the history of cultural tradition by merely claiming to have done so.

My point has been that the semiotic universe of signs and representations that Western culture inhabits pervades all its practices. Moreover, because of the might of Western economies, technologies, weapons development, and communication systems, Western culture permeates the globe, with its mark leaving its own tattoo on social practices around the world.[58] Resorting to fantasies of resistance and agency or imitations of the "primitive" cannot change this condition any more than attempts to refuse negative representations by denial can reverse the overdetermined meaning and legacy of these signs.

The allegation that representations may be recuperated—seized from the histories in which they originate and with which they are in dialogue—is misguided, and it becomes little more than inflammatory rhetoric in the publications of such writers as Camille Paglia.[59] Paglia's idol, Madonna, equally falls prey to these illusions. Madonna's book *Sex* is nothing if not a compendium of the most audaciously gullible, simplistic, immature, self-destructive, and ultimately exploitative assertions on behalf of the notion that anything goes—including sexism, racism, self-abuse, masochism, and sadism—as long as the perpetrator claims its value as self-representation.[60] To say this is not to "loathe Madonna," as Paglia claims that those who criticize Madonna do. I watch and listen to Madonna with the same fascination as anyone interested in the paradoxes and spectacles of entertainment culture; I even enjoy Madonna.

Paglia and Madonna are only the most flamboyant examples of those who claim to control all aspects of their representation. They are joined by numerous academics who theorize that both the construction and reception of conventional signs may be subverted by projections of self that emanate from a spectrum of individuated needs and desires ranging from the butch-femme aesthetic to the heterosexual straight, from blacks (Michael Jackson often the example offered here) to browns and whites.[61] Without belaboring the argument, my point is this: In an effort to posit agency outside of history, to escape history, a spurious kind of independence folds back on itself, creating a double indemnity; one has been damned to damn oneself. The effort to deny the interconnectedness of historical representations is akin to sleepwalking through time. It may be done, but at what expense?

While this response may seem to suggest a futility in altering history and asserting agency, the situation is not wholly unredeemable, even if I am pessimistic. What I do insist is that certain kinds of historically loaded representations cannot be reversed without a thorough understanding of their embeddedness in a complex overlapping cultural network of experiences, contexts, and conditions. That Ishmael Reed could advocate shaving the heads of black feminists who collaborate with white feminists might be related to the punishment of French women who slept with Germans during World War II and the penalties imposed on German women who slept with Jews during the same period. The fact that skinheads, who promote white supremacy, are also part of this matrix indicates a dense web of shared violence and ugliness that few imagine can be aggregate. The idea that a woman or a man who elects to shave her head also participates in this configuration is even more odious to him or her. I suppose this is why the three women who could "see" me "getting shot" for saying these things imagined such a violent reaction to my supposition: people share the space and continuity in time with this historical structure, despite their loftiest aims.[62]

The other two questions require only a brief response, and the answer to the second one is an emphatic "no." All generalizations are dangerous, and at the beginning of this essay I cautioned about the use of terms. The concept of trauma must be used judiciously. I offer it only as a model for examining cultural configurations and representations if one remembers not only the wide range of traumatic experience that is possible, but also the differences in intensity and duration between these experiences. Each trauma must be examined in and for itself; and in theorizing "cultures of trauma," I struggled to clarify that my examples are limited to themselves. Moreover, they are also limited to the Western Judeo-Christian tradition. I cannot and would not attempt to speak about pre-Columbian, African, or Asian instances of shaved heads, as I have been asked to do. But on the subject of monks, nuns, and other members of religious orders who shave their heads, it is prudent to point out that this practice usually signifies submission to a higher authority. That trauma is involved is entirely a different question.

Finally, in no way do I pass moral or ethical judgment on anyone who chooses to shave her or his head or wear a tattoo. Both my scholarship and artistic practice have been devoted to trying to understand the social structures and cultural representations that invent and perpetuate destruction and violence, that destroy and harm identity, that strip agency from human will, and that leave a legacy of despair in the world. Those are the subjects of this essay. To attempt to decode these structures by describing them is very different from passing judgment on individuals who, in their effort to resist these negative histories, may appropriate aspects of them. Rather, if there is a qualifying feeling that comes from my work, a personal opinion about the people who shave their heads or tattoo their bodies as signs of difference and self-empowerment, it is that I have empathy for the struggle.

In trying to make a contribution to that struggle, this essay aims to underscore the dangers of unconsciously perpetrating negative traditions. The examples of shaved heads and marked bodies were selected because of their contemporary popularity and the connections between the current historical moment and the histories and practices of Western culture. No argument is perfect. Mine is flawed. But these imperfections spring from an imagination that seeks to contribute to the construction of a more humane interaction and responsible relationship to history, the present, and the future.

# Remembering Invisibility: Documentary Photography of the Nuclear Age (1998)[1]

*We knew every feature of the terrain over which we would be flying. And now the Japanese landscape was unfolding below us just as the pictures had promised. . . . Our I.P. [initial point], an easily identifiable landmark that stood out in the aerial photos, was 15 1/2 miles east of the point in the heart of the city which was to be our target.*

PAUL W. TIBBETS, JR. *The Tibbets Story*[2]

## INTRODUCTION

Paul W. Tibbets flew the plane with a payload aimed at Hiroshima on August 6, 1945. The aerial photographs had been precise, and his target was as visible as the bomb was lethal. The explosion vaporized two hundred thousand people. The flash from the blast lasted one fifteen-millionth of a second, long enough for the light to tattoo the warp and woof of woven kimono fabric onto flesh. It also bleached the stairs around someone sitting at the entrance to the Sumitomo Bank 250 meters from the epicenter, leaving only a shadow of the atomized body on the pavement.[3] When Yoshito Matsushige, a thirty-two-year-old cameraman for the Hiroshima *Chugoku* newspaper, attempted to photograph the melee on Miyuku Bridge a few hours after the bomb was dropped, radiation speckled his film. Matsushige remembered the light of the bomb:

> I had finished breakfast and was getting ready to go to the newspaper when it happened. There was a flash from the indoor wires as if lightening had struck. I didn't hear any sound, how shall I say, the world around me turned bright white. And I was momentarily blinded as if a magnesium light had lit up in front of my eyes. Immediately after that, the blast came.[4]

Similarly, radiation burned the emulsion on Berlyn Brixner's film when, three weeks earlier, standing in the North Shelter some ten thousand feet from the explosion, he photographed Trinity, the first atomic test, detonated July 16, 1945, at Alamogordo Air Base in New Mexico.

The imprints of radiant energy certified a technological act, punctuated a turning point for humanity, and constituted undeniable evidence of the unprecedented capacity to annihilate life, a lethal power that would soon be augmented by the risks of nuclear energy and expanded weapons production. The imprints of the bomb's light resemble the heliographic "sun prints" first identified and explored by British potter Thomas Wedgwood just before 1800. In fact, the term "photography," coined by astronomer Sir John F. W. Herschel, came from the idea of "writing with light," the heliographic process that anticipated photography, ominously forecasting the atomic and nuclear technology that enabled the bomb to inscribe the index of war indelibly on Japanese bodies and cities.

Photography was also crucial to the precise targeting of the atom bombs that destroyed Hiroshima and Nagasaki—such that paradoxically, photography *of* the nuclear age is equally indispensable to addressing the violent threat of living *in* the nuclear age. I contend that photography can play a vital role in the survival of the planet by enabling the visual knowledge necessary for remembrance, the prerequisite for agency. Photography can represent the micro and macro conditions of the nuclear age, depict the hidden places and conditions of nuclear weapons manufacture and storage, and display nuclear energy industries, as well as record humans, animals, and the environment damaged by radiation and fallout. Yet, despite the wide range of photographs that depict the nuclear age, the unfathomable power and awesome beauty of the billowing mushroom cloud remains the icon of the age. A photograph, taken by an anonymous US government photographer, of shot Mike, a thermonuclear test conducted at Enewetak Atoll on November 1, 1952, is paradigmatic of the image that is indelibly imprinted in the minds and identities of billions of people on the planet. Yet, while the nuclear age and its images are a part of the psychological structure of populations throughout the world, and while its production, protection, and potential use shape global policies, the concomitant reality of its effects are repressed in the defense mechanisms of denial and disavowal. These dissociative behaviors only increase the imperceptibility of the nuclear age, resulting in psychic numbing and forgetfulness.

These unprecedented conditions and unequaled images need a new vocabulary in order to make them concrete and bring the impact and threat of the nuclear age back into the foreground of discussion and policy. I suggest *nucleography* for the unparalleled visual traces of the bomb's light, *nucleographic* for documentary photographs of the nuclear age, and *nucleocide* for that war that is its legacy, war that is ever in the process of becoming. The abstract prints of nucleography are the first visual records of the invisibility of radiation in the nuclear age. They are also what I would describe as a new kind of war in which bombs fall and light is discharged, not on a battlefield but in the circumstances of everyday life. The overt aggression of dropping such weapons directly on civilian populations has not been perpetrated again since the bombing of Hiroshima and Nagasaki—at least not in the same way. So then, what more is to be said about nucleographic images? I would argue that the prints made by the bombs' light are records situating nucleography as a branch of documentary

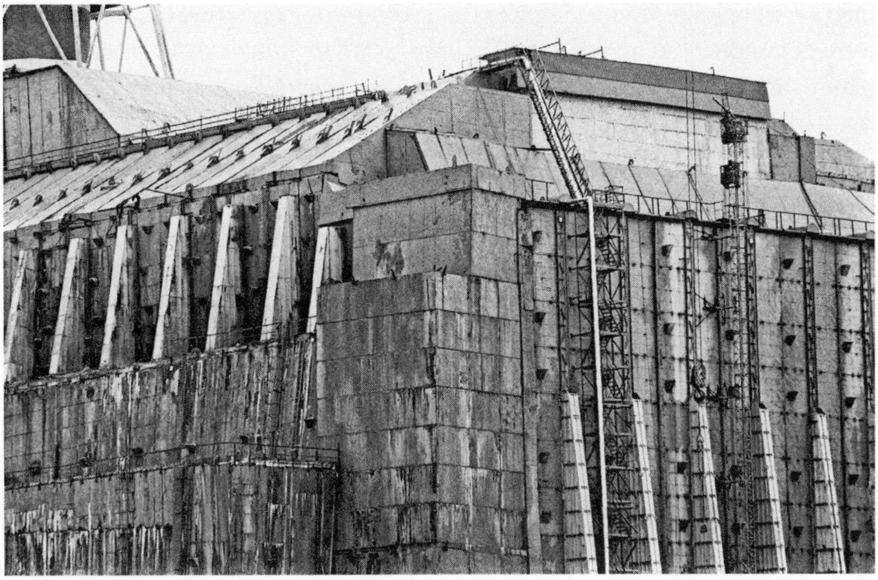

FIGURE 8. © James Lerager, *Chernobyl Sarcophagus*, 1991. All Rights Reserved. Courtesy of the artist.

photography, to whose illustrious and troubled history I shall return. Documentary photographs of the nuclear age constitute a category of photographs that require special attention and need to be distinguished from other kinds of evidentiary images. For documentary photographs of the nuclear age bear visual witness to a new kind of continuous war, born on July 16, 1945, and named "Trinity," cynically evoking the Christian doctrine that defines God as the hypostasis of three states: Father, Son, and Holy Spirit. If the atomic bomb gave birth to "Trinity," its progeny is nucleocide.

The term *nucleocide* names the unabated nuclear assault on the planet. Robert Jay Lifton and Eric Markusen described the psychological response to the nuclear age as "genocidal mentality."[5] Drawing on and amplifying the concept of genocide to include the destruction of the entire planet, I propose the term "nucleocide" to describe the defense and energy practices of advanced industrial nations around the global that produce nuclear weapons. While "genocide" refers to wars of race and national identity, "nucleocide" refers to war against life: human, animal, and plant.

James Lerager's photograph *Chernobyl Sarcophagus* (1991) is a visual record of the site of the worst nuclear accident to date. A reactor at the Chernobyl Nuclear Power Plant in Ukraine, then part of the Soviet Union, suffered a catastrophic increase in power that led to explosions in its core on April 26, 1986 (figure 8). The hulk of the partially destroyed plant at Chernobyl depicted in Lerager's photograph is a monument to the immediate death of thirty-one individuals; the acute radiation sickness of more than two hundred people in the accident's immediate aftermath; the widespread pollution of lakes, rivers, reservoirs, and ground water that contaminated the food chain; the animals that died or stopped reproducing after the accident (for example, the horses that were abandoned on an island in the Pripyat River four miles from the power plant, and which died when their thyroid glands were destroyed by radiation); the four square kilometers of pine forest directly downwind of the reactor, now called the "Red Forest," which turned reddish-brown and died; and the global radiation patterns and the spread of radioactive contaminants into the atmosphere, which were extremely high in countries bordering on Ukraine, such as Poland and northern Romania. The contaminants reached as far north as Scandinavia; as far west as Greenland, Iceland, and northern Canada; as far south as Turkey and parts of the Middle East; and far into the east, where Soviet and Chinese records have not been released as of this writing (1998). The aftereffects of Chernobyl were expected to persist for one hundred years but decline over time. All this is to say nothing about the future cancers and genetic effects on humans as well as fauna and flora, and the enormous economical costs of the accident. This is the legacy of nucleocide, and the invisibility of radiation that the nucelographic photograph assists us in remembering. What follows is a deliberation on how such photographs visualize this new kind of war and its nucleocide; how they contribute to common knowledge of the nuclear age; how they may engage viewers in becoming more responsible in the nuclear age; how they may help humanity to understand its own unity under radiation; and how the nuclear age renders all discussions of difference in a postmodern world merely academic, as radiation and fallout do not discriminate, but transform us all into a global "we."

The effects of the arms race did not end with the fall of the Berlin Wall on November 9, 1989. The violence of the Cold War only went underground, becoming more dangerous not only in terms of nuclear contraband and the potential for dirty bombs and terrorism, but also because the threat of the nuclear age continually recedes in public memory as the standoff between the United States and the former Soviet Union has ostensibly concluded. For example, think only of the unfortunately titled Peacekeeper W87/Mk-21 reentry vehicle, armed with nuclear warheads, which Paul Shambroom photographed at Warren Air Force Base in 1992. Such weapons are stored in remote places that are inaccessible and invisible to the public, where they are kept ready to deliver their deadly cargo. Equally obscure and further masking the danger of the end of the Cold War are the secured locations where the production, storage, and potential use of both nuclear weapons and nuclear energy occur. Indeed, the Cold War policy of mutually assured destruction (MAD) remains as descriptive of the technologies, procedures, the aim of the nuclear age today as it was forty years ago, making MAD a vivid metonym for the mentality that creates weapons of mass destruction for the maintenance of peace.

## PURE WAR

Before the end of the Cold War, Paul Virilio described "pure war" in a 1982 discussion with literary critic Sylvère Lotringer, a conversation that resulted in the book *Pure War*, published by Semiotext(e) in 1983. Pure war, Virilio explained, is "military space . . . having its own characteristics,"[6] is a war of "chrono-politics,"[7] and is an "a-national logistical revolution" that follows what Virilio describes as "a statement by the Pentagon from around 1945–50 which is extraordinary: 'Logistics is the procedure following which a nation's potential is transferred to its armed forces, in times of peace as in times of war.'"[8] Pure war is the war machine that invades all aspects of everyday life. In pure war, episodes of actual war are not as significant as are the tendencies to produce war. Such tendencies infiltrate all ordinary ways of seeing and contrive a global vision based in the logistics of military perception. Pure war is "the doctrine of production [that] has replaced the doctrine of use on the battlefield," and in which "the computer already has the last word."[9] Pure war is the war in which "the use of weapons is no longer taught . . . because the time for decision is now insufficient."[10] Pure war is the

> suicide State [that] no longer needs men, and that's why it's pure. It doesn't need the human war-machine, mobilized human forces. . . . We are facing a cult. . . . Pure War is the absolute idol [in which] the scientific progress of nuclear energy is bringing idolatry in place of ideologies. Because nuclear war is an idolatry. Pure War is a situation which is entirely comparable to that of the idol in ancient societies. We have come back to the supreme idol.[11]

Television viewers witnessed just such a war eight years after Virilio and Lotringer's book was published, when they watched "smart bombs" during the 1991 Gulf War. Such is also the war in which electromagnetic waves are being developed and deployed by the US Department of Defense, in its so-called "non-lethal weapons" program.[12] Pure war has advanced for fifty years, and it presents an unprecedented, unparalleled form of aggression on noncombatant civilian populations throughout the world by the "military-industrial-congressional-complex" about which former President Dwight D. Eisenhower warned in his farewell address from the White House Oval Office on January 17, 1961.[13] Eisenhower's cautionary words come to life in Robert Del Tredici's aerial image *Rocky Flats* (1983), which depicts a daunting and vast complex in Colorado, a site that handles more plutonium than any plant in the Western world. So, too, does Paul Shambroom's camera bear witness to the invisible reality of the nuclear age as seen in his image of the *Poseidon Submarine Control Room, USS Calhoun, Naval Submarine Base Kings Bay, GA* (1993). Such photographs behold the otherwise inaccessible (and therefore relatively invisible) yet concrete sites at the intersection of defense and industry about which Eisenhower warned:

> This conjunction of an immense military establishment and a large arms industry is new in the American experience. The total influence—economic, political, even spiritual—is felt in every city, every state house, every office in the federal government. We recognize the imperative need for this development.

Yet we must not fail to comprehend its grave implications. Our toil, resources and livelihood are all involved; so is the very structure of our society.

Pure war is also about the invisibility of terrorism and the sudden surprise of terrorist acts—a first incident of which, Virilio argued, was the capture of Beirut Airport by Israeli paratroopers in 1982. These ever-increasing incidences of terrorism represent "the art of deterrence [and] *acts of war without war* [Virilio's emphasis]."[14] Pure war is also about the disappearance of what Lotringer described as "place and individual," to which Virilio added:

> There we have a modernity, a refusal of citizenship, of rights, of *habeas corpus* . . . spreading all over the world. It's easier to make people disappear . . . than to shut millions up into camps, as they did in Nazi Germany. Even if Gulags and concentration camps still exist—and they do, alas—disappearance is our future."[15]

Pure War is about a "perspective of the end,"[16] and its very means are invisible, subsumed in the absolute speed of nuclear weapons and their absolute destruction. With this development in the human capacity for destruction, the planet has arrived at a "mega-interruption":

> Individual death founded all of religious, mystical and magic thought. From the recognition of the death of tribes, of the group, they then arrived at the idea that civilizations, too, are mortal. With nuclear weapons, the species is now recognizing the possibility of its own death. Nuclear holocaust reintroduces the question of God—no longer on the scale of the individual or of a chosen race, but of the species. It reinterprets man's role.[17]

Virlio correctly concludes, "The true enemy is less external than internal: our own weaponry, our own scientific might which in fact promote the end of our own society."[18]

Terms like "pure war" enable a grasp of the global conditions of the social and technological production of contemporary war: its scale, speed, power, and potential for absolute, final, destruction. However accurate and prescient the analysis and naming of pure war is, the term also denotes an abstract concept that runs the risk of rendering further invisible the materiality of the nuclear age. The term "nucleocide" demarcates the precise cause, situation, and global result in which massive death on earth is the result. World War II established the foundation for nucleocide with the United States as the perpetrator. The Cold War amplified nucleocide in the race for nuclear weapons. Pure war is the ubiquitous result that promises disappearance. With the continual attempts by non-nuclear countries to become nuclear, the massive increase in nuclear contraband, the threat of aging nuclear power plants, and the sudden and surprising promotion of the nuclear industry by George W. Bush and Richard Cheney, nucleocide is increasingly possible.

## NUCLEOGRAPHY

The denotative banality of nuclear age photography belies its source in the connotative symbols, icons, and foundations of pure war, and in its narration of human and environmental tragedy. This is because nuclear age photographs are of the ordinary invisibly transformed into the extraordinary. They are genre pictures in which the memento mori foretell a future of suffering and death. Documentary photographs of the nuclear age witness a new kind of militaristic circumstance: war with no conventional troops or battlefields, just commonplace human beings, animals, and the environment left invisibly damaged. Four aspects of nuclear age photographs stand out. First, pictures of the nuclear age require extensive description as they cannot visualize radiation, and the sites of production and storage are so remote and protected that they remain unseen by the public. Second, some of these photographs record the otherwise uncommon fact that the nuclear age is about civilian conditions of war, a concept that eludes citizens and about which most people dissociate throughout the world. Third, and most elusive, many of these nuclear age photographs, or war images, are primarily pictures of ordinary people, places, and things: portraits, landscapes, and genre pictures that belie the violent content of warfare. Fourth and finally, some of the images show visually repugnant and emotionally horrific scenes, environments, and events that have the power to elicit very direct emotional response and which are therefore avoided.

The photographs of Robert Del Tredici, a Canadian artist and photographer, are exemplary of the educational value of nucleography. In 1989 Del Tredici founded the Atomic Photographer's Guild, a loose association of photographers concentrating on nuclear age subjects.[19] Two years earlier he had published *At Work in the Fields of the Bomb* (1987), a comprehensive visual study of the varied sites of the nuclear age. Five of the photographs in this book capture the power of nucleography. Drawing attention to the microscopic aspects of the nuclear age in the photograph *Particle of Plutonium in Lung Tissue* (1982), Del Tredici pictured the cancerous effects of plutonium-239 deposited in the lung tissue of an ape and magnified five hundred times over a period of forty-eight hours.[20] Plutonium-239 is the transuranic element used for nuclear weapons and energy; it has a half-life of 24,400 years.[21] Taken at the Lawrence Radiation Laboratory in Berkeley, California, on September 20, 1982, Del Tredici's photograph shows tracks made by the alpha rays emitted from a particle of plutonium. Furthermore, his photograph of *Strategic Weapons Facility Pacific* (November 2, 1984) pictures an aerial view of what Del Tredici captions as the "Naval Submarine Base Bangor, Hood Canal, Puget Sound." The image includes two types of strategic weapons bunkers in the facility: sixty-four closely spaced bunkers, which store propellant for Trident missiles, and twenty-one bunkers spaced farther apart, which store Trident warheads.[22] Together with his field notes, Del Tredici's photography brings the vast, inaccessible space of nuclear-age technology into a human range, and condenses the incomprehensible complexity of the nuclear weapons site into a compact image that nevertheless remains abstract in its implications about the effect of the site on human life and on the planet.

In an entirely different context, on August 25, 1986, Del Tredici took a picture entitled *Stanrock Tailings Wall.* It depicts a barren landscape of dead trees and a wall of white sand comprised of radioactive mill wastes from uranium mining in the region of Elliot Lake, Ontario.[23] This example of nucleography bears witness to the millions of tons of tailings that have been deposited directly into the environment and carried by the Serpent River System into the Great Lakes, where they will remain unmarked and hazardous for hundreds of thousands of years. Such destruction of the environment extends to animal life and the food chain. In Swedish Lapland, Del Tredici photographed *The Becquerel Reindeer* (December 3, 1986), which depicts reindeer carcasses in a slaughterhouse freezer at Harads Same-Produktor.[24] The animals had eaten lichen contaminated with cesium-137, material carried in the wind from the Chernobyl meltdown. Cesium-137 can be introduced into the environment either by nuclear bomb explosions or by leakage from a nuclear power plant. Since the first nuclear weapon tests released cesium-137 and other radioactive nuclides into the environment, those materials have been absorbed into leaves and roots that serve as reservoirs for them. Such a process became especially vivid in Sweden, where "the maximum radiation allowed in meat [was] 300 becquerels per kilo [and the reindeer measured] as high as 16,000 becquerels per kilo."[25] Workers there named the radioactive carcasses "the becquerel reindeer." Ciguatera poisoning in the food chain, especially among fish, has also been reported in the Pacific Marshall Islands, where the United States tested at least sixty-six atomic and hydrogen bombs between 1946 and 1958, and in French Polynesia, where the French tested nuclear weapons.[26] Del Tredici's photograph *Marshallese in Washington, D.C.* (April 23, 1987) shows a delegation from the Marshall Islands "that sued the U.S. government for $5 billion in radiation damages. *U.S. Court of Claims, Washington D.C.*"[27] Two Marshall atolls—Bikini and Rongelap—remain uninhabitable.

These photographs picture what cannot be seen. The second aspect of nucleography is how it necessitates verbal description. As theorists of photography have long pointed out, without discursive anchoring, the meaning and subject matter of photographic images are unstable. Couple the invisibility of radiation with the elusive content of pictures, and it becomes possible to imagine the demanding task of visually narrating the nuclear age. Such otherness is vivid in *Yucca Pass*, a photograph of a place in Nevada, made by an anonymous photographer working for the US Department of Energy. Few citizens outside the Southwest and the US military realize that Yucca Pass is the gateway to Yucca Flat, one of the most frequently used weapons test sites in the United States. The photograph depicts a sign with the international symbol of radiation, which warns of the dangerous and toxic environment. Remove the double admonition—the sign and symbol—and nothing separates the viewer, hiker, or visitor from the imperceptible dangers that wait along a perimeter that is not and cannot be dotted with such signs. Since the international symbol is not universally known, it may not alert someone crossing into this territory. Another photograph by James Lerager, *Nuclear Lake in Kazakhstan* (1992), shows a body of water with a backdrop of the sky at sunset. How is the viewer to know that this body of water is so thoroughly contaminated by irradiated nuclear waste that someone ingesting its fluids would die within forty-five minutes? Even the photograph's title functions only as a clue to the real threat that only a caption can more adequately convey. The violence immanent in these two pictures is the mayhem of nucleocide and the technologies of pure war that only nuceography can capture.

The images of the nuclear age plunge viewers into and require ekphrastic discourse. As Roland Barthes has pointed out, photography is evasive and viewers impose rhetorical and aesthetic narratives on it. Narrative description of photographs of the nuclear age is especially demanding because the photographs' very subject matter, radiation, is invisible to the naked eye. W. J. T. Mitchell has argued that the goal of ekphrasis is to overcome otherness.[28] Nowhere is this more central than in photographs of the nuclear age that present images of an elusive, but paradoxically constantly present, otherness, precisely because *what* the photographs depict is too often the presence, threat, and progressive destruction of radiation. As the ekphrastic condition of the photograph is well known, I turn my attention to images of the nuclear age that witness pure war and its nucleocide.

## NUCLEOCIDE

Nucleocide is the subtext of all photographs of the nuclear age. James Lerager's *Children's Home in Western Ukraine* (1991) pictures youngsters genetically damaged by fallout from the nuclear explosion at Chernobyl. Lerager's *Kazakh Herder* (1990) shows a man in a Soviet hospital ward being treated for cancer, another victim of the nuclear arms race ravaged by radiation. These pictures, which Lerager considers examples of "engaged photography," have a targeted emotional plea, rallying activism by appealing simultaneously to viewers' fears, fascination, and repulsion. Similarly, in *2-Headed Calf* (1989), Hiro Toyosaki depicts an animal born nine miles from and seven years after the Three Mile Island nuclear power plant accident in Harrisburg, Pennsylvania, which occurred on March 28, 1979. Like Lerager's *Cyclops* (1992), a photograph of a fetus preserved as a medical specimen in a jar at a hospital in Kazakhstan, such images bring the often indiscernible, emotionally disturbing, and therefore repressed effects of the environmental contamination of nucleocide vividly to the fore.

Some photographs of the nuclear age, such as Dorothea Lange's *Newspaper Stand in St. George, Utah* (1953), record this war more clearly than others. Lange's image depicts huge headlines on a daily newspaper in a newspaper box at the small town of St. George, Utah. The headlines announce the first test of a hydrogen bomb, or H-Bomb, by the former Soviet Union. The picture also draws attention to St. George, the epicenter of fallout from the Nevada testing grounds. In this way, the photograph of a newspaper stand in a small American town is a picture of war, illustrating another historical moment in which the arms race, as well as pure war, threatens a civilian population by exposing it to radioactive contaminants. The photograph raises the question: Which superpower is the villain of St. George? Pure war and nucleocide are as much embedded in Main Streets throughout the world as they are in St. George, and as much as they ever were in a battlefield. Lange's photograph belongs to what I am calling the nuclear age category of "ordinary images": simple portraits, landscapes, and genre pictures. They are prosaic pictures whose mundane appearance makes them so threatening. Lange's *Corner of Main Street* (1953) and *St. George Boulevard in St. George, Utah* also qualify as pictures of the commonplace incidents of war that were made in her effort to signify irradiated land and an irradiated town in the United States merely by picturing its everyday life. Similarly, Lerager's *Kazakhs Herding Sheep* (1990) was taken near the former Semipalatinsk in Kazakhstan, the site where the former Soviet Union tested the greatest number of nuclear weapons, and where a pastoral people and their animals now continue to live and graze, irradiated.

In addition to these genre or landscape pictures, there are portraits like Lerager's *Reason and Lois Warehime* (1985), which portrays an apparently ordinary man and his wife. But Warehime is an "atomic veteran," one of the American military personnel exposed to nuclear fallout in Japan and later in Nevada. Warehime joined the Marines at age sixteen in 1943, fought in Saipan, and landed in Nagasaki shortly after the atomic bomb was dropped. "Bulldozers [ran] most of the time," he said. "It was dry, dusty—lots of dust—we were sleeping in bags on the ground in pup tents. Nobody mentioned radiation. We stayed two weeks." Ten years later, Warehime was assigned to Nevada and participated as a platoon leader in shot Simon (a fifty-kiloton bomb). He estimates that his platoon was 2,500 yards from the explosion, and that eight officers were five hundred yards closer:

> You could see your bones, your whole body was compressed. The fireball was straight up and really big. The dust was so thick you couldn't see the guy next to you. When it cleared to 50 yards we moved in skirmish lines to our objective, through dead and blinded jackrabbits and coyotes. On the way back, a jeep with two safety monitors ordered us to get out. When we got back to our trucks we were dusted off with brooms. One hour after the shot everyone was sick and throwing up—54 guys. They took us to showers, ran Geiger counters over us, destroyed all our gear. We had diarrhea something awful. Two days later they sent me back to Fort Knox. My teeth came loose. I had to have them out. My hair fell out, then grew back. This shot ruined my military career. I've been tired ever since.[29]

Warehime's life story is poignant, sobering, and infuriating, an enraging example of pure war. Moreover, the invisibility of the effects of radiation in such nucleographic portraits evades even Roland Barthes' concept of the *punctum*, the term he used to theorize how viewers respond to some photographs that "prick" their consciousness and emotions long after they have been seen.[30] Viewers may find their own individual *punctums* in nucleographic images, but the invisible pathologies embedded in the bodies, environments, buildings, fauna, and flora, which are indexed by such photographs, elude even the prick of a *punctum*, and must be imagined and conceptualized by the viewer. Nothing prepares a viewer to know, for example, that the people swimming in the foreground of Kenji Higuchi's photograph *Mihama Reactor* (1982), in Japan, are being contaminated by water that contains the deadly substances cobalt-60 and manganese-54. Viewers cannot know that the mother in J. Pat Carter's portrait *Mother and Child* (1979) is in an evacuation center after the Three Mile Island disaster in March of 1979.

These nucleographic photographs signify the absent sign of nucleocide and its hidden markers of death and destruction. The ability to visualize the ever-present haunting of the nuclear age is the *punctum* of nucleographic photographs. "To live in the nuclear age is to be a part of and within the threat of 'the Real,'" John Whittier Treat writes in his extraordinary book on Japanese nuclear age literary criticism and poetry, *Writing Ground Zero: Japanese Literature and the Atomic Bomb*, adding that this "Real" is "historical, political, and *lived*."[31] Nucleography contributes to making the "Real . . . *lived*" conditions of the nuclear age visible to be witnessed, despite some significant critics' deferrals. Treat points out that Jean Baudrillard, "in his highly influential 1981 work *Simulations*, declares that 'the nuclear is the apotheosis of simulation. . . . a performative feigning' (58)";[32] Jacques Derrida described nuclear war as the "impossible real," further suggesting that "the nuclear age has always been with us" and that there is "no radical new predicate in the situation known as the nuclear age."[33] But, as Treat insists, Derrida was able to make such a claim *only* by failing to mention the destruction of Hiroshima and Nagasaki.[34] The Austrian philosopher Karl Popper's 1982 observation is worth recalling here, as he pointed out that "any argument against realism which is based on modern atomic theory—on quantum mechanics—ought to be silenced by the memory of the reality of the events of Hiroshima and Nagasaki."[35] Treat expands on this comment, noting that the bombs dropped on Hiroshima and Nagasaki altered the history of the world forever, and "split human history into halves . . . the first [dedicated to] our survival as a species [which] had nothing to do with our will to survive; the second in which survival is *all* it has to do with."[36]

The unseen real is what John Hooton evinces in his photograph *Minuteman Missile Silo* (1989), which depicts an intercontinental missile silo in Montana, one of the many such silos that dot the American West. The real is also what Del Tredici photographed in *Minuteman II Missileers Lieutenants Lamb & Goetz* (November 21, 1984), a picture of two of the men who keep watch as part of the US Air Force intercontinental ballistic missile launch crew at Ellsworth Air Force Base, Rapid City, South Dakota. Del Tredici quotes a Lieutenant Goetz, who explained the procedure for launching a group of missiles:

> It takes two launch votes. One is transmitted by two men from this capsule, and another control center does the same thing. So there are quite a few safeguards that we have to go through before we can launch a sortie.[37]

The "real" of nucleocide is what N.R. Farbman depicted in *Technicians Putting on Protective Suits*, shot at the Hanford Atomic energy plant in 1954; it is the war tested repeatedly in the desert of Nevada, where Richard Misrach photographed *Aerial View of a School Bus* (1987), which depicts a vehicle used for bombing practice; it is the *B-2 'Stealth' Bomber* (1993) that Paul Shambroom photographed at Whiteman Air Force Base in Montana; it is the airspace reserved for military use alone in Nevada; and it is "the areas of the continental United States crossed by more than one nuclear cloud from aboveground detonations" that nuclear age photographer Carole Gallagher pictures in a diagram on the page facing the table of contents in her book *American Ground Zero: The Secret Nuclear War* (1994).

This new invisible war may also be scrutinized from the vantage point of what Carol Cohn, a feminist political analyst, has theorized as the "technostrategic languages" that defense intellectuals use to make the language of war invisible. Cohn cites such phrases as "friendly fire," for firing on one's own troops, and "collateral damage," for the killing or harming of citizens. "Technostrategic discourse," she writes, creates "a conceptual system . . . that enables weapons of mass destruction to be translated into power . . . legitimating the very existence and proliferation of nuclear weapons themselves, as well as the entire regime of nuclear-armed organized peacelessness built around them."[38] But the abstract terms of technostrategic discourse linguistically reshape descriptions of mayhem as benign and increasingly imperceptible.[39] Alfred Eisenstaedt's 1954 photograph of the first Atomic Energy Commission, with commissioners Sumner T. Pike, Lewis Strauss, Robert F. Bacher, William W. Waymack and David E. Lilienthal, reveals a site and the individuals responsible for the technostrategic language of command, control, communication, and computer information.

The Cold War was, and pure war remains, fundamentally covert. Governments from Washington to Moscow, London, Paris, New Delhi, Jerusalem, Pretoria, and Beijing continuously wage such wars on their own and other civilian populations: the billions who comprise the brigades witnessed by nucleography are you, me, we, globally. An example of this simple yet monstrous reality is a classified document that Gallagher quotes in her magnificent book: "In one 'top secret' AEC [Atomic Energy Commission] memo, the people living downwind of the Nevada Test Site during the atmospheric testing era were described as 'a low-use segment of the population.'"[40] This government document attests to the fact that in pure war, some are more expendable than others. In Del Tredici's photograph *Bernard Benally* (August 18, 1982), a Navajo Indian, pictured stoically standing with his wife Jeannette, reminds viewers that Native Americans living and working in the Southwest were a segment of that population considered by their government to be "low-use." Benally, a uranium miner, now lives with lung cancer on Red Rock Navajo Reservation. When Del Tredici asked him whether he knew "what they use the uranium for," Benally responded: "All I know is that they used it for something like a gun."[41] The former Soviet Union also clearly discriminated against certain minority and tribal populations, especially in Kazakhstan, as two photographs by Lerager of Kazakhs exposed to radiation (1990) suggest. Such political policies typify the global scope of pure war with regard to the use and abuse of citizens worldwide.

Moreover, the effects of pure war do not end with the first generation exposed to radiation, for genetic damage is passed on to future generations. Gallagher's photograph *Robert Carter* (October 1988) shows Carter holding across his chest a large photograph of the platoon of soldiers with whom he served. The photograph depicts the moments before they witnessed shot Hood, the largest atmospheric shot ever tested in Nevada, detonated on July 5, 1957. In the photograph, dozens of soldiers are seated on the ground facing the massive explosion, with nothing to protect them but their hands, which, to a man, they hold up to cover their eyes, as if this futile gesture could protect them. The image is tragic. Gallagher's field notes tell the reader that Robert Carter was seventeen when he saw shot Hood. At forty-nine, his spine had already deteriorated and he had experienced debilitating muscle weakness for years. Carter's two sons also have genetic problems, as do many of the survivors of Hiroshima and Nagasaki as well as the children and grandchildren of atomic veterans. Who knows how many citizens all over the world, over whom contaminated winds from nuclear testing have deposited "hot spots" on the earth, have cancer and will die from fallout?

Dale Beaman, pictured by Lerager in *Dale and Doris Beaman, son Doug*, is another atomic veteran. Beaman participated in Operation Crossroads on the Bikini Atoll in 1946. He was eighteen years old. He has "colon cancer . . . migratory muscle spasms, and musculoskeletal deterioration"; he has had kidney surgery and "suffers from diabetes and hypertensive heart disease"; his "son Doug, 18, has severe musculoskeletal and connective tissue abnormalities, [resulting in] numerous operations especially to his legs and knees," and is "mentally retarded"; and "Dale's daughters have congenital joint abnormalities."[42] The cruelest effect of nucleocide is its genetic toll on multiple generations, and the near impossibility of tracing disease to its source.

As if the impact of all these conditions is not relentless enough, after the Atmospheric Test Ban Treaty was signed in 1963, the United States, the Soviet Union, and the United Kingdom (all signatories to the treaty) simply moved their tests underground, which made testing more forgettable. Almost overnight the nuclear fear seemed to disintegrate, giving way to the illusion of increased safety while radiation continued to be vented into the atmosphere. Yet unsanctioned photographs such as Del Tredici's *Minor Scale Unofficial Portrait* (June 27, 1985), taken from a press bus just four minutes after the test blast at White Sands Missile Range in New Mexico, reveal a different story of how underground tests "vented" into the atmosphere. While some countries went underground in 1963, France continued atmospheric tests until 1974, and China continued them until 1980. Neither country has yet made public this information about fallout, hot spots, or irradiation from its atmospheric nuclear weapons testing programs. France continued testing in the oceans into the late 1990s, and both India and Pakistan conducted tests in 1998. Moreover, in December 1993, US Secretary of Energy Hazel R. O'Leary unveiled some 204 previously unreported nuclear tests undertaken by the United States. No one knows the actual statistics on Israeli testing—or, for that matter, on testing by the former Soviet Union and China. When Benjamin A. Goldman and Kate Millpointer published *Deadly Deceit: Low-Level Radiation High Level Cover-Up* in 1990, they pointed out that since 1945 fallout globally had been "equivalent to 40,000 Hiroshima-sized bombs."[43]

Although the bomb has not been used as an overt weapon since August 1945, such overt and covert military testing has continued worldwide ever since. Del Tredici's 1987 photograph of the Perimeter Acquisition Radar Attack Characterization System (PARCS) shows an early warning attack facility headquartered in Colorado Springs, established in 1985 to oversee military use of space. Furthermore, under the auspices of nuclear energy, the use of plutonium in weapons manufacture has continued throughout the world. Nuclear waste from nuclear energy plants has polluted the environment, fouled water sources, seeped into and fallen on crops, and been ingested by animals whose milk and by-products are consumed by human beings. Containment and management of nuclear waste is perhaps the central issue of the nuclear energy industry. At Hanford alone, Alexander Wilson writes, "at least 800 billion liters of liquid wastes have been dumped . . . over the years, most of them directly into the soil—with few records kept."[44] Dan Budnik's photograph *Rusting Barrels of Radiated Mill Tailings*, taken in the Colorado River tributary area of the state of New Mexico, bears witness to the domesticity of death in the environment, just as Hiro Toyosaki's photograph *Radiation Cleanup* attests to a project undertaken in September 1978 at Eniwetok Atoll, where the United States tested bombs in the Pacific between 1954 and 1955. A photograph by the US Department of Energy shows an unlined trench for nuclear waste created at Hanford in the 1950s. The photograph depicts cardboard boxes filled with transuranic waste, a substance with an atomic number greater than that of uranium. When the cardboard deteriorated, the waste contaminated the soil and leached into the groundwater.

The nucleocide of pure war is always in the processes of being waged and of becoming, and always bringing with it the inherent, dormant, suspended, and potential promise of death in the domestic sphere, and in the environment. One of the few distinguishable conditions of pure war may have been the dismantling of nuclear stockpiles following the economic and political demise of the Soviet Union in 1991. The resulting chaos has made plutonium and uranium by-products, as well as nuclear devices, a commonplace thriving business in terrorist contraband, undertaken often by Soviet nuclear experts, among others.[45] Robert L. Gallucci, a special envoy appointed by the US Department of State to deal with weapons of mass destruction, confirmed this fact in a talk he gave at Duke University in 1998. He put the gravity and extent of the problem very bluntly: "We are like a drunk looking for his keys under a streetlight because that's the only place he can see."[46] Even the United States—putatively believed to have the most secure control of any country over the weapons-grade material in its nuclear stockpile—has admitted that there are unaccountable losses in its inventory. For example, the director of the weapons security evaluations office of the US Department of Energy observed that there are "security lapses involv[ing] quantities of plutonium greater than 4½ pounds, enough to build a nuclear bomb."[47]

Caches of unprotected highly radioactive materials turn up regularly throughout the world, as this 1992 report in the *New Scientist* confirmed:

> On 9 October [1992], Frankfurt police found lead containers filled with caesium 137 and strontium 90 [components from which nuclear weapons can be constructed] in a luggage locker in Frankfurt's main railway station, and in the boot of a car with Polish license plates.[48]

To make this threat even more comprehensible, *The Economist* reported in 1993 that "the world probably contains about 250 tons of . . . [weapons-grade] plutonium and 1,500 tons of the uranium. To lose one bomb's worth from the stock is the equivalent of losing a single word from one of three copies of *The Economist*." At the time of this writing, more recent estimates suggest that in the former Soviet Union alone, there are one thousand tons of highly enriched uranium and two hundred tons of plutonium, enough to create between three and six thousand nuclear weapons.[49] These estimates are from declassified reports. One can only imagine what the real numbers might be; and if the thriving business in plutonium and uranium contraband is not chilling enough, we do well to remember the accidental launch of nuclear weapons that nearly occurred on January 25, 1995, in northern Russia, as was reported in the *Scientific American* in November 1997.[50]

## CONCLUSION

Paul Shambroom's photograph *Joint Chiefs of Staff Room, the Pentagon, Washington, D.C.* (1993) is an image of death deferred, the result of what is known as "command, control, and communication (C3)," an information strategic and tactical system employed within a military organization. Shambroom's photograph embodies the vacant harbinger of death that Siegfried Kracauer identified in 1927 as the structure, effect, and reception of photographs in general:

> That the world devours [photographs] is a sign of the fear of death. What the photographs by their sheer accumulation attempt to banish is the recollection of death, which is part and parcel of every memory-image.[51]

Kracauer's view of photography as conveying something gone, a moment vanished, and time elapsed has been elaborated continuously ever since. Barthes explored the theme of death in the "having-been-there" of the photograph; Susan Sontag popularized this notion in the early 1970s; and Thierry de Duve argued in 1978: "Seen as live evidence, the photograph cannot fail to designate, outside of itself, the death of the referent, the accomplished past, the suspension of time."[52] A decade later in 1988, John Tagg insisted that "the unconscious signified (of the photograph) must always be the presence of death."[53]

If Kracauer and his followers are correct, as I think they are, then death must be acknowledged and understood as the defining latent content of every photograph. As such, the photograph's inherent morbidity bears a symbiotic connection to the actual deaths perpetrated in conventional war, the potential deaths by nucleocide, and the psychic numbing (death) and denial of the fear of the nuclear age and pure war. Only a photograph is equipped to record the nuclear age: twice over, as an object and as a subject. In this symbiotic function, the capture of death in nucleography may equally exercise a form of reversal, becoming a form for retrieval and remembering. Remembering invisibility is the key to altering the fate of the "we." It is the beginning of a confrontation with the trauma of daily existence in a terrain of ever-threatening death that immobilizes and deadens individual response and produces psychic numbing, as a result of our incapacity to feel that "we" can resist and our subsequent refusal to know. Remembering, then, is the initial step in altering such psychological responses.

Only through recuperation of memory can healing, agency, and eventual empowerment begin. Healing requires a witness; it cannot take place in a vacuum. To witness does not mean to provide evidence, as to document; to witness is to acknowledge and empathize. The importance of the photograph is its role as witness to the condition of nucleocide and its effect of psychic numbing. I write this in full awareness of the broad and valuable critique of the "truth" of photographs, and of the ability to manipulate images digitally and in the darkroom. The critique of photography was overdue and justifiable, but a cynical approach to nucleographic photographs might only redouble the thanatotic aspects of the nuclear age: "we" need nucleography, and the principled photographers of the nuclear age, for their invaluable civic function.

Let me close with Carole Gallagher's image *Ted Przygucki* (July 1986), whose subject holds a second picture within the picture (a structure similar to that of Gallagher's photograph *Robert Carter*). The photograph of Przygucki is one of military personnel participating in the "Buster-Jangle" series of tests that included what is euphemistically referred to as "Dog Test," November 1, 1951, which involved a 21.5-kiloton device dropped from a B-50 bomber, which exploded 1,417 feet (432 meters) above the Przygucki's platoon. "Dog Test" was not the only test Przygucki witnessed; he was also present at the explosion of twenty-two atomic bombs between 1952 and 1956. In his own words, he saw pigs, chickens, rabbits, and donkeys "all burned to a crisp." He was twenty-eight years old and a master sergeant, as well as "the army truck master of Survival City," which the Associated Press in May 1955 described like this:

> Immediately after the blast, a vast cloud of dust welled up from the desert floor, covering the test town like a brown shroud. White fire seemed to jet soundlessly from the dirt you were staring at. Civil Defense experts prodded into the shredded wreckage of this atom-blasted town and learned where and how you would die–or survive—in a nuclear attach. C[ivil] D[efense] workers started probing into basements of damaged and destroyed buildings to see whether mannequins left in bomb shelters would have escaped. Ripped and crumpled debris made clear that none would have lived. The mannequin families in them "died"—to a man. In the two flattened homes, four shelters were uncracked. . . . Photos showed a two-story brick house on Doomsday Drive, 4,700 yards from Ground Zero in a shambles. This was the Darling family home."[54]

The results of being exposed to all these tests were, for Przygucki, devastating: "My teeth fell out about 1956. I could pull them out myself. . . . Every year after I would get a bad case of laryngitis until 1976 [when] I had cancer of the larynx."[55] Gallagher adds:

> Sergeant Ted Przygucki has a visible hole in his throat, the hallmark of a laryngectomy. In it is a little metal button with a screen to let air in and keep dust and water out. "If I get any water in me I would drown, because I haven't got the strength to cough water up, or liquids." And his buddies from the Nevada Test Site? "Most of them are dead." Przygucki is a diminutive man who never married, and whose cancer took him by surprise.[56]

Visual knowledge of the nuclear age is crucial to remembering the hiddenness of Przygucki's experience of pure war. "We"—the only global "we" that cannot be denied—must imagine the vision-destroying bomb, see the negative effects of radiation from bombs and nuclear energy plants on humans and fauna and flora alike, testify to how defense industries throughout the world hide the sites of the nuclear age from our vision, and pledge to become witnesses.

# II. Double

# The Ideal Gifts and *The Trinity Session* of Istvan Kantor (2014)[1]

Istvan Kantor shares many characteristics with Ulrich, the antihero of Robert Musil's trilogy *The Man without Qualities* (1930–42). Not the least of these is a genealogy rooted in the Austro-Hungarian Empire and its waning days, which were plagued with what Musil describes as "a mysterious disease of the times [in which] blockheads played a leading role and men of great talent played the part of eccentrics."[2] Not only would Kantor inherit the historical legacy of that empire, he would also contract its disease as a supremely gifted artist turned oddball: in his words, a person making "trans-ultra-terrorist hyper-radical post-neo-popo-corn-porn-zero-art."[3] Kantor attributes his self-characterization to one of his many "noms de plume," adding: "hahaha."[4] All this in addition to having been born into a country belonging to the bloc dominated by the totalitarian regime of the Soviet Union, itself an outgrowth of the Russian Empire. Kantor would equally have the misfortune of maturing in the era of "globalization" under yet another empire, the United States. Thrice the subject, if not the object, of empires teetering on the brink of chaos, Kantor is well aware that the most recent conflation of world orders compacts aspects of both communism and capitalism, superficially differentiated while dispensing nearly identical effects around the world.[5] Of this condition, Kantor declares, "Communism sucks! Capitalism is the source of misery! Democracy is a lie!"[6] Kantor would also link his contempt for the ideologies of supremacy to derisive scorn for the numerous cultural descriptors of this period of empires, from modernism and postmodernism to posthumanism and "the contemporary." To wit, Kantor's response to the query "How does your work relate to the whole spectrum of contemporary art?" is: "Next time I'm in jail, I'll think about this question."[7]

In this answer to the question that he, in fact, put to himself, posing as an interviewer with the appropriate pseudonym of "Indi Anna Police," Kantor offers a sardonic yet oblique reference to the many arrests he has provoked and endured as the result of his "ideal gifts" to art and society.[8] Summoning the confining space of a jail while metaphorically scratching graffiti on its walls, being caged is for Kantor the prime moment for contemplating his place within art. Such incarceration exemplifies the constraining principles to which empires subject thought, a condition in which the "spectrum" of the spectacle of contemporary art is itself also entangled. Kantor, like Ulrich before him, recognizes this conundrum: Captivity is the truth of the mental prison to which cultural institutionalizations submit citizens. As Homi Bhabha would observe, empire is also "a potent apparatus for looking, viewing, and gazing—an act of surveillance, an art of regulation, and a profound shaper of visual culture."[9] It is against these "shapers" that Kantor unceasingly fights. Like Ulrich, "alone and left to gnaw his lips,"[10] Kantor rejects how "ideals and morality are the best means of filling the big hole that one calls the soul";[11] and, like the "fools" whom Musil describes as "the mentally deranged and the people with *idées fixes*," Kantor is among the few who "unceasingly endure . . . the fire of the soul's rapture."[12] How? By calling for blood.

From 1979 to the present, Kantor has maintained his *Blood Campaign* (late 1970s to the present), which includes the vandalism of art museum walls, and arrests in Canada, France, Germany, Hungary, Italy, Romania, the former Yugoslavia, and the United States. A second decade into this activity, in 1991, he was forcibly removed from the National Gallery of Canada after performing *Ideal Gift*, an action in the series *Blood Campaign* that consisted of hiring a nurse to extract his blood into six vials, which he then carried to the gallery, where he splashed a bloody X on the wall of the Marcel Duchamp room. Anticipating his own arrest, he was nonetheless grabbed by the guards before he could complete the performance and read his manifesto against the Gulf War, "Sweet Blood of a Dead Pigeon Manifesto: Additional Interpretation to *Ideal Gift* Jan 30, 1991," which begins:

> The function of *Blood Campaign* is to subvert culture, to question the very validity of established culture that is always corrupted by profit and controlled by censorship, to question the order of priorities, and especially the fact that property always seems to have priority over people and people's lives and needs. As I am reading this manifesto, thousands are being killed by the greedy, corrupt and murderous machinery of total censorship: war.[13]

The histrionic tone of this text recalls *Bloodbath*, undertaken by the Guerrilla Art Action Group (GAAG), comprised of Jean Toche, Jon Hendricks, Raphael Montañez Ortiz, and Poppy Johnson. On November 18, 1969, in a protest against the Vietnam War at the New York Museum of Modern Art, the members of GAAG famously threw blood on each other and sullied the museum's entrance hall. *Blood Bath* and *Ideal Gift* are acts of defiant anger as well as therapeutic deeds, the latter calling to mind Homer's designation of Paean, the physician of the Olympian gods summoned to heal the wounded. In the context of *Bloodbath* and *Ideal Gift*, "the wounded" are the institutions of art implicated in war and, by association, the social diminishment of art itself. The insubordination expressed in an art action like this simultaneously testifies to artists' challenges to and encounters with power. Artists' initiation of these kinds of conflicts must be evaluated not only for the unsettling, destructive, and aggressive means employed to emphasize crisis, but also for the urgency they express about caring for the world. In this regard, Kantor denies that his gifts of nearly thirty-five years compare to those of Hermann Nitsch, whose *Orgies Mysteries Theater*, since the early 1960s, has been drenched in blood as the mortal signifier of an aesthetic discourse about life, death, and the destructive histories of Western culture. Differentiating his actions from Nitsch's rituals, Kantor claims that his "blood performance has no relation with collective catharsis"; has "nothing to do with the subconscious, sexual repression, genetic codes and ancient rituals;" "is very individualistic"; and is an action that "anyone on this planet who [has ever] had his/her blood taken" understands.[14] For Kantor, "blood taking" is the "message" that confirms: "I am the one who deals with this world [using] blood [as] the vitalizing stream of social stupidity."[15]

Stupidity brings us back to Kantor's *doppelgänger*, Ulrich, who is similarly riveted to the question of human folly, as Musil points out: "The long and the short of it is, there is no important idea that stupidity does not know how to make use of, for it can move in all directions and is able to wear all the garments of truth, [whereas] truth . . . has only one garment and one road and is always at a disadvantage."[16] There is, likewise, no question but that Kantor wears one cloak of truth, the disadvantage of which is his raw harshness, his unequivocal hostility to stupidity, and the excess of his aesthetic response to the idiocy of cultural institutions. Speaking of "idiots," Musil writes that they "possess something, in the simple concreteness of their mode of thought, which is generally observed to make a mysterious appeal to the sentiments."[17] Neither a cretin nor an idiot engaged in sentiments or sentimentality, Kantor tames his truth by playing the fool—"hahaha"—in the timeless role of the sage. A jester who outwits the crowd with wily intelligence and shrewd cleverness, Kantor takes the temperature of the era and its wars with the sensitivity of a wounded animal. He acts alone—if one is alone while simultaneously inhabiting multiple identities—not giving a damn about the consequences, all the while being steeped in compassion and repeatedly draining blood from his body to metonymically "deal with the world."[18]

It is to such charged art actions and mental states that I have been called to turn my attention in this essay, diagnosing the patient, as it were, by answering the following questions put to me by Linda Feesey: "What is the evidence of the role of trauma—cultural, political and social—in the work of Istvan Kantor? . . . What does this [his] trauma convey? . . . According to its presentation, what is its origin?" My qualification for responding to these questions, I am told, is that in 1993 I wrote that some "art not only bore witness to survival strategies by converting invisible trauma into a representation, but, more immediately, into a presentation."[19] Before analyzing Kantor's art through the lens of extreme experience, it must be said that a case could be made for the proposition that the conditions of empire are enough to have already plunged entire world populations into states of rebellion, dissociated distraction, and numbness, all part of the etiology of trauma. Given this triangulation of reactions to strong emotions, few possess the creative means, energy, or courage to convert them into rational ends for social purposes, as Kantor certainly has done. Having acknowledged that his is not an isolated case, let us return to Kantor to investigate his case further, shadowed as always by Ulrich.

Taking ordeal as the site of an overwhelming accumulation of everything, which produces the nothingness often described as the black hole of trauma in which memory is suppressed, then Kantor is the embodiment of Musil's point that "there is as much lack of everything as of nothing," and that this condition "is as though the blood or the air had changed."[20] Since Kantor is full of blood, and Ulrich is only air (a figment of Musil's novel), we might think of Kantor's mortal condition as lacking everything by comparison to Ulrich's imaginary state, which lacks nothing. In this way, they complete each other. Each, for example, searches for life, which he cannot sense; each grasps at reality, which eludes him; each is indifferent to conventional morals, which are, for both men, without meaning. Even as Ulrich's disposition is passive and without passion, and Istvan's temperament is aggressive and full of feverish fury, these are but two sides of a unified character that is indifferent to and yet consumed with the self in the world.

Musil's phrase "The Like of It Now Happens," the subtitle to the second book of *The Man Without Qualities*, could be said to describe divided states. This curious condition is somehow analogous to a fugue, which is a state of being "like" something that "happens," as a fugue entails a period of loss of awareness, short-term pathological amnesia from which one eventually emerges, returning to a normal state of mind. Perhaps Kantor often lives in something akin to a fugue state, taking into account his many noms de plume, his actions as Monty Cantsin, and especially his claim to have been rescued from anonymity by finding the word "amen." As Kantor has explained, "One day I awakened without memory [and] simply adopted a name found on my clothing, 'Amen.'"[21] For a brief time in the early 1990s, Kantor lived under the sign of "Amen.," punctuated by a period. His life as "Amen." was consistent with the phenomenon of fugue in that it was short-lived, it occurred only once, it might have been the result of acute distress, and it included wandering with his identity and memory clouded and confused, all the while functioning perfectly well in the everyday world, and eventually returning to his given name, Istvan Kantor, who then stated: "History and identity are total mysteries to me."[22]

As an alias, the name "Amen." denotes a form of agreement: "You said it." "I'll say." "You bet." "Yes, indeed." "Amen" is also an exclamation related to a creed, and it testifies to belief in something, as in the ending of the Lord's Prayer: "For thine is the kingdom, and the power, and the glory, for ever and ever. Amen." Amen is similarly a proclamation marking the end of something, a conclusion or a finality signifying, "so be it." Simultaneously an abrupt interjection of approval or an admission that something *is* so, this name connotes the grave authorization that it also *be so*. The period after "Amen." equally announces Kantor's full stop, a break with and in his life: a fugue. Yet this breach indexes the condition he continues to embody in the irreconcilable interstice between being and ending, or an existential end of being. Concurrently alive and dead in the fissure separating a fully realized life from a dissociated numbed existence, Kantor endures while repetitively recapitulating the same acts and using the same materials, blood and fire, to recuperate his death.

When and where did Istvan Kantor die? Probably he perished between November 4 and 10, 1956, when the Russians sent a massive force into Hungary to quell the revolution that had begun on October 23. Kantor was six years old, having been born in Budapest on August 27, 1949. Never mind the fact that this psychic death actually took place two months after his seventh birthday, when the Hungarians began their spontaneous revolt against the tyranny of the despot Mátyás Rákosi, the "monster" at the helm of "the most oppressive dictatorship in the Eastern bloc" at the time.[23] What is important is that Kantor was present at "the defining moment of the Cold War," as the eminent Hungarian-born historian Victor Sebestyen has written, "when the Soviet Union showed, beyond doubt, that it was prepared to use overwhelming force [and] barbaric measures to keep its empire, and the West was content to let it do so," standing by while "the Hungarians were brutally crushed; their capital . . . devastated; thousands of their people died; [and] their country was occupied for a further three decades."[24] The Soviet Union's overwhelming display of force, weaponry, destruction, noise, fire, and blood broke the boy's concept of himself in half, severing the child from the safety of his youth and plunging him to the ever-after uncertainty of an adult.

According to one of his biographers, Cassandra Sung-Hyan (another of Kantor's noms de plume), Kantor experienced all this while living with his family in a Budapest bunker, where he remembers arming himself with the toy wooden gun his grandfather had carved for him, running into the street to join youths throwing Molotov cocktails and shooting at armored cars, and being chased by a soldier who dismounted from a tank and followed him.[25] In another account Kantor explained, "I often lie about my birth, in fact I like to say that I come from nowhere . . . and always say that I was 6 when the Hungarian Revolution happened, because that was my greatest performance piece and you do your best work when you are 6, hahaha, (I ran out to the street with my toy gun and stopped a soviet tank convoy by pointing it toward them from behind a tree . . .)."[26] This kind of parthenogenetic narrative is similar to Kantor's "discovery" of his identity as "Amen." and it belongs to the category of origin myths that artists tell, and historians recount, to construct the glamour and mystery surrounding them. These explanations have ancient pedigrees, beginning with the Greek legend of the contest between Parrhasius and Zeuxis, which established the long tradition inherited by Giorgio Vasari when he wrote his hagiography of the Renaissance, *Lives of the Most Eminent Painters, Sculptors and Architects* (1550). This folkloric emphasis on the heroics of the artist endures in celebrated tales like that of Vincent Van Gogh severing part of his ear, Jackson

Pollock pissing in a fireplace, and Joseph Beuys's fable of being a JU-87 bomber pilot during World War II. Importantly, some aspects of all the stories are true, even if the legends are exaggerated and some of the facts are wrong. Moreover, most of these tales are shorthand for communicating about a troubled or traumatic past: Van Gogh's madness, Pollock's alcoholism, Beuys's participation in World War II on the side of the Third Reich.

In Kantor's case, the repetition (with variations) of his story of the wooden gun establishes his psychological concept of himself as six-year-old soldier fighting for Hungarian freedom. But this history must also be understood as a helpless child's empowerment tale, and as a screen memory shrouding even harsher realities. What is at stake in the narrative is how the events of 1956 structured Kantor's subsequent ideations of himself, his art, and his worldview, as well as their entanglement and mutual hostility. For whether true, false, or partially confabulated, Kantor's lore is embedded in the actual historical experience of a ferocious revolution witnessed by a profoundly threatened child who wanted to fight back and who, as a martyred heroic adult warrior, reenacted the revolution's most salient phenomena in his art: its drama, noise, aggression, destruction, violence, fire, and shedding of blood for the nation.

Kantor's nation is art. This, in part, accounts for his continuous war on its institutions. Recreating the intensity of those six days when the tanks rolled into Hungary, Kantor continually revives the most concentrated moment of his awareness of the intensity of life on the brink of death. At the same time, he is able to re-experience his metaphorical death and his image of himself as having "basically . . . done everything when I was six years old."[27] This mental construct of a fully formed and accomplished individual affirms his sense of no longer being completely alive after the age of six. A partial death is the result of dissociating (metaphorically dying) from the threat of the event, a symbolic death that shrouds parts of the memory of the actual experience, making it inaccessible and causing the shocked child/artist to repeat signifying elements associated with the original events. Kantor's repetition is manifest not only in the duplication of materials and actions, as noted above, but also in the sensations of violation and suffering and his continuous attempt to recuperate the part of the lost/dead child who perished at age six.

Death is the singular ideation of trauma, and the first aspect of its paradoxical etiology. For one remains alive after a part of the self has died, living the death of aspects of the self that have had to be repressed in memory so that one can survive the trauma of the experience in life. In other words, to save the self and endure the crushing emotional impact of a life-threatening experience, one dissociates to circumvent mental collapse. Dissociation preserves the ego by burying parts of the psychological assault in a kind of black hole that is inaccessible to the mind. Dissociative experiences commit the individual to a continuous and primarily unconscious effort to retrieve the lost or dead parts of the self in which one, in contradiction, continues to reside while struggling to reenact trauma's shattering in order to live with and beyond it. The second feature of trauma's paradox is that, as full information about the experience is absent, elements of its narratives are inevitably partial and often incorrect. Ironically, however, circumstantial and incomplete evidence provides traces of the otherwise irretrievable proof that dissociative memory protects the mind from what the body knows. Critical to understanding the function of trauma, then, is to grasp that the precise elements of the truth of the event almost always elude accurate description, while expressing its exact reality despite confusion of the facts.[28]

Such is how time works for the traumatized, stopping at the point of crisis and forever repeating in the effort to recuperate the whole self partially buried in the silence of corporeal knowledge. In this regard, Kantor appears to fight the eternal war he can never win, symbolized in all the wars he has attempted to resist by presenting his "absolute alienation from the ruling value systems of the post-modern cultural establishment and the related business/military political-complex."[29] When he claims that he lives "in the never ending present, a timeless zone where it's always six o'clock," what he announces is the collapse of his world in six days at the mental age of six.[30] This survival story is additionally propped up with his "theory of accumulation," which includes the idea that this endless "six o'clock" time zone is a site of "vertical expansion" where "the accumulation of everything as the same time" occurs.[31] Underpinning Kantor's account of time is his interest in the British physicist Julian Barbour's book *The End of Time* (1999), in which Barbour asserts that time is an illusion, and argues that no evidence of anything but the present exists.

Barbour's theory would be compelling were it not for the fact that memory is not simply a psychological phenomenon of the past and an imaginative "belief" in the future, but a physiological fact based in the inextricable relationship between nurture and nature, each altering the other over time and pitting the body against memory while simultaneously supporting it. Thus does the impact of traumatic experience effect changes in the brain, and developing research on this phenomenon increasingly demands rethinking of the ways in which history must be written in order to accommodate this more fulsome understanding of traumatized time: time and memory caught, as it were, between the physical and mental experience and memory of events. For the "now" of a traumatic present is always the "then-when" of something that occurred; something that changed reality forever; something that opened a chasm in memory for events that could no longer be fully be retrieved; and something out of focus that repeats and repeats in the body, gathering momentum and requiring response.

The "something" that was the Hungarian revolution is not the only source for the evolution and traumatic content of Kantor's art. The overlapping, interconnected, and overwhelming number of double messages that he received as a child and as a young man growing up in the communist system must be considered as contradictory injunctions which ensnared him in the emotionally distressing "double bind" that can lead to schizophrenia or the splitting of a personality, as the anthropologist and social scientist Gregory Bateson and his colleagues theorized fatefully in 1956, the very year of the Hungarian revolution.[32] Kantor writes cogently about these contradictory messages when he describes how he was "a normal child, clean, orderly and obedient," but lived in the "post-war era in a land of devastation and hopeless misery"; he also lived with a "loving family in a country populated by dictators, rebels, traitors, assassins, police informers, double agents, second-hand dealers, knife-sharpeners, dog-catchers, and child molesters." While he came from "an intellectual, middle-class family with aristocratic roots," they lived in an environment of "bombed out buildings overgrown with weeds, and dark basements exhaling the stench of poverty." He spent his childhood wearing "crisp uniforms [including] a red tie, white shirt, badges, membership ID, the propaganda language and the gestures [of] ceremonies and celebrations," while all around him the "decadent scene of decay, rubble, scrap and junk produced the background for the Orwellian atmosphere of personality cult." Exacerbating these contradictions was the difference between public and private life, he commented:

> What meant Soviet Liberation in school was called Russian Invasion at home. We celebrated the People of the Great Soviet Union in school and at home we listened to Radio Free Europe's sermon about American Freedom. At school I learned about atheism and at home I took private religious lessons. In school we were taught that collectivism was above all while at home family values ruled our life. Living with double standards was confusing and conflicting.[33]

As Kantor's personal history constitutes the conditions of the double bind, his art actions and personae counterbalance the duplicitous aspects of art institutions that pay homage to the rhetoric of interactivity, participation, and political and social engagement while capitulating in silence to war, violence, and political and social ills.[34] The "aim" of his blood paintings is to compensate and offer recompense for this hypocrisy by making "a dramatic statement [and] radicalizing an empty white wall with the simple means of a symbolic gesture."[35] Kantor's ideal gift, then, is an X, the sign of cancellation endorsed in his own blood and a denunciation representing his indictment of the whole cultural fabric. His donation of the bloody X, often placed between two famous paintings, is his effort to create an "open-situation that is both an impulse for communication in a repressive social reality and a conceptual work of art that negates repression."[36] Of course the ideal fails, for Kantor's means are desperate.

But consider what might happen if the Musée d'art contemporain in Montréal, to take one example, had accepted his gift and left the bloody X to dry on its walls; had framed the marked space; had put up a wall text that named the artist, the title, the date, the medium, and the donor; and had celebrated this conceptual act in the tradition of Duchamp, in whose designated cultural space Kantor acted? Ulrich has an answer to this, our knotty question:

> It would instantly be made plain . . . that life's requirements are different from those of thought. What happens in life is, roughly speaking, the opposite of

> what the trained mind is accustomed to. In life the natural differences and likenesses are very highly esteemed. Whatever exists . . . is to a certain extent felt to be natural, and there is a disinclination to tamper with it. The changes that become necessary only come about slowly and as though trundling first this way and then that. And if someone were, from a pure vegetarian conviction, to say 'ma'am' to a cow (bearing in mind that one is much more likely to behave inconsiderately to a being that one addresses as "hi, you!'), he would be regarded as a . . . madman—but not on account of his animal-loving or vegetarian convictions . . . but on account of their being directly applied to reality. In short, there is an elaborate compromise between the mind and life . . . ."[37]

To Ulrich's observations, Kantor might respond with an apparent non sequitur, that is also intentionally a related metaphor:

> Two policemen fighting with a cripple sitting in a wheelchair. This could be a great title for a Neoist?! Poem.[38]

To Kantor, Ulrich might answer with an equally poetic, encompassing response:

> Funny! If you look at it all with a bit of detachment, you can't help being reminded, in a way, of starlings—you know the way they flock together in fruit-trees, in the autumn."[39]

So might the endless doubling of meanings and messages in Kantor's art go, including doppelgängers and double binds. Able to condense and displace a host of ordinary and extraordinary factors, from empire to art-as-nation, Kantor's art recharges his blood as much as our air by operating with the conscience of graffiti to redress abuses of power with aesthetic signs of the strength and determination of the powerless. Sounding an alert about the consequences of trauma in the context of culture, Kantor demonstrates its aftereffects in art. Meanwhile, as Ulrich notices that "at times he felt . . . as though he had been born with a gift for which at present there was no function," and as Musil cautions that "one can't be angry with one's own time without damage to oneself,"[40] Kantor sings on: "I come from nowhere. What is the aim of art? Where are we going? My blood keeps flowing, keeps flowing, keeps flowing . . . ."

## *THE TRINITY SESSION* (2009)[41]

Istvan Kantor's *The Trinity Session* (2001) is terrifying and absurd (figure 9). The work presents orgasmic, climactic sexual response enabled by technology, itself aligned with the psychic torment of reason embodied in the institutional trappings of such unlikely things as office furniture! Both kitsch and high art, Kantor presents opposition, contradiction that British literary critic Terry Eagleton equates, in another context, to tragedy.[42] Kantor's tragedy, however, contains no

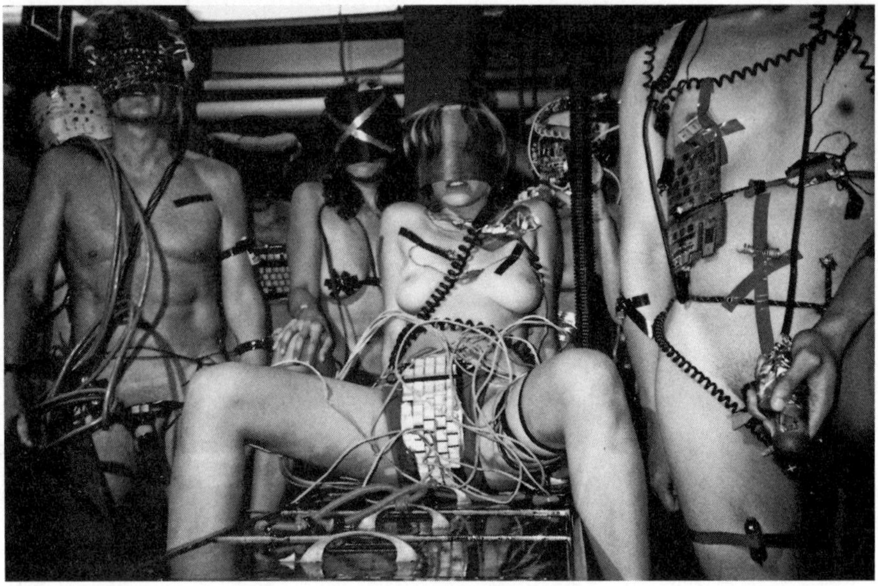

FIGURE 9. Istvan Kantor, video still from *The Trinity Session*, 2001, featuring the technological media work of MachineSexActionGroup. The video was produced for the TransSexTech residency project at Trinity Square Video in Toronto. Courtesy of the artist.

heroic fall from grace, but rather slams headlong into craven power and social malaise, which he dissects with simultaneous perverse pleasure and virtuous condemnation, showing how human dignity may easily be subverted. The acrid aesthetic result is a picture of human isolation, aloneness so absolute that mere loneliness appears saccharine. *The Trinity Session* exacerbates emotional emptiness with a spectacle of participatory interaction conjured with cold, calculated precision, and it plays a serious game of earnest sorrow, pivoting between dread and wit.

One is able to witness *The Trinity Session* in the form of a video performed by Kantor's MachineSexActionGroup (MSAG), all the members of which appear naked with their heads and faces covered by various kinds of technological paraphernalia, which primly (perhaps judiciously) masks the identities of the individual participants. Everyone is strapped into masses of machinery attached to their genitalia and other erogenous zones to stimulate orgasm mechanically. Female participants have their nipples taped over in ironic, if not disdainful, complicity with hypocritical regulations regarding public nudity. One woman with a computer keyboard mounted on her vulva rapidly fingers the keys covering her clitoris, simulating cybernetic masturbation while also performing it. She is part of the group of anonymous performers who writhe and fuck robotic mechanisms in a sea of cables and cords. Endlessly humping and grinding in ferocious intensity and speed, the performers build toward their own blindingly explosive, spastic climaxes—multiple orgasms that make even the most straitlaced viewer envious.

As the absurd circus of pounding sounds and gyrating bodies mounts, ecstatic celebrants are doused with buckets of blood, transforming the erotic machine play—with all its self-conscious, outlandish, and tasteless trappings of benign, consensual S&M—into a war zone that robotically disrupts the boundary between Eros and Thanatos such that desire dissolves into sexual mayhem on the brink of a great, computerized chasm of violence, solitude, and silence. "Let him who has something to say step forward and be silent!" wrote the Austrian critic Karl Kraus on the eve of European Fascism.[43] In fact, Kantor grew up with that authoritarian, hierarchical formation of consciousness translated in his native Hungarian communism into the communitarianism that cynically produced parallel constructions of mind, thoroughly disciplined into brutal symbolic forms of fantasy production, which his work displays and to which it attests.[44]

Kantor describes *The Trinity Session* quite differently than I have done here. He writes: "MachineSexActionGroup . . . explores the socio-physical aspects of trans-kinetic ecstasy and the techno-orgasmic ambiance of high-speed information exchange through a site-specific machine-cult performance focusing on robotic stimulation, desktop eroticism, office furniture-sex and cybersportecstasy."[45] However intellectualized Kantor's anesthetized description of the performance, a vivid disconnect remains between his ekphrastic verbal description and his visual representations. Kantor unknowingly conjures the ever-burgeoning bourgeois Internet trade in techno-pornography calibrated to titillate the body in high-speed information and virtual exchange. *The Trinity Session* renders palpably visual this narcissistic excess and the desperate need for psychic and physical connection that cannot be assuaged either by technology or by sex. Kantor frames the overwhelming presence of media and computer information in a fanatic narrative of "office furniture ecstasy, file cabinet orgy, office robot rebellion, and executive machinery seizure" as if the eroticized workplace might bring ecstasy and salvage the individual and "cybersport," a banal extension of sports-as-entertainment.[46]

Kantor's title—*The Trinity Session*—is itself sardonic, calling to mind the overlap between the eroticism of violence and acts of public ferocity such as "Trinity," the code name for the US test site for atomic bombs dropped on Hiroshima and Nagasaki in 1945, vicious events that changed history and inaugurated the nuclear age with its infinite desecration and obliteration of humans and the environment. Kantor's title also summons religious rhetoric used to shield acts of mechanical mass murder, such as the destruction of the World Trade Center towers and the US response in an orgy of "shock and awe" [and the final killing of Osama Bin Laden in May 2011] that constitute equivalent crimes against humanity. Kantor's title seems as well to be a mocking prelude to the sadistic pornography Mel Gibson depicted in his putatively religious film *The Passion of the Christ* (2004).

Kantor's *The Trinity Session* is also an apt description of an entirely different kind of excess: the "market economy" that first swept the planet in intemperate consumerism and information gluttony, only to result in the very failure of the markets and worldwide recession, if not depression, of the first decade of this century. Kantor's work further suggests that while the trinity of techno-info-orgasm is profoundly seductive, its rapture is artificial. While being collective, it is equally individualistic and separate, ultimately failing either to ameliorate boredom, confusion, anger, and psychic despair or to reform culture, society, and politics. Kantor's ideology, however, is never as literal as these examples; it remains ambivalent, aesthetic, and sinister.

In *Eroticism: Death & Sensuality*, Georges Bataille argued that eroticism presupposes humans in conflict with themselves, a discord that emerges from the fact that "sexuality is limited by taboos, and the domain of eroticism is that of the transgression of these taboos."[47] Kantor reproduces such conflict, using and enjoying eroticism as his means of attack. The brilliance of *The Trinity Session* is his juxtaposition of bathos and pathos, recalling Bataille's observation that "we cannot avoid dying nor can we avoid bursting through our barriers, and they are one and the same."[48] *The Trinity Session* succinctly represents how Kantor's oeuvre "bursts through" not only sexual taboos and psychic death but the very existential dilemma of the nature of freedom that he has continually deconstructed in endlessly changing artistic production, which includes paintings, sculpture, performances, installations, videos, a vast corpus of writings, and the neo-Dada persona "Monty Cantsin." All of this work testifies to Kantor's mad, uncompromising genius, perhaps best represented in the sign of the stamp of an iron, which he burns on many of his works, and the huge X scrawled in his own blood on the walls of galleries, museums, and buildings. Kantor's burned and bloody symbols simultaneously mark and cancel out what they signify: the artist and the brand of the abuse of power on and in his life.

Kantor's shameless abandon displays a morbid pathology determined by growing up in the Eastern bloc, where he endured the stamp of the brutal Hungarian revolution and learned the language of violence, isolation, and silence. He not only inherited this historical surfeit; he escaped it, only to accede to the aesthetic extremes of twentieth-century art.[49] Notably, Kantor came of artistic age during the punk movement, with its anarchistic disdain of cultural expression vivid in his adaptation of neo-Nazi, Soviet, and Chinese nationalist icons.[50] Kantor both commemorated and mocked these ideologies, equally scorning the double standards, social inequalities, and pretense of democracy and grasping the reciprocity of totalitarianism and capitalism in both modernism and postmodernism.

Kantor arrived at this fertile representational territory in the mid-1970s after emigrating to Canada, where he began to fuse the visual signifiers of capitalism, fascism, and communism, making it impossible for the public to determine his own ideological beliefs.[51] He summed up his inscrutable politics in the term "Neoism," a concept that referred to his intent to confuse ideology after having it "forced fed *ad nauseam*, even though . . . I don't believe in any of it." His response was to "puke out [ideology] in the form of Neoisim, and to plunder from many sources other than just political demagogy."[52] With Neoism, Kantor attacked the problem of "bourgeois humanism"—that "honourable but spineless critique of fascism,"[53] as Terry Eagleton would describe humanism thirty years after Kantor began his assault on "that criminal" concept.[54] Kantor's violent response to ideological false consciousness resulted in the artist being frequently arrested and jailed as a maniacal cultural outsider.

The significance of Kantor's work, including performances like *The Trinity Session*, derives from the ontological depths to which he has pushed art in an effort to articulate and present truths about contemporary social calamity. Kantor's work is cruel in the tradition of Antonin Artaud; slapstick in the habit of Charlie Chaplin; and of a high seriousness that grates "on the postmodern sensibility, with its unbearable lightness of being,"[55]—all the while feigning, while portraying, the substance of cultural tragedy.

# Franz West's Dialogic *Paßstücke* (2003)[1]

You begin. "I want to talk about Franz West's *Paßstücke*, a word that means 'adaptives' in English. (The German singular is *Paßstück*.) These odd objects call to mind the one in the double, or the one in the many [fig. 10]. They suggest both Louis Lavelle's philosophical considerations of the similarities between Narcissus and Pygmalion (in his 1939 *The Dilemma of Narcissus*), and Paul Ricoeur's meditations in his 1990. . ."

"Hold on," I break in, arresting your rush to discuss West's work in relation to these two French philosophers. "Why bother with 'the one' in a postmodern age of rhizomes, autopoesis, epigenetics, string theory, and other system approaches to the entanglement of life? And let's not forget the large number of multiple personalities flooding psychiatric offices these days—a veritable 'epidemic' in the United States and Holland, if one is to believe Ian Hacking," I laugh (but not at the multiples).[2]

You laugh too. "Because West's objects begin with the body, that singular center . . ."

"Wait," I interrupt again. "Before you proceed, please describe a *Paßstück*."

"But of course." You take a deep breath. "West began making the *Paßstücke* in 1973. They are curious semiabstract forms that suggest vaguely identifiable objects, but whose identity is undecipherable. They have a strong surrealistic character, something like a wrapped object by Christo or Man Ray, or like a found object that Miro might have assembled into a sculpture. West made the *Paßstücke* predominantly in wire, plaster, papier-mâché, and polyester. He constructed the earliest *Paßstücke* with bandages he had found in his mother's dental office, and these particular *Paßstücke* might suggest wounding and healing. But I do not want to overstate this, as the *Paßstücke* seem more whimsical and mysterious than traumatic. In his exhibitions, West often installs the *Paßstücke* on the floor or hangs them from the wall. Sometimes he places them on pedestals, which gives them a distinctly sculptural presence. All are white. While some have complicated shapes, others are quite simple. Most importantly, he encourages viewers to wear them."

"Wear them?" I wonder.

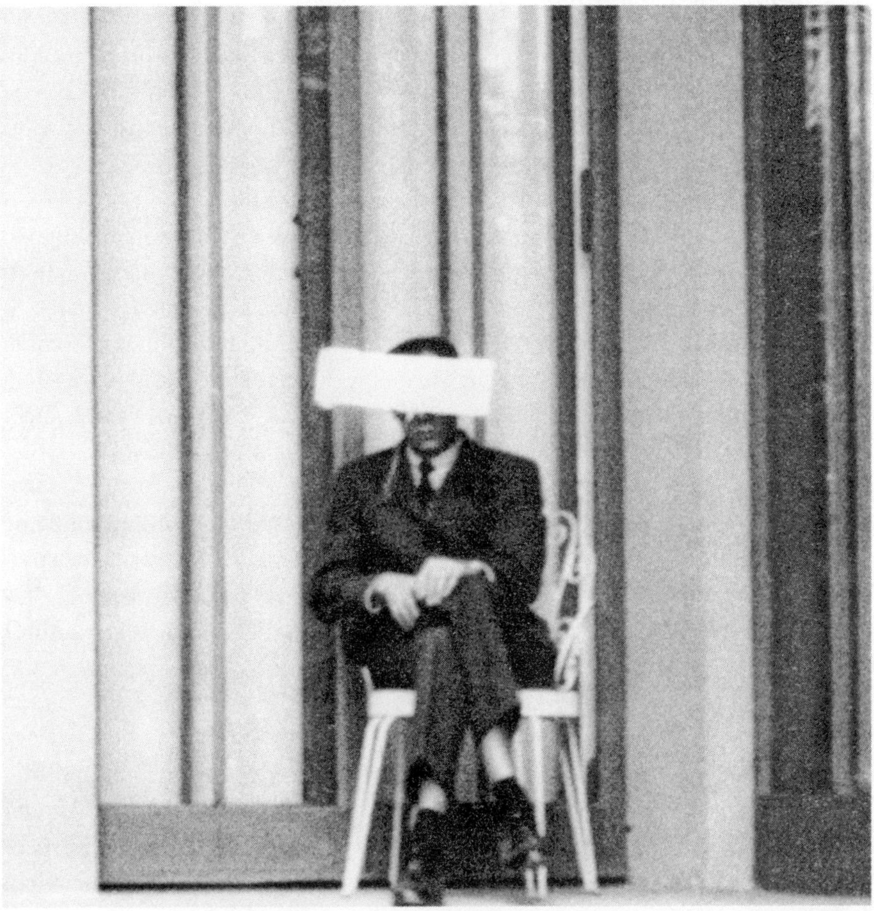

FIGURE 10. Franz West, *Paßstücke*, ca. late 1970s. Performed by Johann Szeni (aka Janc Szeni and Janc Sceniczei) at the Wittgenstein House, Vienna. Bandage, wire, plaster, papier-mâché, and polyester. Photographer unknown. Courtesy of Archiv Franz West, Vienna.

"Yes," you answer. "For example, one rectangular *Paßstück* is rather flat, about sixteen by six inches with a protruding wire used to attach it to one's body. Photographs show people wearing it in front of their eyes as a mask or a kind of screen. Another *Paßstück* resembles a large oar. It is well over five feet in length, with protrusions on each end. I have seen someone carry this *Paßstück* over his shoulder like a very large tool, while another person relates to it quite differently, hugging it close to her body like a beloved person."

When you pause, I encourage: "Please continue."

"West wants viewers to handle the *Paßstücke*, to move them around, to carry them, or to wear them like prostheses. Critic Achim Hochdörfer offers an excellent description of this process: 'The visitor is invited to place a *Paßstück* in any desired relationship to his or her own body. These fragile, rather awkward objects do not fit the body in any organic way that would engender a relaxed atmosphere. On the contrary: the "actor" is actually compelled to assume a pose that robs him or her of any natural poise and not infrequently leads to comical contortions. The piece inhibits, disrupts and caricatures the natural movements of the body. Handling West's *Paßstücke* has some of the paradoxical quality of being told to "be spontaneous".'"[3]

"Oh yes!" I exclaim with gusto. "I once saw a photograph from 1975 of West standing on a very low plinth, a kind of pedestal. He was holding an arc-shaped *Paßstück* over his head like a halo by inserting the index and little finder on both hands into holes positioned at either side of the arc's midpoint. He then balanced the *Paßstück* in the middle of his forehead, from a hornlike protrusion that extended from its back. The image is memorable. West looks like a devilish angel, distinctly impish and almost childlike in his delight both in his object and in its use. It is the way that he appeared in relationship to the *Paßtück* that convinced me that I would like him as a person."

"In fact, you have touched on a key aspect of the *Paßstücke*." You suddenly become all business. "*Paßstücke* communicate something of the nature of a personality. West himself observed that 'if one could visually perceive neuroses they might look somewhat like *Paßstücke*. In other words, the *Paßstücke* are anthropomorphic representations of neuroses, capable of motivating a person to perform certain types of movements.'"[4]

"Neuroses? Certain types of movements?" I ask.

Your patience seems to be wearing thin with my interruptions, but you continue to explain. "In psychology, the word 'neurotic' has come to be associated with anxiety disorders.[5] For West, the *Paßstücke* can visualize aspects of a wearer's anxiety, stress, and phobias, all of which distort the patterns of so-called normative behavior. Hochdörfer considers the *Paßstücke* to be 'deeply unsettling presentations of the individual's own attitudes, habits and desires. . . . reveal[ing] the unbridgeable divide between an inner state of mind and a socialized behavior pattern.'[6] In addition, neurotic (or anxiety) symptoms may be characterized by a wide variety of somatic and mental symptoms, many of which evolve from dissociation. In dissociation, specific mental processes (memories, ideas, feelings, and perceptions) are lost to conscious awareness and become unavailable to voluntary recall. Dissociation provides a mechanism for displacing unpleasant, painful, and anxiety-provoking concepts and memories from consciousness. Such lost memories, feelings, and perceptions may return symptomatically in one's interaction with the many in the one revealed by the *Paßstücke*."

I am suddenly reminded of the lifesize doll of Alma Mahler that Oskar Kokoschka made in 1919. After the end of their love affair, he carried the doll around Vienna in his carriage and took it everywhere with him. So I note, "While the *Paßstücke* are not explicit in the same way as Kokoschka's ersatz lover, the doll he made of Alma Mahler revealed his neurotic obsession with her. Thus, West's *Paßstücke* analogously function as that kind of surrogate object."

"Well . . ." You appear hesitant to agree. Nevertheless, you tolerate my point and caution: "But the *Paßstücke* have another function, that of adapting wearers to their internal psychological conditions. Remember, *Paßstück* means 'adaptive' in English. As a tool for adaptation, the *Paßstück* may express neuroses *and* simultaneously accommodate wearers to their anxieties by externalizing stress and phobia in the form of this odd material alternative for invisible suffering. Or, as you pointed out about the picture of West wearing one of his *Paßstücke*, they might help to exhibit one's sense of humor, one's appetite for play, the qualities of one's imagination, etc., etc. In short, wearing the object, I could confront multiple aspects of myself."

"While it is obvious that clothing expresses one's personality, how does interaction with objects do the same?" I ask.

"The use of any everyday object can, but does not necessarily, reveal aspects of identity. The very enigmatic qualities of the *Paßstücke* emphasize personality traits not otherwise readily apparent in our use and manipulations of normal objects. What I mean is that because of their special status as art objects (which traditionally have been, by definition, without utilitarian use), the *Paßstücke* can operate without reference to everyday objects. Their significance resides in *how* they visualize what we *already* know about the interrelationship between the psyche and its objects. Moreover, the meaning of any particular *Paßstück* depends on how it is perceived and potentially changes each individual user. Such use may exaggerate the unconscious relationships and interactions that she or he has with all objects."

"For Wittgenstein," I reply, "meaning and use must not be conflated but are determined in some sense by each other. In this regard, West's objects might be understood as visual corollaries to Wittgenstein's argument that the rules of ordinary language are neither right nor wrong, nor true or false, because meaning derives from use."

"Correspondingly," you echo, "as language is a game for Wittgenstein, the *Paßstücke* suggest a form of play in which a wearer's idiosyncratic interaction with it individually determines meaning." You seem relieved by the sudden turn of our conversational direction. "Desire to use a *Paßstück* clearly motivates action, and action tautologically determines use."

This last point concerns me, and I reply, "Then use of the *Paßstücke* expose wearers by visualizing their neuroses?"

You confirm that this is true in a certain sense, and add, "But 'expose' may be too strong a word. One could argue that the psychological function of the *Paßstücke* is to provide a corporeal representation of an individual's inner life. Speaking linguistically, *Paßstücke* are to objects what the pronoun 'I' is to 'myself.' They are the same but different, and they offer not a mirroring relationship, but a more substantive reflective distance. One sees 'the one' in its multiplicity, and that multiplicity throws doubt on the 'one.' This brings me back to Ricoeur, whom I cited at the beginning of our dialogue. Among other things, Ricoeur's project—succinctly expressed in the title of his book, *Oneself as Another*—was to examine the opposition implied in the concepts of 'self' and 'I,' to demonstrate the presence of the one in the double (or many), and to raise the existential dilemma inherent in the conception of God."

I am flabbergasted that we could have moved from the curious *Paßstücke* to God, "God!?"

"God."

Your certainty piques my interest.

You proceed: "Pondering Descartes, Ricoeur points out that it is our cognition that invents God for itself. Ricoeur writes: 'By a sort of rebound effect of the new certainty (namely that of the existence of God) on that of the cogito, the idea of myself appears profoundly transformed, due solely to my recognizing this Other, who causes the presence in me of its own representation.'"[7]

"The recognition of its creation of God," you continue, "forces consciousness, according to Descartes, to assume 'the second ontological rank' below God, since cogito, being finite, understands itself to be less than its own creation/awareness of the infinite God."[8] You pause in excitement.

I, too, find these ideas stimulating, especially since the implication is that a mere object—a *Paßstück*, which is the extension of human creation, production, and cognition—may be understood to contain qualities of the infinite. This brings the concept of "God" closer to a kind of universal energy with which I feel more comfortable. But I keep the conversation centered on the *Paßstücke*. "I understand why you raise Ricoeur in relation to West's *Paßstücke*, because although he began as an existentialist philosopher, Ricoeur now consistently rejects it, as well as Cartesian claims for an absolute transparency of the self to itself that would render self-knowledge independent of any kind of knowledge of the world. Moreover, the *Paßstücke* throw into question any stable identity by constantly altering one's relationship to notions of 'self' through changing interactions with the object."

You ignore me and return to God. "Ricoeur explains human self-doubt when faced with its consciousness of God by quoting Descartes: 'Thus the [notion] of the infinite somehow exists in me prior to the [notion] of the finite, that is, the [notion] of God exists prior to the [notion] of myself.'[9] The result, according to Descartes, is that I (or anyone, for that matter) perceive my likeness to God 'by the same faculty through which I perceive myself.'"

I interrupt again. "What initially appears to be a linear, logical chain of creation, is really a loop of logic."

"Yes," you answer. "Ricoeur argues that because God maintains me in existence, it is God who 'confers on the certainty of myself the permanence that it does not hold in itself. The idea of God is in me as the very mark of the author upon his work, a mark that assures the resemblance between us.'[10] Ricoeur returns to Descartes to deliver his conclusion: 'I perceive this likeness . . . by the same faculty through which I perceive myself"."

OK, if you insist, I think to myself. I will try to address the issue of God and the *Paßstücke*. But this seems more than inappropriate. I respond: "May we conclude that West's *Paßstücke* is to our neuroses what God is to our sense of being the 'other'? In other words, we may ignore the problem, but we must find some relation to it—the 'problem' being that being is simultaneously oneself, 'other,' and God along a scale that ranges from apathy to agnostic to atheist to believer. In whatever way we react, we reveal ourselves."

You plunge on without commenting on my point. "Ricoeur does not leave the matter with Descartes. He draws on Malebranche, Spinoza, and the entire movement of idealism (through Kant, Fichte, and Husserl) and then moves on to Nietzsche and what he calls 'the shattered cogito,' namely, Nietzsche's attack on Cartesian thought and the idealists' notion of 'I think.' For Nietzsche, language is deceitful and paradoxical, an unreliable 'illusion' serving as an 'expedient' on behalf of preserving life.[11] Everything that reaches our consciousness is utterly and completely adjusted, simplified, schematized, and interpreted; the actual process of inner 'perception' the relation of causes between thoughts, feelings, desires, between subject and object, is absolutely concealed from us, and may be purely imaginary."[12]

I drop God and move on to Nietzsche, not missing the irony of my swift passage from one to the other: "This is how Nietzsche argued against positivism, which says, 'There are only facts,' whereas Nietzsche says, 'There are no facts, only interpretations.'"[13]

You finally answer me directly. "Right, and there is no 'I,' only an interpretation of causes . . ."

This brings us right back to West's *Paßstücke*. I try again. "On the one hand, we might conclude that these objects concretize the complex interrelationship between the linguistic multiplicity of 'me, myself, and I,' and that which is always already the intricate condition of consciousness responsible for a sense of God (the 'other') against which we judge ourselves 'the other.' On the other hand, the *Paßstücke* equally exhibit how one might imagine an 'I' and a 'myself' only through interaction with an object."

You pause for a moment to think. "In which case, West's *Paßstücke* confront the wearer unpretentiously with an aspect of the Western philosophical tradition of subjectivity, but without the Nietzschean 'lies' of language, and in the deconstructed phenomenological context of Nietzsche's 'hyperbolic doubt' about the truth of object relations. Through this process of thought, we arrive at the inherent multiplicity of the subject as an hermeneutics of the self." You relax now, as you imagine that you have worked this teaser out.

"So what are you proposing?" I ask. "That West's *Paßstücke* thrust the user into an hermeneutic circle, in which it becomes impossible to understand the work until one grasps its relationship to oneself and vice versa? Or that the unidentifiable, elusive shapes of the *Paßstücke* and our interactions with them are somehow metaphors for our relation to the concept of God? Or, that this conversation is as ridiculous as the *Paßstücke* themselves are as objects? Or . . ."

"Yes."

I become tense and retort, "I feel suspended in the ekphrastic gap between language and object (or image), that verbal representation of visual representation.[14] Philosophical discourse may be a means of representing the meaning and function of the *Paßstücke*, but it is also simultaneously inadequate and overbearing because the objects are so unassuming, even humble, like the objects associated with *Arte Povera* . . ."

"That's true," you add. "In addition to bearing a remote similarity to the objects of *Arte Povera* (in being of common materials and unassuming forms), the *Paßstücke* exhibit the legacy of what Lucy Lippard in 1966 called 'eccentric abstraction,' a term she used to describe post-minimalist, process-oriented art like that of Eva Hesse . . ."[15]

"Well they certainly are eccentric," I agree. "What about Pistoletto's 'Minus Objects'?" I leap at the opportunity to mention those brilliant amusing works that Pistoletto began to produce in the early 1960s. "The 'Minus Objects' are idiosyncratic products of Pistoletto's imagination and his paradoxical strategy to rid the world of one less (minus) object by making another one!"

"Many of Pistoletto's 'Minus Objects' were performative," you add.

"Yes," I confirm. "If we think about the function of the *Paßstücke* mandating performative conditions of art, then they require interaction that ultimately displays the spectator as the work-of-art-in-process. In this sense, the objects are props, like those that appear in happenings or Fluxus events. The *Paßstücke* testify to the continuation and permutation of the long pedigree of the goal of interactivity in art."

You become playful. "Think of Marinetti's challenge to Futurists' audiences: 'Throw an idea instead of potatoes, idiots.' There is continuity here, speaking of interactivity, between the Futurists and the provocative actions of the Viennese Action artists in whose context West matured. In 1963, at the age of sixteen, West witnessed Hermann Nitsch's infamous 'Festival of Psycho-physical Naturalism' in Nitsch's Perintegasse studio in Vienna. Art historians have frequently noted that the disemboweled lamb and blood that Nitsch used in this action, as well as the physical violence of the performance, left West in such a state of agitation that he made the decision to leave school. West felt that the impact of Viennese Actionism was so immense in Austria at that time that 'the only alternatives were to become either "a model [for Nitsch, Otto Mühl, or Rudolf Schwarzkogler; Günter Brus did not use models] or a follower."'[16] West became neither. Five years later, in June of 1968, West ingeniously responded to the scatological and antisocial acts that members of the group performed on a stage at the Vienna University—acts such as masturbating and vomiting while singing the Austrian national anthem. West had the extraordinary presence of mind and penetrating intelligence to stand up amidst the shocked and disgusted audience and comment wryly: 'Thank you very much, I enjoyed your performance enormously.' Next, he turned to the audience and said: 'I think these gentlemen have earned a round of applause.'[17] And he led the applause. In other words, with composure and irony, West threw an idea instead of a potato, which is fundamentally the essence of his art in every medium."

"Exactly. His calculated cool demeanor deflated the aura of putative anarchy, and revealed these acts to be a kind of postadolescent rebellion."

"As objects, the *Paßstücke* must be considered in light of this history. In contrast to the kinds of materials used by the Viennese Actionists—blood, animal viscera, everyday objects that could be sadistic and masochistic (razor blades, knives, pins, etc.)—West produced objects that more ambiguously conjured the fetish and 'provoke psycho-physical gesticulations and poses in the user.'[18] Moreover, as West wrote (with poet Reinhard Priessnitz), the *Paßstücke* had 'a certain similarity to the cult objects people wear in Africa, a typical material from here, and it's not an art-object but a neurosis that you get here, which has much the same origins.'"[19]

I become lost in thought, comparing the *Paßstücke* with cargo cult–type fetishes. By drawing this analogy, West implies that the fetish, although made from First World materials, becomes an object of art in Third World countries even as it remains merely utilitarian in Western society. In addition, in terms of their everyday use, Western objects function as tools that disclose our anxieties. The question then remains whether West's *Paßstücke* would be valued as cargo cult fetishes or as works of art in a Third World context.

You break in on my silent ruminations. "No wonder that in 1982, West began to make *Paßstücke* in the form of furniture pieces for the public to sit or recline on in his exhibitions."

"What do you mean?" I am startled back to an awareness of you.

You answer, "He staged viewers within his exhibitions by inviting them to sit or recline on his objects, a strategy consistent with the disciplined humor he displayed in facing the Viennese Actionists' 1968 performance *Art & Revolution*, which we have just discussed."

"I see. With the furniture (*Paßstücke*), West can transfer the psychological dimension from the artist-as-maker to the spectator as wearer-performer, converting viewers into works of art. In other words, he transmogrifies the narcissistic aspect of art into the Pygmalian complex!"

"Well," you say, "finally we come full circle to Louis Lavelle and the point with which I opened this conversation. In *The Dilemma of Narcissus*, Lavelle suggests that the opposite of narcissistic self-love is the Pygmalion dream of giving life to an image by willing or desiring it. Their 'tragic similarity,' Lavelle argues, resides in the fact that while 'Narcissus sees nothing but his own image,' Pygmalion can only love a life that 'is one which must first give itself being, before it can give itself to him.'"[20]

I understand your point immediately. "In the *Paßstücke*, West makes art about the self making itself, with shades of Narcissus *and* Pygmalion insofar as all objects reflect their maker. But the *Paßstücke* remake viewers by externalizing representations of their internal mechanisms. The *Paßstücke* bring an aspect of the viewer to life, Pygmalion-like. Does this mean, then, that West can only enjoy his works—they can only 'give' themselves to him—if the internal personality characteristics of a viewer are animated? If so, the *Paßstücke* are a generous gift and, at the same time, the wearer of a *Paßstück* functions as the nymph Echo to West's narcissistic impulses."

"That is what I was thinking," you declare. "But the issue is again more complicated. Lavelle theorized a 'doctrine of participation,' which suggests that while God is the absolute, or pure act, we are a 'participant' of that divine act; God *is* and we *are* from the act. Human essence is *in* God, while existence is *from* God. Participation occurs across the 'interval' between essence and existence."

"I wonder if West's requirement that viewers participate with the *Paßstücke* makes the *Paßstück* an 'interval' between artist (essence) and viewer (existence)?" I query, with some sarcasm prompted by the return of God.

"Perhaps." You consider the point. "But let me finish. For Lavelle, to know what we *are* means to know what we must *do* to make our existence worthy of its essence. Ego can glimpse the spiritual conditions of being only fleetingly and always beyond the self, leaving the human longing for more . . ."

"But ego is also the source of neuroses and desire, and is exacerbated by materialism. We are back to the cargo cult, wherein the market for objects (the 'art world') is a fetish that West seems to mock in the *Paßstücke*."

"Yet," you conclude, again summoning Lavelle, whose ideas are beginning to try my patience. "Without ego there would be no appearance at all, nothing to awaken us to the beauty of our own unknown selfhood beyond the self we take ourselves to be."

"Which self?"

"The you, me, myself and I we experience in Franz West's *Paßstücke*."

# 1.1.78—2.2.78: Lynn Hershman's *Roberta Breitmore* (1978)[1]

*Eventually she began to swallow solid foods*
*and improve her interpersonal relationships.*[2]

JANUARY 1, 1978

Peripheries are the edges of experience. Edges point to centers.
Roberta Breitmore is an indistinct character existing on our perimeter. As a
Persona, she has no comprehensible beginning; her contemplated end in
Suicide exposes her unknown but threatening dilemma. She appears and
We meet her in the city only in moments. She enters and is an exit without
Destiny. Erratically surfacing, she is a vacant participant in psychotherapy,
Art openings, EST, Zen Center, Weight Watchers, her own neighborhood. In
Employment she is absence. Roberta is calculated and artificial. Contrived
Testimony to her reality exists in documents, evidence of 20th century
Existence: driver's license, checking accounts, charge account plates,
Social security cards. Legitimacy is proffered as to her biological
Authenticity in the form of electrocardiograms, fingerprints, blood count;
Psychology accounts for her verity through psychiatric reports. Proof of
Being surfaces in residual objects: clothing, make-up, an apartment. Her
Home in Baker's Acres is her socioeconomic face, quarters for a middle-
Class transient. Her objects reflect class lines and female preoccupations. The
Theatre of her arbitrary reality poises pathetically in materials from our
Stage. Yet the disguise is acceptable in an uncanny way. Only part of the
Act, an outline entity without substance, a multilayered shadow, spirit
Prop in our vast production, Roberta seems disturbingly similar. In her,
We meet ourselves. She has established our legitimacy by assuming the social
Identity. Our rift is exposed. For in her nebulous context, she becomes
Colleague to the whole, without her and Others, we dissolve as a total
Unit. Her sequential narrative exists simultaneously with our own. Narrative
Enclosures describe her experience of life. Human meaning comes only through
Events. Spatial description but temporal fragmentation from her splintered

Biography. Random and dissipated, life seldom coalesces. Eventually, only
Moments separate void. Yet, in the randomness, a momentary rapport exists between
Things and relationships stand out with such clarity, they can illuminate life. The
Uncanny, Freud said, is something secret, a familiarity emerging after
Repression.[3] Disconnection, the pathetic truth we only murmur, Roberta represents.

## JANUARY 5, 1978

I know Roberta sort of started out gradually. I mean, she just had a
Beginning when she emerged from the secrecy of Lynn's basement. She rode on
Buses then. She had no real destination. Like everybody, she traveled in
Anonymity. You know, when you just look at people and they can look back at
You. Nobody gets too threatened because nobody knows anybody or cares. Her
Neighbors didn't know her either, even though she knew who they were. In fact,
Everybody keeps to themselves in that neighborhood; you know, social/physical
Boundaries are observed to protect people there, against what, I don't know. That
District was a good place for Roberta 'cause anonymity permits freedom. Same thing for
Passengers on the buses; momentarily everybody exchanges roles, displayer and
Looker. Everybody is isolated in the game, enclosed by the absence of
Involvement in the risk of human engagement. But these are lonesome mental
Distances. Ultimately Roberta wanted more involvement, so she started going to
Bars, Churchill's over on Clement Street. There she could have a little deeper
Participation without exposure. She put ads in papers so that she could meet
People, and she went to social activities. All these activities insured her
Safety to continue to look and show without revealing. Later, in New York
City, she was really brave, showing off and watching from Bonwit Teller's
Windows. Seeing and exposing, she enacted our subtle social conventions.
Parties were her favorite. I say, guts! when she started going to Lynn's
Art events, openings and stuff like that. She expanded from the bus stage to the
Social gathering. Then somebody recognized her at an art opening. Of course her
Persona had to disappear, for her desire to look and experience, as well as to
Show, could only be fulfilled incognito. To be acknowledged in her acts of
Voyeurism and exhibitionism frustrated this drive because it differs from other
Desires in that it is dependent upon lack.[4] The anonymity of the voyeuristic
Performer must be preserved. Since Roberta was exposed, she multiplied into
Other look-alikes. "Roberta would do anything to get noticed," Lynn said. Several
Pair of eyes see more than one. Six experiences multiply the vicarious
Invasion. Just about everybody accuses Roberta of self-indulgence in foolish
Acts. We pretend we are innocent in her doubling exchange, as we struggle for
Communication too. But our social separation keeps us in the subject/object
Paradox.[5] Our chasm is deep. In obscurity and human insecurity, we find
Identification through our acts. As mutual participants on her stage, we are like Kabuki
Actors, where: One feels like the bamboo when one looks at the bamboo.[6]

## JANUARY 9, 1978

Voters define San Francisco as a split city. It is a socially segregated
City, separated politically, artistically, ethnically, racially, sexually. City of
Cults, fads and revolutions, an anchor for poets, metaphysical speculation,
Mecca to the religious, goading sexual experimentation. On the very
Edge of the continent, she offers geological faults. Transients and
Dream seekers experience both the promise of infinite possibility and a
Freedom with intensity. At the same time, people meet with disillusionment,
Limitation and bitter, pitiless isolation. Physically beautiful, for the
Insane and mellow, she is a mineral bath. Like the Montgomery Street weekend
Hippie, not only she but many wear two faces. Schizophrenia metaphorically is
District City, San Francisco. Roberta is an object contained both by the city's
Space and the locale's time. She does not pretend to change the conditions of
Life around her. Rather, she is an empty center around which the city's
Skin is articulated. As a passive collage, she is not subversive, but only a
Receptacle, the tribal container—symbolizing social psychosis, a microscopic
Metaphor. Through actions, her physical transformation exceeds symbol. She becomes a
Link between the city she represents and the meaning she presents. This is a
Metonymy.[7] Carrying on the concept, separation, through her chain of continual
Proximity, Roberta successively displaces the city's disconnectedness. Her
Imitation is accomplished through spatial contiguity. Our cleavage is replaced by
Duplicity. Miming our collective separation and condensing our individual
Unity, she becomes a unique connector of opposing forces. Ultimately her
Performance creates a whole when the distant points along her horizontal
Axis of metonymy and her vertical axis of metaphor are connected. From her
Capsule, she functions as both reflection and object. Showering back shattered
Images from the glass of Victorian leaded and beveled panes, Roberta is a
Crystal with facets like our own.

## JANUARY 13, 1978

Dresses for $7.98, I'm sure. Nobody can get things that cheap. In thrift
Shops, maybe. Roberta always wears the same outfit, she thinks it fits her
Image. She used to change all the time till she got comfortable. Images have
Importance, they project who you are. I mean, short miniskirts are tacky now.
Femininity is in. And Punk Rock. Schizoid, isn't it. I mean long, soft
Skirts and frilly peasant blouses simultaneous with leather and safety pins in
Cheeks, weird. (The thesaurus lists Double as a synonym for Weird.) Roberta's
Fashion sense is certainly not very keen. And, she lives in that classy area;
Paradox isn't it? But then, maybe she is smart like those secretaries—you know,
Women in the Financial District who realize that it is the girls with lots of
Leg showing that catches husbands. Brave, also cunning, but then what is important?
Style or men? Roberta doesn't attract the guys who go in for fashion. Her
Sexuality in the short skirt is her asset. And her advertisements in papers,
Come-ons, probably helped. That guy I_____, the one who thought she was a
Beauty, probably also thought she was a Hot Ticket. Apparently that strange
Outfit of hers didn't bother him. Neither did that ratty raincoat covering her fashion
Sin: FAT. Roberta eats a lot when she gets depressed. You know, she has this
Ideal that everybody will be really nice, and she'll meet a man hoping he'll fit her
Dream. Then she gets disappointed and eats. Disgusting. She should learn the
Adage, "You can't be too rich or too thin." She sort of tries by going to
Weight Watchers and living in Pacific Heights. She aims for the "better
Life." Anyway, I_____ didn't even notice her fat. Maybe fat doesn't matter? The
Prostitute recruiters noticed only her short, tight dress and interpreted that she'd sell
Sex rather than style. Anyway, sex and loneliness, they often go hand in
Hand with Roberta. And I_____, too. I mean, he wasn't too proud to write
Her. She probably could have invited him to EST, another kind of cure for
Loneliness. I_____ wasn't afraid to show his need for love; neither were those
Other guys she met. All of them so anxious. Kind of like some organic
Specimens demonstrating cultural desperation. I_____'s letters were sincere, fragile.
Roberta observes and unmasks human vulnerability from her silent, fortified
Distance. Her scrutiny emphasizes her specimen's singularity against her own
Plurality. Anyway, guys who hang around Fern Bars, looking for a little
Love, wouldn't have dared answer her ad or take her out. After all, fashionable
Ladies would point and say, "Look at her, she looks marked down from $1.98." Her
Accusers would only be $6 off.

JANUARY 17, 1978

Social usage bestows multiple connotations upon pure matter then makes
Bundles of collected myth.[8]

> Blonds have more fun. If I have only one life to live, let me live it as a blond. Blond is goodness and purity. Blonds are beautiful. Blond angel. Gentlemen prefer Blonds. Shallow like a blond. Vacuous blond. Dumb blond. Only her hairdresser knows. Blonds age quickly. Men date blonds, then they only marry brunettes.

Blond implies intensification of social experience, sexual adulation and
Companionship, even curiosity. The myth is so pervasively powerful, blond issues
Magic. Roberta treats these myths as commodities purchasable with her yellow
Wig. Yet, the attraction to becoming a blond weds a diabolical double bind. The
Mystique incorporates inevitably a profound contradiction. Simultaneous with
Glamour is deep suspicion that deception and ignorance root under the
Surface of the golden fibers. Colors of dual personality alter under the
Mask as Roberta changes. Make-up too, swathes a path of fraudulence. A
Mirage swabbed with color creates exaggerated bone structure where her
Reality offered other contours. She gleans these tricks from the perfected
Mannequin. But both men and women scan body and beauty books admiring false
Bulges and hollows. She devours these same books, today, searching for the key to
Androgyny. Roberta's bouts with weight demonstrate her longing for the
Cultural ideal sylph, a mortal, slender Being supposed to inhabit the air, but totally
Soulless. Swollen curves of the Fredericks of Hollywood women now come to represent
Mass, a density undesirable. Anonymous perfection in fashion magazines entice
Camouflage. "Everyone loves the clean fresh clarity of the
Face of an innocent girl." We admire the wrinkles on the aging man as earned
Marks of distinction and character. But Roberta faces disparate cultural
Values that seek to neutralize her identity behind the mask. Reconstructing
Images, she exposes a geosociological map. She represents a grotesque, sad
Parody portraying a social treachery so split and frayed it prevents any unified
Whole to emerge.

## JANUARY 21, 1978

Man, is Roberta sexy. You can really see it in the sneaky way she uses
Colors. Wow! She always chooses reds. She varies the tones from
Pink, rouge, blush, and peach to deeper, lustier scarlets, violets, and
Purple. Colors, you know, have their own myths. I guess it's based on
Reality, however. Like, Fire = orange/red = heat/danger. So the myth of
Red emerges from the truth of the flame. We come to know red as representative:
Life, blood, energy, warmth, danger. You know, everybody's got their own
Meanings. But just about everybody thinks of red and sex, like thick red
Lips, as Roberta's. Red advances; it is the color of experience.[9] Odd that
Roberta pretends to be shy, demure, reticent, like she says in her scribbled
Writings on the portraits. Then there are the entries in her diaries,
Self-descriptions in which she divulges the sexual nature of her mental
Portraits. Descriptions in her journals about her body bare the inner
Soul of a Romantic constructing caverns of pleasure from her own form:

> Mouth: deep pink leans against a pale rounded shape anchoring into a
> pearly yet dull hemisphere. The flesh is moist and fragile.
> Eyes: . . . depths of water . . . morose swellings
> Body: . . . milk white . . . rounded shoulder raises up from the darkness
> outspread fingers stretch to the floor.[10]

Boy, Roberta sure writes sensual things about herself. Her attitude about
Survival is even mixed with a kind of sexuality, like when she described the
Technique for tackling life in California as "Getting it on in California."
Everybody knows what "Getting it on" means. She animates a lot of stuff with
Eros. Like, "Cool fog travels like an unwanted lover beneath the
Edge of her raincoat." Fog, sleep, sheets, and a sculptor, even
Morning curving through her own cloudlike being are transformed objects and
Phenomenon, displacements of her erotic Imagination:

> Sleep that night came upon Roberta like a divine favor. She barely felt the cool sheets land on her bare skin, or the heavy moisture seep through the crack of her window when a pandemonium of dreams ensued. Her peaceful breathing belied the endless fatigue . . . Roberta awoke . . . Around her like a puddle lay deep darkness . . . (seconds) chipped away one by one like a sculptor pummeling marble . . . morning curved through violet clouds swelling like an archer's bow . . . she wondered if death was absolute.

Sex is overwhelming. She condenses it into a climatic symbol representing life and
Death. I'd say that deep in Roberta's character hides a tender, dreaming sensation
Seeker. A person longing for experience, for intensity and gentle romance.
Masks allow theatrics forbidden either by mores or by personal inhibition.

Freedom is conferred by masks. But lurking below their boundaries are subtle
Truths about exploring without risk of discovery. Seems to me like she wants
Experiences without having to suffer from their realities. I guess when
We stand looking at her, we perform a similar act. Seeking sensation, we wear
Masks retaining our anonymous, uncommitted, and irresponsible position as
Spectators.

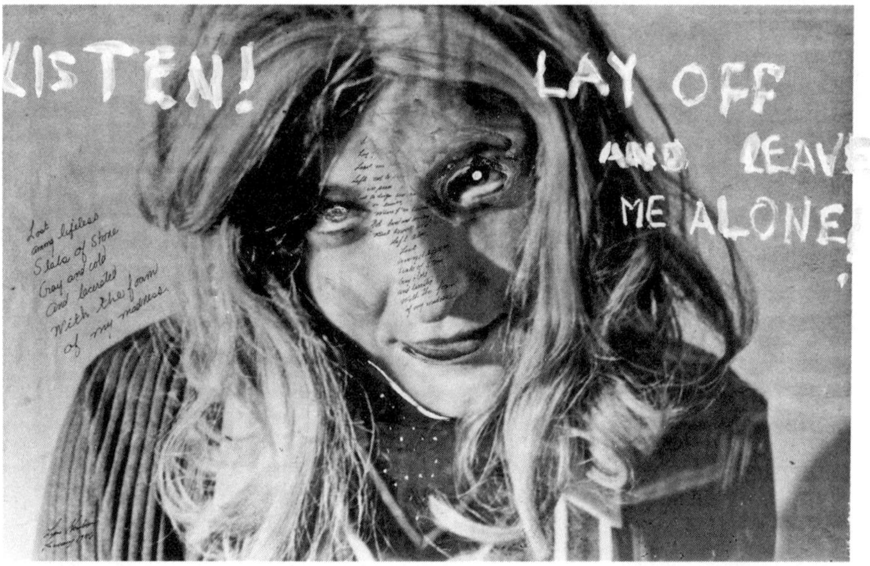


FIGURE 11. Lynn Hershman, *Roberta: External Transformations (Lay Off and Leave Me Alone)*, 1976. C print and acrylic, 30 × 40 in. Photograph by Edmund Shea. Courtesy of the artist.

FEBRUARY 29, 1978

Roberta's got this idea about having the crazies. You know, she thinks she's
Schizophrenic. Let's face it, her interests are all pretty ordinary, like the
Mirror reflection, the shadow and the soul. Anthropologists say that the
Idea of the soul came from the conception of the doubling image of one's own
Shadow.[11] From this arose the idea of guardian spirits and finally we got
Souls. Presto! This scared the ancients. I mean, the fear of multiple
Selves created all kinds of taboos. Whole societies have forbidden the
Name of a person to be uttered by that individual for fear of the resulting
Confusion of the self. Anyway, Roberta calls her own doubling, Schizophrenia, a
Representation that is pretty much the popularization of one version of
Madness. Everybody knows what a Schizophrenic is, you know, like three
Faces of Eve. There's a lot more to being schzo than doubling. Seems more like
Narcissism to me. Narcissus would have no other lover than himself. And her
Persona is the androgynous fusion of two separate sexualities, Robert/Roberta.
Lover and beloved. Narcissus and the Schizophrenic share similar
Characteristics. In Roberta's version of Schizophrenia, a frightened
Personality splits. R. D. Laing's popular illustration, Self = (body-world), is an
Equation of this breach.[12] In it, the body is in touch with outer reality, the
World, but the Self becomes sealed off from the bodily experience. Roberta has both
Feelings, a self that is removed from the world and a self that is lost in the pool's
Reflection. She equates this feeling with falling into the abyss, the Black
Hole of physics that constantly collapses inward. She proposes the cleansing
Act of suicide to rid herself of the circularity of the Narcissist. I guess premature
Death always lurked in her future. Without a center, her contrived
Reality could only spiral into an abyss. Besides, maybe she got sick of being
Herself. Anyway, all I know is that her Shrink said she wasn't too nuts.
I am no doctor, how am I supposed to know? Only seems to me, and perhaps to
You, that if she got away from that mirror she'd be fine. Nietzsche said:
"Man's shadow, I thought, is his vanity."[13]

## JANUARY 25, 1978

Meetings with Roberta primarily occur photographically and textually in the
Context of a still or moving picture. Simultaneously, she is seen to be a
Woman both here and then. The photographic function displays a place that is
Present but a time past: a space within our space, but a temporal sequence in another
Space.[14] Receptacle of paradox, Roberta pictures a corporeal being then in a visual
Now. The uneasy balance of absence/presence diminishes her photo's credibility.
Suspect! Pictures collaborate in contrived connotations through their
Vulnerability to alterations. Therefore, our alliance is a skeptical one of
Acquiescence. Roberta's photographs contain additional variables that complicate
Confidence. Manually manipulated, unabashed alterations defy the eye's
Negligence. Raw marks of violent confusion conceal surfaces, leaving a finish of
Intensity dressed with scratches, mars, and blotches of pure pigment. The face is a
Distortion of bizarre configurations, contortions containing conflict. Screeching
Writing demands, "LAY OFF AND LEAVE ME ALONE." Fragmented penmanship forms
Words that reflect the meaning of the language used (figure 11). Thus, the text
exaggerates
Connotations of the photographic gestures; for example:

> (She writes) . . . crouched over, her head barely 9″ from the paper . . . holding the pen very tightly. A rigid jaw is invariably present . . . lack of alignment between the head and the rest of the body. The head is often carried at an angle to the trunk . . . she draws back slightly. . . . There is something strange and dreamy about her. When she is greeting you she reaches out the tops of her fingers, which are cold and transparent. She smiles confusedly, distantly, and uncertainly. The dissociation between the smile and the mouth and the lack of expression in the eyes is typical of the schizoid personality. The schizoid mask is not removable at will. It is frozen by an underlying terror.[15]

Verbalism and visuality conspire to construct the portrait of psychic abyss.
Roberta proudly displays the image of her madness. She flaunts her
Fabrications in the written-over, painted-over gesture. Everything is a
Forgery, an artistic lie. We are asked to accept the lie and abandon our
Skepticism. Doing so, we submit to the symbol being offered as representation.
Meaning is discoverable at this point.[16] Roberta becomes a sign framing a
Signification. Now, the drama of the origins of this double begins. We accept her
Lie as a sign for the reality of a truth in another situation. Referring to the
Fact of imbalance in the reality being symbolized, her sign becomes a form of
Projection. Our indictment generates from the suspicion that the signs are a
Performance precisely produced to proclaim their creator. Accusation of the
Artist follows. Receptacle of the reality being represented, the artist must be
Mad.

## FEBRUARY 2, 1978

District City, San Francisco, Roberta implicates you.

> Everywhere we look there is tension between the past and the future, between a pessimism we cannot shake and an optimism we cannot quite believe in. The present is thus a turmoil of understandable nostalgia, crippling indecision and bewildering negativism, a general disorientation. —John Noble Wilford, *San Francisco Chronicle*, Wednesday, February 1, 1978:

Symptoms of contemporary social distress confess a disturbed psychic situation:
Feelings are incapable of being aroused, persistent sense of illegitimacy, a
Sense of feeling dead in the world.[17] We are the "Me" generation. The "I" cult reaches
Adulthood and, there, gains increasing numbers of adherents as self-awareness,
Consciousness-expansion, and self-improvement concerns expand to an epidemic
Stage.[18] Narcissism in the '70s is even an intellectual fad. Roberta's
Emotions parallel the culture: "Achieves no orgasms . . . seeks a permanent room
Mate to help share costs and cut loneliness . . . no spontaneity of gesture . . .
Tensions in deep muscles of her skull."[19] Although Roberta represents a shallow
Parody, a superficial surface along the brink of our own Being, she is not the
Advocate of our slender subsistence in place of a more profound vision. As
Mirror, she betrays the center. Roberta mimes. "The single most important social
Quality of emotional expression is . . . the capacity of emotions to take on
Characteristics of populations."[20] Seventy years ago it was a form of social
Hysteria; today it is Narcissism, and twenty years hence, Sado/Masochism.[21] So
I say, "Don't dare call yourself I. Only I am I, and you are only you."[22] When
You become Roberta, we reject her. She is always and forever, Other. But in the
Glass, you and I shift constantly, exchanging identities with impunity, a doubling
Reflection, projection of who I am and what you want to be. Mirrors are
Justification, continually. "I" and "you" are interchangeable; they signify the same
Function, intermittently, of different subjects.[23] Jeer, dismiss, or pity Roberta. But
Roberta. Be frightened or amused or bored. She is mad and you, of course, are
Sane. But Roberta forces the core to the boundary by being the beginning of our
Loci. Every center shifts between its edges. Every edge has two faces.

The individual becomes conscious of himself as being this particular individual with particular gifts, tendencies, impulses, passions under the influence of a particular environment, as a particular product of his milieu. He who becomes thus conscious of himself assumes all this as part of his own responsibility. At the moment of choice he is thus in complete isolation, for he withdraws from his surroundings: and yet, he is in complete continuity, for he chooses himself as product; and this choice is a free choice, so that we might even say, when he chooses himself as product, that he is producing himself. —Søren Kierkegaard

# Larry Miller's *Mom-Me* (2003)[1]

Larry Miller was born in 1944 while his father was away, serving in World War II. His parents divorced soon after his father's return, and his father moved to Oregon only to return to Missouri to kidnap Larry, now two years old, who was rapidly returned to his mother. Years later, Miller's natural father became a born-again Christian with whose fundamentalist beliefs he disagreed. Miller's mother then married a man whom Miller described as intellectually backward, a "hillbilly," who regularly beat his mother and sometimes assaulted Miller until he ran away from home at the age of thirteen. "The psychological trauma was unspeakable," he remembers.[2] "I really thought he would kill us."[3] Miller's stepfather also took him to the basement of their home on many occasions to show him pornographic photographs of naked women in various positions, as well as pictures of piles of dead bodies from the Holocaust that he had somehow obtained during the war.[4] Miller's emotional conflict about his troubled childhood included anger at his mother for not protecting him, an overwhelming sense of powerlessness as a child, and guilt about his inability to defend his family against his stepfather. Miller overcompensated for his home life by excelling in school, which he believes was his "salvation."

Miller's dysfunctional family and the events of his childhood critically shaped his work for, as he recalled, he lived in a violent environment in which the violence itself often took place in a sexualized context:

> He did variously kick me, hit and throw me around when out of her [Miller's mother's] view, especially in the basement, as I said. But I cannot say I was punched full force in the face with a closed fist repeatedly like my mother. She was the regular victim of [his step-father's] pitiful, severe beatings to the face and body. It was sickening and she took it like a martyr . . . It might ultimately have caused her breast cancer. As for me, at age four I somehow "knew" he was perverted and dangerous. It was like an animal sense; I was repulsed, scared and protected myself by trying to be scarce, and rightly so. So I saw my mother as the Victim—and my younger sister and brother (his children) [also as victims]—[but] not myself.[5]

Although Miller did not at the time understand his various psychological strategies for survival, his four-year-old instincts are in keeping with the ability of even small infants to be cognizant of moral issues. Ronald Batson, a psychiatrist at Duke University specializing in incest and trauma, observed that "the pictures of naked women and dead bodies that Miller was coerced to see constituted a form of sexual aggression, and contributed to what is described in the pathology of incest survivors as an 'incestuous environment.'"[6] Miller became hypervigilant in order to ward off and avoid his stepfather's violence, and he dissociated himself psychologically from the memories of his past; both behaviors are similar to the patterns of individuals who have experienced actual sexual abuse. Miller continues to suffer nightmares to this day.[7]

Miller's video installation and performance *Mom-Me* (1973) is the principal subject of my investigation here; it consists of photographs, texts, and a ninety-minute video documenting the artist's attempt to inhabit his mother's psyche while under hypnosis. In *Mom-Me*, Miller aimed to grasp aspects of his mother's concept of him and of his relationship with her. Yet *Mom-Me* contains no references to Miller's traumatic childhood. In viewing the work, I recognized the signs of Miller's traumatic subjectivity and questioned him about his childhood. Miller is extremely reticent about discussing his past and cautious not to overstate his childhood situation, fearing especially that his biography might interfere with the public's ability to view his work in and for itself. Moreover, Miller has long psychologically suppressed the traumatic content in *Mom-Me*. Nevertheless, that content was vivid to me in its absence, quite simply because of its symptomatic references. Thus did I solicit Miller's biographical recollections, and what follows is my reading of the various substrates of *Mom-Me*.

The initial indicator was Miller's work on anomaly and psychic phenomena, which suggested a traumatic background, as those with post-traumatic stress disorder often recount paranormal experiences, and researchers on anomalous experiences are familiar with the capacity of traumatized subjects and artists, as well as artists who have been traumatized, to test high in psychic abilities.[8] Miller reports having had paranormal experiences since childhood, especially precognition, dreams, and psychokinetic abilities in the late 1950s and early 1960s. In the mid-1960s he began more serious study of psychic phenomena, and tried consciously to produce it.[9] He eventually looked for artists historically who had dealt with psychic phenomena, trance, and hypnosis:

> I saw myself in relationship to Dada, Surrealism, and Pollock. I saw hypnotism in relationship to automatism. I was trying to innovate. But at the same time, I was trying to do something that was not imitative. I didn't know anyone who had done anything with psychics; the Surrealists must have done something with hypnosis. I wanted to bypass the conscious mind. Certainly my acquaintance with people from Fluxus was a kind of underwriting of, "Go for it". . . . Today I am an interested skeptic.[10]

Among artists like Miller who associated with Fluxus, trauma is frequent, as in the cases of Yoko Ono, Henry Flynt, George Maciunas, Wolf Vostell, Nam June Paik, David Tudor, and others. Fluxus artists embraced anomaly, and that openness contributed to an environment in which Miller could freely explore the paranormal. But while Miller was associated with Fluxus, he also pursued body art, performance, and video, and considered "psychic medium as a pun for artistic medium" in the Duchampian sense.

In 1967, Miller began systematically to include the paranormal, telepathy, and psychokinesis in some of his art. The first artwork that he made using psychic material was *Stone* (1967–73), which commenced when he consciously began carrying a stone he found by a river in Missouri. Three years later, in 1970, his fascination with a display of moon rocks exhibited at the Smithsonian Institution in Washington, DC, inspired *Stone*. George Brecht's *Chair Event*, the "chair with a history" that Brecht began to explore in the early 1960s and whose history continues to develop, also influenced Miller. In addition, Miller was interested in the negative space that Henry Moore created in his sculptures, as well as the importance of the concept of "nothing," central to Lao Tzu's thought.[11] After carrying the stone in his pocket for six years, Miller submitted it to readings by nine psychic mediums, asking each of them to relate information about its energy. The transcripts of these psychometric readings cohere around the themes of historical antiquity, religion, power, and blood, subjects that the psychics felt reflected the history of the rock, Miller's relationship to it, and Miller himself.[12]

A second project, *Lines to Grow*, begun in 1973, continued to occupy Miller for decades, and evolved from a spontaneous psychic reading of the lines in his palms made by one of the psychics with whom he was working on *Stone*.[13] The psychic noted that the lines of his left and right hands represented two divergent psychological states of development, and she told him that he "must" work on developing the lines in order to become a "less self-destructive" individual. Miller responded by concentrating psychically upon growing the lines in his hands, and he has since made casts "every ten years to allow for significant changes in morphology."[14] Thus far he has made four sets of hands, with the fourth set completed in January 2005. The lines in his hands "are growing well," according to the original psychic, whom Miller consulted again in the mid-1990s.

Also during this period, Miller made a video entitled *Jim The Wonder Dog* (1978). This video documentary is about an extraordinary telepathic dog, "Jim" (1925–37), a Llewellyn English setter that lived in Marshall, Missouri, where Miller was born and grew up. Owned by Sam Van Arsdale (who ironically also owned the Hotel Ruff in Marshall, and whose name sounds like the terrier breed Airedale), Jim performed feats of psychical knowledge by answering questions posed to him by Van Arsdale.[15] For example, Jim picked Kentucky Derby winners correctly for seven years in a row, and he was able to respond to questions put to him in five languages, as well as in Morse code and shorthand.[16] Jim became so famous that he was tested for his telepathic abilities at the University of Missouri, where he correctly responded to every question asked of him. (A request from the University of Missouri for Jim's brain was denied after Jim's death.) For his documentary on the dog, Miller undertook research on "thinking animals," interviewing Laura Dale of the American Society for Psychical Research in New York City. Miller's video, *Jim The Wonder Dog*, is an unprecedented documentary on the subject of animal psychic powers.[17]

All of the works Miller realized on anomalous forms of knowledge are fascinating. But *Mom-Me* is especially arresting for Miller's use of hypnosis as the medium for retrieval of psychological material, and as a vehicle for connecting psychically with his mother's concepts of him. In order to realize this work, it took a year for Miller to find a willing and capable hypnotist. He first approached a psychiatrist well known for his therapeutic use of hypnosis. But this doctor refused to participate in the artwork, advising Miller that such a process might be dangerous to him, and that he might suffer serious psychological damage by dislodging psychic material with which he was not able, or ready, to cope. Miller persisted and found a hypnotherapist who would work with him; they had six sessions together, five of which were audiotaped and the sixth and last of which was videotaped. Miller believes that in the last session he assumed his mother's identity.

As the videotape begins, Miller explains in a voiceover why he is being hypnotized:

> I wanted to know what it would feel like to become my mother, to lose consciousness of my own identity through hypnosis and to believe for a while that I was Mom. In six weekly sessions with a professional hypnotherapist, I was able to enter into progressively deeper hypnotic states until I become Mom in mind and body. During this ninety-minute session, Mom was casually interviewed to evoke her persona, her concept of self, of me, and of our relationship.

Once Miller is hypnotized, the therapist establishes that he is speaking to "Mom" and begins to interview Miller-as-Mom, asking her about her children and focusing on her son Larry. Upon seeing a family photograph of his mother holding him as a child, Miller—now speaking as his mother (Miller-as-Mom)—describes her child as a "chunky baby who cried a lot." But he was "a good kid." The therapist then asks Miller-as-Mom to draw a life-size picture of herself. Miller-as-Mom makes a very realistic drawing of herself but leaves off her hands, an action that is accompanied by the statement: "Maybe I'll just leave the hands off" (figures 12–15).

In the second phase of the interview, the questions and photographs are directed more precisely to Mom's view of her relationship with her son. In a voiceover, Miller says that "talking about herself had seemed manageable," but that in discussing "the mother-son relationship she becomes disturbed and frequently escapes into a sleep state." In other words, Miller-as-Mom is unable to maintain

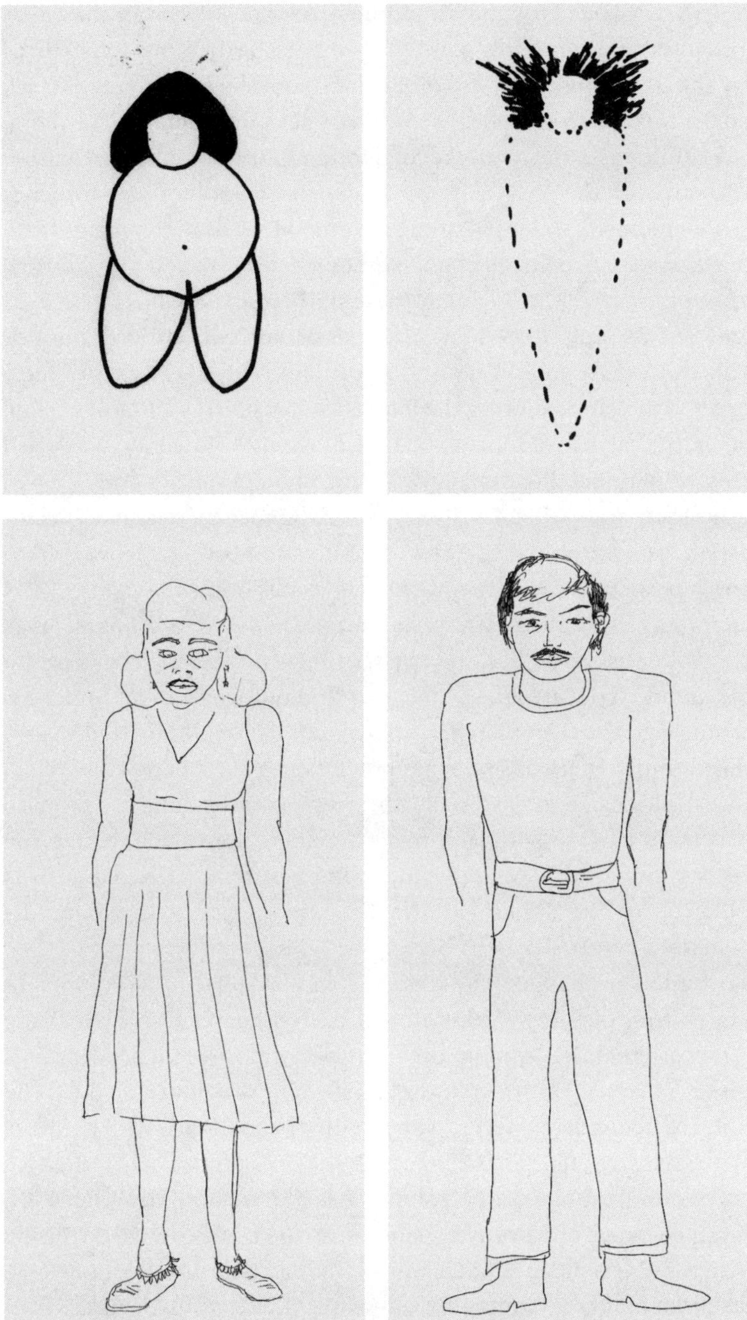

FIGURES 12–15. Larry Miller, *Mom-Me*, 1973. Top: drawings by "Larry" of Mom and Larry; ink on paper, 9¼ × 8 in. and 11 × 7¼ in. Bottom: drawings by "Mom" of Mom and Larry, ink on paper, each 72 × 32 in. These four drawings are components of a larger installation that included two panels with family snapshots, photographs by the artist, video stills with the text of the video transcript mounted on board, life-size portraits, post-hypnotic ink drawings on paper, and a fifty-three-minute video documentary of Miller's hypnosis. Courtesy of the artist.

consciousness when asked to discuss his mother's relationship to her son Larry. Recognizing that the relationship is painful for Miller, the therapist tells him as "Mom" that if she is "bothered" by any of the questions she should merely flick her wrist, and the therapist will not continue that line of questioning. The therapist then shows Miller-as-Mom a number of photographs that Miller had earlier selected and brought to the session. Regarding a photograph of his mother at about the age of eighteen, Miller-as-Mom remarks, "This reminds me of Betty Grable." About a provocative image of his mother in a bra-top and a grass skirt, Miller-as-Mom comments: "Clyde sent us these skirts from Hawaii. . . . I'm fond of that picture." The therapist also shows Miller-as-Mom a conventional portrait snapshot of his mother and one of himself in the late 1950s. Miller's strikingly handsome image strongly resembles the famous sultry portrait of James Dean. Miller had taken the picture of himself in 1966 at the age of twenty-two, when he was "interested in projecting thought 'into' the photograph."[18]

Next the therapist asks Miller-as-Mom if she feels that there are any "similarities" between "you and him." Miller-as-Mom responds that she wanted to say something but is unable to remember what it was, and she begins to flex her wrist dramatically, signaling extreme discomfort. The therapist asks, "Was it important?" Miller-as-Mom flicks her wrist again. The therapist asks again: "Do you want to talk about it? Do you want to find out what it is?" Miller-as-Mom does not answer. The therapist then asks what Miller-as-Mom thinks Larry might have been thinking about in the picture. Miller-as-Mom answers: "Well, it's hard to say, it's kinda serious." Finally, the therapist asks Miller-as-Mom to draw a life-size picture of her son Larry to accompany the realistic picture she has already drawn of herself. Miller-as-Mom complies, but states, "Oh, this is silly. I don't like it too much," as she draws. Though the picture is realistically drawn, it also has no hands.

After several more exchanges, the therapist wakes Miller up and immediately asks him to draw pictures of himself and his mother. Unlike the realistic figurative pictures that Miller-as-Mom drew during hypnosis, Miller's drawings after hypnosis are abstract. He draws himself first, using disconnected dots. The figure resembles a cocoon-like mummy shape with a head topped with hair that stands out like radiant, energy-filled tentacles. Next Miller draws his mother. He depicts her as a round, fat figure with tubular legs and a round head. This is a particularly strange image of his mother, since in all the pictures he used during the session she is quite slender. What is most striking about Miller's drawings, however, and the element that unites them with the drawings made under hypnosis, is that they, too, do not have hands. When I pointed out this obvious detail to Miller he was surprised, and he stated that in all the years since making *Mom-Me*, neither he nor anyone else had ever noticed this correlation.

Let us recall that Miller-as-Mom consciously, even under hypnosis, decided, "Maybe I'll just leave the hands off." "Hands off" is a powerful subtext of *Mom-Me* that suggests a sublimated relationship to his and his mother's hands. Hands prevail throughout Miller's entire oeuvre, beginning with *Revivified Self-Portrait*

*No. 2* (1967–96), and *Lines to Grow*, and continuing with *Finger Exercise* (1983), *Astro-Genetic Landscape* (1989), and *Geonomic License Series No. 6* (1995). *Finger Exercise (Transplant)* (1990–95), in which Miller attaches a fingernail clipping, removed from his hand, onto the finger of an audience volunteer, is a continuation of Miller's activity of collecting both his own and his mother's nails. (Miller also collected hair and other bodily samples from his mother, who, as he explained, enjoyed "the special attention.")[19] Of particular interest is the dialogue between Miller and his mother in *Mom's Feet: My Hands* (1972–74):

LARRY MILLER: What do you think about feet?

MOM: Feet don't do anything for me . . . Now hands fascinate me . . . Hands can tell you a lot.

LM: Like what?

MOM: Oh I can tell one thing about your hands. You have a weak spot—but you don't like to show it.

LM: A weak spot?

MOM: Just the way your fingers are structured. You're holding in to something tight—things that you should be letting out. You got emotion that you hide. It's a security form, a way of holding onto something or holding in something. Turn it loose, I say.

LM: You're saying that from the hands, or from having raised me?

MOM: No, the hands. Now that's what I'd say.

LM: What do you suppose I'm holding in?

MOM: I wouldn't know.

LM: Well, you reared me, so . . .

MOM: Well I was busy rearing you. I didn't have time to study you too.[20]

This conversation between mother and son brings closer to the surface the discussion of the meaning of hands that is pending between them. It haunts the artist's work like a fetish, or a force of conscience, as with Shakespeare's Lady Macbeth, who obsessively washes her bloodstained hands. In his essay "Some Character-Types Met with in Psycho-Analytical Work," 1916, and in his book *Civilization and Its Discontents* (1946), Sigmund Freud identified a sense of guilt (as associated with hands) as the most important problem in the development of civilization. *Mom-Me* has many suppressed oedipal and familial layers implied in Miller's use of hands, and the avoidance and sublimation of hands suggests traumatic experience played out in his interest in the anomalous and the paranormal. Miller's desire to "become whole" evinces the fragmentation associated with traumatic subjectivity.

As already noted, Miller used photographs (some taken when he was a baby and some shot by him of his mother and of himself) as "pre-existing ready-mades" in *Mom-Me*. He also used drawings to make portraits that he described as being seen through "another's eyes" (namely the persona he assumed when he became "Mom" in thc hypnotic trance). In both the photographs and the drawings, Miller dealt with portrait images, ostensibly from both his conscious mind (the images he brought with him to the session) and his unconscious psyche (the images he drew while hypnotized). These photographic and graphic references point to the shifting positions of subject-object and creator-viewer, suggesting how identity is both self- and socially constructed in the maturation process. *Mom-Me* can be compared to the artistic tradition of self-portraiture, Miller has pointed out, with the addition that these portraits attempt formally to materialize some aspect of the artist's dissociated mind, and therefore, do not purport to represent only physical appearance.[21]

*Mom-Me* also tries to visualize some aspect of the mind of someone other than the artist: Miller believes that he did enter the mind of his mother and that she drew herself. Whether Miller realized his aim—whether these drawings actually *are* pictures created by his mother and communicated by his hands—is not the point. Even if actuality were to concern us, it could not be proved. What must oblige consideration is the truth of Miller's desire to make such an image, and his belief that he accomplished his aim. Miller shifts attention from his intentions to the history of self-portraiture (in the autobiographical tradition from Rembrandt to Duchamp) and astutely points out that it hinges on an identification of a factual observation of a psychic creation. These psychic creations to some degree reflect oedipal relationships, especially with the mother. Indeed, Miller's intelligent title—*Mom-Me*—signifies the interconnection between "me" and "mom" that adheres for most in the appellation "mommy." While *Mom-Me* is resoundingly personal to Miller, many universal aspects of it visualize the ways in which the oedipal construction of personality operates in self-identity.

Miller further argues that "the degree to which the application of autobiography pertains to an understanding of *Mom-Me*, seems to balance on a scale with 'factual-events' and narrative located at one pole and 'internal projection' and pictures at the other." In this way, Miller's work summons considerations of Henri Bergson's concept of *durée*, which posits a continuous field of experience wherein no perception exists that is not full of memories.[22] Miller writes:

> *Mom-Me* is autobiographical at both ends. . . . We have a person sketching autobiographical pictures, but from a removed vantage point in the unconscious through hypnosis. This means that the only factual biography present was in the family photographs and the only factual autobiography present was the self-portrait photographs. The form and the content was reflected by surrogates.

To claim that a "surrogate" enacted his performance implies that Miller actually made psychic contact with and became his mother, which, again, is impossible to prove or disprove. In the absence of such evidence, *Mom-Me* actualized something akin to a visual depiction of the resolution of the false binaries that Bergson found in the operations of memory. The philosopher's concepts of the integral relationship between memory and consciousness suggests how mental binaries (inside/outside, part/whole, subject/object, and viewer/maker) might disappear at points in the time-space continuum where the extendedness of images and the lack of extension of ideas merge. Freud echoed this theory three years later in his essay "Screen Memories." In both Bergson and Freud, consciousness and the psyche appear to operate at cross-purposes, apparently in order to maintain equilibrium in the mind/body, space/time duality, and to preserve psychological balance between the ego functions of consciousness and the pathologies of unconsciousness. In both models, consciousness balances opposing states, operating like dissociation (which permits both blocking of some memories and access to other memories).[23] Reconstruction and reintegration of memory is the aim of trauma therapy. *Mom-Me* functioned in this sense as a healing agent for Miller, who claims that his relationship with his mother and his memories of his family life improved after completing the work. That he was unable to draw hands and continues to be concerned about hands in his works of art suggests another area of psychological research for the artist.

*Mom-Me* might also be seen as a working model of the site where a picture is exchanged over the shifting image/screen of the gaze and the subject of representation discussed by Jacques Lacan.[24] *Mom-Me* draws viewers (and Miller himself) into the moment in which images pass into memories and vice versa, in the same way that identities merge on the plane of psychical construction. Miller compares *Mom-Me* to "elective surgery" in which he voluntarily opens his psyche and removes his mother, who in turn then takes a look at him and at herself. Miller wanted to make "an object" within the psyche both accessible and external. He intended to make the psyche an object for contemplation of the construction of self, and, thus, he used hypnosis to make psychic contact with internalized notions about his mother's views of herself and of him. In his attempt to inhabit his mother's psyche, Miller visualized his projection of an internalized image of his mother and his longing for an understanding of her, for a grasp of what she thought of him, and for closure of his dissociated relationship with her.

Dissociation is key here. Often described as "the compartmentalization of experience, identity, memory, perception, and motor function," traumatic dissociation truncates aspects of consciousness from normative experience and memory, producing unconscious or sublimated memories that reappear or are enacted in altered forms.[25] Dissociation is frequently the primary instrument for survival from trauma, providing a form of cognitive homeostasis (however fragile) that enables severely traumatized individuals to live with experiences otherwise too painful for consciousness to acknowledge. Among many cognitive behaviors, dissociation includes de-realization, depersonalization, amnesia, confusion, and alterations in identity in which various parts of the subsystems of mind "disconnect in terms of information exchange or mutual control."[26] This is especially true of dissociative identity disorder (DID)—formerly called multiple-personality disorder (MPD)—a psychological behavior that is primarily attributed to childhood sexual abuse. Dissociation is a survival mechanism that protects the psyche from exposure to distressing memories and experiences. Moreover, traumatic subjectivity and dissociation are interconnected to problems of memory.

Dissociation is associated with pathology, or survival mechanisms, and with creativity, and is part of the artistic process itself.[27] In this regard, dissociation is a cognitive behavior that is coded in the unconscious positively (when it is associated with art and creativity) and negatively (when it is associated with traumatic subjectivity and survival). Artists are often described as "losing" themselves in their work, which comes to "speak" for them. This is especially true for artists with a traumatic history.[28] Many artists testify to this dissociative process, whether or not they have been traumatized. Arthur Rimbaud, Friedrich Nietzsche, and Rainer Maria Rilke all accounted for their artistic abilities *as if* they had been "spoken by another." Rimbaud observed, "Je est un autre"; Nietzsche's "es denkt" names something "thinking in" him; and Rilke wrote, "Where there is a poem, it is not mine but that of Orpheus who comes to sing it."[29]

Dr. Colin A. Ross, founder in 1995 of the Colin A. Ross Institute for Psychological Trauma, notes that "complex relationships among hypnosis, dissociation, absorption, fantasy-proneness, somatization, and paranormal experiences" exist in both artists and traumatized people.[30] In fact, researchers at the Stanford Research Institute found that "artistic talent, visual-spatial intelligence, and creativity all tended to be associated with high remote-viewing [psychic abilities such as clairvoyance and telepathy] scores."[31] My twenty years of research on destruction, violence, and trauma in art corroborates connections among creativity, trauma, and multidimensional aspects of consciousness (the anomalous or paranormal); I have theorized that traumatic subjectivity resides at the phenomenological center of performance art, of which Fluxus is a genre.[32]

For thirty years, Miller's work on psychic phenomena has been doubly coded; it is both an expression of traumatic subjectivity and a powerful form of creativity harnessed as a survival technique. *Mom-Me* is the most extensive work of art on anomalous knowledge in the body of Fluxus works, although several Fluxus-associated artists—Ono, Robert Watts, Carolee Schneemann, Geoffrey Hendricks, Nye Ffarrabas, Robert Filliou, and others—have used psychic phenomena in their work.[33] When Miller created *Mom-Me*, however, he knew nothing about Fluxus artists' use of psychic phenomena in their work. He sought hypnosis first as a means to produce a unique work of art, and second as a means to quiet his own mind. Finally, he also felt that "something 'therapeutic' seems to transfer to certain people from this piece."[34] Louise Bourgeois may have been one of those people.

Miller first exhibited *Mom-Me* in 1973 at 112 Greene Gallery in New York, where numerous artists saw it, including Al Hansen, whom Miller met there for the first time, and who told him: "Everybody is talking about your show!" But significantly, it was Louise Bourgeois who showed the most interest in *Mom-Me*, Miller remembered: "She was one of the few people that sat through the hour and-a-half video." She also encouraged him to continue his work with hypnosis, and even discussed "the possibility of a collaboration" on several occasions.[35] The following year, Bourgeois made *Destruction of the Father* (1974), a sculpture that marked a turning point in her work, and she began systematically to depict the ambiguous and conflicting relationship she had to her father and the network of childhood relationships that motivated her art. What may only be described as a higher level of self-consciousness about the relationship between her art and her past, Bourgeois noted in her diary on April 1, 1974: "The search (pushing on) for truth is what has kept me going. The secret of my anxiety. What is it since childhood? It has to do with hostility—what is wrong with me?"[36]

In December of 1974, Bourgeois exhibited her new work at 112 Greene Gallery, the same gallery where a year earlier she had seen Miller's *Mom-Me*. In 1975, Lucy Lippard began to write about the sources in childhood of Bourgeois's imagery. Lippard's views exemplified the critical reception of Bourgeois's new sculptural direction, especially in feminist quarters where the exploration of physical and sexual violence against women had been a key trope since the end of the 1960s.[37] Eight years later, at the age of seventy-one, Bourgeois created *Child Abuse (Portfolio)* (1982). This photographic and textual spread in *Artforum* was one of the earliest personal artistic presentations of incest.[38] Although Bourgeois does not mention the impact of *Mom-Me* in the development of her work, it seems to have stunned her with its invisible dissociated violence hovering below its surface. *Mom-Me* is an extremely sensitive and courageous work, and it may have played a pivotal role in helping Bourgeois to recognize her own dissociated consciousness, thereby giving her permission to address it more directly in her art. *Mom-Me*, then, may be understood to have built upon and expanded feminist discourses about psychological and sexual abuse.[39]

While he acknowledges that the process gave him some "personal benefit," as I have noted above, Miller does not feel that an examination of his biography is "really necessary to the 'art-construct' presented to the viewer."[40] Moreover, though he views his own "hands . . . as a work of art in progress," Miller has "tried to minimize personal biography in these kinds of works," and he views art as indebted to "a collective intelligence—therefore one's personal history and expression are secondary to more universal interests of art."[41] Clearly, I disagree.

The eccentricity of *Mom-Me* demands contextualization within the psychodynamics of the artist's life, in order for its strange focus and material (psychic phenomena and hypnosis) to make sense in terms of his trauma. In addition, an artwork such as *Mom-Me* provides critical aesthetic research on the interrelation between art and healing, and therefore it is vital that its sources are clear. Miller's poignant, intrepid, and unprecedented effort to unify his emotional/mental construct of "Mom" (with his sublimated and dissociated familial experiences and oedipal relationship to her) is singular in the history of art in its form and content, and in its voracious will to reconstruct memory. I know of no other portrait in the history of art that purports to be an actual psychic representation (or self-portrait) of another person's mind that is simultaneously made by that person who is inhabited by an artist. In both these respects, *Mom-Me* deserves a great deal more attention in the history of art.

"There are 'tones' of mental life," Henri Bergson observed; "our psychic life may be lived at different heights—now nearer to action, now further removed to the degree of our *attention to life* [author's emphasis]."[42] Miller's attention to anomaly represents not only an extraordinary attention to life, but also a will to live in and through art.[43]

## AFTERWORD

Consciousness cannot be adequately explored until more expanded conditions of knowing become commonplace territories of research. In this regard, Robert G. Jahn and Brenda J. Dunne, scientists associated with the Princeton Engineering Anomalies Research (PEAR) Laboratory, opened in 1979, have called for a "science of the subjective":

> The particular form of human observation, reasoning, and technical deployment [that] we properly term "science" has relied at least as much on subjective experience and inspiration as it has on objective experiments and theories. Only over the past few centuries has subjectivity been progressively excluded from the practice of science, leaving an essentially secular analytical paradigm. Quite recently, however, a compounding constellation of newly inexplicable physical evidence, coupled with a growing scholarly interest in the nature and capability of human consciousness, are beginning to suggest that this sterilization of science may have been excessive and could ultimately limit its epistemological reach and cultural relevance. . . . Huge anomalies . . . cannot, in principle, be accommodated by conventional, orthodox models [of science]. They require a break with current [scientific] thinking."[44]

Fluxus provided remarkable models for a "science of the subjective" in visualizing anomaly in works of art and artistic processes, even if in its early years Fluxus men often avoided acknowledging the very anomalous underpinnings of their own work. The failure of some Fluxus artists to endorse such operations has many sources, not the least of which is the connection between gender and expression associated with women. Yoko Ono confirms the interconnection between anomaly and gender:

> In those days, in Fluxus, it was not "cool" to use anything that had to do with human psyche. I think I am the first one who used things like "Kehai" (music of pure vibration created by human psyche) in her work. It's [the reason for excluding such material in Fluxus] to do with John Cage, who was more interested in mushrooms, nonsensical events and chance. Consequently, he broke down dramatic sequencing of sounds and created chance music, which basically had nothing to do with human emotion, which relies on emotion created

in result of sequential events. I was criticized for being too emotional, dramatic and uncool, so I might as well give you this side of the story, too.[45]

In other words, both anomaly and emotion were deemed too female. Some older male Fluxus artists could not become involved in the paranormal or admit (as Miller did) their own personal expression of sexuality, which they could only visualize through related or distant nonpersonal, sexist subject matter. The radical shift that younger artists like Miller brought to Fluxus in the late 1960s and early 1970s was to make anomaly and sexuality the very materiality and content of their work. It took a gay man (Geoffrey Hendricks) and a traumatized man (Larry Miller) to do so. Hendricks and Miller were men willing to abandon the patriarchal codes of control and machismo, who dared to go where Fluxus women had often been. Miller and Hendricks have both created works in a heroic directness and naïve openness. They risked what earlier Fluxus artists guarded, even when, as in the case of Dick Higgins and Pauline Oliveros, they were openly gay, or, as in the case of Schneemann, the art was full of the paranormal but carefully controlled and presented so as not to appear "too crazy."[46]

Miller and Hendricks altered Maciunas's Fluxus canon by exploring the private existential conditions and complex psychosexual and social dynamics that Fluxus women had long entertained. In doing so, they also reflected the historical and art-historical feminist tenor of the late 1960s and early 1970s. The fact that such aesthetic concerns were sanctioned in their work, and not in women's art, suggests the underlying sexism in Fluxus, regardless of the fact that it was one of the most socially, sexually, and racially tolerant of all avant-garde movements.

In closing, it is good to remember the words of Terence McKenna, who once commented humorously on how the scientific model has failed to account for the normativity of anomaly in everyday life:

> No less a founder of modern scientific rationalism than René Descartes was set on the path toward the ideals of modern science by an angel who appeared to him in a dream and told him that the conquest of nature was to be achieved through measure and number. This enunciation, which is really the battle cry of modern science, first passed through the lips of an angel!. . . . This aspect of science, the fact that much of its premises have been transferred to mankind from the hidden realm of higher intelligence, is completely suppressed in its own official story. The official history tells the story of rational thought, of conquering the dark world of superstition.[47]

# Unbosoming Lennon: The Politics of Yoko Ono's Experience (1992)[1]

I

On the album *Double Fantasy*, recorded just before his murder in 1980, John Lennon publicly avowed his difficulty in being able to "hardly express" that "woman . . . I'm forever in your debt."[2] In the song "Woman," Lennon continued: "Woman, I will try to express my inner feelings and thankfulness for showing me the meaning of success." On the same album, in the song "Watching the Wheels," Lennon imputed the notion of attaining success, which was for him merely "playing the game." He described the process as "wheels going round and round"; and, as the most infamous bread-baking, child-rearing househusband in the world, Lennon said he simply "really loved to watch them roll." But he was equally content, he crooned, "to watch shadows on the wall." For "I'm no longer riding on the merry-go-round," he sang; "I just had to let it go." In these songs Lennon rejected the conventional codes of the male rock 'n' roll star's measure of achievement. He also abandoned the caricature of the swaggering, crotch-bulging, thick-lipped, Mick Jagger-like, hard, wet, womanizing, musical cock of the rock, jazz, and country music business. He confessed, "Woman, I know you understand the little child inside your man. Please remember my life is in your hands."

In his unabashed and unembarrassed acknowledgment of woman, Lennon sang to Yoko Ono. Euphemistically, he made "a clean breast" of his thoughts and promised her, "I'll try to express my inner feelings." In short, Lennon "unbosomed himself." Both references to female mammary glands—unbosoming and making a clean breast of something—are synonyms for the verb "to acknowledge," when used in the context of disclosure. Lennon publically unbosomed himself in oracular confession and corporeal display. His disclosures simultaneously manifested the site of manhood and allowed Lennon to divest himself of traditional masculine control. His psychic and physical disrobings and his awkward but sincere embarkations into women's spaces offered an implicit critique of male behavior, which in turn provided a powerful impetus for the ridicule heaped upon him when he retreated from public life.

A source for Lennon's uncommon proclamations, the public reports on his psychological state, may be found in the lyrics Ono sings in "Beautiful Boys," a cut on *Double Fantasy*, the album on which Lennon's song "Beautiful Boy (Darling Boy)" also appeared. In "Beautiful Boys," Ono instructed boy-men to invert and, thereby subvert, their culturally determined control. She urged them: "Never be afraid to cry. . . . never be afraid to fly . . . never be afraid to go to hell and back. . . . [and] never be afraid to be afraid." The attitudes Ono expressed in such songs, along with her art and proto-feminist philosophy, dismantled the stereotypical masculine facade of one of the most beloved and powerful international heroes of pop culture. She offered him an alternative epistemological frame through which to experience sexual difference, through which to begin reconstituting himself along the lines of women's experience and, perhaps in part, through which to rechannel some of the dominating repressions of his own Eurocentric, patriarchal experience. Lennon listened. Moreover, he listened conscientiously. Then he admitted, "Yoko changed me. She forced me to become avant-garde and take my clothes off when all I wanted to be was Tom Jones."[3]

None of the legendary heroic or villainous accounts of Ono or Lennon have probed the content and structure of this couple's contribution to cultural formations. But their union provides a unique cultural model for ways in which gender and racial equality may be constructed in heterosexual relations. In large part, the means by which they architected this political and social practice are to be found in the body codes Ono helped to pioneer in happenings and Fluxus, codes and practices that empowered both artists individually and in union with each other. Their struggle reveals a passionate will to fulfill need with desire and to transform anger, emotional pain, and suffering into a model for interpersonal and multinational love. Furthermore, the psychophysical permissiveness, which is a quality of performative art, played a critical role in determining Lennon's ability to rehabilitate his gender identity and to redefine himself continually as the more complete artist that he aspired to be. As an artist, he became confident enough to display his own self-reconstruction and renaissance.

This essay is an attempt to convey some of the ways in which Ono's avant-garde performance work helped nurture the architecture of LENONO, the neologism they coined for a record label.[4] This fused identity also appears in the photomontage of their two faces created for the poster for Ono's 1971 exhibition *This Is Not Here* at the Everson Museum of Art in Syracuse, New York. Three aspects of LENONO deserve exploration: first, the biographical and artistic origins of Ono's art actions and her protofeminist concerns as they contributed to Lennon's entrance into the avant-garde; second, the ways in which the history of avant-garde performance helped Lennon to articulate his own male space for feminist practice; and finally, the ways in which together Ono and Lennon utilized the vehicle of live performed art to realize the activist potential of their union in popular culture beyond the insularity of the art world.

Redirecting attention to the biographical and artistic aspects of Ono's development as the foundation for LENONO must not diminish the uniqueness of Lennon's ideals or his courageous public displays of personal struggle. Rather, such an alternative view may revive long-neglected aspects of Ono's artistic contributions, sharpening the focus on her as the artist Lennon referred to as "the most famous unknown artist in the world." For even the numerous exhibitions of and articles on her work have failed to probe the germinating role her art played in Lennon's transformation. Moreover, scholars have neglected to grapple with the substantive value and quality of the way she constructed and then directed her art to address difficult social dilemmas. Finally, the performative dimension of her contribution to social formations has been neglected until recently.

## II

Together, in the domain of physical and emotional disclosure, Lennon and Ono created a wedge in social, political, racial, and sexual discourses of their era. Already in November 1968, with the release of the album *Unfinished Music No. 1: Two Virgins*, under whose cover Lennon and Ono appeared as two naked lovers gazing into the eyes of the music consumer, Lennon had entered Ono's double articulated cultural space—the space of woman, and ethnic other, and the space of an Asian woman. Ono not only represented woman and other, but was publicly seen as "the other woman," the adulteress who wrecked Lennon's marriage and the concubine who ruptured the Beatles.

A redoubling and consequent intensification of the spaces of otherness and womanness occurred in Lennon's own masculine disrobings. In his nakedness, his public exposure, Lennon entered woman's space, where he exhibited himself as an object for the male gaze. The intense reluctance of many men to expose their intimate physical or emotional self is culturally supported in the stereotype of the "strong and silent man," a prototype to which playwright Vaclav Havel, who would later become president of Czechoslovakia and of the Czech Republic, gave poignant testimony in letters to his wife Olga written from prison in 1981. Havel explained, "My aversion to 'disrobing in public' was a factor in my decision to stop writing poetry and start writing plays, a genre in which the persona of the author is best concealed."[5] In spite of his own aversions, Lennon literally confronted entrenched constructions of masculinity. He rendered himself multiple and vulnerable by appearing naked in public and, thereby, magnified his rejection of the ubiquity of the masculine cover.

The "change" that Lennon felt Ono had occasioned when he "took his clothes off" might be understood as an analog to the culturally circumscribed female space where emotion is possible to unbosom. Stripped of his clothes, Lennon symbolically prostrated himself before the world, shedding the protective masculine skin of his prior model, Tom Jones, in order to experience the political dimension of the feminine in his own male body. Lennon's naked public exposure helped him to understand how the body might become a cultural medium or, as feminist philosopher Susan R. Bordo writes, "operate as a metaphor for culture."[6] Equally, Lennon's unbosoming was his public manifestation of his private need and desire for the utopian condition he repeatedly called "love." This act may be understood, retrospectively, as a reaction to what feminist anthropologist Murial Dimen has described as "the intransigence of the patriarchal state":

> The intransigence of the patriarchal state is the reason that we must maintain a utopian vision of a society in which desire is empowering, not weakening, in which all parts of the self can come out of the closet—passion and need, will and empathy, the anger that, through a paradoxical love, can make our society realize its ideals of democracy and decency even while hell-bent on betraying them.[7]

Lennon's desire for Ono empowered him to abandon certain elements of patriarchy. Supported in his partnership with Ono, he repeatedly "came out of the closet" with a utopian social program of love envisioned in the imagination and enacted before the world. Lennon considered such actions, his public disrobings, to be gestures of submission, of "surrender," the word Lennon and Ono repeatedly selected to describe their united state of nonresistance.

Moreover, appearing naked in public also qualified Lennon, he felt, to be "avant-garde." For Lennon associated the avant-garde with the codes of happenings and Fluxus, avant-garde practices to which Ono had contributed, and to which she had introduced him, but also genres in which the nude figure often appeared as the principal material of expression. Thus, Lennon's nudity not only accrued the power to "change" him, but also was coextensive with his conception of the "avant-garde."

Lennon and Ono's achievements were neither ubiquitous nor without problems. Certainly, in the popular press they depicted their journey as fraught with pitfalls that initially caused strains and then temporarily ruptured their marriage. In Lennon's words, his separation from Ono "started in '73," a complex time in which at one point he "ended up as part of mad, drunk scenes in Los Angeles," and which, he remembered, he "finally finished . . . off on me own."[8] One of the most telling incidents in Lennon's struggle for identity, within and outside of his relationship to Ono, is described in the account he offered of an event at the Troubadour nightclub and restaurant in Los Angeles, when he emerged from the toilet with a Kotex sticking to his sweating head. A reporter recorded that Lennon supposedly asked a waitress, "Do you know who I am?" Lennon remembered the event differently:

> If I'd said, "Do you know who I am?" I'd have said it in a joke. Because I know who I am, and I know she knew because I musta been wearing a Kotex on me head, right? I picked up a Kotex in a restaurant, in the toilet, and it was clean and just for a gag I came back to the table with it on me head. And 'cause it stuck there with sweat, just stayed there, I didn't have to keep it on. It just stayed there till it fell off. And the waitress said, "Yeah, you're an asshole with a Kotex on."[9]

However, far from "knowing" who he was at that time, by his own admission, Lennon floundered in his separation from Ono. His question—"Do you know who I am?"—and his simultaneous assertion of that identity—"I know who I am"—reveal the ways in which he displaced his transforming male identity. The phallic-shaped cultural object, the Kotex signifying woman and menses, paradoxically became the symbol through which he represented the woman—Ono—responsible for reshaping his identity.

This event provides a humorous but very touching example of the personal conflict Lennon waged in his effort to redefine himself within the confines of conventional patriarchy. For Lennon repeatedly admitted his stake in culturally defined norms of masculine order. Months before his death, he stated in a *Newsweek* interview:

> I was a working-class macho guy who was used to being served and Yoko didn't buy that. From the day I met her, she demanded equal time, equal space, equal rights. I said, "Don't expect me to change in any way. Don't impinge on my space." She answered, "Then I can't be here. Because there is no space where you are. Everything revolves around you and I can't breathe in that atmosphere." I'm thankful to her for the education . . . . It's like a play—we wrote the play and we're acting in it. It's John and Yoko—you can take it or leave it . . . . Being with Yoko makes me whole.[10]

Ono took a wider, more compassionate view of Lennon's gender identity:

> I know the kind of machoism that he was surrounded with . . . in his environment—his nature itself was not very macho, he was a sweet, sensitive person but he was in that society so he didn't know any better—and when he met me, and when he saw society attacking me, I think his sort of knighthood side came out. . . . He observed it all, so then he realized what it is for women in this world. And that did a lot of good really—for him to understand feminism. He was a real feminist, you know, and he read a lot of books about it.[11]

I do not mean to present an unproblematized view of Ono's cultural position. In terms of the stereotypes for "feminine" behavior, the press and sometimes even other artists described her as stubborn and willful. Clearly she refused to be ignored either in the new music arena, in happenings and proto-Fluxus circles of the avant-garde, in the pop culture of the Beatles, or in the business world.[12] While such assertive behavior is rewarded in men, it is typically vilified in women. The press converted Ono's determination into a representation of aggression, and portrayed her persistence as opportunistic. Having suffered the abuse heaped upon her in the popular press, it is a remarkable testimony to her strength of character and vision that she continued to work.

Furthermore, in the 1970s, when Ono's protofeminist position was channeled into the organized forum of the burgeoning feminist movement, her behavior proved equally problematic. For although she was acknowledged as a feminist, and even invited to perform for an international conference sponsored by the National Organization for Women (NOW) in 1973, she continued to flaunt her sexuality by appearing in erotically titillating clothing—hot pants and low-cut blouses—and refused to behave in a politically submissive manner.

Later, as an established businesswoman, she equally disrupted convention. For it appeared to the public that Lennon had complied with what was perceived as her dominating personality by remaining at home to assume the primary childrearing role. In all of these examples, her public image was that of an uncontrollable woman, someone who defied social norms. Cultural retribution for such women is swift. They are frequently cast into the role of the *vagina dentata*, the fatal woman so vividly and maliciously depicted by Picasso and de Kooning. But, regardless of the painful personal repercussions, Ono continued to challenge and remove obstacles to her desire, confront repression, and publically denounce sexism, and by being her uncompromising self, she became what the public considered a profound nuisance.

## III

By the time Ono met Lennon in November 1966, she had pioneered and realized many of the variegated aspects of 1960s event art in performances that ranged from happenings through Fluxus to agitprop actions, body art, and conceptual art. It is well known that she entered the New York art world by way of new music circles, with her first husband, Toshi Ichiyanagi, and that John Cage was the critical influence in her development.

Ono's work evolved in the interdisciplinary, collaborative, and participatory environment of the burgeoning movement of happenings, which were characterized by their nonmatrixed juxtaposition of events. Yet, even in her earliest events, Ono's concentration upon the phenomenological and psychological content of solitary actions was clear. For example, in *A Grapefruit in the World of Park*, one of a series of "operas" she presented on November 24, 1961, at Carnegie Recital Hall, she lit the stage so dimly that participants had to strain to see. The darkness allowed her to emphasize silence and, quoting Cage's attention to silence, Ono reframed it so as to illuminate the physical sensation of alienation. In this sense, while some of her early works (such as *A Grapefruit in the World of Park*) included the simultaneous presentation of unrelated events, her works seldom had the disparate baroque *Gesamtkunstwerk* theatricality of the happening. She was not interested in exploring what she described as the happening's "assimilation of the arts," but, rather, she was concerned with the "extrication of various sensory perceptions"—not, in her words, the "get togetherness . . . but a dealing with oneself" because "life is like that."[13] She wanted the participants in her work to "start to see things beyond the shapes . . . [to] hear the kind of sounds that you hear in silence . . . to feel the environment and tension and people's vibrations . . . the sound of fear and of darkness . . . [and] of togetherness based on alienation."[14]

Ono's attention to simplified, repetitive formal structures and the use of common objects in concentrated, short events drew her into an alliance with artists with whom she helped to formulate the emergence of Fluxus. This milieu witnessed La Monte Young and Jackson Mac Low's proto-Fluxus publication *An Anthology of Chance Operations*, which was published in 1963. The volume also reflected experiences by many of the contributing artists who had participated in Cage's legendary class on musical composition at the New School for Social Research (1958–59). The performances Ono and Young sponsored in her Chamber Street loft, beginning in December 1960, were critical to the later development of Fluxus, and were attended by many artists eventually associated with that group—most importantly, its founder and principal organizer, George Maciunas. At this time, Ono joined the manipulation of objects with the use of her body as both a material tool and psychological agent of process, anticipating body art, as the artist Willoughby Sharp would define it in 1970.[15]

In 1964, Ono published her book *Grapefruit*, which contains sections on music, painting, events, poetry, objects, film, and dance. These scores for events consistently demonstrate the relationship between the physiological and the psychological. *Laugh Piece* and *Cough Piece* (both 1961), call for the performer to "keep laughing a week" and "keep coughing a year." In her *Pieces For Orchestra* (1962), the performer must "tear, touch, and rub." In *Body Sound Tape Piece* (1964), Ono focused on the sound of emotion through the ages of human development. In 1963 she emphasized the heart and the circulatory system in *Pulse Piece* and *Beat Piece*. *Beat Piece* was quietly performed in 1965 when members of the audience came onto the Carnegie Hall stage and lay down on each other's bodies to listen. The most eloquent and moving performance of *Beat Piece*, however, was internationally felt and transmitted when the work appeared, transformed, on Lennon and Ono's album *Music No. 2: Life with the Lions* (1969), as a recording of the heartbeat of their fetus, the baby Ono later miscarried while Lennon camped at her bedside on the hospital floor.

Ono's multisensual works and her acute attention to touch anticipated not only aspects of essentialist feminism of the early 1970s and cultural feminism of a decade later, but also equally the theorization of certain elements of biological determinism in the poststructuralist theory of the French feminist Luce Irigaray. In 1981, Irigaray described women's pluralistic eroticism in this way: "Woman has sex organs just about everywhere."[16] Her multiplicity of sexualized zones, Irigaray noted, creates a plurality that is based on the primacy of touch. While Ono's score for *Touch Piece* preceded Irigaray's theory by twenty years, *Touch Piece*, which reads simply, "Touch," reinforces Irigaray's claim for this polysensuality. In her song "Kiss Kiss Kiss," on *Double Fantasy*, Ono described a polyphysicality based on individual need, the attempt to "deal with the self." She sang:

> Kiss kiss kiss kiss me love . . .
> I'm bleeding inside
> It's a long, long story to tell
> And I can only show you my hell

Touch touch touch touch me love . . .
Just one touch, touch will do . . .
I'm shaking inside
Its that faint faint sound of the childhood bell
Ringing in my soul.

Ono exaggerated and highlighted physical intimacy in her *Bag Piece*, a process sculpture that eventually became the model for a series of works she began to realize in the early 1960s, but which would also appear later in her collaborations with Lennon. "Bagism" called for a single performer to get into a large black muslin bag, remove his or her clothing, and either put the clothes back on or simply sit silently to create a static silhouette that resembled a large rock. Sometimes the work was called *Stone Piece*, a title related to Ono's exhibition *The Stone* at the Judson Church Gallery in 1966.[17] A variation of the *Bag Piece* might be performed by a couple who get into the bag and do various actions that include sex. All versions of the work produced a quixotic kinetic form. Paul Krassner, editor of the *Realist* during the mid-1960s, was reported to have remembered that Ono and Tony Cox performed something similar to this piece at a macrobiotic restaurant, the Paradox, where Ono worked in 1966 as a waitress.[18] Krassner said:

> I'd been to the Paradox and I'd met Yoko and Tony. There was this tiny, tiny, stage in the back room, and they'd get into these big black bags and fuck, or not fuck. It was a very strange phenomenon. I was intrigued. So I gave her two thousand dollars—to fuck, or not fuck, in a bag.[19]

A tantalizing advertisement for this "show" that appeared in the *Village Voice* on July 14, 1966, announced: "New York is a Stone Summer Festival"—a not too subtle allusion to being "stoned." The ad continued:

> Let the others go to Fire Island, the Berkshires Provincetown. While they are away relaxing in the sun (spending lots of money) you can beat them to the cocktail hour conversation draw by dropping down to the Paradox, 64 E. 7th St. to participate in the *Stone*—art form of the future. Is it psychedelic? Is it avant-garde? Is it Zen? Whatever you think about it, you will have something to talk about. Everybody else is. Stop in any day 1–11 PM and spend an hour cooling out . . . Anthony Cox and Yoko Ono know.

Once Ono and Lennon coupled, in 1968, they employed the bag as a multivalent form of personal and public defense. The *Bag of Laughs* mocked war, and "Bagism" embraced peace and gender equality. At the same time, the couple could be seen to have publicly "bagged it," in the vernacular of the period. In other words, together they made a performance of surrender by refusing to "play the game."[20]

The content of Ono's works originated in her self-professed hunger to be touched and kissed, expressions of physical intimacy that she hoped would cauterize her bleeding inside and quell the shaking of the little girl whom she frequently described as inhabiting her when she recounted her own lonely childhood.[21] The centrality of touch as a theme in her art and its relationship to her biographical history is critical, as a series of studies undertaken immediately following World War II on the significance of touch in human development demonstrate.

At that time, the pioneering Viennese child psychoanalyst René A. Spitz wrote a paper entitled "Hospitalism: An Inquiry into the Genesis of Psychiatric Conditions in Early Childhood."[22] In his work, Spitz discussed the high mortality rate and incidence of severe developmental and psychiatric problems in individuals who, as infants, suffered from lack of physical stimulation and absence of the mother. Spitz pointed out that crib deaths resulted from a lack of affective interchange, from a lack of touch, even though the babies had been well fed and lived in clean environments. Those infants offer powerful evidence to the life-supporting primacy of touch.

Considered in the light of Spitz's work, Ono's own childhood during World War II in Japan, where she experienced deprivation, poverty, and a prolonged separation from her father, provides a stark background for the development of her art. Her emphasis on touch, and her repeated removal of herself and her lovers to a dark inner sanctuary where she might hide with them, constituted an effort to metaphorically and physically continue to exist within the sensual motion of the womb. Equally poignant was Lennon's retirement to a similar place of removal, the Dakota building in New York, in the mid-1970s. One might argue that he was metaphorically bagged away in the protected womb of his wife. Lennon's difficult working-class background in reconstructionist Britain provides ample evidence for his psychological need for the reassuring protection of a hidden space within which to heal.[23]

Ono's work originated not only in her fascination with kinesthetic and sensual experience, but also in her rejection of patriarchal domination. She manifested her defense against phallocentricity in humor and in metaphors of violence and destruction. In a brief 1967 essay, Ono wrote:

> I wonder why men can get serious at all. They have this delicate long thing hanging outside their bodies, which goes up and down by its own will. First of all having it outside your body is terribly dangerous. If I were a man I would have a fantastic castration complex to the point that I wouldn't be able to do a thing. Second, the inconsistency of it, like carrying a chance time alarm or something. If I were a man I would always be laughing at myself. Humor is probably something the male of the species discovered through his own anatomy. But men are so serious. Why? Why violence? Why hatred? Why war? . . . Men have an unusual talent for making a bore out of everything they touch. Art, painting, sculpture, like who wants a cast-iron woman for instance.[24]

Later, continuing her critique of penial culture, Ono and Lennon held the phallus up as an object for examination and ridicule—a humor tinted with mockery, as in their film *Erection* (1971). In *Erection*, they record the construction of a building, with its steel girders and supports, by filming it from the same point of view over a period of time. Commenting on the film, critic John Hanhardt described the gradual evolution of the structure on an empty lot as an "organic form 'growing' before our eyes."[25] Hanhardt's formalistic description of the process, however, fails to stress the ideological statement Ono expressed in the selection of an architectural metaphor for the rigid phallus. Here, the erection of a building parodies the cultural construction of phallic identity embodied in the edifice of erection. In *Erection*, Ono and Lennon cleverly satirized, by juxtaposition, the false symmetry of culturally constructed nature/culture dichotomies in the identification of gender.

Even before 1967, Ono had created protofeminist art actions that commented on women's submissive domestic roles. For example, in 1961 Yvonne Rainer performed Ono's event *A Piece for Strawberries and Violins*:

> Rainer stood up and sat down before a table stacked with dishes. At the end of ten minutes, she smashed the dishes. Her action was accompanied by a rhythmic background of repeated syllables, a tape recording of moans and words spoken backwards, and an aria of high-pitched wails sung by Ono.[26]

Four years later, in 1965, Ono offered one of her paintings as a critique of suburban female etiquette when she laughed, "I can just see a Bronxville housewife saying to her guests 'do add a circle to my painting before you have a drink.'"[27]

Ono rejected normative gender roles very early, and such works laid the foundation for the more aggressive feminist position both she and Lennon asserted in the 1970s. They coauthored and recorded the song "Woman is the Nigger of the World" (1972), which appeared on the albums *Sometime in New York City* and *Shaved Fish*. In this song they publicly acknowledged the repression of women and owned up to the psychological and social state of denigration shared between women and blacks. In this way, they used the term of black defilement, "nigger," to reclaim for women and for people of color (like Ono) a place where the injustice of language and the epistemological systems that underpin that language might be confronted.[28] They sang:

> Woman is the nigger of the world . . . think about it . . . do something about it. We make her paint her face and dance. If she won't be a slave, we say that she don't love us. If she's real, we say she's trying to be a man. While putting her down we pretend that she's above us. If you don't believe me, take a look at the one you're with. Woman is the slave of slaves.[29]

The kind of gender suffering described in "Woman is the Nigger of the World" runs throughout Ono's work. It erupted early in angry scores such as

**CONVERSATION PIECE**

**Bandage any part of your body.**
**If people ask about it, make a story and tell.**
**If people do not ask about it, draw their attention to it and tell.**
**If people forget about it, remind them of it and keep telling.**
**Do not talk about anything else.**

**1962 summer**

FIGURE 16. Yoko Ono, *Conversation Piece*, summer 1962. This text first appeared in Yoko Ono's *Grapefruit* (Tokyo and Bellport, NY: Wunternaum Press, 1964). Courtesy of the artist.

"Wall Piece For Orchestra to Yoko Ono" (1962), in which she instructed the performer simply to "hit a wall with your head." Ten years later, in 1972, she again expressed this self-destruction in her song "I Felt Like Smashing My Face in a Clear Glass Window," on the album *Approximately Infinite Universe*.

But in 1962, Ono wrote the score for *Conversation Piece*, which emphasized the necessity for human beings to narrate individual pain, to "tell," share, and communicate even in the face of public indifference (figure 16). Ono invented bandaged wounds to articulate her psychophysical pain. This impulse to narrate suffering, to describe the unspeakable conditions of interior life, is central to finding a voice through and by which to repossess and recover a sense of the concreteness of personal experience and, certainly as urgently, to communicate that autobiographical experience to someone else. In this sense, Ono's work anticipated by several decades what Mae G. Henderson described as the "body as historical text" in her brilliant analysis of Toni Morrison's novel *Beloved*. Henderson wrote that Morrison's task was

> to transgress, discursive boundaries by setting up a complementary and dialogic relationship between the "interiority" of her own work and the "exteriority" of the slave narrative. . . . To the degree that (Morrison's) work is intended to resurrect stories buried and express stories repressed, Morrison's relationship to the slave narrators, as well as the relationship of her text to its precursor narratives, can be profitably compared not only to the relationship of the historian to his or her informant, but also the analyst to the analysand.[30]

Ono's *Conversation Piece*, like many of her scores, may be understood as a kind of autoanalytic, autobiographical transformation of an essentially private knowledge into a public aesthetic form, through and in which others might find a vehicle to a personal voice. Ono's ability to create models from personal and intimate experience for public and social actions is critical to the radical social content of her art and of her impact on future actions with Lennon.

Ono's suffering represented her need to be loved and touched as much as it equally reflected her experience as a woman. She needed to "tell," and that telling bespeaks something of women's experience as described by Dimen, who observed:

> Every time a woman goes for a walk, her mind and her body are invaded by a social definition of her femininity that threatens to disconnect her from her own experience. This is the experience of domination, the loss of one's sense of and wish for autonomy, as a result of processes that play on one's doubts about the reality and validity of one's self, one's perceptions, and one's values.[31]

Indeed, Dimen's evocation of the violence that women experience when simply walking on the street was a theme that Ono explored in 1969 with her film *Rape*. In this film, the camera (operated by Nic Knowland) and the sound (produced by Christian Wangler and Ono) relentlessly follow a woman (Eva Majlath) on the street, pursuing her aggressively into her apartment. As Hanhardt has written, the camera becomes a "transgressor of privacy, an invader of the human body and thus an extension of the male film crew and of ourselves as viewer-voyeurs."[32] *Rape* also proclaims the cultural domination of women, escape from which preoccupies many women to the extent that little energy remains for the validation and development of self. As Dimen notes:

> Individualizing is a mainstream cultural ideal. Connoting autonomy, agency, and singularity, it also suggests the kind of adult who is responsible for himself and no one else. . . . Relatedness, then, connotes the personal and the interpersonal, the particular and the pragmatic, care and nurturance, and invisible, ephemeral processes and feelings . . . .[33]

Feminist scholar Susan Gubar has pointed out that "woman's image of herself as text and artifact has affected her attitudes toward her physicality and she argues how, then, these attitudes in turn shape the metaphors through which she images her creativity. . . . Women have had to experience cultural scripts in their lives by suffering them in their bodies. . . . For the artist, this sense that she is herself the text means that there is little distance between her life and her art."[34] In this sense, Ono made her art a way to narrate her life. She provided scores and scripts for her viewers to use to tell their own intimate experiences and keep telling them until the repetition had dimmed not only the meaning of the tales but also the feeling of pain.

In *Women's Ways of Knowing: The Development of Self, Voice, and Mind*, the editors point out that sociolinguists have observed "a tendency for women to ground their epistemological premises in metaphors [that] suggest [that] speaking and listening [are] at odds with visual metaphors that scientists and philosophers most often use to express their sense of mind."[35] These theorists also note that women's emphasis on speaking and listening posit a different kind of knowledge and construct a different state of mind: "Visual metaphors encourage standing at a distance to get a proper view, removing—it is believed—subject and object from a sphere of possible intercourse."[36] However, these feminist theorists have also observed that in women's emphasis on speaking and listening, a different kind of knowledge and mind is constructed, for "unlike the eye, the ear operates by registering nearby subtle change. Unlike the eye, the ear requires closeness between subject and object. Unlike seeing, speaking and listening suggest dialogue and interaction."[37]

In her work, Ono sought to redress alienation precisely by plunging experience into the unstable space of auditory sensory intercourse. Her film *Fly* (1970), for example, featured a continuous shot of a fly traversing the nude body of a woman, accompanied by a soundtrack from Ono's record of the same name, which featured "a 22-minute long series of alternately soothing and gratingly raw, but elemental female vocal noises—sighing, screeching, pathetic humming, and childlike crying, burping, choking, etc."[38] This film highlighted both the tactile and the auditory elements found in *Conversation Piece*, where Ono stressed the "telling" and "telling again" of pain, a "telling" that brought the individual in contact and touch with several other individuals.

The theme of relatedness that runs throughout Ono's work, her need to tell, her compulsion to scream—that scream that appeared in what Lennon called her "sixteen multitrack voice," and which surfaced again in the Plastic Ono Band and anticipated the dissonant sounds of punk—appeared most powerfully in her action *Cut Piece*, realized in 1964 in Japan, on March 21, 1965, at Carnegie Hall in New York, and again in 1966 before an international gathering of artists in London at the Destruction in Art Symposium (DIAS). In *Cut Piece*, Ono sat motionless on the stage after inviting the audience to come up and cut away her clothing. Both in New York and in London, when she performed *Cut Piece* she covered her breasts at the moment of unbosoming. *Cut Piece* entailed a disrobing, a denouement of the reciprocity between exhibitionism and scopic desires, between victim and assailant, between sadist and masochist, and ultimately of man and woman and the unveiling of the gendered relationships of subject and object. *Cut Piece* also recalls her psychic experiences, intimate sensations she expressed in this statement:

> People went on cutting the parts they do not like of me finally there was only the stone remained of me that was in me but they were still not satisfied and wanted to know what it's like in the stone.[39]

*Cut Piece* is an intervention that went beyond social, political, and gender issues to aesthetic concerns. It also deconstructed the subject/object relationships that reside behind the edifice of art—the often-presumed opaque neutrality of the ubiquitous art object and distant art observer. In *Cut Piece*, Ono demonstrated the viewer's responsibility for the condition, reception, and preservation of art objects by addressing the destructive side of creation.

Ono felt that it was precisely the kind of relentless psychological and psychic feeling she typified in *Cut Piece* that marginalized her work in the art world. Her explanation was reasonable. She said her work was "not well accepted even in the avant-garde because the New York avant-garde was into cool art, not hot"; she continued, "What I do was too emotional. In a way they thought it was too animalistic."[40] In the post-abstract expressionist school of Beatnik cool that in New York had hardened into the ice of minimalism, Ono's work was felt to be too much. Indeed, both Ono and Carolee Schneemann, two women whose work dealt with visceral expression of sexuality and emotion, felt ignored within their own milieu, despite being invited to exhibit and perform. Schneemann has described the experience as one of simply not belonging to the "men's art team," despite their pioneering work.[41] A telling reflection of the differences between European and North American tolerance for and interest in erotic and expressionist work is, however, the fact that both Schneemann's and Ono's work was supported more readily in Europe than in the States, even though the art "scenes" on both continents were equally male-dominated and gender-exclusive.

While Ono was part of the aesthetic artistic underground in New York, her involvement with the political underground dates from her European period, beginning with her participation in DIAS. DIAS, in fact, set the stage for Ono's introduction to Lennon. Immediately following DIAS, in November 1966, she held an exhibition at Indica Gallery, then in Mason's Yard near St. James' Picadilly in London. Indica was housed in the same building as the British underground newspaper the *International Times* (*IT*). Miles[42] not only served on the editorial staff but had also been part of the DIAS honorary organizing executive committee. In its November issue, *IT* advertised Ono's historic Indica exhibition. Ironically, the ad announced an "ONO-WOMAN SHOW" and went on to explain that this "one-man show" would consist of "Instruction Paintings" and was "the first showing of her works outside the U.S. and Japan . . . in which the audience will be directly responsible for the construction of the paintings."

Even before her Indica exhibition, Ono had identified herself with the radical counter-culture in subtle but unmistakable ways. Notes to her program of DIAS performances explained that "the bicycle used in 'Bicycle Piece for Orchestra' is one of the original White Bicycles made by the PROVOS when they were brought here to London earlier this year by DIAS." In this manner Ono linked herself, through DIAS, to the agitprop happening events originated by the Dutch PROVOS in Holland, who since 1965 had sparked demonstrations by workers and students that resulted in riots and incidents provoking and challenging the Dutch government.[43]

The infamy Ono earned in Europe was derived principally, however, from her *Film No. 4 (Bottoms)*. While the first version of the film was made in New York in 1966 and was included in Fluxfilms, Ono shot a longer version of *Bottoms* the following year with Tony Cox in London, where it gained its notoriety. Stylistically a minimalist film recalling Warhol's many early films of 1963 (*Kiss, Sleep, Haircut, Eat, Blow-Job*, among others) and 1964 (*Empire, Harlot, Taylor Bead's Ass*, among others), *Bottoms* featured the silent movement of 365 naked London bottoms, often of famous people. *Bottoms* failed to pass the British Board of Film Censors at the time.[44] Ono continued to encounter problems with *Bottoms* in Belgium when in the summer of 1967 she was invited to enter the film in a festival of experimental films in Knokke-le-Zoute. Once there, however, despite censorship, she participated in a scandalous protest-happening by appearing together with many other artists naked in the "Election of Miss Festival," an agitprop action orchestrated to protest a nearby military installation. The action was calculated to outrage the Belgian minister of justice, who was presiding over the film festival.[45] Jean-Jacques Lebel, a French painter, poet, pioneer of happenings, and political activist, staged the event, which briefly landed him in prison after he was found guilty of insulting public morality. Ono's association with him only added to her pedigree as a participant in the radical artistic underground. Although much has been written about Lennon's associations with radicals such as Jerry Rubin, Ono had prepared the ground for such interactions several years before their pictures were taken with Rubin in 1971 on their way to a benefit for Attica Prison.

While it is unlikely that Rubin and other political activists would have ever sought out Ono without her connection to Lennon, her experience in the environment of the international activist underground helped her to refocus the happening as a political action into which she later drew Lennon. In this regard, *Cut Piece* is critical as a transitional work, not only for the resonance it had in the international underground, but for the way in which she transformed the aesthetic event into a socially critical work. For although *Cut Piece* remains tied to her own private struggles to find a tactile outlet through which to voice a language for pain, *Cut Piece* was equally social commentary and an unbosoming of the complicit relationship first between individuals and secondly between the individual and the social body, its constructs, and its collectivized behaviors.

## IV

Once Ono began to live with Lennon in 1968, their collaborations served as a model for the extension of performance from the private, egocentric sphere of personal body-action (with its communication of a self-reflexive psyche) to a performative act, self-consciously realized in the public arena as collective social intervention and political action. In March 1969, when Ono and Lennon married, they immediately moved into the Amsterdam Hilton for their honeymoon. There they converted the ubiquitous 1960s gathering-of-the-flock, the "Be-In," into a weeklong "Bed-In" for peace. During this event they conducted interviews ten hours a day, they explained, "to protest against any form of violence." They noted: "Bed-Ins are something that everybody can do and they're so simple. We're willing to be the world's clowns to make people realize it."[46] In May of that year, in Montreal, they repeated the "Bed-In," conducting more than sixty radio interviews. The "Bed-In" anticipated an art of electronic and global dimension fifteen years before Nam June Paik used satellites to connect his internationally televised program *Good-Morning Mr. Orwell* of New Year's Day, 1984.[47]

The use of the "Be-In" as an aesthetic strategy had already appeared in Ono's work before her union with Lennon. In the August 1967 issue of *Art and Artists*, an announcement publicized a "Be-In" in London by Ono. The ad for this happening-transformed-Be-In read:

> Yoko Ono, whose now famous "bottom" movie is being shown to the general public at the Jacey Cinema, Charing Cross Road, is holding a weekend of Events at the Midlands Art Centre in Birmingham on October 14th. She is planning to present a "be-in," lectures, two film showings, a concert and whatever else might flash into her ever-active mind. The Brummies may not realize what hit them until after the event—Miss Ono being noted for the enigmatic quality of her work.[48]

The mystery and enigma inherent in Ono's earlier work became overt and accessible in her collaborations with Lennon, as when they revised Ono's *Beat Piece* and recorded the actual heartbeat of the fetus she eventually miscarried. The "Bed-In" extended the "telling" and "touching" implicit and explicit in all of her art from the private intercourse of the nuptial bed to a discourse with the public. In the "Bed-In," the couple allowed themselves to be seen and, more importantly, to be heard in the promotion of a personal will for the public construction of what they called "peace and love." Moreover, in the "Bed-In," Lennon and Ono defied racism and classicism in their presentation of an aristocratic Asian woman in bed with an English working-class man and international celebrity. The "Bed-In" undermined sexism in the representation of a marriage of equality. It subverted conventional as well as radical politics by fusing the public art-event, the happening or "Be-In," with the private events of the human body. In this way, Lennon and Ono returned politics to the bedroom, site of private neuroses, battleground of the sexes, and territory of their possible recovery.

Furthermore, Lennon and Ono transformed her artistic "Be-In" into their joint political statement, a paradigm for public action. The "Bed-In" represented a powerful plea for international peace, symbolized by love and signified in the matrimonial bed. It located Ono and Lennon at the popular cultural center of the international pacifist movement. But the legacy of these events resides in

Lennon's name alone. For example, John Bushnell cites one aspect of the international impact of Lennon on pacifism in his book *Moscow Graffiti*. Bushnell points out that all branches of the Soviet counterculture identified with Lennon:

> Counterculture pacifists were, from the beginning, prolific graffiti writers. The pacifist message lent itself to clear statement more readily than did the diffused ideas of the hippies. . . . [For] hippies, intellectually committed to disengagement from the world, did not seek to spread their views, [while] pacifists, by contrast, were determined to address Soviet society.[49]

Furthermore, Bushnell notes:

> Lennon has become the patron saint of the Soviet pacifists, as the annual memorial observances of his death would indicate. In 1983, pacifists in Riga asked to be officially registered as the John Lennon Peace Committee. [But even earlier] memorial meetings on the anniversary of John Lennon's death were held on the Lennon hill overlooking Moscow. The very first of these memorials was in fact held immediately after Lennon was gunned down in December 1980.[50]

These are just two of numerous examples in which Lennon, not Ono, has been credited and associated with worldwide pacifism until recently, when Ono has begun to be acknowledged as equal to Lennon in her work for peace.

As the "Bed-In" linked sexual union with political and social intercourse, Lennon and Ono clearly rejected violence and destruction as effective models for the resolution of conflict. This position signaled an important clarification, if not shift, away from the element of violence and destruction that had been present in Ono's work since the late 1950s. Such scores as her *Blood Piece* (1960), for example, had called for the performer to

> Use your blood to paint. Keep painting until you faint (a) Keep painting until you die (b).

Tony Cox discussed the destructive aspects of Ono's work in the article he wrote for the special issue on "Auto-Destructive Art" that *Art and Artists* published in August 1966, an issue which anticipated DIAS. However, although Ono recognized the affinities that her work shared with destruction as it was used to create art, and although she participated in DIAS, she had also relentlessly separated herself from the actual violent and destructive expressions she encountered there. Raphael Montañez Ortiz, a Puerto Rican artist and DIAS participant, recalled that after he performed *Chair Destruction* at one of the earliest DIAS press conferences, Ono took the podium and announced: "I don't think destroying a chair is destruction art. I don't think throwing blood around is destruction art. It's much more subtle than that."[51]

The point is that although Ono's work contained both conceptually masochistic and violent elements, these functioned as imaginary techniques for communicating and confronting pain, frustration, anger, and sorrow. Ono employed these elements to express the inexpressibility of pain. In her score for performances, many of which can be found in *Grapefruit*, she refers to destruction and violence as an aspect of imagination, asking the performer to think pain into objecthood. In this state of imagining, one may literally objectify that which has no objective reality, and by so doing move toward not only sharing but enduring, and perhaps even overcoming, that pain. In 1970 Ono wrote, "Violence is a sad wind that, if channeled carefully, could bring seeds, chairs and all things pleasant to us."[52] She also observed, "The job of an artist is not to destroy but to change the value of things."[53] Together with Lennon, Ono was able to dispense with the masochistic, self-destructive elements in her work; Lennon's well-documented aversion to violence should not be underestimated in the healing and refocusing of her art.

After the "Bed-In," Lennon and Ono continued to condense personal issues into a public discourse on broad political concerns. In a Montreal press conference on December 15, 1969, at the height of the Vietnam War, they launched a Christmas peace billboard campaign:

WAR IS OVER!
IF YOU WANT IT

They strategically installed their billboards in urban centers around the world: Times Square in New York, the Sunset Strip in Los Angeles, and Shaftesbury Avenue in central London. Then, holding up a black bag they called the "Bag of Laughs" (again a transformation of Ono's *Bag Piece*) at their Montreal press conference, they simultaneously signaled the folly of war and the joy of peace. They laughed in the face of institutionally circumscribed "states of war," and insisted that responsibility for change and peace was lodged in the individual, "if you want it."

Their billboards were located not simply in major cities but in entertainment districts: the film industry of Hollywood; the theater, literary, and art district of London around Shaftsbury. In those locations the public announcement linked entertainment-as-spectacle with the theater of war in which art actions might intervene. Times Square provided a densely populated stage set for the conjunction of art and politics, an arena other artists would soon mine.

*War Is Over* was immediately followed in January 1970 with an action in which the couple got radical haircuts, which in their severe style anticipated punk in the midst of hippie hair fetishism. This action functioned as a metaphorical protest, an inversion of the culturally proscribed, a critique of conformity within even radical ranks, for the length of one's hair still signified the credentials of youth, rebellion, and alternative values. In addition, the sale of the hair trimmings had an important economic function. Ono and Lennon donated the funds to Michael Abdul Malik, also known as Michael X, a radical black poet and human rights activist from Trinidad. Michael X used the proceeds to start up the Blackhouse, a black culture center in London. He had been earlier involved in the Free Playgrounds, a community-based attempt to clear and rehabilitate remaining bomb sites left from World War II in London's underclass and working-class neighborhoods. One of these playgrounds, significantly, became the primary site for DIAS. The Blackhouse burned down months after it was begun. Michael X was later arrested for robbery, and in 1973 he was convicted of two murders. In 1975 he was hanged—a death sentence that artists and activists throughout the world vigorously protested.[54]

Such media events and involvement with the underground of the late 1960s served as volatile material evidence that was eventually used against Lennon by the US government against his attempts to immigrate. These efforts occupied Lennon's attention until 1975, even though the government's case against him was based upon little more than a 1968 conviction for possession of marijuana.[55] Given Ono and Lennon's many years of litigation against the US government, one might speculate that such associations formed the background for the curious absence of critical attention given to some of Ono's most provocative process and action-oriented work. A public image seems to have been architected very carefully to distract from the most compelling aspects of her art and its history. So, for example, in a later interview (1986), when she mentioned the Knokke-le-Zoute festival in Belgium, where she and Tony Cox had appeared nude and Jean-Jacques Lebel had been arrested as organizer, she explained merely:

> There was a film festival in Belgium in 1967, the Knokke Film Festival and they invited me to show the "Bottoms" film. You're supposed to sign some document to register for the festival first, and I forgot that part of it. So I went to the festival, and they showed my film and some of the judges came from America obviously, and they said, "We were determined to give you a prize, but we can't because you didn't register."[56]

In addition, the pamphlet accompanying Ono's exhibition at the Whitney in 1989 only mentioned her DIAS participation in a brief sentence: "She was invited to participate in the 'Destruction in Art Symposium' in London, a conference of some fifty artists from around the world.'"[57] Such references discreetly distanced Ono from the more controversial and politically volatile elements of the 1960s counterculture. Certainly, from a legal standpoint it became not only reasonable but also expedient and advisable to do so. For while struggling to be accepted as an artist—an acceptance she found, ironically, in the radical underground—she also needed to carefully construct a context for the reception of her work in a manner that suited her evolving social position as much as Lennon's legal situation. Nevertheless, this period in Ono's life and art was pivotal to the impact both she and Lennon had in the public.

The London art critic Jasia Reichardt observed that Ono's influence operated by infiltration.[58] Infiltration by diffusion made it possible for Lennon and Ono to couch the category "art" in the vernacular activity of the period, the "Be-In," and to transform that action into a "Bed-In" of international political significance. Infiltration by diffusion was also the agent of Lennon's change.

## V

In *Madame Butterfly*, Pinkerton describes his geisha as fluttering "like a butterfly" with a "divine sweet little voice." He states:

> I cannot say whether it's love or caprice. Certainly I know she has seduced me with her ingenious ways. . . . I am seized by a wild desire to pursue her, even though I should crush her wings in doing so.

*Madame Butterfly* condenses a patriarchal Western narrative of authority—the ability to possess, use, abuse, and finally discard the seductress whose ingenuity is blamed for boiling wild passion in the man—a tale of power based upon the control of obedient, submissive women that was exercised in Asia before and during World War II. This is the narrative the public employed then, and continues to employ now, to strip Ono of her authenticity and originality and to vilify her. The opera condenses this Western male desire then displaces and reconstitutes it in the arena of least resistance: the cliché of the Asian woman as the ultimate object, a being of fragile vulnerability and bound feet, the victim of sadism who is then presented as a willing masochist. *Madame Butterfly* is a drama of female powerlessness and male authority over the ethnic female other.

Yoko Ono posed a deeply threatening challenge to this stereotype and the structure of power upon which it rests. For what was the public to make of this delicate, small, Japanese woman with her childlike voice, shy demeanor, and breathless personal style—the perfect Butterfly—who nevertheless defied these concepts and whose famous and publically adored husband subjugated himself to her by sleeping at her feet and admitting, "I'm forever in your debt"?

Hounded, mocked, and discredited, John Lennon authorized male feminism in his exemplary existence with Ono. However, rather than understanding the serious psychological and ideological statement that Lennon's transformations represented, fans, the media, and even Lennon's friends commonly dismissed his actions as excess and eccentricity. His struggle to divest himself of traditional gender and cultural categories, his househusband phase, was even rumored in popular culture to be a guise behind which he hid an addiction to heroin. Lennon's valorization of women's activity earned the vibrant Ono the deadly epithet "dragon lady." A reference to the role of the castrating female, the term "dragon" (a metonym for Asia) revealed the thinly disguised specter of Western racism: the fear of the mythic "Yellow Peril," the continuing repressed fury over the indignity of Pearl Harbor, and the deeply rooted Western stereotype of the Asian as devious and secretive. Ono's public rebellion, her rejection of Japanese customs and manners, and the rigid conformity demanded by the aristocratic tradition into which she had been born added to the confrontation she posed to Western concepts of a Japanese woman.[59] Thus, in the United States her ethnic identity was collapsed into that of the "alien culture" that had contributed to World War II, had survived to produce electronic wonders like portable radios and Instamatic cameras, and was the exotic source of an industry that swelled the market with colossal quantities of commercial kitsch. It should not be forgotten that in the cultural climate of the 1960s, all of these associations would have formed the subtext of Ono's identity. They all clashed with the network of aesthetic practices espoused by the bohemian, intellectual milieu of the art world to which she belonged, and the working- and middle-class values of the pop music milieu from which Lennon had emerged.

The blame projected onto Ono for Lennon's transformations stripped him of the responsibility he took for himself in choosing the multiple factors that empowered and liberated him: feminism, otherness, and the naked body on public display. In this way he was deprived of the honor he might have claimed for his rejection of the position of dominance, his exemplary support of a woman, and his adaptation of feminist principles that became the foundation for his music and lyrics in the 1970s. Ono, too, was systematically negated: robbed of recognition for her unique contributions to art, for her part in Lennon's liberation, and for her joint authorship of LENONO. In the end, not the public but the internal politics and institutions of criticism in both the visual arts and pop music contributed most substantially to dispossessing Ono and Lennon of their achievements in each other's cultural and sexual domain.

While Lennon remained at center stage during his life, Ono's prior work formed the foundation and architecture of their activities. She had clearly observed the distinction between art and life and did not share the naïve, universalizing view that the two might merge, contrary to what many artists and critics have maintained. Already in 1966 she had written: "Art is not merely a duplication of life, to assimilate art in life, is different from art duplicating life."[60] She realized that the radical element in presentational art is the difference it demonstrates between art and life, constructed on the distance across which the performance conducts a metonymic transit that momentarily reveals the contingency between culture and body. Like a synaptic impulse, presentational art communicates from the metaphoric to the actual, and from the simultaneously individuated and constructed conditions of the personal to the collective.

Ono elaborated her emotive ways of knowing by pioneering techniques and methods of performance that conveyed the feminist ideology and politics that feminized Lennon. Through Lennon, her art and philosophy diffused into world culture—that imaginary space about which Lennon sang in "Imagine" (1971): a place without geographical, national, racial, or sexual boundaries. Ono described this space when she wrote, "A dream you dream alone may be a dream, but a dream two people dream is a reality."[61] Together, Lennon and Ono repeatedly sought and explored ways to be the producers of their own discourse and the authors of a state they might claim as authentic. They reinvented themselves continually, from their beginning in *Two Virgins* to their primal scream regression therapy, and in songs such as "(Just Like) Starting Over."

Together, with the structural support of the aesthetics of performance, Ono and Lennon anticipated an alternative model for experience, something akin to what the Scottish psychoanalyst R. D. Laing identified in 1967 as "the politics of experience," or what feminists described when they insisted, "The personal is the political."[62] Their continual reinvention, redefinition, and restatement of the conditions of felt experience was employed not solely for the purpose of narcissistic self-fulfillment, but as a process connected to both the social and political climate of their historical moment, and most importantly, to a history they actively participated in constructing.

Lennon and Ono continually confronted or refused to be complicit in the construction of stereotypical roles other than the ones they had invented—except, most significantly, the institution of marriage. Indeed, marriage provided a culturally defined form in which they ironically defied social mores and undermined class divisions and cultural racism. The marriage pledge legitimized the much debated and contested state of their union. In other words, they used the institution of marriage against the racism of the very society that had established it as an institution.

From the public's perspective, Lennon seemed to have nothing to gain from his marriage to Ono. But his actions repeatedly demonstrated that it was not the public sphere that he honored but the private, that space traditionally consigned to women. Upon the site of this woman, Yoko Ono, Lennon constructed something of a self that resembled the self he identified as John Lennon. He repeatedly acknowledged his need for and love of Yoko Ono, which in large measure seems to have fortified his will to forge circuitous paths, however unstable, toward his own authenticity, an authenticity and freedom he identified as coextensive with Yoko Ono. Just before his death, he made this experience clear when he sang on *Double Fantasy*:

Even when I'm miles at sea
And nowhere is the place to be
Your spirit's watching over me dear Yoko . . .
After all is really said and done
The two of us are really one
The goddess really smiled upon our love dear
Yoko.

This essay has been an attempt to account for an aspect of the critical exchange with social and cultural formations that John Lennon and Yoko Ono undertook in the 1960s and 1970s. In exploring the biographical and cultural events that belong to the various histories that have been narrated around this couple, I have sought to recover and situate their vital interchange in the context of the theory and practice of live performed art. The ideological and formal elements of happenings and Fluxus contributed an important share in providing them with an alternative structure through which to redefine ways not only of being in the world, but also of affectively intervening in the world. In this sense, as a link in the complex chain of changes that have transpired across the twentieth century, performance art in all its various manifestations continues the utopian aim of early-twentieth-century artists to intervene in life and alter it. This genre of visual art has always been revolutionary and controversial because at its structural center, the presentation of the body is a moral and ethical act that comments upon the ideological space that impinges upon that body. As the material of such a living art is the human body, as the material of performed art is human action in real time and space, and as the content of live art is human experience, the political dimension of the body in a social nexus is thus always manifest in this art.

The visual art event, with its emphasis on the body, permitted Ono and Lennon to use their bodies as the primary site for the construction of social and cultural change. They literally became acting agents able to demonstrate the relationship, interconnectedness, and contiguity of acting and viewing subjects. Moreover, as an international celebrity, Lennon already belonged to the public, thus making his work with Ono and their collective ideas more acceptable to the public. But, beyond the limited confines of aesthetic discourse, Ono and Lennon as acting subjects could transgress the philosophical alienation existentially experienced between human subjects by demonstrating their connectedness. In their public actions they functioned as human material, paradigms through which the value of social exchange could be forged. They not only offered an example for human reciprocity between genders, classes, races, and nationalities, but also provided a model for how to negotiate a responsible interaction in the political order. Ono realized this dimension of her aesthetic practice, and she taught it to Lennon, who himself experienced aspects of the power of the presentation of the body in his musical performances.

Drawing upon this history and elaborating it with the mutual appropriation of aspects of each other's gender experience and identity, this remarkable woman and man created a transgressive opening in culture internationally. Their opening in the social should not be described as a rupture in the usual radical sense of the avant-garde. Rather, it was a blossoming, an unbosoming, that continues to constitute an example of a liberating experience. Their struggle is pre-paradigmatic of a new epistemology of human interaction that is the task and challenge of the twenty-first century.

# III. Shooting Range

# Burden of Light: Chris Burden (2007)[1]

*Swear on your eyes . . . to the truth.*
JOSÉ SARAMAGO, *Blindness*

Light pervades Chris Burden's work, from the glint of a bullet to that light emitted by solar rays, fire, and electricity, and the refracted luminosity of materials like glass, nickel, water, gold, and diamonds. Titles such as *Icarus*, *The Speed of Light Machine*, *The Fist of Light*, and *Urban Light* attest to four decades of Burden's fascination with the capacity of light to elucidate aspects of human experience and consciousness. Rather than being used as a medium in and of itself, light becomes a multifaceted signifier for a wide range of meanings and subjects in his work, including myths and metaphors for knowledge; the authority of institutional practices, especially those of science and technology; the politics of social space and war; the mysterious energies of natural forces; and questions of morality, ethics, and the obverse, as darkness partners equally with light in Burden's art. His work with light can be sinister and foreboding, plunge viewers into pitch-blackness, expose the lethal and life-giving potentialities of light, and juxtapose visibility and invisibility. Light bears a singular task in Burden's art: to manifest and communicate the ancient concepts and qualities of *lux* (symbolizing "the light of ideas, speculations, inference, revelation and divine illumination") and *lumen* (related to knowledge gained from empirical evidence in the observable dimensions of light).[2]

Light figures in more than fifty works in Burden's art in a range of media. Yet, despite its physical, physiological, and psychological centrality to Burden's practice, art historians and critics have uniformly neglected light as a crucial dimension of his oeuvre. This is due in no small measure to the critical hyperbole that has plagued his reception and interfered with an appropriately scholarly consideration of his work's semiotics. An example of this sort of criticism is a 1974 review by James Collins, who charged Burden with "game-playing" and "tokenly dangerous" acts, as well as with "raging for chaos."[3] Erroneously claiming that Burden shot "himself in the arm" in his performance *Shoot* (November 19, 1971), Collins then linked this inaccurate account to the equally erroneous story that Austrian artist Rudolf Schwarzkogler had "sequentially mutilated his own penis."[4] Such criticism unfairly discredited performance art and justifiably dismayed Burden. "I didn't do performances for that many years [because] the press was too distorting," he said. "I would read what they had written and [think], 'My God! Who are they talking about?!' "[5] In contrast, more thoughtful criticism has noted a range of significant conceptual and historical themes in Burden's work, including a "will to power,"[6] the pursuit of "self- and situational control,"[7] "danger, risk, and unexpected survival in the cosmos of technology,"[8] masochistic extremes,[9] and "pure renunciation."[10] These subjects are qualities and conditions of Burden's art, but such descriptions miss a quintessential philosophical dimension of his work: the sculptural role that light plays as it shapes Burden's viewers' psychological and psychophysical experiences, and as it both transmits and sustains Burden's own unique aesthetic vision and the principled concepts represented in his art.

Nevertheless, it is true that danger distinguishes the material conditions of many of Burden's works. Burden calculates unleashing violence as a means to oblige himself and his viewers to act with mutual responsibility and trust. So that while one may justifiably point to unprecedented fearsome aspects of his work, no other artist has so consistently trusted the public to react to dangerous and challenging situations and to treat the artist and his artworks with such responsibility. In short, Burden trusted viewers *not* to electrocute him in *Prelude to 220, or 110* (1971) and *220* (1971); *not* to kill him in *Shoot* (1971); *not* to starve him in *Bed Piece* (1972) and *Doomed* (1975); *not* to abandon him in *Deadman* (1972); *not* to permit him to be severely burned in *Icarus* (1973); *not* to let him drown in *Velvet Water* (1974); *not* to permanently damage his body in *Trans-Fixed* (1974) and *Back to You* (1974); *not* to destroy buildings in *Samson* (1985) and *Exposing the Foundations of the Museum* (1986–88); *not* to let technology overpower reason in *Big Wheel* (1979); *not* to neglect cultural heritage in *Urban Light* (2005); *not* to forget the transgressions of power in *The Other Vietnam Memorial* (1991), *America's Darker Moments* (1994), *Hidden Force* (1995), *The Mexican Bridge* (1998), and *L.A.P.D. Uniforms* (1993); and *not* to forget the possibility of nuclear holocaust in *A Tale of Two Cities* (1981). Given this litany of ways in which Burden has activated the conscience and ethics of viewers, the time has come to shift the discourse about his art away from its more spectacular aspects to its experiential depth where *lux* and *lumen* unite in trust.

## BLIND TRUTH

In *White Light/White Heat* (February 8–March 1, 1975), Burden remained invisible on an elevated platform in the Ronald Feldman Gallery in New York for twenty-two days without seeing nor speaking to anyone or coming down from the platform (figure 17). Burden based his title on Lou Reed's 1967 song about heroin addiction, sung by the Velvet Underground.[11] In part, the endurance aspect of his performance obliquely referred to the physical effects of heroin, in-

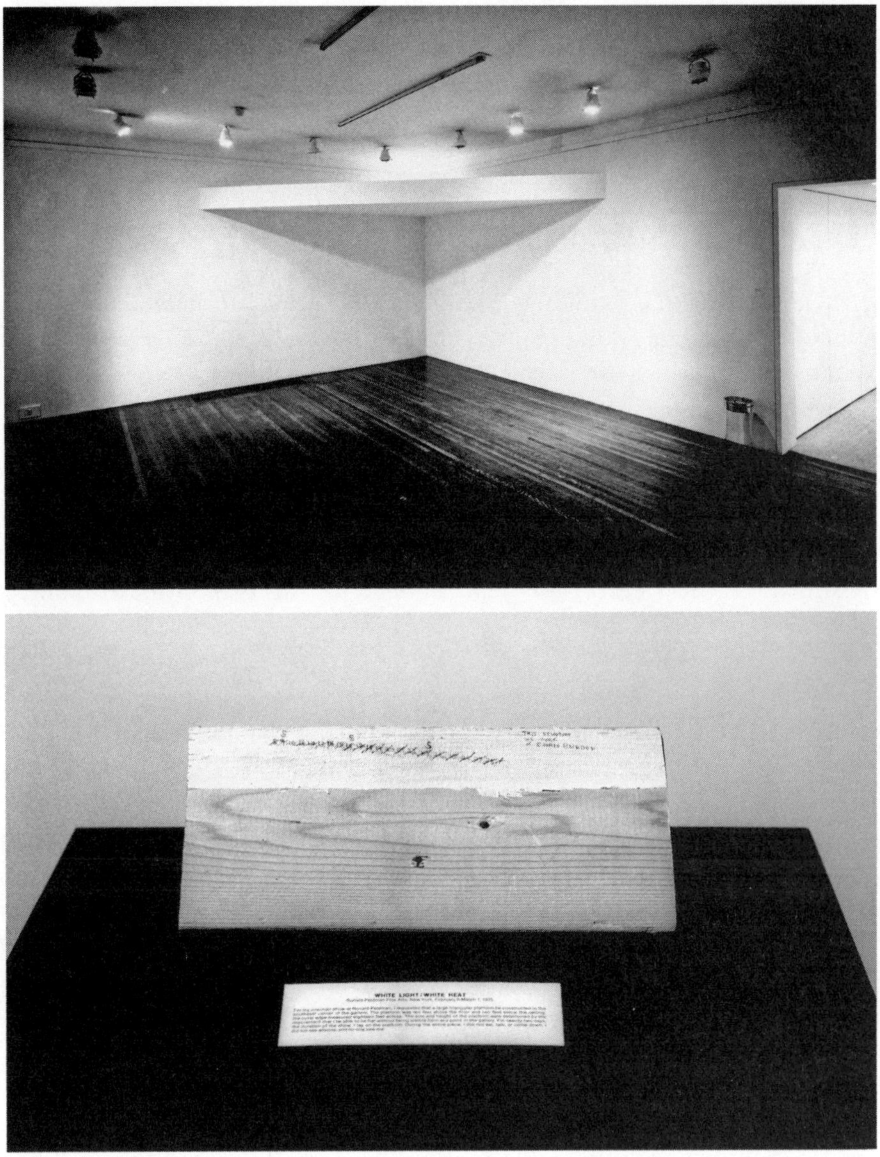


FIGURE 17. Chris Burden, *White Light/White Heat*, February 8–March 1, 1975, Ronald Feldman Fine Arts, New York. Statement by the artist about his performance: "For my one-man show at Ronald Feldman, I requested that a large triangular platform be constructed in the southeast corner of the gallery. The platform was ten feet above the floor and two feet below the ceiling; the outer edge measured eighteen feet across. The size and height of the platform were determined by the requirement that I be able to lie flat without being visible from any point in the gallery. For twenty-two days, the duration of the show, I lay on the platform. During the entire piece, I did not eat, talk, or come down. I did not see anyone, and no one saw me." Courtesy of the artist.

cluding the ways in which heroin slows respiration and heart rhythms, lowers the body's temperature, constricts the pupils, and also makes one indifferent to pain, grief, fear, hunger, and cold, all of which result in feelings of sensory deprivation and physical isolation. Burden achieved a similar although non-narcotic state, reproducing some of these effects by remaining isolated, fasting, and drinking nothing but one six-ounce glass of celery juice a day (a liquid known for its utility in lowering and maintaining blood pressure and for its calming effects) during the entire three-week period.[12]

Read through the normative conditions for seeing art, *White Light/White Heat* offered viewers nothing to look at but a stark minimalist structure in an architectural and institutional setting saturated with light. With nothing to see, visitor's perceptions were submitted to the contemplation of that which could not be witnessed, yet with the pledge that Burden inhabited the space. Burden's visual inaccessibility required viewers to experience the art through means other than mere looking, and to conceptually connect visibility to invisibility.[13] By restricting what spectators could witness and validate as truth, Burden expanded the necessity for them to attend to other corporeal perceptions, and heightened their senses to discern his presence in the gallery and "feel that something was wrong."[14]

The fact that Burden used his body to enhance feeling over seeing emphasized physiological over visual methods of knowing, thereby activating viewer proprioception, or what neurobiologist Paul Grobstein has referred to as the "I-function."[15] Proprioception is a mechanism of the central nervous system that governs one's awareness of self, most significantly through determining which senses identify environmental stimuli and enable the decision making that is necessary for well-being. Grobstein coined the term "I-function" in order "to refer to those aspects of brain function that support/create 'consciousness' (as opposed to the much larger sphere of brain function that supports behavior without consciousness). . . . In this regard," he maintained, "proprioception . . . represents an enormous and continual barrage of incoming information that greatly influences our behavior but that we have little or no direct access to."[16] Moreover, as Alain Berthoz writes in *The Brain's Sense of Movement*, proprioception is about kinesthesia, a characteristic feature of which "is that it makes use of many receptors, but remarkably it has been forgotten in the count of the senses." Berthoz adds that one "plausible explanation" for the neglect of proprioception "is that it is not identified by consciousness, and its receptors are concealed."[17] To make this point even more clear, a familiar example of the operations of proprioception is how the mind produces the sensation of pain in an absent limb.[18]

In *White Light/White Heat* Burden produced an experience akin to that of the phantom limb by making himself visually unavailable and leaving viewers to sense that something was amiss in the gallery. One critic described the mild psychological disturbance that this sensation induced as the room being "haunted . . . by the vacuum of [Burden's] withheld presence."[19] Such sensations put the body on alert. In this way, Burden's work illustrated how proprioception is a key survival mechanism of the body.[20]

Few researchers have considered the role of survival as an aspect of proprioception in discussing the central nervous system's commands for movement to the muscles. But in a truncated comment Berthoz posed a provocative point, explaining that while muscles are slow to contract, "eighty milliseconds is a very long time if you are trying to get away from a predator."[21] What is clear from this point is that one of the roles of proprioception in the central nervous system is to alert the body to danger.[22] In this regard, Burden's use of the body as an aesthetic medium in *White Light/ White Heat*, as in many of his performances, presented the public with a subtle but vital discourse on, and experience of, the conditions of survival.

Comments by Noel Frackman, a critic who witnessed *White Light/White Heat*, reinforce the point that proprioception is a survival mechanism:

> The very air was molecularized by the unseen presence of Burden. The cool Minimal piece had living, breathing human content. There was never a question in my mind as to whether Burden was really there: he had to be there. Otherwise the piece would have no integrity. . . . Those who think of Burden as an exhibitionist in art are going to be disappointed when they see *White Light/ White Heat*, [which] is full of astonishing implications.[23]

One of the most surprising implications of Burden's piece may be understood through an event that occurred two years before he performed this work, when he was featured in the May 1973 issue of *Esquire* magazine, together with seven other people described as "touchstones by which we know that . . . something new is happening."[24] One of these individuals, Neil E. Miller, a professor of physiological psychology at Rockefeller University, worked on experiments aimed at "educating the autonomic nervous system . . . to follow the instructions of the brain," and predicted that research in this area would "enable us to lower our blood pressure by an act of will, just as today we ask our hands to scratch an itch."[25]

Miller's experiments on the brain and nervous system paralleled Burden's aesthetic experiments in body art, insofar as both sought to harness the body/ mind relationship for the enhancement of physiological experiences and as such research (whether scientific or aesthetic) informed the ways in which the body responds to survival needs through proprioception. Moreover, *White Light/ White Heat* supplanted viewers' knowledge by sight in order to awaken psychophysical felt relations to presence in place, space, and time. Alerting visitors to unseen conditions in the gallery, Burden's work prepared them to be more attuned to the surrounding world, and in this way it contributed to preparing the mind to assist the body's ability to become alert in extreme circumstances. Such a physiological operation recalls Claes Oldenburg's desire for art to function like "the conversation between the sidewalk and a blind man's metal stick."[26] Like

Oldenburg's click of the stick, Burden's activation of human proprioception prepared consciousness to connect to social and environmental factors at the same time as it offered viewers an experience akin to Burden's own while enduring the performance.

What one critic called the "rarely equaled wholeness"[27] of Burden's art derives explicitly from its capacity to kindle proprioception as a localized response. *White Light/White Heat* achieved Burden's aim of interrupting the "distance between me and the audience," as "the audience was part of the work" due to physiological exchange.[28] In this way, Burden also assisted people in "question[ing] what kinds of experiences are possible."[29] This restrained action resoundingly rejected the aspect of spectacle with which Burden had become associated by 1975, in favor of the nonvisual, perceptual, emotional, and intellectual qualities of aesthetic experience that the light-drenched white gallery and proprioception evoked.

Galvanized by the combination of their uncomfortable proprioceptive perceptions and their cynical disbelief and irrepressible curiosity about the artist, some viewers felt compelled to confirm what they could not see by jumping up and down to catch a glimpse of Burden. One visitor became so anxious that she succeeded in peeping in on and photographing Burden through an extended lens.[30] The media also responded to his provocation, and CBS television news attempted to film him descending from the platform at the end of his vigil.[31] But Burden's art dealer Ronald Feldman intervened, rejecting the idea as irrelevant to and even destructive of Burden's intention, which had less to do with the proof of presence than the experience itself. Others simply refused to believe that Burden had remained on the platform for twenty-two days.[32] Such incredulity is ironic, given the fact that in *I Like America and America Likes Me* (May 23–25, 1974), Joseph Beuys tricked the public into thinking that he had lived with a wild coyote for three days at the René Block Gallery in New York. Even today, few realize that Beuys did not remain in the gallery with the animal for twenty-four hours a day, but left the gallery each day after closing hours. In contrast, Burden did indeed live on his platform for twenty-two days, twenty-four hours a day, without eating or drinking anything but the small amount of celery juice.[33]

Suppositions of Burden's putative duplicity fail to reckon with the fact that in order to dupe the public, he would have had to deceive himself. Burden would not cheat himself of the wisdom he gains from the truths he discovers in his art, truths that provide the inner strength upon which the ethical foundation of his work is based and the bond of trust he creates with his viewers. Peter Clothier astutely identified these personal character traits when he observed that Burden's "uncompromising . . . engagement with social reality" depends upon his ability "to share in the common responsibility and his willing acceptance of that load."[34] To suggest that Burden "ignores conventions and obeys no moral or behavioral code," as a critic once proposed, is to fail to understand the moral purpose underlying his belief in ethical action.[35] Burden's aesthetic rests on such conviction and is an ethic of corporeal knowledge based on the truths of experiential insight.

There is something rather poignant about how Burden's sincerity translates into the production of knowledge. For example, what is seldom discussed in considerations of *White Light/White Heat* is that Burden encouraged his friends to come into the gallery and talk to him during the performance. He asked them to keep him company:

> Even though I couldn't see, I could hear . . . . I would be really exhausted just from the activity down below. Ron was the only person who was really able to come in and talk to me. It's really hard to talk to somebody if they don't answer and you don't see them. . . . People would come in and would try to talk, stumble, and leave. Ron Feldman would come in kind of like NBC News, yap away, and leave.[36]

Although Burden attempted to augment social engagement, he also isolated himself so successfully that he precluded the possibility of exchange, denying himself that which he most wanted. Howard Singerman believed that "the more the audience needed Burden, the less Burden needed them."[37] But while Burden did become increasingly psychologically removed as the work progressed, [38] it is equally true that what he reported learning from the action was that "human beings really need other human beings."[39]

Such interpersonal need relates to Burden's biography, which critics and art historians almost never consider and which he seldom discusses. But in understanding the psychological conditions from which *White Light/White Heat* emerged, it is useful to know that at the age of twelve in 1958, Burden moved to the isle of Elba in Italy, where he lived off and on into the early 1960s with his mother, brother, and sister while his father worked in the United States. During this period he spent some nine months in bed after a small Vespa truck in which he was riding flipped over and crushed his foot.[40] Kathy O'Dell is the only art historian to have theorized (even without knowing of this event) that Burden's bed pieces (she includes *White Light/White Heat* among them) feature what she perceptively called "a home-sited mnemonic device and a manipulation of distance."[41]

*White Light/White Heat* may be described as just such a "mnemonic device," which calls forth Burden's psychophysical memories of months of solitude and convalescence, and which contributes to the creation of art that reflects that distant experience on Elba. In this sense, *White Light/White Heat* not only is a key work in the history of performance art for activating viewers' visceral, proprioceptive survival responses, but also reflects Burden's life and relates to the very foundations of why he decided to become an artist:

> For me [the Vespa accident] was an isolation period, and I actually attribute that to when I became an artist. I started taking pictures. My grandmother had

given me a Brownie camera for my twelfth birthday [and] my mom let me use the Rolleiflex, this really fancy German camera. . . . So I started taking pictures. When my foot got crushed, I saw this big fancy book, *The Family of Man*, and I wanted to take pictures again.[42] I would go out with this camera when I was recovering with my limpy leg and I had this wicker basket—because I was a kid, I could get away with carrying a fancy camera and taking pictures undercover, hiding my camera in the basket. It was about not wanting to invade people's privacy even though I was taking their picture. I wanted to be low-key and not annoy people. I would take bus trips, and I was trying to take pictures like *The Family of Man*. I have a whole body of work that I took. I didn't have any friends. My brother and sister were real social because they were younger and going to local school. I was this freak that was lying in bed with, you know, a big crushed leg. Then the spring came and I was taking all these pictures. That's how I kept myself entertained. I remember one time I went to the photo lab in the main town, which was about an hour and-a-half bus ride away. As the clerk was going through photos, I saw a couple of images. I did not immediately recognize them as being my own, as I took rolls and rolls of film. I initially thought that someone else was taking photos that were similar to mine.[43]

Rather than someone else, however, the person who Burden found was himself. He also discovered the will and the capacity to engage the world alone as an artist:

> That was when I think I became an artist. . . . I wasn't conscious of it. . . . It was a turning point, because that's what made my life have meaning. I got on a bus or my bicycle and went out into the country, or I cruised the docks and took these pictures. That gave me reason to get up the next morning.[44]

This period served to exaggerate Burden's need to connect with others, and he answered that call by taking photographs that pictured humanity. Some forty years later, as a continued response to his concern for social interaction, Burden would purchase and renovate more than one hundred stately 1920s Los Angeles cast-iron street lamps with art nouveau globes in an installation entitled *Urban Light*. These elegant street lamps cluster together, as if to recuperate the human scale that Burden imagines made past nocturnal urban experience more congenial. In salvaging these artifacts of light, Burden thinks of himself "as a preservationist," one who saves "part of the infrastructure that makes a city a city" in order to provide "some California light" wherever the work is exhibited.[45]

Burden has consistently harnessed sculpture to light the darkness with aesthetic objects that also provide inner revelation (*lux*). Burden's idealistic concept of social sculpture is also vivid in the installation *The Hidden Force*, in which a large magnet, roughly the size of a human body, floats in each of three reflecting pools at McNeil Island Corrections Center, a prison near Steilacoom, Washington. In Burden's words, the work constitutes "a metaphor for the 'right direction' or the 'right way,'" and his "hope [is] that the inmates might make the connection between this unseen, but internalized, force of nature and unseen human values . . . that they must also internalize."[46] *The Hidden Force*, with its concerns for universal moral law, and *Urban Light*, with its consideration of how scale and quality of light affect human behavior, both connect to *White Light/White Heat* insofar as Burden learned in this performance that rather than food or water, he missed human contact. He longed for the very sight of others: "Actually seeing other people. Seeing them. Seeing other human faces. . . . [What] I've learned most, is that people need people."[47]

## MUTE TRUTH

The color white dominated the perceptual conditions of *White Light/White Heat*. It produced a visual vacuum of achromatic light, like a blank sheet of paper on which an inscrutable event in the course of becoming was yet to be written. Burden considered *White Light/White Heat* to be a "refinement" of *Bed Piece* (1972), in which he had similarly remained in a light-filled gallery for twenty-two days in a white-sheeted bed. But in this performance he stayed under the watchful eyes of viewers with whom he had no verbal contact. Burden dressed all in white for three more unnerving performances, using white as a color to signify ritualized danger and/or isolation. In *T.V. Hijack* (February 9, 1972), he held a knife to the throat of the woman interviewing him on television; and in *Jaizu* (June 10–11, 1972) he wore sunglasses with lenses painted black on the inside. The glasses rendered Burden virtually blind, and confounded the very communal experience he appeared to be soliciting, sitting silent in front of two pillows and a bowl of marijuana cigarettes that visitors who had come to chat with him were invited to enjoy while he looked on, mute and blind. The color white also dominated *Oh, Dracula* (October 7, 1974), which took place in the foyer of the Utah Museum of Art in Salt Lake City, in a room of Renaissance religious paintings. There, Burden had himself suspended in a chrysalis-like white sheet after having placed two lighted white candles on the floor, one under his head and the other under his feet, changing his envelope-like cocoon into an inverted altar.[48] Without narrative or pictorial content, his living presence presented the actual embodiment of the representational sacral subjects depicted in the paintings around him. While he hung silent in his shroud, Burden's title prepared the public to consider its own Draconian voyeuristic complicity in visually sucking the life-blood from the art "object."[49]

Burden revisited his implicit indictment of viewers' interactive responsibility to art in *Samson* (1985), an installation with the capacity to split the architecture of display asunder when a 100-ton jack pushed two large timbers and steel plates against the weight-bearing walls of a building in response to the movement of visitors passing through the entrance turnstile. Burden's title linked Samson's fatal flaw (his erotic attractions) to art lovers' search for visual pleasure (scopophilia). The installation examined the ways in which the interrelationship between the display of art and the compulsion to see (as sensual gratification) endangers the very capacity of art to exist.[50] Indeed, Burden's work is replete with the theme of viewer responsibility across the division of visibility and action. He addressed this topic again in *Velvet Water* (May 7, 1974) when he positioned himself behind a partial wall constructed in the same space as his audience and attempted to breathe in water. The audience could see Burden on a video monitor and could actually hear him choking and gagging behind the wall. Confronting viewers with their complicity, Burden enabled them to watch and listen to what was taking place in the same space in which they failed to intervene in a potentially life-threatening action. In *Velvet Water*, as in other potentially lethal performances in which he staged suffocation and dehydration, Burden again wore white clothing.

While white summons concepts of purity, awe, and reverence, it also signifies death, as in snow and in the end of life symbolized by the death of nature in winter. White is also the funerary color in Asian cultures, unlike black, which is the more immediate symbol of death in the West. In a blacked-out room for audiences limited to four, Burden hung more than five hundred miniature model spaceships and performed *The Citadel* (August 8–12, 1978), illuminating each tiny object one at a time with the light of a white candle. An audiotape accompanied his action of slowly lighting the elements of the scene; it played the sound of a rocket blast and a message about the end of the universe. *The Citadel* belongs to a number of works the artist has produced on the subjects of war, apocalypse, and radiation.[51] Moreover, at least seventy-five works in his oeuvre juxtapose good and evil, life and death, and connect these concepts to aspects of light and dark, black and white.

*The Fist of Light* (1993) is an important and extreme example of Burden's ongoing interest in the physical effects of light on human physiology and emotion. The installation consisted of a rectilinear aluminum room covered on the inside with 112 metal halide high-intensity lamps that saturated the interior with direct and reflected light, generating enough heat to strip paint off the walls of the building in which it was exhibited; and, more ominously, to potentially blind an observer. From the exterior, the room resembled a metal cube with large cooling air ducts running over its surface, providing air conditioning that lowered the interior temperature and prevented the system from overheating. Burden imagined this piece "like a clenched hand poised to strike at New York."[52] In this way, *The Fist of Light* deployed light augmented by technology as an instrument of power to illuminate and destroy. Left out of control, the installation could have generated enough electrical energy to cause a blackout in lower Manhattan.[53]

In part, *The Fist of Light* represented Burden's comment on the work of such artists as James Turrell and his teacher Robert Irwin, both of whom use light as a medium. "By pushing to an extreme what is conventionally viewed as a benign and positive material, I altered light into an unconventional hazardous and powerful force," Burden explained.[54] Discussing the negative potential of a putatively benevolent medium, Burden joined the notion of *illuminati*, or enlightened souls, to the diabolical dimension of light as fire, as represented in the concept of Lucifer. Indeed, the signification of light as a representation of virtue is undermined to reveal the potential danger of energy and its connection to chaos, vice, and destruction. Such a work summons the dazzling experience of light in book 10 of Plato's *Republic*, in which a column of light stretches "over the whole of heaven and earth," and in the middle "hangs the spindle of Necessity, by means of which all the revolutions are turned."[55]

Works of psychological and sensorial intensity such as *The Fist of Light*, *Samson*, *Oh, Dracula*, and *White Light/White Heat* attest to how Burden's physical ordeals and sculptural installations critique both the institutions of art and the behaviors they reinforce. One of the more ingenious examples of such a critique is *Exposing the Foundations of the Museum* (1986–88), a work in which Burden literally "brought to light" the very foundations of the Temporary Contemporary building of the Museum of Contemporary Art in Los Angeles by removing a fifty-two by sixteen-foot section of concrete floor from the northeast wall and excavating a trench nine feet deep near columns supporting the structure. In exposing the institution's foundation, he exposed the site where art depends upon the meeting of nature and culture to sustain it. Burden performed similar exposés in *Full Financial Disclosure* (1977), in which he made his gross income public; in *Working Artist* (November 22–24, 1975), during which he worked in a gallery treating visitors as guests; and in *Honest Labor* (March 26–30, 1979), for which he spent five days digging a deep ditch from 9 a.m. to 5 p.m. in a vacant lot in Vancouver.

Burden has also used light to contrast the spiritual with the dark side of human nature in the convergence of cultural and political affairs. One of his first youthful encounters with this dichotomy was on Elba, where in 1980 he recalled the vivid impression of opening his bedroom curtains on the first morning after his family's arrival on the island the night before:

> On one side of the brick building [next to his building], painted by hand with red paint, [was] a swastika four stories high. Four stories high in red paint! I knew what a swastika was. I'd seen them in France or in books. But I'd never seen one four stories high, graffiti-style, bright red. As a little kid, I remember looking at that and looking at that brand new mayor's building painted all white and thinking, "This is not an accident. This is an official statement of policy."[56]

Burden's childhood awareness of the political intricacies of interpersonal relations (*lumen*) imprinted him with concepts of good and evil as primary forces of social life and led to his juxtaposition (in literal and metaphorical uses of light and dark) of moral principles of conduct (*lux*) with questions of individual and collective responsibility. The legacy of these critical moments of conscience is represented most profoundly in his infamous performance *Shoot*, which is particularly relevant in this context, insofar as for this event Burden "found a friend

. . . willing to 'graze'" his arm with a bullet from a distance of about fifteen feet "while others watched the 'crime.'"[57]

Burden had been thinking about what it would feel like to be shot ever since the US National Guard had opened fire on students at Kent State University in Ohio some eighteen months earlier, on May 4, 1970. Four students had been killed, one permanently paralyzed, and eight wounded.

> Kent State was a bigger deal to me [than the Paris protests of May 1968] because everybody was rioting all the time [in those days]. But all of a sudden US troops were shooting at protesting students. It's like: "Uh ha, that never happened before!" [The police] would beat them up, club them, and mace them, but they didn't actually whip out the guns and level a volley at people who were unarmed. All of a sudden [the violence] . . . took on another dimension.[58]

Burden's new perspective on the immediacy of political violence took the form of a question that he posed to himself. He wondered what would happen if, during a period when "everybody's trying to avoid being shot, I flip it over and do it on purpose?" His answer: "I'd be right there in that weird gray area."[59] What Burden meant by the "weird gray area," I think, is that his actions would inhabit the ambiguous interstice between perpetrator and victim. As such, *Shoot* could exhibit the state's responsibility to care for and protect its citizens, the general accountability required of citizens in any social context, the interpersonal duty one person has to another and to the self, and the precarious balance between responsibilities.

The very values Burden examined and established for himself in *Shoot* would be challenged thirty-three years later in November 2004, when one of his own graduate students, in a class taught by visiting artist Ron Athey, staged a classroom performance. The incident has been reported as follows: "The student withdrew a revolver from a paper bag, loaded one bullet into the chamber, and, in a classic act of Russian roulette, spun the chamber, held the gun to his head, and pulled the trigger. The gun did not fire a bullet, and the student abruptly fled the classroom into the night. Seconds later, the students in the classroom heard the gun being fired in the parking lot."[60] Burden was not present, and he resigned his twenty-eight-year teaching post after learning that the university refused to discipline the student. Significantly, in 2002, one year and several months before this incident took place at UCLA in 2004, Burden had explained why he had chosen not to perform *Shoot* on the campus of the University of California, Irvine, during a Duchamp symposium in 1971:

> There was kind of a buzz. You know, there was a conference and people were going to do things. But then I started thinking about it and I thought: "Guns on campus; that could be problematic." It would have been a crisis with the chancellor. It's not about testing the University or anything like that. I thought doing it in a university context could be problematic for the university. I'd already

thought about shooting and being shot, and so I thought this would be a perfect place to do it and then I thought better of it. Which I think was a wise decision, because the campus police would have been involved.[61]

Moreover, a letter Burden wrote on the day he performed *Shoot* in 1971 explains how he came to the strategic decision not to perform such a work in a university context. To the editors of the avant-garde publication *Avalanche*, he wrote:

> I was going to do a piece during the Duchamp Festival. I changed my mind and the piece is being done tonight at F Space. I will be shot with a rifle at 7:45 p.m. I hope to have some good photos.[62]

Rather than highlight the sensational aspects of his deed, Burden focused on the aesthetic result of his act and its photographic documentation. This is not to say that Burden was not aware of the wider ramifications of his performance, or that he did not do *Shoot* to draw attention to his work. He was, and he did. But Burden limited his audience to a handful of close friends, performed the act in an obscure alternative space that he and fellow artists opened and managed, and ethically avoided any confrontation with police or the university. What must be understood is that what would become the spectacular reception of *Shoot* did not occur until two years after it was performed, when *Esquire* magazine featured Burden in the article discussed above. It is important to put this history of *Shoot* in perspective, especially for younger artists (such as Burden's student) who may not grasp the ethical conditions under which Burden responsibly performed the piece. Moreover, in a period when the histories of performance art are increasingly distorted by critics lacking direct knowledge of its complexity and historical circumstances, by art historians inventing theories about it that are not based in the work, and by the media and Hollywood making a spectacle of performance to sell books and movies, careful examination of the origins of such renowned and controversial works as *Shoot* is even more pressing.[63]

## SENSATE TRUTH

In addition to explorations of personal responsibility, questions regarding the ethical practices of art institutions, and the moral responsibilities of viewers, Burden's work also contains overt Christian references, as in *Doorway to Heaven* (November 15, 1973), *Trans-Fixed* (April 23, 1974), and *The Visitation* (November 9, 1974). Not coincidentally, the impressive spectacle of salvation and damnation so often conjured in the liturgy and practices of the Catholic Church had an impact on Burden in his youth. "My best friends were Catholics," he recalled, as were "my brother and sister . . . for a couple of years or so when they were going to a local school in [Elba,] Italy."[64] Burden remembered, for example, how his brother marched in church at the head of "a [church] procession with the old banner swinging," and how he thought, "Oh man! They are going over; they are passing over to the Catholic side."[65] Yet Burden's own performances, sculptures, and installations rehearse a secular "passing over" from transgression into a different order of consciousness, a transition often expressed through and/or experienced as light in a manner that recalls Christian liturgy. While Burden has never made such references himself, the symbolic and psychological use of illumination in his work evokes the figure of Christ as "the light of the world" in John 8:12. Christians celebrate Easter, in particular, with fire and light rituals, and "the equation of God with the Absolute and the pure light essence finds expression also in the creed where the Son (Christi) is defined as 'God of God, Light of Light, very God of very God'."[66]

In Burden's art, such a view of light assumes an entirely different character, as in *Trans-Fixed*, where, nailed Christlike to a Volkswagen, Burden surged from a dark garage into the sunlight on a car that he described as "screaming for me."[67] While the title involves a word play with the term "transportation" and the idea of being fixated on the local culture of Los Angeles, with its cult of the car, it also implies the transfixing effect of Catholicism as a conveyor of meaning about life and death:

> I didn't grow up as a Catholic; I was aware of Catholic practices. . . . The darkness of those cathedrals is something you don't forget. They are dark and dank. Those things are spooky. It's the absence of light . . . Death. Those cathedrals are about nothing but death, aren't they? I think so—and how your life is transient and inconsequential in terms of the greater whole. . . . *Doorway to Heaven* was about doing this thing that should kill you but isn't going to because you figured out how to escape. . . . So the spark is a metaphor for life, if you want. . . . *White Light/White Heat* was a paradigm for life and for death. What seems infinite at the beginning, towards the end seems transient and brief.[68]

*Death Valley Run* (October 14, 1976) also took life and death as its subject and cast the drama in the bright burning light of the desert, which also recalls the sites of Christ's torments. In this work, Burden rode a bicycle eighty-four miles for seven hours through the scorching heat of a mirage-filled desert in southern California, wearing all white (and an orange vest to alert motorists to his presence on the road). This action and its title suggest efforts to outrun death and to pass through the valley of death as conceived in the Psalm 23, where one "fears no evil." As in *The Fist of Light*, riding through Death Valley exposed Burden to the dangerous aspects of light and heat that permeate his art. In another work, *B. C. Mexico* (May 25–June 10,1973), Burden similarly exposed himself to the elements, especially the lethal aspects of light, by paddling in a small canvas kayak from San Felipe, Mexico, to a remote island beach in the Sea of Cortez. Again, in the white light and heat of sky and sea, Burden survived for eleven days with only water to sustain him in a daily average temperature of 120 degrees. The title, *B.C. Mexico*, inverts the artist's initials, drawing the subject of the work into the deep time of the earth itself as it stretches at least 4.5 billion years into the past. The reference to Mexico before the birth of Christ evokes advanced civilizations that thrived long before the Conquest, which brought with it decimating diseases and its limited historical perspective.

Taking to the sea again in a canvas kayak in *Solaris* (October 23, 1980), Burden floated several miles west into the Pacific, into the glare of the setting sun, becoming progressively more invisible to viewers on shore, who could only see him through a powerful telescope that distorted his image and made him appear as though he had entered an otherworldly realm of light. This work recalls Russian filmmaker Andrei Tarkovsky's *Solaris* (1972), a film suffused with a mood of foreboding, uncertainty, pain, and grief, that tells the story of a space station designed to study the sentient ocean of a distant planet and that thematizes the failure of humanity to grasp the nature of creativity, the futility of technology to increase human understanding, and human "arrogance and faith in its own paucity of knowledge."[69] Burden situated his own *Solaris* in the context of the Cold War space race, invoking the US space program and using walkie-talkies to communicate with "Mission Control." Excerpts from the tape he presented during the performance suggest that he, once again, sought to enter the "gray area": "C.B. to Mission Control, Houston. / I am out here. / I am on the edge. / I am an Astronaut. / Rotation 12 over 30, 39 over 52. / 14 over 23. / Vector .027. / Hull temperature 273. / Over and out."[70]

A comment that Burden once made, in which he considered the function of his performances to be a "sort of training for some sort of . . . outer space program," is relevant to this performance, as Burden's art prepared him to encounter the edges of known experience in a material universe of infinite possibility.[71] Another example of this aim might be his sculpture *The Speed of Light Machine* (1983), in which he studied the problem of light travel with the thought that he was preparing to "travel to the distant stars."[72] Devising original methods for the rigorous physical and mental training necessary to encounter, recognize, and communicate about the unknown in itself, Burden's art-making process and works of art represent a non–religiously based spirituality dependent upon light as a fundamental means of communication of moral concepts. While Burden does not purport to have religious beliefs attached to a particular doctrine, the values of Christianity appear to have determined his moral stance, even if his practices also suggest Eastern philosophy, especially Zen and Tao.[73]

Fire is another source of light in Burden's work, important for its underlying secular spirituality and sensuality. Fire figures in *Match Piece* (March 20, 1972), *Dos Equis* (October 16, 1972) and *Oh, Dracula* (October 7, 1974), as well as in *Dreamy Nights* (October 15, 1974) and *The Visitation* (November 9, 1974), to name just a few performances. Additionally, many of the photographs Burden meticulously selects to represent his work often feature firelight, most notably *Deadman* (November 12, 1972), *Fire Roll* (February 28, 1973), and *Icarus* (April 13, 1973).[74] Fire played a key role in Burden's installation *The Reason for the Neutron Bomb* (1979), which contained some fifty thousand matchsticks, suggesting the potential for global conflagration when taken in conjunction with the work's title.[75] Among the four classic elements, fire is considered to represent a living force and is related to processes of transformation and purification. Moreover, fire is the light that signifies the active, masculine, yang principle in Chinese symbolism, and is often understood in the West as the symbol of emotion and sexual power. In *The Psychoanalysis of Fire* (1938), the French philosopher Gaston Bachelard similarly linked fire with heart, love, hate, and vengeance, drawing its semiotics into the domain of Eros and Thanatos, or the intertwining of sexuality and eroticism with mortality.[76]

Many critics have written about Burden's masculinity, sometimes diminishing its artistic expression as the production of "boys' toys."[77] Such comments overlook the sexual magnetism that energizes Burden's art and its resulting hold on his viewers, trivializing the erotic attraction of his art in mere gender stereotypes. The raw eroticism of Burden's art derives as much from his use and control of volatile materials (like fire) as it does from his personal fortitude, his fearless approach to danger, and his intrepid willingness to tolerate and survive peril. Moreover, Burden's ability to summon, endure, and check intense experience, as well as to harness explosive and evocative materials and respond to and manage unpredictable audiences, unites his art with both mythic and actual powers of sexual energy and spiritual renewal.

Burden imbues his objects and actions with an aloof poise that is simultaneously quiet and full of metaphorical fire. Fiercely autonomous, Burden's work is nevertheless connected to the viewer in ways that are simultaneously cool and hot, simple in form and dense in meaning, darkly dangerous and radiant, unyielding and forgiving, and wholly inculcated with the physiology of the muscular that is generally associated with the masculine. Finally, although personally charming and affable, Burden's trenchant refusal to court an audience—or at least to court it only on his own terms—creates a distance that neither requires approval nor is moved by censure. Such a position renders his work psychologically seductive for the ways in which it expresses his independence from the art world, at the same time as he makes his work available to the very institutions from which he remains aloof. Such qualities are the foundation of his work's sensual pull, an erotic dare that cannot be separated from the force of the ethical will behind it which sustains it.

## LIGHT TRUTH

While Burden does not deny the metaphysical or metaphorical implications of his art, he also does not solicit such readings. Many critics support him in this effort, believing, as does Paul Schimmel, that Burden's works are "uncluttered with religious, literary or historical references."[78] For his part, Donald Kuspit has considered Burden's themes of transcendence only in relation to the artist's association with what he calls "the 'mystical' character of the machine."[79] Howard Singerman has identified Burden's "quest for experience and knowledge," and quoted Robert Horvitz, who saw Burden's "invitations to activity" and "experience" as his work's key focus rather than the "metaphors [and] meaning" sought by the public.[80] Unquestionably, Burden is a skeptic, uninterested in "dogma and propaganda" and wary of divulging his spiritual concerns, even though his work is saturated with characteristics that recall meditation, asceticism, and mysticism.[81] He prefers to refer to his position as that of "free physics," which, given his educational background in science, I interpret as a manner of working that seeks to translate data from the interactions of matter and energy in both nature and culture into visual models.

Burden channels his work through a rational analytic process grounded in a quality of conscience that includes principles of reason, ethics, morality, and emotion. Decidedly not pious in any institutionally religious sense, Burden's vision expresses the fundamental principles of the energy that animates nature:

> When I got my new puppy, I would take her on long evening walks and try to photograph her. Invariably, by the time I had aimed the camera and pressed the button she was out of the picture frame. When I first saw this photo, I couldn't believe I had captured this nearly impossible and fleeting image of my exuberant little dog and the new moon rising. In this photograph I saw the incarnation of God.[82]

The reflection of light on the moon and the bursting life of a young animal constitute rich sources for Burden's imagination. Founded in active empirical investigations and pragmatic deliberations on material conditions, light—with all its multiple and far-ranging symbolic potentialities—carries the metaphysical weight of Burden's art. Rather than producing art that is dependent upon sight for truth, Burden unites the conceptual illumination of *lux* to the empirical understanding of *lumen*.

Attempting to capture such qualities of light, physicist Arthur Zajonc wrote in *Catching the Light* that "the lights of nature and of mind entwine within the eye and call for vision."[83] Indeed, Zajonc continues, light informs the theorist and the scientist, as well as "the artist and the monk," as "both know that through a disciplined practice they can internalize nature so that they can realize new capacities of mind."[84] Burden has labored in light for more than three decades.

Burden's art enables insight into hidden forces at the cusp of normative and mystical experience. At this nexus, Chris Burden's ineffable intelligence saturates his art with substance, integrity, and peerless lucidity.

# *Teaching A Dead Hand To Draw*: Kim Jones, War, and Art (2007)[1]

## I

Basic training psychologically authorizes people to kill before combat even begins (figure 18). One Vietnam veteran remembered that his "drill sergeant forced the squad to crush kittens to death in their hands," reported clinical psychologist Edward Tick in *War and the Soul* (2005). When this soldier was unable to do the act and broke down, "declaring that it was wrong," he was "shamed until near breaking." Then, he killed his kitten. He "cried over the kitten's death," but was later able "to kill people without remorse."[2] This soldier killed with a "dead hand"—a term that Kim Jones, also a Marine and Vietnam veteran, would later coin in another context.

Jones arrived at this association in an artist's book/sculpture he made by hand, entitled *Teaching a Dead Hand to Draw*, begun in 1976 and not completed until 1995—an object to which I shall return in the conclusion. For now, I wish only to introduce Jones's title as the pretext for pointing out that the hand that draws an image from the imagination (whether in pictorial, sculptural, or performative language) is also the hand that draws and fires a gun. Moreover, a "dead hand" is a corporeal instrument able to extend the psyche trained to kill into the act itself. The relationship between a dead and a live hand is the generative operation at work in how Kim Jones translated the language of war trauma into the languages of art.

*Khaki Marine Shirt* (2005) is a stunning demonstration of Jones's decoding. This composite object is simultaneously a wearable shirt of Marine military issue and a drawing/sculpture. On the back of the shirt, Jones drew graphic symbols of troops and movements on a ground painted white. The drawing depicts the opposing forces of a battle in spare black graphic signs of *X*s and dots, as well as rectangles for tanks and fortresses; lines for tank movement, combat, and containment; and directional forces in a "war that never ends . . . an X-man, dot-man war game."[3] As Jones explains:

> They have no gender. They're *X*s and dots. They're symbols. They're erased to show movement. I'll draw a tank, or I'll draw an *X*, and erase it, then re-draw it in a different position. Or I'll make a line of tanks that shows them moving

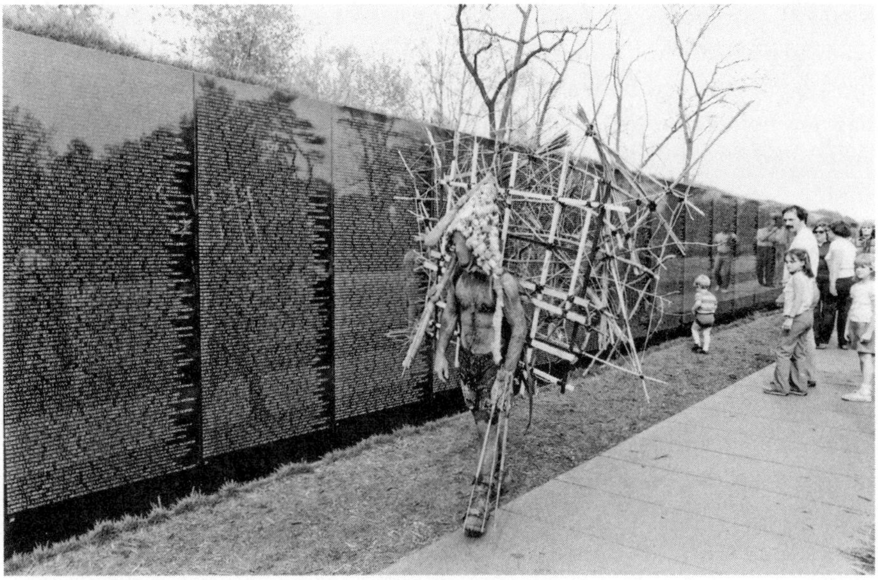

FIGURE 18. Kim Jones, *Walk from WPA to White House to Vietnam Memorial*, April 30, 1983, Washington. Performance sponsored by Washington Project for the Arts. Photograph © Mark Gulezian, Quicksilver Photographers. Courtesy of Kim Jones and Pierogi Gallery, Brooklyn, NY.

through their two-dimensional world. But when they're killed they're erased and that leaves a ghost image. So the erasing is a very important element of the war drawings. . . . The important thing is that it's always changing.[4]

Jones augmented the drawing by adding a wood frame on the middle of the back, which is also overpainted in white with line drawings that continue the action. The frame is embedded in the shirt and projects from it, isolating a section of the larger drawing that appears overall to be a circular encampment. Framed as such in the middle of the back, this part of the drawing also doubles for and looks like a target, marking its wearer as the object of assault. In addition to its original function as a shirt, the framing device enables the shirt/drawing/sculpture to be converted into a tabletop/cover that stabilizes the object flatly on a surface where the drawing may be observed more closely, as if by those who would plan battle strategy. Thus does *Khaki Marine Shirt* serve multiple purposes, as do many military items carried into the theater of battle.

Photographed wearing this drawing/sculpture/tabletop object, with his head covered in pantyhose, Jones became a generic Marine with the burden of battle born on his back, targeted for death. Jones has noted that his war drawings are "like a diary—like a writer keeping a daily diary."[5] In this way, the very shirt on his back records a daily meditation on his inner life, his memories as a Marine, and his continued sense of self as a soldier. But the photograph also attests to the fact that it sits uneasily on his back, as the embedded frame distorts the shirt, forcing Jones's body into an unnatural pose. Jones's naked arms extend awkwardly from the garment's short sleeves, and his "dead hand" dangles, ready to do battle and draw the war of which it is a specter. *Khaki Marine Shirt* must be understood both as a work of art and a relic of the Vietnam War that has never ended for Jones, whose art must be considered the precise aesthetic expression of the Vietnam War for how his unique language of artistic forms simultaneously indexes and expresses its physical conditions and psychological toll.

## II.

The kitten story recounted above amplifies Jones's *Rat Piece*, carried out in the Union Gallery at California State University, Los Angeles, on February 17, 1976. At the beginning of this event and in the company of viewers, Jones transformed himself into his persona that became known as Mudman. Disrobing and covering parts of his naked body in mud, he then pulled pantyhose over his head to cover his face and strapped onto his back a towering macabre sculptural apparatus made of (among other materials) twigs, foam rubber, and mud lashed together with electrical tape. Spotting a photographer taking pictures of his action in the gallery, Jones asked if any had been taken before he had donned the mask. When the answer came back negative, Jones is reported to have commented: "Good, because I don't want my face in this."[6] As "performance is not acting" for Jones,[7] his insistence on visual anonymity reinforced an aesthetic determination to draw the representation of a "mudman" such that actions undertaken as that icon would stand in for the experiences of others.[8] Jones then read a text that referred to a range of emotions, which one viewer described as "feelings about his nakedness, the structure on his back, reactions to his performance and to himself as though the structure were part of his physical being, feeling like a mad thing caught in the wind, trying to escape and to identify his feelings."[9] Another witness remembered that the performance had "a theme of needing recognition."[10] Following his verbal commentary, Jones doused three rats confined in a cage with lighter fluid, and burned them alive.[11] The rats screeched as they burned, and Jones bent down and screamed along with the tortured animals.[12]

In this tragic action, Jones pictured the viciousness of war and its haunting residue in his imagination, conduct, and very ability to endure senseless brutality. In his screams, Jones dislodged parts of the radical intrusion of the imprint of war and death on his psyche that is the legacy of trauma, defined succinctly as a normal response to extreme stress resulting in chronic anxiety. Jones also presented the public with a faceless apparition able to carry out such violence—violence as a means in itself, and violence as a force to conjure the mayhem of the Vietnam War. Mudman is he who came out of the mud and marched into a world that did not want to see what he had lived: flesh-burning napalm; relentless rain and monsoon-drenched red soil that rendered survival as tenuous as it eliminated difference and reduced soldiers to hulking fly-ridden beings; labyrinthine tangles of jungles, hills, and mountains that hid unremitting threats of attack—the legacy of guerilla war; and the constant delivery of bodies to death in bloody, rotting corpses, burned and smelling of shrapnel and gun powder.

As much as Jones created a metaphoric representation of the lived conditions of Vietnam, he also reenacted an explicit behavior that he and other soldiers had performed in Dong Ha, where they were stationed. In his words:

> vietnam dong ha marine corps our camp covered with rats they crawled over us at night they got in our food we catch them in cages and burn them to death I remember the smell
> some enjoyed watching the terrified ball of flame run
> vietnam dong ha marine corps feel sorry for one and let it go my comrades attack me verbally
> vietnam dong ha marine corps guard duty it was my turn to sleep a duck was quacking bothered me threw a rock at the duck hit its head next morning it was staggering around crippled I couldn't kill it a friend crushed its head with his boot[13]

As this remarkable narrative of war attests, *Rat Piece* revived actual events and presented metaphoric qualities of the extremes to which Jones and others had become accustomed in a situation of survival where sensitivity to crushing a duck's head or to burning rats alive were themselves acts of mental and emotional survival in a context of uncontrollable threat.

Jones' nakedness in *Rat Piece*, as well as his use of women's pantyhose as a mask, also summoned the eroticism of both sex and death that hung over Vietnam, which, together with alcohol and drugs, momentarily tranquilized and sedated anxieties and tensions as much as it fed despair.[14] Indeed, "acting out through rageful and violent expressions, including during sexual activity, often became a source of shame, guilt, and self-degradation years later [for Vietnam veterans], and a source of preoccupation with fear that one might once again become 'evil' or violent as one did during the war."[15] These aspects of Mudman return in Jones' erotic drawings, which he reworked decade after decade, changing, updating, and redrawing, or repainting. In many of these works a composite surrealistic creature—half human, half beast—presides in a wide range of sexual activities and postures, simultaneously perpetrator and victim, predator and hunted. Male figures, split in half, appear in landscapes of sandbags; blood and demons issue from mouth to penis and anus; entrails double as bamboo. Such drawings often picture a gigantic phallus: vehicle of orgasm, signifier of pleasure, and object of threat in the larger landscape of Thanatos, where the primitive impulses for destruction, decay, and death, or what Sigmund Freud theorized as the "death wish," coexist with the life instinct. (The French refer to this death within the Eros/Thanatos dyad as *le petit mort*, or the "small death" that occurs at orgasm.)

Eros and Thanatos are even more explicitly rendered in *Self Love*, a drawing/painting/photograph from 1986. Nude, but wearing the "walking sculpture" of *Rat Piece*, Jones eradicated his own face and amplified his walking sculpture by drawing over the photograph with a graphic tangle of what appear to be hybrid organic forms that fuse entrails with roots. A kind of stump appears around his legs, over which Jones has penned phrases such as "self love" and "love of self." This work recalls the narcissism that Freud identified in his study of World War I combat neuroses in *Beyond the Pleasure Principle* (1920). Such self-love (narcissism), Freud argued, is a traumatic manifestation of "intense, unmanageable self-directed sexual energies," or what psychiatrist Robert Jay Lifton, reading Freud, called an "internal narcissistic conflict" that is leveled at the self in direct proportion to unexamined traumatic experiences that make up the life/death paradigm and symbolization of the self.[16] Evidence of this complex interweaving of self and other is particularly heightened in Jones's overdrawings of illustrations of pinup girls from "girlie" magazines. These drawings catch the partially naked women in a webbed labyrinth that resembles Jones's walking sculpture.

In a telling comment made in 2005, Jones noted that his walking sculpture was also like a "skeleton outside my body."[17] The skeleton has been associated with the personification of death, but also with suffering and the reaper, who culls life unto death. The image of the skeleton equally signifies Chronos, who in Greek myth is included as one of the Orphic triad: Phanes (or Eros), Chaos, and Chronos (or Time). Together, the members of the triad emanate from unknowable worlds to create change and transformation.

Space does not permit deeper consideration of the significance of the ancient triad in Jones' work, but this relationship is part of the structure through which Jones moved from Chaos through Eros over Time toward healing. The photographs of women's bodies in his drawings appear to be metaphoric representations of Jones himself, sexual objects enclosed in his own exoskeleton: these are self-portraits, albeit projected, altered, and hybrid.[18] What I have been describing is how Jones drew himself as the "mad thing" that he became in and after Vietnam, and which he described in his spoken/read narrative during *Rat Piece*. This is the naked man who is simultaneously soldier, Mudman, and skeleton, and who asks for recognition of nightmarish war experiences; for acknowledgment of the psychological torment of returning to a hostile nation after sacrificing his youth; for admission that veterans were forced to forfeit a burgeoning, once innocent, sexuality; and for acceptance as the social misfits veterans understood themselves to be in the wake of experiences that only other veterans could share.

Furthermore, in the drawing/photograph *Self Love*, Jones holds a small sculptural skeleton made of sticks and twigs: the figure also wears a walking sculpture on its back. Mimetic, but not a mirror image, the skeleton doll represents a lifeless yet differentiated double of the artist: a skeletal echo in which death is inextricably conjoined with life as a narcissistic extension of self and self-image. In turning his skeletal self inside out and wearing it on his back, and in re-creating a skeleton to hold in his hands (itself wearing a skeleton on its back), Jones visualized interior emotions as multiple representations of psychic death in an agonizingly negative self-image that pictures the skeleton not twice but thrice. This visualization draws out as an image "the extreme fear and terror that many combat personnel have experienced, [which] almost never was disclosed during war duty," and the self-condemnation for feeling fear, as well as fear "that others might be cruelly and brutally condemning of the emotional states produced by difficult situations."[19] The body's skeletal frame doubles as icon of death and inner numbness, depicting Jones's inner psychic structure as a vehicle for exhibiting his inner feelings.[20] Displacing the skeletal frame and emotions onto an external source, Jones's skeletal double echoed the self exhibited in the drawings, which was embellished to read as contaminated and overgrown, the site of exposed guts.

The walking sculpture-cum-skeleton might be said to function as a metaphorical Möbius strip, drawing a line from interior to exterior life, a line that connects as much as it depicts the continuity between inner and outer modes of dissociation.[21] Jones's post-traumatic stress disorder is especially vivid in terms of psychic death, numbing that reflects "internally directed rage and blame, . . . impacted grief, and profound fear—fear of 'going crazy' over a seeming inability to forget the immersion in death trauma."[22] To make the psychological complexity of these experiences more difficult, combat troops are trained in psychic numbing and denial, training that includes dehumanizing the enemy as a tactic for killing "it." In the Vietnam War, such tactics were epitomized by "repeating the mantra, 'Fuck it, it don't mean nothing.'"[23] Jones's drawings especially visualize this separation of mind from experience: the traumatic discontinuity and rupture that is nevertheless part of an unremitting metonymic continuity that extends to, and is embodied in, his art.

## III

Jones had already made the rat his moniker several years after returning from Vietnam, repeatedly revisiting this sentence in his writing: "vietnam dong ha marines its summer time 125 degrees heat sweat like pigs work like dogs live like rats red dust covered everything."[24] Such a description of living like rats summons the widespread negative cultural concept of the rat as a vicious, unclean, parasitic pest that steals food and spreads disease. This view of rats signals, in part, the legacy of the black rat that carried parasites on its back, vermin that in turn bore the Black Plague bacillus, causing the fourteenth-century Black Death, killing millions.[25] Central to this image is the rat as the intermediary for the death of millions, a representation that recalls statistics of the Vietnam War in which US veterans were themselves made to be the medium through which nearly two million Vietnamese, two hundred thousand Cambodians, and one hundred thousand Laotians died. Adding to these overwhelming statistics, more than three million Vietnamese, Cambodians, and Laotians were wounded, and some fourteen million people were displaced as refugees. At the same time, the veterans were also victims of the war machine that killed or maimed its own forces: more than 58,000 US soldiers died; nearly 304,000 were wounded; and some 33,000 were paralyzed. In addition, some 110,000 veterans died from unspecified "war-related" problems; 35,000 civilians were killed as noncombatants; and nearly 2,500 soldiers remain missing in action today.[26] These statistics of great carnage remain unconsidered in the very psyche of the United States itself, which has still not come to terms with its role in the Vietnam War.[27]

While Jones materialized the underlying cultural psychosis related to the Vietnam War in *Rat Piece*, his book *Rat Piece* documents the cultural response to the work, systematically detailing the sequential unfolding of the performance, beginning with his own statement and moving to announcements by the gallery of his show, news articles about it, and responses by the art community (which never mention Vietnam or the fact that Jones was a veteran). The book also records the repercussions of *Rat Piece* in the legal system and how money changed hands, including fines for undertaking the action and fees to attorneys. *Rat Piece* shows how Jones was vilified as "sick"; how the police and the courts prosecuted him for cruelty to animals; how Frank Brown, who organized Jones's performance at the Union Gallery, was fired by the university; and how some powerful voices in the art world found Jones's performance "sensation-seeking rather than art" (the opinion of Marxist critic Max Kozloff, then executive editor of *Artforum*). Lacking insight into a quintessential representation of the Vietnam War by one of its veterans, Kozloff refused to publish images of *Rat Piece*, which he deemed "cruel theatricalism," while paradoxically acknowledging the photographs of Jones's performance as "quite arresting."[28] For his part, Robert Hughes, then art critic for *Time* Magazine, pointed out:

> Nearly ten years ago on the first night of *US*—Peter Hall's [sic][29] celebrated play about Vietnam—when members of the cast burned live butterflies on stage. At this point dozens of people rose to protest about cruelty to animals, before storming indignantly out to supper in restaurants where they ate the force-fed, diseased livers of geese and the flesh of large slaughtered mammals.[30]

Hughes, of course, was right about the hypocritical public response.

The book *Rat Piece* concludes with three documents. The first is a prayer to St. Jude that appears as a photocopy of a small prayer card from the National Shrine of St. Jude in Chicago. It beseeches the saint "of hopeless cases, of things almost despaired of," to pray for the supplicant.[31] When one "send[s] . . . prayers and petitions to the National Shrine of St. Jude, they are incorporated into the Masses, prayers, and good works of the Claretians in Chicago, and [in the prayers of those] in more than sixty countries around the world."[32] St. Jude cured the leper. That Jones selected this saint for his book is evidence that he identified with the pariah, experiencing intense isolation and misunderstanding for his art and his participation in the Vietnam War.

The back of the page dedicated to St. Jude corroborated this identification with the outcast. A letter from the dean of Otis Art Institute of Los Angeles County, James G. Souden, written to Jones in 1972, explains that should the artist continue working on filming the death of a "white rat doused in lighter fluid and set afire" (a film Jones was making in 1972, nearly four years before performing *Rat Piece* and four years after being honorably discharged from Vietnam), the faculty council (to whom the letter was copied) would "not countenance this kind of action." The dean closed with the suggestion that Jones might consider continuing his "graduate work at another institution."[33] Initially threatened with abandonment by the society he loyally served in Vietnam, Jones also was threatened with being forsaken by the very art institutions in which he sought succor. Four years before the diagnosis of PTSD, in 1980 no one could understand that Jones's sacrificial act (burning of rats) in the name of art released anger and mourning in the name of war, discharging traumatic pain as a means to live.

The last entry in *Rat Piece* is titled "Kali-Yuga," the name of the period in Hindu and Buddhist calendars characterized by the spiritual degeneration of civilization, or the "age of darkness." It is also the Buddhist term for the current period, and worth citing in full:

> the date authoritatively recognized as the beginning of this
> kali yuga of ours is February 17, 3102 bc
> krita yuga ideal and perfect age 1,728,000 years
> treta yuga one quarter less virtuous 1,296,000 years
> dvapara yuga another quarter gone 864,000 years
> kali yuga our own age the worst 432,000 years
> the sum of all four is 4,320,000 the length of the great yuga
> at the end of that time the sun's heat will supposedly ignite everything
> and a cosmic deluge dissolve all back into its source the cosmic sea
> **RATS LIVE ON NO EVIL STAR**
> A PALINDROME ON THE SIDE OF A BARN IN IRELAND.

Such a closure to Jones's performance and book draws the work into a larger frame of guilt, confession, redemption, and forgiveness, as well as the cosmic cycle of creation and destruction that brings renewal even for the despised rat, part of the minutiae of matter that makes up the "cosmic sea" of stars. A palindrome is the linguistic equivalent of a no-win situation, wherein one remains within its defining perimeters between paradox and contradiction. That Jones has maintained this palindrome as a key representation of self/rat/Mudman/skeleton signifies the depth of his understanding of the social, political, cultural, and existential situation in which the negative and positive poles of rats and stars circulate as metaphors of good and evil, as well as of injustice and its opposite: the dispassionate principles of moral right in which fairness and truths about the real nature, causes, and circumstances of actions may be gained (or, in the case of Vietnam, never were).

While Jones never named Vietnam directly in the performance or book, he nonetheless documented the hysteria by which the public displaced its metaphors as a way to avoid examining the impact and lasting effect of Vietnam on veterans of that war.[34] Vietnam veterans were put in the position of the "double bind," or the communication of contradictory messages. Anthropologist Gregory Bateson coined this term and used it to theorize such messages as a factor contributing to schizophrenia. Taking up the psychological and social ramifications of double bind in relation to the cultural expectations of the social contract in "said/meant" relationships, Kathy O'Dell has pointed out:

> By 1970, it had become clear in the context of the Vietnam War that there was a growing discrepancy between what was fact and . . . *represented* as fact by individuals in positions of power. As people followed the war from home (on television or in the newspaper), they became aware that body counts were being inflated and that atrocities such as the Mỹ Lai massacre were common. The gap between "what was said" by those in power and "what was meant" grew wider and wider, [leading to] erosion of faith in the allegedly consensual relationship between the citizen and the state in the early 1970s.[35]

O'Dell further argued that as a result, some performance artists of the 1970s took suffering upon themselves. While O'Dell cited artists who did not fight in Vietnam, such as Chris Burden (to whom Jones dedicated his book *Rat Piece*) and Vito Acconci, her observations are doubly true for an actual veteran like Jones.

Jones must have been contemplating what he would do in *Rat Piece* when he performed *Wilshire Boulevard Walk* nearly two weeks earlier, on January 28, 1976. Walking from sunrise to sunset the length of Wilshire Boulevard in Los Angeles while wearing the walking sculpture, Jones simply "walk[ed] in an out of" the lives of people he met on the street.[36] Walking in his combat boots with his body smeared in mud, Jones appeared as a phantom of Vietnam, not unlike Ho Chi Minh, the great Vietnamese statesman and leader of Vietnam independence, who wrote "Endless Rains" in his *Prison Diary* while incarcerated in China by the British during the 1930s for his labor activities:

> Nine days of rain, of sunshine one day:
> Really the sky above has shown no feeling.
> Tattered shoes, muddy road, legs caked in clay!
> Still, tirelessly I must keep slogging.[37]

Jones and other veterans would not have been able to read Ho's diary in the late 1960s in Vietnam.[38] They were not told that Ho was the revolutionary who founded the Viet Minh independence movement in 1941 and established Communist control in northern Vietnam in the 1950s only after President Harry S. Truman refused to answer eight letters in 1945 from Ho requesting further assistance from the Central Intelligence Agency and the US government (which had helped him resist Communist Chinese domination in Vietnam in the early 1940s). Jones would only have been taught that the president of North Vietnam (from 1955 until his death in 1969), along with his Viet Minh and Viet Cong soldiers, was to be vanquished as a "gook" or "slope," the racist expressions brought to Vietnam by Korean War veterans and used to refer to anyone of Asian origin.[39]

It is not inconsequential that Jones performed *Wilshire Boulevard Walk* and *Rat Piece* ten years after he had volunteered in 1966 for military service when his draft status came up 1A. Only nine months before he performed these actions, Saigon fell to the North Vietnamese on April 30, 1975, and the last Marines were evacuated from the rooftop of the US embassy in that city. Six months after Jones performed these two works, North and South Vietnam united to form the Socialist Republic of Vietnam on July 2. Ten years later, in 1986, Oliver Stone, himself a Vietnam veteran, brought out the film *Platoon*. Unlike Jones, whose courageous work was not understood, *Platoon* would be hailed for the very realism for which Jones was maligned—for "its feeling of verisimilitude for the discomfort, ants, heat, and mud—of the jungle and brush: the fatigue of the patrols, the boredom and sense of release of base camp, the terror of ambushes, and the chaos and cacophony of night firefights."[40]

## IV

Kim Jones never killed anyone in Vietnam. Stationed just a few miles south of the Demilitarized Zone (DMZ),[41] in Dong Ha, he delivered the mail. This job, which for some would have been a relief from direct combat, humiliated Jones, who descends from a long line of soldiers.[42] The area where he was stationed witnessed some of the fiercest battles of the war: Quang Tri, Con Thien, Camlo, Camp Carroll, the Rockpile, and Hamburger Hill. Khe Sanh, where a bloody battle began on January 21, 1968, was only forty miles from Dong Ha.[43] To make matters worse, Jones was shipped out of Vietnam on January 28, 1968, days before the infamous and deadly Tet Offensive began (on the night of January 30, 1968; it lasted until early June 1969). Dong Ha, Jones's home base, was totally destroyed in April 1968. That Jones missed these battles is part of the burden Mudman carries on his back: a weight of skeletons, sorrow, anguish, unfocused fury, and guilt. When asked about his guilt, Jones responded that "probably, maybe" he did feel such emotions, and added:

> But there was this other guy that I knew with 3rd battalion 4th Marines H & S company. I came over from Okinawa . . . with them, and they were right in the middle of Operation Hickory attacking these hills in Khe Sanh. There was a lieutenant who hated my guts and he took me aside and said, "I'd really like to send you out to Hill 881 South and 881 North[44] but we are short on postal clerks. If I send you out and you get killed I'll be in trouble." But there was an office typist, and they sent him out; they had extra typists, they needed people. There were the black guys and Hispanics who were protesting. The black guys

were better organized and refused to go. Some of those battles were pretty fierce. So there is guilt about that—not being sent out to those places. It wasn't something that I would volunteer for. I give a lot of credit to people who were really into it. I do think there is a certain kind of heroism in them. I have a lot of respect for those guys and I have a lot of respect for those who protested too.[45]

Jones strongly discourages romanticizing his experience in Vietnam, considering his service lowly when compared with the heroism of other Marines. But one cannot look at his art without seeing the scenes of carnage that have come to memorialize the violence and destruction represented by the war in Vietnam. For Jones was also sent on convoy missions while delivering mail to places near Dong Ha, eleven miles from the DMZ; Camp Carroll, a key Marine base to which Jones often refers, was near Khe Sanh. Moreover, as Jones recalled, "the base at Dong Ha was always getting hit by rockets and artillery; they [the National Liberation Front (NLF) and Vietcong (VC)] were all around us; you had to stand guard duty, go on the convoys, burn your shit."[46] But while Jones experienced some of the worst fighting in Vietnam, he realized that he was perceived as expendable because he was, in his words, "a fuck-up."[47] So when a shortage of mail occurred, Jones and other "non-essential" soldiers were sent straight to the DMZ to "stuff sandbags." He explains that the soldiers "hung out . . . just waiting for them [NLF and VC] from December 1967 to January 1968—like speed bumps to slow them down."[48] Jones emphasizes that he and his fellow GIs were "not heroes, just people the military could spare and didn't need."[49] Jones' sentiment was shared by hundreds of thousands of veterans unwilling to assume the mantle of hero when they had been "scared to death; never a hero," in the words of John Ketwig, another veteran.[50]

Upon his return to the United States, Jones immediately began to grow his hair long. He kept it like that for more than a decade, understanding what he had missed of the legendary Sixties while in Vietnam, not wishing to be identified with the vilified veterans by deeply engaging in art. But he finally cut his hair in 1981, and remembered that not long after that "I started making those *Star* sculptures in about 1984–1985 with black electrical tape and tree branches."[51] He made "hundreds and hundreds of them, but ended up throwing them away"—not before, however, giving his sculptures what he described as "a haircut." "They all look like they have butch haircuts, like hippies going into the Marines," he commented.[52] Jones treated the *Star* sculptures as metonymically coextensive with himself, giving them a physical identity like that of a Marine, an identity that he would himself reassume in 1981 and keep until today. About his relation to the Marines, Jones has noted that it is "a very controlling organization" that he was relieved to get out of, though at the same time they could "be *comforting* because everything is more or less taken care of for you; you don't have to make decisions."[53]

The *Stars* appear again in other situations, among them two untitled installations, one at Lorence Monk Gallery in New York in 1990 and the other at P.S. 1

Attic in New York, for the exhibition *Out of Site 1990–1993*. A photograph of the first installation shows the artist dressed as Mudman and wearing his walking sculpture. He kneels in front of a wall and windowsill, dripping with black mud, among numerous scattered *Stars*. For the P.S. 1 installation, Jones covered the floor of a stark white room with newspapers and then splattered the entire space—furniture, floor, and windowsills—with tar-like black mud, strewing the spiky spidery *Stars* (also besmirched with black) about the room. When I described this installation to Jones as a massacre scene, he responded that he found it "comfortable" and "familiar." "It's like the mother of the serial killer," he explained. Asked if he was the serial killer, Jones answered, "I'm not; I'm just speaking about how my work looks; it's scary . . . it is noisy in a certain way."[54]

Jones' mention of the "serial killer" suggests a relationship between the repetition compulsion of the serial killer to kill and the expectation and requirement of a soldier to kill in an environment bordering on bedlam. The word bedlam comes from the Bethlem Royal Hospital of London, the world's oldest psychiatric hospital (variously known as St. Mary of Bethlehem, Bethlem Hospital, Bethlehem Hospital, and Bedlam). Long associated with the uproar and confusion of the lunatic asylum, war similarly is a situation of madness and chaos. This is the muddy embattled world in which the *Stars* are "comfortable." Indeed, many of Jones's untitled war drawings, especially of battles like those in *Khaki Marine Shirt* or *Puffy Jacket* (2005), exhibit grounds filled to overflowing, a situation referred to in art historical terms as *horror vacui*: fear of empty space. Such overexcited cramped fields are often related to drawings and paintings associated with "outsider" art or the art of schizophrenics.[55] When I pointed this out to Jones, he responded that his war drawings began in the 1950s as a teenage boy's game that he kept private for decades. When asked why he secreted them away, and if he was ashamed of his game, Jones answered:

> Maybe—it was a little too strange. At that time it didn't seem like artists did things like that. . . . Maybe it was too personal, too close to like the inside of my brain.[56]

Then, in response to the suggestion that his drawings resemble *horror vacui*, best experienced in schizophrenic's drawings, Jones recalled his surprise when he had first learned of the works of artist Mirit Cohen:

> She committed suicide around 1990 by jumping off a building; she bought a bunch of roses and jumped off a building. She was Israeli and did these drawings that fill up all kinds of space. Her drawings are very *horror vacui* like Paul Klee and they fill the space. I saw them and thought, "Holy shit! There is someone doing work like mine."[57]

While Jones acknowledges the visual similarity between his work and that of a troubled artist like Cohen, who could not endure her demons, or the schizophrenic, who translates messages from unknown sources into the visual world of the psyche, Jones's war drawings are of a completely different order.

Jones replays, restages, rethinks, and rearranges the site of his traumatic experiences, gaining control and mastery over that which eluded him in Vietnam. When I asked if the drawings were a response to the many wars that followed Vietnam, Jones replied, "No, and they are not about Vietnam."[58] Nevertheless, in this regard, combat maps of Vietnam military campaigns that bear an odd resemblance to those made by Jones are available for purchase over the Internet. They include topographical and tactical maps, diagramming battles in which "one grid square equals one kilometer."[59] While Jones is aware of such maps, he never used them:

> People often think the War Drawings look like some place—i.e., Los Angeles, London, Paris, etc.—but they are all places in my head. They look like maps but they are maps that are constantly changing. To me they are alive. I DON'T DENY that they are also drawings, and that the shapes in them come from various art historical references.[60]

What the Internet site demonstrates is how consumed the public in general remains with the Vietnam War in particular, constantly replaying its battles, which remain as "alive" for them as they do for Jones.

Returning to the *Stars* that Jones scattered about in the P.S. 1 installation, he commented further:

> They are watching you and it's their world, and you are allowed to walk through it. It feels like if you ever turn your back on it, it moves. Rats are real survivors.[61]

Rats are opportunistic survivors, existing with and in close proximity to humans. In this regard, survivors of traumatic experience lead lives akin to that of a rat, to say nothing of one who pictures himself as a rat, as Jones does (he once wrote, "I need to live with rats").[62] The traumatized understand themselves to be close to, but not really a part of, everyday human intercourse. This is precisely how Jones experienced himself upon his return from Vietnam, feeling more comfortable with those on the margins of society: the homeless, the addicts, the street people.[63] To be sure, Raymond Monsour Scurfield, a specialist in war trauma, has observed: "Vietnam veterans, especially in the several years immediately following their service in Vietnam, denied and avoided directly talking about their war experiences with most everyone, [as they were] embarrassed, fearful, ashamed, enraged, or ignorant of the link between postwar problems and the war itself; many men and women withdrew and became psychologically isolated."[64]

Being an artist, Jones creatively addressed his isolation by assuming the identity and behavior of the rat, at the same time communing with and drawing out the hidden underbelly of war and society in actions, sculptures, drawings, and installations. As early as 1973, he began showing work on the street:

> There was no place to show work at that time. It was a comfortable thing to do. I started out in Venice where I knew people and it was comfortable going out on the street and showing my art. It started out with the foam rubber room installation in 1973–74, [in a place] on the boardwalk in Venice that I took over [for] about $25 a month rent. . . . I covered the space with sand and foam rubber. In April of '74, I made another foam rubber room. . . . It was very comforting. I did several pieces when I was in there. It was like a nest or a cave. There was this one older homeless woman who moved in when I left for a week. She had her bags and stuff. It was easy to walk in. I told her to get out and she sort of grumbled and got out.[65]

Asked about the significance of the foam-rubber room, which in photographs appears claustrophobic and manic, Jones replied:

> It was a social piece for me—a way of meeting people like David Hammons [who] loves to go out after 12:00 midnight and he feels comfortable. That's the same way I felt in Venice at that time. It was a way of making my sculpture without having to deal with someone telling me what to do, like a gallery or museum. There is a kind of a freedom in doing that.[66]

## V

In addition to hanging out on the streets late at night and in the early mornings, Jones developed the character Spit, about whom he wrote in a self-published text titled *Spit* (1981).[67] This surrealistic tale narrates an encounter with a street person who compulsively spits—at people, places, and things. Spit is simultaneously someone else (an actual person that Jones observed on the street) and Jones himself. The spitting reflex appears to be a reaction to the state of the world, self, and cosmos in general, as Spit expectorates even at stones. Each page of the story is surrounded by drawings that resemble Jones's walking sculptures. The drawings meander, taking the form of soft entrails and bony structures as well as rootlike hybrids similar to those Jones drew on his photograph in *Self Love*. In *Spit*, however, these forms morph into crosses, telephone poles, ducks (a duck is killed in the story), trees (transformed into "upside-down nude women with their legs spread apart"), and both rigid and limp phalluses.[68] The strange tale describes a violent journey with Spit that ends in an eerie account of an operation (one Jones actually did undergo around the time he wrote the piece) that—like *Spit*—has been altered to fit an hallucinogenic nightmare-like chronicle.

This story is, like so much of Jones's art, a testimony to the artist's unparalleled ability to draw art from traumatic experience using a variety of media. Another important text that deserves more attention than I can give here is *A Life of Secrets* (1994), in which Jones narrates a powerful dream/history of US Marine recruit training in San Diego, where he sees a novitiate nearly drown during an exercise in which the men are required to "leap, boots first, into the 12-foot-deep pool. . . . slip off boots and float to the top."[69] The recruit "sinks to the bottom," is pulled out, and lies "like a wet sack of laundry" before "two hands push down on his chest," causing water to squirt "from his mouth like an uncorked champagne bottle." This introduction to drowning in basic training is immediately followed by a description of the "rainy season in Vietnam," which transforms the environment into a kind of "moonscape" near the DMZ. "Damp heat surrounds" the twenty-three year old Jones, who is "tired" as a result of rockets having fallen all night, but also "bored." He spies a "baby rat sitting under a piece of cardboard" and rescues it, only to put it in a puddle and watch it "frantically" swim to the edge "keeping its head above water." Jones continues his narration:

> Finally the child-rat reaches dry land. It looks exhausted. I pick it up and place it in the middle of the pool of muddy water again. The rat sinks to the bottom and drowns.[70]

This tale of a tortured baby rat, irrationally sacrificed, is the dream of the veteran who has been shocked by basic training, shattered by war, and psychologically damaged by leaving comrades and by surviving, and who therefore feels comfortable in the context of the outcast and outsider, as well as in spaces of visual turmoil that recall the site of the original trauma, which he reenacts daily in both his conscious and unconscious mind. This is the profile of the traumatized survivor. It is a picture of the psychological pattern that prevails throughout the history of war in which veterans "cannot leave war's expectations, values, and losses behind, [and for whom war] becomes the eternal present"—veterans for whom a "frozen war consciousness" (associated with PTSD) is comfortable.[71]

Roméo Dallaire, the Canadian lieutenant-general force commander of the United Nations Assistance Mission for Rwanda between 1993 and 1994, suffered similarly. Unable to use his force to prevent the genocide in Rwanda, despite his now-renowned heroic attempts to intervene without support from the United States or the world community, Dellaire has compellingly written about his subsequent PTSD, alcoholism, low self-esteem, and identification with the social outcast in his memoir *Shake Hands with the Devil* (2003).[72] For such soldiers, the psychological pain of war never ends. Indeed, "of the 3.14 million Vietnam theater veterans who served in the war zone . . . between 1964 and 1975, it is estimated that 15.2% currently have complete PTSD, [and] an additional 11.2% currently have 'partial PTSD,' that is, one or more PTSD symptoms, but do not meet full diagnostic criteria."[73] These figures reflect "the most comprehensive and sophisticated psychiatric epidemiological survey ever conducted on veterans of any era of service in the United States," and they show that "over one-fourth of the entire Vietnam veteran population have war-related problems some seventeen years since the last U.S. troops were evacuated from Vietnam."[74]

What these studies further demonstrate is that before examining the histories of Vietnam veterans, "psychoanalytic theory did not consider either the environment or adult experiences to be central to personality development in the life span. In terms of adult traumatic reactions, it was presumed that emotional distress would dissipate and hence that postwar psychological sequelae would be transitional in nature."[75] It should not, however, be surprising that many veterans of various wars, including the Vietnam War, "vigorously deny the validity of PTSD as a valid condition in order not to admit to themselves their own problems that may be at least partly war-related" and that they fear being the carrier of the "death taint which is aversive to others."[76] Moreover, environmental factors are central to trauma and to personality development throughout life, including long-term and potentially permanent neurological effects; traumatic reactions do not necessarily dissipate, nor are they transitional in nature; and the psychobiology of the individual is an important factor in whether one will be affected by traumatic stress.[77] As Harry A. Wilmer, a Vietnam veteran, put it:

> It seems to most of us that Vietnam was a long time ago, that it is past history. It is not. It still lives in the nightmares of combat veterans and the collective unconscious of us all. It is an illusion to declare that the Vietnam Syndrome is over. Denial never killed anything.[78]

Regardless of the fact that the memory of the Vietnam War could not be killed, "it was common for Americans . . . to confuse their feelings and perceptions about the Vietnam War with their feelings about the warriors who fought in it, [and] many ordinary citizens and veterans of earlier wars scapegoated Vietnam veterans," calling them such pejoratives as "'baby-killers,' 'losers,' 'crybabies,' and 'walking time bombs.'"[79] To some degree, these are the terms in which Vietnam veterans' emotional problems are still perceived, as witnessed by the character Lester Farley in Philip Roth's book *The Human Stain* (2000). Roth described Farley as "a trained killer [who was] not supposed to come back."[80] Farley kills his former wife and her lover, and the book ends with the veteran sitting on an upturned bucket while ice fishing alone on a frozen lake in the middle of a vast landscape. It is an astonishing representation of the Vietnam survivor's icy rage and frozen loneliness, of the person who feels more comfortable apart from others, and who—like Farley—describes himself as having already died in Vietnam: "I am a man who fucking died."[81]

## VI

Jones typed the text for his artist's book *Teaching a Dead Hand to Draw* on an old manual typewriter. Later, he cut up this text and collaged it onto pages that look burned and are heaped with layers of objects like twigs and sticks, giving it a heavy thick appearance, a visual look that is augmented by black tar–like paint that covers the book's exterior and much of its interior decoration. Tiny repetitive grids of black decorate full pages, with a small bit of color in the center of each. Other patterns and abstract drawings fill many of the book's few thick pages, over which the collaged bits of text articulate the narrative. The overwhelming appearance of the book is one of a scorched remnant, Jones's visual aid in teaching a dead hand to draw. For the title of his book, Jones borrowed from Joseph Beuys's famous performance *How to Explain Pictures to a Dead Hare* (1965). While Beuys, a voluntary soldier in Hitler's Luftwaffe, displaced his wartime experience onto the form of a dead animal (to whom he "described" his own drawings, images presumably descriptive of heinous wartime deeds), Jones incinerated his own animal persona, the rat, killing himself metaphorically in order to teach his own "dead hand" to draw—that is, to live.[82]

While dressed as Mudman in his walking sculpture and pantyhose mask, Jones performed the narrative of *Teaching a Dead Hand to Draw* in an action that was videotaped in his studio in 2001. The video is striking for how Mudman stands passively, numb before the camera. After a moment or two, a voice (presumably the cameraman off screen) instructs Jones to "reach over and pick up the book." Jones then walks over, picks up *Teaching a Dead Hand to Draw*, and begins reading. The first sentence is the leitmotif of his art: "vietnam dong ha marines it's summer time 125 degrees heat sweat like pigs work like dogs live like rats red dust covered everything." The story continues, describing rockets, artillery, and mortar attacks on the Marines, who "jump in our rat holes" and "live in a constant state of tension and anger" without "hamburgers or ice cream." Jones drones on without emotional affect: "They are playing a game, but what game is it?" At the end of the performance, Jones recites the dates on which he worked on the book: "1976, 1987, 1988, 1995." Anyone familiar with the artist's work will immediately recognize the text of *Teaching a Dead Hand to Draw* to be comprised of fragments culled from his statement at the beginning of his *Rat Piece* book. This, and Jones's continuous working and reworking of the book *Teaching a Dead Hand to Draw* (like so many of his drawings and sculptures) attest to how his art cycles through and back to the key tropes of his life and art, decade after decade: killing, the killing of animals, being an animal, the brutality of killing and of being an animal—erotic and, paradoxically, numb.

In the video, Jones also shows other books that he has made and comments that "stories are hidden inside," so that this book, the one holds, would have to be "destroyed" so that one can find the stories. Jones then describes as a kind of "skin" the cover of the very book that would have to be destroyed so that its secrets could be learned. Thinking about skin as an organ of communication, O'Dell has noted (following psychoanalyst Didier Anzieu) that skin

> is the body's only "external sense" that functions reflexively. Touching oneself, Anzieu writes, renders the sensation of "being a piece of skin that touches at the same time as being a piece of skin that is touched. . . . It is on the model of tactile reflexivity that the other sensory reflexivities (hearing oneself make sounds . . . looking at oneself in the mirror), and subsequently the reflexivity of thinking, are constructed.[83]

O'Dell further observed that the experience of "it's me" is a "quality of the body [that] is particularly palpable" in some kinds of very intense artistic performances.[84] Maurice Merleau-Ponty summoned thoughts similar to those of Anzieu in his notion of "coiling-over" in *Le visible et l'invisible* (1964).

Extrapolating the meaning of skin as a medium of self-reflexivity, of knowing oneself, it is possible to understand that, in part, Jones grasps the skin of his book as a metaphorical cover that stands in for the suppressed memories that bind his life in layers, and which, if known, threaten his destruction. This metaphor suggests that Jones fears that the knowledge of his stories (memories) would destroy him because the book (his body) is more than a metaphor—it is his skin, a surface connecting to him and to his life, which extends from the artist as a shadow to Vietnam: different, but the same.

This discourse on skin suggests that teaching his "dead hand" to draw represents a powerful encounter between Jones's artistic identity and his soldier self: the artist grasps the core of his own being as at once dead and alive, and has the wisdom, courage, and self-respect to coach life back into the traumatized shell of the veteran. In this respect, Jones has endured to teach himself to survive through a wide variety of forms, none as poignant and powerful as "a dead hand." This very act of endurance requires patience and fortitude, and recalls comments by Robert Jay Lifton:

> Survivors can go one of two ways, or usually both ways: one is, having touched death, they can close down and remain numbed and really be incapacitated by what they've been through. Or they can confront, in some degree, what they have experienced and derive a certain amount of insight and even wisdom from it that informs their lives. I think that great achievements have occurred in relation to survival, including spiritual and religious moments. And so there's another dimension of the survivor. . . . The general idea is that one can use a death encounter and re-create oneself in relation to it.[85]

Jones has had the temerity and exceptional force of temperament, personality, ingenuity, and originality to teach his hand to draw. Through that act, in all its aesthetic variety, he continually overcomes the grief and memories of experiences beyond comprehension that are the legacy of the Vietnam War, and of which Kim Jones is the consummate artist.

# Jean Toche: Impressions from the Rogue Bush Imperial Presidency (2009)[1]

## I

Documentary photography bears witness to moments in history, and art photography of the body depicts intimate life, including sexuality, identity, family relations, privacy, and one's association or disconnection to the self. These two truisms about photographic genres are related to questions regarding the purpose of photography to capture appearances or to transform the world in what Louis Ducos du Hauron, a French pioneer of color photography, called "transformism" in 1889. Anticipating such techniques as the retouched photograph and the unprecedented ability of the digital to undo and remake the appearance of the real, "transformism" is today thought of as art photography, a genre that differs from documentary realism for its illusionism and recourse to idealism. (The art photography of Surrealism is an obvious case in point, including all of its manifestations from Hans Bellmer to Joel-Peter Witkin and Cindy Sherman.) Of these two photographic approaches (realism and idealism), documentary photography is often considered to be the more "potent and radical," as Graham Clarke puts it, for its indexical relationship to "emotional and harrowing experiences: poverty, social and political injustice, war, crime, deprivation, disaster, and suffering."[2] (Jacob Riis's photographs in *How The Other Half Lives* [1890] remain paradigmatic of this approach, for their presentation of "private lives in a public context.")[3]

The work of Jean Toche in *Impressions from the Rogue Bush Imperial Presidency* belongs both to the potent/radical documentary category of photography (for its sociological and political content) and to the illusionism of art photography (for its manipulated personal matter). As such, Toche's photo/texts maintain a tension between genres, throwing into question the false polarity of realism and idealism and the artificial binary of the intimate body and the public document. In this body of work, Toche takes his place on the barricades of political events at the intersection of personal opinion and public debate while preserving a determined dialogue with aesthetic practices. In the tradition of conceptual art, for example, he uses textual documents to comment on, among other topics, George W. Bush's two-term administration (2001–8) while simultaneously drawing on performance art by performing explicitly for the camera. His contribution to the lexicon of conceptual and performative photography, then, is to present corporeal metonymies of his confrontational and controversial cultural views.

Yet, seen in the context of the traditions of documentary photography, Toche's self-portraits often appear as visual non sequiturs, insofar as their precise semiotic relationship to the political content of his texts is difficult to discern. In this way, his photographs disrupt the dynamics of documentary photography (and the history it purports to depict), all the while remaining evidence of his responses to current newsworthy events. Sometimes, Toche's disordering of the relationship between image and text is perplexing, as in the pairing of a photograph of his cat with a text of his moral outrage over the US bombing of a mosque in Fallujah, Iraq, in his work *April 20, 2004*. The subtle link between the two may reside in the metaphor of a lurid, unnaturally colored cat that represents the despicable bombing incident itself. In such a case, the disconnect Toche achieves becomes so extreme as to suggest the impotency of any image or text to capture events and effect change, even as his art undeniably awakens viewers' consciences to the very same incidents.

At other times, Toche presents his body as a direct link to current events. In *April 26, 2004*, he manipulates the photograph to make his face a brilliant red. Potentially signifying righteous indignation (metaphorically "seeing red"), the artist glares at the viewer through huge glasses that exaggerate the intense blue of his eyes, above a text that reads: "Executions and murders carried out by governments, be it the death penalty, political assassinations, mass executions of civilians or prisoners, genocide, are never justifiable and never acceptable in any civilized society." Reinforcing the connection of emotion and thought to events, Toche strengthens the content of his message that executions and murders are savage under any name. But in this work, the artist also situates his art within the history of the European avant-garde, summoning the techniques of artists (like Henri Matisse), who were named Fauves in 1905 for their use of brilliant color for visual effect. That Toche appears in *April 26, 2004* with a bright red face, before an equally bright blue wall of arabesque-like flowers, is an unmistakable reference to Matisse's *The Dessert: Harmony in Red* (1908), a painting in which the background printed wallpaper and table laid with dessert fuse as one blue floral design on a red plane. By quoting Matisse, Toche signifies the relationship between his dramatic visual commentaries and revolutionary art.

For more than fifty years, Jean Toche has made art from a position of moral and ethical indignation, expressed openly and without reservation against political corruption, social hypocrisy, and human rights abuses throughout the world. His target has been especially the United States, beginning in the 1960s, when he first began protesting its war in Vietnam, Laos, and Cambodia (1959–75). The exhibition *Impressions from the Rogue Bush Imperial Presidency* brings together a selection of Toche's works on this subject from 2004.[4] Toche chose the title of this body of work as a mark of his indictment of the deceitful, empire-building Bush administration and how it operated with criminal villainy.

Among many examples of this "rogue" behavior is Vice President Dick

Cheney's oversight role in the Bush administration's surveillance program, which sanctioned the waterboarding of terrorist suspects, a technique condemned by the signatories to the United Nations Convention Against Torture adapted by the UN General Assembly in 1984. Another, among a host of egregious examples of rogue behavior, was the Bush administration's suspension of Article I, Section 9 of the US Constitution (concerning the writ of habeas corpus), an act that the Supreme Court ruled unconstitutional on June 12, 2008, ending the indefinite detention of "enemy combatants" without charge or trial at the US military base at Guantanamo Bay, Cuba, and upholding detainees' rights to challenge detention in civilian courts. Today, Toche persists in tracking how the Bush administration's arrogant contempt of the Constitution continues to be unmasked, and in many ways perpetuated, by the Obama administration.

In addition to the methods and policies of the United States in war, terrorism, and torture, Toche has condemned corporate negligence, citing, for example, the 1984 industrial disaster in Bhopal, India, when lethal gas escaped a Union Carbide plant (a subsidiary of Dow Chemical Company), killing 2,500 and injuring thousands.[5] His work has also addressed such subjects as the physical and sexual abuse of prisoners in US jails, the gutting of the statutory separation of church and state, the violation of gay rights, the ban on embryonic stem cell research, creationism versus evolution, the challenging of abortion rights, and the censorship of art. In *August 19, 2004*, Toche questioned the silence of the art community about "the viciousness of Attorney General John Ashcroft" when a "German curator [was] twice denied authorization to board an airplane for the U.S.A."

Toche has railed against cultural, social, and political conditions around the globe, writing about various European countries in *March 8, 2004:*

> President Chirac insists that to mention the existence of anti-Semitism in France is an attack on the honor of France. **"DEFENDING THE HONOR OF . . ." simply means: "WE WILL NOT PERMIT CRITICISM, QUESTIONING AND CHANGES." Honor is a phony word used by pompous idiots, patriots, fascists, militarists, ethnic cleaners, xenophobes, racists, sexists and perpetrators of other forms of bias of intolerance, by opponents of same-sex marriage, by religious leaders, by muzzlers of free expression and of civil rights, by flag bearers, by those government officials who bulldoze artists and art works, by demagogues, by the upper crust, by chief executives of corporations and other crooks . . . NB: Anti-Semitism and demonization of Jews is fast rising in Europe. In Antwerp, Belgium, incidents of hate are daily occurrences.**

The Taliban, too, have been the target of Toche's recrimination. Eighteen days after the World Trade Center bombing, in *September 11, 2001*, Toche wrote:

> Crimes against Humanity.
> Why do they keep happening?
> Mostly because we are indifferent

to what is taking place.
Women, under the Taliban's rule,
have been reduced to silence and degradation.
Women, under the Taliban's rule,
are routinely abused, physically and verbally.
Women, under the Taliban's rule,
are routinely beaten up like cattle, brutalized.
Women, under the Taliban's rule,
have been reduced to 3/5 of a person.
But we, as artists, are silent.
This silence is frightening.
What is happening to our own humanity?
Is anyone listening?[6]

*Impressions from the Rogue Bush Imperial Presidency* proves that some are listening.

## II

These works belong to the long history of Toche's social and political engagement, but this particular series began in 2001. Its first iteration took the form of letters printed on a variety of decorative papers. As Toche created as many as six hundred letters a year, and mailed sometimes more than one letter to fifty people a day, the process became quite expensive. In 2003, the artist consolidated the letters into a journal titled *Of Piss @N' Pus*, each issue of which contained all of his letters for the month.[7] At this time Toche also began to produce photographs with texts in an 8″ × 10″ format, a body of work that eventually morphed into the current series of 4″ × 5½″ works with a photograph (usually a self-portrait) at the top and a text below. In 2008, Toche began to print images and texts in scrolls as large as 2 × 15′. In addition, each of the 4″ × 5½″ works contains a notice on the back for free use, urging recipients to circulate the information and encouraging their appropriation with a promise that mocks capitalist economies while heckling them: "Hey! FREE GIFT!"[8] To complete these works, Toche signed and numbered each on the back and mailed the limited edition in a stamped envelope through the postal system.

The process of making the photographs includes digitally manipulating the images to introduce vivid expressionist color. Toche believes that this body of work has returned him to his "roots as a painter, working in an abstract expressionist style."[9] The photographs also contain art-historical references ranging from the off-register bleed of Andy Warhol's silkscreen prints of celebrities to the scatological and playful humor of Marcel Duchamp. In *February 23, 2004*, for example, it is just possible to make out a photograph of George W. Bush pasted to the inside of Toche's toilet seat, conjuring Duchamp's *Fountain* (1917), the urinal he turned upside down, signed, and presented as a sculpture.

In *November 26, 2004*, Toche displays his naked buttocks, "mooning" the viewer below a T-shirt bearing the sarcastic emblem "UTOPIA." In his work *March 27, 2004*, wearing a shirt, tie, and jacket and sporting a blue hat, Toche is nude from the waist down, demurely covering his genitals while addressing questions of censorship, and responding to what he describes as the authoritarian "trampling of artistic freedom" in the United States under the Bush administration. With this gesture of modesty, he requests: **"PLEASE, TEACHER, MAY I STAY IN THE ROOM?"** In such works, Toche nods to the theater of the absurd, exemplified in Alfred Jarry's play *Ubu Roi* (1896), which opened with the infamous salvo "Merdre!" (an intentional misspelling of the French word for "shit"), and in Piero Manzoni's *Merda d'Artista* (1961), ninety cans of the artist's excrement on sale for the daily price of gold on the stock market and proudly held up for the camera by Manzoni himself, standing in a bathroom. Such works also bring to mind Chris Ofili's *The Holy Virgin Mary* (1996), a picture to which balls of elephant dung are attached, along with collaged genitalia from pornographic magazines. This kind of locker-room humor runs throughout Toche's works. In a particularly funny piece, *January 26, 2004*, Toche stands naked, his backside reflected darkly in a mirror. He wears a terroristlike black ski mask and holds a photograph of President Bush. In the text below, Toche asks: "Who is the idiot who sent HIM a signed, dedicated photo of the President?"—"him" being a reference to Toche, as if the artist himself were a terrorist.

In staging himself, Toche's photographs recall the Polaroid *Auto-Portraits* of Lucas Samaras (from the 1970s to the present), as well as the work of many artists who since the 1960s have used photography to picture the body.[10] What is particularly unique about Toche's work, however, is the aggressive quality of the image/text that animates the act of viewing. Toche enlivens beholding through the combination of insistent, pointed remarks and close-up physical confrontation with his own body. In *December 7, 2004*, he is pictured in black and white; the camera angle looks up at his nose and eyes from below while the artist peers down at the viewer above a text that reads: "Why is everybody silent while Pres. Bush continues to destroy Iraq, stone by stone at great cost to human life?" Together, this text and Toche's direct stare compel response, whether of agreement or disagreement. When asked about the claim that some consider such an approach to be "angry," Toche responded:

> It's a way to bring attention to the point—if you don't do it like that, no one will read it. Sometimes it's a logical and sometimes it's an absurd way to get the point across; but it's absolutely not personal, it's a bombastic style. I am not an angry person myself. My response is to humanity. It goes back to when I was a student at the University of Brussels, when I participated in strikes and demonstrations. What is taken as my so-called anger is my feeling that corporations, universities, governments, and so on need to be taken to task, and that takes a lot of energy.[11]

What Toche describes as "energy," here, is the exertion of the intellectual, emotional, and ethical force of conviction.

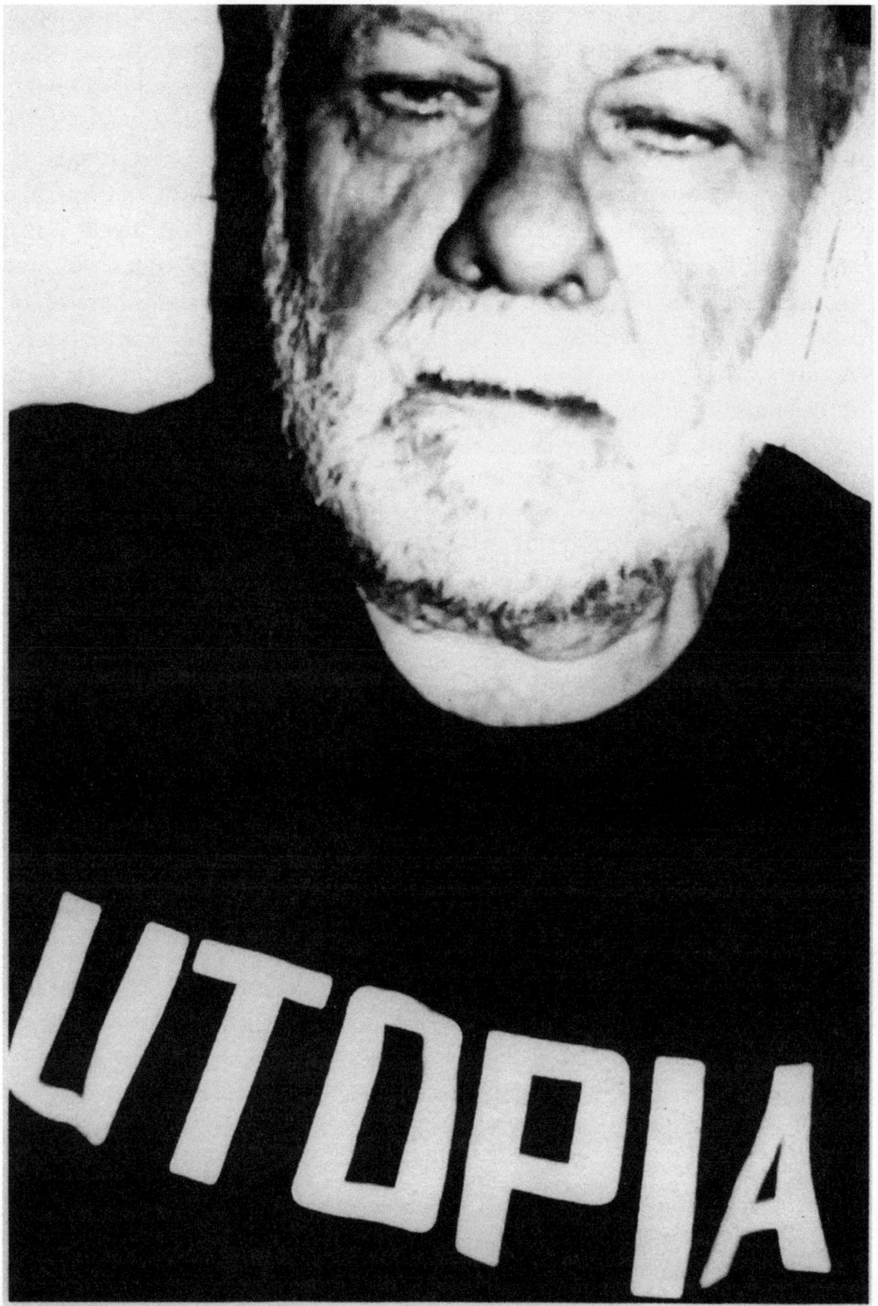


FIGURE 19. Jean Toche, *May 21, 2004*, 2004. Polaroid photographic self-portrait, 4 × 5½ in., with text. Courtesy of the artist.

Toche's cultivation of an appearance of belligerence must be understood as an aesthetic of aggression—a formal technique that is purposively antagonistic and meant to engage viewers directly. Toche revealed the ethical underpinnings of this aesthetic in his manifesto "AGGRESSION ART," October 9, 1969. In this tract, he responded to what he described as the "invasion" by artists (including himself) of Ward Island in the East River bounding New York City while participating in Charlotte Moorman's seventh annual "Avant-Garde Festival." When "hoodlums"—the term of thinly disguised bigotry that local newspapers used to describe the Puerto Rican youth of the island—damaged some of the art, Toche responded to the newspaper's use of the term by critiquing the artists themselves: they had produced "white arrogant decadent Kultuur" in the form of an "abstract and totally irrelevant language called 'Art,'" which they "imposed on the . . . community."[12] Toche then called for the

> absolute necessity for the artist to become more relevant to his [or her] environment and to the social struggle going on in the world, if art is to survive as a meaningful force. To express and not repress. To involve oneself in reality and human crisis instead of playing irrelevant and indifferent abstract games. To try to understand what is around us instead of patronizing and telling it to the people.[13]

By more than a quarter of a century, as this text shows, Toche anticipated the so-called social turn of art in the 1990s toward engaged community interaction and participation—art that has been hailed as dialogic, interventionist, and research-based. He was also consciously emphasizing an ethical approach to art decades before the alleged "ethical turn," which was attributed by some art critics in the 1990s and 2000s to the writings of Jacques Derrida, Emmanuel Levinas, Giorgio Agamben, Slavoj Žižek, and Jacques Rancière, among others.[14]

Nevertheless, critics continue to pit supposedly activist art against ostensibly aesthetic art, but such divisions are usually artificial.[15] Toche collapses that divide in his application of aggression as a formal technique into his aesthetic use of photography as a medium. To arrive at his aesthetic of aggression, he drew on Konrad Lorenz's book *On Aggression* (1966) in his 1967 manifesto "MANIFESTO 2 FOR A THEATER OF HUMAN DESTRUCTION." Lorenz, a Nobel Prize winner and a founder of ethology, argued that aggression must be perceived not only as negative, but also as serving positive functions in survival and natural selection, as well as playing a central role in animal communication. Extrapolating such theories to human interpersonal contact and exchange, Toche's outrageous pronouncements open a space in the interplay between his antagonistic texts and assertive photographic presence, where viewers' retorts manifest a desire to assert their own views.[16]

Roland Barthes, writing in another context, theorized how such an interstice is opened in photography and operates in the function of the photographic *punctum*, "as a kind of subtle *beyond* [Barthes's emphasis]—as if the image launched desire beyond what it permits us to see."[17] Applying to Toche's work Barthes's idea of how photographs initiate desire "beyond" what is visible, it is possible to recognize that the form assumed by that "subtle *beyond*" is aggression: Toche's aggression and the perception of his views and behaviors as a threat produces "desire" as a primal *need* to react, a latent survival response in the human animal. This necessity may be further theorized, if one considers what the apophatic dimension of Toche's art. *Apophasis* is the Greek word for the figure of speech that alludes to something by denying that it will be mentioned: "I will not mention your lack of political uprightness." The apophatic, thus, states without stating and, in Toche's visual production, visualizes without visualizing. Aggression in his art assumes the apophatic function; it is the "subtle *beyond*" that is nonetheless present in the work, and to which viewers respond for how it implicates them: "I won't mention your lack of moral integrity and ethical response to the social world." Toche produces not only desire and need, but also the obligation to react.

The spectator's strong response to Toche's work is the result of his working method. Identifying such formal constructs in Toche's work is not to argue, however, for a formal interpretation of his deeply passionate, socially engaged art, but to underscore how his aesthetic imbricates aesthetics and activism in form and content, a combination intrinsic to any substantive art. Or, as John Dewey put the subject in 1934: "Whatever path the work of art pursues, it . . . keeps alive the power to experience the common world in its fullness . . . by reducing the raw materials of that experience to matter ordered through form."[18]

To arrive at this delicate balance, Toche culls his commentary from everyday television footage and newspaper articles, especially *The New York Times* and *The Wall Street Journal*. He reads "both newspapers at breakfast"; finds what he "wants to talk about"; quotes a paragraph or a few sentences, "but not the whole article"; and always "gives credit," but does "not ask permission" from the author.[19] He particularly admires the journalism of Paul Krugman and Bob Herbert, and the general accuracy of *The New York Times* and *The Wall Street Journal*, upon which he depends because he is "not equipped to do that kind of research."

Toche appropriates material from the public domain for its relative objectivity. At the same time he also believes that it is not incumbent on an artist to pretend impartiality or to produce pseudo-objective commentary, a point that raises the much-debated question of the relationship between social responsibility and artistic freedom.[20] Toche has always answered this dilemma directly. By maintaining complete independence from public funding and by paying for his own art, he can speak up without reservation. The result? Acerbic, sardonic, and pointed commentary that is always infused with irony and humor, as in *July 17, 2004*, where Toche appears smiling in an impressionistic-like self-portrait, under which in Comic Sans SM font he comments: "**THIS IS NOT A WAR HEAD**." In *October 8, 2004*, Toche parodies Vincent Van Gogh. Wearing a yellow straw hat and holding a knife in his teeth, he makes an irreverent reference to the celebrated incident of Van Gogh mutilating his ear, and adds the text: "'IT'S HARD WORK TO BE THE IDIOT OF THE VILLAGE,' PRES. BUSH SAID." To this observation, Toche responds, again in Comic Sans SM font: "**LUNATIC WITH RESOLVE**!"

As these examples show, working with newspaper and textual commentary engages Toche with choices of typeface as an element to assist in triggering viewer interaction. Toche uses the computer's arsenal of fonts for its immediacy. In *September 29, 2004*, he chose a bold sans serif to quote George W. Bush, as if he were shouting in response to a question asked at a press conference about violence in Iraq. Emphasizing how Bush shifted the topic away from the query, Toche focused on how he condemned Americans for being unable to make sound judgments, the putative result of a dependence on Hollywood-produced television. Retorting to Bush, Toche chose Times, an ostensibly more objective font, given its source in *The Times* of London. But in an unexpected turn, Toche seemed to concur with the president, blaming this clouded vision on muddied "eyes and soul." Toche's irony served as self-mockery, as he became a US citizen in 1997, thereby implicating himself in this critique. This may explain why the artist places his forefinger to his mouth in a sign of "don't tell."

Again relying on the visual power of a font, in *July 19, 2004* Toche ridiculed the hypocrisy of the Bush administration's rejection of gay marriage, selecting a typical wedding invitation script to announce the bogus marriage of President Bush to Vice President Cheney. Appearing without his shirt, in shocking pink and red, with a smug grin but unsmiling eyes and a bushy white beard, Toche is of indeterminate sexuality, but his politics are not indeterminate. Toche used a bold headline type in *October 12, 2004* to emphasize the sadism of a few US soldiers who, following orders from "the highest level" in the Bush administration, tortured Iraqi prisoners at Abu Ghraib Prison in Baghdad. In disgust over these incidents, Toche whispers in tiny Times Roman: "President Bush . . . will eventually be indicted." Above this text, seen behind bars in a very dark black-and-white photograph, the artist screams.

Carrying on multiple, overlapping conversations in *09/11/2004*, Toche again uses a sans serif typeface to narrate part of the history of US interference in Middle Eastern affairs. He particularly cites the role of the United States in the 1953 coup d'état in Iran, which overthrew the democratically elected government of Prime Minister Mohammed Mosaddegh. This notorious incident, Toche rightly points out, has been conveniently forgotten in the current antagonism between the United States and Iran. Then, commenting in the American Typewriter font, which suggests that he is typing on an old-fashioned typewriter, Toche carries on a kind of solitary dialogue with Osama Bin Laden, who appears as a ghostly apparition above the text. The image of Bin Laden is an unmistakable reference to the Shroud of Turin, on which an image of Jesus of Nazareth is said to appear. In this context, Toche folds the image of the martyrdom of Christ into the political positions, beliefs, and acts of Bin Laden—a comparison that some Christians and Muslims might consider blasphemous. At the same time,

Toche rebukes Bin Laden for the atrocity of 9/11, writing: "Personally, I oppose the killing/maiming of civilians."

In *October 30, 2004*, Toche explains, with a facial expression as emphatic as his bold type, that his work "is one example of how to speak up," but adds, "There are many other ways." The urgency of the responsibility to "speak up" is vivid in Toche's stress on the importance of moral social conduct, where he states:

> **STOP RAMBO. STOP INTOLERANCE. STOP LIES. STOP THE JAILING OF REPORTERS. RESTORE BILL OF RIGHTS. STOP THE MILITARY OCCUPATION OF IRAQ. PUSH BUSH OUT. ABSOLUTELY.**
> We must stop this run-away train: it will crash and kill everyone.

Because of his incendiary commentaries, Toche has experienced public scorn; he has often been fearful in his home on Staten Island, which has been attacked; he has been followed and verbally abused by people in his neighborhood; he has had his mail tampered with; and he has been watched by governments from the United States to Belgium.[21]

## III

Jean Toche was born in Bruges on August 15, 1932. World War II broke out in Belgium on May 10, 1940, when he was eight years old. His father "became one of the officers in command at the time and we went with him wherever he went: north toward the coast of Belgium where I spent the night in a house that burnt and many were killed."[22] Toche remembers his mixture of "fear and defense" during this period:

> There would be an alert in the middle of the night. I was used to getting up and hearing air raid sounds. A V1 bomb came down and there was something wrong with its motor. It had a flame in the background. I saw it at my eye level, up close. It went crashing down and destroyed a house on the other side of the valley. It shook me up—I was about ten. I am antiwar because of what I saw: the burning of trucks and tanks; soldiers burning. I saw the troops burning. The thing I always remember is the stench of the burning tires.[23]

As a child witnessing such events, Toche had no agency. As an adult, he "tried to stop that brutality from happening again."

On March 11, 1959, he married the American ballet dancer Virginia Poe (1922–2000). One of the most poignant works in this series, *July 31, 2004*, is "In Memoriam," which commemorates the fourth anniversary of the death of his beloved wife. Virginia was, according to Toche's text on the card, a "pure atheist (not even baptized) and a gypsy dancer, from Cincinnati, Ohio, the heartland of the USA." The couple met in Belgium in 1958 when Toche was, in his words, "very wild, rebellious and self-destructive." He credits Virginia with "patiently nurtur[ing]" him to become "what I am today," and also identifies himself as "her creation."[24]

Toche and Virginia arrived in New York City on July 5, 1965. There they entered a circle of artists involved in "destruction in art." In September 1966, Toche participated in the "Destruction in Art Symposium" (DIAS) in London, organized by Gustav Metzger (see "Survival Ethos and Destruction Art," in this volume). The work of those who participated in DIAS represented a broad, cross-cultural, transnational response to the Cold War, the civil rights movement, liberation movements in Africa, and the antiwar and ban-the-bomb causes, as well as the psychological and social causes of violence in society and the family.

Toche's first performance in New York City, *I ACCUSE* (May 10, 1968), took place at the Judson Memorial Church in Greenwich Village, where the artist Jon Hendricks worked as the director of the gallery.[25] Affiliated with the American Baptist Churches USA and the United Church of Christ, the Judson was renowned for its senior minister, Howard Moody, who continued the church's legacy of advocacy for civil rights and free expression. The Judson was an early supporter of controversial causes like the right to abortion and the decriminalization of prostitution, and it also presented experimental art, allowing Hendricks to exhibit artists associated with happenings, environments, assemblage, and Fluxus, and especially artists involved in community action and political protest.[26] Hendricks hosted several exhibitions at the Judson related to destruction in art, as well as *I ACCUSE*, which Toche performed five weeks after the assassination of Martin Luther King Jr.

Sitting in the basement of the Judson under a huge electric bulb, with a siren blaring, Toche charged the public (as well as himself) of prostituting to a "trivial culture." He called for "total change," concern with human "development, not . . . exploitation," and described his action as a "LIGHT SIT-IN," a reference to the intense spotlight he used in the event, as well as a pun on light as "lightweight," of lesser consequence than the historic events of the day.[27] In an exhibition of his work that opened in Brussels in March 1968, Toche described his use of light as: "Light = Conditioning; Light = Provocation; Light = Aggression; Light = Destruction."[28]

A little over a year later, on October 15, 1969, Toche, Hendricks, and the artist Poppy Johnson founded the Guerrilla Art Action Group (GAAG).[29] Toche's wife, Virginia, participated in some of GAAG's activities, as did the artist Joanne Stamerra (Hendricks's future wife). Although Toche and Hendricks continue to issue periodic statements on behalf of GAAG to this day, GAAG's principal actions took place between 1969 and 1976. The acronym GAAG functioned as a reference both to the word "gag" and to the control of free speech. Typical of the kinds of early actions GAAG staged was one performed on the steps of the Metropolitan Museum of Art during a banquet. With Toche as "the artist" lying in a trunk on the museum's grand entrance steps, Hendricks, acting as "curator," celebrated Toche by pouring milk over him and rubbing caviar into his hair.

Their sardonic action was aimed at drawing attention to the failure of museums to address social and political problems, particularly the war in Vietnam, while carrying on their usual cultural activities. In another action, at the Museum of Modern Art in 1969, Toche, Hendricks, Johnson, and Silvianna[30] attempted to force the museum to remove the Rockefellers from its board because of their involvement in the manufacture of weaponry used in the Vietnam War; the artists did this by staging a scene of carnage, including spilling cow's blood and fighting with each other inside the museum lobby. Other more conceptual works included actions like the letters GAAG wrote to President Richard Nixon, Vice President Spiro Agnew, Attorney General John Mitchell, Secretary of Defense Melvin Laird, and Secretary of State Henry Kissinger. The letter to Nixon is as instructive an antiwar protest today as it was in 1971:

> Guerrilla Art Action, to be performed every day, from May 1 through May 6, 1971, by Richard M. Nixon, President of the United States of America:
> EAT WHAT YOU KILL

## IV

A public issue that Toche considers pressing today is the Second Amendment right to bear arms. While opposed to guns, Toche is nevertheless "very wary about changing the U.S. Constitution," and finds himself in a "situation of contradiction."[31] Having studied the Constitution closely, he holds it to be both a remarkable document and to contain "basic flaws in how it formed the U.S." Choosing the First Amendment as an example, Toche points out: "It came about because Catholics in Maryland were afraid that Protestantism would be an imposed religion." One of the Constitution's key defects, then, is how Congress and the states enforce the First Amendment and ensure regulation of the separation of church and state. Not only can Toche not abide religious intolerance, which is the source of so many wars; he also rejects religious censorship, especially of art and literature:

> I am not a religious person. I am tolerant as long as [Congress] doesn't try to legislate it; if they do I am going to fight about it. I was raised as a Catholic and studied in seminary and then quit and went to public school. My mother never forgave me. The teaching in seminary put me off: you start with a list of books you were not supposed to read: [André] Gide (my father was a friend of Gide); [Paul] Valery, and so on.

Toche is also unforgiving of what he considers criminal acts by the state, and thinks that a general lack of historical knowledge and national willingness to forget the past, both of which are prevalent in the United States, lead to "the repetition of mistakes." He offers the example of similarities between the war in Iraq and the war in Vietnam, and accuses the public of thinking, "Let's move on and forget about the criminal actions of Bush, Cheney, and Rumsfeld." While Toche believes that the Republican administration of George W. Bush "created enormous crimes," he "stopped being a Democrat when Nancy Pelosi said the Congress would not try them," stating categorically: "I will not join again until they go to the [International War Crimes Tribunal] in The Hague."[32]

How these alleged war crimes are handled also implicates the Obama administration, as during his campaign Obama discussed whether he would pursue criminal charges against the Bush administration if elected. In April 2008, *The Philadelphia Daily News*, for example, reported Obama's pre-election comments on the subject:

> What I would want to do is to have my Justice Department and my Attorney General immediately review the information that's already there and to find out are there inquiries that need to be pursued. I can't prejudge that because we don't have access to all the material right now. . . . If crimes have been committed, they should be investigated. You're also right that I would not want my first term consumed by what was perceived on the part of Republicans as a partisan witch hunt because I think we've got too many problems we've got to solve.

Obama continued:

> Are there possibilities of genuine crimes as opposed to really bad policies. . . . One of the things we've got to figure out in our political culture generally is distinguishing between really dumb policies and policies that rise to the level of criminal activity. . . . Now, if I found out that there were high officials who knowingly, consciously broke existing laws, engaged in cover-ups of those crimes with knowledge forefront, then I think a basic principle of our Constitution is nobody above the law.[33]

Critical to Toche's examination of the Obama administration is that Obama and Attorney General Eric Holder "have said they don't favor prosecuting lawyers who wrote legal justifications for interrogation methods that the president and his attorney general have declared to be torture," and that they "have sought to protect CIA officers who followed the legal guidelines."[34] Furthermore, the comments by Obama quoted above also pertain directly to the June 2009 revelations of a secret CIA counterterrorism initiative with "presidential authority to capture or kill al Qaeda operatives, directed by Vice President Cheney, who instructed the CIA to withhold information about this measure from Congress for eight years, his two administrative terms."[35]

Nevertheless, Obama's careful language constitutes what Toche both respects and continues to analyze. Toche voted for Obama, acknowledges that Obama's election was "a great historic moment" for the United States and the world, and (at the time of this writing, in 2009) remains "enthusiastic" about

Obama's promise. What Toche insists, however, about Obama's decisions is that they need "scrutiny," and he gives the example of Obama's choosing the homophobic minister Rick Warren to give the invocation at his inauguration. Toche "reserve[s] judgment about the progress of the Obama administration, in part, also because it includes so many individuals from other administrations." Accordingly, in appraising the level of change the Obama presidency has brought to the United States, Toche remarks: "Change yes, and no."

V

The art critic Max Kozloff once wrote, in an essay on the relationship between representation in painting and photography, "Historical knowledge, unaided by moral consciousness, cannot redeem tragedy."[36] Charging that narrative painting, especially history painting, presents an "idealist vision [that] tends to dissociate us from a feeling not only for foreign locales, but for our own, in its historical moment,"[37] Kozloff observed that "it fell to scientific culture and historical sense,"[38] through the technological development of photography, to enable viewers to become "witness to their 'otherness'"[39]—that is, to how individuals *in* history are aware *of* history "only after it has occurred."[40] Toche's work maintains a balance between the two in the knowledge that how history is made, represented, and reflected upon depends on this unstable equilibrium.

The artist and art historian Michael Corris remembered that in the 1970s, in a conversation with him and the conceptual art group Art & Language, Toche observed: "It is the journey, not the destination, that is important."[41] Then, commenting on Toche as an artist and revolutionary, Corris quoted Slavoj Žižek: "A true revolutionary is one for whom the process of revolution is the excitement, as well as the nagging doubt that the revolution will never be realized fully."[42] The truth of Corris's insight may be found in Toche's *May 21, 2004*. There, Toche appears with downcast eyes, wearing a T-shirt imprinted with the word "UTOPIA" (figure 19). The work suggests that the artist soberly contemplates the denial of history with which conscience—or the principles that govern one's thoughts and actions in response to history—requires him to grapple. In response, Toche put his body (in photographs) and mind (in texts) on display, to be judged for how he wrestled with key ethical issues of his time.

# IV. Corpora Vilia

# Cloud with Its Shadow
# Marina Abramović (2008)[1]

## EXTRACTS FROM AN AUTOBIOGRAPHY

Marina Abramović first performed *The Biography* in 1993. This work in progress synopsized her life, using lists of names, places and events as verbal cues for recovering memories, which she then paired with extracts from her performances. Six years later, French filmmaker Pierre Coulibeuf produced the film *Balkan Baroque* (1999), synchronizing clips from a history of her performances with her voice-over narrative.[2] Describing the film as Abramović's "autobiography, both real and imaginary," Coulibeuf suggested that her history was partly invented. But this comment is misleading: few artists have as directly or as candidly based so much of their art on the history of their lives, or have presented their biographies with such astonishing frankness. Moreover, scrutiny of the historical facts of her life, as well as her performances, writings, interviews, and teaching generally supports her representations.

*The Biography* unmasks the foundations upon which Abramović would practice art and suggests how she would eventually transform her life in order to live her art "in the here and now."[3] Brief extracts in the artist's voice provide the foundation for the following survey:

> '46 Born in Belgrade. '48 I refuse to walk. '50 Fear of dark bedrooms. '51 See father sleeping with a pistol. '53 First jealousy attack. '56 Violent fights between mother and father. '57 Traumas: dreams of jumping out of the window. '59 Parents divorce. '60 Unhappiness. First migraine attack. '61 First menstruation. I start to paint my dreams. '62 First exhibition. '64 Drinking vodka. Sleeping in the snow. My first kiss. '65 Father gives me a pistol for my birthday. Teach me to shoot. Games with knives. '66 I join the Communist Party. '69 I don't remember. '72 I start using my body as material, blood, pain, watching major operations in hospitals. Pushing my body to its physical and mental limits. '74 Reading Dostoyevski, Marina Tsvetaeva, Rilke, drinking Turkish coffee, singing sad Russian songs. '75 Meeting Ulay, strong attraction. '77 Male and female energy are united to produce hermaphroditic state of being. '79 Fear of nature, acceptance of nature. Gobi Desert, Thar Desert, Sahara. '80 Mental transformation. Stillness. '81 Meeting Tibetans. Be quiet, still and solitary. The world will roll in

> ecstasy at your feet. '87 Everything is going wrong. Problems with our relationship. Feeling unwanted, ugly, fat. Burning my possessions. '88 I stop liking his smell. '89 Growing my hair, buying my own house. Need for change, laughter, pleasure, and glamour. Bye bye togetherness. Bye bye intensity. Bye bye structure. Bye bye Tibetans. Bye bye solitude. Bye bye danger. Bye bye jealousy. Bye bye unhappiness. Bye bye tears. Bye bye Ulay. '90 Working in the mines of Brazil. Waiting for an idea. '92, War in Yugoslavia. Trip to Belgrade. My father's sadness. Questioning my responsibilities. Smell of Turkish Coffee. Grandmother. Snow. Neša.[4] Knez Mihailova.[5] Memories. Proust. Kafka. Forgotten music. Forgotten language. Ash. War. Poverty. Blood. Mourir. Pistol shot. The poor. The guilty. Everything is going to the devil. '94 Working with rats. Meeting mother and father again. Illusions and disillusions. More and more migraine attacks. Over worked and over-exposed. I'm tired . . . I want to go away somewhere so far that I am unreachable by fax or telephone. I want to get old, really really old, so that nothing matters any more. I want to understand and see clearly what is behind all of this. I want not to want anymore. I'm looking at you. You are looking at me. This is not the past. This is not the future. This is here and now.

Abramović's pronouncements in *The Biography* testify to the coextension of her art with her past, particularly in terms of the formation of her youth in a family and nation (Yugoslavia) where control of the body also required mental submission and where "a culture of heroism and sacrifice," to which she continues to feel bound, shaped her relationship to public mores and personal ethics.[6] An understanding of her work depends in part upon learning that although she internalized the necessity for adherence to severe disciplinary measures at home and to communist principles in the public sphere, Abramović also externalized their psychosomatic affects in body actions for others to witness.

In addition, Abramović's presentation of her body as the primary material of her art and as a "straight dialogue of energy" with the public is a hallmark of her work and a legacy of body art.[7] She belongs to a small number of artists throughout the world who pioneered body art and who established many of its aesthetic criteria: the use of the body as a tool;[8] the body's physical action as a primary form of visual communication; bodily endurance of physically painful events to visualize psychic pain; the body as a medium for understanding space, time, duration and memory; the body as a witness to history and a vehicle for offering corporeal testimony to psychological, social, cultural and political experience; the body as an intermediary for psychophysical exchange of energy with other bodies; and the nude body as a medium through which somatic conditions of truth may be sought and visualized.

Understanding how Abramović arrived at "the here and now" is as crucial to grasping the import of her work as it is to how she changed over time. Through determined philosophical study and reflection, spiritual learning and meditation, mental and physical exercises for self-development and self-control, Abramović altered her behavior and emotions, using her own body/mind as the agent of that change. In this regard, Abramović once quoted Mircea Eliade, the Romanian philosopher and historian of religion, who observed that "to be human is to be initiated." To this idea, she added, "But to be a creative human is to be self-initiated."[9]

## II: SACRED CONTACT

In *Cleaning the House* (1996), Abramović sat in the middle of a heap of bloody cattle bones, carefully picking the meat off and washing the huge femurs. Several months earlier, in *Cleaning the Mirror I* (1995), she thoroughly scrubbed a human skeleton. In both actions she wore white, her garments becoming progressively soaked in blood and creating a spectral presence that appeared to mourn the wrenching breakup of her native country. Her action paralleled successive wars in Yugoslavia, beginning with the Croatian War of Independence (1991–95), overlapping the wars in Bosnia and Herzegovina (1992–95), and ending with the war in Kosovo (1996–99). By washing away destruction (signified by the bloody bones) and death (represented by the skeleton), she seemed to atone for the catastrophe of the Serbs who engaged in ethnic cleansing, wholesale rape, and the incarceration, torture, and murder of thousands in death camps—the first in Europe since the Holocaust. Such violent interethnic fratricide was rooted in World War II, when the Independent State of Croatia was established in 1941 under the fascist Ustaše, and Croats began massacring Serbs en masse, hiding their remains in caves where pigeons nested. Moreover, Serbs fleeing the Ustaše joined communist partisans who, in turn, took vengeance on the Croats. In the 1980s, Yugoslavia banned a play on the subject, entitled *The Pigeon Cave*, for fear of Serbs' reprisals. In 1990 these facts became widely known, and villagers began exhuming the bones from one site described as a "40-meter-deep cavern, piled with killing-field relics."[10]

Given this history of fratricide, Abramović's performances incriminate everyone in the former Yugoslavian nation, yoking intimate acts of purification onto the polluted social body to insinuate that the crimes of the state are also those of its citizens. "To clean" also means to eradicate, obliterate, and annihilate, acts often accompanied by abrogation of responsibility. To her sorrow and guilt for the sins of the nation exhuming its genocidal past, Abramović added, in both *Cleaning the Mirror I* and *Cleaning the House*, an element of "sacred contact," calling upon ancient Slavic traditions in which the bones of the deceased are exhumed and washed. Such rituals were practiced in Montenegro, the artist's paternal ancestral home and a land to which she has many deep emotional and historical ties. Similar to ritual washings in many religions, double burials (the inhumation of bodies and exhumation of bones to be washed) exist in religions throughout the world.[11] In Slavic traditions, male relatives often unearth the coffin and "women wash the bones with water and wine, before putting them in a white, clean handkerchief."[12] The custom, called *po adetu* ("according to the custom"), represents the hallowed preservation of the memory of the deceased that connects them to the living,[13] providing them with "a peaceful transition to the next life."[14]

Also in 1995, Abramović performed two additional versions of *Cleaning the Mirror*, both of which accord with the custom of sacred contact. In *Cleaning the Mirror II*, she lay nude for ninety minutes on a white sheet with a skeleton on top of her so that it moved to the rhythm of her breathing as if animated by her breath; in version III she attempted to communicate psychically with objects placed before her in the Pitt Rivers Museum, Oxford, an ethnographic and anthropological museum known for its international collection of "masks, magic and ceremonial objects, tools and weapons, war trophies," and so forth.[15] These iterations of the performances could be said to represent an effort to communicate across the divide between life and death. As such, *Cleaning the Mirror* evokes the ancient theme of *vanitas* in which the mirror foretells the future of the self as death, as well as the modern theme of the inextricability of the life force (Eros, or libido) and the death drive (Thanatos), which Sigmund Freud theorized as the primary structures of human nature and the complexion of human desire.[16]

The dyad of Eros/Thanatos pictured in *Cleaning the Mirror II* became explicit ten years later in Abramović's *Balkan Erotic Epic* (2005), which circles back to the themes of war and religion implied in *Cleaning the House*. A multiscreen video installation, *Balkan Erotic Epic* was based in part on Abramović's extensive research on Balkan erotic pagan and folk rituals. It consisted of numerous segments that depicted fertility rites either in animated drawings or actual re-enactments, erotic acts used as healing agents for the body, animals and the earth, and rituals for the insurance of agricultural fecundity. Between each section, Abramović lectured on such customs, presenting herself as a caricature of academic authority by dressing in a black suit, her hair pulled back in a bun, and wearing glasses. Sections of *Balkan Erotic Epic* included nude men copulating with the earth, women dressed in folk costumes massaging their breasts, and women exposing their breasts and genitals to the earth in a rainstorm. One segment depicted men in Yugoslavian national folk costumes, standing motionless on a stage covered with a red cloth that was embroidered in black folk patterns found throughout the Balkans, their erect penises jutting out of their trousers.[17] Abramović remembered being "overwhelmed" by this representation of erotic power and suggestion of "national pride, [and] the idea of muscular energy, touching the idea of sexual energy as the cause of war, as a cause of disasters, as a cause also of love."[18]

Accompanying the scene of male erection, the renowned Yugoslavian film star Olivera Katarina is heard singing "My People Sleep a Deep and Lifeless Sleep." The song contains the lines: "The war is our eternal cross. Long live our true Slavic faith." Abramović 's decision to include it plunged the work into the exceedingly convoluted historical machinations of Balkan religious and secular politics: the song's title and lyrics are derived from Petar II Petrović-Njegoš's play *The Mountain Wreath*, a verse epic published in 1847. Sometimes called the

Shakespeare of Montenegro, and best known for his poetry and philosophical literature, Petrović-Njegoš took up in *The Mountain Wreath* the complexities of nationality, ethnic cleansing, and religious struggles, borrowing his theme from conflicts between Serbs and the Ottoman Empire that led to the extermination of many Muslims in Montenegro at the end of the seventeenth century. The play called for tolerance between Christians and Muslims, lamenting, "O my wretched Serbian nation snuffed out!"[19] *The Mountain Wreath* was read throughout Yugoslavia when Abramović was in school, and was still required reading in all Yugoslavian schools in the period before the 1990s war.[20]

This classic work of Serbian literature assumes even greater import in light of the fact that Petrović-Njegoš belonged to a dynasty of prince-bishops who governed the largest diocese of the Serbian Orthodox Church in Montenegro. Appointed to the throne of the official Archimandrite in 1831, Petrović-Njegoš contributed to the eventual transformation of Montenegro from a theocracy into a secular state. This modernization of the region led directly to the death of Abramović's maternal grandfather, Petar Rosić, who was "tonsured to the monkhood with the name Varnava," and who from 1930 to 1937 was patriarch of the Serbian Orthodox Church.[21] Abramović tells how Varnava died before she was born, poisoned for refusing to unify the Catholic and Orthodox churches: "The king's personal doctor put crushed diamonds in his food."[22] Varnava's death remains shrouded in myth and mystery.[23]

Abramović's narrative implied that her mother rejected the Church and the monarchy in protest against the murder of her father. But this history is more complicated: Patriarch Varnava was a known Nazi sympathizer in a Serbia that itself had increasingly become virulently anti-Semitic during the 1930s. In January 1937, Varnava "met German journalists to express his 'vivid interest' in the new Germany and to praise Hitler for leading 'a battle which serves all of humanity.'"[24] Historian Philip Cohen continues: "Varnava also stressed his sympathy for the Führer's fight against the Bolsheviks . . . [and] in April 1937, an official publication of the Serbian Orthodox Church explicitly identified the Jews as the hidden force behind freemasonry, capitalism, and communism, the world's 'three great evils.'"[25] The state would eventually canonize Varnava as a saint of the Yugoslavian Orthodox Church. By the end of July 1937, Varnava was dead and his daughter would become a communist. Since Abramović's mother came from a "bourgeois and religious family," in the context of the Eastern Orthodox Church her action could not have been more blasphemous, even if Marx was "public" and God was "private" in the lives of most Yugoslavians.[26] Abramović's mother forsook her faith and her parent's teachings for a materialist conception of history and the individual's rights and roles within it, also rejecting her father's anti-Semitism and politics.[27]

After enrolling in the Communist Party, Abramović's mother joined the resistance during World War II, becoming a major in the Army and meeting Marina's father Vojin Abramović, who served as a commander of the 13th Montenegro Division. Both were considered heroes in Yugoslavia, and both became ranking members of the Yugoslav Communist Party. The story Abramović tells of her parents' meeting is as romantic, but partial, as her narrative of Varnava. Vojin found Danica "among a group of sick and wounded partisans and took her to a hospital on his white horse; later [Danica] saved his life when she found him lying unconscious among other heavily wounded soldiers."[28] But when asked about the origins of her name Marina, Abramović answered, "My father was in love with a Russian soldier called Marina. Grenade hit her, and she literally exploded in front of his eyes and die. Because he was in love with her he gave me her name. My mother was always unhappy about his decision."[29]

For the artist herself, this name established a double Oedipal triangle, adding to the normative configuration—mother/daughter/father—a second complexity—mother/lover-daughter/father—in which Marina was always both daughter and the "other woman," the embodiment and memory of her father's beloved lover. In other words, Marina personified a woman who had died young and therefore remained ideal, and with whom her mother could never compete and of whom she would always be jealous—a jealousy that the mother projected onto her daughter. This dilemma produced a transgenerational behavioral model that Marina herself inherited, documenting that she had her "first jealousy attack" in 1953 at the age of six, an emotion that she would combat throughout her life.[30]

One of the ways in which Abramović may have addressed the pain and rage of jealousy was by channeling it into art. In one instance, she perfected the Argentinean tango *Jealousy*, which she first performed in a section of *Modus Vivendi* (1981) with Ulay (Frank Uwe Laysiepen), the artist with whom she lived and collaborated between 1976 and 1989. The term *modus vivendi* connotes a compromise that permits adversaries to live together temporarily, as Abramović and Ulay would, as did her parents until her father left when Abramović was a teenager and her parents divorced. Furthermore, jealousy and death commingle in a work that anticipated *Cleaning the Mirror I and II*, in which Abramović and Ulay used a photograph that Ulay had taken in Amsterdam of the connected skeletons of Siamese twins. "At that time, we identified ourselves strongly with this image," Abramović has written.[31] In other words, the couple, both born on November 30, felt joined to one another organically in a manner that would hold them together into and beyond death. In this way, *Cleaning the Mirror I and II* must be understood to have interconnected with and referred obliquely to Abramović's past relationship with Ulay.

The foregoing interwoven and webbed histories are the substantive subtext of Abramović's art, but especially *Balkan Erotic Epic*, a work full of striking images and actions that has rightly been described as a "quasi-documentary . . . recreation of ancient ceremonies . . . within a grand tradition of European painting devoted to role-playing."[32] No image from this theatrical production, however, is more arresting than a photograph of the artist herself. Nude from the waist up, Abramović stands before the red tapestry with black Balkan folk embroidery. Her hair hangs over and hides her face, accenting her full breasts and objectifying her body. In the video, Abramović slowly and repeatedly knocks a human skull against her rib cage just below her breasts. This knocking of death on the fulsome body of the artist is very moving, and recalls her understanding that "the crucial moment in a lifetime is when you accept your own mortality."[33] Appearing to offer the skull like a gift, Abramović's gesture shifts the objectification of and desire for her body, keeping lust at bay and providing the gift of death that Jacques Derrida aptly described as "sacrifice, vengeance [and] cruelty" bound up in the "history of God," as well as the "moral genesis of responsibility and moral conscience."[34] Such are the metaphysical subjects that Abramović's work suggests, enjoining eroticism, violence, destruction, war, and death in the service of spiritual reconciliation with loss and with healing.

## III: TRUTH SETTING ITSELF TO WORK

These varied perspectives and multiple interpretations demonstrate how open Abramović's performances can be to non-specific readings, even as they are resolutely and specifically autobiographical. Such is the case with *Balkan Baroque* (1997), the third performance in what must be considered a trilogy (together with *Cleaning the Mirror I* and *Cleaning the House*). Comprised of several parts and created for the 47th Venice Biennale, *Balkan Baroque* opened with a performance similar to the one in *Cleaning the House*. Wearing a long, voluminous, white gown, Abramović sat amidst an enormous pile of 1,500 fresh beef bones, which she washed and cleaned while continuously singing folksongs from her youth in her throaty, seductive, sorrowful voice. Abramović performed this action in front of an installation of three videos she had filmed earlier, including one of each of her parents that flanked one of herself. In the videos, her parents discussed their lives in response to questions Abramović had posed to each separately. Mirroring these parental voices, in her own video Abramović performed two different roles that appeared to be personifications of her parent's individual traits and qualities. Images from all three were reflected in three water-filled basins made of copper, a metal noted for its ability to heal the mind and body through energy-conducting properties.

In the first section of her video, Abramović dressed in a white lab coat to tell a story of the Balkan wolf rat.[35] She began by noting that "rats will never kill or eat the members of their own families." But they can be made to do so by being starved until their teeth grow long, after which "the rat catcher . . . takes a knife, removes the rat's eyes and lets it go." In "outrage" and "panic," the rat dives into the hole, kills all but the strongest rat, which in turn kills it. "This is how we make the wolf rat in the Balkans," Abramović ends her tale. A key source for her allegory of Balkan familial sadism, social violence, and genocide[36] was no doubt *The Ratcatcher* (1925), by the Russian poet Marina Tsvetaeva (1892–1941), a writer whom Abramović greatly admired and had read in the early 1970s. Just as Tsvetaeva drew political parallels between rats and revolutionaries, so Abramović's wolf rat story functioned as a metaphor for the pathological history of Balkan xenophobia and the attempts to eradicate ethnic outsiders as if they were vermin.[37]

As the narrator of the wolf rat tale, Abramović mimed her mother, whom the artist always described as a "severe authoritarian," and who, as the director of the Museum of Art and Revolution in Belgrade, was also a commanding and accomplished woman (figure 20).[38] This persona appears in a number of guises throughout Abramović's work, including the academic narrator in *Balkan Erotic Epic*.[39] In her second role in the video, Abramović removed the lab coat to reveal herself seductively dressed in a black slip-like dress, her long, thick, hair hanging loose. She then danced to folk music indigenous to "the regions of Eastern Serbia and Romania," brandishing a red scarf in imitation of a Balkan tavern singer.[40] This sultry and playful persona seemed to signify an internalized manifestation of and relation to her father, the tall, dashing man whom the artist remembers as vigorous, down-to-earth and life-embracing, but at the same time always associated with the military, violence, and war.[41]

Abramović's theatrical performance *Delusional* (1994, curated by Charles Atlas) anticipated *Balkan Baroque* in its emphasis on the artist's parents and association of them with rats. In part I, "The Mother," Abramović danced wildly over plastic rats that squeaked when she stepped on them. Then she lay on a bed of ice, sat on an iron stool, and leaned on a window while telling stories about her miserable childhood. A video image of Abramović's mother telling her own life stories preceded these actions. In part II, "The Rat Queen," Abramović revealed four hundred live rats below the stage while a video played with the image of a rat doctor narrating a story about rat hygiene, rat sexuality, and rats' parenting skills. Part III, "The Father," included a video of Abramović's father telling war stories while Abramović performed a striptease that began with her wearing military fatigues before stripping down to black bra, panties, garter belt and stockings. Eventually taking off all her clothes, she ate a raw onion that caused her to weep. In Part IV, "The Rat Disco," loud techno music was played, causing the rats to scurry in fear and confusion. Finally, in the "Conclusion," Abramović, still naked, entered the area with the rats while telling a story of her image of happiness, which included being pregnant and married. At the end of the performance, she violently smashed the glass division between the upper and lower stages, as if breaking free of the contaminating environment of her youth.

*Delusional* is a distressing picture of the artist's troubled relations with both parents, but as a subtext for much of her art, no association is more disquieting than the one that Abramović drew between herself and her father. For while she has consistently represented him as a hero and demonized her mother, in *Delusional* the incestuous drama of their relationship is vivid in her striptease, nakedness, and eating of the tear-inducing onion. Such unsettling actions are also stark in *The Hero* (2001), which the artist dedicated to her father, who died the year she performed the piece. Abramović sat astride a white horse holding a large white flag, a symbol of surrender. But *The Hero* was to have been "a two-part piece in which the artist faced a mirror image of herself seated on a black horse," which "was later edited out in order to focus on the 'hero' aspect of the work."[42] This would have juxtaposed traditional symbols of good and

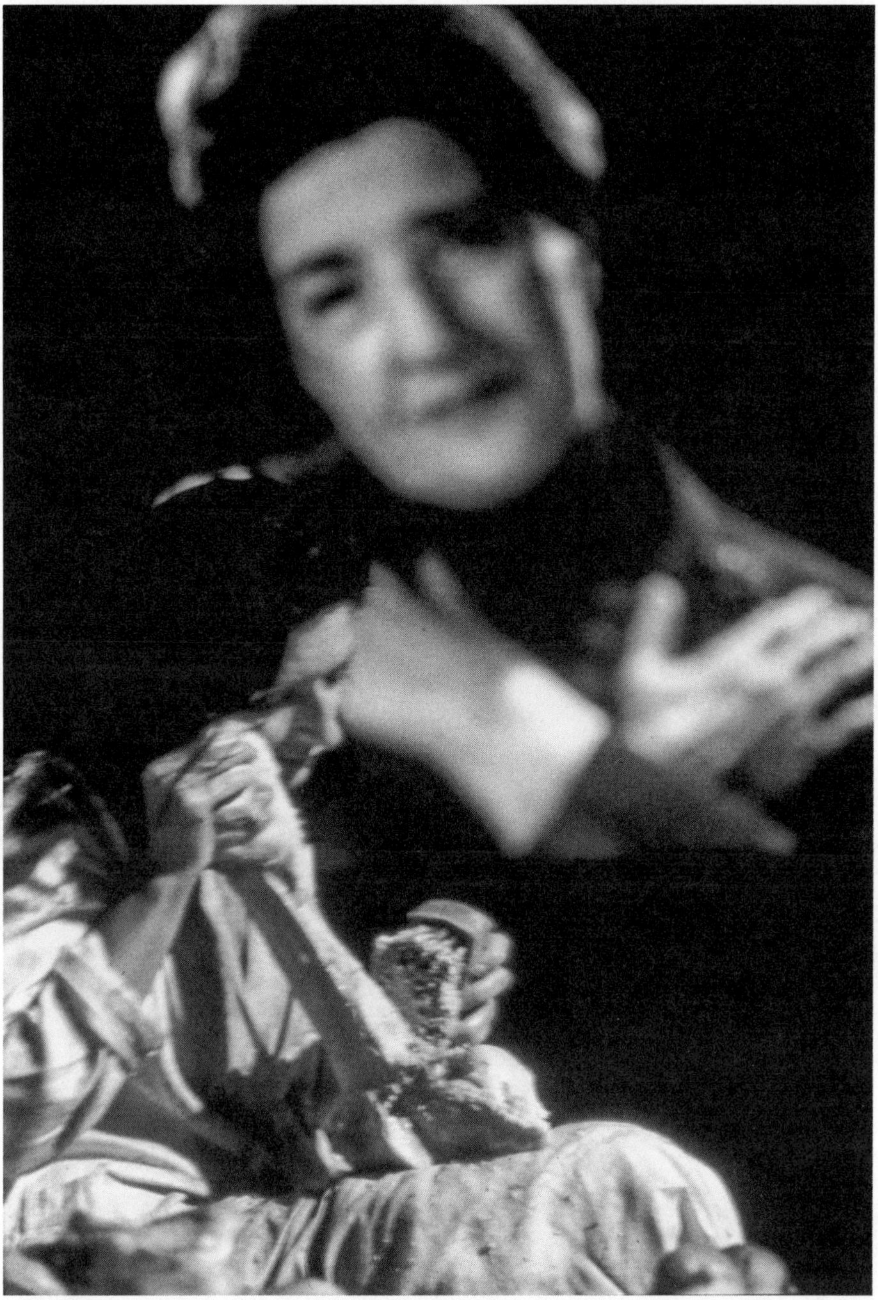

FIGURE 20. Marina Abramović, *Balkan Baroque* (performance-installation detail), Venice Biennial, June 1997. Photo by Elio Montanari. Courtesy of the artist.

evil in the white and black horses. As the black horse, Abramović was "Marina," the lost personification of her father's dead lover and, therefore, the seductive, bad daughter. Thus, while Abramović used the white flag to represent how her father, in her words, would "never surrender," the flag equally suggests her submission to him.[43]

*Role Exchange* (1975), in which Abramović switched places with a prostitute in the red light district of Amsterdam, sheds further light on her relation to her father.[44] She has explained that *Role Exchange* initially reflected her reaction to the red light district, which "shocked" her as someone "coming from a communist/socialist country" with its puritanical moral demands, and from a family where her mother was always "talking about morals, what was right and what was wrong."[45] But Abramović has also noted her interest in the "moral aspects of the architectural spaces" of the brothel, which for her had "the appearance of military spaces," where "everything is utilitarian," "every object has a function," and "everything is geared toward work."[46] Conflating the space of the brothel with that of the military, *Role Exchange* may have been an unconscious counter-commentary on her father's militaristic world. This interconnection indicates the depth of the oedipal conjunction of sexuality and violence, as well as order and control in the shared tropes of both the brothel and the military.

Abramović played out her paternal drama in yet another way, with her mother as the villain. But, as Judith Lewis Herman has pointed out in *Father-Daughter Incest*, when a daughter is "drawn into the marital conflict in the role of mother's rival," she can please her father "only at the expense of alienating [her] mother," who is often blamed for the daughter's misery and for not protecting her against the father.[47] In Abramović's case, her mother's dominating and demanding personality made her an even more accessible target. Abramović expressed the emotional results of this oedipal double bind in her proposal for *Untitled* (1970), an action that would have ended with the artist playing Russian roulette with a loaded pistol; its score reveals why the action was never performed.[48]

> I stand in front of the public dressed in my regular
> clothes. At the side of the stage there is a clothes rack
> on which hang the clothes that my mother wanted me
> to wear. Slowly I take the clothes one by one and I change into
> them. I stand facing the public for a while.
>
> From the right pocket of my skirt I take a gun.
> From the left pocket of my skirt I take a bullet.
> I put the bullet into the chamber and turn it.
>
> I place the gun to my temple.
> I pull the trigger.
>
> This performance has two possible endings.[49]

In addition, in a drawing accompanying the text Abramović listed the garments and accessories that made her want to shoot herself:

> heavy brown pin for the hair; white cotton blouse with red dots; light pink bra 2 sizes too big; heavy flannel slip, dark pink, three sizes too big; dark blue skirt, mid-calf; heavy synthetic stockings, skin color; heavy orthopedic shoes, with laces.[50]

In response to her mother's imposition of taste and style, Abramović felt "very ugly and I would often cry. . . . To revenge her, I collected one hundred pots of cheap brown shoe polish and I smeared it all over the walls and the windows of my room."[51] The memory of sullying her room with symbolic excrement exhibits the depth of Abramović's hurt, manifest as anger and rebellion, as well as her desperate attempt to communicate with her mother. This childhood response to loneliness and longing may be traced to the fact that immediately after her birth, Abramović was placed in the custody of her maternal grandmother, returning only to her parental home when she was six.[52] This longed-for reunion occurred just two hours before her newborn brother, Velimir, was brought home from the hospital. The anticipation of finally reuniting at home with her mother and father, and the simultaneous competition for their attention posed by the new baby, threw Abramović into what can only be described as a kind of hysteria: she developed a rare bleeding disease and was confined to bed for nearly a year.[53] Regardless of being bedridden, Abramović described this period as the "best time in my life," because for a brief period she was at the center of her parents' attention.[54]

In short, Abramović grew up in a family on which the public spotlight shone, but the beautiful, brilliant, and privileged child of the communist apparatchik class remained alone. Her solitude was aggravated by her mother's constant rivalry, vivid even late in life when in the 1990s she told Abramović:

> As for pain, I can stand pain. It is a rare case, especially in a woman giving birth, that the whole hospital doesn't hear her screaming. I never let out a single sound. When they were taking me to the hospital, they said: "We shall wait until you start screaming." I said: "Nobody has, and nobody will ever hear me scream." I had my teeth pulled out without an anesthetic on two occasions.[55]

Here Abramović's mother competes with her daughter's renowned ability to endure physical suffering, and also attempts to surpass her childless daughter's understanding of pain. Abramović's mother's determination to control her feelings is further reinforced by her response to her daughter's question: "Why, when I was a child, did you never kiss me, ever, or hold me?" Surprised, she answered, "But my mother never kissed me!" Then, reining in her emotion, Abramović's mother added, "Of course, not to spoil you."[56]

Abramović's work is thoroughly infused with her effort to cope with such conditions. Her mother also once told her that she had always been "very proud" to be pregnant with her first child, "but just before my little girl was born, [I dreamed] that I was giving birth to a huge snake. I was terrified and I woke up."[57] The "little girl," of course, was Marina, who eventually included this statement in her monologue for *Delusional*. While Abramović has drawn no direct relationship between her mother's comment and her work *Dragon Heads* (performed several times between 1990 and 1994), it is striking that in one of its iterations Abramović sat on a hospital bed for more than an hour with five pythons moving over her body. She has always associated *Dragon Heads* with the end of her relationship with Ulay, choosing to accompany the performance with Verdi's aria from *La traviata*, "Un dì felice eterea" (One day a rapture ethereal), which referred to eternal love. But *Dragon Heads* must be seen also as a representation of her mother's view of her as a snake—an image clearly communicated when Abramović allows the pythons to cover her head. The work is also an allusion to both Ulay and her mother, insofar as it is a metaphor for the artist's longing for unconditional love. Abramović transformed the absence of such love into inspired and moving imagery whose distinguishing fierce and forceful character are accomplished through the very behavior that her mother had taught her: disciplined restraint.

While the works discussed above may seem a long way from *Balkan Baroque*, the histories supporting them disclose the array of Oedipal dramas that Abramović conflated with the legacy of Balkan turmoil. Translating family and nation into a visually magnificent work of art, *Balkan Baroque* pictured a woman cleansing death, flanked by narcissistic parents, aptly reflected in tubs of water, talking about themselves. This image communicates the very essence of aloneness, an existential truth that Jean-Paul Sartre described at the end of his autobiography *Les Mots*: "I know very well that no one is waiting for me."[58] *Balkan Baroque* rendered explicit what was implicit in *Cleaning the Mirror I and II* and *Cleaning the House*: Oedipal representations must be read as metaphors for nationality and genocide, condensed and displaced in the wolf rat story and delivered as sound through the nostalgic folk songs, as well as a way of mapping familicide onto genocide in order to rid the nation of vermin, much as the family destroyed itself. In its psychologically insightful visualization of the aesthetics of pain, and in its collapsing of private torment into public shame, *Balkan Baroque* may be compared to Goya's series *Disasters of War* (1810–20).

Placing Abramović's performances and multimedia installations in this broader conceptual arena opens them to even wider historical readings as spiritual meditations on the state of the planet. For example, she performed *Cleaning the Mirror I* just months after news of the 1994 Rwandan civil war broke, during which conflict nearly a million people were killed in one hundred days. Similarly, *Cleaning the House* summons reflections on the mad cow disease crisis that led to the slaughter of more than 2.5 million cattle in Great Britain between 1986 and 1995. Given these worldly contexts, Abramović's performances register the grief and horror of heaps of human skeletons left by the Rwandan genocide, and the shock of mounds of burning carcasses in the British countryside, the latter disaster embedded in human hubris and the former in colonialist practices in Africa. But the commanding power of Abramović's work is how open it remains to multiple interpretations.

Furthermore, the generative symbol of bloody hands and ritual cleansing in Abramović's trilogy also reside squarely within classic representations of guilt, shame and purification, recalling Lady Macbeth's renowned command, "Out, damned spot!"—the directive that, even in sleepwalking, betrayed her bloody hands as responsible for murder. Through Lady Macbeth's soliloquy, Shakespeare introduced themes of guilt and expiation, summoning biblical connotations of the sin represented in Pontius Pilate's need to wash his hands of the decision to crucify Christ. If a tragic theater exists today, Abramović's trilogy must be acknowledged as its exemplar. Her actions perform the political and psychic conditions of the body in relation to essential conditions of life and death determined in the family (*oikos*) and society (*polis*), explored from Greek tragedy to Shakespeare and beyond. Similar psychopolitical drives that organize society later propelled Antonin Artaud to write his 1932 manifesto "Theatre of Cruelty," which called for the enactment of the "magical connection with reality and with danger . . . halfway between gesture and thought" and aimed to assault false reality to reveal inherent spiritual and physical truths.[59] Three years earlier, Martin Heidegger had anticipated Artaud's quest when he argued that art itself is a catalyst for truth: "In the artwork, the truth of what is has set itself to work. . . . Art is truth setting itself to work."[60] Abramović's trilogy functions as tragedy in all of these ways, not only through its commanding, turbulent compositions, baroque staging, and intense emotional content that visualize the territory "halfway between gesture and thought," but also through her visual meditations on the conflict at the intersection of relations between the family and nation.

In her art, Abramović deploys the body as an index of experience embedded in and shaped by public and private relations and events. While ritual is widely acknowledged in her performances, most viewers and critics have missed her work's outwardly directed social content.[61] Setting art the task of visualizing the interconnection between the individual and collective, Abramović has realized what few performance artists have achieved: the ability to focus corporeal action on the social conditions of the historical body in its cultural circumstance without claiming to be politically active. As I have written in another context, the principle material of such a practice is the artist's body, and its site is the social body.[62] Abramović's performances translate history into art while not permitting either art or history to become mimetic of the other, and without identifying with political movements (especially pronounced in this regard is Abramović's disavowal of being a feminist while supporting feminism). Abramović's art embarks on a journey of energy and mind but does not abandon commitment to the body, matter, collectivity, or history, drawing viewers into visual actions and participation with objects in ways that elicit dynamic creative energy as it metaphorically determines the world and metonymically connects experiences and events to biography. Such are the aesthetics of truth setting itself to work.

## IV: THE STAR

No works in Abramović's oeuvre better exemplify the psychological negotiation of a subject within her social and cultural situation than *Rhythm 5* (1974) and *Thomas Lips* (1975). In both actions, she makes the star simultaneously a symbol of place and a marker of identity. For example, in *Rhythm 5* she nearly suffocated while lying inside a five-pointed star that she had filled with one hundred liters of gasoline and ignited; it consumed the oxygen around her, rendering her unconscious until a viewer dragged her from the burning star. In *Thomas Lips* she ate a kilo of honey, drank a liter of red wine, broke the wine glass with her hand, whipped herself, and lay on a cross constructed of ice blocks with a heater suspended above her. But, most commanding of all, she cut a large five-pointed star on her belly with a razor blade. Later, in both *The Biography* and *Seven Easy Pieces* (2005), she reenacted a section of *Thomas Lips*, again cutting the star on her stomach.

The alarm of these spectacles has caused few to notice their most salient detail: the five-pointed star has been the symbol of universal communism and socialism since Karl Marx and Friedrich Engels used it as an emblem. Russia adapted it in 1918 as a symbol of the Red Army. Along with the hammer and sickle, it represents the sign of the Communist Party. The five-pointed star was positioned in the center of the Yugoslavian flag before the breakup of the country's former republics and autonomous provinces.[63] In communist nations, the star symbolized the five fingers of the worker's hand, the five continents where communism could grow, and the five social groups leading to communism: youth, the military, industrial laborers, agricultural workers or peasantry, and the intelligentsia.

This red star also appears on Abramović's birth certificate,[64] which she included in *Communist Body / Fascist Body* (1979), performed with Ulay.[65] She and Ulay invited eleven friends to their Amsterdam loft, requesting that they arrive at 11:45 p.m. on the eve of the artists' birthday, November 30. Upon arrival, the guests found the two artists asleep. One table had been set with food and champagne from Yugoslavia, and another with food and champagne from Germany. On a desk, the artists' birth certificates lay "joined together with tape."[66] While Abramović 's document bore a star, Ulay's bore a swastika. Ulay was born in 1943 in Solingen, Germany, the birthplace of Obersturmbannführer (Nazi SS Lieutenant Colonel) Adolf Eichmann, who managed the mass deportations to extermination camps in Nazi-occupied Eastern Europe, where Abramović's parents had fought the German fascists, but also where her maternal grandfather had been a Nazi sympathizer. Embroiling the couple's art in the psychic affects of the war, the performance linked their art to the body politic, or the ways in which society indoctrinates and modifies corporeal and social experiences, manifest in the former Yugoslavia's celebration of "'biologistic' metaphors such as 'the body of the institution,' 'state organs," or 'the hand of justice."'[67] Similarly, the language of Fascism had indoctrinated the young Ulay, and he would spend his youth in the aftermath of Germany's defeat.

Thus, while marked at birth with the star and the swastika, and while performing *Communist Body / Fascist Body* during a period in which the ideological struggle of communism and fascism resulted in the Cold War impasse of communism and capitalism, Abramović and Ulay slept together under a bright red blanket. Ironically signifying both Nazi fascism and worldwide communism, they presented themselves united by a color that would otherwise symbolically separate them while at the same time being the unifying color of blood. In the most vulnerable, intimate, and nonaggressive of all acts—sleep with another person in the presence of others—Abramović and Ulay neutralized culturally explicit and destructive ideologies and nationalisms through two requisite actions for life: rest and food.

Thus, the star Abramović cut onto her body confirmed the centrality of the state and the ideology that had so profoundly shaped her, and to which she had pledged the first twenty-four years of her life. The first time she cut the image onto her body, she positioned it upside down. Viewed from the artist's standpoint, the star appeared as the five-pointed star of communism; from the viewer's vantage point, it resembled a pentagram.[68] In both the second and third cuttings, Abramović flipped the star, emphasizing its original communist and nationalist connotations to viewers. In whichever orientation, the testimony of the star on her body was bleak, signifying a marked body, enunciating the silence that is a rudiment of trauma and a source of the destruction of identity, and offering a sign of a visible wound and a mark of honor, a symbol of resistance and an icon of marginality, and a signature of capture that both designated and disguised identity.

Abramović's connection to and simultaneous wounding by life under the five-pointed star continued to prevail in her adoration for Josip Broz Tito, leader of the Socialist Federal Republic of Yugoslavia from 1945 until his death in 1980. Her attachment is exemplified in a photograph of Tito in her New York office, which she hugged to her body in 2007, proclaiming continued "love" for the renowned leader of her childhood and young adult life[69] who was "passionate in everything—food and drink, love and hate, decision making . . . who behaved as if there was no distinction between his love life and important Party business."[70] In her book *Balkan Epic* (2005), Abramović even included a photograph of herself entitled *Portrait with Tito* (2004), in which she stands in black pantyhose with black high heels, legs spread, holding a photograph of Tito over her bared breasts. The image visualizes the thin divide between identity and nation and between sexuality and politics, and her stance and costume bring to mind her striptease in *Delusional*, making the father of the nation synonymous with her own father as another erotic figure dominating her life. The necessity of transforming the wounds of the star, which signified a place of death, persecution, disillusionment, and unhappiness for the artist, was indispensable for self-healing.

During this period, Abramović also produced *Count on Us* (2003), a multi-screen video installation in five parts. The most commanding image of this work featured children wearing black, lying on the ground in the formation of a five-pointed star. Abramović, also dressed in black, lay in the center with a skeleton covering her body from head to outstretched arms and legs (an image that may also have referred back to *Rhythm 5*). While Abramović maintained that *Count on Us* represented her aggrieved response to the decimation of the infrastructures and economies of the Balkan countries and "false promises from the European Union and the USA for help,"[71] the alignment of the star with images of death vividly testified to the Balkan's oppressive ideologies.

The star appears again in a photograph in *Private Archaeology* (1997–99), a large wooden construction with shelves that when pulled out can be read like the pages of an "object/book." The photograph is of the star on Abramović's belly in *Thomas Lips*; on each of its five points Abramović has written: "ENTER TO THE OTHER SIDE; PLACES OF POWER; FOOD; PREPARATION TO ENTER; DEATH." These phrases encompass a range of activities related to measures preparing Abramović to pass from life through places of power, with the sustenance of food, to death. Just as she had transformed the historically specific content of *Balkan Baroque* into a universal image of the relationship of the body to death, in this representation of the star, Abramović converted definite meaning to indefinite inference. The star, while metonymically connecting her body to Yugoslavian communism in the past, might be understood metaphorically in the present as an intermediary, a celestial force that lights the darkness, altering a symbol of nation and ideology into an emblem of radiating energy.

In 1975 Abramović was already well on her way to becoming a star herself. In 1973 she had performed *Rhythm 10* at the prestigious Edinburgh Festival, where she met Joseph Beuys. In 1975 she participated in Hermann Nitsch's *Orgies Mysteries Theater*, and in the following year, 1976, photographs of four of her performances appeared in the influential special edition on Eastern Europe of *Vision* Magazine, edited by the conceptual artist Tom Marioni and published by Crown Point Press in Oakland, California.[72]

Moreover, Belgrade was anything but a backwater removed from international experimental art, and the audacity of Abramović's work rests on solid foundations in Yugoslavian modernist movements from Cubism, Futurism, Dada, and Belgrade Surrealism to the internationally recognized neoconstructivist New Tendencies Movement that emerged in the late 1950s and early 1960s in Zagreb.[73] New Tendencies organized international exhibitions of kinetic, geometric, systems, and op art, and also had strong ties with many European avant-gardes, such as the German ZERO group, the French Groupe de Recherche d'Art Visuel, and the Italian Gruppo N and Gruppo T throughout the 1960s and 1970s.[74] During the same period, conceptual and body art also developed throughout Eastern Europe, and information from the West was not nearly as scant in Yugoslavia as it was in other Eastern European countries like Romania and Albania, due to Tito's special relationship with both the West and with Russia. In addition, Yugoslavia opened up even more during the period of the Prague Spring, which resulted in the relaxation of strict communist control. The "spring" that had spread throughout Eastern Europe came to an abrupt end in

August 1968 when the Russians entered Prague with tanks. Yet, however progressive Yugoslavian art was, the secret service remained powerful and present.

International interest in Yugoslavian artists, especially those from Belgrade, also reflected the founding of what eventually became the renowned Student Cultural Center (SKC) in Belgrade. It opened in 1970 and, under the art direction of Dunja Blazević, attracted artists, critics, and art students from around the world.[75] Ironically, the events surrounding the founding of the SKC led to Abramović's break with communism, her subsequent artistic development, and her eventual departure from Yugoslavia. In 1968, Abramović was the president of the communist art students' party, which protested for more space, art supplies, and a place to exhibit, as well as more fundamental rights, including free speech. Tito gave the students a building formerly belonging to the secret service—it became the SKC—but he failed to acknowledge their other demands. Shocked and disillusioned by the capitulation of her student peers to Tito's response, Abramović burned her Communist Party card.[76] This decisive moment marked a turning point in her relation to the nation, even if she gained much from the new Student Cultural Center in terms of the development of her life and art. In fact, the SKC was a gracious, accommodating space, with excellent rooms for installation and performance: "They made a café, a movie theater, a bookshop, a library; everything was there. So I started practically living there."[77] Abramović made her first sound installations in the SKC, and there the important Group of 70 was formed, emerging as the first avant-garde in Yugoslavia to explore performance, installation, and video. It included Raša Todosijević, Ero Milivojević, Urkom Gergelj, Zoran Popović, Neša Paripović, and Marina Abramović, the only woman in the group.

## V: CLOUD WITH ITS SHADOW

Abramović once wrote: "I dream that I wake up in another dream talking to my shadow."[78] Her statement suggests that she is thrice removed from the reality of her body, existing in a dream of a dream, where, in talking to her own shadow, she converses with the incorporeal, ephemeral extension of that absented body. As a child Abramović painted her dreams; in her teens she painted clouds; later, she painted car and truck accidents. The continuity between the dream, the cloud, and the accidents exhibits lines of connection among a disembodied, dreaming self (its dissociated cloud, or shadow self), and the self-realization that may be augmented through violence and in pain. The first work of art that Abramović made after she stopped painting at the age of twenty-four, *Cloud with Its Shadow* (1970), was a small collage consisting of a peanut shell divided horizontally with each half pinned to a white sheet of paper. One half of the shell was empty, exposing its two-celled structure; the other side contained the two nuts, whose soft meat Abramović pierced with a straight pin to secure it to the paper. The shape of the peanuts on their white ground suggested a cloud: a diaphanous, boundary-lacking shape-shifter anchored to the context of art where it cast its shade. This early work anticipated Abramović's first realized actions: by presenting the body as a material from life placed into the context of art; by articulating the specter of the body as an artifact of processes, substances, and memories; and through the metaphorical role of the pin (in a wide variety of subsequent painful forms), which lances feeling and experience to secure a surface for visual representation.

The theme of the cloud and the shadow is present throughout Abramović's work in many different forms. Four years after making *Cloud with Its Shadow*, for example, she performed *Rhythm O* (1974) in Italy, lining up seventy-two objects on a table and instructing the audience to use them on her "as desired." "I am the object," she explained. "I take full responsibility." The action lasted six hours. One photograph near the end of the performance depicts the artist, stripped to the waist by the public, eyes brimming with tears, holding a set of Polaroid pictures, which someone had taken of her during the event and placed in her hand. Again, thrice removed, Abramović became the object, shadowing others' actions, shadowing the function of the objects, and shadowing her own photographic shadow. At one point, a man took the gun Abramović had left on the table and pointed at her head but the audience grabbed it and threw the bullet out of the window. The performance ended much later, precisely at 2 a.m. as Abramović had planned. Only then did she begin to move about on her own, a transformation from object to subject that frightened the audience, who "literally ran out of the space," she remembered, because "they could not stand me as a person, after all that they done to me. Abramović contined: "The Gallerist gave me a ride to the Hotel. As soon as I arrived in my room, I took a look at myself in the mirror and I realize I get a big piece of white hair. That's how *Rhythm O* ended."[79] *Rhythm O* represents the ghost of a zero-sum game in which one can only gain if another suffers an equal loss. Exhibiting the depravity to which most people will stoop when given control over another person, Abramović was one of the few who maintained responsibility for, and dignity throughout, this action. *Rhythm O* recalls Stanley Milgram's famous experiments on the ethics of conscience, coincidentally published in December 1973, just months before Abramović 's action. Milgram concluded that cruel authority over others "won more often than not" over morality.[80]

Five years later, in *The Brink* (1979), Abramović would walk back and forth on the shadow line of a wall on top of which Ulay simultaneously walked. She shadowed Ulay, shadowed the wall, and cast her own shadow. The performance lasted until the sunlight diffused the shadow line, leaving only the wall and artists as objects in space.[81] Four years later, as part of their performance *Anima Mundi* (1983), Abramović and Ulay would stand "with outstretched arms on a spacious, sun-drenched staircase in Thailand imperceptibly inching towards each other in time with their own shadows . . . until the tips of their shadows touch."[82]

Given these shadow works, the poignancy of a photograph taken of Abramović while walking the Great Wall of China in *Lovers* (1988) is heartrending. It depicts Abramović alone, her isolation doubled in the long, solitary shadow that her body casts against the wall of a cliff that she passes as she marches nearer to the end of her creative and amorous journey with Ulay. Having started from opposite ends of the wall, each walked ninety days and each covered more than 2,500 kilometers "to say goodbye" when they met in the middle.[83] A photograph of *Lovers* anticipates the image of surrender in *The Hero*. Abramović stands on the Great Wall wearing a red jacket and holding a large red flag. Rather than denoting surrender, the color red in China is associated with love and weddings, as well as with funerals, thereby indicating her passion unto death for Ulay.

Five years later, in her sculptures entitled *Mirror for Departure* (1993), Abramović pressed the faces of volunteers into red clay discs framed in iron to create ghostly imprints, shadows reminiscent of Roman death masks; and in performance workshops with students, she required each apprentice to gaze at his or her own reflection in a mirror that she held for five minutes. In all these works, the shadow functioned as a metonymic extension of the artist. The existential condition of shadows contributes to what Tina Ballantine has described in another context as a "metaphysical and intellectual understanding of 'self' ":

> Stripped of excess and filed to spareness, [the shadow] unveils the painful yet exquisite core of human experience: the knowledge that the very characteristic that grants human beings their unique position on the planet—the singular ability to identify the "self" as separate, thinking, and individual—is . . . an artificial construction. To abandon possession of the "self" as a marker of being human is to lose a sense of grounding, but if at the same time that the "self" as possessed "self" disintegrates, we also discover ourselves as connected to others, we then find new moorings more various and numerous that are, ultimately, more stable and useful.[84]

Abramović's "self" had first to disintegrate into shadow before she found moorings in the "here and now." For the body thrice removed shadows itself and is a numbed body in escape from a "self" that it neither knows nor understands. Such a body must be penetrated or punished to feel and encounter itself. The oscillation between pain and punishment (also to be understood as a form of discipline) and dissociation (or mental absence from the body) occurs in many of Abramović's performances, especially in the early years. In her first action, *Rhythm 10* (1973), for example, the twenty-six-year-old artist applied polish to the nails of her left hand and then, kneeling before an array of twenty knives in different shapes and sizes, splayed the fingers of her left hand on the floor, picked up one of the knives in her right hand, and began stabbing between the fingers on her left hand. Conceiving of the varying sizes and sounds of the knives as "rhythms," she recorded the process on a tape recorder, only stopping each time she cut herself to rewind the tape, pick up a different knife, and begin again. After she had used all the blades, Abramović rewound the tape, listened to the first action, and then attempted to repeat the performance in the same rhythm, sequence, and manner of lacerating herself. That she would convert such violence into a musical metaphor related to rhythm summons the fact that her mother had "forced me to play the piano even [though] I didn't have any ear for music."[85] Replaying that obligation in its most painful literal manifestation, Abramović punished the fingers that had struck the notes without joy or talent for what she perceived to be their clumsy failure. This aesthetics of pain visualized a somatic memory of emotional suffering disengaged from the source of its wound, even though Abramović has insisted, "I was never interested in shocking. What I was interested in was experiencing the physical and mental limits of the human body and mind. I wanted to experience these limits together with the public. I could never do this alone."[86]

While many different kinds of performance developed throughout the world beginning in the early 1950s, the aesthetics of performance in Europe and Eastern Europe were strongly inflected by an expressionistic style derived from the combination of the influence of Georges Mathieu and Yves Klein (both tutored by Dali), the Viennese action artists (influenced by Mathieu), and Joseph Beuys, coming out of happenings and Fluxus. By the early 1970s, all these impulses had converged into body art, whose means were increasingly spare (reflecting the aesthetic of Arte Povera and Minimalism) but whose content became explosive. Abramović's work is exemplary of this synthesis. On the one hand, the expressive European approach to the body provided her with a means to articulate pain visually, and simultaneously to relieve her own psychosomatic symptoms. Self-flagellation and self-cutting reoccur in Abramović's art, especially in *Thomas Lips* and later in *Dissolution* (1997), in which she whipped herself "until I no longer feel any pain."[87] On the other hand, when she began to work with Ulay, their performances became pared down and minimal. In the 1980s they started to travel extensively, learning about spiritual practices in other cultures, meeting with spiritual leaders, and understanding a connection to pain that had not initially informed Abramović's work:

> Much later when I got into other cultures, when I went to Tibet, met the Aborigines and was also introduced to some Sufi-rituals, I saw that all these cultures pushed the body to the physical extreme in order to make a mental jump, to eliminate the fear of death, the fear of pain and of all the body limitations with which we live. We in the Western society are so afraid. Performance was the form enabling me to jump to that other space and dimension.[88]

Bojana Pejić, a Yugoslavian art historian and longtime friend of Abramović, has argued that "the self-infliction of injuries is the way in which Abramović arrives at the state of being-in-her-body, in which the mind is freed from the fear of pain."[89] However, Pejić does not situate Abramović's pain in the initial context of her attempt to numb emotional suffering, but rather in her retrospective view of her own process, acquired in spiritual journeys and mapped onto her earlier habit of using pain to dissociate. But in order to appreciate the extent to which Abramović has grown as an artist, this early context must be restored. To return to *Rhythm 10*, for example, Abramović has noted that "the mistakes of the past and those of the present are synchronous" in the work, suggesting that she continued to punish herself for her perceived bad behavior, which, while attributed to her mother's constant criticisms, must also have included her father's contributions to the oedipal triangle.[90]

While Abramović's most intense experiences of her body have been in performance, she more often invoked and solicited escape in performative sculptures and installations. In *Escape* (1997), visitors were required to commit to twenty-five minutes of restraint in steel constructions with leather belts, their ears covered to block out sound so that they might access desire for evasion through mechanisms associated with torture and sadomasochistic eroticism. In *Inner Sky* (1991), viewers were asked to remain motionless with eyes closed under an amethyst geode suspended in an iron sculpture, escaping the body into the mind's eye. In such works, Abramović drew on the medium of performance art as both an explanation for and a source of her self-harming practices, explaining:

> As a performance artist, I faced enormous obstacles, and one of the biggest obstacles was my own mind. I don't see it as real but more like an echo of the universal mind. It's a feeling, which you have best when you force your body to experience pain. Essentially, you're causing the physical pain in order to define limits and to increase those limits to the maximum. Senses are inherent to the mind, senses are a part of the mind, they are not independent. Once your state of mind emerges and is expressed through senses, you cannot stop the process. But I want to stop it, to control it, to have power over my own mind.[91]

Abramović's comments summon a history of emotional deprivation whose traumatic symptoms include self injury in the forms of stabbing, cutting, pinching, hitting, scratching, burning, picking at the skin, head-banging, hair-pulling, and self-poisoning.[92] While self-injury is no longer considered suicidal or masochistic, it often becomes compulsive, an addictive effort to manage anxiety, self-loathing, perfectionism, and psychic pain. Attempting to escape the body is a dissociative response that produces a mental effect similar to that of self-inflicted pain, since the body in pain is a body without verbal language, even though pain's language is visually expressive.[93] For Abramović, performance itself provided a means of escape. In response to the question, "Who are you?" Abramović answered, "I don't know; I learn about myself through work, not through my life."[94]

While she was not alone in exhibiting the body in pain, Abramović's early self-harming works became exemplary of body art in the popular imagination, among younger artists, and even among many scholars. As a result, the idea that harming oneself demonstrates the aims of body art has led to great misunderstandings and distortions of the medium, as well as of the intentions of most body artists, including Abramović. She has become increasingly uncomfortable with the abuses of the body and threats to the public performed in the name of body art, as have other pioneers of the medium, and she refuses to mentor students who are "bulimic, anorexic, take prescription drugs, have depression," or use performance in self-destructive ways:

> I will never do anything to hurt them in any way, and I will never propose a situation where a group can get hurt. Because if I do performances on me, that's my problem, and I am dealing with that. But even if they get extreme ideas, they can't do it if I'm present; they can do it during their own lifetime as independent artists, and take their own responsibility, but not while they are also called my students.[95]

Abramović's workshops teach participants "endurance, concentration, perception, self-control, and willpower," as well as "confrontation with their limits mental and physical" without self-harming activities. An example of such an exercise is: "Taking a bath in the ice-cold water of the river or sea, [which] helps us reinforce our physical strength."[96] Her aim in such work, especially in the Independent Performance Group (IPG) that she founded, is to work more with specific students and explore her "role . . . as a curator, and as a connector, to give information."[97]

Abramović has referred to herself as one of "the grandmothers of performance art," suggesting that she accepts the reception of her work as paradigmatic of a number of directions in performance art, including her history of performing violent and self-harming works. At the same time, different historical eras require dramatically different responses, have different implications, and necessitate different boundaries that function both to counter and to replicate different historical contingencies and social and political formations.[98] It remains to be seen how long the self-harming model's distortion of the history of body art will prevail. But if Abramović's early performances, growth, and personal development are its measure, then her example of research, problem-solving, and healing will replace violence as an aesthetic paradigm.

Good art responds to and comes from good art, but unique art absorbs the lessons of art history and at the same time communicates original ideas and forms. Such is the case with Abramović's *The House with the Ocean View* (2002).[99] In this performance, Abramović fasted for twelve days, only drinking water, while living at the Sean Kelly Gallery in New York. Her environment included three platforms comprising a bedroom, sitting room, and bathroom, all open to the public. In front of the space, a series of ladders with rungs made of butcher knives, sharp edges turned upward, prevented her from descending and the public from ascending. The rooms were sparsely furnished and contained very few objects. But one object was of particular significance: a metronome that ticked, as if keeping time, but actually regulating silence. Abramović kept the metronome going during most of the performance. The odd presence of this object in a performance devoted to a kind of meditation, together with the ladder rungs made of knives, recalls the artist's failed music lessons, as well as her performance *Rhythm 10*, and suggests a relationship to the past that Abramović attempted to heal in the piece.

Moreover, Abramović made her every action available to public scrutiny by equipping viewers with a high-powered telescope. This extreme form of exhibitionism simultaneously serviced and exposed the public's voyeuristic appetite.[100] The more closely viewers looked, the less they could see what Abramović presented: a fully integrated, self-possessed artist who could only be encountered through an exchange of psychic awareness. Her ability to focus out from her body, beyond herself, no longer required the body's shadow. Moreover, without the infliction of pain, or psychological flight, she tutored the public in the consequences of one's will to enhance empathic interconnection. Through a meditative focus, she offered the public a view of the sublimity of the infinite, metaphorically instantiated in "the ocean view."

Indications of mental healing from the shadows of pain, punishment, and escape had begun to appear in Abramović's art at least a decade earlier, as her installation *Double Edge* (1995) proved, and to which *The House with the Ocean View* was in part indebted. *Double Edge* featured four ladders with rungs consisting of stainless steel knives, heating elements, cooling elements, and wood. An attempt to climb one of the dangerous ladders would have resulted in punishment: being cut, or being burned by either searing hot or frigid temperatures. Making the correct choice, climbing the ladder with wooden rungs, one could ascend without injury. Thus, climbers were required to think carefully about the consequences of their decisions, to contemplate the results, and to move with wisdom towards a goal that would protect and honor the body.

Since the late 1980s, Abramović's sculptures, such as various versions of *White Dragon* (1989), *Chairs for Departure* (1990), and *Crystal Cinema I* (1991), have encouraged viewers toward such goals. Her *Soul Operation Room* (2000) even includes a *Reprogramming Levitation Module* (2000), among other apparatuses, to reconfigure the mind constructively and homeopathically. In all of these works, viewers remain in meditative states accentuated by the healing properties of crystals or, as in *Reprogramming Levitation Module*, dried chamomile flowers, copper, and quartz. Abramović's site-specific project *Dream House* (2000) in Echigo-Tsumari, Japan, encompasses all these qualities. There, spaces for instruction and dressing, a bathroom and kitchen, a dream library and dreaming rooms, and a spirit room were furnished with unusual objects and clothing for participants to encounter, engage with, and even wear. Enhanced with magnets and mineral stones, the spaces were open to visitors to spend the night, where they could discover new levels of ability while exploring the potential of the house to affect their mental relationships to space and time and, consequently, their dreams.[101] "This is my continuing attempt to create a cultural dialogue about and to reconnect with our need to ritualize the simple actions of everyday life," Abramović wrote. Among these rituals she included "writing, thinking, walking, standing, sitting, lying, eating, washing, drinking, dressing, undressing, sleeping, dreaming."[102]

Abramović has worked studiously on an integrated sense of self through years of philosophical and spiritual study, begun in the late 1970s with Ulay, nurtured in travel to spiritual centers throughout the world, and enhanced by work with spiritual leaders and healers such as the Dali Lama. She has spent decades learning to understand the body as a medium of visual communication and energy exchange wherein meaning resides. The body as site for the creation of meaning can be considered a "commissure."

## VI. ABRAMOVIĆ/ULAY: COMMISSURE

Few images of male and female unity and division are as commanding as *Relation in Space*, which Abramović/Ulay performed in July 1976 at the thirty-eighth Venice Biennale. The action was simple: The two naked artists walked toward each other, passing but barely touching, turning as they reached the wall and then repeating the process. After each turn they increased their pace, eventually running at high speed and repeatedly colliding. Jaap de Graaf's photographs captured the action of the couple's slender, lanky bodies; their long, flowing hair; the tension in their faces and arms; the hands that did not touch as the bodies crashed; the swinging penis and bouncing breasts; the hard abdomens; the couple's palpable attraction and tension' the accidental, then purposeful, meeting and eruption of bodies. Nothing in this action was prurient, including their nearly identical, ideal bodies. No wonder that the prominent fashion photographer Steven Meisel failed in his imitation of de Graaf's pictures and Abramović/Ulay's actions when he created the cover for the November 1998 issue of *Vogue Italia*. Meisel photographed his models semiclothed in high-fashion garments. But while the models' body positions and hair copied those of Abramović/Ulay, their haughty, disinterested poses had neither the powerful psychic magnetism shared by the artists nor their magisterial concentration, neither their dignity with grace nor their external authority and internal might.

Abramović/Ulay's action cannot be copied, repeated or reenacted without losing its historical integrity and aesthetic elegance, for it was a moment shared and created between two artists, their public, and a camera. This work belongs to the 1970s, when the mere presentation of the nude body in a simple action within an art context could elicit authentic excitement and even awe as the public confronted for the first time the radical possibility of the body's visual, nonverbal, nonnarrative communication. *Relation in Space* took fifty-eight minutes to perform, and remains a singular, unforgettable event in the history of art, a work that even Abramović/Ulay could not recapture in actions such as *Interruption in Space* (January 1977) or *Expansion in Space* (June 1977), which duplicated many of its formal elements. *Relation in Space* is one of a handful of unsurpassed actions in the history of body art.

It was also the first visual expression of Abramović/Ulay's call for a vigorous life, lived in the present as a critical act of survival. They indicated this aim in their manifesto:

> *Art vital*
> no fixed living place
> permanent movement
> direct contact
> local relation
> self-selection
> passing limitations
> taking risks
> mobile energy
>
> no rehearsal
> no predicted end
> no repetition
> extended vulnerability
> exposure to chance
> primary reactions

Fifteen months after *Relation in Space*, in October 1977, Abramović/Ulay performed *Relation in Time* at Studio G7 in Bologna, Italy. For seventeen hours the couple sat back-to-back with their long hair tied into a continuous bun, linking the backs of their heads together and holding them fast to each other. During the final hour an audience was allowed in to observe. The sequence of photographs of this action shows how over time, through weariness, gravity and loss of concentration, their neatly roped hair gradually pulled and tugged until it showed signs of strain, eventually slipping out of the knot that held them together. "This ligature of hair was not an object that could be exhibited, bought, or sold but it was, nonetheless, an artificial thing created as a point of juncture across which the artists visualized qualities of their exchange."[103] In its eventual unraveling, the increasingly disheveled band of hair exhibited physical properties of force, movement, and tension—the invisible dynamism and magnetism that drew the couple together and eventually set them apart.

In such acts, Abramović/Ulay exhibited what I have theorized as a semiotic feature of body art: the cultural function of the commissure, which signals the dual operations of linkage at a juncture; as well as trust, or the delivery of self into another's charge. The word "commissure" is derived from the Latin *commissura*, to join together or connect, and it denotes the place where two bodies or parts of one body meet and unite in a joint, seam, closure, cleft, or juncture. In this sense, "commissure" refers to the corporeal slit separating both the eyelids and the lips, and to the band of nerve tissue connecting corresponding parts of the right and left halves of the brain or spinal cord. Such physical functions make commissure a useful concept for considering the operations of metonymic interconnection enabled by body art in which the subject-to-subject exchange between the performer and the audience marks their bodies' interconnected corporeal contingencies.

The word "commissure" is also related to the term *committo*: to unite, connect, entrust, or perpetrate. It may, therefore, signify the interval that joins subject to subject in a metonymic exchange that stages and displays intersubjectivity. In this way the presentation of the body in art vividly manifests the contextual yet invisible covenant between doing and seeing, and between seeing others doing and seeing. Moreover, incorporating trust differentiates the meaning of commissure from Maurice Merleau-Ponty's concept of "chiasma," which attends to the interconnections among linkage, differentiation, and unification, but not trust.[104]

One of the most moving aspects of Abramović/Ulay's work was the way in which they entrusted themselves to one another, a quality exemplified in *Breathing In, Breathing Out* (1977). This performance had the artists kneeling, coupled together, with Abramović's knees inside of Ulay's kneeling but spread thighs. With their mouths pressed together, their noses blocked with filtertips, Ulay commenced breathing in oxygen and breathing out carbon dioxide. The remainder of the nineteen-minute event had Abramović/Ulay both breathing carbon dioxide in and out. A contact mic attached to Abramović's throat transmitted the sound of their breathing. Like all of their art actions, this work could be said to have existed in and across the commissure of trust wherein they exchanged the very source of life: breath. Yet the action also risked surrendering life, even as it created an image of the ideal couple locked in a deeply sustained kiss. As the artists' bodies gradually used up all the oxygen in that single lungful of air, their action enacted the breathless, all-consuming, dangerous side of the juncture (the commissure) that passion can become.

*Imponderabilia* (1977) is perhaps the most obvious demonstration of the function of the commissure in which bodily action exhibited its relatedness to its object, namely the audience. For ninety minutes, the artists stood naked facing each other on either side of a doorway at the Galleria Communale d'Arte Moderna in Bologna. Their position within the door frame forced visitors to enter sideways through the small space between them and to decide which artist to face, a decision that raised sexual and gender anxieties and desires in relation to the experience of art. While some have interpreted *Imponderabilia* as "the staging" or "stubbornness" of "sexual difference,"[105] others have noted that Abramović/Ulay considered their work a negation "of the general idea of man and woman," in an effort to create "a more complicated notion of sexual difference."[106] The very title *Imponderabilia* suggests that the answer to these various points of view is undecidable.

Abramović/Ulay's work together consistently required viewers to imagine the space of connection between human beings in which the boundaries of what constitutes the other dissolve in conditions of human resemblance, interaction, need, and trust. In *Talking about Similarity* (1976), for example, Ulay held his mouth open until he began to drip saliva, after which he sewed his lips shut and departed from the exhibition space. Taking his place, Abramović answered audience questions about Ulay's action in an attempt to speak for him, until she made a "mistake" by speaking for herself. In *Light/Dark* (1977), the artists kneeled opposite one another with their faces lit by two strong lights, and alternately slapped each other's faces until one of them stopped. In *Rest Energy* (1980), Abramović/Ulay delivered themselves into each other's charge: Abramović surrendering to the possibility of mortal injury, and Ulay to the possibility of murder. Both leaned back while Ulay—holding an arrow by its nock as Abramović held the bow taut—pointed it at her heart. For an excruciating four minutes and ten seconds the two artists remained in this tense and difficult muscular suspension, staring at each other while small microphones attached to their bodies recorded their increasing heartbeats.[107]

*Rest Energy* was one of four actions (together with *Point of Contact*, *Nature of Mind*, and *Timeless Point of View*) that Abramović/Ulay performed under the title *That Self* in August 1980. In order to perform these works, Abramović/Ulay undertook training in hypnosis, investigating the link between material and psychic knowledge and energy, an exploration that would shape and characterize their art and lives together for the next eight years. They established and sustained the duration of the pieces and the images in *That Self* through the accumulation of individual and collective energy. In *Point of Contact*, they stood for an hour pointing and looking at each other, their fingers millimeters apart. In *Nature of Mind*, which lasted only nine minutes, Abramović stood on the edge of a ledge over a body of water as Ulay fell from above, momentarily lying across her body as he dropped into the water. Finally, in *Timeless Point of View*, Abramović rowed a boat out into the sea, disappearing on the horizon while the sound of her rowing was transmitted to Ulay on the shore. The image for *Timeless Point of View* came to Abramović in a dream in which her body was understood "as a boat that shelters being."[108]

All of the above works materialized the function of the commissure in different ways. In *Talking about Similarity*, Ulay sewed up the space of commissure, shutting off both bodily functions and language while Abramović attempted to open that space through empathic speech. *Rest Energy* visualized the dynamic psychophysical, chiasmatic crossing that exists in all relationships at the otherwise invisible interstitial space of interconnection. Commenting upon the action, Ulay once noted that the arrow was also pointed at his heart, identifying the site of the powerful emotional impact the action would have had if he had lost control of the arrow. And the unusual group of performances constituting *That Self* asked viewers to envision opposition and union in energetic exchange. Thus, in *Point of Contact* the artists pointed their fingers, visualizing the space of synaptic transfer that united them, and in *Nature of Mind* they portrayed the nanosecond of space-time in which physical connection ignited the fleeting electrical charge of touch. Rather than a "metaphysics of action,"[109] Abramović/Ulay's performances visualized spaces of connection to communicate the very real materiality of presence in the uniting site of the commissure.

While Abramović/Ulay described the first period of their collaboration as one of "the Warriors," in which their actions were often heroic, exploring conditions of conflict, aggression, difference and defense, *That Self* must be considered as a transitional series anticipating their second period, "the Saints," a name that derived from their focus on repetition, endurance, meditation, silence, and the exchange of energy in the creation of knowledge. Writing about *That Self*, Abramović/Ulay noted:

> At the beginning of our Relation Work
> we considered vitality as an energy
> for physical motion, with the effort
> to direct movement towards physical limitations.
>
> Our approach to concrete physical matter
> changed gradually by the influence
> of our executed vital work.
>
> Now we consider vitality as an energy of sensitivity
> for inner and outer dialogues.
> Such a dialogue depends on the speed of sensitivity.
>
> This movement gives to us a greater opportunity
> towards the opening.[110]

*That Self* also paved the way for what Abramović/Ulay called "the opening," which took place in the Australian outback, where they learned "to be-in-the-body by being in nature."[111]

"Opening" is a mystical concept found in many religions, from Buddhism and Hinduism (the Buddha's enlightenment and Shinyata emptiness) to Judaism (the Kabbalah and the Zohar), Christianity, Islam, and Sufi and Native American practices, among others. For Abramović/Ulay the searing summer heat of the Australian desert, their uncanny psychical experiences there, and their eventual interaction with Aboriginal culture precipitated a crossing into the domain of awareness by sitting silent in isolation for long periods of time during their three months there. "In the desert you think ten times before moving," Abramović remembered, "[and] the company of a lizard is enough [just] to watch its throat pulsing." Ulay professed: "Motionlessness is the best thing I have done. It synthesizes everything. It is the homework."[112]

The artists translated their insights into conditions of pure timeless presence in their epic performance *Nightsea Crossing*, which they described as follows:

> Presence.
> Being present, over long stretches of time,
> Until presence rises and falls, from

Material to immaterial, from
Form to formless, from
Instrumental to mental, from
Time to timeless.[113]

Abramović/Ulay performed *Nightsea Crossing* twelve times between 1980 and 1987. The formal elements of the piece were spare. In its first manifestation, at the Sydney Biennale, Ulay (dressed in red) and Abramović (dressed in black) sat for sixteen days, seven hours a day, without moving, gazing at each other across a table on which they had placed a diamondback python, an Aboriginal boomerang covered with 24-carat gold leaf, and 250 grams of gold they had found in the Australian desert.[114] In *Nightsea Crossing* they always used their own dining table, which was shipped to them for each performance.[115] In *Nightsea Crossing Conjunction* (April 1983), they performed at a table four meters long that they had covered in 24-carat gold leaf for the occasion of performing with Ngawang Soepa Lueyar, a Tibetan Lama, and Watuma Taruru Tjungrrayi, an Australian Aborigine. While Abramović/Ulay realized the first performance of *Nightsea Crossing* with no barrier separating them from the public, subsequent performances took place in theaterlike settings to prevent interruptions to their concentration.

Mental disciplines like raja yoga abetted the couple in performing such a work as *Nightsea Crossing*, and body art made possible the visual representation of their cerebral concentration and mental exchange, which they performed, paradoxically, in uninterrupted stasis and lack of interaction. Corporeal stillness activated the psychic linkage in their analytical and nonanalytical mental operations, exhibiting the embodied if otherwise invisible conditions of presence. In 1983 Thomas McEvilley identified Abramović/Ulay as "Tantric collaborators" influenced by Tibetan Buddhism, Theosophy, and alchemy, and intent on visualizing the "mystical-philosophical approaches to the concept of the two-in-one, the mutual dependence of opposites [and] the interchangeability of opposing forces" that have informed a wide range of religious and philosophical traditions from "Sumerian religion [and] Classical Greek and Indian thought [to] occult traditions and initiations in the West."[116] McEvilley compared their *Relation in Movement*, performed at the 1977 Paris Biennale, to "Plato's teaching that all eternal things move in circles . . . and Aristotle's mind-that-knows-itself, endlessly circling in its self-awareness."[117] In *Relation in Movement*, Ulay drove their van for sixteen hours in a circle while Abramović, in the passenger seat, counted the number of circles: 2,226. Following numerology, when added together these numbers make twelve, which is further reduced by adding together one and two to equal three. After *Relation in Movement*, the artists had the number three tattooed on each of their middle fingers in red ink as a marker of the number of their mutual birthday (30 November).[118] Two years later, on their birthday, Abramović/Ulay performed *Three*, together with a snake. This performance came five months after the performance of *Kaiserschnitt* (Caesarean; 1978) at the renowned Vienna Riding Academy with a white Lipizzaner horse. As in *Three*, in *Kaiserschnitt* they invited the intrusion of an animal, reinforcing the raw force of nature on the events of life and the impact they had on one another.[119] These often overlooked performances anticipated *Nightsea Crossing* in its diametrical play of forces and its numerology (performed 12 times = 3).

Perhaps no work better exemplifies the "image of similarity" that Abramović/Ulay achieved in their performances than *Nightsea Crossing*. While they augmented such perceptions in both the content and the form of their work, as well as in their striking physical resemblance to each other, Abramović insisted that the couple also presented an image of "invisible difference." By this she meant that if one closely observed their responses, their ability to endure, their self-control, and a host of other characterological traits, it would be possible to see how they were quite dissimilar. Speaking about these differences and their diverse performative abilities, interests, and approaches, Abramović observed: "We begin in a sort of synchronized similitude . . . and then we arrive at the level in which each of us functions alone. At that moment, there is not more contact . . . but within, there is a separation."[120] This statement anticipated the end of their relationship. For over the years, Abramović/Ulay changed in their physical appearance, increasingly competed over their varying abilities to endure their prolonged physical aesthetic project, and grew apart. When they walked the Great Wall of China for three months from opposite ends in *The Lovers*, in the hope of closing the chasm destroying what had once been the erotic, aesthetic commissure of Abramović/Ulay, the connection ended.

## VII: BRIEFLY RE RE

The meaning of the prefix "re," which when added to a root word means "back" or "again," is useful in thinking about Abramović 's *Seven Easy Pieces* (2005), the series of actions in which she reenacted both her own *Thomas Lips* and performances by Bruce Nauman, Vito Acconci, Valie Export, Gina Pane, and Joseph Beuys, as well as performing *Entering the Other Side*, a new work, at the Solomon R. Guggenheim Museum in New York. Commenting on the series, Abramović stated, "I will never repeat ever again, it's once in a lifetime."[121] She further observed:

> I am doing [the reenactments] because I feel that I am the only one left of my generation who is still performing. . . . I want to set history straight, because there are so many commercial rip-offs . . . Theatre also rips off performance like you can't imagine; and of course this happens in art too. A lot of kids are doing copies. So my attitude is if you want to do a performance originally done by someone else, it's fine if you treat it like, say, a musical score. But you have to have a few rules. For my re-enactments I have asked the artists or their foundations for permission.[122]

Believing that these repetitions had to be re-realized "in the spirit of the original performances," Abramović chose works that she had never seen performed, but which "fascinated" her, and with which she hoped to connect emotionally and physically by sharing the other artist's "energies" in the act of reperformance.[123] She also wanted to pose a series of questions to the history of art, and eagerly anticipated the response of artists, critics, art historians, and the public. Among her questions were: "Are we allowed to do it? Is it something new? And if we are doing it, is it correct to do the piece that has been done once and maybe should not be repeated? And if we decide to repeat it, what are the conditions under which it must be done?"[124]

Response to her performances was rich and varied. Much centered around the role that spectacle plays in an imperative for repetition, and the ways in which repetition "challeng[es] and reassign[s] the authorial agency of the (re) performed works. . . . potentially eclips[ing] the works,"[125] and how it thereby "transforms performance into vapid simulacra to re-place the 'real' Being of the original work."[126] For some critics, reenactment was seen to be a "reactionary nostalgia for an idealized . . . unmediated, live experience, [which] reifies performance, aligning it with the demands of the market for reproducibility," while also being "celebrated as a means of interrupting the march of time as progress and or rewriting canonical history against the forces of power and capital."[127] Other writers cited past critical and philosophical positions on repetition, pointing out how live performance is always already mediated in a "mutual dependence . . . with mediating technologies,"[128] how repetition "perverts" history "from within . . . creating the 'pseudo-cyclical time' of spectacle,"[129] and how repetition of the past decenters the notion of "original myth,"[130] in contrast to Friedrich Nietzsche's insistence upon "eternal return."[131] Still another critic observed that "if apparent newness can disguise repetition, a literal repetition can produce difference."[132] Although unrelated directly to Abramović's Guggenheim series, a comment by theater historian Joseph Roach captured her wish to make her own and other artists' past actions "live," in her words, so that performance art would not "die."[133] Roach wrote that theatrical practices represent a "necrophilic" impulse that seeks "to preserve a sense of the relationship to the past by making physical contact with the dead."[134]

In this regard, it is worth noting that Abramović began to produce ever more theatrical realizations of her visual concepts, as well as distinctly autobiographical works, after the death of her relationship with Ulay in the early 1990s. Staging her own life, Abramović felt that she could also "stage my pain and then play it in front of an audience," as a means to "liberate myself from it because I would really be able to see it."[135] While Abramović believes that in "playing somebody else," theater makes biography "false," paradoxically she also thinks that theater enabled her to be "totally open and vulnerable to the public," permitting her to achieve "distance" from herself in order to understand herself through consideration of aspects of her personal history and the reenactment of her art.[136] Abramović's attitudes to the different capacities of theatre and performance to display "reality" divulge how her work is constructed around a pair of complementary but conflicting beliefs about the nature of truth and representation, illustrated by how she simultaneously exhibited her life and mentally distanced herself from it in order to confront and alter it in her art.

Moreover, Abramović associates the one-time body action of an artist with the production of a singular work of art. "I am a performer," she has stated, "not an actor."[137] In this orientation to her work, she emphasized body art's insistence on the real-time action of the artist who creates a unique work of art available to the future only in documentary photographs, video, and film. Such work is different from theater insofar as theater places greater emphasis on script, role-playing, staging, and repetition. While *Seven Easy Pieces* was realized in a series of singular events that Abramović performed, and thus was reminiscent of body art, it also represented theater in its representational modes. Ironically, in themselves or even in the hybridity Abramović brought to the combination of body art and theater, neither genre of presentation could recapture the real time of the original or the context of the originating artist or actor's personal performance, despite her revitalization of the body works or her forceful, sometimes gripping reperformances. This very hybridity, however, raises constructive debate for the future over the fine line between the nature of presentation and representation in body art and theatre, even if re-presentations of body art are at best nostalgic and at worst kitsch.

## VII: CONCLUSION

In a letter to her brother of 1991, Abramović confessed what she deemed to have been the failure of her spiritual efforts, while at the same time acknowledging her joy in finding what she considered to be the spiritual source of her future work, namely "chemical transformations of the body":

> My path in life is not clear to me. I feel a force which arouses my desire to reveal the secret of spirit and body. I was seeking, trying to get that knowledge from people I respected, but I failed. I tried to get it from tribes in the desert and from monks in Tibetan monasteries. I talked to so many holy people in India, but I always had that feeling of incompleteness. Now I know why I couldn't succeed. I was asking for the truth of others, but truth has to be realized directly . . . After all these years, I'm positive that a state of illumination is nothing other than a chemical transformation of the body in which energy is crystallizing . . . This is the secret entry to cosmic transconsciousness.[138]

Abramović visualized her experience compellingly in minimalist sculptures with maximalist potential, which she called *Transitory Objects for Human Use*.[139] Such works as *Black Dragon* (1994) instructed viewers to "press your head, heart and sex against the mineral pillows."[140] *Red Dragon* (1989–90) instructed, "Sit on the copper seat. Rest your head on the mineral pillow until its energy is transmitted."[141] But her exquisite performance *Dozing Consciousness* (1997) seems closest to capturing what she meant by "cosmic transconsciousness." Here, Abramović simply lay on the ground on her back for thirty minutes, her face buried in slender, semiclear quartz crystals. As she breathed, the crystals shifted positions, brushing together to make a gentle tinkling sound in response to her body's movement. This performance exhibits how she came to understand and then visualize how the body as matter responds in modes of excitation to the tension of particles, playing the musical notes of the elementary strings of the universe.

Abramović's performances are distinguished by their conceptual clarity, physical concentration, emotional complexity, and insistent spiritualism. For more than thirty years, stunning and unforgettable photographic and video documents of her actions have attested to the unmatched quality of her art. This is an exceptionally rare accomplishment in any medium, but especially so in one where the body is called upon to enact demanding physical events, the psychophysical strain of which causes most artists to stop performing within a decade. In addition, Abramović's corpus of installations and sculptures provoke meditation, intuition, and dreams. Her accomplishment is considerable. It is consummately visual and corporeal, dealing with her own body and its histories in her performances, and with the bodies of others and their histories in sculptures and installations. Her actions, images, and sculptures are direct, uncluttered, honed to emotive essence, and steeped in historical conscience, research, and personal experience. Her art is unrivaled in its unique representation of the intersection of an artist's art and life, situated in the world around it and in energetic relation to its viewer.

This survey essay began with excerpts from Abramović's *The Biography*; it ends with an autobiographical note that demonstrates with poignancy and prophecy how she achieved living in the "here and now" for herself, and which might also be considered a model for thinking about the future of the planet:

> When I was on a very small island in south Thailand, only one kilometer long, I discovered that there were no shells there. So that the so-called "naked crabs" had no houses. Normally they would find small shells, use them as houses and carry them around. Because they couldn't find shells, those hermit crabs would go into Nivea containers. . . . [that] tourists would leave . . . on the beach. . . . and carry them on their shoulders as their own houses. I found it so sad that three hours later, I took a boat to another, bigger island, where natives were selling shells to the tourists. I bought three kilos of small shells suitable for houses for the little crabs and I went back to the small island by boat. All day I was trying to teach one particular crab to take off the Nivea container from his back and put on a real shell, but every time he went back to the Nivea container and, you see . . . evolution. In the end they love plastic better. You see how far we've gone in changing nature.[142]

# Thunderbird Immolation: William Pope.L and Burning Racism (2002)[1]

I

What's the word?
Thunderbird.
How's it sold?
Good and cold.
What's the jive?
Bird's alive!
What's the price?
Thirty twice.

Americans recognized this advertising jingle in the 1960s as the commercial that the Ernest and Julio Gallo Winery ran on the radio to sell Thunderbird, an inexpensive fortified wine that it developed in the 1950s. When William Pope.L performed *Thunderbird Immolation* in 1978, however, he did not know that Gallo had created the beverage especially for inner-city blacks, whose habit of mixing large quantities of forty-proof port with sugar and lemon juice was the inspiration for its taste. Aiming to become the "Campbell Soup of the wine industry," Gallo sold some 2.5 million cases of Thunderbird in its first year of production.[2] Ernest Gallo, who had capitalized on this extremely lucrative market, also delighted in telling the story of how he would drive through skid-row neighborhoods, spot someone on the sidewalk, roll down his window, and call out: "What's the word?" The immediate answer came back: "Thunderbird."[3]

Pope.L did not need to know the historical minutia of capitalist exploitation, class arrogance, social difference (and indifference), and racism that characterize Gallo's tale, because it is the story of his life. The artist's depiction of the poverty of his family is best exemplified in his memory of his grandmother and aunt's plight:

> My grandmother would walk into stranger's yards uninvited, pull up their weeds and call it dinner. In her own yard, at dawn, my Aunt Jenny clubbed possums on their heads and called it dinner. . . . I can't stand an empty cupboard. I think it's immoral. At bottom, I think it's scary and lonely.[4]

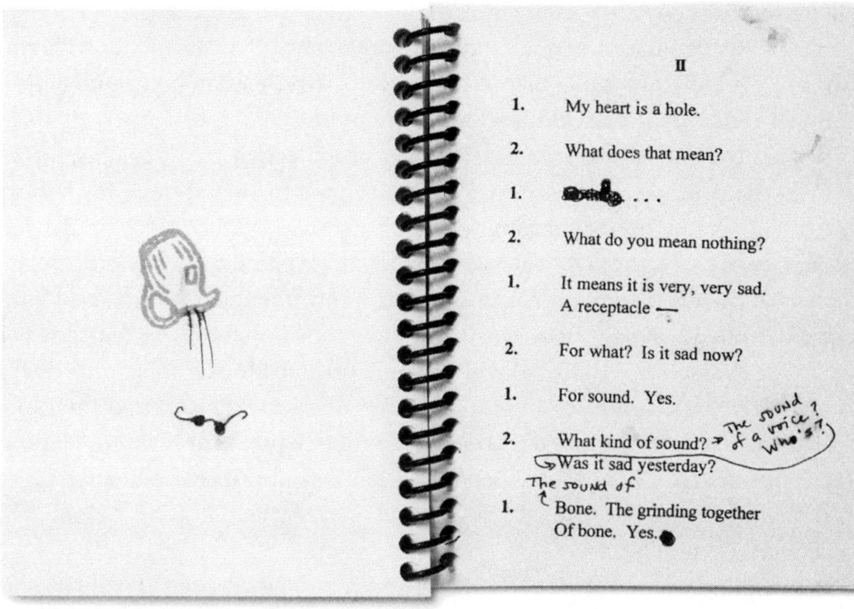


FIGURE 21. William Pope.L, excerpt from *Hole Theory, Parts: Four & Five*, January 2002. First published in *William Pope.L: The Friendliest Black Man in America*©, edited by Mark H. C. Bessire (Cambridge, MA: MIT Press, 2002). Courtesy of the artist.

"Scary and lonely" are attributes of those scurrilous human beings whose very existence is socially made to be felt as an affront, an insult, to others. This is the psychic territory to which Thunderbird beckons as an aid to numbing and, simultaneously, the will to self-destruction. Pope.L narrates the somatic affect of this history of cause and effect when he writes:

> I am always afraid. I am always American.
> I am always black. I am always a man.
> The ghost inside the claim.[5]

This is the voice of an indomitable and exquisitely poetic spirit (figure 21).

Pope.L chose a place outside of the entrance to 420 Broadway, then home to such famed New York galleries as Castelli and Sonnabend, to perform *Thunderbird Immolation.* There he disgorged, appropriately from a brown paper bag, objects of his performance: two bottles of Thunderbird, a bottle of Wild Irish Rose, a can of Coca-Cola, a yellow plastic cup, and a box of wooden kitchen matches. These he placed on a yellow square cloth on the sidewalk. Taking off his shoes, he seated himself on this yellow curbside dais, removing his glasses and putting them before him next to the cup. He then encircled himself with matches, staging an arena for his action. Throughout the event, he spoke to no one. He also used the matches to write out letters, forming words on the edge of the cloth in front of him. His only form of verbal communication, therefore, transpired through words created from the same tools that suggested his possible end. His language insinuated not only the spark of a corporeal conflagration, but the inflammatory state of his speech. Together, language and action established a visually volatile street situation.

Pope.L then began to meditate, sitting cross-legged in a yoga-like pose. He used the color yellow as a formal device to punctuate and unify his performance. Yellow functioned for him in a distinctive and symbolic way (in the yellow square of cloth, the yellow plastic cup, and the yellow socks) to indicate, he suggested, the color symbolizing wisdom in "tantric religion," while the Thunderbird recalled the magical symbol for thunder and lightening, or the power of nature for Native Americans.[6] Having established for himself this atmosphere of meditative wisdom, from time to time he mixed the alcohol and the Coke together, never drinking a drop, and poured the mixture over himself. The impression must have been that his immolation was imminent. When a gallery official came out to request that he leave, Pope.L gathered up his belongings and departed immediately.

Out of place in the center of the white international art trade, Pope.L represented himself as the quintessential crazy street person who is bad for business. Stationed near the entrance to fashionable mercantile establishments, this apparently itinerant black man reeked of alcohol, appeared to be ready to set himself aflame, and, probably most importantly, intimidated customers and drove away business. *Thunderbird Immolation* (and other street works like *Roach Motel*, 1978, in which the artist crawled the streets with the insect killer box attached to his nappy head) is socially aggressive and confrontational in the manner of Adrian Piper's early *Catalysis* pieces.[7] Pope.L was not only not welcome to sit in front of chic commercial art galleries, where he was making a scene, but his mode of scenic production—performance art—was itself not recognized as a serious aesthetic form of representation outside of the marginal circumstances of alternative spaces at that time. Both the artist's person and his style of art threatened the aesthetic, economic, and racial status quo.

## II

Pope.L has said that his performances aim to "rub myths together [to] try to make fire."[8] Visually presenting himself as an animated tableau, a living picture, Pope.L represented an aesthetic metaphor for the negation of American liberal democracy, standing for equality and justice; he also embodied the hypocrisy of these claims, metonymically being linked to the oppressive, separatist, and exploitative conditions of both his artistic and his social cultures even as he countered and exposed them. In short, Pope.L presented himself as "the ghost inside the claim," or what Kobena Mercer has described in another context as one of the "'invisible men' of the late-capitalist underclass . . . [who] have become the bearers—the signifiers—of the hopelessness and despair of our so-called post-Modern condition." These men are over-represented in statistics on homicide and suicide, misrepresented in the media as the personification of [alcohol], drugs, disease and crime[;] such invisible men, like their all-too-visible counterparts, suggest that black masculinity is not merely a social identity in crisis. It is also a key site of ideological representation, a site upon which the nation's crisis comes to be dramatized, demonized, and dealt with . . . .[9]

The inflammable performance of Pope.L's black male body doubled and intensified the representational power of this presentational situation, contaminating both the myth of art as a universally transcendent vehicle for personal transformation and the myth of American culture as universally democratic.

While performance art is fundamentally a figurative practice deeply intertwined with the development of figurative painting, sculpture, and photography from history painting and various types of social realism to documentary, Pope.L's performative intervention in the spaces of the elite Soho commercial art market also realized a high level of conceptual abstraction. For *Thunderbird Immolation* rendered perceptible and palpable a moment in the alienation of a subject reduced to an object that contemplates this affect in a determined act of self-representation. Aesthetic actions, realized within such eruptive contexts, characterize the social criticality of performance art and establish its efficacy at the juncture between culture and real-time politics.

Pope.L's dress for the performance reinforced his vivid understanding of this interconnection: he wore a neat white pressed shirt, a small black bow tie, and black trousers, establishing his conceptual and ideological connection to the impeccable appearance of his self-selected mentors: Malcolm X, Patrice Lumumba, and William Wells Brown (the latter widely considered to be the first African-American novelist, playwright, and historian). Like them, Pope.L took pains to display his intellectual cultivation through the sanctioned trappings of white gentlemanly attire, wearing a costume that bespoke his internal dignity and personal achievement. Thus he mixed his art and social activism with the visual decorum of white patriarchy, only to disturb the impression of balanced reason by pouring the degrading and volatile fortified wine over his body.

There is much to be said about the careful formal elements in *Thunderbird Immolation*, formal elements that conceptually reinforce the socially critical message of William Pope.L's art. The square shape of his yellow mat, for example, recalled the monochromatic minimalist painting that played a key role in his development as an artist, and, in particular, his abiding interest in the white monochromes of Robert Ryman. Indeed, a comment by Pope.L about Ryman must be considered central to a broader understanding of *Thunderbird Immolation*:

> As the son of Robert Ryman, it is my job to walk in his footsteps to the front door of the family mansion and burn it to the ground; then claim that the conflagration is not so much a rejection or celebration but a negotiation-worth-

having, which must be lived consciously *in the space between contradictions*. In this sense, there is no such thing as contradiction, only the fire that burns amidst the networks made up of them [author's emphasis].[10]

Pope.L's anger and incisive intelligence is as unmistakable here, as is his penetrating insight into the deeply interrelated conditions and histories of painting and performance. The statement demonstrates how the artist transmogrified painting into performance through a stunning articulation of poetic and artistic logic:

> I could never see myself throwing that much white (weight) around. . . . He must think he's some kind of super-hero who only eats white food and only helps white people by making only white culture. . . . [H]is was a sociology of painting (whether he was hip to it or not).[11]

Pope.L had already performed *Thunderbird Immolation*, a work of art that provided his means to realize the somatic dimension of this "space between contradictions," twenty-three years before he offered this astute interpretation of the patriarchal and racial (white) authority that underpins the audacity of Ryman's white monochrome paintings (and I, for one, shall never see Ryman's work the same again).

Pope.L expresses his fury, symptomatically enough, in what is best known as "black humor," wherein the insensitivity, paradox, and cruelty of experience and existence are displayed in ordinary characters or situations that are morbidly and absurdly exaggerated far beyond the limits of normal satire or irony. As LeRoi Jones (known later as Amiri Baraka) pointed out in his discussion of the black minstrel tradition in *Blues People*, the "darky" is perfectly poised to present black humor, and was, "at his most human excursion into the mainstream of American society, . . . a comic figure."[12] The "darky," or black man (for black women have historically been invisible), is the prototype for the grotesquerie associated with "black" humor, whose devices are that of tragic farce. Pope.L's humor inhabits this domain, investigating pathos and pushing it to the existentially absurd. For what is more extreme and ludicrous than a human being driven to douse himself in liquor while sitting on the curb? As Samuel Beckett once proclaimed, "Nothing is funnier than unhappiness, I grant you that."

## III

Pope.L matured in a cultural climate where one watched nationwide race riots and the burning of the inner cities on the nightly television news. This was the technology that also brought home other such incendiary acts as that of the Buddhist monk Thích Quảng Đức, who immolated himself on June 11, 1963, at a busy intersection in downtown Saigon in protest of the American-sponsored government treatment of Buddhists. In October, 1967, some ten years before

Pope.L began his *Crawl* pieces, the works of art in which he "lowered" himself to the street in order to bring attention to what he calls "a troubled site," John A. Williams published his extraordinary book *The Man Who Cried I Am*, a novel that narrates the story of 1940s segregation, interracial love, African-American expatriation, and CIA racial intrigue. This critically acclaimed volume was described as a "seething, angry book," and as "intensely American."[13] The man who is forced to cry "I am," is what Pope.L lowers himself to sense; "I can smell it," he wrote, describing the scent of fear at the level of the street.[14] Thelma Golden has described this place as "the most despairing level [of] 'extinction.'"[15] These are what are now called the "homeland" sites and backgrounds that must be born in mind to understand such an "intensely American" performance as *Thunderbird Immolation*. It should also be noted that Pope.L performed *Thunderbird Immolation* during a period in American history when rates of violent crime (murder, rape, and robbery) increased dramatically in urban areas, when the phrase "law and order" increasingly filled the empty discourse of presidents and politicians, when the death penalty was reinstated, and when record numbers of black men began to be incarcerated.[16] Also in the mid-1970s, the white supremacist group Aryan Nations appeared as the influence of the David Duke–led Ku Klux Klan waned. *Thunderbird Immolation* and the *Crawl* pieces, from the late 1970s to the present, were anything but safe art performances, then or now.

Pope.L's performances belong to the mental, social, and political theater of the absurd. Few artists in any medium have been able to capture existential absurdity with the acute accuracy of Pope.L's performances, except perhaps William Wegman. As in some of Wegman's early video performances, Pope.L visualizes poignant existential turmoil, then adds the incomparable dimension of racism. In the end, his work is a form of revenge against the abuses that society supports without appearing to break any laws. As Lenny Bruce once noted, "Satire is tragedy plus time." Pope.L's humor is akin to that of Lenny Bruce in his ability to conjoin rage with farce. Bringing humor into the context of racism reflects as well what Greg Tate observed about the liberating cultural impact of black self-confidence that was inspired by the civil rights and Black Power movements:

> [They] freed up more black artists to do work as wonderfully absurdist as black life itself. The impulse toward enmeshing self-criticism and celebration present in the most provocative avant-garde black art of the '70s and the '80s . . . owes a debt to [those who made] so much noise about the mythic beauties of blackness that these artists could traffic in the ugly and mundane sides with just as much ardor.[17]

A long history of art in the street stretches from Dada to the International Situationists, happenings, Fluxus, agitprop and guerrilla actions, performance, and so-called public art. Pope.L 's performances occupy a special place within this history that belongs to those artists who hope to heal, or, in Pope.L's words, "bring attention to . . . a situation taken for granted and needful of restoration."[18] His performances point to the gap between prosperity and the dispossessed. In *Singing*, for example, the artist performed at a men's shelter on 3rd Street between Second and Third Avenues in New York, close to where his family lived, and where "several family members probably were housed or participated in programs. . . ."[19] His aunt stayed at "the women's shelter nearby." Thinking about the context of this environment, Pope.L observed:

> Whereas the women's shelter was always quiet, the men's shelter was a real hangout. Every day guys would sit on picnic tables in the courtyard and talk aloud and share information about where to get food, clothing, a drink . . . the men's shelter could be a raucous site. A site of laughter. A site of violence. *Singing* brought the show to the show, if you will. It was the overplaying of mirth against a backdrop of greed, need, and struggle. The acting out in *Singing* was analogous to the acting out in the courtyard at meal times, as if to say: "Fuck it, I sing if I wanna sing, dammit. Come what may. And it will.

There is a difference between Pope.L 's work and the histories of live, performed art, especially by whites. As Richard Powell has pointed out about black diasporal cultures, there seems to be present a "structural dependence upon an acknowledged collection of life experiences, social encounters, and personal ordeals, the sum of which promotes a solidarity and camaraderie that creates community."[20] Powell further notes that diasporal culture is "characterized by forms that are not only alternative to mainstream counterparts, but proactive and aggressive in [their] desire to articulate, testify, and bear witness to . . . cultural difference."[21]

I have focused on *Thunderbird Immolation* because it embodies the range of themes William Pope.L has explored in his performances for over two decades, and finally because two photographs of the performance contain clues to the cumulative purpose of his work. When one studies a documentary picture of *Thunderbird Immolation*, it is possible to discern the following letters spelled out in wooden kitchen matches: "KE ART WONDE. . . ." In another photograph of the performance, one can decipher the word "MAKE." Today, Pope.L no longer remembers what he wrote. But thinking about the fundamentally desperate content of his performances, the cruelty of US culture, and the survival issues of his life, is it too far-fetched to suggest that in the midst of threatening his own self-immolation, Pope.L was writing: "MAKE ART WONDERFUL?"

# Barbara Turner Smith's Haunting (2005)[1]

"I tried to avoid the fact that I was shocked by the impact of the news all the time," Barbara Turner Smith commented, referring to daily media reports of human misery and suffering around the globe.[2] Conscious of her "capacity to feel the pain, grief, and suffering of people I do not know," Smith concluded: "We can experience the depth of the human condition without it's being personal; that's the kind of haunting I have." Haunting permeates and informs Smith's art and life. From her early Xerox photocopy books and black paintings to performances that celebrate sexuality, sacrifice, spiritual quests, growth, and giving, her haunting signifies a pervasive yet generative consciousness of death that is the source of her deep sense of contingency and responsibility. Smith's awareness of the fragility of being—her inner gnawing and its link to interpersonal accountability—constitutes a self-regulating and self-reflexive aesthetic practice that entails both personal reflection and interdependent care.

In early 1965, Barbara Turner Smith proposed to Gemini G.E.L., the Los Angeles-based artists' press of hand-printed limited edition prints, that she make a lithograph there. The print would have been an image of a gravestone about the size of the lithography stone. It would have been "chiseled looking," with a text that read "HERE LIES." A real flower would have been pressed into the surface of the print, obscuring the name of the dead person. The flower would have represented for her how "real life . . . goes on and on." Smith's print would have been "a print of a stone on a stone with life in between." This would-be print anticipated much that followed in her art.

Smith had been working in the print collection at the Pasadena Art Museum since 1960, and she was excited about the possibility of realizing a print of her own. Informed that "Joseph Albers is busy at work at Gemini," Smith went home "fuming":

> Anyway, lithography was the print medium of the 19th century and not the media of NOW! What was the medium of our time, I asked? Copy machines! Which type was a truly new technology? I phoned around asking how mimeographs, photocopy machines, ditto, blueprints, etc., etc., were made. The only

one that was truly different was Xerox. The image is made by electronically charged particles falling on the paper in the same configuration as the original on the plate above. These particles are plastic and need to go through a heating process to bond to the paper. The heat sinters, slightly melting the beads of plastic and they merge with the paper. So I rented the 914 Xerox machine and went nuts with it for months.

Smith had recently read Marshall McLuhan's *Understanding Media* (1964) and recognized the importance of new technologies in the creation of knowledge.[3] It may be difficult to recall today, when photocopy technology is taken for granted, that there was a culture without copy machines, or to appreciate the sense of unlimited possibilities to share information that they promised. But the shift from more traditional print technologies to copy machines was nothing short of revolutionary, and Barbara Smith was one of the first artists to realize its aesthetic potential.[4] "I knew it was the future of communication, because once you get these machines out in every corner of every city, information transfers and people can write and self-publish their own books," she said; "and I am a populist."

Smith achieved her "endless ideas" by leasing a copy machine manufactured by the Xerox Corporation. She began making photocopy books in 1966, laying real things on the copy plate: natural forms, like leaves, and found objects, like lace and fringe, that produced intricate hazy patterns. Smith then juxtaposed these images with copies of photographs, frequently of herself and her three children. In *Broken Heart* (1966), for example, Smith conjoined images of the organ of the heart (recto) and a picture of her daughter overlaid with geometric lines and a bisected circle (verso). In another work, *Bond* (1966), she photocopied the wrapper for the paper she used to make the books (recto) and contrasted that page with copies of photographs of her daughter and son (verso). Attentive to wordplay, Smith gave her book a title that simultaneously indicated its medium—Xerox on bond paper—and her more personal union with her children. As these titles also suggest, Smith produced her Xerox books during one of the most difficult periods in her life, a time that led to separation from her husband and children and her eventual divorce in 1968. Literally coming to her rescue—like a deus ex machina, the Greek god that intervenes in a crisis—photocopy technology provided Smith with multiple possibilities to picture her tumultuous inner and outer worlds.

During this period, Smith dedicated herself to becoming the artist that she told her husband she would be when, in the 1950s, she informed him that she would "paint." She only realized the full measure of this promise when the couple dissolved their marriage after nearly two decades. The transition from housewife to artist provoked prolonged anxiety for Smith, who had enjoyed the security of a conventional upper-middle-class family life. But the role of traditional homemaker had also been a suffocating one—a role that Betty Friedan had brilliantly described as "the problem that has no name" in *The Feminine*

*Mystique* (1963). Friedan's book contributed to launching the feminist movement, which would sustain Smith and to which she would contribute. In a work simultaneously symptomatic and declarative of her journey toward independence, Smith preemptively recorded her liberation in *Coming Out Party* (1966), a paired set of images in one of the Xerox books. Standing coquettishly nude behind a gossamer cloth, and literally coming out naked and performing nude before an unseen viewer, Smith asserted her bodily independence from the social and religious mores and traditions to which she had been committed. She also invited her husband to collaborate in making erotic images, but when he declined she made erotic prints of herself.

In the two-page layout called *Undies* (1966), Smith lay on top of the machine in bikini underpants, photocopying her lower torso and upper thighs. On the left-hand page, the weight of her body against the glass reveals the fold in her panties as they press into her labia, while on the facing page the inverted lace V-panel of her bikini points both up to her exposed navel and down to the cleft between her thighs. In *Do Not Touch* (1966), one photocopied page shows Smith's two hands and fingers, festooned with rings, seductively holding her labia apart to expose her clitoris pressed against the glass copy plate. She paired this image with a photocopy of her crotch, sitting astride the machine to expose pubic hair, labia, and upper thighs. While these body representations are sexually explicit, the blurry black-and-white technology of the photocopy veils the picture and prevents direct visual access to the kind of graphic display favored in pornography. The pictures in the Xerox books signal Smith's first attempts to use her body to make art and, thus, belong to the early history of actions created solely for the production of photographs.[5] Moreover, they may be the first vaginal pictures staged for a camera in the history of body art;[6] and Barbara Smith is certainly one of the first artists to use photocopy technology specifically for performative ends.[7]

Copying her body directly was only one of the ways in which Smith made images for the Xerox books. She also used the machine to duplicate photographs or magazine imagery, removing the copy two or more times from its original source. Photocopying the photocopy, Smith created cumulative facsimiles in a process that enabled her to explore more fully the photocopy machine's innate capabilities of reproduction and recombination. Smith enhanced the indistinct visual qualities of her pictures to achieve hazy results by "going directly into the machine to mush around the toner before it had been sintered." In addition, recombination and reprocessing increasingly diminishes the clarity of the original, and that trait enabled Smith to transform the actual image into an apparitional one.

Smith had anticipated this haunted presence in a series of body-sized (about four by five feet) black paintings on Masonite that she began in 1965. She made the black paintings by mixing a color, such as cobalt blue or a dark green, with enough black to make the painting read as a rich black monochrome. She then painted on this surface a minimalist shape.[8] Next, she framed the black paintings and covered them with glass:

> These were essentially conceptual paintings in as much as the viewer would immediately believe s/he was coming up to a real painting, but the mirroring effect was so powerful that not only did you see yourself, but it was also difficult to see the "said" painting. You suddenly really only saw the world around you.

Unlike the black paintings by Robert Rauschenberg, Ad Reinhardt, and Mark Rothko that absorb viewers into their surfaces, the reflective glass over Smith's black paintings replicated observers, thus resembling Michelangelo Pistoletto's paintings on reflective surfaces in the early 1960s.

Smith's black paintings raise questions about the nature of reality by mirroring a shadowy observer who appears as if a projection of a Platonic ideal. In contradiction, they also draw observers into the picture by reflecting them situated in the environment of the reflection where they become part of, and interact with, the painting. Viewers literally become figures on the ground of the painting, simultaneously part of the surface and part of their own surround. In this way, Smith created performative surfaces across which the play of the gaze could see and be seen. This interactive constellation for viewing recalls Jacques Lacan's observation:

> The eye sees only from one point. But in existence I am looked at from all Sides. . . . The split is not between the visible and invisible, but that of the gaze and its "strange contingency". . . . Something is always eluded in it . . . [that] belongs to the phenomenon of mimicry.[9]

In this way, Smith's black paintings can be said to have anticipated her performances by the ways in which they summoned the "strange contingency" of the intersubjective viewing conditions of performance art. Producing images in the Xerox books and reflections back from the black paintings, Smith deferred access to the original, while simultaneously connecting viewers to the work itself, duplicating her own haunting.

## II

An intriguing aspect of the Xerox books is the way in which Smith conceived them: "These books are all coffins," she said, "my father was a mortician."[10] The Xerox books can now be understood as a haunting of a fugitive reality that Smith entombed in art-turned-sarcophagus, and one that connects her art to her relationship with her father and his profession. I do not mean to imply that either the Xerox book images or the black paintings picture actual repressed memories; they clearly do not. Rather, these images are indices of dissociation that would lead to performances in which Smith duplicated her haunting in metaphorical acts of death, loss of identity, and expression of emotional hunger. Smith's startling triad of associations—coffin, father, mortician—deserves considerable attention for how these words join her artistic production to a traumatic scenario.

Smith explicitly enacted such a traumatic scene in *Piercing the Corporate Veil* (1980). In this performance, she installed a coffin on a catafalque in the center of a small room in which she fasted and meditated. She then lay down in the coffin, dressed in "a beautiful pink dress . . . symbolic of the pink dress my father gave me in high school." She added:

> He was inappropriately focused on me. He was devoted and gave me all his attention. It was great fun, but my mother became very jealous. In some sense I was a mistress. In high school, he took me out to buy my dress for the prom—this beautiful pink dress. When my mother saw it, her face just fell. I got the sense that she had never had such a beautiful dress. It was not right. She should have had that dress.

During the nineteen to twenty hours that Smith lay silently in her coffin, she attempted "to psychically penetrate certain kinds of boundaries . . . to go somewhere beyond death," where she might contact her father and "redress the situation, ridding myself of his possession and my complicity." This narrative cites "the situation," Smith's deep need to alleviate her father's "possession," her guilt for enjoying his attention (expressed as "my complicity"), and her just desire to move beyond her psychological pain, to get "to the other side of it."

The "situation" Smith intended her performance to "redress" resembles what Harvard psychiatrist Judith Lewis Herman describes in her book *Father-Daughter Incest* as an "incestuous environment," which results from a seductive parent demonstrating "intrusive sexual interest" in a child, a circumstance that is "a form of covert incest."[11] Smith's response to her father's "inappropriate focus" identifies an improper and seductive display of affection that emphasized her sexual desirability and put Smith, as a child and teenager, in a competitive "situation" with her mother. Such covert seduction may result in emotional turmoil similar to that experienced by children of actual incest. The psychological effect of inappropriate sexual attention in both overt and covert incest is a breach of parental boundaries and childhood sexuality, the consequence of which may be memory disorders and dissociation. Traumatic dissociation splits memory, compartmentalizing it into units of experiences too painful to acknowledge. Walled off, these memories become unavailable to consciousness and may leave a void, or the sense of non-being. This inner numbness is often reported to feel like death.[12] Paradoxically, while traumatic subject matter may not be recoverable to memory, it is extant, and identity may be literally haunted by the void left by the dissociated content.[13] The felt absence is actually present, but is inaccessible to memory.

*Piercing the Corporate Veil* represents a vivid display of dissociation, or "a deformation of memory [that] cannot be attributed solely to the content of an occurrence or to the subject's predisposition to such mnemonic derailment."[14] In her action, Smith attempted to ameliorate dissociation, by breaking through the blocked mental processes in order to convert haunted absence into presence. The pink dress and the coffin functioned as metonymic links to Smith's father and to her childhood past, while the ritual action transported the artist to a psychological and corporeal state through which she might safely confront the impact of these events.

In addition to works like *Piercing the Corporate Veil*, Smith's performances have dealt with other structures of traumatic memory, in particular feelings of loss of self-control that are symptomatic of the responses to domination, sex, and sexuality that are paradoxically both the origin of childhood trauma and the vehicle through which victims of both incest and incestuous environments reenact it. In such circumstances, where "physical displays of affection [encourage] the romance between father and daughter," children learn that sexuality is a means to gain attention.[15] Repetition of the traumatic scene in later life is frequently an attempt to overcome the sense of nonbeing experienced by the child, the result of selfish domination by the abuser of the child. Adult survivors often turn to sex and sexuality (the very dissociated content of their experience) to fill that void. Smith reconstituted such emotional hunger and loss of identity—what she called her "non-being"—in many ritual acts of giving associated with food and sex. In these performances, Smith seems to have countered her own psychic deprivation by bestowing sustenance on others.[16]

*Feed Me* (1973), is the most notorious of these performances, and one in which Smith sought direct nourishment for herself. As she permitted one person at a time to enter a room in which she waited nude, a tape loop of her voice repeatedly commanded: "Feed me, Feed me." Once in the room, Smith provided her visitors with accoutrements of intimate pleasure such as a mattress, a rug, pillows, books, food, wine, water, teas, body oils, perfume, music, flowers, shawls, and beads. The visitor could "choose anything he wanted to use as a medium of interaction" as a way to "feed" her, including sexual intercourse. In this instance Smith's stark juxtaposition of periods of human development was stunning, as "Feed me, feed me" is an utterance one associates with a child in need, while intercourse belongs to adults. Significantly, however, while Smith used desire and sexuality as means for structuring her action and gaining nurture, she was not helplessly compliant and passive. Rather, she actively negotiated with her visitors, and their actions required her permission before anyone could "feed" her.[17] Smith's insistence on agreement, then, must be understood simultaneously as expression of traumatic need, as a marker of her burgeoning feminist politics, as sexuality used as a substitute for appropriate care, and as a force through which she could garner responsible interaction and concord. In addition to reflecting her past, this action, in Smith's words, "displaced the way I had been treated by men (originally I suppose by my father, yet most especially since my divorce, but not entirely so) with what I wanted: some sort of civility, control and complexity, and not mere fucking."

While Smith's audacity in *Feed Me* has been celebrated in the history of performance art, art historians have uniformly overlooked how her work in general, and *Feed Me* in particular, fused Eros (life, creativity, and growth) and Thanatos (homeostasis, dissolution, negation, and death).[18] Writing about the life and death impulses in his book *The Birth and Death of Meaning*, cultural anthropologist Ernest Becker theorized that the human drives of sex, aggression, acquisitive accumulation, will to power, and mimetic desires (e.g. artmaking) represent historically and culturally shaped expressions of a deeper ontological need to deny death—and, significantly, that such denials may be culturally "generative."[19] Moreover, in her model of traumatic subjectivity, cultural critic Ruth Leys observed that theories of traumatic subject formation oscillate between mimetic and antimimetic:

> Mimetic theory holds that trauma, or the experience of the traumatized subject, can be understood as involving a kind of hypnotic imitation or identification in which, precisely because the victim cannot recall the original traumatogenic event, she is fated to act it out or in other ways imitate it. . . . Antimimetic theory also tends to make imitation basic to the traumatic experience, but it understands imitation differently . . . in the sense that [the traumatized subject] remains a spectator of the traumatic scene, which she can therefore see and represent to herself and others.[20]

Smith's artistic representations are themselves split into mimetic and antimimetic tropes: mimetic in terms of her performances and reflective black paintings, and antimimetic in terms of her Xerox books. If one considers *Feed Me* in particular, then Smith may be thought to have condensed and relocated the psychic death caused by covert incest (and the resulting need for authentic sustenance) into mimetic actions.

Using culturally generative means, Smith could be said to have restaged traumatic subjectivity in terms of both Eros and Thanatos while at the same time continually working through her trauma before a witness in performance. The medium of performance art seems to have appealed to Smith specifically for its immediacy, for the opportunity to reenact repressed symbolic material in concrete terms, and for the witness.[21] As she has stated:

> Performance has been the central orientation of my life since the mid-sixties when I . . . stepped out of conventional life into this art reality. From that new stance, my entire milieu became my art and all the things I do and make as well.[22]

The "art reality" of performance facilitated and, in Smith's words, "forced" the restaging of her "entire milieu," and also permitted her to inhabit that milieu. Thus, it is not inconsequential that many of Smith's performances are durational, lasting over many hours and over several years. A parallel exists between the ability to endure prolonged events and the protracted experience of trauma, and in some ways this equivalence accounts for the unusual number of artists who have performed durational works and who themselves have been traumatized.[23] Indeed, traumatic subjectivity resides at the phenomenological center of the majority of actions and events realized in performance art;[24] and sex and death are core motivations in durational performances, and are essential to understanding Smith's work.

Returning to *Feed Me*, it could be said that Smith sought to gain the love of agape, the spiritual connection represented in the unconditional love of a good parent for a child, a parent who protects boundaries and nurtures a sound identity. Such a notion of pure love is conventionally associated with the love of God for humankind, and is rehearsed in both the Jewish Chaburah and the Christian Eucharist.[25] In this regard, Smith's Presbyterian upbringing is relevant, as Christian mysticism augmented her interest in mystical traditions in general. Smith has stated:

> I was pretty much, from the outset, a mystic. People who affected me were those who had actual [mystical] experiences. They carried the mysticism involved in Christianity . . . . Presbyterians do not talk about mysticism. For example, I had Sunday school teachers who had a baby die . . . and they started talking about this mystical experience with the death of their baby. This couple was completely unique, and I felt they made the rest of the adults around nervous because no one talked about such things.

No doubt in a climate where metaphysical concepts were not discussed, talking about "such things" would have had a powerful impact on Smith. Mystical traditions held the promise of a love akin to agape, in which the unity of care, devotion, and empathy exceeded the mere pleasure and immediate satisfaction of Eros. But talking about "such things" may also have given Smith permission to ponder the metaphysics of her sense of death and its attendant mourning. As Thomas McEvilley pointed out more than twenty years ago:

> The public performance of taboo acts is also an ancient religious custom with roots in shamanism and primitive magic. Both art and religion, through the bracketing of their activities in the half-light of ritual appropriationism, provide zones where deliberated inversions of social custom can transpire; acts repressed set loose for their power to balance and complete the sense of life, and held safely in check by the shadow of reality of the arena they occur in.[26]

Mysticism and interest in states of nonbeing also relate to the dissociated blanks of Smith's own traumatized psyche.[27] For, on "one or two occasions," Smith felt a sense of "identity erasure [that] did scare me."[28] She recalls that during the experience of "erasure," she "momentarily . . . would suddenly lose my immediate identity"; this represents another consequence of traumatic dissociation. Although Smith "rarely [knew] ahead of time much of what these pieces [would be] all about," she directly enacted her sense of erasure, her loss of identity, in some performance pieces. None of these were more powerful in their effect on Smith than *The Way to Be* (1972; fig. 22). This performance began when she commenced a trip from San Francisco to Seattle with two male

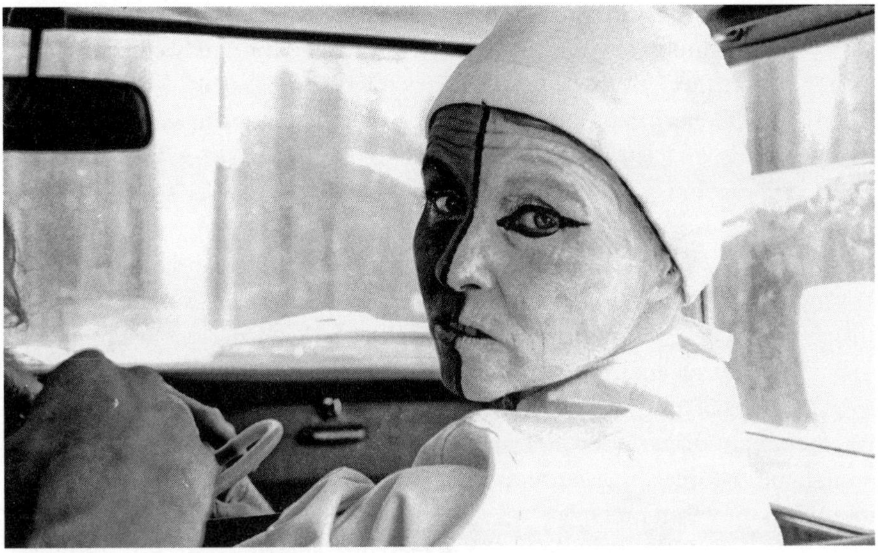

FIGURE 22. Barbara Turner Smith, *The Way to Be*, 1972. Artist photographed on a car trip from San Francisco to Seattle, during which she performed at various locations. Courtesy of the artist.

friends. Throughout the duration of their trip, Smith tried to "erase" all aspects of her identity by dressing in white, covering her hair, and painting her face half white and half black:

> I would never speak to anyone. I was a puzzle to people. I didn't try to act. People would try to guess. The two guys would photograph and interview people, who wondered whether they should call the police. It was very, very scary. I kept a journal. *I had to give up all interior structures of my own. It felt like I was screwing around with my psyche. I gave up my identity and was walking around like this nut case.* I didn't realize how screwy it was until I was doing it. First, we went to a winery, and it was just like I was in some other reality because the guys pretended that they didn't see me. That's how erased I was. I was completely gone and, at the same time, I was there in the most bizarre way [author's emphasis].

In her title *The Way to Be*, Smith insinuated that through self-imposed acts of erasure she might free herself of the burden of the past and of her own body. A lovely, blond, blue-eyed, vivacious woman, Smith represents the epitome of Western beauty. By camouflaging the embodied signs and values of canonical Western desire, Smith might escape from, and absolve herself of, the social pressure to perform the roles culturally proscribed by the body that had been the source of her distress. Like the visage that she divided into black and white, that Janus-faced persona signified good and bad, split between interior and exterior.

Tampering with identity can be a dangerous proposition when that identity has already been compromised by trauma. When Smith attempted her own "erasure," she did in fact experience the panic and terror that accompanies the elision of presence.[29] Altering, or playing with, identity has been celebrated as a trope of postmodern culture in cultural theories that have been widely rehearsed in many fields, and especially in the analysis of performance art.[30] But while the political project of post-structuralism, to deconstruct unitary epistemologies, has been vital to rethinking power relations and diversity, it has offered little assistance to those whose identity and sense of stability in the world is in danger.[31] In a global circumstance where cultures of trauma have increased exponentially, the understanding of traumatized subjectivity continues to remain a blind spot of post-structuralism. Destabilizing identity is almost always counterproductive to the healing of trauma, and it may even be dangerous to those who are already fragmented by dissociation and who require the reconstruction of identity with a modicum of unity in order to function in the world.[32] In her own battle with identity, Smith's attempt to go "back to a primordial space . . . a black void" represents a powerful, generative exertion of will to confront and heal the empty space of psychic death.

## III

Smith approached such a renewal from a point of constructive origins in her durational performance *The 21st Century Odyssey* (September 26, 1991–September 26, 1993). This performance unfolded in epic vignettes emulating Homer's adventures in the *Odyssey*, and began when she and her partner at the time, pathologist Dr. Roy Walford (a diet, aging, and life extension scientist), decided to remain in contact via e-mail and interactive hookups[33] while he worked as a medical officer in Biosphere 2 and she traveled the world.[34] In thinking through the parallel between the journey on which she was about to embark and the story of the *Odyssey*, Smith conceptualized herself as a female Odysseus, and Walford as the male counterpart of Penelope, "caught inside the Biosphere" and waiting for Smith to return. Only after traveling to India, Nepal, Thailand, Australia, Hawaii, California, London, and finally Oslo did the intensity of her odyssey reach a psychological ending. There in Norway, Smith began to feel the weight of her past and of her performative journey, a work of art that had been challenging, draining, expensive, and lonely, as well as exhilarating and instructive. Smith faced the fact that the relationship she sought with Walford had "failed to become what I had wanted it to be," and she began to contemplate how the blind prophet Tiresias guided Odysseus into Hades to face death before he could return "home," the metaphor both for mortality and the symbolic return to the self.[35] She then performed Odysseus' Blind Date (1993), an action that included exploring Oslo with a small group and performing various roles in the myth, eventually having herself tied to a great Yggdrasil tree, the huge ash that her Viking ancestors called Yggdrasil, or Tree of Life, linking earth, heaven, and hell. This symbolic act liberated Smith "to surrender control and . . . also give up my dream of this piece." Concession to "failure" entailed understanding that her "longing for connection. . . . [and] real love" could not be found in another person, but only in herself.[36]

During this period she read about Norway's ancient past and mythology, especially the god Odin, chief divinity of the Norse pantheon, god of war and death, poetry and wisdom, and this knowledge led to consideration of her own "psychic state." Such reflections recall what the Hungarian psychoanalyst Franz Alexander called "corrective emotional experience," namely re-exposure under favorable conditions to a past overwhelming emotional situation that offers a corrective to trauma.[37] Smith's genealogical home enabled her to put aside a desire for "real love" (eros) from Walford, and a lifelong craving for unconditional paternal love (agape). Through the concept of Odin ("all father," or god the father), she could discover agape in herself. Such iconographical complexities represent Smith's "imaginatively generative" response to death: in her own words, "mythic archetypes . . . where surrender and insight resides."

Thinking further about Smith's *The 21st Century Odyssey*, Max Horkheimer and Theodor Adorno's essay "Odysseus or Myth and Enlightenment" comes to mind. The two Marxist philosophers posited that Odysseus may "no longer be celebrated," as he is merely a "proprietor," who "manages" his affairs so that—like the "bourgeois subject"—he may "sleep with a quiet mind."[38] "Odysseus," they argued, is "a prototype of the bourgeois individual . . . compelled to wander, [acting] as sacrifice and priest at one and the same time."[39] They further observed: "It is homesickness that gives rise to the adventures through which subjectivity (whose fundamental history is presented in the Odyssey) escapes from the prehistoric world."[40] This battle for subjectivity is a struggle against nature (the prehistoric world) and for reason (the myth of enlightenment). Horkheimer and Adorno identify the birth of bourgeois subjectivity as inequity, and its repetition and endurance as a form of sacrifice, writing: "The venerable belief in sacrifice [enacted in the *Odyssey*] is probably already an impressed pattern according to which the subjected repeat upon themselves the injustice that was done them, enacting it again in order to endure it."[41]

Although Smith's haunted subjectivity was the initial motivation for her odyssey, she enacted her anguish not to endure a martyred sacrifice, but to arrive at responsibility.[42] In *The 21st Century Odyssey*, Smith met face-to-face the secret undercurrent of traumatic repetition (impressed pattern) that animated both her life and the ancient Homeric story. Her identification of "failure" may be seen as the failure of a conclusive teleology, and that recognition must be honored for her uncommon perception into the odyssey of her life, enacted through her art. With customary candor, Barbara Turner Smith did not present herself as the heroine of her own story, a tale with a happy ending. Hers was a search that did not arrive.

Smith's realization of her inability to achieve her goals is the very embodiment of self-reflective, self-reflexive growth away from the myth of enlightenment and toward ethical expansion. What I mean by ethical expansion is a closer understanding of self in relation to others and the world, an understanding that has become responsibility simultaneously to self and to others in the world. Responsibility signifies an alternative to individual enlightenment, even if "responsibility" is a problem of "the experience of singularity," as Jacques Derrida has observed, locating the conundrum of contemporary bourgeois existence in his book *The Gift of Death* (1992). In this intricate consideration of the sources, aims, and duty of religion, Derrida further notes: "My first and last responsibility, my first and last desire, is that responsibility of responsibility that relates me to what no one else can do in my place."[43] Derrida's premise is, thus, that "everyone" must take upon him or herself his or her own death, and in this very act axiomatically assume relational responsibility:

> The sense of responsibility is, in all cases, defined as a mode of 'giving oneself death' . . . Everyone must assume his [or her] own death, that is to say *the one thing in the world that no one else can either give or take: therein resides freedom and responsibility* [author's emphasis]."[44]

Smith continually entered the void of herself, giving herself the gift of death in all its excruciating regret, sorrow, and mourning—and, with that pain, the freedom that results from such incalculable accountability. This is not to say naively that Smith (or anyone else for that matter) is "free," but rather to honor the odyssey of her journey towards knowledge and understanding. In this meaningful sense, Smith's art is in itself an act of giving, an aesthetic practice of both personal reflection and interdependent responsibility.

# The Aesthetics of the Misfit: The Case of Henry Flynt and David Tudor (2004)[1]

*All of a sudden you are giving yourself a freedom of interpretation, which you didn't have before.* DAVID TUDOR, on his experience as an interpreter/performer[2]

*I've always felt that there's a point where a piece seems to be alive, that is, living. And that's the point where I know the composition is finished, even though I might have designed the procedures so that it could change, you know. But there's a point where the composition is alive, and it doesn't need any more . . . culture.*

DAVID TUDOR, on his experience as a composer[3]

David Tudor expressed similar aims for his dual roles as a composer and an interpreter-performer of other composers' scores. As an interpreter-performer, he valued and sought out the instant when, in his words, "all of a sudden you are giving yourself a freedom of interpretation, which you didn't have before."[4] As a composer, Tudor explained that he imagined finding "a point where a piece seems to be alive, [when] it doesn't need any more . . . culture."[5] Clearly, Tudor trusted in and aspired to the moment when in following a score he could unexpectedly depart from it, reaching a point of independence and sovereignty in the creative act. Drawing on interviews with and statements by Tudor and other artists, this essay triangulates Tudor's artistic aims with those of John Cage and Henry Flynt in order to reappraise Tudor's aesthetics as a performer and composer. Although Tudor was the consummate interpreter of Cage's work, his own aesthetic interests diverged considerably from Cage's rejection of self-expression, his pursuit of anonymity in the work, and his notions of freedom. Tudor's wish for his work to no longer "need culture" parallels similar aesthetic theories articulated by Flynt, an artist-composer who, like Tudor, was associated loosely with the circle of Fluxus. Tudor might be viewed through different standards of representation both as a person and as an artist, a proposition that may lead to fresh ways of regarding his aesthetic attitudes, processes, and aims, and to a more expansive view of his art, both as a composer and as an interpreter of other composers' works.

## "THIS IS HOW I KEEP YOU ENTERTAINED"

In the quotations opening this essay, Tudor stated his aesthetic intentions to arrive at an instant of recognition that would emerge unexpected from both his own conditions of being and from the conditions of being creative. He sought to discover rather than orchestrate such a point, and he wanted to set himself free from other composers' compositions while simultaneously being immersed in and connected to them. Such aims differ widely from the ways in which his fellow artists perceived him, and from the putatively anti-expressionist modes of presentation attributed to both new music and Fluxus-type performance. Representations of Tudor by his colleagues invariably follow this canonical view, exemplified in Alison Knowles's opinion of his performative style and personality, which is worth quoting at length:

> David Tudor had a neutral personality. He looked not extraordinary in any way. He was medium build, a nice looking guy, and he understood how to go right to the work and just do it with no self-presentation, just to do it like the score says. . . . The attitude in performing art or music that is non-descriptive in the notation, by that I mean the author doesn't specify dynamics or emotive stance, that attitude is all important. In this David was a master. It is understood [in Cage-influenced and Fluxus works] that emotive material in the producer-performer is not needed, feelings like anger, ecstasy, etc., are not written-in because they are undesirable. In so far as they exist naturally in the performer, they are felt anyway in the gait, the hand, the hair, in the natural attitudes that pervade our bodies as we approach the piece. Nothing is desired that is not naturally inherent. No attitude or interpretive mode is expected or hoped for. For this reason remarks from the spectators such as "But nothing is going on," or "How am I supposed to feel?" are heard. We are naturally programmed to expect theatre and performer interpretation in all the arts. When Fluxus and new music bypassed theater, it picked up such magicians as David Tudor. No one could do 4 minutes 33 seconds like he could. He could stand naturally, sit as if he was in a railroad station waiting for a train, and turn the pages as if he himself was quietly waiting for something like the rest of us. Whether it was one's own art or someone else's doesn't matter. This neutral stance which is so desirable is hard to achieve, and he was the master.[6]

Knowles's understanding of Tudor's immaculate execution of the aesthetic values embedded in Fluxus musical performance exemplify how artists perceived his work as an interpreter of new music.

Carolee Schneemann considered how Tudor's views differed from this general understanding of his work described by Knowles and others, and she explained that no one guessed or observed Tudor's desire to grant himself freedom in his interpretation of someone else's score. In addition, Schneemann had been unaware of his simultaneous interest in making the work come alive so that it would no longer "need any more culture." I asked Schneemann, "How could such a deeply utopian, expressionistic, and earnest investment in the life of art and its performance escape notice?" She responded:

> He was the most reticent person in the world; he wasn't quite alive; he was transparent, like Warhol. You heard him. You almost didn't see him. He was like a small color. He had no charisma, which was his charm. He disappeared into the work. He was really so unique in this way. He was a musician's musician. He had no way of dramatizing his deep merging with the material. The audience was just enveloped with what they heard. There was no way to know it [these intentions and feelings]. There was no gesture. [His performance] merged into the very first notes because there was no gesture. He was always so within what he was bringing forward. Really you thought of the music, not of him, to an extent that it was really different than with other performers. You never knew he had drama, or lovers, or anything. He was quiet and incredibly modest.[7]

Similarly, John Cage also referred to Tudor's private life and characteristic reticence when he recounted that once, sitting apart from guests at a party, Tudor was asked to join the group. He responded, "I haven't left it. This is how I keep you entertained."[8] Merce Cunningham repeated Cage's story at Tudor's memorial at the Judson Memorial Church, September 17, 1996. Quite simply, Tudor was understood, categorized, and mythologized by his peers in this way. But Tudor's own statements suggest that the man keeping everyone entertained desired also to astonish himself, and that he granted himself permission for such a moment of amazement. Tudor's ability to be present and attentive to himself enabled him to become unencumbered by, and free of, the score that he both conformed to and interpreted. In other words, he gave himself permission to escape himself in order to become "free," even as he found himself in the performance of another composer's work.

Such aims differ considerably from those of Cage and his renowned legacy, as Cage eschewed notions of "freedom" and "self-expression," positions manifestly evident in two stories he recounted in his well-known 1958 lecture "Indeterminacy." In the first narrative, Cage describes how Morton Feldman (in response to artists' discussions of freedom, and the idiom "free as a bird") went to a park to watch birds and returned with the following comment: "You know? They're not free: they're fighting over bits of food."[9] In this story, Cage recasts the simile "free as a bird" into a competitive principle of survival in order to undermine the concept of freedom. On the subject of "self-expression," Cage remembered:

> One of Mies van der Rohe's pupils, a girl, came to him and said, "I have difficulty studying with you because you don't leave any room for self-expression." He asked her whether she had a pen with her. She did. He said, "Sign your name," she did. He said, "That's what I call self-expression."[10]

In this brief story, Cage fashions authorial presence as the narcissistic performance of one's signature.

But, for Tudor, freedom and expression were far from being expressionistic gestures of self-interest. It was possible for Tudor to achieve these goals only in the interpretation of and interconnection and communion with another artist's creative act. What Knowles praised in Tudor's "neutral stance" was actually the freedom he gave himself to empower his individuality in union with the values of his community. Community in Fluxus, happenings, and the new music circles to which he belonged was everything. Likening this communal experience to a Quaker church, Schneemann explained:

> It was simple. It's partly how we made the work and shared the work. Many of his [Tudor's] concerts were in these small out of the way places; you'd hear these amazing experimental works with twenty people that really mattered. Each art configuration had its own audience context around it. . . . You found your source of study and inspiration in the community.

In part, Tudor's sense of self and freedom is firmly embedded in German Romantic traditions, especially in the thinking of theologian and philosopher Johann Gottfried von Herder, who believed that the distinguishing feature separating humans from animals and nature is self-awareness and the self-reflective ability to mirror the self within the self. Anticipating Nietzsche and Bergson, Herder argued that the human sense of freedom derived in no small measure from being always in a state of "continuous becoming," for in a state of incessant action, one knows oneself to be alive—and vividly. The pursuit of art and life as a vital force, a "continuous becoming," is apparent in Tudor's interest in identifying the instant when "all of a sudden you realize that [the composition] has a life of its own."[11] Paradoxically, in Tudor's anthropomorphic aim to give life to art in the animation of another composers' work, he gained insight into his own creativity, and observed that such recognition made it necessary for him, eventually, to acknowledge the authorship of his own compositions. When he acknowledged himself as a composer, he seemed astonished: "It occurs to me that it's I who have done that. . . . I have given life to this configuration."[12]

Thus did Tudor's stance represent a deeply human sentience, experienced in the ability to lose one's "self" in the interaction, interconnection, and interdependence with another. Secondly, Tudor's sense of self was gained in combination with the empathic act of entering into and becoming one with the creative art of another, such that in this absence of self he was able to find himself. Thirdly, Tudor's great talent was in being able to appear to others as neutral, all the while enabling himself to become "free," precisely because he recognized his interrelation with his community of artistic peers. In other words, his community required the appearance of neutrality even though, paradoxically, it also required freedom in interpretation. Tudor was able to combine both. "Free" for Tudor meant something akin to enlightenment, namely insight into the paradoxical isolation and interconnection of life. This enlightenment, or way of being, is very different from the Western Enlightenment paradigm of human self-sufficiency that also was foundational in his approach. Tudor's form of wisdom is also, in part, akin to the Zen-like state of egolessness (freedom) embraced by Cage. Tudor's freedom came from being literally in concert with another, and in full acknowledgement of his own personal will to originality, such that he could proudly say, "It's I who have done that." In this way, Tudor combined the Western tradition of freedom, as manifest in romantic expressionism, with the Eastern tradition of freedom, defined by selflessness. In speaking about his aim as a composer to have his work arrive at and inhabit a place bereft of "the need for culture," Tudor referred to culture in the sense of high art, as the general development of intellectual, spiritual, and aesthetic inherited values and qualities sanctioned by a cultural elite. In these aims, Tudor clearly looked to his Fluxus colleague Henry Flynt, who was well known for commenting on just this subject in his public lectures from the late 1950s to the mid-1960s, lectures in which he often railed against "serious culture." Thus did Flynt's theories of art and culture illuminate Tudor's aim to rid himself of the accreted representations and practices of culture.

Compared to Cage and Tudor, Flynt is little known and less understood. He is rarely discussed except for being a fine country and blues musician and for having authored the prescient essay "Concept Art" in 1961, which he wrote while fully engaged in the new music and proto-Fluxus New York environment at the end of the 1950s and early 1960s.[13] The broader scope and impact of Flynt's unorthodox art practice and critical aesthetic views has been largely ignored. Yet Flynt's ideas are relevant to Tudor's aesthetic aims. They also played a little-known but central role in shaping the social and aesthetic identity of Fluxus through their influence on the politics of George Maciunas, the self-appointed leader of Fluxus, whose friendship with Flynt enabled him to absorb Flynt's anti-European cultural stance. Flynt's leftist ideas filtered into Fluxus and its collective ethos through Maciunas, contributing directly to the public image of Fluxus as a radical social movement.

The civil rights movement and African American and regional music had powerfully affected Flynt, a Southerner; and these singularly American traditions contributed to Flynt's rejection of the cultural imperialism of inherited European cultural traditions.[14] Flynt's social position and self-evaluation as a cultural outsider, a North Carolinian living in New York and studying at Harvard, caused him to consider himself a "creep" in the vernacular of the 1950s, a social position that Tudor may have silently shared.

## THE "BREND" OF A CREEP

On May 15, 1962, composer Christian Wolff, then a student at Harvard, organized a lecture by Flynt, then a twenty-two-year-old from North Carolina, a Harvard mathematics major who had dropped out (figure 23). In his lecture, Flynt

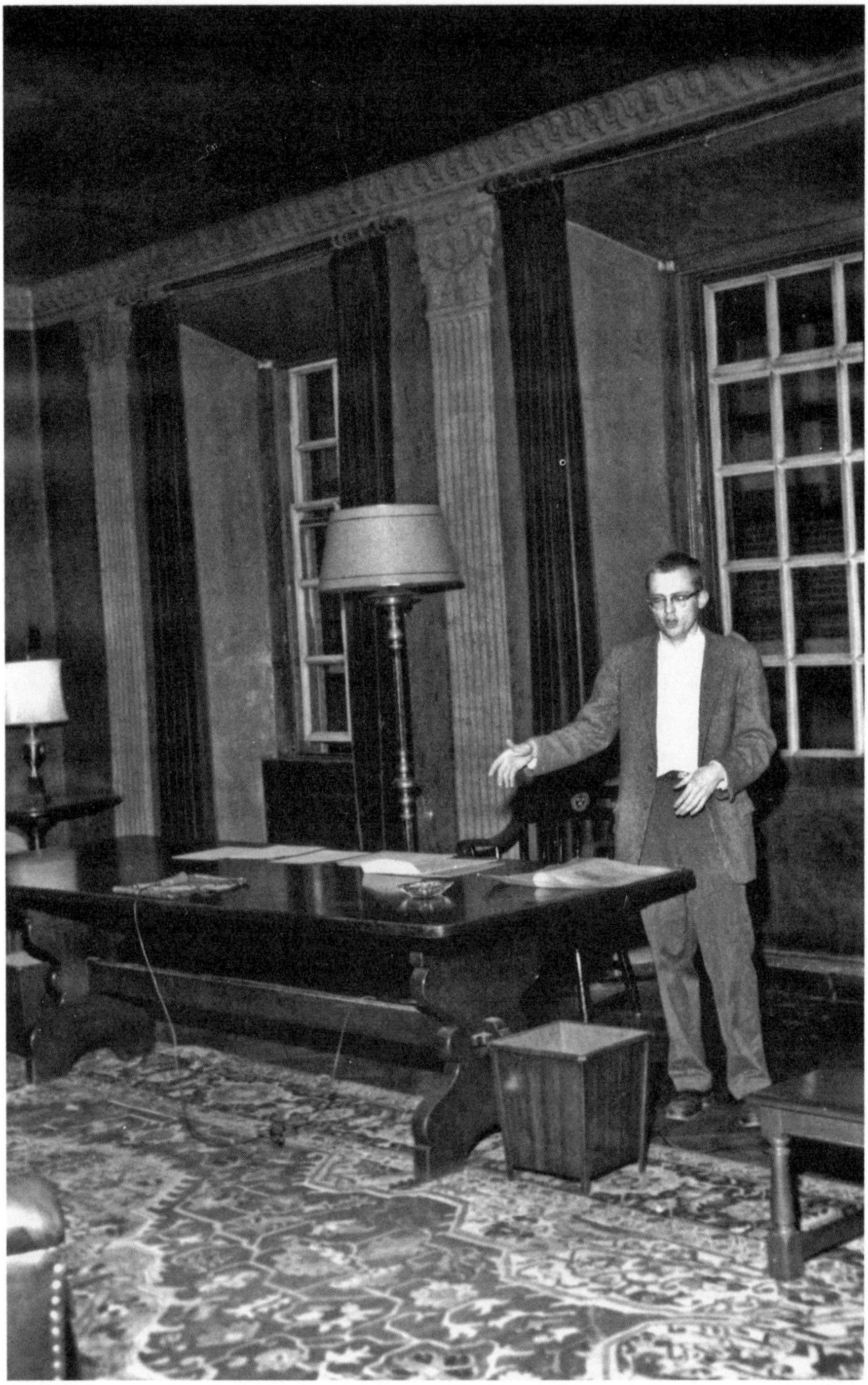

FIGURE 23. Henry Flynt presenting *Creep Lecture*, May 15, 1962, in the Upper Common Room, Harvard University. Photograph by Tony Conrad. Courtesy of the artist.

analyzed the social misfit known at the time as the "creep."[15] A veritable personification of a creep himself, Flynt delivered his talk, "The Important Significance of the Creep Personality," in the august upper commons room of Harvard's Adams House while standing before a massive library table situated authoritatively on an oriental rug. Flynt began his lecture by defining "general acognitive culture," a phrase he invented to describe the social conditions and norms that contribute to the traditional definition of "culture" as "knowledge, the fine arts, peripherally amusement and quality of life."[16] Flynt explained that he sought "to repudiate and discredit . . . certain [adult] human activities" in order to expose what he considered to be the inauthentic origins of institutionalized culture, organized recreational and entertainment activities. Such activities, he claimed, produce homogenized, conformist behavior, and are the source of frustration and loss of individuality.[17] The second part of Flynt's lecture was entitled "Creep"; in it, he linked his repudiation of "serious culture" to the ways in which cultural norms contribute to the formation of standardized personality types.

Flynt began the "Creep" lecture by formulating the general principles of his theory of the creep personality. He had begun working on this idea five years after Helen Lefkowitz, a fellow student at the National Music Camp at Interlochen, Michigan, had rejected his teenage advances (Flynt was seventeen at the time) by describing him as "such a creep." Recoiling from his personal humiliation, Flynt began his systematic investigation of "the creep problem." Flynt defined "creeps" as creative and intelligent, although regarded by the public as abnormal because of being generally shy; unstylish; socially unassertive; often lacking in self-confidence, poise, and sophistication; and commonly sexless and awkward, especially in habits of courtship.[18] Flynt argued that the social isolation of creeps is a critical part of their evolution and unique behavior, and evolves as such because they are treated with "condescending scorn, amusement, or pity."

Flynt further explained that submission to involuntary seclusion and a solitary existence is precisely what allows creeps to develop "the morale required to differ." Lack of conformity and concomitant marginality, Flynt claimed, increased the possibility for the formation of authentic desires and the ability to live an extremely rich fantasy life. In other words, the ability to cultivate an authentic personal culture is nurtured in solitude, where an exaggerated imaginative sphere compensates for an absence of interpersonal experiences. Because of their involuntary social isolation, creeps reject notions of maturity that enforce the childhood/adult dichotomy, that require sexual sophistication as a criterion for maturation, and that lead to the development of a military personality. Flynt argued that this childlike resistance to specialization itself could become a precondition necessary for the rejection of social regimentation, the principal component that leads to the negative militarization of adult life.[19]

Flynt's discussion of the social construction of culture and personality evolved into a philosophical theory of opposition, for which he coined the neologism "brend" in 1963. "Brend" stood for a utopian aesthetic of pure subjective enjoyment, unrestrained by convention, objective standards, or intersubjective value. "Brend" required the cultivation of one's own individual idiosyncrasies and preferences, which Flynt defined as a "contentless model" for arriving at one's "aesthetic self" by bypassing socially inscribed pseudoculture, or "pseudo-'brend,'" and reaching a point where one's own individual "just-likings" could be found. In Flynt's words. "brend" encompasses the things that one simply does because "you just like it as you do it . . . These doings should be referred to as your just-likings. These just-likings are your 'brend.'" "Brend" was an umbrella term for a simultaneous critique of social conformity and model for the defense of social misfits like himself.

Flynt's lectures in the early 1960s became topical enough to attract such composers as Cage, Virgil Thomson, and David Tudor, all of whom attended at least one of the talks. Flynt's struggle to articulate an alternative aesthetic represented his response to the "tremendous peer pressure [to have] new concepts" that he felt was exerted in the new music circles to which he belonged at Harvard and in the Fluxus milieu. Flynt was especially alienated by the aura of celebrity surrounding Karlheinz Stockhausen, and he organized a legendary protest against the German composer on February 27, 1963. Together with his Harvard friend Tony Conrad and the filmmaker Jack Smith, Flynt picketed against Stockhausen's musical form of "serious culture." They had earlier marched with placards outside of the Museum of Modern Art, the Philharmonic Hall at Lincoln Center, and the Metropolitan Museum of Art (where the *Mona Lisa* was then being exhibited to record numbers of visitors) on February 22, carrying signs bearing slogans: DEMOLISH SERIOUS CULTURE! DESTROY ART! DEMOLISH ART MUSEUMS!

The following evening, at Walter De Maria's loft, Flynt delivered the fifth lecture in his series, titled "From 'Culture' to Veramusement," adapting and inventing the term "veramusement" from the Latin veritas and the English "amusement" to signify the truth of enjoyment in personal kinds of pleasure (pure recreation).[20] During the lecture, Flynt condemned human "suffering caused by serious-cultural snobbery," while standing before a large picture of the Russian poet Vladimir Mayakovsky. The audience was ushered into the room by having first to step on a print of the *Mona Lisa* used as a doormat. Flynt's lectures were of great interest to numerous artists, some of whom even took the time to write to him to discuss the content of his talks. Among those epistolary responses were letters from composers Terry Riley and Cornelius Cardew, poet Diane Wakoski, and artists Walter De Maria and Robert Morris. Morris wrote to Flynt at least twice, in August 1962 and again in March 1963. His letters are particularly interesting in what they reveal about how Flynt's concepts shaped Morris's later thinking, articulated in his celebrated series of articles, "Notes on Sculpture."[21]

Flynt's militancy and self-conscious anti-art position came about through his emulation and misinterpretation of the aims and values of Duchamp and Cage. For example, Flynt believed the myth that Duchamp had ceased making art, and after reading a *Time* magazine article of March 21, 1960, he came to believe that Cage, too, would "move away from art" and cease composing. Flynt remembered, "The idea that there would be some kind of utopian evolution in which art—in the sense of museum art—would disappear, I took that seriously. I thought that was really profound."[22] Wishing to follow his self-selected mentors (Duchamp and Cage), Flynt naïvely and systematically destroyed much of the work he had made in the late 1950s and early 1960s in an attempt to practice the purity of his ideals. "Brend" was part of Flynt's strategy to move toward the liquidation of art.

George Maciunas spread Flynt's ideas, sometimes even adapting his language, as the following letter of November 3, 1964, to Wolf Vostell attests:

> Fluxus opposes serious art or culture and its institutions, as well as Europeanism. It is also opposed to artistic professionalism and art as a commercial object or means to a personal income; it is opposed to any form of art that promotes the artist's ego. Fluxus rejects opera and theater (Kaprow, Stockhausen, etc.), which represent the institutionalizing of serious art, and is for instead of opera and theater, vaudeville or the circus, which represent a more popular art form or totally nonartistic amusement (which have been considered false by "cultivated" intellectuals).[23]

Maciunas (himself a European immigrant to the United States from Lithuania) directly adopted Flynt's language of opposition to inherited European aesthetic conventions and practices. He also applied Flynt's emphasis on popular culture and his notion of veramusement to describe the goals of Fluxus as he, Maciunas, would theorize them.[24] Through Maciunas, Flynt's emphasis on the development of both creep subjectivity and one's individual "brend" entered into and informed Fluxus values.

"Brend" would counter "serious culture" and the impact of imperialist European aesthetics, and affirm personal "just-likings," at the same time as it allowed for a whole range of difference, namely complementary and conflicting values of individual expressive "just-likings" and practices. Cultural value would be understood in the widest sense, ranging from the worth attributed to all means of exchange, utility, and feeling or emotion. Such a definition represented an early attempt to acknowledge the interchange between the individual and the collective and the inextricable link between culture and its commodification as "Art" with a capital A.

## THE TRAUMAS OF CREEPS

Returning to Tudor, enough is known about his biography to postulate the conditions that led to his sense of isolation, ability to concentrate deeply, and appearance of solitude even in the midst of friends. Tudor had all the makings of a "creep." He was born when his father was fifty years old. He was traumatized when he was young by his mother's suicide, a trauma that was exacerbated by his father's subsequent lack of interest in the boy. It seems that in the early 1960s, Tudor suffered some kind of sexual dysfunction, as letters written to him by his wife, M. C. Richards, suggest.[25] All of these experiences imply that Tudor's affectless self-presentations represented a mode of dissociation, a traumatic interiorization of feeling resulting in his extraordinary ability to appear to do nothing at the piano, all the while exuding compelling expressivity in the slightest movement or gesture of his body. Tudor's desire to avoid the "need" for culture in the production of art, and his resistance to the social conditions that shape notions of originality, may have been the environment necessary for the creative growth that Flynt theorized.

While the two artists' aesthetic objectives bear comparison, my approach to an account of Tudor's special qualities should not be understood to be an argument about direct influence. According to Flynt, he and Tudor did not "fraternize," even though they belonged to similar new music and Fluxus circles and Tudor attended Flynt's first concert at Yoko Ono's loft on February 25, 1962, which he later described to Christian Wolff.[26] Rather than a study of influence, our concern here is with the cultural formations that result from traumatic subjectivity. Both artists were outsiders. Both organized their notions of cultural meaning, and found other peripheral groups with which they could identify from that position of marginality.[27] Both artists searched for a unique place of "freedom" (or "brend") unfettered by received culture.

Tudor's artist colleagues described him as "secretive" and "solitary"—as precisely the kind of individual able, according to Flynt (and trauma theory), to develop the morale required to be different. Recalling Cage's anecdote about Tudor, Tudor even understood his ability to "entertain" his friends by remaining distant—outside of their social interaction. Tudor's particular gift was his capacity to live an extremely rich fantasy life in his own work, unrestrained by "conventions" and "objective standards," at the same time as he would appear to conform to the Cage- and Fluxus-influenced convention of neutrality. Indeed, it could be argued that Tudor performed in his empathic performance of his peers' works in accordance with Flynt's directions for arriving at one's "brend." Flynt wrote:

> Consider the whole of your life, what you already do, all your doings. Now please exclude everything which is naturally physiologically necessary (or harmful), such as breathing and sleeping (or breaking an arm). From what remains, exclude everything which is for the satisfaction of a social demand, a very large area which includes foremost your job, but also care of children, being polite, voting, your haircut, and much else. From what remains, exclude everything which is an agency, a "means," another very large area which overlaps with others to be excluded. From what remains, exclude everything which involves competition. In what remains, concentrate on everything done entirely because you just like it as you do it.[28]

Something similar to this instruction for finding one's "brend" occurred when Tudor disappeared into his interpretive performances of other composers' work. What many have described as his nonattitudinal, neutral position was in fact a very distinctive approach and attitude, something akin to his own "brend." Tudor's ability to assume such a disposition seems to have represented his "just-likings." He was simultaneously immersed in the pursuit of his independence from inherited cultural traditions and conventions, and in a process of the discovery, assertion, and empowerment of his own individuality as "freedom" in union with the values of his community. An enumeration of the aspects of Tudor's "brend" will enable future scholars, especially musicologists, to think about how these values and "just-likings" may have shaped his compositional practices as well as his interpretation of other artists' work.

1. Tudor used interpretation and performance as interstices (between his extreme sense of isolation and sociability, between being a solo performer and a collaborator, and between insisting upon privacy and cultivating community) for opening a space in which he and the music could "come to life."
2. He employed composition, interpretation, and performance as a means for teaching and learning about both himself and others.
3. He reintroduced personality, subjectivity, originality, and authorship as emotive material, which Cagean aesthetics had expunged, by attending (in the extreme) to the interiority of his own imagination and his ability to convey that vision in the most subtle, rigorous, and minimal use of his body and virtuoso musical discipline.
4. He solicited new material from his composer friends as a means of constantly reinventing himself in community with his peers.
5. He cultivated "freedom" in what appears to have been his will to reconfigure cultural codes and relationships to materials and events. He did so in order to bring them under his control, only to release them again into new and surprising configurations that provided listeners and viewers with new modes of art and music.

Such are the aesthetics of the misfit found in the margins of work by artists like Flynt and Tudor, themselves at the borders of Fluxus, itself a misfit and liminal even among avant-gardes until the 1990s.[29] The techniques that Flynt articulated for the eccentric are guides to the social construction, psychological proclivities, and creative survival of the outsider and his or her proposition for reordering the world through embodied works of art. Tudor achieved this aim, remaking his world moment by moment.

# Notes on Rudolf Schwarzkogler's Images of Healing: A Biographical Sketch (1990)[1]

Rudolf Schwarzkogler was born in Vienna on November 13, 1940. He studied graphics at the Graphische Lehr-und-Versuchsanstalt (Pedagogical and Experimental Institute for Graphics) between 1957 and 1961, where he befriended fellow artist Heinz Cibulka one year after meeting the artist Hermann Nitsch. In the autumn of 1963, Nitsch introduced Schwarzkogler to the artists Günter Brus and Otto Mühl.[2] That November, Schwarzkogler met the graphic artist Edith Adam at the now defunct Café Sport, a Viennese coffeehouse once frequented by artists.[3] Schwarzkogler and Adam began living together in the fall of 1964 while Schwarzkogler was working as a commercial artist for Koreska, a firm that made ribbons and correction fluids for typewriters. Schwarzkogler quit his job in late September 1965, and Adam supported him for the rest of his short life. That same year, Nitsch, Brus, and Mühl began plans to found *Das Fieber* (The Fever), a magazine with a cover designed by Schwarzkogler. While the publication never appeared, *Das Fieber* served as a catalyst for the foundation of what would become Wiener Aktionismus (the Vienna action group).[4]

After Schwarzkogler met Nitsch, Brus, and Mühl, he destroyed most of the abstract graphic works that he had made on transparent paper between 1962 and 1963, works showing his interest in Marcel Duchamp, Kurt Schwitters, and Yves Klein.[5] But several untitled assemblages, paintings, and drawings from the mid-1960s survive, and are characterized by Schwarzkogler's severe formal simplicity, purist aesthetic, and use of monochrome with surfaces purged of extraneous elements including gestural strokes. From 1965 to 1966, Schwarzkogler realized six actions, including two performances with an audience and four private action tableaux made for the photograph. In the last two years of his life, 1967 to 1969, he returned to drawing and sketching, concentrating on picturing an imagined ritual space he called *The Consecrated Austrian Pavilion*, and drawing objects related to that space, which he called *Consecrated Things*. He also drew images for a playground, executed spare line drawings of heads and bodies resembling the Buddha, and wrote short theoretical statements.

Schwarzkogler began participating in the happenings of the Viennese actionists in October 1964 when he appeared in Mühl's *Luftballon Konzert* (Balloon Concert), *Mühl's Materialaktionen* no. 13. Several months later, on January 16, 1965, Schwarzkogler assisted Nitsch in his *7. Aktion (für Dr. Tunner)*, a private event celebrating Nitsch's friend Wolfgang Tunner, who had just received his doctorate.[6] The action took place both in Nitsch's studio, at no. 132 Brünnerstraße, and in his apartment, at no. 171 Jedlersdoferstraße, and it was attended by Tunner and his two brothers, Nitsch's wife Eva (a psychologist), Edith Adam, the Austrian filmmaker Peter Kubelka, and the Austrian poet Reinhard Priessnitz.[7] Schwarzkogler then served as the model in Nitsch's next four actions between January 22 and June 30, 1965.[8] But despite this intense period of collaboration, Schwarzkogler did not travel in September 1966 with Nitsch, Brus, Mühl, the Viennese filmmaker Kurt Kren, and the Austrian artist Peter Weibel (then only twenty-two) to participate in the Destruction in Art Symposium (DIAS) in London. DIAS was the first time the Viennese action artists had performed outside Vienna, and Schwarzkogler's inability to attend estranged him further from the activities and cohesion of the group.

Upon their return from DIAS, the artists staged a happening, *Action Concert for Al Hansen* (October 29, 1966), at the Galerie Nächst St. Stephan for the American pioneer of happenings, artist Al Hansen, who had accompanied them from London and DIAS back to Vienna. Schwarzkogler did participate in this event, but while the others performed energetically around Hansen, Schwarzkogler withdrew into a small cardboardlike cage that he had earlier installed in the middle of the gallery.[9] From that time forward, Schwarzkogler's sense of isolation and rejection by the group grew steadily. Nevertheless, when plans for DIAS/USA were under way in the United States, Schwarzkogler wrote to the artist Raphael Montañez Ortiz (then known as Ralph Ortiz) requesting an invitation as a member of the Viennese "Direct Art Group" (the title Mühl and Weibel had concocted to secure funding from the Austrian state to attend DIAS in London, explaining that he wanted to participate).[10]

In 1968, Schwarzkogler appeared in two films: Mühl's *With Verve* in the New Year and Brus's *Satisfaction*. But by the end of that year, he had stopped communicating with almost anyone, and had become so withdrawn that Edith Adam, Nitsch, and Nitsch's wife, Eva, suggested treatment by a well-known Munich psychoanalyst.[11] This plan was never carried through, and Schwarzkogler plunged to his death from his second-story apartment window in Vienna on June 20, 1969, three years after his last action.

## II

Schwarzkogler began what would be his short corpus of actions in the summer and fall of 1965. His first four actions took place in his friend Heinz Cibulka's apartment. Schwarzkogler performed in the first action, *Hochzeit* (Wedding), which featured him as a groom and Anni Brus (Günter Brus's wife) as a bride. Like Nitsch, and no doubt following Nitsch's method, Schwarzkogler understood "the process of painting [as] strongly associated with ritualistic and sacred ideas," which he attempted to communicate using symbolic materials: a black mirror; a knife; a pair of scissors; glasses containing red, blue, yellow, and white chemical substances; glasses with blue paint; a yellow bath sponge; eggs; a chicken; a brain; and so on. These elements fused materials associated with the objects and substances employed by the other action artists: Brus's use of tools that could wound; Nitsch's use of visceral animal materials; and Mühl's use of foodstuffs in the creation of material actions. When Anni Brus's dress caught fire during the event, Schwarzkogler abandoned live action until he appeared alone in his last work, *6. Aktion* (1966).

Between *Hochzeit* and *6. Aktion*, Schwarzkogler worked with Cibulka, posing him as a "passive actor" in a series of four different photographic tableaux simulating castration and healing. He initially titled these four actions, made for the production of photographs, *Aktion mit einem menschlichen Körper* (Action with a Male Body).[12] Schwarzkogler himself did not photograph the tableaux that he designed with Cibulka as his model, but collaborated with the Austrian photographer Ludwig Höffenreich, who had photographed for Nitsch since the early 1960s. In other words, Schwarzkogler designed the tableaux and positioned Cibulka; Cibulka posed in the tableaux that Schwarzkogler orchestrated to appear to be live actions; and Höffenreich took the photographs of Cibulka, creating stills that simulated real life events.[13]

In these four actions in which Chibulka's body is the model, each action comprising numerous Höffenreich photographs, Cibulka's body is frequently shown only from below the neck to the lower part of the torso, with the focal point being on the genitals, often wrapped and bandaged in gauze or hidden by flayed fish that appear to be his penis, opened and bloody. When Schwarzkogler organized Cibulka's upper torso or entire body to be displayed, he often covered Cibulka's eyes with gauze bandages. In *4. Aktion* (1965), simulated blood appears to ooze from under Cibulka's gauze-covered head and right eye. In another image, Cibulka's head is bound and covered with net and string. Whether Cibulka's head or penis is bound, Schwarzkogler has attended carefully to isolating the figure in white space, which frames the wounded, bleeding, and apparently healing body. Schwarzkogler has created the wound aesthetically and antiseptically wrapped, repaired, and sutured, marking areas of the body with chalk lines, points and planes of potential future violation. Höffenreich's black and white photographs are sometimes overexposed, flattening the image and contributing to the illusion that they are documents of a surgery.

To repeat: Schwarzkogler's series of four staged actions for the camera took place in private studio sessions without viewers. He created the mise en scène for which Cibulka was the model. Höffenreich took the photographs under Schwarzkogler's direction. These private studio works did not include developmental action through time, were not happenings or live actions, and were strictly arranged by Schwarzkogler as discrete tableaux created for the production of photographic images. The resulting fictive constructions were seductive, symbolic, simulated constructions of imaginary events. However much they have been interpreted as believable documents of actions in real time, they are not. They were the product of pure aesthetic artifice, serving only as an index of and metaphor for possible wounding and healing. After Schwarzkogler's death, Nitsch would describe his work as "Apollonian," or abstract and conceptual, as distinguished from the other Viennese actionists' "Dionysian," expressive actions.[14]

In 1972, a selection of Höffenreich's photographs of Schwarzkogler's tableaux featuring Cibulka's body were exhibited at Documenta 5 in Kassel, Germany, but the wall texts identified neither Höffenreich nor Cibulka as having participated in the construction of the image (figure 24). No wonder Robert Hughes, then a journalist for *Time* magazine, believed the images to be true and circulated the myth that Schwarzkogler had died from castrating himself. Hughes wrote in *Time*:

> Those interested in the fate of the avant-garde should reflect on a Viennese artist named Rudolf Schwarzkogler. His achievement (and limited though it may be, it cannot be taken away from him; he died, a martyr to his art, in 1969, at the age of 29) was to become the Vincent van Gogh of body art. As every moviegoer knows, van Gogh cut off his ear and presented it to a whore. Schwarzkogler seems to have deduced that what really counts is not the application of paint, but the removal of surplus flesh. So he proceeded, inch by inch, to amputate his own penis, while a photographer recorded the act as an art event. In 1972, the resulting prints were reverently exhibited in that biennial motor show of Western art, Documenta V at Kassel. Successive acts of self-amputation finally did Schwarzkogler in.[15]

Hughes confused the fictional with the documentary, a seductive trap that continues to plague the reception, meaning, and contributions of performance art to the history of art. But Schwarzkogler did not die in a body action; he did he castrate himself; and he did not even appear in the staged photographs that spawned the myth of his self-castrations.[16]

Thinking about the proximity of truth and fiction that Schwarzkogler's images orchestrate, it is worth remembering Umberto Eco's observations about the semiotics of theatrical performance:

> An object, first recognized as a real object, is then assumed as a sign in order to refer back to another object (or to a class of objects) whose constitutive stuff is the same as that of the representing object. . . . The very moment the audience accepts the convention of the mise-en-scène, every element of that portion of the world that has been framed . . . becomes significant. [T]he actor who is making a performative statement—"I am acting."—. . . . tells the truth since he announces that from that moment on he will lie.[17]

The truth of Schwarzkogler's work resides in the photograph's blatant black and white lie, which succeeded as an index to produced belief in an originating refer-

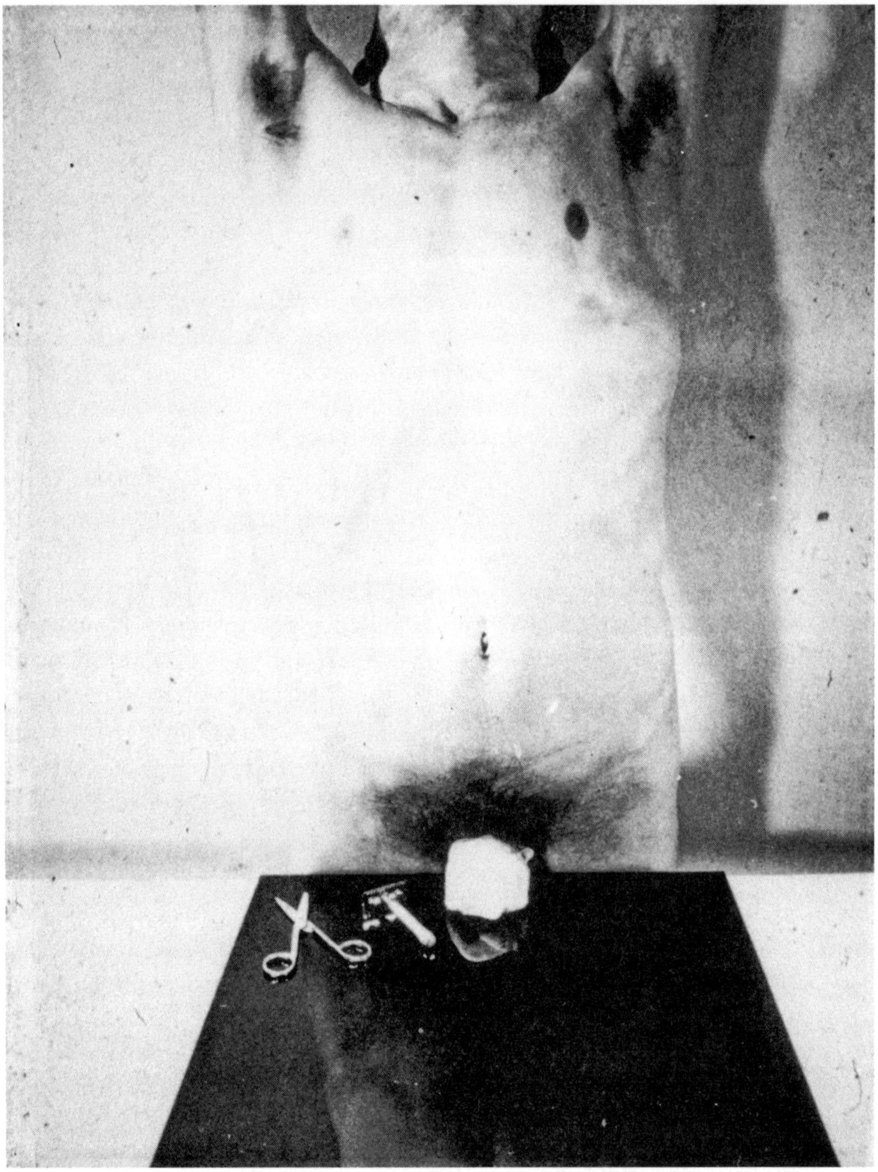

FIGURE 24. Rudolf Schwarzkogler, *2nd Action*, 1965. Photograph of Heinz Cibulka in the role of the actor. Photograph by Ludwig Höffenreich. © MUMOK, Museum Moderner Kunst Stiftung Ludwig, Vienna, on loan from the Österreichischen Ludwig Stiftung. © The estate of Rudolf Schwarzkogler, courtesy Gallery Krinzinger, Vienna.

ent that never existed. Schwarzkogler's simulation of corporeal pain and mythic castration offers such an image of suffering that it has been taken to be truth.

## III

Very little is known about Schwarzkogler's childhood, except that he was separated from both of his parents at an early age, that his father was a medical doctor who died when he was a small boy, and that his mother was a cosmetologist. When Edith Adam met Schwarzkogler, he was living with his grandmother. A wealth of oedipal content in the artist's photographic tableaux calls for a psychoanalytic reading of his work, which is beyond the aim of this sketch, even as the tools of his parents' trade appear as materials in his actions, photographs, and writings. In addition to making these references to his parents' professions, Schwarzkogler often visited the Vienna Institut für Geschichte der Medizin der Universität Wien (Institute of the Medical University of Vienna) at the Josephinum, where he studied wax anatomical and obstetric models that Emperor Joseph II had commissioned when he founded the academy for the purpose of training army field surgeons in 1785.[18]

The figures in the academy's collection are disturbing. Each is life-size or larger than life and looks strikingly real, except for the fact that the skin is made to appear to peel away from the body to reveal particular organs, systems, and structures such as the skeletal or muscular system. In several cases, the genitals are displayed prominently with surface skin and pubic hair intact. These macabre, uncanny figures are strangely erotic, and stand or recline in enormous glass vitrines as if resting. One female figure, a Venus-like mannequin with a wig of blond flowing hair, is open from the base of her throat to her vagina, and her breasts are peeled back to reveal her internal organs. The installation of the mannequin in the vitrine is distinctly misogynistic and sadistically erotic. This museum served Schwarzkogler and all of the Viennese action artists as a primary source for their work. A general reconstruction of the Josephinum was carried out from 1962 until 1966, during Schwarzkogler's most active period.

Combining his father's medical profession with the images he found in the collections of the Josephinum, Schwarzkogler collapsed disparate experiences and memories into a hybrid art form engaged with the Freudian discourses of repression in which he and other Viennese action artists were interested. Schwarzkogler's portrayal of a bandaged, wounded, and possibly castrated body represented indexes of the Freudian castration complex embedded deep in the Western imaginary and psyche. Jacques Lacan observed that Freud "went so far as to suggest in *Civilization and Its Discontents* that the castration complex is a disturbance of human sexuality, not of a contingent, but of an essential kind."[19] Schwarzkogler directed his fabricated tableaux precisely at this "essential" social pathology.

## IV

Three years after he produced his last photographic action tableaux and his last action, Schwarzkogler fell to his death from his second-story apartment window on Doblergasse in the 7th district of Vienna. Whether the artist actually fell, jumped, or attempted to fly (under the influence of Klein's Leap into the Void [1960]), will never be resolved. But what can be said is that by 1969, Schwarzkogler had begun to experiment with various physical health regimes with which he hoped to cleanse and purify his body and calm his mind. At the time of his death, however, he had arrived at a prolonged state of extreme agitation, the result of his self-imposed strict regime of milk and bread, a diet described as "die Milch-Semmel Diat" (Milk-Small Bread Rolls Diet) by Dr. Franz Xaver Mayr in his work on the digestive system, a book that Schwarzkogler had in his library.[20] Edith Adam remembers that during this period Schwarzkogler experienced severe hallucinations that at times led him to cower in his room, imagining himself surrounded by snakes. She remembers that on the day Schwarzkogler died, he had been experiencing a period of severe hallucinations and was sitting in the window of their apartment while she worked in another room. It is Adam who conjectures that he either fell (owing to his altered mental state), jumped (in a suicide that resulted from his depression), or attempted to fly (like Klein), consequently falling to his death.

Schwarzkogler had read widely in European and Far Eastern mysticism, and had sought to create an "art of painting as an art of healing."[21] At the time of his death, his library included texts by various swamis and yogis on healing and the religious practices related to Hatha Yoga, as well as introductory texts on Hinduism and Zen Buddhism.[22] The library also contained a number of texts on esoteric health practices and self-curative programs. In addition to these titles, forming a sort of textual bridge between them, Schwarzkogler owned and read Heinrich Däath's Medizinische Astrologie (Medical Astrology), originally published in English in 1914 and in German in 1926.[23] This book describes the relationship between the anatomical and planetary powers and the principal biodynamic effects of the various signs of the zodiac.

The attributes that Däath related to the zodiacal sign of Scorpio, Schwarzkogler's sun sign, bear a strong relationship to Schwarzkogler's symbolic vocabulary. For example, Däath identified Scorpio with "procreation, readaption, and . . . the reproductive and destructive forces in life."[24] Many areas of the body that Däath identified as being governed by Scorpio are identical to those areas of the body to which Schwarzkogler drew aesthetic attention: the pelvis, iliac regions of the groin, scrotum, and sexual organs. Däath also identified Scorpio professionally with the soldier, the surgeon, the butcher, and the worker with edged tools, geometry, and the angle.[25] Surgery and blood could be said to have functioned as exterior and interior symbols linking the life of the private body to the practices of the social body in Schwarzkogler's work. Writing on Schwarzkogler, Herbert Klocker has observed:

> Whereas in the explosive orgy of Nitsch's concept, man is to be reconciled with being through the automatism of the frenzied ecstasy, Schwarzkogler's action-aesthetic seems to reflect salvation through the slow suspension of the corporeality . . . [by] freezing the hoped-for aesthetic concentration in the picture, making it more controllable and more conscious . . . thus he developed in the course of the six actions a perfectly aestheticized body and object language.[26]

## V

Walter Benjamin's "The Work of Art in the Age of Mechanical Reproduction" (1936) was a primary source for Schwarzkogler. But contrary to Benjamin's view that reproducible objects lose their "aura" and thereby unpack the economic and ritual basis of art, Schwarzkogler's photographic works—informed as they were by an awareness of the ideological function of ritual within the social field—achieved an aura, the dimensions of which have reached cult status. It may well be that his use of photography was a response to Benjamin's interest in the political efficacy of photography as a reproducible and widely disseminated medium. Reconsideration of what constitutes aura and the conditions under which it is produced is long overdue, considering the enormous impact on the history of performance art that the myth of Schwarzkogler's self-castration spawned at the precise moment when it had became clear that Andy Warhol's photographically based silkscreen works had already undermined Benjamin's theory.

Schwarzkogler's works were also catalysts for recasting the ancient, patriarchal castration theme as a contemporary metaphor. Communicating the story anew in the chemical and mechanical language of the photographic apparatus, Schwarzkogler revitalized an arena of corporeal and psychic anxiety that had slipped into the history of myth. The public desire to believe his photographs as actual images of castration, violation, wounding, and hospitalization testifies to their quality and effectiveness as images and to the apparent need or desire at this juncture in Western history to reengage the dynamics of a cultural discourse related to tropes of castration.

In another context, Schwarzkogler's work reflects on the history and traditions of medicine that originated in the cult of Asklepios, the hero physician who served humankind as a doctor, who has been described as making people "right again with the knife," and who died in his efforts to conquer death in resurrection and healing.[27] At the site of Asklepion in Corinth, excavations unearthed hundreds of terra-cotta anatomical fragments that archaeologists have suggested symbolize the aim to heal the body parts of believers who presented themselves at the temple. Life-sized votive objects representing limbs and organs exist, including more than one hundred hands and feet of men and women, dozens of breasts (offered singly or in pairs), and male genitalia.[28] A description of the votive objects representing male genitalia recalls the images Schwarzkogler produced:

> Most of the eighteen complete examples of male genitals found were coloured red, though one was gilded, with red, black or blue pubic hair, mounted on white plaques, with red or blue borders. The offering of these may most often have been in gratitude for a return of potency.[29]

Visitors to the Asklepion temples often slept in the shrine, where it was believed that their dreams functioned in conjunction with the god's curative powers. Archaeologists recount one such dream:

> A man [had] a stone in his penis. He saw a dream; he seemed to lie with a handsome boy and having a seminal discharge, he ejected the stone and, picking it up, walked out with it in his hands.[30]

In addition to being an agent of healing, Asklepios was also associated with sacrifice, which was symbolized after a "night of dreaming in the shrine," and which seems to have "brought the cure, signaled and symbolized, in the cock's crow."[31]

While nothing in the Schwarzkogler archive suggests that he had knowledge of the Asklepion myths and traditions, from the beginning of his practice as an artist he was strongly influenced by Nitsch's penetrating and extensive research and study of the mythic underpinnings of European culture. Moreover, Schwarzkogler's brief career was spent in the midst of a group of intensely self-mythologizing artists. In this regard, the history of myth and the resulting mythic history cannot be detached or expunged from the record of Schwarzkogler's work.

Schwarzkogler performed his last action, *6. Aktion* (1966), without the participation of Cibulka and in private with Höffenreich taking photographs. Schwarzkogler began by wrapping his entire body in white gauze bandages before carrying out a number of esoteric actions: he held the socket and cord of a burning hot lightbulb at his open mouth; he tied a cable around his head; he touched a chicken on the floor "from whose beak an electric cable" extruded; he placed the white-hot lightbulb on the chicken; he lay down on the floor and performed various actions with cables and the chicken; he stabbed the chicken (then lying in his lap) in the beak with a knife, tied it to his body where it hung in front of his genitals, and held it by the leg with his teeth; and he lay on the floor with the cord of a stethoscope leading "from his ears to a white ball," among other actions.[32]

This last action suggests that Schwarzkogler knew of the role of the cock in ancient Greek medicinal practices. The ancient agency of sacrifice symbolized by the cock was also transformed in Eastern European mythology into aspects associated with mistletoe, which was sacred to the Greek god of medicine (Asclepius) for how it "hangs from the esculent oak,"[33] Robert Graves explained, adding:

> Mistletoe was regarded as the oak tree's genitals, and when the Druids ritually lopped it with a golden sickle, they were performing a symbolic emasculation. The viscous juice of its berries passed for oak-sperm, a liquid of great regenerative virtue.[34]

Simultaneous emasculation and regeneration is part of the cosmogonic scenario of revitalization to which such legends of the snake and other ithyphallic imagery belong. Mircea Eliade observed that these rituals reactivate the creative force in cosmic renewal. But he also pointed out:

> This world is no longer the atemporal and unchangeable Cosmos in which the immortals dwelt. It is a living world—inhabited and used by creatures of flesh and blood, subject to the law of becoming, of old age and death. Hence it requires a periodic repairing, a renewing, a strengthening.[35]

Regeneration requires destruction, as Eliade contends: "Every eschatology insists on this fact: the New Creation cannot take place before this world is abolished, once and for all."[36] For Friedrich Nietzsche, affirmation is born of reconstitution through perpetual "becoming," a rejuvenation that redetermines the nature of being. The cruelty, negation, and destruction essential to this process is—as described by Jacques Derrida, following Antonin Artaud—"a necessary affirmation that can be born only by being reborn to itself,[37] at "the limit of representation."[38] Commenting further in his essay, "The Theater of Cruelty and the Closure of Representation," Derrida added:

> Theatrical art should be the primordial and privileged site of this destruction of imitation: more than any other art, it has been marked by the labor of total representation in which the affirmation of life lets itself be doubled and emptied by negation.[39]

In highly compacted arcane signifiers of regeneration and transformation, Schwarzkogler opposed death with the fragility of mortality, seeking to redefine fragmentation in terms of the contingency of suffering bodies in strange forms of resurrection that anticipated Derrida's observation: "Cruelty is consciousness, is exposed lucidity."[40]

# V. Terminal Culture

# Rauschenberg's "Gap" (2014)[1]

During an interview with Robert Rauschenberg and his dealer, Leo Castelli, in 1977, the writer and impresario Barbaralee Diamonstein slowly read aloud Rauschenberg's famous 1959 statement from the Museum of Modern Art's exhibition catalogue for *Sixteen Americans*: "Painting relates to both art and life. Neither can be made. (I try to act in that gap between the two.)"[2] Diamonstein's dramatic reading perhaps reflected her respect for the definitive role that the twenty-one-word statement had on art and its histories. By 1977, Rauschenberg's "act in the gap" had become a maxim for experimental art—from assemblage, happenings, Fluxus, body art, and process art to art and technology in the 1960s, and from performance and installation to pluralism in the 1970s. Rauschenberg's appropriated imagery, combined with photography and painting, would soon also be recognized as the antecedent for visual aspects of postmodernism, especially neo-expressionist painting, in the 1980s;[3] and his worldwide travel and insistence on collaboration and interactivity would inform "relational aesthetics" in the 1990s and collectivity in the 2000s.[4] But after reciting Rauschenberg's words, Diamonstein just looked at him.

Rauschenberg picked up the conversation in his careful manner, speaking with determined forethought:

> I don't think that any honest artist [pause] sets out to make art. You love art. You live art. You are art. You do art. But you're just doing something. [pause] You're doing what no one can stop you from doing. And so, it doesn't have to be art. And that is your life. [pause] But you also can't make life. And so there's something in between there that, because you, you flirt with the idea of that, that it is art.[5]

Diamonstein interrupted him to ask, "Are you saying that art, painting, rests more in ideas than the painting itself?" Rauschenberg answered:

> No. I think the definition of art would have to be more simple-minded than that, and it's about how much use you can make of it. Because if you try to sepa-

rate the two, art can be very self-conscious and a blinding fact. But life doesn't really need it. So it's also another blinding fact.[6]

After his introspective analysis, which was full of many thoughtful pauses, Rauschenberg stopped talking. Diamonstein avoided, or did not grasp, the sweeping implications of his arresting commentary and, failing to explore its philosophical depth, ironically followed up with a question about his approach to "surface."

Diamonstein was not the only critic, just the first, to miss the broader implications of Rauschenberg's thought. Curiously, it appears that no scholar has remarked on his 1977 comments. Despite its omission in the abundant literature on the artist, Rauschenberg's 1977 amplification of his 1959 statement provides his most expansive explanation of his process in the interstice where he "just" did "something" that "no one could stop [him] from doing." Rauschenberg's 1977 commentary is also his most incisive remark on artistic integrity in the act of making,[7] the clearest identification of his emotional states in the gap, and the most commanding example of his conviction that the significance of art resides in its "use" value. This essay explores these lines in Rauschenberg's thought, attending closely to the meaning implied by his process in the gap, the site of his sense of immediacy between the incommensurability of one blinding fact (art) and another (life).

In 1949, a full decade before Rauschenberg articulated the gap as the space within which he did "something," the artist Susan Weil introduced him to the process of creating monoprints on blueprint paper.[8] Exposing the paper to the ultraviolet light of a sunlamp turned it a rich ultramarine blue, leaving the covered areas of underexposed paper in the varied tones of pale blue to white. Using this paper, Rauschenberg made striking blueprint images of his friend Patricia Pearman, who posed nude in various positions, one picture of which *Life* magazine published in its April 9, 1951, issue, along with images of Rauschenberg and Weil making other types of blueprint images.[9]

The famous photographs that Hans Namuth took in 1950 of Jackson Pollock standing over and on his canvas while painting on the floor appeared for the first time a month later in *Portfolio* magazine, as well as in the May 1951 issue of *Art News*. Harold Rosenberg's theory of action painting followed in the December 1952 issue of *Art News*.[10] That same year, Georges Mathieu began having himself photographed while painting, and he would soon begin to perform action paintings publicly. In October 1955, the Gutai artist Kazua Shiraga would perform *Challenging Mud* in Osaka, Japan, wrestling on the ground in viscous pigment mixed with mud; and on June 5, 1958, Yves Klein would begin experiments using a female nude model who, after immersing herself in his patented International Klein Blue paint, made prints of her body on canvas placed on the floor of his friend Robert Godet's Paris apartment.[11] As *Life* was distributed worldwide, it is certain that Mathieu knew the images of Rauschenberg working with the nude model, and it is highly possible—even probable—that Klein and

Shiraga had also seen the images at some point. In this regard, an historical relationship exists between Rauschenberg's concept of using a live nude to create images, and artworks that followed throughout the world.

While describing his artistic process in 1959 as an effort to "act" in the gap, Rauschenberg did not align his approach with the history and theory of action painting,[12] or with the events just cited. He rejected the notion of art and life collapsed into an undifferentiated unity, and instead marked out a place that distinguished the two even as it imperceptibly interconnected them. In the 1949 blueprint works, Rauschenberg remained the maker, not the work itself, even as he posed in several of the monoprints.[13] His conceptually nuanced position vis-à-vis the fusion of art and life would earn him the sharp criticism of John Cage. "I think there's a slight difference between Rauschenberg and me," Cage explained in 1968. "And we've become less friendly, although we're still friendly. We don't see each other as much as we did."[14] Cage explained the breach this way: "I have the desire to just erase the difference between art and life, whereas Rauschenberg made that famous statement about working in the gap between the two. Which is a little Roman Catholic, from my point of view."[15] When the interviewer, Martin Duberman, an authority on Black Mountain College, asked Cage what he meant, Cage responded, "Well, he makes a mystery out of being an artist."[16]

Cage's comments reflect his own unease about how Rauschenberg had, in only a few words, unsettled the idea of either the unity or the dualism of art and life, fundamentally exposing the claim for unity as utopian, and for dualism as falsely oppositional and potentially hierarchical.[17] Instead, Rauschenberg would "try," as he wrote, to establish his own position, one of presence between the blinding facticity of art and life.[18] "I am in the present," Rauschenberg stated in a 1961 interview, "with all my limitations but by using all my resources."[19] In *Autobiography* (1968), his more than sixteen-foot-tall, three-panel lithograph, Rauschenberg ends the spiral text in the middle panel, which also resembles a thumbprint, by stating that he is "creating a responsible man working in the present."[20] Read in this context, the blueprint works anticipated Rauschenberg's identification of the gap, which both constituted the site of presence and provided the resource of an open space where he was neither completely in art nor in life. As for Cage's characterization of Rauschenberg's thought as "Roman Catholic," and his mendacious charge that Rauschenberg "mystified being an artist," Cage knew well that both were untrue.

## RAUSCHENBERG'S ETHICS

Rauschenberg expressed an abiding personal judgment that ethical principles prevail in making "something" when, in his initial retort to Diamonstein's reading of his 1959 statement, he said: "I don't think that any honest artist sets out to make art." His first and next fourteen sentences on the topic deserve closer attention. The following interpretation seeks to contribute to a better appreciation of the stakes for Rauschenberg when he positioned the "act" of making something in the gap, as well as of the meaning of his art in general.

The historical context for his insistence on artistic integrity, the honesty of the artist, is worth considering here. Rauschenberg entered the art world during the height of what he called the abstract expressionists' "self-confession and self-confusion," a mode of existence he rejected for himself.[21] He was instrumental in bringing about the shift from what he understood to be egocentrism to the ambiguous social commentary of pop art, from whose equivocal cultural positions he also removed himself. He was internationally renowned by the late 1970s when postmodernist irony arrived as the cultural iteration of poststructuralist questioning of inherited beliefs and structures of knowledge. But while Rauschenberg would remain distant from the extremes of postmodernist radical relativity, his art modeled aesthetic paradigms for radical visual relativity and respect for difference.

Among the many works that exhibit traits associated with postmodernism are *Solar Elephant* (1982), or what Rauschenberg called a "free-standing picture" (another term he used for Combine) with its juxtapositions of technical drawings, organic forms, and objects from popular culture; and his four-paneled, feverish *Pneumonia Lisa* (1982) a ceramic version of Leonardo da Vinci's *Mona Lisa* (1503–17) that Rauschenberg superimposed with a variety of images, from a horse and the face of Venus in Sandro Botticelli's *The Birth of Venus* (c. 1486) to a motorcycle fender decorated with a Mickey Mouse decal.[22] These works evince the narrative instability characteristic of postmodernism, as well as what Sam Hunter described as Rauschenberg's "mercurial consciousness."[23] Rauschenberg would put it this way in 1963: "My fascination with images . . . is based on the complex interlocking of disparate visual facts . . . that have no respect for grammar."[24] Five years later he would observe: "Now we have so much information. A painter a hundred or two hundred years ago knew very little. . . . It wasn't natural for him also to take into consideration cave painting and fold it into his own sense of the present."[25]

Despite Rauschenberg's proto-postmodern consciousness of the random function of images in contemporary society, his unrestrained appropriation of images, and his careful juxtaposition of seemingly unrelated images, some observers might view his steadfast insistence on "honesty" as old-fashioned, particularly in cultural circumstances favoring irony. This would be true especially for those who claim that they no longer know "what art is,"[26] no longer "believe in" the values once attributed to art,[27] or find such principles laughable in the context of the soaring global market for art, which transmogrifies the Nietzschean "transvaluation of values" into its obverse: rather than exalt life and creativity, the market reduces everything to capital.

"Once irony is admitted," conceptual artist Michael Asher noted in 2009, "nothing can be innocent."[28] Rauschenberg was anything but innocent. Yet while he deployed paradox in his work, he did not share the pervasive cynicism of the late twentieth and early twenty-first centuries, as a letter he wrote in 1999 regarding *The Happy Apocalypse*, a project he undertook for the Vatican, makes clear. Firmly declaring the purpose of his art, Rauschenberg wrote:

> Healing with faith is paramount. My art work is filled with hope, courage, and strength; it will work to support inspiration and life."[29]

Asher did not refer to Rauschenberg when he wrote the following, but he may as well have been describing Rauschenberg's stance as an alternative to the insouciance of our era:

> It takes a strong act of will to reassert that a certain phenomenon—a painting, a gesture, a dumb object—is just what it purports to be. . . . Once one reinvests art with some consideration to the real, this yawning from one extreme to the other [high vs. low and art vs. life] has to cease. The specific relationship between work and viewer reasserts its importance, as the body becomes the site of a different kind of interplay between the visceral and intellectual aspects of the experience.[30]

Rauschenberg demonstrated strong acts of will at an early age. As "a shy child [who] often hid from people,"[31] he survived his father's "physically violent, abusive and alcoholic" behavior;[32] and, as an adult, endured "his father's dying words: 'I never did like you, you son of a bitch.'"[33] Biographers seldom reveal these unsavory details of his life, or the fact that when Rauschenberg returned home from military service in World War II, his family had moved to another town without telling him or leaving a forwarding address. Usually Rauschenberg's decision to change his first name from Milton to Bob is attributed only to the moment he determined to become an artist and entered the Kansas City Art Institute in 1947, rather than to the fact that he bore his father's name, an identity he shed in order to leave his past behind. Yet, to the question, "How much of your work is autobiographical?" Rauschenberg replied: "Probably all."[34]

What is often repeated about his biography is that during his teenage years, Rauschenberg began rejecting the religious dogmas of his Texas fundamentalist Christian community and the Church of Christ, especially the taboos against dancing. But one anecdote—which underscores his loneliness—is not often told. Rauschenberg explained that when he was just fifteen, in response to a preacher insisting that the Bible advocated marrying a virgin rather than a widow, he "stood up in church," he remembered, "and flung my arms out and said, 'Why? You can't help but sometimes be a widow!'"[35] Forty-seven years later he was still upset by the idea and remarked to Barbara Rose: "How could God say something like that? People get lonely."[36] They do, and he did, often referring to the "loneliness of painting," which, in part, accounted for his devotion to collaboration in art and technology, and his decades-long participation in dance and theater.

In college, after refusing to kill and dissect a frog, Rauschenberg was expelled. When he entered the Navy at eighteen and announced that he was not going to kill anyone, he was trained as a neuropsychiatric technician, running three different wards with only one doctor. "No, I was not forced to fight," he said. "What I witnessed was much worse. I got to see, every day, what war did to the young men who barely survived it. . . . Every day your heart was torn until you couldn't stand it. And then the next day it was torn up all over again. And you knew that nothing could help. These young boys had been destroyed."[37] Rauschenberg also compared his psychological state at the time to those of his patients: "If an analyst had written mine down, I would have been right on top."[38] To these experiences add his self-doubt, rooted in severe dyslexia; his bisexuality; his voracious appetites; and his alcoholism.

Then consider his many accomplishments and high international profile in the media, from newspapers and popular magazines to art journals and television. His prominence makes it easy to understand that Rauschenberg's strong will could cause friction and even provoke jealousy.[39] After all, as one of his high school teachers said, Rauschenberg was "a DEFINITE leader. . . . He always had ideas: Milton always had some solution to suggest."[40] Ileana Sonnabend described him as a "strange mixture of boastfulness and humility, depression and high spirits," and she especially noted "a spiritual quality in his works, as well as a poetic and ephemeral quality." Finally, she observed an aspect of his personality that unsettled some: "People like to hold on to what they know. Bob likes to shake them out of their habits."[41]

I recount these and other biographical factors for how they inform about Rauschenberg's concept of "honesty," which comprised his determination to be truthful to himself as a maker of "something," forthright in his devotion to the object in all its material complexity, committed to engagement with everyday realities, and dedicated to the interplay between the visceral and intellectual aspects of viewers' experiences. Rauschenberg best expressed this honesty when he commented in 1963: "My morality is not to walk in my own footsteps."[42] What he meant by this poetic statement was that, while "all" of his work was to some degree autobiographical, the integrity of his art depended upon bringing the viewer into the work.

Thinking of not walking in his own footsteps, Rauschenberg incorporated his classmates into his work in 1949 while a student at the Art Students' League in New York by putting canvas on the floor at the entrance and recording everyone's footprints as they entered the room. Two years later, he painted his series of modular *White Paintings*, which, Walter Hopps observed, were "of acute importance" to Rauschenberg for how they "became palpable objects subject to ambient light and shadows."[43] What the *White Paintings* pictured for Rauschenberg was the presence of anyone and anything in the room, shadows that captured a quixotic and ephemeral history of everything that had once been there. What is also fascinating about the *White Paintings* is that under certain light conditions, one can see one's own shadow, as well as a faint double of it.

In 1952–53, during what he called his "nine-month trip to the Mediterranean and into North Africa," Rauschenberg made boxes and "Constructions," later exhibiting them at the Galerie L'Obelisco in Rome, which titled the works *Scatole Personali* (Personal Boxes) and *Feticci Personali* (Personal Fetishes). In his exhibition statement, Rauschenberg wrote that he had chosen the materials for the "Constructions" for "the richness of their past . . . or for their vivid abstract reality," and he suggested how to interpret and use both the boxes and the constructions:

> In other [boxes] one or several compartments are left empty for you to add bits of your own choice, to rearrange the contents, or to leave them in their emptiness which signifies unknown possibilities. . . . A hanging construction of mirrors to mirrors is visual infinity. Other stringlike totems hang pretentiously boasting of their fictitious past. A contemplative instrument is made with a bead on a coil of wire. You may develop your own ritual about the objects. The order and logic of the arrangements are the direct creation of the viewer assisted by the costumed provocativeness and literal sensuality of the objects.[44]

To photograph the *Feticci Personali* in 1953, Rauschenberg suspended his works from trees and statuary in a park, a temporary installation that anticipated the Japanese Gutai's eccentric structures and first outdoor exhibition in 1955. The *Feticci Personali* also suggest the "poor," or nonaesthetic, materials and modes of presentation that interested artists associated with the Italian art movement Arte Povera, founded in 1967.

*Scatole Personali* and *Feticci Personali* were also foundational for Rauschenberg's own series of *Elemental Sculptures*, made in 1953 after he returned from Italy to New York. Some of these works are uncompromisingly minimal in structure and brute in materials, like *Untitled (Elemental Sculpture)*, with its bricks, mortar, steel spike, metal rod, and concrete. But others in the series are more yielding and interactive, consisting of found blocks of wood and rounded stones often tethered together with twine. Rauschenberg encouraged the public to manipulate the component parts of such works, and a photograph of him sitting irreverently, but with a solemn expression, on one of the *Elemental Sculptures* suggests the interaction with these works that he sought from the public. He exhibited the sculptures together with a black monochrome and a matte-black monochrome painting, and two *White Paintings* in a two-person show with Cy Twombly at the Stable Gallery in New York in September 1953.

Whereas the *Elemental Sculptures* ask for actual physical involvement, all of Rauschenberg's art requires a highly active visual engagement with his superimposed and transposed images, words, and signs. But his most aggressive, inescapable technique for including viewers in his work was his extensive use of mirrors and reflective surfaces: works like the *Carnal Clock* series (1969), which included mirrored Plexiglas, and *Wild Strawberry Eclipse (Urban Bourbon)* (1988), which, like many of his painting series of the 1980s and 1990s, featured polished enameled and mirrored aluminum surfaces.

Considered together, these three means of enticing or capturing viewers—cast shadows on paintings, actual manipulation of objects, and mirroring or reflecting in sculptures or paintings—relate to what seems to have been three primary objectives for Rauschenberg: to offer the possibility to viewers for an exchange of fields of vision; to activate viewers by bringing their presence into the work; and to emphasize the present, whereby one literally enters into the charged space Rauschenberg himself has inhabited, the gap to which the public literally contributes through its presence in the works, bodily reminders that reinvigorate the immediacy and constantly changing imagery in his art. As he said in 1960: "Immediacy, the only thing you can trust."[45] Once bodily engaged in the operation of a sculpture, or virtually embodied within the mirrored surface of a painting or sculpture, viewers have no choice but to be "honest," in the sense that in the now of the present, any act or image is what it is: one cannot hide from or alter one's reflection or shadow or action. In these ways, Rauschenberg's concept of the gap existed apart from art and life, while enveloped in it; the gap was an interstice like that between water and air.

## LITERCY

Many of these elements come together in *Litercy (Phantom)* (1991; figure 25). Like so many of his works, *Litercy* feels monumental but is human-sized, modest like Rauschenberg himself. A silvered monochrome, resembling grisaille, *Litercy* includes photographs and silvered pigments that Rauschenberg transferred onto its mirrored aluminum. The work brings viewers into direct contact and interaction with images, signs, and texts, more so than do most of Rauschenberg's works on reflective surfaces; and it is for this and many other reasons that I explore this work in depth, proposing that it is the quintessence of Rauschenberg's relation to the gap, and of how he brought the world into that fissure in reality that is art.

A brief introduction to *Litercy*, from left to right, will help. On the left a man, paints the word "Wate[r]"; ghostly shadows of trees appear in the middle ground; and on the right a building strewn with pennants also sports a sign that reads "Bob's," as well as the word "Hand," and the sign of a hand with its index finger pointing painted on the side of the building. The latter doubles the concept of "hand" while visually reinforcing the word and creating continuity and difference through word and image. This is just the first of many doublings in the work. Standing and moving before the painting, one sees oneself reflected near, or on top of, the figure, words, and images. A riveting overlap occurs when the viewer comes into contact with the words "Bob's Hand," which then form a textual allusion to the artist and the appendage responsible for the work's making.[46] Accordingly, as we become part of the image and make contact with the words in *Litercy*, we enter a sea of sign painters: first, in the literal figure of the man painting the sign; second, in the metaphorical figure of Rauschenberg, the maker of signs; and, third, in the form of one's own reflection as it joins the sign makers who create and comprise the content of the painting. Seen in

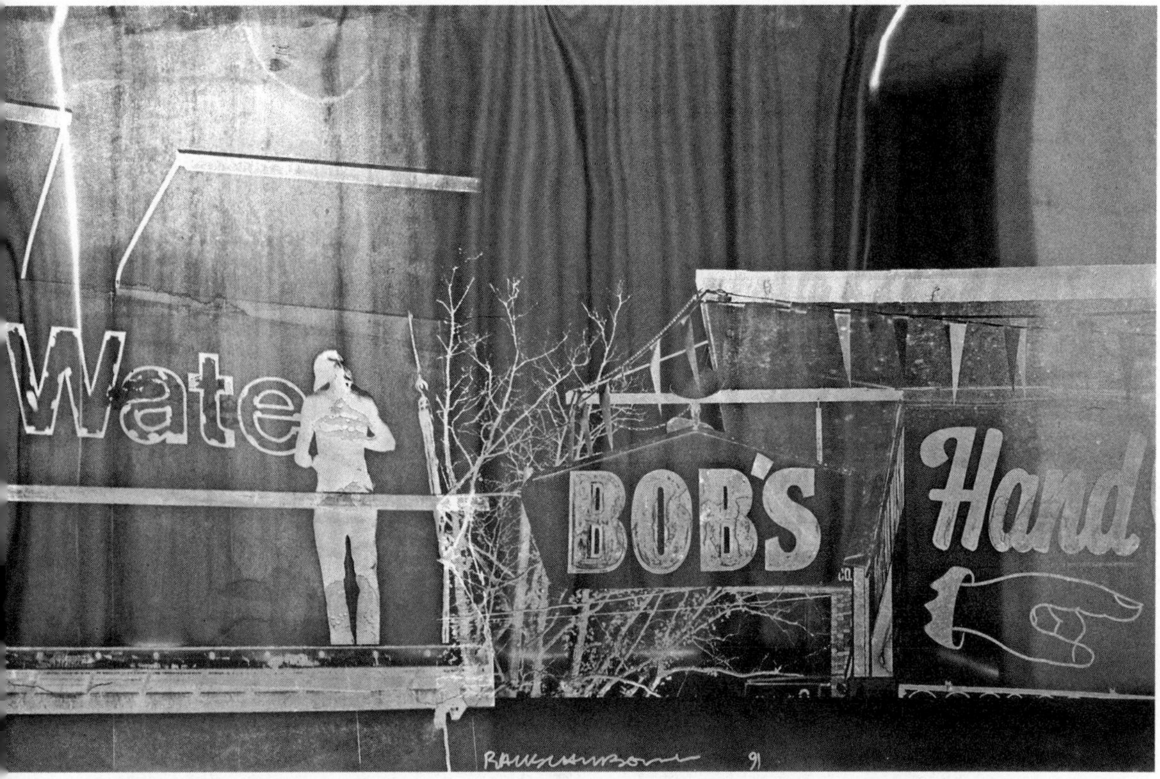


FIGURE 25. Robert Rauschenberg, *Litercy (Phantom)*, 1991. Pigmented varnish on mirrored aluminum, 49½ × 85 in. (125.7 × 215.9 cm). Robert Rauschenberg Foundation, New York. © Robert Rauschenberg Foundation. Licensed by VAGA, New York.

the space with the hand of the maker, the viewer's action is doubled: one becomes simultaneously the object of one's own gaze and that of the gaze of other viewers, as well a creator of the picture.

The symbol of the pointing finger continues the multiplication of signifiers, as its gesture summons one both into the space where the painting lives, and out beyond its parameters. While reflected in the painting, a viewer may reach out virtually to touch the pointing finger, fingertip-to-fingertip, as if reenacting God's finger touching Adam's finger in Michelangelo's *The Creation of Adam* (1511–12) on the ceiling of the Sistine Chapel. Yet this pointing finger is not that of God, but only the deictic sign of a command to look—but not to just look and not to just look anywhere. Pointing from inside the picture to outside its frame, the finger returns viewers to the space of the museum, to art, and to life. Thus can Bob's hand be said to touch the viewer and to signal, or indicate, his or her exit from the painting by pointing beyond it. In this way, the pointing finger is an overt directional guide that may be understood to refer to all aspects of Rauschenberg's concepts in his 1959 statement: art—try to act in the gap—life.

As long as viewers move before *Litercy*, they continue to act upon its imagery, maintaining its liveliness in the present. But as soon as they depart from the space of the painting, *Litercy* becomes an obdurate object, a datum in the territory of the blinding fact of art and the blinding fact of life. Rauschenberg had already identified the facticity of an object in 1958, when he commented upon and described "an Etruscan hand," which he owned, as "that's just that. It's just so literal. It's a fact. A hand."[47] Rauschenberg's fascination with this Etruscan hand resurfaces in the reference to three hands in *Litercy*: the sign painter's hands, Bob's hand, and the hand with the pointing finger. Rauschenberg explained that his paintings "are all facts [that] your mind . . . adds up to something."[48] These facts are literally visual or invisible (as are the sign painter's hands), and they play off one another to awaken the viewer's imagination to the liveliness of the gap, the space in which one participates in contributing to the life and imagery of the painting. This process is something akin to how Rauschenberg described his practice: "I work very hard to be acted on by as many things as I can. That's what I call being awake."[49] However intriguing the vitality of *Litercy*, the painting is much more than a tutorial in Rauschenberg's effort to "try to act in the gap," or in how he involves viewers in and awakens them to that site.

*Litercy* is, to my mind, one of the great (overlooked) paintings of the twentieth century, an assertion that becomes clearer when the painting is placed first in conversation with René Magritte's *The Treachery of Images*, more commonly known as *Ceci n'est pas une pipe* (1928–29) and, secondly, when it comes into dialogue with Velázquez's *Las Meninas* (1656). Beginning with Magritte, as in *The Treachery of Images*, so it is in *Litercy*. Neither the images nor the words represented are what they appear to be. The painted representation of a pipe is not a pipe; the digit pointing is not Bob's finger; the words "Bob's" and "Hand" are not Robert Rauschenberg or his hand. *Ceci n'est pas un homme ni une main*. In addition, the exterior world that appears in *Litercy* or, for that matter, in the *White Paintings* is not the thing itself. The former is only a mirror reflection, the latter a shadow diffraction that even doubles itself under certain lights. Diffraction is the action of light as it bends in passing around an obstruction or through a slit to become an indistinct form. Deploying such operations in painting, Rauschenberg takes *Litercy* to the depths of the chicanery that Magritte identifies in his title *The Treachery of Images*.

In a 1966 letter to Michel Foucault regarding the philosopher's meditations on the relationship between words and things in his book *Les Mots et les choses* (1966), Magritte concentrated on the difference between the words "resemblance" and "similitude," as well as on how painting brings viewers into a confrontation with the slippery interrelationship between the visible and invisible.[50] "Things do not have resemblances, they do or do not have similitudes." Magritte announces, and proceeds:

> Green peas have between them relations of similitude, at once visible (their color, form, size) and invisible (their nature, taste, weight). It is the same for the false and the real, etc. . . . Only thought resembles. It resembles by being what it sees, hears, or knows: it becomes what the world offers it. It is as completely invisible as pleasure or pain.[51]

*Litercy* is a visual symphony of reflected and diffracted similitudes that render viewers present in the painting. Like green peas, we bear similarities (or not) in color, form, and size while retaining our invisible nature, thoughts, pleasure, and pain. "But," Magritte cautions, "painting interposes a problem" for the visible and invisible, since

> there is the thought that sees and can be visibly described. *Las Meninas* is the visible image of Velázquez's invisible thought. Then is the invisible sometimes visible? On condition that thought be constituted exclusively of visible images."[52]

Again, *Litercy* not only proves but augments Magritte's thesis by further throwing realism into question and unraveling representation through visible paradox and contradiction.

Rauschenberg constitutes thought in two visible ways in *Litercy*: first from within the work proper, as the painting requires viewers to think through what they see in words ("Wate[r]," "Bob's," and "Hand") and in images (sign painter, shadows of trees, building, sign of a pointing hand), and to think of these words and images through and in relation to Rauschenberg's actual production of the painting; and, secondly, from without, by bringing viewers and their worlds into the work with all the attendant invisible thoughts and emotions that surface as we see ourselves constituted as signs, and as we act in and think about the psychological and conceptual significance of our experiences in that space. Thus does Rauschenberg increase in manifold ways the consequences of the concepts in *Ceci n'est pas une pipe*. No one would "seriously argue that a word is what it represents—that the painting of the pipe is the pipe itself," as James Harkness observes in his introduction to Foucault's *This Is Not a Pipe*. "Yet," as Harkness adds, "it is exactly from the commonsense vantage that, when asked to identify the painting, we reply, 'It's a pipe.'—words we shall choke on . . . ."[53]

All this makes perfect sense until Rauschenberg throws down the gauntlet to both Magritte and Velázquez. What if what we see in *Litercy* is what it represents? This is my hand reaching out to touch the pointing finger, and so on. Here the discussion turns to *Las Meninas* (1656) for how Velázquez staged the viewer—in view—by painting a representation of a mirror in which two figures standing outside the picture look into its scene and become part of the events that the painter himself is still painting. If, following Harkness, we ask, "Is that the king and queen?" the answers might be "Yes, certainly," or "Perhaps people of the court?" More words to choke on. But what if one asks, "Who is that in *Litercy*?" We would have to acknowledge that they are we. This is I standing near the sign painter's scaffolding, and it is also me as a representation, a mirror image, that is neither here nor there. This is the territory of heterotopia where, as Foucault notes, things become "disturbing, probably because they secretly undermine language, because they make it impossible to name this and that. . . . and are part of the fundamental dimension of the fabula."[54] In these many ways,

Rauschenberg's interests dovetail with Magritte's fascination with verbal/visual non sequiturs, with Foucault's conceptualization of heterotopia, and with Velázquez's distortions of space, time, and politics. Such a space for Magritte was the epitome of the surreal. For Foucault, it was the nonhegemonic space of utopia. For Velázquez it held the enigmas of representation and the illusions of identity. For Rauschenberg it was the space of now, the intangible crack between artifice and reality, which throughout his career he insisted we must inhabit with him, even if only momentarily.

Rauschenberg's title, *Litercy*, could equally be said to entertain Magritte's terrain of revelation and concealment, insofar as it could be seen as a trope of the visible and invisible. We might assume that Rauschenberg's initial misspelling of the word "literacy" was an unintentional dyslexic mistake, but it was a spelling error that eventually he intentionally decided to retain. Suggesting this order of intentionality is not just guesswork: Rauschenberg was fanatical about using the dictionary to correct his many spelling errors.[55] Thus, in maintaining the misspelled title, Rauschenberg pointed (like the pointing finger in *Litercy*) to the fact that literacy, or the assumption of education, competence, and knowledge, may reveal nothing of the invisibility of education, competence, and knowledge. In other words, good spelling can hide ignorance, just as bad spelling may have nothing to do with intelligence.[56] Litercy could also be seen as pointing its finger at the visually illiterate, just as the finger was pointed at Rauschenberg for not being textually literate. Apropos of Magritte's words, "Painting interposes a problem," *Litercy* hangs as visible evidence of otherwise invisible thought.

Magritte's position is further borne out in Rauschenberg's non-singular act of elision: The deletion of the "a" from his title *Litercy* echoes the absence of the letter "r" in the sign painter's "Wate[r]."[57] Viewers and readers fill in what is missing with their experience and knowledge; or, as Magritte adds, a painted image is "intangible by its very nature" and thus "hides nothing, while the tangibly visible object hides another visible thing—if we trust our experience." He then reminds us that while the invisible "hides nothing . . . the visible can be hidden."[58] Magritte is simultaneously talking about the arbitrary condition of signs, what can be immediately known, and what may be discovered in the interrelationship of thought, trust, and experience.

For Rauschenberg, experience was everything: "I put my trust in the materials that confront me, because they put me in touch with the unknown." Only then does he "begin to work," and only "when I don't have the comfort of sureness and certainty." But how does he arrive at such a mental condition? He answers:

> Sometimes Jack Daniels helps too. Another good trick is fatigue. I like to start working when it's almost too late . . . when nothing else helps . . . when my sense of efficiency is exhausted. It is then that I find myself in another state, quite outside myself, and . . . things just start flowing and you have no idea of the source.[59]

In other words, to become fully conscious Rauschenberg lost himself in any number of techniques, from inebriation and exhaustion to the prudent abandonment of the pesonal arrogance of "efficiency" and "sureness and certainty." He claimed that only by becoming "quite outside" himself could he open his consciousness to the "unknown."

Care must be taken here, as Rauschenberg exaggerates. The fact remains, however, that his "trust in materials" anchored him to the facticity of things, and that facture tethered him to reality, not unlike how the rocks and other objects he fastened to his paintings, sculptures, and Combines secured the work to the world around them. These objects might be considered metaphors for Rauschenberg's effort to reach out of the gap and into the world through his work, ultimately securing it (and himself) to art and to life. With the rock that secures a suspended rope to the floor in his sculpture *Untitled (Venetian)* (1973), or with the coconut that serves as the severed head of a martyred saint in *San Pantalon (Venetian)* (1973), Rauschenberg met reality.

Perhaps the most subversive tactic that Rauschenberg marshaled in *Litercy* was the visualization of the phenomenon of similitude in the relationship between the painting's reflective surface and the sign-painter's unfinished word: "Wate[r]." Like water, the surface of *Litercy* shimmers. The painting is elusive, furtive, and seemingly transparent and liquid, so much so that it is almost impossible to photograph. Like water, *Litercy* has the capacity to plunge viewers into a tenuous, vague space: the pool of Narcissus, where one is split from oneself and others, but is incapable of leaving the mesmerizing reflection of one's own presence in the painting. The missing "a" and the missing "r" in *Litercy* play another role in this context: both omissions may be understood as forms of diffraction that reinforce the action of the surface of the painting itself, its watery condition. Accordingly, *Litercy* carries within it—just as the shadows of Rauschenberg's *White Paintings* do—consequential visual, psychological, and narrative meanings, as well as the invisible history of all that has passed before it: its invisible sociological record of art and life.[60] Or, as Rauschenberg stated in 1987 about his abiding "obsession" with reflection, mirroring, and projected shadows: "I don't want the piece to stop on the wall. And it has to somehow document what's going on in the room and be flexible enough to respond."[61]

## (THEREFORE IT IS)

While it may seem that we have traveled a convoluted path, seemingly far afield from the question of honesty and what is at stake in Rauschenberg's act in the gap, *Litercy* takes us to the core of the matter. It sets in motion all that occurs in the gap before the decision is made to regard the "something" that Rauschenberg makes as art, and before that art becomes institutionalized as Art. Such circumstances require another detour.

Rauschenberg knew very well the difference between "something," "art," and "Art," as a letter he wrote, postmarked October 18, 1951, to the New York art dealer Betty Parsons, proves.[62] Writing in the Blue Ridge Mountains of North Carolina, only four days before turning twenty-six, Rauschenberg explained that "since putting on shoes" he had "sobered up from summer puberty and moon-lit smells."[63] The poetry of his opening line refers specifically to his first series of black paintings, works like *Untitled (Night Blooming)* (ca. 1951). With its thick sticky surface, pitted with gravel from being pressed wet against the ground, the painting displays a tiny waning crescent moon barely visible above dashes of white paint that symbolize the fragility and brevity of the petals of the night-blooming cereus.[64]

The lyricism of Rauschenberg's opening line is followed by the power of his next: the *White Paintings* were "almost an emergency." After acknowledging that his monochrome paintings were "not Art" because their status as "art has not been" recognized, Rauschenberg asserted that the series was original and "deserves . . . a place with other outstanding paintings" in the history of art. Seizing the moment with youthful confidence, Rauschenberg expressed an urgency to exhibit these paintings "this year." As part of his persuasion, he boldly risked never exhibiting again in the gallery that prided itself on such artists as Barnett Newman, Clifford Still, and Ad Reinhardt. He promised to forgo any future exhibition in Parson's gallery if she would show the new works within the next two months. She did not. Rauschenberg had to wait another twenty-three months before the *White Paintings* were exhibited at the Stable Gallery in September 1953.

Why did Rauschenberg throw his fate to these works that were not-yet-art, rather than join the vaunted group of abstract expressionists? He grasped the immanent honesty and uniqueness of his work, writing to Parsons that they "take you to a place in painting art has not been." He followed this declaration with two stunning sentences:

> (therefore it is) that is the the [sic] pulse and movement the truth lies in our pecular [sic] preoccupation.[65] they are large white (1 white as 1 GOD) canvases. . . .[66]

In making these enraptured pronouncements, Rauschenberg uses parentheses twice, in the only place where they are used in the entire letter. The parentheses mark off a break from the rest of his thoughts. The sentence "(therefore it is)" heralds another: "(1 white as 1 GOD)." This is the same parenthetical technique that he used in his famous statement "Painting relates to both art and life. Neither can be made (I try to act in that gap between the two.)" In his use of parentheses, Rauschenberg could be said to have introduced a textual device for framing and for offering readers a visual means through which to enter the gap with him.

Several sentences after "(therefore it is)" and "(1 white as 1 GOD)," Rauschenberg becomes perfectly clear about the task he has set for the *White Paintings*: "They are a natural response to the current pressures of the faithless and a promoter of intuitional optimism." Testifying without ambiguity to the role of faith in his life as the source of "intuitional optimism," Rauschenberg names joy, brightness, and positivity—precisely the same qualities he was continuing to promote forty-eight years later, in 1999, when he explained that his life came from a place of "hope, courage, and strength" in order that his art "support inspiration and life."[67] Rauschenberg never deviated from the aim he expressed in 1951. The *White Paintings* have proved to be momentous for numerous reasons over time, but they must also, and perhaps above all, be understood as the artist's manifesto of faith and a foundation from which he never wavered, notwithstanding the preponderance of critical and art-historical ink to the contrary. Rauschenberg's unshakable faith and intuitional optimism appears to have embarrassed many critics, art historians, and curators, who tend to find ways to discuss his works without addressing the potent conviction represented in them. Walter Hopps associated the *White Paintings* with "rectilinear minimalism and flat surface articulation," even as he admitted, albeit with a caveat, that in Rauschenberg's earlier *Crucifixion and Reflection* (c. 1950), the artist may have suggested "a reconsideration of the iconic meaning of the cross as an abbreviated reflection."[68] Hopps also summons comparisons to "Abstract Expressionist art of this time," and, most curiously, writes about another early work, *Mother of God* (ca. 1950):

> Although Rauschenberg had no direct connection with the contemporaneous Beat (as in spiritually beatific) world of Jack Kerouac and Allen Ginsberg, this work resonates synchronistically with their mix of seriousness and wildness, spirituality and play, as well as their explicitly American wanderlust. The work reveals that Rauschenberg sees urbanity as part of nature.[69]

The strained effort to transform Christian references into "urbanity as part of nature," as well as to connect Rauschenberg to the Beats, with whom, Hopps admits, Rauschenberg "had no direct connection" in 1951, is proof enough of the lengths to which Hopps felt he needed to go in order to disassociate the artist from the spiritual sentiments he expressed in his letter to Parsons—the letter that, ironically, Hopps reproduced in full in the very book in which he distances Rauschenberg's work from such intentions.[70]

Susan Davidson associates early works like *Crucifixion and Reflection* and *Mother of God* with abstract expressionism, avoids engagement with Rauschenberg's religious concepts, and calls the *White Paintings* "proto-Minimalist statements."[71] She remains resolutely noncommittal when she comments, "No single interpretation of these works suffices."[72] Sam Hunter writes off the Christian content of the work altogether; "Rauschenberg's role in [the *White Paintings*] is more medium than creator," he states, crediting Cage's "non-volitional esthetic" for the direction that Rauschenberg's work took, even while acknowledging that while Cage and Rauschenberg met in 1951, they did not become friends until the summer of 1952, and Cage was not at Black Mountain when Rauschenberg made the works in 1951.[73] For her part, Mary Lynn Kotz ignores the religious connection to the pre-white and *White Paintings* altogether.

Only Barbara Rose, Rauschenberg's close friend for decades, is unapologetic. She notes that Rauschenberg's depiction for the Vatican of God as a satellite dish, in *The Happy Apocalypse*, was his effort to show that this object represented "the sacred receiver and broadcaster of all communications."[74] Rose further asserts that all of Rauschenberg's prolific production, "this manic activity . . . is a vast idealistic project." His "penchant for ringing certain images with painterly frames" may be nothing less than a way of creating "haloes for what the artist considers sacred." Moreover, his "acts of the salvation of the humble, the mutilated and the discarded are not arbitrary," but rather are deeds of "a poet who can barely read, a preacher whose sermons are his life and work." Though he "tried," Rauschenberg "failed to save the world." Instead, he "put his best efforts into saving the grand manner and the great tradition of painterly painting."[75]

A more moderate position is that of the art historian Branden W. Joseph, who addresses the religious issues in Rauschenberg's letter to Parsons, even while citing "unpublished notes" from a 1991 interview with Rauschenberg by Hopps that has Rauschenberg testify against himself to a "short lived religious period" in the early 1950s. (Oddly, Hopps does not quote this comment in his book on Rauschenberg.)[76] Joseph acknowledges that a number of the pre-white and *White Paintings* seem to be symbolic of the divine, with Rauschenberg's paintings representing a sort of "incarnation," a term Joseph credits to the art historian Thierry de Duve.[77] Despite admitting the symbolic "divine" in Rauschenberg's *White Paintings*, Joseph concludes that the works represent only "the residual traces of religious implications," and then presses forward with a "modernist" interpretation of them.[78]

Rauschenberg's "urgency," Joseph is at pains to explain, "seems also to have resulted from a newfound engagement with the developmental logic of modernist painting."[79] Joseph then describes Rauschenberg's "parenthetical, elliptical reminder '(therefore it is)'" as Rauschenberg's confirmation that the works belong to avant-garde canons of transgression that Joseph argues are confirmed by the rest of Rauschenberg's sentence: "that is the pulse and movement[,] the truth of the lies in our pecul[i]ar preoccupation."[80] This conclusion leads Joseph to interpret the *White Paintings* as evidence of the specter of Clement Greenberg's 1950 lectures at Black Mountain, which Rauschenberg did not hear, as he was not in attendance at the college at that time. Finally, Joseph reads Rauschenberg's interest in the monochrome as belonging to the modernist "zero degree of painting."[81] This deduction is based on Rauschenberg's explanation to Parsons that he was "dealing with the suspense, excitement and body of an organic silence, the restriction and freedom of absence, the plastic fullness of nothing, the point a circle begins and ends." But Rauschenberg followed this sentence by stating that the *White Paintings* "are a natural response to the current pressures of the faithless and a promoter of intuitional optimism, thoughts that have nothing in common with formalism or the "logic of modernist painting."

Finally, like so many before him, Joseph presumes from Rauschenberg's language:

We must look. . . . to the context of Rauschenberg's collaborative relationship with John Cage—whom he met in 1951, but would come to know only in the summer of 1952—. . . to understand this transformation in the discursive framework surrounding the *White Paintings*.

It is not only Cage whom Joseph recommends, but also Cage via Henri Bergson and Antonin Artaud, among other individuals and philosophic traditions. Just as Hopps joins Rauschenberg to the Beats while acknowledging there is no connection, Joseph links the *White Paintings* to Cage, whom Joseph acknowledges only came into Rauschenberg's life in a substantive way a year after the paintings were made. It was during this period in the summer of 1952 that Cage, so rapt with the *White Paintings*, composed *4′33″*. Not only impressed by Rauschenberg's accomplishment, Cage felt that he "must" compose *4′33″*, the composition that emphasized what Rauschenberg had identified in the *White Paintings* as their "organic silence." Otherwise, Cage explained, "I'm lagging."[82]

Such distinguished authors as Hopps, Davidson, and Joseph display similar discomfort or ideological conflict with the artist's determined spiritual relation to his art. But it was Cage who first commandeered Rauschenberg's art away from his faith or his spiritual purposes, to judge from the leaflet Cage wrote and had passed out during Rauschenberg's 1953 exhibition at the Stable Gallery. It read:

To Whom
No subject
No image
No taste
No object
No beauty
No message
No talent
No technique (no why)
No idea
No intention
No art
No feeling
No black
No white (no and)
After careful consideration, I have come to the conclusion that there is nothing in these paintings that could not be changed, that they can be seen in any light and are not destroyed by the action of shadows.

JOHN CAGE

Hallelujah! The blind can see again: the water's fine.[83]

Rauschenberg seems never to have commented on Cage's leaflet. Regardless, it is hard to overlook Cage's pervasive pejorative tone, or his disparagement of Rauschenberg's black-and-white monochromes and *Elemental Sculptures* as "No talent," "No idea," "No art," "No feeling," "No black," and "No white."[84]

Rauschenberg's passion and the innate sophistication of his monochrome works defy Cage's description, and it is difficult to imagine that Rauschenberg appreciated the leaflet. He was more likely perplexed, perhaps even hurt, by its terminology and implications, which were so far from his own aims. Furthermore, as Cage's list includes "No message" and "No intention," these terms imply that Rauschenberg's art had none. What could be further from the goals of the artist who pondered "(therefore it is)," who conceptualized "(1 white as 1 GOD)," who was concerned about "the pressures of the faithless," and whose outlook was informed by "intuitional optimism"? Moreover, what could Rauschenberg have thought of the discussion of his 1959 statement in Cage's oft-cited 1961 essay, "On Robert Rauschenberg, Artist, and His Works"? There, Cage continued in the vein of the 1953 leaflet, describing the "gap" as "the nothingness in between . . . where for no reason at all every practical thing that one actually takes the time to do so stirs up the dregs that they're no longer sitting as we thought on the bottom." As if this was not insulting enough, Cage added: "All you need to do is stretch canvas, make the markings and join. You have then turned on the switch that distinguishes man, his ability to change his mind."[85] Given Cage's deprecation of Rauschenberg's reverent approach to art and life, Rauschenberg must have suppressed his spiritualism in the composer's (and others') company. It may be telling, however, that in 1965, following his break with Cage in late 1964, which had accompanied Rauschenberg's resignation from the Merce Cunningham Dance Company, Rauschenberg purchased an orphanage at 381 Lafayette Street in New York and made its chapel his studio.

Cage's insistence upon inserting himself into the arena of Rauschenberg's art succeeded in shaping the reception of Rauschenberg's work. Much more research needs to be done to untangle Rauschenberg from Cage, but in the meantime it is unconvincing to suggest that one must "look. . . . to the context of Rauschenberg's collaborative relationship with John Cage" for an understanding of Rauschenberg's work. On the contrary, what must be considered is how Cage shifted the meaning of Rauschenberg's intentions away from Rauschenberg's purposes, even as, or perhaps because, Cage knew very well that Rauschenberg often disagreed with him. Merce Cunningham offers a ready example of Rauschenberg's resistance to Cage's interest in the application of the workings of chance to painting. "You can't use chance in painting without turning out an intellectual piece," Rauschenberg told Cage. "You can use it in time, because then you can change time."[86] Given such wrangling, it seems unlikely that Rauschenberg was the artist interested in Cage's 1953 leaflet.

I think that the artist who was especially drawn to Cage's text was Ad Reinhardt. Cage's leaflet reads like notes for what would become Reinhardt's famous "Twelve Rules for a New Academy," published in the May 1957 issue of *Art News*.[87] In earlier publications, however, the date 1953 is given for the inception of "Twelve Rules."[88] In Reinhardt's many versions of his biographical

"Chronology," for example, one dated ca. 1966, lists 1953 as the year in which Reinhardt "paints last paintings in bright colors,"[89] while another version, ca. 1965, adds that in 1953 he "gives up principles of asymmetry and irregularity in painting."[90] What is particularly interesting about the ca. 1966 version is that it lists for 1956 the following:

> Is called by Emily Genauer "a frightening example of a man of talent but with so much ego as to insist that what he refuses to do is more important than what other artists do."[91]

Genauer was none other than the critic who had published Cage's leaflet "in its entirety" in the *New York Herald Tribune* on December 27, 1953, and she was clearly someone whom Reinhardt had enough interest in to add to one version of his chronology.[92]

No one has commented, to my knowledge, on the close relationship between the Cage and Reinhardt texts, and early writers on Reinhardt, like Lucy Lippard, take pains to distance his later monochromes from Rauschenberg's antecedent monochromes of 1951–53. For Reinhardt, according to Lippard, Rauschenberg's monochromes were merely "suggestive, but not necessarily seminal to Reinhardt's project," because they "were a kind of skeptical nihilism."[93] Lippard closes this commentary by pointing to the fact that "Reinhardt makes no mention of Rauschenberg's matt black work."[94] I have also found no mention of the fact that Reinhardt's four-panel painting *Black Quadriptych* (1955) is identical to Rauschenberg's four-panel *White Painting* (1951); both works join four identically sized canvases together in a larger square. Perhaps more importantly, Lippard insists that "a distinction should be drawn between the significance that the monochrome held for these artists in the early 1950s." She concludes: "In contrast to Rauschenberg's neo-Dadaist gesture, Reinhardt's monochromes are constructive."[95] But the association of Rauschenberg's monochromes with "neo-Dada gesture" has to do with the reconfiguring of their reception in Cage's leaflet, and nothing whatsoever to do with the actual content of Rauschenberg's *White Paintings*, or with the context he intended for his works. As a photograph of his installation at the Stable Gallery proves, this context was anything but "neo-Dada," and Reinhardt knew that too.

In 1964, Reinhardt mentioned in an interview: "Even when I was writing "Twelve Rules for an Academy," and I was setting up the—it was sort of humorous because there was only one artist that was qualified to be a member of this academy."[96] Reinhardt never explained what the "the" was, nor did he identify the "one artist," and neither did he ever mention Rauschenberg in the interview. But could the "one artist" have been anyone other than Rauschenberg, even if by 1957 he had left monochromes long behind? If not Rauschenberg, the "one artist" must have been Reinhardt himself. Rauschenberg later remembered, no doubt with pointed irony, that Barnett Newman "hated" his *White Paintings* and that Reinhardt "hated" his black ones.

Though it is well known that Rauschenberg wanted to be a "preacher" when he was a boy, and though his dealer Leo Castelli claimed at one point, "He still is [a preacher]," what I want to insist is that Rauschenberg was simply a man of faith. As he matured, he drew sustenance from every living creature and every produced thing. The world and everything in it served to increase his endless source of belief that, as he expressed it to Monsignor Mario Codognato in August 1999, "healing with faith is paramount." Early on, he set apart a space to enact that faith, between the otherwise overwhelming circumstances and demands of art and life, which he later understood as "blinding fact"—a phrase that suggests the more common expression "brute fact," meaning something that cannot be explained, that contradicts the principle of sufficient reason. A statement Rauschenberg made in 1991 pushes that understanding in yet another direction, one that expands on what "blinding fact" might have meant to him. "Understanding is a form of blindness," Rauschenberg observed. "Good art, I think, can never be understood."[97]

Blinded by the infinite possibility of the fact of art (in its abstract, visible invisibility) and the fact of life (in its literal, experienced reality), Rauschenberg sought ways to get outside, but also remain in proximity to, these inscrutable totalities, not only for himself but also for his viewers. At the same time, he invented ways to keep the act of "making" a vital pursuit and to bring viewers into the genesis of the "something" that he "tried" to make happen in the gap, with the poignant "understanding" that his and their "acts" might eventually lead to blindness as well.[98]

I have now come full circle, back to Rauschenberg's 1977 comments to Diamonstein. Especially critical are the next four sentences he uttered after first establishing his view of the honesty of the artist: "You love art. You live art. You are art. You do art." At this moment in the interview the cadence of his speech changed, and as Rauschenberg spoke these short declarative sentences, he seemed to chant, clapping quietly in time to the sound of each verb: "You love art. You live art. You are art. You do art." This is the most intimate statement that Rauschenberg ever made about his state of mind in the gap. In 1991, he would observe: "Whether I am working in shadows or silks or atrocities or just the street corner, it's headed toward . . . a realization of 'you are here.'"[99] Focusing on the behavioral and emotional forms of process in life, rather than on its objective ends, Rauschenberg's clapping enacted the affect that took over when he loved, lived, was, and did "something" in that space where "you're just doing something [that] no one can stop you from doing," because it "is your life" and it "doesn't have to be art." Taken together with his further observation that "you can't make life," Rauschenberg separated the process of making an object from that of making a life. At the same time, he acknowledged that doing is your life, because that is where you love, live, are, and do (in his case) "art." Rauschenberg's "act in the gap" thus denotes the distinction of loving, living, being, and doing art, and the disparity between being in life and making life; and he succinctly identified the intersection of mental states in the "act" as differentiated from the social conditions of the ends of production—that is, "how much use you can make of" art.

Many intriguing accounts exist of Rauschenberg in the studio, but none is more exhaustive and comprehensive than the valuable contribution of Robert S. Mattison, who explains in detail how the artist drew on the "constant running banter [and] jokes" of his studio assistants to arrive at associations and solutions in his art through "small talk [that was] seemingly unrelated and apparently inconsequential to his immediate activity,[100] but whose "common energy" was essential to "his creative process."[101] Mary Lynn Kotz quotes Stanley Grinstein, an art collector, who recalled witnessing Rauschenberg's energy while working and participating in his own late-night habits, which made "every day . . . like a party. Rauschenberg with a contingent of friends, everybody helping, everybody laughing."[102]

Juxtaposing this festive atmosphere with the importance that Rauschenberg gave to organization—"Everything I can organize I do, so I am free to work in chaos, spontaneity, and the not yet done."[103]—provides a fuller picture of the care that he put into systematic organization in order to free himself to see "the not yet done." To the best of his ability, in other words, Rauschenberg tried to live daily life as if in the gap, in order to find what had not yet been discovered or "done." To reinforce his aim to dwell in the constant present, Rauschenberg kept virtually no earlier examples of his art either at his studio or at his house, explaining, "What interests me is the here and now. . . . Reality is you and I here at this moment."[104]

"Few people have the imagination for reality," Johann Wolfgang von Goethe observed. Rauschenberg was one of those few. For him, being in reality was like a creed. "To break down barriers [and] see as an alien does," he advised, "to get lost in the city, or the country, to see things . . . that maybe you are blind to."[105] Here are the stakes of the gap for Rauschenberg: "I am in the present. . . . The past is part of the present."[106] Dave Hickey would keenly observe that Rauschenberg "invariably devoted all his generosity" to the "task of inventing the present."[107]

Overfamiliarization with the conventions of living, even with seeing his art hanging on the walls of his own home, threatened to become stultifying to Rauschenberg by proximity. The best example of how anesthetized routine and destruction of imagination both horrified him and affected him emotionally comes from his experience in China in 1982, only six years after the soul-crushing Cultural Revolution had ended with Mao Zedong's death. Shocked by what he experienced in China, Rauschenberg reported: "I think [the Chinese] really were just beaten down. They had exhausted any initiative, any hope of anything changing. Once you kill the curiosity, everything else goes."[108] What devastated him even more than witnessing desire and inquisitiveness drained from so many people was "this big water buffalo [working a water wheel] walking around and around and around blindfolded with an old dirty rag. That was his life. If one isn't moved by that. . . ."[109] Rauschenberg never finished his sentence. As his own existence depended on sight, witnessing the huge beast of burden blindfolded and wounded, psychologically distressed and depressed Rauschenberg.

Rauschenberg felt that everything required his keen attention, so that he might unlock the simplicity of something's deceptive complexity, or vice versa, and thereby discover its mystery. This is why, when Diamonstein asked him if he thought that art rested "more in ideas" than the thing itself, he answered: "The definition of art would have to be more simple-minded than that, and it's about how much use you can make of it."[110] For the writer Stephen R. Dolan, Rauschenberg implied that "if you can't make art, you can't destroy it; that "creating with the intent to create limits creativity; and that "it is the action that counts as opposed to its being." Dolan concluded about Rauschenberg's aim: "Art's 'use' is in the mileage you get out of leaving what you have made out there for others: that's where your act is its most effective."[111] The "use" of art, for Rauschenberg, required not sequestering it as Art outside of life, which would render it a "very self-conscious and a blinding fact," as its vaunted social position and prestige as Art would strip art of its life. Rauschenberg's last sentence on the matter delivered a coup de grace: "Life doesn't really need it [art]. So it's also another blinding fact." With this closing sentence, the Diamonstein conversation veered off in another direction. But Rauschenberg never had the hubris to believe that life needed the "something" that he made, so he preserved the "gap."

Rauschenberg once said: "Being a painter, I probably take a painting more seriously than someone who drives a truck or something. Being a painter, I probably also take his truck more seriously."[112] Far from making an imperious statement of superiority, Rauschenberg took "seriously" the act of concentrating on and thinking about all things in themselves and in relation to each other, in order to become one "who could see." Perhaps, as Rauschenberg might say, the message is more "simple-minded" than that: it is about looking long at, and thinking hard about the gift of the world. Or, to quote Rauschenberg: "It was not until I realized that it is the celebration of the differences between things that I became an artist who could see."[113]

# Warhol's "What?" (2016)[1]

Many in the 1960s dismissed Andy Warhol as a mere product of Madison Avenue advertising and capitalism.[2] Even as recently as 2005, Carolyn Christov-Bakargiev, the art historian and curator for Documenta 13, seemed to blame the artist for how "large exhibitions at times become cynical, postmodern visions embracing a pop Andy Warhol attitude."[3] Already in 1970, Rainer Crone's book *Andy Warhol* attempted to right this perception of the artist. Crone insisted that Warhol had "revolutionized traditional aesthetics" by uniting silkscreen, painting, and photography; following Walter Benjamin, Crone also pointed out that mechanical reproduction enhanced Warhol's "criticism of bourgeois aesthetics" by transforming art's "authenticity" and "ritual" into "politics."[4] While Crone did not avoid the central role of Warhol's personality in an analysis of his art, he emphasized the artist's formal and aesthetic achievements and quoted a number of critics in support of this view. Warhol was praised as having "scraped off the terrifying lies of civilization—of Kultur, of history, of politics, and of art itself" (Clair Wolfe); as being "one of the most thoroughly organized and consistent, modest, and self-effacing geniuses in the entire history of art" (Kurt von Meier); as someone who "will probably turn out to be one of the most influential artists of his generation" (Alan Solomon); as "one of the principal didactic artists of our time" and an artist who revealed "the nightmare that the American Dream has become" (Barbara Rose); as the artist who proved that "Elizabeth Taylor is a commercial property, as commercial as a can of Campbell's soup" (Paul Bergin); as "totalitarian" in how the public consumed everything he produced (John Leonard); and as an artist whose "work looks forward" and is "not" Pop (Henry Geldzahler).[5] Such laudations recall how, in his series of interviews with Pop artists, Gene Swenson framed Warhol's aims:

ANDY WARHOL: No one would know whether my picture was mine or somebody else's.
GENE SWENSON: It would turn art history upside down?
ANDY WARHOL: Yes.[6]

Warhol assented, as he did to many interpretations of his work.

By contrast, Steven Koch presented Warhol as the cruel and poignant icon in his book *Stargazer: Andy Warhol's World and His Films* (1973), describing the artist as someone who had "acquired . . . a capacity not to be moved";[7] who, especially in his film *Sleep* (1963), achieved "the dissociation of time in the name of a hypostatized quietude";[8] who, as a voyeur . . . absents himself" while keeping "his distance"; and whose "passion and patience stand in a murderous equipoise."[9] The voyeur, Koch continued, possesses "a sexuality in which nothing is shared . . . desire is peculiarly abstract, [and] by defining himself as someone whose presence must remain unknown, as one who is not there . . . his depersonalization is complete."[10] In considering the role of Warhol's psyche and sexuality in relation to his art and to the world, Koch concluded with cold precision: "Though he speaks like a child, he does not see with a child's eyes. He sees with an intellectually airtight, very perverse, utterly mechanistic mockery of that childlike newness."[11]

Koch's original and groundbreaking analysis was prescient, if unsettling, and although persuasive, his conclusions about Warhol's identity also felt somehow slightly off the mark. I read the book in 1976 and it perplexed me for years. Not until the early 1990s, after learning about the etiology of trauma and post-traumatic stress disorder, did I come to believe that what Koch had articulated in his identification of Warhol's "narcissism" was an affect that could be theorized as a self-protective, albeit partially unconscious, behavior that screened and thereby protected Warhol—and others—from identifying an originating trauma or traumas. In this way, and following Freud's pivotal "Screen Memories" (1899),[12] it could be argued that Warhol's supposed narcissistic behavior "owe[d] its value as a memory not to its own content but to the relation existing between that content and some other, that has been suppressed."[13]

I shall allude throughout this essay to Warhol's traumatic subjectivity, but in 1993, in an effort to articulate this insight, I gave a talk titled "Warhol's Shadow" at the symposium "Re-Reading Warhol: The Politics of Pop" at Duke University. I suggested that Warhol "evinced trauma in his metonymic identification with shadows," a trope that may have emerged during the years he listened to the radio play *The Shadow* from his sickbed. The precocious child was, I thought, fascinated with the idea of a doppelgänger, a man/shadow with "the power to cloud men's minds so that they cannot see him," and who knew "what evil lurks in the hearts of men."[14] I pointed out that in September 1937, when Warhol was nine and suffering from what he once described as his second "nervous breakdown" (having had one-a-year at the ages of eight, nine, and ten),[15] Orson Welles assumed the role of "the Shadow." Cautioning listeners in his booming baritone, Welles recited the famous phrase "The Shadow knows!" This declaration was followed by explosive, threatening laughter and a roiling section of Camille Saint-Saëns's *Le Rouet d'Omphale*. No doubt Warhol, like everyone else who ever heard it, never forgot Welles's sonorous voice, as four decades later Warhol would depict himself as "the Shadow" in his 1981 *Myth* series. Some of the earliest documented examples of Warhol's multiplication of his self-presentation in self-portraits date to the late 1950s, when he began using the coin-operated photo booth. Thereafter, he continued to double, quadruple, multiply, and screen his self-portraiture, right up to 1986, when he overlaid a photograph of himself with camouflage print. In this unresolved effort to articulate trauma as the subtext of Warhol's work, I strayed too far from the interests of the Duke symposium organizers, and my essay was not included in the book that followed.[16] Regardless of my interest in Warhol, I turned to what I named "cultures of trauma" in "Shaved Heads and Marked Bodies" (1993) (in this volume) and put my work on Warhol aside for the next fifteen years.

Then, in 1996, Hal Foster published "Death in America," a decisive, insightful, now canonical essay that extended his reading of Warhol's traumatic imagery to a broader analysis of art. Foster began by noticing that Warhol deferred discussion of "death" in *The Philosophy of Andy Warhol* (1975), saying only:

> I don't believe in it because you're not around to know that it's happened.
> I can't say anything about it because I'm not prepared for it."[17]

According to Foster, the source of Warhol's "stony demurral" ("can't say anything") may have been "an experience of shock or trauma, an encounter where one misses the real, where one is too early or too late (precisely 'not around,' 'not prepared')."[18] Foster explained that he focused on "this idiosyncratic passage because . . . it encrypts a relation to the real that suggests a new way into [Warhol's work], especially into the 'Death in America' images from the early 1960s," as well as into "all Pop images [and] postwar art based in photography" that otherwise inevitably falls into a "reductive" critical binary, and which is read either as "referential or as simulacral."[19] At the beginning of his essay, Foster included an illustration of Richard Avedon's 1969 photograph of Warhol's chest, scarred by the surgery that followed being shot three times by Valerie Solanas on June 3, 1968. At the end of the essay, he included a photograph of a poster of Warhol holding up a bottle of Vidal Sassoon hair spray. The poster had been partially destroyed by one of Solanas's bullets, which pierced a hole through the illustration of Warhol's left eye. Together, these two images insinuated Foster's identification of Warhol's near-death experience as his trauma.

Foster then turned to Warhol's "compulsion to repeat" as proof of his desire to operate and be perceived as "a machine." He argued that Warhol's pronouncement represented a "performance" aimed at revealing "a society of serial production and consumption [such that] if you enter it totally, you might expose it; that is, you might reveal its automatism, even its autism, through your own excessive example."[20] Reiterating his consideration that Warhol's claim was "a performance, of course," Foster added: "There is a subject 'behind' this figure of nonsubjectivity who presents it [nonsubjectivity] as a figure."[21] This comment defers a decision as to whether Warhol was actually traumatized, an ambiguity that Foster maintains when he adds abstrusely:

Otherwise the shocked subject is an oxymoron, for, strictly speaking, there is no subject in shock, let alone in trauma. And yet the fascination of Warhol is that one is never certain about this subject 'behind': is anybody home, inside the automaton?"[22]

Leaving behind this irresolution, Foster writes that Warhol's repetition of motifs is "not restorative," and is "not about a mastery of trauma," but about "an obsessive fixation on the object in melancholy."[23] Not wholly satisfied with his description, Foster restates his thesis: Warhol's "repetitions not only reproduce traumatic effects; they produce them as well (at least they do in me)."[24] The result of these "several contradictions" is the way in which Warhol's work succeeds in a "warding away of traumatic significance and an opening out to it, a defending against traumatic affect and a producing of it."[25] Such simultaneity leads to Foster's theory of "traumatic realism" based in "repetitions that fix on the traumatic real, that screen it, that produce it," and that are the basis of the "Warholian paradox . . . not only of images . . . but also of viewers that are neither integrated . . . nor dissolved."[26] The "subject-effect" of the artist's work is, for Foster, epitomized in Warhol's statement: "I never fall apart because I never fall together."[27] This indecisive resolution "resonates in some art after Pop. . . . [in which] there is a genealogy of traumatic realism."[28] Foster concludes by giving Warhol the last word in an uncustomarily long commentary (for Warhol) on the indivisibility of watching television and living life, feeling and not feeling, and continuing to reside "in pain."[29] Although Foster never acknowledges Koch's work, Koch too emphasized Warhol's "yearning . . . ache of pain."[30]

Everyone has his or her Warhol. This essay is about my Warhol, especially in conversation with Crone, Koch, and Foster. An indefatigable, elusive man in pain, Warhol was much admired, celebrated, and flattened into a caricature. In what follows, I read Warhol's behavior not as a "performance" but as a performative manifestation of traumatic subjectivity, the affect of Warhol's severely dissociated personality. My Warhol is also the Warhol whom Arthur Danto described in 1999 as someone whose "philosophical intelligence [was] of an intoxicatingly high order. . . . touching the very boundaries of . . . thought about art."[31] This is the Warhol whom I especially pursue in this essay, beginning with his oft-repeated question "What?"

## WARHOL'S "WHAT?"

The last sentence in Andy Warhol's *The Philosophy of Andy Warhol (from A to B and Back Again)* (1975) is: "Forever what?" This question appears at the end of "Underwear Power," the book's final chapter, ostensibly devoted to his "favorite thing. . . . underwear."[32] That the question may have expressed Warhol's philosophical worldview is anything but apparent, folded in as it is with jockey shorts. Warhol begins the chapter with a discussion of the various merits of different brands of underpants, while at the same time cajoling "B" to go shopping with him at Macy's. B begs to go to Bloomingdale's, but Warhol prevails. After browsing in Macy's and heading for Gimbels, they "cut through Woolworths," prompting Warhol to mention associations brought on by the smell of frying chicken. "I almost bought some even though I don't like fried chicken," he quipped, before reflecting on class relations: "In high-class stores they sell through 'display,' [but] in low-class ones they sell through 'smell.'"[33] Warhol then asks whether B is "glad" to have been "born rich," while musing to himself that B "is so . . . lucky he wasn't born in a five-and-dime family," as Warhol had been.[34]

Leaving Woolworths for Gimbels, B pleads to go to Bloomingdale's or Saks, alternately whining for "old jewelry" at Cartier. Warhol's response is swift and punitive:

> Cartier's! . . . Listen, B, I think we should do this every day. It would do you a lot of good, coming out into the world and seeing what life is all about. It doesn't start at Saks and end at Bloomingdale's. It's not a YSL boutique. Maybe you should spend more time getting underwear and socks and going to the dime store. . . . This is what real life is, B![35]

Smarting from the scolding, B retreats to inspect school supplies while Warhol examines Gimbels' "used jewelry," searching for a ring with "a big big stone." Returning to regale Warhol with memories of "the big amethyst" they saw in Paris, B coos over "how purple" it was—"Siberian, not South American"—and how it had "belonged to the Imperial Family." As Warhol listens to B, he notices that the stones he is scrutinizing "look smaller and smaller."[36] But when B asks why he "likes jewelry so much," Warhol snaps: "I don't like jewelry so much. Let's go buy some Dr. Scholl's Footsavers. Jewelry will never replace Dr. Scholls."[37] B sniffs: "I'd rather have jewelry." "Why?" Warhol asks. B retorts: "Because a diamond is forever."[38] Unseating this recitation of a trite marketing slogan for diamonds, Warhol demands: "Forever what?"—his final comment in the book.

Warhol's denouement plunges the conversation into the domain of philosophical speculation, leaving readers to ponder how objects, ideas, events, and even people accumulate worth; how value remains perpetually in question; how a shopping culture naturalizes the accretion of the quality of "forever"; and what "forever" might be worth. Warhol's inimitable ability for what I call "circuitous inversion" was his strategy for destabilizing interlocutors, whether in art, writing, or interaction. While appearing to be fully immersed in trivia, Warhol could displace minutiae with luminous insight and, just as quickly, return to everyday froth. I think that Warhol deployed circuitous inversion as a distancing mechanism, aided and abetted by his oft-repeated question, "What?" which had an unsettling effect on his interlocutors.

Rainer Crone writes that Warhol learned methods for creating "alienation" from Bertolt Brecht's *Verfremdungseffekt*, which Warhol learned about while designing sets for a small Off-Off-Broadway theater company on the Lower East Side between 1953 and 1955. Crone (who was close to Warhol from the mid-

1960s on and was one of his earliest biographers) explains that Warhol, together with members of the theater company, "concentrated on plays after Franz Kafka and of Bertold Brecht,"[39] especially "Brecht's Caucasian Chalk Circle and The Good Man of Szechuan."[40] Warhol "acquainted himself with Brecht's didactic plays during the long and exhaustive discussions about content and technique of presentation that these works demand," and confronted "Brecht's definition of realism and the instructive value of his theory of alienation."[41] Crone especially identified instances of "Brecht's 'alienation-technical moments' (*verfremdungstechnische Momente*)" in Warhol's films as early as 1966, when the artist began using "structurally analytic methods—strobe cut, a blank film frame which gives a short flash on the screen when the film is running."[42] Such techniques alert the viewer to the making of a movie, creating a distance within which the viewer becomes critical.

Adaptation of estrangement as a critical method for art—to which I would add the Warholian technique of disrupting an interlocutor with "What?"—may have also served Warhol as a conceptual aid for working with the separation he experienced from others and from himself. "Working with," meaning using, is not the same as "working through," a phrase often colloquially connected with undergoing psychotherapy. Furthermore, I do not mean to suggest in any way that Warhol defaulted to techniques for distancing as a psychotherapeutic aid or tool. On the contrary, he employed it as a way to keep the world at bay. At the same time, augmenting his capacious curiosity, Warhol's "What?" served to unnerve those engaged with him for a time long enough to create an opening out of ordinary perception to consider philosophical conjecture regarding how meaning, value, and purpose are produced. "What?" may have also been Warhol's most successful strategy for circuitous inversion, as he could interrupt a moment with this spontaneous query and then immediately retreat to his favorite camouflage: banality. Warhol's "What?" exhibited not only his keen insight and perception, but also his method for manipulating others, all qualities that remained, throughout his art and life, predictably unpredictable. Such Warholian elements would lead the artist and filmmaker Julian Schnabel to comment in 1989 that Warhol's work required physical and mental "space" in order for one to grasp "the sublime gesture of its diamond bullet to the brain."[43] The "bullet" of Warhol's sagacity is never more manifest than in the space he created with his "What?"

Following his mother's habit, Warhol habitually uttered the word "What?" Apparently, this is the only word that Mrs. Warhola spoke in the last known video recording that the artist made of her—in February 1971, the year before she died, and a mere three years before he brought out *The Philosophy of Andy Warhol*, ending in "What?" The bedridden Julia makes a cameo appearance in this video while she and Andy watch the televised third moonwalk, which he is also in the midst of videotaping. Invisible behind the camera, Warhol can be heard calling, "Mom?" She answers, "What?" Wayne Koestenbaum writes, "This is. . . . her last word to Andy as far as his art knows."[44] Koestenbaum conjectures that Warhol frequently used the word "'what'. . . . either because he didn't catch what the other person was saying, or because he sought confirmation, or because he liked repetition, and wanted to hear the same comment twice, with the hope that the second time around it might metamorphose into something strange." He also posits that Warhol asked "What?" when he tried to "make sense of heard speech and because he needed time to come up with a coherent response."[45]

Having ruminated on Kostenbaum's observations, my sense is that Warhol's "What?" was his way of opening up an opportunity for examining the facticity of things, and that if he was hoping for "something strange," it was to investigate further the conditions of the psychological and social reality that, curiously, rendered them oddly authentic. In this regard, Warhol's mode of inquiry calls to mind the first of Wittgenstein's seven propositions in *Tractatus Logico-Philosophicus* (1922):

1 The world is all that is the case.
 1.1 The world is the totality of facts, not of things.
 1.11 The world is determined by the facts, and by their being all the facts.
 1.12 For the totality of facts determines what is the case, and also whatever is not the case.
 1.13 The facts in logical space are the world.
 1.2 The world divides into facts.
 1.21 Each item can be the case or not the case while everything else remains the same.[46]

Given Wittgenstein's concepts, Warhol's "What?" could be said to have been his inherent method for questioning both the totality and the division of facts, insofar as the world itself leads to the determination of "all that is the case." In examining the conditions under which any fact could or could not be the case, Warhol asked "what" its specificity was, and how it came to be so while everything else remained the same. A word, a thing, or a person was for Warhol a fact that filled a logical space in the world.[47] Thus, his question, "Forever what?" was not about whether a diamond could last "forever," but about what facts make diamonds consequential and what values endure from these facts.

Scrutinizing everything from a dollar bill and flowers to a race riot, and from a Brillo box to a blow job, Warhol's "What?" demonstrated that anything and everything becomes a "fact" for philosophical meditation and picturing the world. But as an artist rather than a philosopher, Warhol contemplated the meaning of a fact's category in a language that was not exactly its own, and for the most part through the visual. In this sense, the task to which he set the question "What?" was to invert circuitously the primary denotations of a thing in order to confound and multiply its connotations. His attitude toward pornography exemplifies this point, at least as he expressed it in a 1977 conversation with the writer Bob Colacello, an indispensable cohort and the editor of Warhol's magazine *Interview* from 1970 to 1982. As Colacello explained, night after night Warhol had been leaving photographs of pornography all over Colacello's desk, where he discovered them each morning upon first arriving at work. Colacello became increasingly irritated, and he finally challenged Warhol, pointing out—and disingenuously shifting the blame—that the images might be offensive to "all the girls who work here." Warhol responded: "Just tell them it's art, Bob [Warhol's emphasis]. They're landscapes." Then, holding up a photograph of "fist fucking," Warhol added, "I mean, it's so so. . . . so abstraaaaact."[48]

This statement amplifies the "What?" that Warhol identified in the photographs. For while being titillating images of sex, they were equally straightforward visual form, abstractions, or "landscapes." Rather than being swayed by socially prescribed responses to representation—which is not to say that the images he photographed were not pornographic—they were also something else in Warhol's mind. His talent for expansive interpretation and visualization permitted Warhol to defer denotative meanings while maintaining paradoxical relationships to the connotations of form.[49] In this regard, Warhol's notorious detachment (from products, people, and sex) goes a long way in explaining the unprecedented contribution he made to the analysis of culture. Warhol could retreat to mental concepts and remain emotionally aloof, a capacity I will discuss as his inordinate faculty for both dissociation and immense lucidity. Warhol comprehended, as few do, that images are just things among the totality of facts. Their subversive psychological power did not deceive him, as that influence was just an aspect of the deep cognitive potential of representation. Warhol discovered more of the nature of the "What?" of appearances, especially pornography, by doing precisely what David Freedberg recommends in The Power of Images: "looking hard" at the "figured material object."[50] Koch called Warhol "the most interesting pornographer of the century," and I would agree.[51]

Warhol's facility for abstracting himself from a fact in order to see the thing-in-itself also permitted him to dissociate from the quotidian, and was the primary factor in his "radical . . . self-denial,"[52] self-abnegation, and asceticism that he balanced with self-indulgent debauchery. Warhol expressed abstemiousness in his minimalist aesthetic, his cool mental remove, his renowned parsimony, his public posture of aloof distance, his economy of dress and speech, and his work ethic, which included volunteering in the Catholic parish where he attended mass every week and fed the homeless in its food kitchen on Sundays. Debauchery could be found most notoriously in his studio, the Factory, or during periods like the late 1970s, when he produced his *Oxidation* paintings and *Torso Polaroid* series. This period, according to Colacello, also found Warhol frequenting gay S/M bars in New York, where "leather and rubber, bondage and discipline, masters and slaves, indeed every sort of kink and fetish known to man ruled from midnight to daybreak," and where the demimonde of "the sexual fast crowd" hung out at the Anvil ("famous for its fist-fucking stage show") and the Toilet (featuring "tubs and troughs where naked men lay for other naked men to urinate on them").[53] Despite the fact that Warhol apparently never went to the bar called the Toilet, and only visited the Anvil "once," Colacello remembered that this milieu was "what was going on [and what] Andy's *Piss Paintings* and *Torso Series* . . . were really all about."[54] As Steve Cox writes,

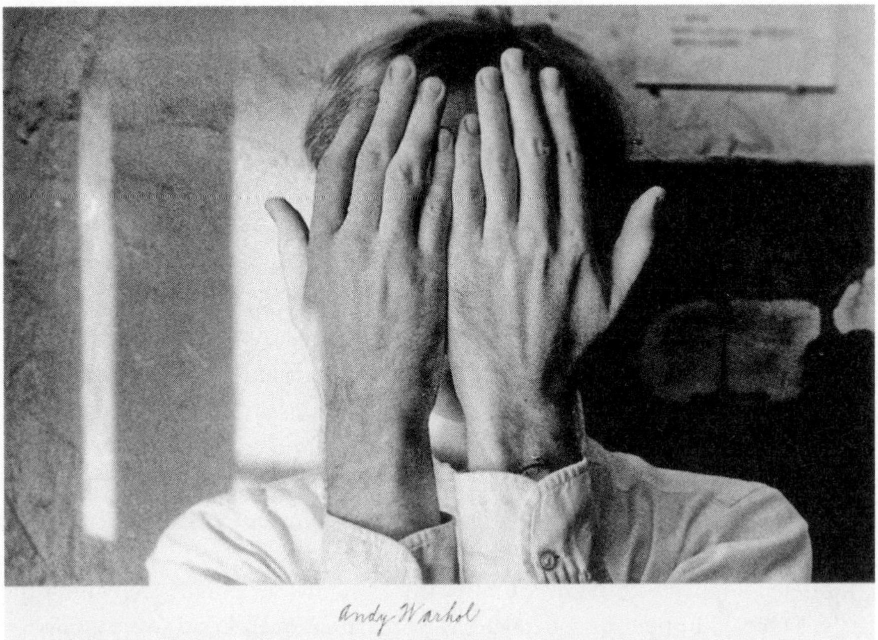


FIGURE 26. © Duane Michals, *Andy Warhol*, 1958. Gelatin silver print with hand-applied text, 9¼ × 14 in., from an edition of twenty-five. Courtesy of Pace/MacGill Gallery, New York.

the seditious qualities of these works allowed Warhol "to deliver the final, Oedipal, coup de grâce to the memory of the swaggering father figures of abstract expressionism while also providing an opportunity to offer a dark glimpse of New York's queer underground."[55]

Yet while Warhol voraciously consumed culture, he left it behind at his doorstep, retreating (no matter how late or early) to the secluded world of his mother, with whom he lived for some forty of his fifty-eight years (fifteen of the eighteen years in which he did not live with his mother were between her death in 1972 and his own death in 1987). This means that during his mother's lifetime, Warhol only lived apart from her for three years (1949–51). With her son sequestered within her maternal fortress, Julia Warhola also contributed to her son's abiding insecurity. In his book *The Life and Death of Andy Warhol*, Victor Bockris notes that she fueled her son's fears of being "ugly" by frequently telling him that he was indeed unsightly, and by holding a grip over his personality to the extent that she "would claim in more than one bitter tirade that she was Andy Warhol."[56] Both cared for and verbally and psychologically abused, Warhol lived with inconsistent messages about his identity throughout his life.

Duane Michals's 1958 portrait photograph of Warhol provides insight into the artist's conflicted identity, especially his anxiety about his appearance—an uncertainty manifest in both his diffident and his caustic behavior, in spite of a confidence about at least one of his physical attributes (figure 26). Pictured from mid-chest upward, Warhol wears a slightly wrinkled but neat white Oxford-cloth shirt that drapes over his thin, small shoulders. He covers his face with his hands. This is the face that shamed him. But most prominent in the photograph are the hands that since his childhood were known to be both elegant and the source of his special talent, as well as the aspect of his body that his mother admired and praised most. Everyone noticed Warhol's hands. He displayed them in very particular ways, even describing them in *The Philosophy of Andy Warhol* as "arresting."[57] Pouncing on the opportunity to taunt Warhol about his one vanity, Silver George, a regular at the Factory, answered its phone one day and, with Warhol looking on, impersonated him while talking to a caller who had phoned to interview the artist. Speaking to the unsuspecting person in an especially fey manner, Silver George explained, "My hands are very nice . . . very expressive. I keep them in repose or touching each other, or sometimes I wrap my arms around myself. I'm always very conscious of where my hands are."[58] Warhol's hands overshadow other details of Michals's picture, such as his watch, barely visible under one shirt cuff; the enigmatic typed note on the wall; what looks like what might be a painting behind Warhol; and even the raking light of the stunning photograph.

Michals appears to be aware of Warhol's hands as shields, screening the artist's face with their long, delicate, sensitive fingers and carefully manicured nails. The series of photographs Michals took in 1958, to which the image in figure 26 belongs, show Warhol posing his hands in various affected ways. Even fifteen years later, in 1973, when Michals again shot Warhol, one of his photographs was just an image of the artist's hands.[59] In the 1958 photograph pictured here, Warhol uses his hands to cover his eyes lest they betray the sharp intellect he hid, and the eyes that could dash efforts to dismiss him as "a Russian village idiot/saint type. . . . a holy fool."[60] These are the eyes whose broad knowledge and piercing countenance Warhol intentionally concealed behind sunglasses in order to con some into describing him as "the great idiot savant of our time."[61] Such comments generally follow what Eleanor Heartney once described as the "well-trodden paths" of presenting Warhol "as a nonintellectual, insecure, status-conscious striver who got his best ideas from others, and whose 'choices' were often in fact happy accidents," as well as someone who "traded artistic audacity for celebrity and financial security, becoming a court painter to the international jet set."[62] Far from being a "saintly simpleton," as art historian John Richardson described him at his funeral,[63] or "never in the least intellectual," as Simon Watney concludes,[64] Warhol was already recognized as different and uniquely talented by his grade-school teachers, who awarded his precocious artistic abilities and intellect by twice advancing him a grade.

Writing about the decisive conditions of Warhol's self-manufacture, Dave Hickey noted: "There is no evidence to suggest that his overriding project was anything more profound than to make the art world safe for Andy Warhol."[65] Hickey continued:

> In its moment, the Factory manufactured sleazy fame by the carload. Later, when Andy was on top of the world—isolated and terrorized by the fame he

> sought to give away—that first Factory remained the only subject upon which he would go misty. . . . The Factory was his baby. It was the best thing he ever made for the best times he ever had. . . . Ultimately, of course, the scene would die of its own success as fame became more interesting than democracy and Andy became the font of celebrity rather than its enabler.[66]

Hickey knows that his account of Warhol is the kind of story Warhol would have concocted in order to mask his adroit mind and rarified sophistication.[67] But it would be difficult to tell if the Factory was the "best thing [Warhol] ever made," or the only subject upon which he would "go misty," for while the Factory may have been the site of Warhol's "best times," Warhol partied throughout his life. As Brian Wallis observed, "Warhol takes seriously the institution of partying," treating it as if he were "a sociologist."[68]

Neither Hickey nor Wallis nor Henry Geldzahler was tricked by Warhol's feigned and misleading naiveté. Then curator of American art at the Metropolitan Museum of Art, Geldzahler wrote in 1964: "The dead-pan, sweet, know-nothing quality of Andy Warhol's personality is continuous with his paintings. He plays dumb just as his paintings do, but neither deceives us."[69] Charles Lisenby, a television set designer with whom Warhol fell in unrequited love in 1954, and with whom he traveled around the world in the summer of 1956, was also not deceived. Lisenby remembered Warhol this way: "People thought he was dumb, but he was anything but dumb, he was more brilliant than even he knew." Lisenby then called Warhol "the most interesting person I ever met, the strangest little guy with an original and unique approach to everything."[70]

Warhol's "unique approach" included such affectations as flaunting his hands, and the gesture of covering his face, which can be seen in Michals's photograph and in Warhol's *Self-Portrait* (ca. 1958), a drawing from the same period. Clearly, Warhol was either rehearsing or repeating the gesture of covering his face with his hands, and, in effect, covering his ugliness with his beauty. But the drawing has a difference: Warhol wears a ring on his little finger, a pinky ring signifying what he called his "nelly" personality, the term he used to refer to his homosexuality. Being nelly was also an affect that Warhol cultivated, according to Koestenbaum, who observed that the artist "infused" his nelly "into every sigh, allowing his emulators to understand that nongenital indulgences . . . emit their own rude erotic charge."[71] Obsessed both with his own "nelly problem" and those of others, Warhol would often ask: "'Does so-and-so have a problem?' . . . hoping the answer would be yes [and] convinced that every married man on Park Avenue had a 'problem.'"[72] Thus does the 1958 drawing flourish what is conspicuously missing in Michals's photograph: Warhol's beautiful hands were the site of his most public display of homosexuality, and the Barthean *punctum* of Michals's photograph was another example of Warhol's "What?"[73] But in Warhol's drawing, his hands become the overt signifiers of his queer identity, which would signal what Michael Moon has identified as "the revisionary queer power of much of his Pop cartoon work."[74]

Michals disliked Warhol, but not because he was nelly. Michals denounced Warhol's fame and the fact that he had become wealthy by making art that the photographer did not respect: "The biggest lie is fame," Michals would explain, "the big success, the dazzling success, the Warhol success, the name-above-the title success which is eventually hollow and fraudulent."[75] Michals' opinion cannot be separated from the fact that he and Warhol were both from the same working-class background but had taken very different artistic paths. Michals explains:

> [Warhol] was born in McKeesport too, and my father was [also] a steelworker. We were from that same milieu. I'm Slovak, and so was Andy, although he used to tell everybody he was Czech because that was classier. He was such an upwardly mobile blue-collar snob. I met him when I came to New York. He was already well known as a graphic designer, and he was very, very ambitious. All his dreams came true, every one he had! Andy wanted to be what he became, a famous artist. Unfortunately he was a terrible artist, and did more to trivialize art than anyone else other than Marcel Duchamp. I always think of Andy as the quintessential American painter of the twentieth century, the same way as Thomas Eakins was the quintessential American painter of the nineteenth century. Andy was a first generation immigrant, he was a victim of violence, he was shot, he was a product of publicity, his work was done in a factory by other people, he was a great manipulator, he stole everybody's ideas, and he ended up being very wealthy. How American can you get? The idea of quality never enters into it, though, and I find his work shabby.[76]

Michals' appraisal of Warhol conveys the two artists' differing valuation and understanding of the history and purpose of art, as well as their dissimilar social ambitions and interest in monetary reward.

Many writers have facilitated the negative view of Warhol that Michals came to hold of him, a view that flattens Warhol, as I noted above, into a caricature of himself. Much of the literature on Warhol does precisely this, and Warhol encouraged such misrepresentations in order to remain elusive and private while being so public. Moreover, such distortions of his personality and intelligence were easy to achieve by merely truncating or selectively quoting from his comments, or presenting his ideas out of context. Consider the case of Alan R. Pratt's introduction to *The Critical Response to Andy Warhol* (1996). Pratt writes:

> Warhol, if nothing else, has played an important role in acquainting us with the seemingly impenetrable ambiguity which is at the center of the postmodern experience. . . . He once told Bob Colacello that 'Criticism is so old fashioned. Why don't you just put in a lot of gossip'.[77]

Pratt quotes this phrase from Colacello's book *Holy Terror* (1990), which is about Warhol. But what Pratt leaves out of Warhol's comment is far more interesting that what he includes. Here is the full story that Colacello told. Colacello had been repeatedly conferring with Warhol about a potential contract from the Dutton publishing house to write a book on Warhol's films. As the self-appointed mentor and employer of Colacello (who was then a recently minted PhD from Columbia University), Warhol considered the project to be "wasting" Colacello's time, and urged Colacello instead to sell ads for *Interview* magazine. "That's the way to become rich, Bob," Warhol advised the younger man.[78] In many subsequent conversations, Warhol continued to resist the idea that Colacello write about his films. When Colacello reminded him that Dutton "wants more criticism" in the book, Warhol responded: "Oh, really. But criticism is so old-fashioned. Why don't you just put in a lot of gossip about Glenn [O'Brien] and Jude." Colacello persisted: "I think they want a lot of gossip about you, Andy." Again Warhol avoided the topic: "Oh, really. So what film did you see today?"[79]

This exchange exposes not only how Pratt edited the Warhol quote to confirm a hackneyed view of the artist as a "postmodernist," but also how he missed the point of Warhol's masterful use of circuitous inversion, his method for arriving at "What?" Leading Colacello in a convoluted dialogue that wrapped back on itself, Warhol suggested writing about gossip as a means to suspend Colacello's request to write about his films—and, while deflecting his attention away from those films, he also asked Colacello about what film he had seen that day, in order to move the discussion away from the publisher's supposed interest in the gossip about Warhol. Such are the means by which Warhol deferred the totality of facts at the same time as he continuously interrogated them. Facts determined what the case might be for him, and "what" it was not.

## AMERICA

"Buying is much more American than thinking and I'm as American as they come," Warhol announced with characteristic irony at the beginning of "Underwear Power."[80] In this statement he reinforced the view, held by art historians, critics, friends, and the public alike, that he was mercenary and superficial. Paul Alexander, one of Warhol's biographers, reinforced this perception when he wrote: "Warhol embraced [a] love of capitalism" and was "possessed by the idea [of] accumulating wealth."[81] If Warhol was a capitalist obsessed by wealth, then that drive must be understood in the context of the real poverty he had endured as a child growing up during the Great Depression. His father worked the coal mines, and after he died in 1942 from drinking poisoned water, the family "existed from that time on or near the subsistence level."[82] When Warhol moved to New York at the age of twenty-one, he continued to live a meager existence through the 1950s, first living with the painter Philip Pearlstein and his wife and then, after his mother arrived in 1952, renting an apartment and, for a time, sharing its one bed with her.[83] At the same time, he worked in the "supremely capitalistic, power-hungry and highly competitive world" of advertising, design, and fashion celebrated in the 2007 television series *Mad Men*. Warhol put it this way: "Life and living influence me more than particular people. People in general influence me."[84] In this environment, Crone points out, "Warhol must have seen how men are used as products—how their characters and values are bought and sold as objects."[85] As for his outlook on buying, comments Warhol made in *The Philosophy of Andy Warhol* suggest that he had a much more negative view of Americans' reputation for buying than has previously been acknowledged; and as Benjamin H. D. Buchloh pointed out in another context, Warhol repeatedly defended "an artistic culture [against] the incessantly expanding and encroaching forms of a proto-totalitarian consumption."[86] That he was "as American as they come" is emblematic of Warhol's gift for saying one thing and meaning quite another.

Something closer to the character of Warhol's inclinations seems to have been that he preferred thinking to buying, and that, as the child of first-generation Eastern European immigrants, he was not so "American" after all. Such inferences become clearer in a few sentences in his chapter "Underwear Power." Warhol begins: "In Europe and the Orient people like to trade—buy and sell, sell and buy—they are basically merchants." Then he adds:

> Americans are not so interested in selling—in fact, they'd rather throw out than sell. What they really like to do is buy—people, money, countries.[87]

Withering and caustic as only he could be, here Warhol bared a deeply disparaging view of Americans as a people for whom buying was a game of menacing acquisition and power, as compared to Europeans and Asians, who, he imagined, traded for the sport of exchange. These salvos might be considered Warhol's shot across the stern, rather than the bow, of his literary ship, firing his truths in the final chapter of *The Philosophy of Andy Warhol*.

However critical of the United States parts of *The Philosophy* are, Warhol especially displayed his acidic view of Americans in *The Andy Warhol Diaries*. For example, in writing about the lack of substantive critical reception for his film *Bad* (1977), he observed:

> The reviews came from England and they were bad for *Bad*. Stupid people like Frank Rich [then film critic for *Time* magazine and *The New York Post*] can write four pages on some nothing movie, but about *Bad* they just describe what it is and leave it at that. Don't they know what their job is? To say what something means?[88]

Here Warhol charged critics to do their "job" properly by directing their attention to the "what" of a work of art. Rather than Warhol's *Diaries* being "bitchy" or merely "gossiping" in tone as many critics have described the book, a closer reading discloses Warhol as continuously searching for the content and value of art, events, and ideas, and contemptuous of those who failed to grapple with their nature, scope, and significance. To wit, he snipped cruelly about Brigid

Berlin (better known as Brigid Polk, one of his "superstars"): "She's so boring to talk to—she never does anything, she never thinks anything, she just lies there in bed in her room at the George Washington Hotel and waits for the fat to roll off."[89] After attending a party at Norman Mailer's home in December 1976, and before going on to list topics of conversation at the gathering, Warhol observed: "Wall to wall, it was an intellectual party like from the sixties."[90] In contrast to those who claim that Warhol barely spoke, or that he conversed only in monosyllabic exclamations, art dealer Paula Cooper described him as "a charming and interesting conversationalist," a view which suggests that Warhol talked when he felt that someone was worthy of discussion.[91]

In addition to being critical of nonthinkers, Warhol derided those whose cultural sophistication did not, in his view, befit their social status. After a visit to Dustin Hoffman's home on December 21, 1976, and a tour conducted for him by the actor, Warhol recounted: "Dustin [was] really nervous about his house, and he was taking me around and showing me every little thing. His taste was oak, but not good oak, so it was funny."[92] For Warhol, who rigorously studied society, culture, and class divisions, "funny" did not connote a benign state of affairs. As Koch once observed, Warhol's humor was "sly."[93] He certainly displayed this cunning in his description of Hoffman, a portrait meant to expose the star as lacking in taste. Furthermore, Warhol also had no patience for a New York society matriarch who demonstrated a lack of discrimination, a woman who was otherwise known for her authority on gardening and was named to the International Best Dressed List Hall of Fame in 1959. "Went out to Westbury to C. Z. Guest's for lunch," he wrote of Christmas Day 1976. "You'd think with all c. z.'s involvement with flowers and gardening that she'd have real stuff, but when you looked close the wreaths and things were half plastic." Examining everything closely, Warhol was repulsed when "C. Z gave everyone her bug repellent for gifts."[94] Warhol's embrace of "good oak" and his desire to experience "real stuff" (even while scavenging for "used jewelry") divulge his search for what mattered, had substance, and promised consequence.

However critical, Warhol saved his full rancor for his penultimate book, *America* (1985), published just two years before his untimely death.[95] *America* also came out during a period during which Warhol's "standing as a 'serious' artist remained problematic" even though the sales for his work were "as strong as ever."[96] The collector Jason Rubell remembers that as a boy, he overheard someone at a party at his parents' home in the early 1980s insisting, "Warhol is no longer making relevant art." For Rubell, this opinion did not match the admiration shown by such young artists as Keith Haring, Jean-Michel Basquiat, and Julian Schnabel, all of whom respected Warhol and sought him out.[97] Nonetheless, the assessment of Warhol during this period has changed little over the past twenty-plus years, judging from comments Helen Molesworth made about the artist in 2012. "By the 1980s Andy Warhol was no longer producing advanced work," she wrote, even if "in 1989 he was the subject of a full-blown retrospective at the Museum of Modern Art in New York."[98] Molesworth dismissed the positive reception of the exhibition "by the 1980s art world" as merely the result of "the Warholian proposition of appropriation."[99] But this view does not account for Warhol's cachet among young, hip New York artists, among whom his unique contribution to the issues raised by appropriation, namely that he had started to plagiarize himself rather than pirate from other artists, was not lost. Warhol's self-appropriation was in direct disapproving response to the way in which Elaine Sturtevant had borrowed his work, beginning in 1965.[100] By appropriating his own art, Warhol resisted Sturtevant's mining of it, and artists of the graffiti art generation admired him for remaking himself by tagging himself.

It was in such a context that Warhol brought out *America*, his photographic essay and text on the nation.[101] *America* features black-and-white photographs that homogenize an otherwise diverse assortment of people and things, images that override the jacket's claim that Warhol had "nothing less than a passionate love affair with the United States." In *America*, Warhol betrays a level of enmity for the country that was seldom more transparent, even considering his 1962 *Death and Disaster* series, or his works from 1963 like *Birmingham Race Riot* and *Electric Chair*. While the chapter titles of *America* are mundane, ranging from "Window Shopping" to "Natural History," the content and inference of his photographs, coupled with his short texts, are anything but genial. While being candid photographs, most of the images are not of celebrities and are far from being "paparazzi-style photographs," as one reviewer described them.[102] Warhol's images in *America* portray a country that is a complex amalgam generally characterized by its lack of dignity, something Warhol abhorred.

In *America*, Warhol pictures gaudy wrestlers and other kinds of garishly dressed entertainers, as well as extravagant sporting events. He exposes the bathing suit–clad buttocks of female beauty contestants lined up like pins in a bowling alley, or like the rows and rows of cheap candy he photographed, from Dots, Whoppers, and PomPoms to CareFree chewing gum. Pictures of ordinary people appear alongside images of actors, artists, and intellectuals belonging to Warhol's circle in the 1980s in places from Montauk and Louisville to Aspen and Hollywood.[103] Dogs also populate the book—Warhol loved dogs—and his photographs of several canines are attentive to the personality of each animal. Race is also a prevailing theme in *America*, as Warhol features images of black and white couples, black and white toddlers, a black toddler wearing a dapper black and white outfit, and a photograph of two black Raggedy Ann dolls. Homelessness is an even more prominent theme in *America*. Warhol begins the chapter entitled "Editorial" with three photographs of homeless people accompanied by the observation: "They guess that there are between 300,000 and two million people living on the streets in America." With typical understatement and characteristic penetrating observation, Warhol added: "A World War II hero froze to death in a park across the street from the White House." Then Warhol gets to his point, the "what" he relentlessly exposes in *America*: "This country is so rich. And I think I see more homeless people on the street every month. How can we let this keep happening?"[104]

The remainder of the eclectic chapter is devoted to money and style, the very preoccupations that occlude attention to issues like homelessness and social isolation. In turning to these topics, Warhol concentrates on outlandish outfits, like that of a man in snakeskin chaps and long fringed gloves, with a huge python draped around his shoulders, and his ass exposed with a G-string wedged between his flexed, muscular buttocks. A naked woman, wearing a transparent net dress and a pair of white gloves, holds an incongruous little black clutch. Where images of the American upper crust appear in this chapter, Warhol presents it as combining tasteless ostentation with displays of exorbitant wealth, celebrity, and power. These photographs juxtapose the nation's tawdry underbelly with exhibitions of raw skin, from overweight and hungry flesh to the hypertrophy of over-exercised bodies. Warhol's parting comment in "Editorial" is on the superficiality of American culture: "I guess nowadays it takes too long to get to know someone's personality and you have to be able to decide fast whether someone's worth your time and trouble."[105]

Warhol opens the book with the sentence "America really is The Beautiful"—a text that appears next to his photograph of a looming, phallic Washington Monument, forecasting the book's overarching attention to sex. The final chapter, entitled "Life," focuses on photographs of children: a white baby with a quizzical expression playing on the floor next to a minimalist sculpture; pictures of infants being held in odd, uncomfortable positions and slumped in strollers; and preschoolers rolling around on the floor of a hallway. One child wears a T-shirt imprinted with Keith Haring's famous *Radiant Baby* drawing, reminding viewers of the path from innocence to AIDS. The chapter ends with twin toddlers seated in a two-seated stroller, looking worried. Their expressions reinforce Warhol's closing text, which is worth quoting in full. Beginning with a deadpan irony that underscores his view of the nation as xenophobic and racist, he comments:

> People have come up to me and said, "You must be the most American artist," and I've read others who think I'm "un-American." Since all of us come from somewhere else—even the Indians came over from Asia a long time ago—I don't see where anybody can draw the line at being "more American," even though they always keep trying with ideas like "I must be more American than she is because my family came over on the Mayflower," or "I'm more American because I'm blonde and blue-eyed and live in the Midwest," or "We're more American than they are because we can speak English." It used to be that we let anyone come to America who wanted to because we needed them to build the skyscrapers and the train tracks and do all the dirty work that the people who were already here didn't want to do. And now they say that with high unemployment we shouldn't be letting anybody else in, and we should kick out anyone who isn't here strictly legally.[106]

The astonishing aspect of this excerpt is how little has changed between 1985, the date of the book's publication, and 2014, the date of this writing.

Following this commentary, Warhol offers an even more unabashed opinion, for one who assiduously avoided communicating his true thoughts:

> But it seems to me that we're still having the immigrants do the work that "Americans" don't want to do. When I was in California I found out that people were learning Spanish so they could talk to their maids, and that all the people doing the really boring jobs in the electronics industry were immigrants. And if unemployment is so bad that we can't really afford the new people coming in, then why are all the maids Spanish, and how come there's a new Korean greengrocer opening in New York every month, and why do the Mexicans keep risking their lives and being thrown in jail to cross the border and get work in the U.S.?[107]

In the second-to-last paragraph, Warhol brings readers close to an understanding of his genuine sense of illegitimacy as an "American":

> I guess it's part of every country that if you're proud of where you live and think it's special, then you want to be special for living there, and you want to prove you're special by comparing yourself with other people. Or maybe you think it's so special that certain people shouldn't be allowed to live there, or if they do live there that they shouldn't say certain things or have certain ideas.

At the close of the last chapter, Warhol repeats his emphasis from the beginning:

> But this kind of thinking is exactly the opposite of what America means. We all came here from somewhere else, and everybody who wants to live in America and obey the law should be able to come too, and there's no such thing as being more or less American, just American.[108]

The rare stridency Warhol permitted himself in *America* exposed his exasperation and disappointment in the United States. His photograph of a huge industrial complex, accompanied by his commentary, especially conveys his disenchantment:

> Now it seems like nobody has big hopes for the future. We all seem to think that it's going to be just like it is now, only worse. But who's to say that this idea is any more realistic than dreaming about robots?[109]

These statements represent another aspect of Warhol's "What?" two years before his untimely death in 1987, when he consigned what had been his hope to the perfunctory reality of "robots." Child of immigrants, Warhol had single-mindedly pursued his hope to make a living in New York, to be accepted as an artist, to become rich and famous, to be loved, and to be "just American." While

Warhol succeeded in many of his "hopes," the last two eluded him. Charles Lisenby rejected his love, and this devastated Warhol, hindering his willingness to be vulnerable to intimacy even with his last long-term partner, Jed Johnson, with whom he spent some twelve years until the early 1980s. Although the critic Marjorie Miller, in a review of *America*, compared Warhol to "Will Rogers with echoes of Mark Twain" for his "truth-telling oratory style,"[110] a description that Tom Crow would repeat a year later in an essay on the artist,[111] these encomiums are about as close as Warhol ever got to being "just American."

## A QUEER RUTHENIAN HOARDER

Neither a Rogers nor a Twain, Warhol was a Ruthenian. "What?" For Warhol, being a Ruthenian meant: "I am from nowhere."[112] He was right. Elaine Rusinko explains, "Carpatho-Rusyns, also known as Rusyns, Rusnaks, Carpatho-Russians, and Ruthenians, are a stateless people, whose homeland today straddles the borders of five countries in east-central Europe—Ukraine, Slovakia, Romania, Hungary, and Poland (where they are known as Lemkos)."[113] Warhol's assertion, she adds, "has become a symbol of the people, who can equally be said to be 'from nowhere'—or at least from no easily identifiable cultural space."[114] "Nowhere" began for Warhol's parents in Miková, a hamlet in the former Austro-Hungarian Empire, then a village in Oslovakia and a town in Slovakia since 1993. This origin story contributed to Warhol's own sense of being odd. His Eastern European Ruthenian roots forever precluded him from being "just American," and equally betrayed his claim to be "as American as they come." Many of Warhol's closest associates suggest that his mother's use of the Ruthenian language in the home accounted for the artist's odd speech patterns and unease in writing and speaking.

A Ruthenian misfit and a visible queer in the homophobic USA, Warhol was a double interloper, as his multiplied self-portraits seem to index. Estranged from America, he continually tried to come to terms with the identity of the nation in his art, as much as he coped with being rejected by gay artists whom he admired, like Robert Rauschenberg and Jasper Johns, who did not befriend him in the late 1950s because he was too "swish."[115] In self-defense, Warhol became even more nelly. Exaggerating what he refused to deny, Warhol paraded his homosexuality and should, I would argue, be acknowledged as a leader by example in the struggle for gay rights.[116]

In this sense, Warhol defied the homophobia of the 1950s, "arguably the single most actively homophobic decade in American history," Jonathan Katz has written, adding, "queers who hoped to survive it had to constantly negotiate the danger of self-disclosure."[117] Steve Cox observed that Warhol as a "homosexual man . . . was always outside, no matter how much the world embraced him."[118] Nonetheless, Warhol's "instinctively insubordinate, transgressive qualities as an artist [shaped how] his (queer) fearlessness in the face of the prevailing heteronormative, macho climate helped to usher in new perspectives in American culture."[119] In the fashionable subculture of 1960s New York, such a "survival strategy," as Simon Watney described it,[120] would be dubbed "camp." "Mr. Warhol is high camp," Marianne Hancock wrote in 1965. "His name pulls."[121] Susan Sontag famously historicized the term in a 1964 *Partisan Review* essay, defining camp as "a certain mode of aestheticism [and of] seeing the world as an aesthetic phenomenon. . . . not in terms of beauty, but in terms of the degree of artifice, of stylization."[122]

Warhol began cultivating this artifice in college, as photographs of him posing with overtly fey hand gestures and carefully struck nonchalant facial expressions suggest. Watney is quick to point out that even though studied, Warhol's behavior was "not altogether voluntary or conscious," but rather the result of "queer experience," dating from his attraction to wearing "his mother's clothes from an early age."[123] In this observation, Watney anticipates what Ann Cvetkovich would later categorize as the behavior of "fellow travelers," who comprise the corpus of "queer theory and trauma theory" and whose "affective experience . . . falls outside of institutionalized or stable forms of identity or politics."[124] Cvetkovich uses the term "trauma" to describe queer experience, a term that only began to appear in the literature on Warhol in the 1990s.

Whether it was the result of his "affective experience" or of the cultural changes in the 1980s, Warhol would, during the next decade of his life, be decidedly alone despite, or perhaps in a manner exacerbated by, his typically heavy socializing schedule. Moreover, according to his archivist John W. Smith, Warhol had taken to "living in two rooms" of his huge townhouse, because his "collection had taken over everything else." Edward Hayes told *New York Magazine* in 1988 that "you had to climb over things" to move through the house.[125] "After a while—especially near the end," Smith added, Warhol "was feeling extremely overwhelmed by all the stuff he had."[126] Smith understood Warhol's collecting to be "a form of artistic practice" with underlying "aesthetic and emotional choices."[127] While it reflected his artistic interests, collecting for Warhol was also intimately related to shopping, which he did during his daily morning walks, strolls that also enabled him to remain apace of local events and to survey the city for what he called his "art projects." Warhol was also a familiar face at auction houses and he frequented antique stores, purchasing all kinds of objects, many selected by category, including photographs of movie stars (which he had collected since childhood), cookie jars, Fiestaware,[128] Russel Wright dinnerware, American folk art, Native American rugs and vessels, Federal-era furniture, Art Deco furniture, silver, and jewelry, among other items. On weekends he went to flea markets. Referring to Warhol's compulsion to collect, Joseph Ketner described him as an "image machine . . . chronically obsessive [and with a] compulsion to produce and to possess cultural artifacts [that] established new extremes of obsessive behavior in the visual arts."[129]

Yet as much as his shopping was a means to evaluate the object-world, Warhol did not respect American habits of "buying," as I have noted above—which makes his compulsive shopping even a more poignant a sign of his loneliness. After his death, it was discovered that he had left many of his packages unopened, merely stashing them in the townhouse. It took "four curators . . . months [to go] through the items, cataloguing more than 6,000 pieces ranging from cookie jars to Salvador Dali and Norman Rockwell paintings."[130] Moreover, Jed Johnson remembered that in 1975, after Warhol purchased his five-story Georgian-style brownstone at 57 East Sixty-sixth Street, he lavished Johnson with funds to decorate their home, and then invited personalities like Truman Capote to dinner parties. Very soon, however, Warhol tired of the parties and told Johnson that having people in the house made him "uncomfortable." As the artist became increasingly private, the "stately rooms increasingly became storerooms."[131]

Given these conditions, it must now be said that Warhol had become a hoarder. His "emotional choices" (as John W. Smith described them) were increasingly dictated by his psychopathology. Far from eager to exhibit his collection, as collectors are wont to do, Warhol was secretive about his hoarding, even failing to enjoy the objects he purchased and leaving them wrapped. In addition, Jed Johnson remembered that Warhol "kept most of the rooms [in the mansion] locked," and that he "had a routine":

> [He would] walk through the house every morning before he left, open the door of each room with a key, peer in, then relock it. Then at night when he came home he would unlock each door, turn the light on, peer in, lock up, and go to bed.[132]

Many of his biographers have described Warhol at this time as "paranoid," increasingly eccentric, and suspicious.[133] Indeed, he also hoarded money and hid stashes of it in the straw mattress that he had especially made for his bed. Warhol told Johnson: "You only feel as rich as the money you have in your pocket or under your mattress."[134]

Rich, Warhol was. Safe, he was not. Although poverty continued to contribute to his fears, Warhol's hoarding of pleasure objects and money cannot only be attributed to the acute deprivation of his childhood, as he also hoarded information, photographs, and ephemera. Few realize that Warhol made photography his central artistic activity during the last twelve years of his life. Most know that he stockpiled audiotapes before he took up the camera, but few know that he then accumulated over more than one hundred thousand photographs as records of the people and places that occupied his daily activities. "With his compulsively collecting eye," William Ganis remembered, Warhol "captured images of hundreds of signs, from storefronts to hand-written posted warnings," and he often would film such things as "every inch of a hotel room, men urinating, snapshots of other framed visual works, and monumental statuary."[135] His "time capsules" were a means to accumulate transient things, a practice that paralleled his compulsive buying routines. Warhol stashed newspaper clippings and photographs related to his art and career in boxes along with "over 99% of all the items that he was constantly being sent or given."[136] He amassed so much in the "time capsules" that Erin Byrne, a researcher working at the Andy Warhol Museum, explained that "it took three weeks, eight employees and over 80 archival folders" to record and file the contents of only "Trunk 1."[137]

As Colacello explained, Warhol's "constant taping and picture taking gave Andy a role to play at . . . parties . . . that put more distance between him and the other players."[138] The result was that these activities "made the stars feel more star-like to have Andy lurking on the edge of the action, stealing glances through his Minox . . . but it also put them off, tired them out, made them weary of Andy and his presumptuous intrusiveness."[139] As I have discussed, despite longing for connection, Warhol was emotionally challenged by interpersonal relationships, and this found him either voluntarily or involuntarily disconnected while constantly surrounded by people. But his ability to be both present and dissociated implies much more. This facility is typical of the precarious balance that trauma poses every day to the traumatized, who may not remember the original trauma, but also may not remember the events of their ordinary everyday lives. Dissociation offers protection and relief from all aspects of reality, and permits a traumatized subjectivity to float in the comfort of not feeling anything, including either pleasure or pain.

Coupling his mania for shopping with his recording and photographing, his "time capsules," and his self-representations as an ephemeral, incorporeal, and simultaneously multiplied being, Warhol's reality suggests just the opposite of Truman Capote's now famous description of the artist as "a sphinx with no secret."[140] On the contrary, Warhol was riddled with secrets and enigmas that perhaps not even he could retrieve or remember. This may have accounted in part for his comment that he "prefer[ed] to remain a mystery," to which he added:

> I never like to give my background and, anyway, I make it up different every time I'm asked. It's not just that it's part of my image not to tell everything, it's just that I forget what I said the day before and I have to make it all up over again.[141]

That Warhol "forgot" what he said from day to day was probably true. A fuller picture of his traumatized psyche appears, especially when considered together with Foster's observation that Warhol warded off "traumatic significance" while remaining "open to it," defended against "traumatic affect" while "producing" it in his art, and avoided speaking about death.[142] All these aspects of Warhol's personality have sources in psychic numbing and detachment, along with the paradoxical aspect of hypervigilance, among a host of other symptoms. Susan Jarosi has analogized the overlapping and contradictory realities of trauma in Warhol's work to the multiple and simultaneous imagery permitted by holography, and she proposed a "holographic model" for reading the ways in which Warhol's work evinces trauma.[143]

Returning to Warhol's hoarding, which seems to have been primarily compensatory, filling in the gaps of dissociation, fragmented memory, and loneliness, it is also critical to acknowledge that in all this forgetting and accumulating, Warhol found an astonishing means to resolve his chronic memory deficits and aloneness. He transferred the work of a damaged memory to the technology of memory production: a tape recorder, a camera, and an archive, using these substitutes as sites of memory. When Sontag asked him why he took so many pictures, Warhol responded: "A picture just means I know where I was every minute. That's why I take pictures. It's a visual diary."[144] Suffering the incapacity to live in his experiences, Warhol did more than merely survive. He persevered as an individual and an artist, deploying intervening mnemonic devices as art, an ingenious technique that enabled him to be present while also being psychologically absent and emotionally numb. This solution protected him against the threat of further psychical pain and disappointment, even as he found a creative means for deflecting his suffering, and even if those means only provided temporary relief and comfort. In what could be interpreted as a related explanation for his habits of hoarding, Warhol explained: "People sometimes say that the way things happen in the movies is unreal, but actually it's the way things happen to you in life that's unreal."[145] "Real life" was for Warhol "unreal." To exist, it had to be amassed. Pictures, voices, objects became metonyms of his life, prompts that reminded him of what had "happened to" him.

Ketner points out that Warhol "began his photographic image diary, his written diary, and his *Time Capsules*, all around 1976,"[146] and that his photographs provided him "with the details of his experiences that . . . act as a catalyst for the mind's eye."[147] This period also marks the aftermath of his mother's death, in late November 1972, and the increase in Warhol's hoarding. Warhol was not present when his mother died, and he did not go to her funeral, explaining to his brother Paul that he wanted "to remember Mother as she was."[148] Having lived with her most of his life, Warhol was adrift in her absence, and his nephew, who went to stay with him for a month after her death, observed:

> He almost had a nervous breakdown. . . . He had a handkerchief of [Julia's] and he didn't want anybody to see him, but he'd take off his wig and he put the handkerchief on his head [and] he was very unhappy. He was like lost.[149]

Warhol never mentioned his mother's death, and even Jed Johnson, who was his partner at the time, did not find out for "many weeks" that she had died, reporting that he had known "Andy for twelve years and he never talked about anything personal to me, ever."[150] When people asked about Mrs. Warhola during this time, Warhol would say something like "Oh, she's fine."

Julia Warhola had provided a conflicting stability for the artist, with a foundation of emotional support that also included verbal and psychological abuse in the form of mixed messages, the kind of contradictory and confusing sense of self that the sociologist Gregory Bateson and his colleagues had described in 1956 as circumstances that could lead to schizophrenia, or to what today would be considered schizotypal thinking, originating in bad parenting, trauma, and other early-life disturbances.[151] It is also not inconsequential that soon after Julia's death, in late 1972, Koch's book *Stargazer* came out in 1973.[152] Compounding the loss of his now disembodied mother, Koch would describe Warhol as a narcissist who was "a phantom,"[153] "who absent[ed] himself,"[154] whose "pain [was] terrible," and who "*experiences himself as an absence* [Koch's emphasis]." That Koch wrote of how the narcissist condemned himself to "the damned"[155] may have further shocked the "exceedingly devout" Warhol, as John Richardson would describe the artist at his funeral.[156] The hoarding was the ultimate sign that Warhol's grip on himself had become increasingly more tenuous. Despite it all, Warhol carried on, and he had the intellectual power to deliver a terse, penetrating, and powerful response to Koch's book, which was printed on its back jacket cover: "*Stargazer* is to die over."[157]

## TO DIE OVER

Warhol did not write the familiar colloquialism "to die for," meaning that something is so good it is worth swooning about. He wrote, "to die over," suggesting that the book's probing invasiveness could cause one to die. Koch's incisive analysis troubled Warhol and may have tapped a part of his traumatic core, the black hole of dissociated memory often referred to in PTSD as a form of psychic death. Given that Koch's narrative brought Warhol to write that *Stargazer* was "to die over" suggests that Koch may have inadvertently authorized Warhol to consider the sources of his emotional turmoil, as the artist discusses his emotions in the first several pages of *The Philosophy of Andy Warhol*, which was published just two years after *Stargazer*. "Some critic called me the Nothingness Himself and that didn't help my sense of existence any."[158] Handling hurt with deadpan humor, and finishing off with a double entendre that hints at his spiritual belief in something other than "existence," Warhol adds: "Then I realized that existence itself is nothing and I felt better."[159] A few pages on, Warhol returns to the issue of existence, quipping that after he looks in the mirror and sees "nothing," he slips into his "BVDs," because "nudity is a threat to my existence."[160]

Undoubtedly, the 1970s were a turning point for Warhol, escalated first by his mother's death and then by Koch's strong critique, both emotionally devastating events—"to die over"—and both precipitated by Warhol being shot on June 3, 1968.[161] While hospitalized after the shooting, Warhol "started to collect things again" after the nuns in the hospital got him "interested in collecting stamps . . . and coins again."[162] Recovering, but in continuous physical pain for the rest of his life, Warhol would describe the 1970s as "very empty."[163] All of these events bring him back, in chapter 1 of *The Philosophy*, to his childhood and the revelation of his "three nervous breakdowns [that] always started on the first day of summer vacation," and which permitted him "to spend all summer listening to the radio."[164] It is at this point that Warhol describes the attacks as "St. Vita-

Dance," the popular name for the involuntary jerky movements associated with what is now known as Sydenham's chorea, an affliction that commonly occurs in children between the ages of five and fifteen, and which presents as irregular, aimless, and rapid contractions of different muscles and excessive movement commonly located in the arm, hand, or face.[165] Although rheumatic fever may contribute to the disease, "any trauma, be it psychic or infectious, may precipitate an attack of chorea."[166] Consistently attributed to "psychical trauma, such as fright, acute worry, highly wrought anticipation, and bodily exhaustion,"[167] chorea has also been ascribed to "emotional stress" manifest in "obsessive, phobic and depressive" symptoms,[168] and compulsive behaviors including "cleaning, checking, repeating, counting, and hoarding,"[169] all of which have equally been diagnosed as "secondary schizophrenia."[170]

What prompted Warhol's original episodes of chorea is unknown, but he experienced many stressful and traumatic events as a child, beginning at the age of two, when his eyes swelled "so badly that his mother had to apply boric acid daily," followed by a fall at age four, which broke his right arm. The fracture went undetected "despite his complaints of pain," and the bone had to be rebroken and set "several months later."[171] That same year, when Warhol was sent to kindergarten, he was slapped by a little girl and became so distraught that Mrs. Warhola did not send him back to school.[172] Warhol became "glued to his mother's side," keeping "his head down . . . as if he were afraid of being hit."[173] Two years later, when he was six, Warhol contracted scarlet fever.[174] At eight he came down with Sydenham's chorea, which gave him the shakes.

> When he tried to write or draw on the blackboard [at school] his hand would shake, and the other boys laughed at him [and] began pushing him around and punching him. Andy became, once again, terrified of going to school. He grew increasingly disoriented, was easily provoked to tears, and found the simplest tasks, like tying his shoes or writing his name, difficult to coordinate.[175]

All of these experiences would have been enough to make a timid child more retiring. But the events that took place every other Sunday would have long-term ramifications. Julia Warhola and the family would visit Julia's sister on Pittsburgh's Northside, and the sisters would sing together and "read their letters from Europe [and] talk about Europe"; but sometimes Julia would begin to "cry [and would] sometimes [come] down with a migraine and [have] to be put to bed."[176] Being exposed to his overwrought mother disturbed the delicate Warhol. But another event he remembered would also traumatize him:

> The first time I ever knew about sex was in Northside, under the stairs, and they made this funny kid suck this boy off. I never understood what it meant. I was just sitting there watching.[177]

Bockris adds, "A friend in the art world would describe Warhol with less ingenuousness: 'Andy was the greatest voyeur I ever met. He was really interested in who did what to whom.'"[178] Warhol himself would quip that he would "rather watch somebody buy their underwear than read a book they wrote."[179]

Warhol's premature exposure to fellatio, to a sexuality that he "never understood" but "watched," is an unquestionable source for his lifelong dissociative behavior. As Freud categorically observed in "The Aetiology of Hysteria" (1896):

> At the bottom of every case of hysteria there are one or more occurrences of premature sexual experience, occurrences which belong to the earliest years of childhood. . . . Since infantile experiences with a sexual content could after all only exert a psychical effect through their memory-traces, would not this view be a welcome amplification of the finding of psycho-analysis which tells us that hysterical symptoms can only arise with the co-operation of memories? . . . The reaction of hysterics is only apparently exaggerated; it is bound to appear exaggerated to us because we only know a small part of the motives from which it arises."[180]

Bedridden with Sydenham's chorea, already traumatized by physical and psychical pain, and having witnessed sexuality that he could not comprehend, the child listened to the radio with "my un-cut-out cut-out paper dolls all over the [bed] spread and under the pillow," and "my Charlie McCarthy doll," elegantly dressed in a black tuxedo, bow tie, and white shirt with wing collar, shoes, top hat, and a monocle.[181] Charlie McCarthy was the dummy of the actor and ventriloquist Edgar Bergen, who had become famous in radio and movies and would later find fame on television. In 1937, Warhol listened to Bergen present new acts that included comedians, singers, rising movie stars, and celebrities including Clark Gable, Ginger Rogers, Barbara Stanwyck, and many others.[182] Movie and radio stars, celebrities, and talking dolls became the constructive mediums through which Warhol further dissociated, disconnecting from and escaping his immediate circumstances and anxiety, and entering the world of his own fantasy and desire. This make-believe surrogate world taught Warhol the art of cultural ventriloquism, minus the monocle.

Bockris described Warhol as a "two-sided character,"[183] and Koestenbaum agreed: "Andy . . . was two people, the invader who walked in, and the exile who walked out."[184] Warhol's friends also identified his duality. The "superstar" Ondine coined the name "Drella" for the aspects of Warhol's personality that combined Dracula and Cinderella. Lou Reed and John Cale used the name on their album *Songs for Drella*, written after Warhol's death and released in 1990. Drawing on personal memories of Warhol's relationship with the Velvet Underground, of the Factory, and of Warhol's life and behavior in general, the songs are stark reminders of Warhol's cruel (vampirelike) personality and its other side: the poor little boy who would become the prince of the art world.

Another source for Warhol's adaptation of dopplegängers was the Polish photographer Weegee (Arthur Fellig, 1899–1968), someone who was also interested in celebrity, violence, secrecy, and eroticism, and who was an Eastern European immigrant. Warhol "came into contact with [Weegee] in New York City in 1949 when he began work as a graphic artist for *Glamour*, *Vogue*, and *Seventeen* magazines," explains Kristen Hope Bigelow, also noting that these publications "simultaneously employed Weegee."[185] Warhol owned Weegee's book *Naked City* (1945), which Bigelow later discovered in the artist's library.[186] Weegee's images of spectacle and disaster appeared in major journals and newspapers, from *Journal America* and *The Daily Mirror* to *The New York Times*. Weegee also maintained a presence in Hollywood, where he made "portraits of film stars and fashionable night spots that he published in 1953 in *Naked Hollywood*." Weegee's publications "catapulted his works to the status of fine art" for his examination of "the glamour myth surrounding the film industry."[187] One of the most influential photojournalists of his time, and an artist obsessed with fame like Warhol, Weegee stamped the backs of his photographs: "Credit Photo by Weegee the Famous." Weegee would write in his 1961 memoir, *Weegee by Weegee*: "Crime was my oyster. . . . I was friend and confidant to them all: the bookies, madams, gamblers, call girls, pimps, con men, burglars and jewel fencers."[188] Warhol, too, befriended the sexual underworld and photographed the rich and famous.

Bigelow perceptively observed: "Weegee's major importance may reside in his influence on . . . Andy Warhol. . . . As voyeurs psychologically inhabiting the margins of society, both Weegee and Warhol paradoxically worked and lived at the cultural center of the social orders and practices they seemed to objectively observe."[189] Biglow also reminds us: "Weegee printed his negatives through screens, kaleidoscopes, and bubbled glass, resulting in a set of distorted images of movie sets and stars."[190] In addition, Weegee understood the power of television, and between 1957 and 1958 he "was a guest on five talk shows," prompting him to produce "a series of distorted photo-caricatures including images of Sid Caesar, Red Skelton, Jack Benny, and Lucille Ball, which were published as a spread in *Look* Magazine in 1957." Weegee influenced Warhol as much as Warhol's childhood memories were confabulations that materialized, in his person and in his art, as hybrids of the characters he adored. But none of these figures captured Warhol's traumatic subjectivity like "The Shadow," a metonymic form of identification that connected to but also screened his traumatic subjectivity.

## WARHOL'S SHADOWS

*Quam multa vident pictores in umbris et eminentia quae nos non videmus. (Painters see more in shadows and protrusions than we ever do.)*

CICERO, Accademica II. 20, 86

Warhol increasingly reproduced shadows. They appeared as heavy materialized shapes in the *Still Life* series (1975), the *Skulls* (1976), and the *Hammer and Sickle* series (1977), and also in his *Self-Portrait* (1978), a silkscreen picturing him from a photographic negative printed in white and gray, which created the impression of shadow twins. Between 1978 and 1979, he also produced 102 silk-screened and hand-painted canvases featuring distorted photographs of shadows. When exhibited at the Hirshhorn Museum in 2005, these works extended some 450 feet around the museum's circular second floor. The abstract forms in the *Shadow* paintings appear against brightly colored matte grounds and conjure the timeless abstraction of the shadow that has been the subject of philosophy at least since Plato.

The source of Warhol's *Shadows* is contested, Lynne Cooke writes, arguing that the most "persuasive" account of this body of works was "given by Warhol's studio assistant at the time, Ronnie Cutrone, who remembers Warhol asking him to take photographs of shadows generated by maquettes devised expressly to create abstract forms."[191] In a footnote, Cooke also states, "Other proposals include the shadow cast by an erect penis or by the Empire State Building."[192] Bob Colacello is the primary source of this latter claim, insisting that the paintings were based on the shadow cast by penises[193]—"erect uncircumcised penises."[194] Undeniably, Warhol was fixated on the penis; he started drawing the form in the 1950s, and photographed the form of the clothed and unclothed organ frequently throughout his life.[195] That the *Shadow* paintings may have represented to him the double of the organ is reasonable, especially recalling his comment that the pornographic photographs he left all over Colacello's desk in 1977 were "abstractions," and owing to the fact that he painted the *Oxidation* series between 1977 and 1978—works that indirectly evoked the phallus for being "piss" paintings.

Warhol may have provided another knowing clue to the source of the *Shadow* paintings when he posed for a photograph by Arthur Tress in front of his first installation of the *Shadows* at the Heiner Friedrich Gallery in New York City, in January 1979.[196] In the photograph, Warhol sits before six of the paintings, five of which were often also referred to as the "Empire State Building" (for their resemblance to its phallic architecture). Seated on a stool, Warhol stares at the camera. His left hand is on his hip, while his right hand holds what looks like a large level for picture hanging. He has positioned the long (perhaps thirty-six-inch), solid metal form between his legs at a right angle from his body, and he grasps it midway with his right hand in a gesture that suggests masturbation of a gargantuan penis. Warhol's expression is deadpan but for the slightest hint of a smirk.

Conflating the idea of the shadow of a penis in his abstract *Shadow* paintings, and then making an erotic gesture while posing before the works, Warhol thrice repeated a reference to the phallus in three different forms: conceptually, visually, and in an action. Such repetition can be associated with the repetition that continually reoccurs until a part of dissociated trauma is identified, recognized, and remembered. Until that moment, an individual often repeats partial and vaguely remembered aspects of the traumatic event in an effort to recuperate its content and experience. While dissociation protects one from the psychic pain of the trauma, it also paradoxically renders one numb for being unable to recover enough of the event to reconcile its elements. In *Beyond the Pleasure Principle* (1920), Freud would describe this pattern of repetition as the subject's obligation "to *repeat* the repressed material as a contemporary experience instead of . . . *remembering* it as something belonging to the past. These reproductions, which emerge with such unwished-for exactitude, always have as their subject some portion of infantile sexual life."[197] Freud further theorized that the "compulsion to repeat" repressed painful experiences remained in conflict with "the pleasure principle," and eventually merged into the "death instinct." Quoting from Schopenhauer's *Parerga and Paralipomena* (Appendices and Omissions; 1851), Freud writes: "For him death is the 'true result and to that extent the purpose of life' while the sexual instinct is the embodiment of the will to live."

Despite Freud's eventual suppression of the "seduction theory," I have drawn on his original identification of the traumatic ramifications of exposure to early sexual experiences, as he was the first to identify the determining role of psychic death in trauma.[198] This focus remains foundational in contemporary trauma theory, especially as pioneered by the psychiatrist Robert Jay Lifton, who explains, in his model of the "*life/death paradigm and symbolization of the self*," that the repetition of "intrusive imagery" is an attempt to resolve the initial experience. Lifton writes: "One could define the traumatic syndrome as the state of being haunted by images that can neither be enacted nor cast aside, and with being 'stuck' or 'trapped in the trauma.'"[199] Repetition in this context is part of "the survivor . . . who has come into contact with death in some bodily or psychic fashion and has remained alive," and who often demonstrates "five characteristics of the survivor: death imprint; death guilt; psychic numbing; conflicts around nurturing and contagion; struggles with meaning."[200] Along with intrusive imagery, "doubling is another expression of these symptoms."[201]

Together with many other authors, I have found the imprint of death and doubling at the core of Warhol's art. I am arguing that primary among the contributing factors that forged his inner void was the experience of watching fellatio under the stairs at his aunt's home, an act that he did not understand as a child.[202] That Warhol was gripped by the concept of a shadow even as a boy appears related to its having become a sustaining metaphor in his art and for himself. Warhol sought out his shadows, became "the Shadow," and repeatedly pictured shadows, such as the shadow of death cast by the chair in his series *Electric Chair* (1964).

Victor I. Stoichita writes that the shadow has been deployed since the Greeks to replace the individual as a possible "mnemonic aid: of making the absent become present."[203] The shadow may be expiatory, having the power to atone for something, as it "projects the model onto the wall and reduces the being to an appearance [which] is not 'the body'[;] it is by double virtue the other of the body (like a 'specter,' like a 'head')."[204] Noting that the Greeks symbolically linked soul and a person's double to the shadow, [205] Stoichita also notes that it was "clearly Plato's intention to place the shadow at the origins of the epiphenomenal duplication, before the image in the mirror."[206] In essence, he adds, for Plato mimesis is nothingness, whether in the painted image, the mirror reflection (*eidola*), or the shadow (*phantasmata*)."[207]

These observations about the nature of shadows, recall Freud's essay "Das Unheimliche" (The Uncanny; 1919), in which he identifies the terror of the double image:

> For the "double" was originally an insurance against the destruction of the ego, an "energetic denial of the power of death," as [Otto] Rank says; and probably the "immortal" soul was the first "double" of the body. . . . Such ideas . . . have sprung from the soil of unbounded self-love, from the primary narcissism which dominates the mind of the child and of primitive man. But when this stage has been surmounted, the "double" reverses its aspect. From having been an assurance of immortality, it becomes the uncanny harbinger of death . . . The "double" has become a thing of terror.

Warhol's shadow was a thing of terror and beauty, his ultimate trope of circuitous inversion for how the shadow embodied his own sense of being a disembodied sign for a sequence of signifiers that became his art. Like "the Shadow," Warhol cultivated the hypnotic ability to cloud minds, drawing attention to himself as a means to draw it away, warding off the "What?" of his own "forever."

# 7:47 a.m. (The Traumatic Visual Vocabulary of Maurice Benayoun's So.So.So. Somebody, Somewhere, Some Time) (2011)[1]

*So.So.So.* takes place at 7:47 a.m., the precise moment when "everything starts to go awry. . . . in a crisis-ridden world seeping into our daily lives," Maurice Benayoun states.[2] The time 7:47 a.m. is "Time," which functions as a verb in the title. It ignites simultaneous but different experiences in three locales: Paris, Rungis,[3] and Praslin.[4] There, somewhere, somebody, and some appear and disappear in overlapping, intersecting, spherical panoramas, a temporality enabled by VR binoculars that visually augment the ambiguous story of people, places, and things that viewers encounter in this interactive installation. As the interweaving of sights and events progresses, diachronic sequencing unexpectedly interrupts the synchronic overlay of visual fragments already seen. These residual images are superimposed from retinal memory like flashbacks on the seminarrative structure of the film, fusing with it to create new hybrid sequences of otherwise involuntary image fragments that reproduce the unique mnemonic vocabulary of each viewer's visual engagement with the work. But the momentarily witnessed flashbacks can neither be sustained nor voluntarily summoned back, and while an image may repeatedly return, the viewer/creator of such memories lacks the power over what will be seen, recorded, or remembered, and what will be witnessed again.

The visual vocabulary of *So.So.So.* establishes an increasingly overwhelming kaleidoscopic pictorial domain that, while being partially of one's own neurobiological responses, is nevertheless completely out of one's control. The only way to turn off the cascading, unpredictable flashbacks is to take off the binoculars. But nine years after seeing *So.So.So.*, I still remember the beautiful bride in an indeterminate context, along with stacks of magazines, cars on a street, and many other images, especially a sandy beach with pristine water that is synesthetically heightened by electroacoustic composer Jean-Baptiste Barrière's music (figure 27). Barrière's otherwise repetitive sound transforms into an evocative sonic mimetics in response to particular sequences, as when footprints in that sand lead the eye to the sea where a man swims. During this moment, something like the sound of waves breaks the abstract music, invoking a hypnotic and seductive experience that simultaneously threatens to produce panic.

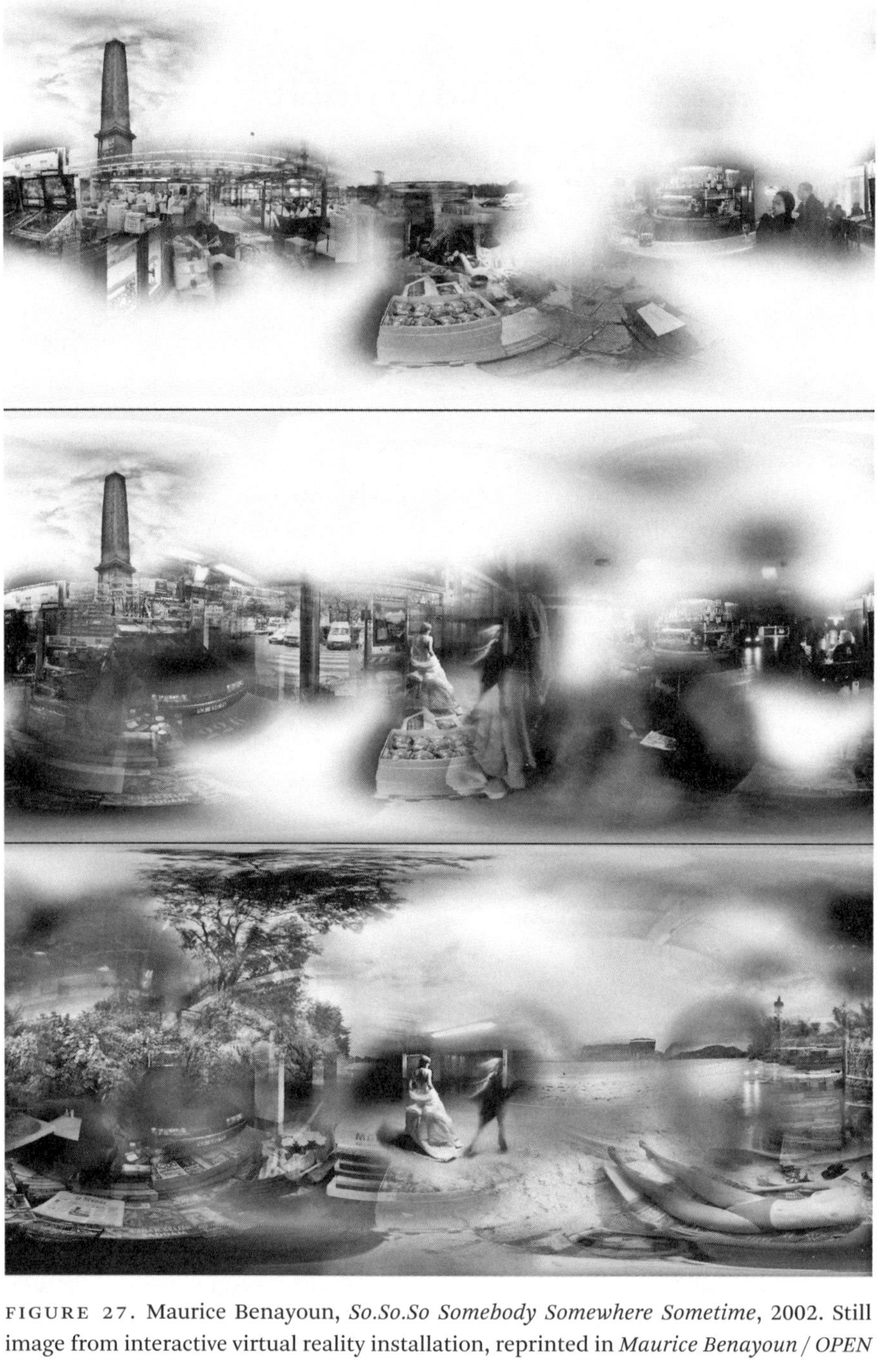

FIGURE 27. Maurice Benayoun, *So.So.So Somebody Somewhere Sometime*, 2002. Still image from interactive virtual reality installation, reprinted in *Maurice Benayoun / OPEN ART 1980–2010* (Paris: CDA d'Enghien and Les Nouvelles éditions Scala, 2011). Courtesy of the artist.

The alarm at 7:47 a.m. reverberates from what can only be described as a kind of claustrophobic agitation, a response to the accumulation of visual sensations and sounds, a response that verges on paranoia. This persecution delusion derives from the events and images, "seeping into our daily lives," that contribute to the discontinuity of the self created from the real fact of being in and yet not a part of the world leaking into and constructing consciousness. Locked in animal being, humanity remembers suffering and pain more than joy: a necessary component of the flight response and survival. Such primal states of mind are triggered in *So.So.So.* as Barrière's sound, coupled with Benayoun's hallucinogenic imagery and the viewer's own flashbacks, excite the unconscious while also awakening the rational mind with intrusive sounds "from far away: a sniper in Washington, Chechens in Moscow, a front page with Saddam Hussein close to the one with G. W. Bush or Charlie Chaplin playing a Dictator for light opera."[5]

Both a finite duration in and of the present and a repetition of the overwhelming infinite being of now, 7:47 a.m. is inescapable. It is also a quality of time "in between, not the night, not the day, not sleeping time, not working time," Benayoun observes.[6] As such, 7:47 a.m. is equally noun and verb, an uncanny juxtaposition of spaces that exist in photographs as places somewhere, in the presence of somebody, perhaps along with some (people), all of whom experience what Marianne Hirsch has called "postmemory" images.[7] Those inescapable pictures that pass from one generation to the next have created memories of events never experienced, but nonetheless remembered. In this regard, Siegfried Kracauer pointed out nearly a century ago that the institutionalization of historicist time was born in the same period as photography with its institutionalization of space. Both signify qualities of what I once termed "terminal culture,"[8] or what Kracauer observed as the way in which the fluidity of memory images is "at odds with photographic representation."[9] Some fifty years later, Roland Barthes would ask, "Is History not simply that time when we were not born?"—and then recall, "I could read my non-existence in the clothes my mother had worn before I can remember her."[10] The only meaning derived from such nonexistent life is that evoked in the photographic "prick," which, Barthes cautioned, "stings" the mind with the combined force of unconscious and conscious retinal memory. Such memory is the material of a psychic grammar, as each viewer's conscious gaze betrays and records his or her scopic desire but cannot contain that which returns as both pleasurable and unsettling visual memories. *So.So.So.* materializes the substance of the historical self as that which one is and is not.

The accumulation of historical time pervades *So.So.So.* as adverbial and adjectival emphasis for how Benayoun uses the English word "so," rather than its French equivalents (*tellement*, *également*, *donc*, *voilà pourquoi*, *ainsi*), to facilitate the work's repetitions and interruptions. "So" may emphasize;[11] describe circumstances;[12] suggest how something may be accomplished;[13] imply elements of degree or extent;[14] posit time, as in "subsequently" or "soon afterward";[15] introduce a logical conclusion;[16] or intensify a truth.[17] When this open, indefinite word "so" is deployed, its meanings multiply the affect of the overlay of images that are equally tripled in the title *So.So.So*. This multiplicity of visual and textual grammars contributes to the construction of the palimpsest that Benayoun builds of the "transient instant." The nature of such an instant can be definitive or ephemeral, that of a breakthrough or of an aporia, either of which appears belatedly and incompletely in the psychological processing of the fragmentary dynamics of traumatic memory.

Just such a definitive event is the crash of the Boeing 747 jet belonging to China Airlines, flight 611, which broke into pieces in midair on May 25, 2002, killing all 225 people aboard. This disaster occurred several months before Benayoun made *So.So.So*. In this sober context the number 747 is not only related to a factual occurrence but also may be linked to the conundrum of the palindrome: a numerical sequence akin to the linguistic equivalent of a kind of Möbius strip. The palindrome's self-referentiality redoubles the operations of traumatic dissociation that somatically stores memories of things seen and experienced. The number 747 may be said, then, to be linked metonymically to the etiology of trauma, as traumatized subjects often exhibit the symptom of repetitive counting, enacted as an obsessive and dissociative but impoverished effort of the unconscious to gain control over the uncontrollable return of distressing memories and images.

Together, the flashback and the palindrome, which are central to the traumatic visual and psychical operations of *So.So.So*., contribute to an archive of images and numbers that brings to mind the "prosthetic memory" identified by Jacques Derrida in *Archive Fever* (1996). But the act of counting and the archiving of numbers, while intended to ward off knowing, are overcome and exceeded by the onslaught of retinal memories in Benayoun's installation. Observing the inscription and residue of what is seen, reseen, and reviewed again in the scopic field, the viewer cannot avoid becoming the Lacanian subject who, gazing back, becomes both image and screen. In these ways Benayoun unseats, and simultaneously evinces, all attempts to avoid the contents of memory, incorporating viewers in a strategic collective experience that is both highly personal and intimately interactive.

Acts of viewing and participating in *So.So.So*. require thoughtful confrontation with the construction and representation of the politics of being at the core of aesthetics, as well as an acknowledgment of the inescapable endogenous and exogenous conditions of becoming, and the increasing traumatic incursion on consciousness of the "crisis-ridden world" that continually contributes to the formation and growth of cultures of trauma.

# Wangechi Mutu's Family Tree (2013)[1]

Listen to Binyavanga Wainaina, Kenyan author and winner of the prestigious Caine Prize for African Writing, commenting after an encounter with Wangechi Mutu's art. "Your power to rearrange what has been presented to control you is your powerful weapon," he explains, "for you can make what you want with your world."[2] While Wainaina implicitly nods to a plural "you," believing "us" able to transform the world, he refers directly to Mutu's resourceful invention of composite portraits of the metaphorical "we" that she continually reforms in images, objects, and actions. Mutu works in every medium to invent this hybrid, from drawing, painting, and collage to sculpture, installation, performance, and film. She cuts into what separates us with the precision of a surgeon before suturing our reconstruction from fragile visual slivers of the wounded family of humankind, already fragmented, deformed, and traumatized. This essay is about Mutu's two-decades-long visual analysis of world culture and its planetary rootedness in racial, sexual, economic, and national divides; war; and the violence of privilege. It is about Mutu's refusal to accept as invincible the conventions of otherness that have been culturally naturalized to isolate and conquer; it is about her exacting reconstruction of shared states of collective subjectivity and cultural agency; and it is about her effort to, in her words, "reclaim an imagined future."[3]

## INTERSUBJECTIVITY

"The idea of clear-cut binaries—African/European, archaic/modern, and religious/ pornographic, I've never really believed in that," Mutu once commented.[4] To undo these binaries, she fuses the history of colonialism and its iconographic shards of diaspora, displacement, migration, and globalization with images of cybernetic, postbiological, hyphenated black, brown, and white bodies. This approach to artmaking belongs to what Mary Louise Pratt described in 1991 as "arts of the contact zones" in which artists attend to the "social spaces where cultures meet, clash, and grapple with each other."[5] Mutu's collage and installation work delivers visual creolization as the corollary of "contact zones." In her construction of hybrid images of the family, Mutu pictures us, figure by figure, as prosthetic animals in all our contemporary creaturehood and bestiality, zoophiles morphed with English roses and African kings in a postcolonial rendition of natural curiosities and unnatural monstrosities.[6] Contrary to the suggestion that she aims to create "something that is whole," Mutu rejects myths of unity and attempts "remaking the world as we once all were/are, animal/ human/ multi-shaded."[7] This comment implies not homogeneity, but rather her acknowledgment of the infinite intertwining and fluidity of life, and it suggests the point of view from which she unites our thick, convoluted history.

Unencumbered by didacticism, and informed by theory without adhering to its dogmas, Mutu works with the cool reason of a world citizen and intellectual whose art embodies the cosmopolitan ideal about which H. G. Wells commented in 1939: "All history is against it. But all reality is for it."[8] What "reality" (namely the multiplicity of truths that comprise the real) is "for" is the ideal of intersubjectivity "across principles of subjectivity," as Peter Hitchcock put it in 2007.[9] Such an ideal is what Gayatri Spivak described when she wrote of a "planetarity" unity realized "through the transforming work of imagining the impossible other as that figured other imagines us."[10] This intersubjectivity is also the I/we that Jean-Luc Nancy has described as "being singular plural," and which Hitchcock has called "the logic of the both."[11] Merging subjectivities might produce the ideal of a multiethnic, multiracial, pluralistic amalgam of imperfect, eccentric composite beings that "the family" already is, but which it has yet to bring to full collective consciousness, social recognition, and political realization. Mutu's art is the pictorial embodiment of this ideal, one that pictures the awkward, failed, but philosophically moving attempt to arrive—even momentarily—at what must and can only be an image of constantly shifting needs, desires, identity, and knowledge in the effort to imagine the other imagining us.[12]

I introduce these diverse theoretical propositions in order to place Mutu's work squarely within the domain of a philosophical conversation on intersubjectivity, as well as to introduce them from the "logic of the both" to suggest that Mutu's art conveys visually how one might appear as concurrently individual and collective—not as collective in a parochial sense, but rather as simultaneously human, animal, vegetable, mineral, and more. At the same time, while it pictures an imaginary "us," Mutu's visual language is critical. Mutu scrutinizes theoretical, art historical, and curatorial traditions, constructs, and practices, and remains a trenchant producer of transracial, transsexual, transnational, cosmopolitan, and urban images of heterogeneity in which intersubjectivity is a give-and-take between singular and plural. In these ways, she avoids the danger of the "elision . . . by Western postmodernist theory of African artists living and working in the Western metropolis," which Okwui Enwezor has identified,[13] and the "mere rehash of entrenched modernist attitudes and methods" cloaked in new theoretical terms, which has been rebuffed by Olu Oguibe.[14] Just to pose the question of where an African artist is born, Oguibe insists, is to raise the specter of colonialism. Still—biography matters. Mutu's life appears embedded in her art, with stealth and multeity, but in her recent attention to the family tree she classifies the origins of her work as belonging definitively to Africa. Born in Nairobi, where she was educated, Mutu attended her last years of high school in Wales, followed by college and graduate school in the United States. Thinking of Kenya as her birthplace, Mutu admits: "When you live in such a country it's easy to dismiss the role it plays in forming your identity. But after you live outside it for a long time, you realize that the big animals that inhabit the not-so-wild wilderness, a few indigenous locals, and sometimes a marathon runner or two are not a sufficient definition of your homeland."[15] Indeed, Kenya is the site of "Turkana Boy," one of the earliest paleontological examples of a nearly complete hominid, the skeleton of which was discovered in 1984 near Lake Turkana. Estimated to be some 1.5 million years old, Turkana proved Kenya, along with other east African countries from Ethiopia to South Africa, to be the site of the origins of *Homo sapiens* and, hence, the family tree. It is this history to which art critic and novelist Simon Njami refers when he writes, "It is impossible to comprehend fully what Africa is [because] none of our pre-conceived notions, certitudes, or intuitions would suffice to account for the schizophrenic reality of this continent";[16] each country has adapted "in their own way" because "Africa is both very old and very young."[17]

All of Mutu's work traverses and conjoins the primordial with the immediacy of the present, laying waste to origins and labels. In this process, Mutu realizes an approach to culture and art akin to what Oguibe advocates when he asserts: "To undermine the idea of the African is to exterminate an entire discursive and referential system and endanger whole agendas."[18] Throwing into question and destabilizing normative categories of race, sex, gender, location, nation, and species, Mutu's art represents a singular effort to dismantle visual regimes that contribute to repression, using our family detritus, duplicity, and inherent capacity for violence against each other, and disclosing our ugly face in all its beauty and grace. In an uncompromising yet compassionate confrontation with what Alain Badiou has described as Europe's colonialist "stranglehold over the entirety of the earth,"[19] and with the world that remains after "the joint disappearances of [the Western concept of] Man and God"[20] and the concomitant rise of fundamentalism in every world religion, as well as with the "triumph of [US] capitalism" and its "wisdom of mediocrity" and exploitation,[21] Mutu insists that we "remain human" even when "at times . . . your humanity is . . . taken away from you."[22]

### *FAMILY TREE*

Eons of successive, dispersed generations of the broken genealogy of humanity appear in each figure of *Family Tree*. Mutu began this series in 2012 when she appropriated imagery from a colonial Spanish publication of anatomical prints, entitled *El cuerpo del hombre*, published in 1843 by one "Dr. Galet."[23] In this body of work, Mutu remakes humankind, reconciling what she has described in another context as "cleavages in our humanity."[24]

Each work comprising *Family Tree* underwent a long series of transformations over a period of months. One of the first works in the series, *Long Gold Fingerlings* (2012), was transmuted through such a process before Mutu eventually withdrew it to stand on its own. A consummate tour de force in the medium of collage, *Long Gold Fingerlings* provides a critical view into Mutu's meticulous working process, and augments understanding of how her painstaking production contributes to the conceptual depth and unique quality of her art. Beginning with a print from *El cuerpo del hombre* that visualized the internal muscular structure of a human body stripped of its epidermal racial signifiers, Mutu initially collaged a figure with the haunted, faded blue eyes of a white man, then replaced it several months later with the eyes of a black man. She then morphed the man's face into the nose of a Surma bride from Ethiopia, her mouth fitted with an orange clay labret.[25] Fashioning the head from male and female parts, Mutu fabricated a covertly transgendered composite figure wearing an animal cape, a multicolored drawn and collaged headdress, and a kind of apron cover-up over its genitals.[26] Ribbons of gold shoot from this eccentric figure's yard-long fingernails like the electrifying rays of a shaman's spell. The figure's ankles and calves are covered in gaiters or medieval-like military greaves composed of an amalgam of textures and technologies. Sitting at the figure's feet is a fantastic animal avatar in the form of a frog, its mouth transformed by a clothespin. Asserting this improbable being's majesty—in all its color, pomp, and ceremony—Mutu imagines something of the deep ancestral and concurrently contemporary "we" that expresses what Nancy describes as "the contact of being with one another [that] is not altruism, nor . . . identification [but] the disturbance of violent relatedness."[27]

No artist better visualizes "the disturbance of violent relatedness" that constitutes and unites the family tree than Wangechi Mutu. In *Family Tree (Original Land)* (2012), Mutu also uses the head of the Surma bride, but emphasizes her piercing, suspicious gaze, a look framed by a high forehead, elongated ears, earplugs, and earrings. Mutu then merges this imposing black woman with a white European man via an aquiline nose, rouged cheeks, and thin lips. A crown, star, or childlike halo cut with many points from simulated wood protrudes behind the compound head, which also sports a saffron toucanet as a hat. While this bird is found in Argentina, Brazil, and Paraguay, the bird-as-hat may also refer to source material that Mutu culled from *African Ceremonies*, a book that depicts (among many other things) male initiation ceremonies of Kenyan Maasai boys, who undergo circumcision when they reach manhood.[28]

In addition, the costume of the magisterial figure in *Family Tree (Original Land)* includes the dress of African kings, British colonials, and Scottish clans. The figure wears a knotted silk neck cloth tied in a bow; a shoulder drape of red satin; and the gray and blue ruffled silk of a European aristocrat. This assemblage appears as something like the right sleeve of the royal robe worn by

Mogho Naba Baongho, emperor of the Mossi, believed to be "king of the universe," whose gown is decorated in exquisitely woven silver threads that Mutu imitates using silver foil.[29] For the left sleeve of this robe, Mutu has collaged the black and white tartan plaid of the tribal dress of the Scottish Menzies clan, and topped the shoulder with the fringed gold epaulets of a general. A tree seems to grow through the center of this magnificent and distinguished figure like a rudimentary scepter, held in place by a royal pearl necklace. Lush green vegetation sprouts from below, establishing the figure as one in and with nature. Regal in this garb of royal pomp and ceremony, assembled from the intermix of fused identities, the transgendered figure melds ritual signifiers of African and European class and power with an equally imposing bird from Latin America.

In this context, Mutu's composite reconstructions of the family are visual exemplars of what decolonialist theorists like Walter Mignolo term "delinking"—that is, the act of uncoupling from imperialist modernity, whether through images or through local practices.[30] In Mutu's hands, collage proves to be the ultimate tool, as well as method, for delinking from the hegemony of Eurocentric imagery, much as the technique of assemblage provided the model for the formulation of the rhizome as an alternative method of writing and thinking history and philosophy.[31] Mutu uses both techniques—collage and assemblage (the latter in installations, as discussed below), augmented with references to multifarious technologies, from motorcycles to cybernetics—to relocate subjectivity in a plurality that could lead to progressive forms of intercultural dialogue.

I have discussed *Long Gold Fingerlings* and *Family Tree (Original Land)* carefully in order to emphasize how Mutu configures and arrives at a new image of humanity in *Family Tree*. Further examination of her rich source material promises to yield much more information about her process and how she shrewdly simulates intersubjectivity by manipulating perceptions of sexuality and queering the image without recourse to rhetoric.[32] This point recalls how she drew on Daniel Laine's book *African Kings* (2000), along with illustrations from porn and fashion magazines, for the *Pin-Up* series of the early 2000s, in which she also introduced transgendered figures. In *Untitled* (2002), for example, Mutu presents a strikingly beautiful brown woman wearing thigh-high leopard stockings. Her introduction of the leopard's skin metaphorically rearranges, while metonymically referring to, African kings who are often pictured as sitting on, and being cloaked in and adorned with, leopard skins—a symbol for monarchy and kingship among many African peoples. (Zulu King Goodwill Zwelithini, the world's longest reigning monarch, is presented as being swathed in leopard skin.) However, the amputated arm of the "pin-up" in the picture, while appearing seductively female, is fitted with a diamond prosthesis that hangs down like a snake or phallus, reiterating what can be deciphered as an erect penis embedded in the painted abstract mottling of the figure's belly. Some critics have argued that Mutu's use of diamonds is an allusion "to the illegal diamond trade and its terrible consequences" in Africa.[33]

Through such refined techniques, Mutu restores the interdependent realities of history that are imbricate, like the modified and overlapping leaves of the pine cone family or scales of a snake. Such comparison of her art to natural structures is not arbitrary or gratuitously poetic, as her work is populated with fauna and flora blended with human body parts and objects, from panthers to prosthetics.[34] *Family Tree (Second Snake Spawn)*, for example, seethes with polytheistic resonance. This sinister being is composed with a serpentine body, a turkeylike head with human lips, and an African female head-as-hat from which a black tail and a brown man (whose form looks like a feather) emerge.

The source for the male figure projecting from this head/hat is a participant in a seven-day Vodun celebration called Kokuzahn, which takes place on the border of Ghana and Togo.[35] Through the inclusion of this figure, Mutu's collage could be said to function as a talismanic magical object with protective powers. This prodigious head sits atop the shoulders of a brown body overpainted in yellow and red. Nestled in the crook of his third arm is another hybrid figure, comprising a white woman's legs and painted red toenails. Her apparently pregnant animal belly recalls a creature from Hieronymus Bosch's *The Garden of Earthly Delights* (c. 1500). She sits in a fantastical chair made up of parts of a flashy red motorcycle and other mechanical parts. Pictured above her (also contained in the brown figure's arms) is the framed image of an aged philosopher sitting at his table with books, paper, pen, and ink before him, resting his hand on a skull, a well-known memento mori (Latin for "remember your mortality") symbol. It is often forgotten that this theme in Western art, from antiquity to the present, is based on the legend of a Roman general who, while parading his conquests through Rome, was cautioned by his slave, "Memento mori": Remember that one day you will be conquered, and that you will die.

Without didacticism, Mutu draws viewers into these multiple worlds of meaning through visual associations and references to cultural history. While close examination of her work offers such rewards, the work does not depend on or necessitate such inspection. But Mutu's skillful production can lull and beguile viewers into only considering its beauty and eroticism. Thus, care must be taken to identify the complicated analysis she undertakes to expose the ideological social function of images, to recuperate bits of memory otherwise inaccessible to recall, and to transform visual language into new content and meaning. The richness of Mutu's art stems from her gift in conveying something of the inchoate noumena of history even as she cements together fragments of its phenomenological past. In integrating the disjointed remains of everything the world is and has ever been, everything it knows and has ever known, Mutu mutates and reassembles "us" in different configurations, one after another after another, world without end—no amen.

## EMPIRE

In 2004, Mutu wrote a text to accompany her collage/painting *Magnificent Monkey-Ass Lies* (2004), a work that features an encounter between a great ape, festooned in feathers, and a spectacular female animal with birdlike feet and a body covered in what appear to be jewels and sores. This being gazes questioningly into the eyes of an androgynous beast, perching but tottering on the stiletto in her hand. The unlikely pair floats in a pink, gray, and white fog that is interrupted throughout with exploding, blood-spurting lesions that counter the potential saccharine overtones of the pastel colors. Together, text and image demonstrate how Mutu marshals her verbal and visual poetics, condensing passages of time from the origins of the family in Africa to the bloody dominion of empire, and into a critique of the social contract. Mutu writes:

> See—long ago around when stories were invented, the Earth spoke mournfully about the age of the monkey and his fuck machine. . . . I mean death machine . . . you know how we play Marco Polo with eyes shut. That's it! That's our social contract . . . this mutha fuckin mess is us. So I was thinking if you were on the auction block would I even bid for your white ass. This cold has made you thin and bitter, but my heart still aches with love, and I remember when animals devoured us and we tasted good to them. Everything I am saying is dedicated to all you magnificent monkey asses, yeah you. Your greatest invention is the desire to own every demon on earth.[36]

Mutu's anger is palpable here. She dedicates this text to all of us monkeys—"yeah you"—but especially those white monkeys who talked with forked tongues, invented the Enlightenment and its death machines, and were determined to return, devour, and enslave the African in acts that expressed our demented self-loathing and fear, or "autophobia," which Frantz Fanon analyzed in *Black Skin, White Masks* (1952) as the "epidemiology of oppression" aimed at the very origins of humankind but projected on black civilization. Mutu continues Fanon's incrimination of racism when she points to the colossal failure ("mutha fuckin mess") of the misbegotten social contract, with its dictate to give up natural liberty and band together for mutual preservation. But let us not forget that if anyone refuses this union, in Jean-Jacques Rousseau's infamous words, "we shall force them to be free." Of course, not all of "them" will be free, only "we," while they—seen through the single gaze by which "Africa and Africans have long been defined"[37]—will be forced to stand naked on the auction block.

Mutu approaches this theme from another angle in her film *Eat Cake* (2012), which calls to mind the famous comment "Let them eat cake." This suggestion that starving peasants should eat cake ("brioche") has been falsely attributed to Marie Antoinette, who was only nine years old when Rousseau originally attributed it to a "great princess" in his autobiography, *Confessions* (1765). Mutu's video performance expands her critique of the social contract. *Eat Cake* opens with a bucolic image of a white swan gliding over water to the soft sounds of birdcalls and wind chimes. Soon an imposing cluster of tree trunks comes into view at the water's bank, followed by the oneiric magical appearance of a colonial-style, spindle-back armchair patterned after an eighteenth-century fan-back Windsor chair. A three-tiered chocolate cake materializes in front of the trees, over which a lace cloth drifts down as a canopy. Mutu then magically appears, standing before the chair and wearing a flowing dark skirt with a white petticoat visible at the hem, a long-sleeved white lace top, a ruffled vest, and clear plastic stiletto sandals with white ankle straps. Her hair is long, unkempt, and as wild as her eyes. She sits. Now, making large, fluid birdlike gestures with her arms, she shakes her hands and flicks her fingers, which have four-inch white nails. After sipping some wine, she ritually pours a little on the ground on either side of her chair. Next she squats before the cake on the ground, carefully removing the lace covering. She begins eating the cake, scooping up handfuls of thick chocolate frosting which smears her hands, nails, face, and hair as she wipes strands blown by the wind out of her face. Still in her squatting position and looking furtively from side to side, Mutu guards the cake as if predators would seize it, gorging herself in the midst of this otherwise pastoral soundscape: the sounds of chirping birds are broken only by the haunting call of a loon and the warning hoot of an owl.

From time to time, Mutu spits out the cake and continues to wipe the thick, gooey frosting from her fingers and hair. With legs spread wide, exposing her crotch in white panties, Mutu lowers her head into her folded arms in a gesture of intense emotion that signifies everything from futility, frustration, and resignation to concentrated introspection. She then rises on all fours and begins squashing the cake, like the dung of history, under her stiletto heels. The last image is of Mutu's hands washing the abject matter from her arms, wrists, fingers, and nails, all of which are adorned with huge rings and dangling bracelets. This primal scene, rife with layers of historical domination and violence, is fully human but also animalistic, invoking both hunter and prey. Among the many allusions this work summons are Mutu as Marie Antoinette, a famished woman-animal, a peasant under the heel of Rousseau's social contract, and a black woman who is potentially the victim of the white man's ravenous greed and lust. In this regard, it is worth remembering that E. A. T. Dutton, upon visiting Kenya's capital, Nairobi, in 1926, described the city as a "slatternly creature," specifically a slut to be exploited.[38] Beyond all these interpretations, *Eat Cake* conveys the will and strength of a powerful black woman who can crush the slime of colonial oppression and wash it from her body.

*Eat Cake* is "bleak," the word Enwezor used to describe Mutu's performances in both *Cutting*[39] and *Cleaning Earth*.[40] In *Cutting* (2004)—realized in the US-Mexico border town of Presidio, "in a desert area that could be anywhere or, more believably, exists nowhere," as Linda Stupart has written—Mutu is seen "methodically hacking at a piece of wood with a machete, a jarring metallic sound accompanying each stroke, her body becoming more silhouetted . . . as the sun sets over the barren wilderness."[41] The video's "ambiguous setting" provides the impression of "uncertainty in time and place [and] a portrait of displacement that subtly and poignantly evokes Mutu's tenuous connection to

Africa and her fragile non-geographical notions of identity."[42] The work seems also to be an homage to the Rwandan genocide of 1994 in which some eight hundred thousand people were killed, most of them hacked to death with machetes in the space of one hundred days.

In another video performance, *Mud Fountain* (2010), Mutu appears nude under "a kind of 'mud rain' [that causes] her to collapse slowly." The imagery and movement are intensified by being projected onto "a monumental wall covered in brownish streaks of paint."[43] This effect evokes a sense of drowning in dirt, as in the metaphorical filth of history and the racist language intended to insult the black body as dirt. This is precisely the racist image that the strategic mantra "Black is beautiful" was invented by the Black Power and Black Panther movements of the 1960s to counter. In a related effort, the anthropologist Mary Douglas coined the phrase "Dirt is matter out of place" in her book *Purity and Danger: An Analysis of Concepts of Pollution and Taboo* (1966), introducing the idea to refer to how "dirt is a by-product of a systematic ordering and classification of matter."[44] Her analysis of social attitudes and values extended to race as well as to the production and destruction of knowledge. Defying racism and white xenophobic bigotry, the Black Power movement reconstituted the very concept of "black," recasting the word as a symbol of the proud, fierce, enduring beauty and power of Africa and black cultural heritage.

Learning from such verbal tactics, feminists in the 1960s also deployed shifts in language to deconstruct the colonization of women's bodies under patriarchy. In this vein, Mutu anticipated *Mud Fountain* with her video performance *Cleaning Earth* (2006), a feminist critique of the abuse of black women's bodies and labor. While *Mud Fountain* shows Mutu simultaneously cleansed with and overcome by the convoluted metaphor of dirt, in *Cleaning Earth* she scrubs a desolate earthen floor in a decrepit room, moving slowly for some twenty-five minutes on hands and knees. For Mutu this work expressed "womanness," "rumination on the black female body," "the massiveness of the tasks we undertake as women," and an effort to convey qualities of a "very basic, mundane activity" that can arrive at a "form of ecstasy."[45] Dirt accompanies a host of materials, such as stiletto-heeled shoes (implying raunchy sexuality) and wine (spilled and overindulged), which form Mutu's visual language. Mutu also attends to an array of subjects and aesthetic qualities, a semiotics that includes (in no particular order): dark spaces and dim monochrome or black-and-white coloration; systematic, repetitive, melancholic corporeal rituals; enticing, magnetic, sultry beauty juxtaposed with desolate, disturbing, often painful existential experiences; the rule and superiority of hubris and the internal pressure to exercise one's will against it; transient, rapidly changing cultural circumstance in which imagery is continually being produced that objectifies and atomizes viewers while simultaneously energizing them; and what Enwezor has described as "the spectatorial aporias that surround the media production and contemporary consumption of images of African and black bodies within the global economy of mediatized signs."[46]

Not only does Mutu stage all of this and much more; she responds by stomping on it with her stiletto heels, indicators of "modernity, urbanization, and 'foreign' ideals of beauty."[47] She also submits her figures' bodies to mutilation and amputation, and depicts them with "diseased skin [that] sometimes looks like bizarre and colorful fabric costumes," in part, she explains, to show how "women's bodies are particularly vulnerable to the whims of changing movements, governments, and social norms."[48] She derives her often cyborglike figures from what she calls the "cosmetic social contract between a primal, pseudo-destructive expression [in] public space and a convoluted paper doll game," a reference to the fashion and pornography industries.[49] She is "obsessed" with "the defacement of posters of celebrities" on advertising billboards,[50] an attraction that bespeaks her appreciation of iconoclastic acts and the role that graffiti can play in wresting control from representations that threaten to obliterate one's sense of self.

Mutu's work is characterized by its deep sorrow as much as by its struggle against the weight of the decentered, deterritorializing ways in which "empire manages hybrid identities, flexible hierarchies, and plural exchanges through modulating networks of command," and the way in which imperialism "regulates human interactions but also . . . rules over human nature."[51] An early response to such emotionally crippling conditions appears in a 1996 drawing in one of Mutu's sketchbooks. The drawing depicts an amoebalike female form with short, spiky dreadlocks sucking one of her own large breasts as she floats in the sky under the eye of a watchful sun while defecating from a hairy anus onto the world (figure 28). Beside this creature, in her small, precise hand, Mutu has written: "their purgatory." In Roman Catholic doctrine, purgatory is not only a place of suffering inhabited by sinners expiating their sins before being elevated to heaven, but also the only state of being that can be altered by the prayers of those on earth, whose appeals raise these suffering souls to heaven. While the exact nature of Mutu's two words might defy explanation, this diminutive drawing strikes me as reminiscent of the "absolute question" of the existential condition of "them versus us" that Njami identified as "the problem of Us in oneself," a phrase he borrowed from the German philosopher Ernst Bloch.[52]

In Mutu's pictorial universe, one is undivided in the world but hybrid in oneself. For example, in the collage/painting *Try Dismantling the Little Empire Inside of You* (2007), a savage figure with motorcycle wheels for feet, prosthetic hands, and a head with one blue and one black eye, topped off with a hat that appears to be a braying horse, crashes through high grass. This scene of mayhem, which includes severed body parts and a blood-spattered background, both the environment of the creature and the title of the work bring viewers face to face with the "s in oneself." Mutu's title implies that the slaughter pictured is as much a continuation of the ravaging empires of the past and present as it is a metaphor for "little empires inside" the psyche that break out in daily violence and petty acts of cruelty such as gossip, envy, lies, dishonesty, and disloyalty. Such is also

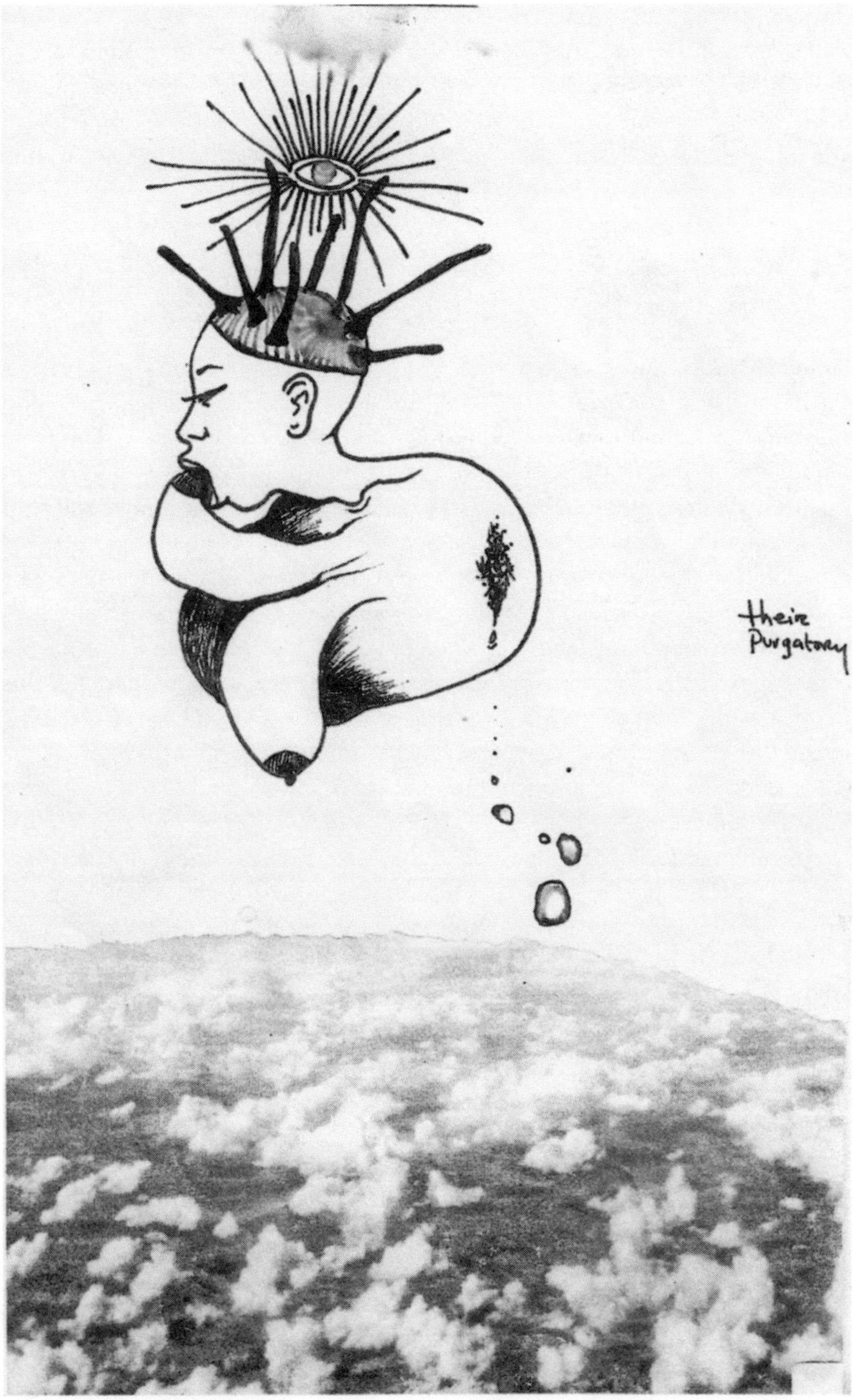


FIGURE 28. Wangechi Mutu, *Sketchbook Drawing*, 1996. Collage and ink on paper, 4½ × 7 in. Courtesy of the artist.

the subject of Mutu's work *Misguided Little Unforgivable Hierarchies* (2005), as well as of works whose titles include Mutu herself in her critique, from *How to Stab Oneself in the Back* (2004) and *Split* (2004) to *My Strength Lies* (2006). Mutu's poetic titles implicate her in the guilt of the family—its histories of imperialism and its collective body saturated in blood. As Mutu observes, "There is this tiny percentage of people who live like emperors because elsewhere blood is being shed."[53]

## TRAUMA AND FEMINISM

Simulated blood and wounded women appear throughout Mutu's work. This is especially true of the many installations in which wine drips from upended and suspended wine bottles into bloodlike puddles. In an early instance of this technique, *Hangin' In* (2004), Mutu painted a pair of flying or floating female figures that explode in red spatters, which stain what she calls the "wounded walls" of her installation, walls that she distressed and scarred with hammer holes before painting the pockmarks red to suggest flesh wounds or bullet holes. She first devised this process of "wounding" a wall in 2004, while on an Artpace residency in San Antonio, Texas. In attacking the wall, Mutu felt that her "body became an extension of the mark-making tool . . . a permanent reminder of this inner rage that probably emanated from feeling uncomfortable as a foreigner in the United States in a time of war and xenophobia,"[54] and fury "about the [US-Mexico] border, about environmental destruction, [and] about waste and human conflict."[55]

Upended wine bottles appeared again in *Exhuming Gluttony: A Lover's Requiem* (2006), a large-scale installation on which Mutu collaborated with the British-Ghanaian architect David Adjaye. In the reworked and retitled *Exhuming Gluttony: Another Requiem* (2011), the bottles, wrapped erotically in fur, drip wine on a long wooden table, progressively stained and mottled its surface, which began to resemble bruised and bleeding skin. On a facing wall, a nearly floor-to-ceiling oval composition of animal pelts hung like a huge sacrificial beast. Mutu explains that *Exhuming Gluttony* was in part a response to the voracious expansions in the art market in the mid-2000s that emerged coincident with the growth of her own career. During this period, the United States was also engulfed in the Iraq War, which she opposed. Given this confluence of events, Mutu and Adjaye wanted to create a "theater of gluttony," making viewers "complicit in . . . a community that had gone viciously wrong."[56]

The wine in these installations again bespeaks Mutu's Catholic upbringing, a reference reinscribed in *Exhuming Gluttony*, where the mandorla-shaped table suggests the form of the medieval aureole used as a framing device for images of Christ and the saints. Wine in the context of dining (gluttony) also evokes the ritual of the Eucharist anticipated in the Gospel of Saint John, in which Christ instructs, "He that eateth my flesh, and drinketh my blood, dwelleth in me, and I am in him" (John 6:56). The Eucharist itself draws on Christ's reported words at the Last Supper. After breaking bread, he says, "Take, eat; this is my body." Then, passing a cup of wine to his disciples, he directs, "Drink ye all of it; for this is my blood of the new testament, which is shed for many for the remission of sins" (Matthew 26:26–28). The performance of a sacred cannibalism of the living body of Christ is consecrated in Christianity in the act of Holy Communion, a practice that anthropologists have traced to both endo- and exocannibalism dating from the earliest history of humanity. Cannibalism proliferated throughout the world, appearing eventually in the pagan rituals of those who practiced Roman Mithraic mysteries that had evolved from Persian and Zoroastrian forms of worship. The continuation of life after death and its connection to ceremonial eating of flesh existed in many religions of Africa, according to the Kenyan religious philosopher John Mbiti.[57]

The installations in which wine is used initiate viewers into such a deep history, as much as Mutu's composite figures conjure up a genealogy of corporeal taboos. Mutu has commented that "blood, waste, and death" are the "rituals of Catholicism [whose] gorgeous, gory, ancient, pagan . . . imagery [is] embedded in me [though it is] hard to figure out whether I am resisting it or embracing it."[58] Mutu also identifies "suffering, penance, and labour"[59] as aspects of her art, a comment that brings to mind one of the seven sacraments of the Catholic Church, namely Penance or Confession, in which one asks for divine mercy for one's sins against God and others in order to be reconciled with God and humanity. Such atonement is a part of many religions and serves to bring individuals into communion with one another, thereby enhancing their sense of being plural.

Enwezor has observed that Mutu's "endless penance," as witnessed in *Cleaning Earth*, "reveal[s] the ravaged body of woman exposed in a context of patriarchal incarceration, social isolation, and implacable vulnerability."[60] Vulnerability as a condition of woman certainly played a role in *The Cinderella Curse* (2007), another installation in which Mutu used overturned wine bottles, this time dripping the pungent fluid onto mounds of blue and white clothing until every fold was soaked with wine and the fabric eventually reeked, sprouting fungus and mold. In the title of this work, Mutu called upon Colette Dowling's bestselling and controversial book *The Cinderella Complex: Women's Fear of Independence* (1981), in which Dowling theorizes that many women experience deep-seated psychological conflict about being emotionally and financially self-sufficient. This dependency is based, Dowling argues, on millennia of social conditioning and patriarchal control that leave many women wishing to be saved and protected but often disappointed when their expectations cannot be met. Such anxiety, dread, and fear of independence can lead to agoraphobia, and may explain why some women remain in physically, psychologically, and sexually abusive relationships.[61]

The theoretical implications of *The Cinderella Curse* are reinforced by Mutu's inclusion of framed collages in the installation from her series *When Sleeping Heads Lie* (2006), collages that evolved from another of her series *Sleeping Heads*

(2006). In both series, the collaged and painted heads appear to be sleeping or fallen, and are portraits that comprise vast numbers of carefully collected bits and pieces of images. Some of the fragments are "so small they often go unnoticed when taking in the whole," Yael Samuel writes, adding, "Bejeweled arms reach out from eye sockets; a breast grows out of a vagina; a tiny curled up body spills out of a nose."[62] Mutu initially installed *Sleeping Heads* in *Hangin' In*, and was astonished when "a very well respected doctor" remarked to her, after seeing the installation, that if he had a patient with such wounds, he would have diagnosed the injuries as "self-inflicted, because they're . . . a sign of a compulsive, monotonous puncturing."[63] Extremely moved, Mutu admitted that "on a deeper level" she may have been "hurting . . . myself,"[64] and that she had stopped making such marks after accidentally injuring herself in the artmaking process.

Mutu's psychic pain is in direct proportion to her empathy for others. She addresses these feelings with a staunch feminist conscience, concerned particularly with the objectification, mystification, and mythification of black women. Mutu distinctly recalls the year when she became a feminist. She was eighteen when the following event catapulted her into consciousness:[65] On July 13, 1991, during the period when Daniel Toroitich arap Moi, then president of Kenya, was "too quickly" combining the government boarding schools (created during British rule) with local schools in the Kenyan educational system, "a group of young men at a co-ed school entered a girls' dormitory, [killing nineteen in the stampede,] and over seventy [girls] were raped."[66] Mutu was shocked that the public trivialized the events as "'Oh, they're just boys, and only a few girls died.'" She recounted that it was then that "my place as a woman hit me. I understood that there was a difference between women's rights and human rights."[67] At this same time, President Moi underwent a transformation "from being a moderate dictator to a pretty vicious one, and freedom of the press was crushed." Mutu witnessed Moi's cruelty via television, including the moment when "a slum was . . . bulldozed with women and children still in the houses, and a day later they [the government] denied that it [the event] had ever been broadcast." Mutu recalls how she felt: "I couldn't believe that these things were happening in my country, and that [experience] fueled the idea that images and art are a powerful way to counter [such abuses]."[68]

Six years later, while working as a graphic designer in Nairobi in February 1992, Mutu witnessed another televised event. A handful of elderly rural mothers were holding a hunger strike in Nairobi's Uhuru Park in an attempt to force the government to release their sons from jail, where they had long been held as political prisoners. President Moi ignored their action until a dramatic of turn of events occurred. Wangari Maathai (1940–2011), the renowned Kenyan environmental and political activist and, in 2004, Africa's first female Nobel Peace Prize winner, joined the women. After Maathai arrived at the park and offered her support, Moi sent police there with tear gas. The police proceeded to club the women, three of whom had to be hospitalized. In the midst of this chaos, Maathai persuaded the women to strip and expose their worn, tired, and sagging bodies to the rampaging police, who fled, shamed by the extent of the older women's desperation and vulnerability.[69]

The extraordnary act of these few elderly Kenyan women fortified and sealed the then nineteen-year-old Mutu's feminism. Later, Mutu's memory of the events in Uhuru Park (since renamed Freedom Park) contributed to the content of her *Pin-Up* series, in which she depicted damaged, mutilated, and hypersexualized black women in imagery that referred to how the Uhuru Park mothers courageously used the authority of their bodies to face their own psychic and physical traumas as well as those of their sons. Mutu has explained that the *Pin-Up* series was also provoked by the atrocities of the civil war in Sierra Leone (1991–2002), during which the government of that country used rape as a technique of genocide, and systematically assaulted women who had been displaced in camps.[70] One of the *Pin-Up* works, *Untitled* (2001), shows a woman with mottled, multicolored skin that ranges from dark brown to white. Her severed left leg is propped up on a wooden pole-like prosthesis, and her right arm, amputated just below the wrist, is inflamed with sores. Nude except for white fingernail polish and net panties, she stares at the viewer with a resigned but knowing acceptance of her body's condition and of her position as a sexual object.

The *Pin-Up* works articulate a reverence for heroines everywhere; they manifest the many ways in which political events seep into and affect Mutu's art, and they testify to the burdens that women's bodies bear. As a transnational feminist, Mutu advocates for women's rights, pointing out, "Anything that is desired or despised is always placed on the female body."[71] The *Pin-Ups* also show Mutu's nonjudgmental and nonsalacious approach to the use of pornography, her insistence on masking titillating aspects of its imagery by collaging over it, and her sustained, layered inquiry into the style and aims of pornographic representations. Mutu's sense of humor about such pictures and her refusal to condemn them demonstrates a fascination with them that coexists with a view of them as repugnant. Her unusual sensitivity and her ability to imagine herself in proximate relation to the traumatized other infuse her work with a philosophical and empathic state that provides viewers with a visual entrée into deeper intersubjective experience.[72]

Underscoring, in her words, "themes of loss, desire, morbid fantasy, [and] the injured body,"[73] Mutu aims to disrupt viewers' prurient interest, instead appending it to traumatic imagery. In this way she subverts illicit eroticism, with its underlying foundation in pain and power relationships, and encourages empathy, without which it is nearly impossible to realize the potential of testimony and witnessing, two essential elements in the healing of trauma. In this context it is especially rare to find someone as empathic as Mutu, who attests to having had no personal experience of traumatic physical harm.[74] Nonetheless, she is capable of deep compassion and she exhibits the empathy of the secondary witness—one who without immediate primary knowledge is able to conceive of the inconceivable suffering of another as that of "Us in oneself." Secondary witnessing, Bettina Stumm writes, "requires navigating between what one already knows . . . and what evades one's knowledge, emotional affinity, and assumptions of personal connection."[75] Mutu materializes what I have described in another context as the cultural signs of trauma, which are highly visible in images and actions that occur both within the conventional boundaries of visual art and in the practices and images of everyday life. She translates these realities into nondidactic art as visual diagrams of suffering, survival, and strength.

Indeed, the very structure of collage, installation, and film—with their disjunction, morphing, and editing of forms and materials—can be theorized as resembling the structure of traumatic dissociation, with its unpredictable and uncontrollable mental and corporeal flow of images, words, smells, sounds, and feelings. By assembling new imagery out of disparate parts, Mutu brings traumatic dissociation to the surface, making her art a veritable metonymy of pain sufficient to testify to "cultures of trauma," especially those produced by colonialism and its attendant racism. This unique capacity to encourage and aid the awareness of states of pain within culture recalls a technique by which Yaqui shamans are able to change reality through shifts of energy. "The point of their focus," brain surgeon Dr. Allan J. Hamilton writes, was "called the assemblage point [by which] they changed their awareness and, therefore, the reality they perceived."[76] Mutu's use of collage, assemblage, and installation, as well as her techniques of film editing (as in *Eat Cake*), may be compared to the Yaqui "assemblage point": she amasses and reassembles imagery in order to draw forth the otherwise submerged experiences of those who have been terrorized, and thereby to transform viewers into new secondary witnesses.

Mutu further achieves this end by inducing in viewers the uncomfortable yet captivating proprioceptive "feeling" that "something is wrong" in and about her collages, installations, and films—a "something" from which it can prove difficult to turn away, as in the visual hypnotics of a highway accident. In this way, her work instigates a chain of signifiers that plunge unsuspecting viewers deep into an abyss, seducing us while saturating and confronting us with corporeal violence. Mutu may as well have been speaking of trauma when she noted, in a reference to severed heads exploding in blood in her mixed-media installation *Our lost mind finding a heart in dutty water* (2007), that part of her visual "strategy" is to "embalm it . . . catch it in time, . . . bronze it to say, 'This is what is happening. This is now.'"[77] This "this" is the catastrophe of culture, and our failure to manage the totality of its abuses of power on all levels. Mutu insists that we imagine the vulnerable, wounded, oppressed, and hounded—the infinite suffering beneath skin and beyond gender. Her art bears visual witness to a being with others that is analogous, according to Emmanuel Levinas, to the call of the "Infinite Other," which can only be answered with the response, "Here I am." This powerful commitment, Stumm explains, "is . . . both an ethical bearing towards the . . . other's infinity" and the capability "to bear oneself ethically towards him or her in a finite way."[78]

Such is the finite humanity of the weeping woman whom Mutu draws in one of her sketchbooks: a semi-prone odalisque-like figure with amputated hands, nappy, kinky-coily hair, and a schoolgirl's sweater, who seems to declare, "Here I am," as she sheds a waterfall of tears for the infinite other.

## FORENSIC ART HISTORY

Mutu's *Forensic Forms* series of the 2000s is her most ferocious consideration of the plight and destiny of us female members of the family, and our growing cyborgian state. In this body of portraits she conjoins collage, ink drawings, and materials such as glitter and pearls with prints from an old medical book on various uterine disorders.[79] *Complete Prolapsus of the Uterus* (2004) presents the puckered lower jaw and wrinkled lips of an old white woman with a short-cropped Afro hairstyle and faded blue eyes. Her expression has been altered by a stinting application of red lipstick that turns her mouth judgmental and her countenance prudish. Above her nose, itself an unrecognizable distortion of flesh, lines suggest African scarification to symbolize strength, fortitude, courage, and beauty. Might such ancient signs usurp the devastating severity of the arrogant white mistress, whose pursed lips appear determined to persevere with ignorant disregard and disdain for African traditions? Does the allusion to a prolapsed uterus, an aging uterus collapsed into the vaginal canal, suggest that the privilege accorded to the white woman has finally failed, and that the black woman will be reinstated at the apex, or head, of society? Or have the two fused together, as in *Ectopic Pregnancy* (2004), in which a hybrid black-white woman labors to give birth through her open mouth, her teeth specked in blood? Is Mutu suggesting that cyborg women will someday give birth to more holistic racial beings, ones steeped in history and sharing in humanity's imbricate knowledge? Viewers will have to answer these and many more questions for themselves.

For her part, Mutu comments that such works challenge the "constant movement towards historicising Africa, turning it into this archaic place," and that she seeks "to envision, not so much blackness as a race, but the existence of African elements in culture in the future and how is that possible."[80] She explains further:

> When I say I'm an African artist, I mean it's part of my practice, part of who I am because I was born and raised there. But often when people say I'm an African artist, it's reductive—it's exotic, it comes from a world that's in the past. Even broaching the idea of race is very complicated because Africans have a different historical experience to those who were abducted and brought here to the U.S.A. [They have] equal senses of alienation and exile but the myth that's loudest is the slave narrative, which doesn't apply to a huge amount of Africans, myself included. I always say that I was racialised in America, I understood my blackness before I got here but not because I was from a black-majority country. We don't break things down in terms of black and white, but we do have the

colonial issue. My work relates to the forced creation story that the colonialists invented for us.[81]

I have emphasized the forensic aspect of Mutu's reconstruction of composite imagery, not only of women but of everyone in the family, to distinguish her work from that of the many other artists using collage to whom she is constantly compared, Hannah Höch, John Heartfield, Romare Bearden, Adrian Piper, Martha Rosler, and Kara Walker among them. To this list Mutu has added her own list of names, including Claude Cahun, Katherine Dunham, and Hussein Chalayan. Moreover, while she admires Höch, Mutu separates herself from her German predecessor, citing Höch's use of "clear-cut binaries—African/European, archaic/modern, and religious/pornographic."[82] Mutu states that she identifies "most with Bearden," whose collages she judges to be "the least reactionary" because of how he summoned photography in "the age of jazz and the Harlem Renaissance . . . to encapsulate truth and time," as well as because of how he employed collage "to create visually stunning narratives of black lives and dreams."[83] But it must be remembered that collage is a time-honored art to which women in particular have long contributed, as Miriam Schapiro and Melissa Meyer have written in "Waste Not Want Not: An Inquiry into What Women Saved and Assembled—FEMMAGE" (1977–78).[84] Thus, limiting comparisons to Mutu's work solely within the history of collage does not begin to communicate the extent of her accomplishments.

While comparing one artist to another inevitably fails, it may be surprising and illuminating to think about Mutu's oeuvre in relation to the conceptual and thematic reach of Matthew Barney's art, in order to reorient a conversation about the scope and depth of Mutu's work. Why? Both artists use figuration to create a vision of futuristic, composite, human/animal cyborg beings situated in lush environments, overburdened with and overshadowed by new technologies. Both artists stage their imagery in theatrical settings that announce themselves as false in order to permit viewers to release their hold on the "real" and become subsumed in the truth of artifice—namely, art itself. Both artists invoke mythic, emotive, poetic, and mysterious transformations. Both emphasize eroticism and open-ended multiple forms of sexuality. Both explore what Freud called polymorphic perverse sexuality and the shattering of taboo; they release and evoke the inherent violence in sex. Both understand the power of the grotesque,[85] the absurd, and the ironic, even if their viewers sometimes miss this element in the expansiveness of their aesthetic range. Both attend to vexing cultural, social, and political questions without the pretense of "being political." Finally, both Mutu and Barney are among the most eloquent artists working today in the legacy of Surrealism. "I think in a surreal manner," Mutu has explained,[86] clarifying her comment with the list of the qualities she most admires in art: a "real sense of personal narrative," "social critique with drama," and "camouflage and mutation."[87] These are all "big themes" in her art, she explains, adding: "We all wear costumes when we set out for battle."[88]

The battle for which Mutu costumes her art is the encounter between the psyche and the everyday world. This struggle between the mind and the quotidian is the profound philosophical territory of surrealism. Seeking to create a more pliant reality by breaking down the separation of matter and mind, as well as by rejecting the constraints of Occidental reason and resisting the artifice of bourgeois culture with its hypocritical morality, the Surrealists invented manifold visual and textual procedures for depicting the surreality invisible to but existing within all aspects of everyday life, and the surreality inherent in animate and inanimate things. Applying an unorthodox approach to Freud's already unconventional theories of the unconscious and his analysis of dream and hypnagogic states, the Surrealists sought to communicate the surreality of liminal stages of knowing, experiencing, and being. Their revolutionary aim was to make surrealism a recognized and active force in all aspects of everyday life and, thereby, to redress fixed perceptions and conventional ways of acting in the world. Moreover, the Surrealists engaged directly in politics, standing with the Algerians, Mexicans, and Haitians, among others, in revolutions to overturn colonial rule.

Beginning in the 1930s, surrealism was the first artistic movement to proliferate worldwide without first being introduced through colonialist art academies. The movement spread quickly, like a virus of liberation, unleashing the imagination to acknowledge the full possibility of human potential. As the Martinique poet Aimé Césaire explained:

> Surrealism interested me to the extent that it was a liberating factor. . . . If I apply the surrealist approach to my particular situation, I can summon up these unconscious forces. This, for me, was a call to Africa, I said to myself: it's true that superficially we are French, we bear the marks of French customs; we have been branded by Cartesian philosophy, by French rhetoric; but if we break with all that, if we plumb the depths, then what we will find is fundamentally black. . . . A process of disalienation, that's how I interpreted Surrealism . . . as a process of detoxification . . . a way of emancipating your consciousness. . . . I felt that beneath the social being would be found a profound being, over whom all sorts of ancestral layers and alluviums had been deposited.[89]

Césaire's words direct us back to the fertile alluvial dirt that Wangechi Mutu introduces into her uninhibited, erotic imagery, a visual poetics aimed at breaking through alienation, restoring the family tree, and bringing us (in oneself) to one in the other. The evocative power of her incomparable titles detoxify stilted ways of thinking and bear the imprint of the liberating absurdity, perceptiveness, and wisdom of dreams. Rather than interpret the unconscious, Mutu inhabits it in a prophetic stream of ideas flowing straight from the stratum of mind to the ancient knowledge of the camel's head, a current of wisdom suggested in her title *The Bride Who Married a Camel's Head*. Thoroughly informed by poststructuralist theory, Mutu updates the twentieth century's vertical orientation of surrealism—from the sub(sous)conscious to super(sur)reality—with imagery that registers time, place, gender, and race in the twenty-first-century territory of the horizontality of the rhizome.

Wangechi Mutu operates as a kind of forensic anthropologist, using composite drawing and image modification to picture the crime scenes of sexism, racism, classism, colonialism, and speciesism, as well as aspects of the economic and technological exploitation of the world. Her forensic pursuits reinforce the very etymology of the word "forensic," which is derived from the Latin *fornsis*, "of or before the forum," pertaining to the Roman forum, where the cases of public individuals were debated. Today the word "forensic" is used primarily in reference to scientific investigations of crimes and the presentation of evidence in courts of law. Mutu presents her visual forensics both in the public forum of galleries and museums and in the court of art history, where her art will be judged in large measure for its contribution to the reconstruction of an intersubjective image of humankind, and for its disassembly of Enlightenment and modernist concepts of a white unified subject in possession of universal truth.

# Notes

INTRODUCTION

1. Ai Weiwei's entry to his blog, August 25, 2006, in *Ai Weiwei's Blog: Writings, Interviews, and Digital Rants, 2006–2009*, edited and translated by Lee Ambrozy (Cambridge and London: MIT Press, 2011), 96.

2. Ibid. For recent research on trauma experienced by animals, see James Dao, "After Duty, Dogs Suffer Like Soldiers," *New York Times*, December 1, 2011. Accessed at http://www.nytimes.com/2011/12/02/us/more-military-dogs-show-signs-of-combat-stress.html?_r=1&hp. See also Mark W. Gilbertson, Martha E. Shenton, Aleksandra Ciszewski, Kiyoto Kasai, Natasha B. Lasko, Scott P. Orr, and Roger K. Pitman, "Smaller Hippocampal Volume Predicts Pathologic Vulnerability to Psychological Trauma," *National Neuroscience* 5, no. 11 (November 2002): 1242–47.

3. Ai Weiwei. Ai Weiwei's Blog, 96.

4. Ibid.

5. *Diagnostic and Statistical Manual of Mental Disorders: DSM-3* (Washington: American Psychological Association, 1980). Clinical psychologists like Charles R. Figley, a pioneer of trauma psychology during the Vietnam War era, define the origins of the term more broadly, identifying its parent fields in psychology, sociology, psychiatry, social work, systems studies, nursing, medicine, and other disciplines. See Charles R. Figley, ed., *Encyclopedia of Trauma: An Interdisciplinary Guide* (Thousand Oaks, CA: SAGE Publications, 2012).

6. Susan Roth, Elana Newman, David Pelcovitz, Bessel van der Kolk, and Francine S. Mandel, "Complex PTSD in Victims Exposed to Sexual and Physical Abuse: Results from the DSM-IV Field Trial for Posttraumatic Stress Disorder," *Journal of Traumatic Stress* 10, no. 4 (October 1997): 539–55. Bruce D. Perry and Maia Szalavitz, *The Boy Who Was Raised as a Dog: And Other Stories from a Child Psychiatrist's Notebook* (New York: Basic Books, 2006).

7. I. Shalev, T. E .Moffitt, K. Sugden, B. Williams, R. M. Houts, A. Danese, J. Mill, L. Arseneault, and A. Cas, "Exposure to Violence during Childhood Is Associated with Telomere Erosion from 5 to 10 Years of Age: A Longitudinal Study," *Molecular Psychiatry* 17, no. 4 (April 24, 2012).

8. Jerry Adler, "Erasing Painful Memories," *Scientific American* 306, no. 5 (May 2012): 56. In 2011 the University of Minnesota's Veterinary Medical Center became the first animal trauma center in the United States.

9. Robert Jay Lifton, "From Hiroshima to the Nazi Doctors: The Evolution of Psychoformative Approaches to Understanding Traumatic Stress Syndromes," in *International Handbook of Traumatic Stress Syndromes* (New York: Plenum Press, 1993): 11–23; Jeffrey

Moussaieff Masson, *The Assault on Truth: Freud's Suppression of the Seduction Theory* (New York: Pocket Books, 1984); Bessel A. Van der Kolk, ed., *Post-Traumatic Stress Disorder: Psychological and Biological Sequelae* (Washington: American Psychiatric Press, 1984); Elaine Scarry, *The Body in Pain: The Making and Unmaking of the World* (New York and Oxford: Oxford University Press, 1985); Kalí Tal, *Worlds of Hurt: Reading the Literature of Trauma* (Cambridge: Cambridge University Press, 1995); Cathy Caruth, ed., *Trauma: Explorations in Memory* (Baltimore and London: Johns Hopkins University Press, 1996); Cathy Caruth, *Unclaimed Experience: Trauma, Narrative, and History* (Baltimore: Johns Hopkins University Press, 1996); Dominick LaCapra, *Representing the Holocaust* and *Writing History, Writing Trauma* (Baltimore: Johns Hopkins University Press, 2000); Francine Shapiro, "Efficacy of the Eye Movement Desensitization Procedure in the Treatment of Traumatic Memories," in Mardi J. Horowitz, ed., *Essential Papers on Posttraumatic Stress Disorder* (New York and London: New York University Press, 1999), 432–57.

10. Yael Danieli, ed., *International Handbook of Multigenerational Legacies of Trauma* (New York: Plenum Press, 1998); Ruth Leys, *Trauma: A Genealogy* (Chicago: University of Chicago Press, 2000); Vamik D. Volkan, *Animal Killer: Transmission of War Trauma from One Generation to the Next* (London: Karnac Books, 2013).

11. Shoshana Felman and Dori Laub, *Testimony: Crises of Witnessing in Literature, Psychoanalysis, and History* (New York: Routledge, 1992); Ernst Van Alphen, *Caught by History: Holocaust Effects in Contemporary Art, Literature, and Theory* (Stanford, CA: Stanford University Press, 1997); Barbie Zelizer, *Remembering to Forget: Holocaust Memory through the Camera's Eye* (Chicago: University of Chicago Press, 1998); Marianne Hirsch, *Family Frames: Photography, Narrative, and Postmemory* (Cambridge, MA: Harvard University Press, 1997).

12. Jonathan Shay, Achilles in *Vietnam: Combat Trauma and the Undoing of Character* (New York: Simon and Schuster, 1994); James Johnson, *Combat Trauma: A Personal Look at Long-Term Consequences* (Lanham, MD: Rowman & Littlefield, 2010); Larry Minear, *Through Veterans' Eyes: The Iraq and Afghanistan Experience* (Washington: Potomac Books, 2010); David E. Lorey and William H. Beezley, eds., *Genocide, Collective Violence and Popular Memory: The Politics of Remembrance in the Twentieth Century* (Wilmington, DE: Scholarly Resources, 2002); Roméo Dallaire with Jessica Dee Humphreys, *They Fight Like Soldiers, They Die Like Children: The Global Quest to Eradicate the Use of Child Soldiers* (New York: Walker & Company, 2010); Philip Gourevitch, *We Wish to Inform You That Tomorrow We Will Be Killed with Our Families: Stories from Rwanda* (New York: Farrar, Straus & Giroux, 1998); Hans-Juergen Wirth, *9/11 as a Collective Trauma: And Other Essays on Psychoanalysis and Society* (New York: Routledge, 2005).

13. Judith Lewis Herman, "Complex PTSD: A Syndrome in Survivors of Prolonged and Repeated Trauma," *Journal of Traumatic Stress* 5, no. 3 (1993): 377–91; Lynn Brunet, *"A Course of Severe and Arduous Trials": Bacon, Beckett and Spurious Freemasonry in Early Twentieth-Century Ireland* (Oxford and New York: Peter Lang, 2009); Lydia Cacho, *Slavery Inc.: The Untold Story of International Sex Trafficking* (London: Portobello Books, 2012).

14. Timothy Murray, *Drama Trauma: Specters of Race and Sexuality in Performance, Video and Art* (New York: Routledge, 1997); Ron Eyerman, *Cultural Trauma: Slavery and the Formation of African American Identity* (Cambridge, UK: Cambridge University Press, 2001); Mitchell Gold and Mindy Drucker, *Crisis: 40 Stories Revealing the Personal, Social, and Religious Pain and Trauma of Growing Up Gay in America* (Austin, TX: Greenleaf Book Group, 2008); Sonya Andermahr and Silvia Pellicer-Ortin, eds., *Trauma Narratives and Herstory* (Houndmills, UK: Palgrave Macmillan, 2013).

15. Jeffrey Moussaieff Masson and Susan McCarthy, *When Elephants Weep: The Emotional Lives of Animals* (Peaslake, UK: Delta Publishing, 1995).

16. Robert Jay Lifton and Eric Olson, "The Human Meaning of Total Disaster: The Buffalo Creek Experience" (1976), in Mardi J. Horowitz, ed., *Essential Papers on Posttraumatic Stress Disorder* (New York and London: New York University Press, 1999), 206–31.

17. Srinivas Aravamudan, *Tropicopolitans: Colonialism and Agency, 1688–1804* (Durham, NC: Duke University Press, 1999); Warwick Anderson and Deborah Jenson, *Unconscious Dominions: Psychoanalysis, Colonial Trauma, and Global Sovereignties* (Durham, NC: Duke University Press, 2011); Walter Mignolo, *The Darker Side of Western Modernity: Global Futures, Decolonial Options* (Durham, NC: Duke University Press, 2011); Ogaga Ifowodo, *History, Trauma, and Healing in Postcolonial Narratives: Reconstructing Identities* (Houndmills, UK: Palgrave Macmillan, 2013).

18. Michel Foucault, *Madness and Civilization: A History of Insanity in the Age of Reason*, translated by Richard Howard (London: Tavistock Publications, 1982), 280. Originally published as *Histoire de la folie* in Paris by Librairie Plon in 1961.

19. Ibid., 281.

20. Sander L. Gilman also discussed the visualization of madness in the seventeenth century, before trauma was understood to be distinct from insanity, and while he did not address trauma directly, he advocated the visual study of how mental illness is visualized and "the insane in the world are described." Sander L. Gilman, *Seeing the Insane* (New York: John Wiley & Sons, 1982), xii.

21. Pierre Janet, *L'Automatisme psychologique (*Paris: Société Pierre Janet, 1973).

22. Much debate surrounds the dating of the paintings at Lascaux, which has been successively corrected. A 1998 radiocarbon result of a sample removed from a fragment of a reindeer antler at the base of the shaft scene places the art between the Upper Solutrean and the Badegoulian, around 18,600 BCE.

23. Recent work on the site at Lascaux conjectures that the consistency of style, technical rendering, and unity of composition may have been the work of a single artist.

24. Margaret W. Conkey, "Images without Words: The Construction of Prehistoric Imaginaries for Definitions of 'Us'," *Journal of Visual Culture* 9, no. 3 (2010): 272.

25. Ibid., 274.

26. Ibid., 275.

27. Ofer Bar-Yosef, "The Upper Paleolithic Revolution," *Harvard Annual Review of Anthropology* 31 (2002): 363.

28. Ibid.

29. Conkey, 276.

30. Jean-Luc Nancy, *Being Singular Plural*, edited by Werner Hamacher and David E. Wellbery (Stanford, CA: Stanford University Press, 2000), 18.

31. Neanderthals used fire for illumination "at least 47,600 years . . . before modern humans reached Western Europe," according to Mark Berkowitz, "Neanderthal News," *Archeology* 49, no. 5 (September/October 1996). Accessed at http://www.archaeology.org/9609/newsbriefs/neandertals.html.

32. Michael Winkelman, *Shamanism: A Biophychosocial Paradigm of Consciousness and Healing*, 2nd Edition (Santa Barbara, Denver, and Oxford: Praeger, 2010), 75. Winkelman quotes Jean Clottes and David Lewis-Williams, *The Shamans of Prehistory: Trance and Magic in the Painted Caves*, translated by Sophie Hawkes (New York: Harry N. Abrams, 1998, 1996). The dead man in the shaft scene is not the only image of a wounded, dying, or dead man in Paleolothic art. There are impaled figures in Cosquer Cave (one dating to 19,000 BCE, and the other to circa 27,000 BCE), in Cougnac (14,000–25,000 BCE), in Pech-Merle (22,000–25,000 BCE), and at other sites.

33. Horst Kirchner suggested that the dead man might be a shaman in a trance in "Ein archäologischer Beitrag zur Urgeschichte der Schamanismus," *Anthropos* 67 (1952):

244–86, as quoted in George Bataille's *Prehistoric Painting: Lascaux or the Birth of Art*, translated by Austryn Wainhouse (Switzerland: Skira, 1955), 140. See also David Lewis-Williams, *The Mind in the Cave: Consciousness and the Origins of Art* (London: Thames & Hudson, 2002). See, in addition, Stanley Krippner and Jürgen Werner Kremer, "Hypnotic-Like Procedures in Indigenous Shamanism and Mediumship," in D. Barrett, ed., *Hypnosis and Hypnotherapy, Vol. 1: Neuroscience, Personality, and Cultural Factors* (Santa Barbara, CA: Praeger, 2010), 97–124.

34. Norbert Aujoulat, *Lascaux: Movement, Space, and Time* (New York: Harry N. Abrams, 2009), 158.

35. Ibid. In addition, the rhinoceros lifts its tail in a manner that some have interpreted as the sign of a female animal in estrus, the meaning of which is obscure, especially in the context of the violence of the shaft scene.

36. Leroi-Gourhan, quoted in Mario Ruspoli's *The Cave of Lascaux: The Final Photographs*, with preface by Yves Coppens (New York: Harry N. Abrams, 1986), 158. See also Arlette Leroi-Gourhan and Jacques Allain, *Lascaux inconnu* (Paris: CNRS Editions, 1979). Richard E. Leakey and Roger Lewin remark: "For the Abbe Breuil, these geometric patterns, or signs, as they are called, were part of hunting paraphernalia traps, snares, even weapons. Leroi-Gourhan included them in his structural duality. Dots and strokes were male signs, he said; ovals, triangles, and quadrangles were female signs. A South African archeologist, David Lewis-Williams, suggests that neither interpretation is correct. They are, he says, images plucked from a mind in the state of hallucination, a sure sign of shamanistic art. His argument is based on a study of San art, in southern Africa, and a neuropsychological model that may be basic to much human image making in hunter-gatherer societies, including those of the Upper Paleolithic." Richard E. Leakey and Roger Lewin, *Origins Reconsidered: In Search of What Makes Us Human* (New York: Anchor, 1993), 328.

37. Aujoulat, *Lascaux*, 158.

38. The literature is too vast to cite here, but it is of some interest that the horse is the animal most represented in Paleolithic painting. At Lascaux, for example, there are 364 representations of horses, "forming 60.2 per cent of all identified animals, followed by stags . . . (14.9 per cent). Auroches, and bison account for 4.6 percent and 4.3 per cent respectively." Norbert Aujoulat, *Lascaux*, 64–65.

39. These archeological-astronomical speculations may be found in Jesper Christensen's "Heaven and Earth in Ice Age Art: Topography and Iconography at Lascaux," *Mankind Quarterly* 36, no. 3/4 (Spring-Summer 1996): 247.

40. Abbé H. Breuil, *Four Hundred Centuries of Cave Art* (Montignac, Dordogne: Centre d' Études et de Documentation Prehistorique, 1952).

41. See, for example, David Lewis-Williams, *The Mind in the Cave: Consciousness and the Origins of Art*. London: Thames & Hudson, 2002.

42. Ruspoli, *The Cave of Lascaux*, 149–50. Bataille refers to the shaft also as "the Well" or "the Crypt"; *Prehistoric Painting*, 110.

43. For example, at Trois Frères a "'sorcerer' or 'god'" figure is painted some "13 feet above the ground, not hidden below" (as in Lascaux). For Trois Frères, see N. K. Sandars, *Prehistoric Art in Europe* (New Haven: Yale University Press, 1985), 136 (originally published in London by Penguin Books, 1968).

44. N. K. Sandars, *Prehistoric Art in Europe*, 135.

45. Bataille remarked that the Lascaux painters "resembled us," and their means for telling us so was to leave "innumerable pictures of the animality *they were shedding*—as though they had felt obliged to clothe a nascent marvel with the animal grace they had lost." The pictures of animals in Lascaux, he continued, "declare that they who painted

them . . . *chose animality rather than themselves* [in order] to give the image that suggests what is fascinating in humankind." Bataille concluded: "What brings us to an amazed, bewildered halt and holds us there is this extreme self-effacement of man before the animal—and of man *just turning into a human.*" See Bataille's *Prehistoric Painting: Lascaux or the Birth of Art* (Lausanne: Skira, 1955), 11. Bataille also wrote: "These non-human figures . . . declare not only that they who painted them became full-grown men by painting them, but that they chose animality rather than themselves to give the image that [which] suggests what is fascinating in humankind." And he identified modern humans as those with ludic capabilities (page 115). Bataille further observed in 1955 that in the atomic age "I am simply struck by the fact that light is being shed on our birth at the very moment when the notion of our death appears to us." See Bataille's *The Cradle of Humanity: Prehistoric Art and Culture*, edited and translated by John S. Kendall and Leslie M. Kendall (New York: Zone Books, 2005), 85. Considering this comment, philosopher Brett Buchanan remarks: "The birth occurs through the passage from animality to humanity, as discovered in art, whereas the death occurs, arguably and no doubt speculatively, through the passage from humanity to animality, as evinced by the sciences of experimentation and war. Through the transformation of humanity in its passion for destruction, self-effacement, and the prospect of absolute death, Bataille hints at a cataclysmic end already foretold within the cave paintings that are taken to be a trace of our beginning." See Brett Buchanan, "Painting the Prehuman: Bataille, Merleau-Ponty, and the Aesthetic Origins of Humanity," *Journal for Critical Animal Studies* 9, no. 1/2 (2011): 13. See also Ian Tattersall, *Becoming Human: Evolution and Human Uniqueness*. New York: Harcourt Brace & Company, 1998.

46. Georges Bataille, *Erotism: Death and Sensuality*, translated by Mary Dalwood (San Francisco: City Lights, 1957), 74.

47. Bataille, *Theory of Religion* (Brooklyn: Zone Books, 1992), 57.

48. Angus McDonald, "Eden/Shangri-la," in Ari Hirvonen and Janne Porttikivi, eds., *Law and Evil: Philosophy, Politics, and Psychoanalysis* (New York and London: Routledge-Cavendish, 2009), 19.

49. Bataille, Theory of Religion, 41.

50. McDonald, "Eden/Shangri-la," 19.

51. Dating is constantly being revised and new sites found. For example, in "Cave Paintings in Indonesia May Be among the Oldest Known" (*New York Times*, October 8, 2014), John Noble Wilford discussed cave drawings in Indonesia found to be 40,000 years old and hand stencil prints at least 39,900 years old, according to a study published in the journal *Nature*. These findings are comparable to the 40,800-year-old red disk from El Castillo, in northern Spain. Accessed at http://www.nytimes.com/2014/10/09/science/ancient-indonesian-find-may-rival-oldest-known-cave-art.html?_r=0.

52. Bradshaw Foundation, "The Art of Chauvet Cave Paintings." Accessed at http://www.bradshawfoundation.com/chauvet/venus_sorcerer.php.

53. Ibid., 19. McDonald quotes from Maurice Blanchot, *Friendship*, translated by Elizabeth Rottenberg (Stanford, CA: Stanford University Press, 1997), 1–11.

54. "Red dots, hand stencils and animal figures represent the oldest examples yet found of cave art in Europe. The symbols on the walls at 11 Spanish locations, including the World Heritage sites of Altamira, El Castillo and Tito Bustillo, have long been recognised for their antiquity. But researchers have now used refined dating techniques to get a more accurate determination of their ages. One motif—a faint red dot—is said to be more than 40,000 years old." See Jonathan Amos, "Red Dot Becomes oldest cave art," BBC News (June 14, 2012): http://www.bbc.com/news/science-environment-18449711.

55. ____. "The Paleolithic Age," for *Essay Web*. Accessed at http://essayweb.net/history/ancient/prehistory_04.shtml.

56. Winkelman., 47–48.

57. Ibid., 48–49.

58. Ibid. Winkelman further points out that "the centrality of shamanic depictions to Middle/Upper Paleolithic representations implies that they were already well-established aspects of human social life," and that the "'wounded man' motif with a penile erection is one aspect that is difficult to explain without reference to the classic shamanic 'death and rebirth' and penile erections associated with dreaming"; pp. 75–76. Post-mortem erection can be the result of trauma to the spinal cord or genital area, damage that causes priapism. This could support a hypothesis that the man in the shaft scene may have been gored by the bison.

59. Ibid., 76.

60. Ibid., quoting Steven Mithen, *The Prehistoric Mind: A Search for the Origins of Art, Religion, and Science* (London: Thames & Hudson, 1996).

61. Ibid., 77.

62. Ibid.

63. Ibid. Winkelman adds: "Totemic thinking involves conceptualizing human intergroup differences and relations in terms of the models provided by the natural world"; pp. 77–78.

64. Ibid. Quoting M. Donald, *Origins of the Modern Mind* (1991), Winkelman notes that "mimetic ability is at the center of the emergence of a symbolic capacity that represents with actions, using the body and its behaviors to represent perceptions of events," and that it "operates on the principle of metaphorical similarity based on perceptual resemblance, providing a representation of the relationship between the self and the external world through movement." Donald, as quoted in Winkelman, 79.

65. Ibid., 80.

66. Ibid., 81.

67. Derick Hodgson and Patricia A. Helventson, "The Emergence of the Representation of Animals in Palaeoart: Insights from Evolution and the Cognitive, Limbic and Visual Systems of the Human Brain," *Rock Art Research* 23, no. 1 (2006): 8.

68. Winkelman, 82.

69. Ibid., 276–77.

70. Regarding the sophistication of painting throughout Lascaux, two bison known as the Crossed Bison in the Nave of Lascaux measure some eight feet in length and were painted in the concavity of the wall in a way that contributed to the illusion that they are galloping toward the viewer. Jean Clotte has written: "Paintings are generally red or black. The reds are iron oxides, such as hematite. The blacks, either charcoal or manganese dioxide. Sometimes . . . drawings [were made] with a chunk of rock or of charcoal held like a pencil. . . . The pigment was then crushed and mixed with a binder to ensure the fluidity of the paint which was then either applied with a finger or with a brush made with animal hair, or blown through the mouth (stenciling). Modern analyses even revealed that in the Magdalenian of the Pyrenees some paintings [at Niaux and at Fontanet] had been made according to real recipes by adding an extender, i.e., a powder obtained from the crushing of various stones (biotite, potassium feldspath, talcum). The aims were to save on the pigment, to make the paint stick better to the wall and to avoid its crackling when drying (Clottes, Menu, Walter 1990). Some images evince different techniques for the same subject: bicolour, joint use of engraving & painting." Jean Clottes, *Paleolithic Cave Art in France*, excerpted in http://www.bradshawfoundation.com/clottes/page5.php.

71. Ai Weiwei, "Spiritual Orientation and the Possibilities of Existence," in *Ai Weiwei's Blog*, 88.

72. Ibid.

73. Jacques Lacan, "The Split between the Eye and the Gaze," section 1 of "Of the Gaze as *Objet Petit a*," in *The Seminar of Jacques Lacan: Book XI, The Four Fundamental Concepts of Psychoanalysis*, edited by Jacques-Alain Miller and translated by Alan Sheridan (New York and London: W. W. Norton, 1978), 72; originally published by Éditions du Seuil, 1973.

74. Ibid.

75. Jacques Lacan, "The Mirror Stage as Formative of the Function of the I as Revealed in Psychoanalytic Experience," in *Écrits, A Selection*, translated by Alan Sheridan (New York and London: W.W. Norton, 1977), 4; originally published by Éditions du Seuil, 1966.

76. Bataille, Prehistoric Painting, 115.

77. See key essays in Paul Mellars, Katie Boyle, Ofer Bar-Yosef, and Christopher Stringer, eds., *Rethinking the Human Revolution*. Cambridge: McDonald Institute for Archaeological Research, 2007.

78. The literature on the subject is distinguished, ample, and growing quickly. See Kathy Rudy's erudite *Loving Animals: Towards a New Animal Advocacy*, University of Minneapolis Press, 2011); Frans B. M. de Waal, "Do Animals *Feel* Empathy?" *Scientific American* 18 (December 2007/January 2008): 28–35; and articles by Jennifer Viegas, a veteran reporter for *Discovery News*, who has written many articles on animal intelligence and empathy, may be accessed at http://news.discovery.com/contributors/jennifer-viegas.htm.

79. Didier Fassin and Richard Rechtman, *The Empire of Trauma: An Inquiry into the Condition of Victimhood*, translated by Rachel Gomme (Princeton, NJ, and Oxford, UK: Princeton University Press, 2009), 284; originally published in Paris by Flammarion as *L'empire du traumatisme: Enquéte sur la condition de victim* (2007).

80. Susan Sontag, *Regarding the Pain of Others* (New York: Farrar, Straus and Giroux, 2003), 114–15.

81. Ai Weiwei, "I'm Ready," in *Ai Weiwei's Blog*, 230.

82. Ai produced *Marble Chair* in a series of white marble sculptures, often with grey or other color veining, as replicas of the Ming and Qing dynasty wooden chairs.

83. A short list of traumatized charismatic figures includes John F. Kennedy, Winston Churchill, Marilyn Monroe, Hayim Nachman Bialik, Maximilien Robespierre, T. E. Lawrence (Lawrence of Arabia), James Dean, Charlie Chaplin, Mohammed, Ruhollah Khomeini, Martin Buber, Al Jolson, William Wordsworth, John Lennon, Paul McCartney, Cary Grant, David Ben-Gurion, Elvis Presley, Ignacy Paderewski, Vladimir Ilyich Lenin, Krishnamurti, Lady Diana Spencer, and Adolf Hitler. See David Aberbach, *Charisma in Politics, Religion and the Media: Private Trauma, Public Ideals* (New York: New York University Press, 1996), and Richard D. Ryder, *Nelson, Hitler & Diana: Studies in Trauma and Celebrity* (Exeter, UK, and Charlottesville, VA: Imprint Academic, 2009).

84. Ai, Ai Weiwei's Blog, 94.

85. Ibid., 75–76.

86. Ibid., 94.

87. Ibid., 72.

88. Jacques Derrida quoted in Emily Easkin, "Derrida: The Excluded Favorite," *New York Review of Books* (March 25, 2013). Accessed at http://www.nybooks.com/blogs/nyrblog/2013/mar/25/derrida-excluded-favorite/.

89. Rosalind Krauss, "Who Comes after the Subject?" in Charles G. Salas, ed., *The Life and the Work: Art and Biography* (Los Angeles: Getty Research Institute, 2007), 32.

90. Ibid.

91. See Henri Zerner's "Crisis in the Discipline," *Art Journal* 42, no.4 (1982). This essay helped to launch the influential "State of Research" series published in the late 1980s by *The Art Bulletin*, which concerned various fields and subjects within art history. These topical articles were followed by a second series in the 1990s: "A Range of Critical Perspectives."

92. Sigmund Freud, *Leonardo da Vinci and a Memory of His Childhood* (New York: W. W. Norton, 1964), and "The Moses of Michelangelo" (1914) in *The Standard Edition of the Complete Psychological Works of Sigmund Freud*, Vol. 13, translated by James Strachey in collaboration with Anna Freud (London: Hogarth Press, 1955), 209–38. See also Jack J. Spector, *The Aesthetics of Freud: A Study in Psychoanalysis and Art* (New York: Praeger Publishers, 1973). During this period, Mary Mathews Gedo brought out *Picasso, Art as Autobiography* (Chicago: University of Chicago Press, 1980), a study widely criticized for using psychobiography.

93. See Jack Spector, "The State of Psychoanalytic Research in Art History," *Art Bulletin* 60, no. 1 (March 1988): 49.

94. W. J. T. Mitchell, "The Pictorial Turn," *Artforum International* 30, no. 7 (March 30, 1992): 89–94.

95. Pioneering scholars on performance in the 1970s and early 1980s include RoseLee Goldberg, Moira Roth, Michel Kirby, Stephen C. Foster, Estera Milman, Bruce Barber, Udo Kultermann, François Pluchart, Catherine Millet, Georg Jappe, Lea Vergine, and journals like *High Performance* (USA), *Flash Art* (Italy), *Performance* (UK).

96. Lea Vergine, *Il corpo come linguaggio (La "Body-art" e storie simili)*, translated by Henry Martin (Milan: Giampaolo Prearo Editore, 1974), 9.

97. Kuspit pathologized Piper, claiming that her art "mask[ed] emotional incoherence" and hid "a somnambulist form of distress" while also being a symptom of it. See Donald Kuspit, "Adrian Piper: Self-Healing Through Meta-Art," *Art Criticism* 3, no. 3 (1987): 10 10. See also, Donald W.Winnicott's famous article "Transitional Objects and Transitional Phenomena," *International Journal of Psychoanalysis* 34 (1953), 89–97.

98. Kathy O'Dell, "The Performance Artist as Masochistic Woman," *Arts* 62, no. 10 (Summer 1988): 96–98. For other essays on this subject matter, see Teresa Opheim, "Self-Mutilation: Pain to Forget Pain," *Utne Reader* (March/April 1987), 21; Mark Selzer, "Wound Culture: Trauma in the Pathological Public Sphere," *October* 80 (Spring 1997): 3–26; and Armando R. Favazza, "The Coming of Age of Self-Mutilation," *Journal of Nervous and Mental Disease* 186, no. 5 (May 1998): 259–68. Favazza's *Bodies under Siege: Self-Mutilation and Body Modification in Culture and Psychiatry* (Baltimore: Johns Hopkins University Press, 1987) was followed in quick succession by Barnet W. Walsh and Paul Rosen, *Self-Mutilation: Theory, Research, and Treatment* (New York: Guilford, 1988); Marilee Strong, *A Bright Red Scream: Self-Mutilation and the Language of Pain* (New York: Viking, 1998); Steven Levenkron, *Cutting: Understanding and Overcoming Self-Mutilation* (New York: Norton, 1998); Caroline Kettlewell, *Skin Game: A Cutter's Memoir* (New York: St Martin's, 1999); and Jane Wegscheider Hyman, *Women Living with Self-Injury* (Philadelphia: Temple University Press, 1999).

99. Kristine Stiles, *Rafael Montañez Ortiz: Years of the Warrior 1960, Years of the Psyche 1988* (New York: El Museo Del Barrio, 1988). Ortiz changed his name first from Ralph to Rafael, and then to Raphael.

100. See Phelan's *Unmarked: The Politics of Performance* (London and New York: Routledge, 1993); and *Mourning Sex: Performing Public Memories* (London and New York: Routledge, 1997).

101. See also Foster's two essays: "Obscene, Object, Traumatic," *October* 78 (Fall 1996): 107–24; and "Death in America," *October* 75 (Winter 1996), 37–59.

102. Griselda Pollock, "Gleaning in History or Coming after/behind the Reapers: The Feminine, the Stranger and the Matrix in the Work and Theory of Bracha Ettinger," in Griselda Pollock, ed., *Generations and Geographies in the Visual Arts: Feminist Readings* (London: Routledge, 1996), 266–88.

103. Ernst van Alphen, *Caught by History: Holocaust Effects in Contemporary Art, Literature, and Theory* (Stanford, CA: Stanford University Press, 1997).

104. Kathy O'Dell, *Contract with the Skin: Masochism, Performance Art and the 1970s* (Minneapolis: University of Minnesota Press, 1998).

105. The list is long, but it would include pioneers like Niki de Saint Phalle, Carolee Schneemann, Yayoi Kusama, Louise Bourgeois, Judy Chicago, Miriam Shapiro, Faith Wilding, Leslie Labowitz, Suzanne Lacy, Lynn Hershman Leeson, Mary Kelly, Valie Export, ORLAN, Ulricke Rosenbach, Ana Mendieta, and many others.

106. *In Context: Yayoi Kusama, Soul-Burning Flashes* (Oxford, UK: Museum of Modern Art, 1989), based on *Soul Burning Flashes*, Fuji Television Gallery, Tokyo, Japan, 1988. Midori Yoshimoto's *Into Performance: Japanese Women Artists in New York* (New Brunswick, NJ: Rutgers University Press, 2005) considers trauma in Kusama's work as well as that of other Japanese artists.

107. Sabine Breitweiser, ed., *Erziehungskomplex/Educational Complex/Mike Kelley's Educational Complex* (Vienna: Generali Foundation, 1997).

108. Dan Cameron, *Doris Salcedo* (Santa Fe: New Museum of Contemporary Art, 1998).

109. See Beatriz Colomina, "The Architecture of Trauma," in *Louise Bourgeois: Memory and Architecture* (Madrid: Museo Nacional Centro de Arte Reina Sofia, 1999).

110. Jill Bennett and Jackie Dunn, eds., *Telling Tales* (Sydney: Ivan Dougherty Gallery, College of Fine Arts, University of New South Wales, 1998).

111. Katrina Brown, Andrew Nairne, and Fiona Bradley, *Trauma* (London: National Touring Exhibitions, 1999).

112. Sabine Eckman, *In the Aftermath of Trauma: Contemporary Video Installations* (St. Louis: Mildred Lane Kemper Art Museum, Washington University in St. Louis, Missouri, 2014).

113. Emily Braun and Megan M. Fontanella, *Alberto Burri: The Trauma of Painting* (New York: Solomon R. Guggenheim Museum, 2015).

114. V. Mohini Giri, ed., *Living Death: Trauma of Widowhood in India* (New Delhi: Gyan, 2002).

115. Eileen M. Murphy, *Iron Age Archaeology and Trauma from Aymyrlyg, South Siberia* (Oxford: Archaeopress, 2003).

116. Francisco A. Ortega, "Trauma and Narrative in Early Modernity: Garcilaso's Comentarios Reales (1609–1616)," *MLN* 118, no. 2 (March 2003): 393–426.

117. Thomas J. Cottle, *Hardest Times: The Trauma of Long Term Unemployment* (Westport, CT: Praeger, 2001).

118. Ann Cvetkovich, *An Archive of Feelings: Trauma, Sexuality, and Lesbian Public Cultures* (Durham, NC: Duke University Press, 2003).

119. Jonathan Shay, *Odysseus in America: Combat Trauma and the Trials of Homecoming* (New York: Scribner's, 2002); and Mark A. Heberle, *A Trauma Artist: Tim O'Brien and the Fiction of Vietnam* (Iowa City: University of Iowa Press, 2001); Stanley Kripperner and Teresa M. McIntyre, eds., *The Psychological Impact of War Trauma on Civilians* (Westport, CT: Praeger, 2003).

120. Yvonne S. Unnold, *Representing the Unrepresentable: Literature of Trauma under*

*Pinochet in Chile* (New York: P. Lang, 2002); and Antonius C. G. M. Robben, *Political Violence and Trauma in Argentina* (Philadelphia: University of Pennsylvania Press, 2005).

121. Susan W. Coates, Jane L. Rosenthal, Daniel S. Schechter, eds., *September 11: Trauma and Human Bonds* (Hillsdale, NJ: Analytic Press, 2003); Judith Greenberg, ed., *Trauma at Home after 9/11* (Lincoln and London: University of Nebraska Press, 2003).

122. Charlotte Pierce-Baker, *Surviving the Silence: Black Women's Stories of Rape* (New York: W. W. Norton, 1998). Pierce-Baker begun to teach about trauma in 1997 at the University of Delaware, when she taught "Black Women Rape and Other Treasons of the Body." She taught "Trauma, Violence and the Lives of Women" in Women's Studies at Duke University in 2001. See also Susan Brison, *Aftermath: Violence and the Remaking of the Self* (Princeton, NJ: Princeton University Press, 2002).

123. Stephen John Morewitz, *Domestic Violence and Maternal and Child Health: New Patterns of Trauma, Treatment, and Criminal Justice Responses* (New York: Kluwer Academic/Plenum Publishers, 2004); and Deborah M. Horvitz, Literary Trauma: Sadism, Memory, and Sexual Violence in American Women's Fiction (Albany: State University of New York Press), 2000.

124. Jason Jacobs, *Body Trauma TV: The New Hospital Dramas* (London: British Film Institute, 2003).

125. Stephanie Barbé Hammer, *Schiller's Wound: The Theater of Trauma from Crisis to Commodity* (Detroit: Wayne State University Press, 2001); Ulrich Baer, *Spectral Evidence: The Photography of Trauma* (Cambridge, MA: MIT Press, 2002); Ulrich Baer, *Remnants of Song: Trauma and the Experience of Modernity in Charles Baudelaire and Paul Celan* (Stanford, CA: Stanford University Press, 2000); Laurie Vickroy, *Trauma and Survival in Contemporary Fiction* (Charlottesville, VA: University of Virginia Press, 2002).

126. Janet Walker, *Trauma Cinema: Documenting Incest and the Holocaust* (Berkeley, CA: University of California Press, 2005).

127. Alan Bass, *Difference and Disavowal: The Trauma of Eros* (Stanford, CA: Stanford University Press, 2000).

128. Lisa Saltzman and Eric Rosenberg, eds., *Trauma and Visuality in Modernity* (Hanover, NH: Dartmouth College Press, 2006).

129. Pollock draws especially on her work on Bracha Ettinger and Ettinger's theories of trauma. See Pollock's "Thinking the Feminine: Aesthetic Practice as Introduction to Bracha Ettinger and the Concepts of Matrix and Metramorphosis," *Theory, Culture and Society* 21 (2004): 5–64; and Pollock's "Art/Trauma/Representation," *Parallax* 15, no. 1 (2009): 40–56.

130. C. R. Figley, ed., *Compassion Fatigue: Coping with Secondary Traumatic Stress Disorder in Those Who Treat the Traumatized* (Philadelphia: Brunner/Mazel, 1995); L. McCann and L. A. Pearlman, "Vicarious Traumatization: A Framework for Understanding the Psychological Effects of Working with Victims," *Journal of Traumatic Stress* 3, no. 1 (1989): 131–49.

131. "Data from large or nationally representative samples [in the United States] suggest that 12% to 53% of girls and 3% to 16% of boys experience some form of sexual abuse during childhood." See Linda J. Koenig, Lynda S. Doll, Ann O'Leary, and Willo Pequegnat, *From Child Sexual Abuse to Adult Sexual Risk: Trauma, Revictimization and Intervention* (Washington: American Psychological Association, 2004), 4.

132. James R. Lewis, *Legitimating New Religions* (New Brunswick, NJ: Rutgers University Press, 2003); Robert Jay Lifton, *Destroying the World to Save It: Aum Shinrikyō, Apocalyptic Violence, and the New Global Terrorism* (New York: Henry Holt, 1999); George Thomas, "Is the Devil Gaining a Foothold in Rome?" *CBN News* (January 1, 2009), http://www.cbn.com/cbnnews/360212.aspx; Vladimir Hernandez, "The Country Where

Exorcisms Are on the Rise," *BBC News Magazine* (November 25, 2013), accessed at http://www.bbc.com/news/magazine-25032305.

133. Samuel Logan, *This Is for the Mara Salvatrucha: Inside the MS-13, America's Most Violent Gang* (New York: Hachette Books, 2009).

134. Robert O. Kirkland, *Drug Cartel and Gang Violence in Mexico and Central America: A Concise Introduction* (San Diego: Cognella Academic Publishing, 2014).

135. Michele Goodwin, *Black Markets: The Supply and Demand of Body Parts* (Cambridge: Cambridge University Press, 2006).

136. Jaye C. Beldo, "Interview with Hakim Bey on Victim Art." Accessed at www.geocities.com/Heartland/Woods/4623/victem.htm.

137. Dennis Cooper, "Trauma Club—Mike Kelley—Modern Sculptor," *Artforum International* 39, no. 2 (October 2000): 124–29. Accessed at http://www.24hourscholar.com/p/articles/mi_m0268/is_2_39/ai_66449491.

138. Popularly known as repressed or recovered memory syndrome, the *DSM-IV* identifies such memory as "delayed onset," describing the phenomenon as memory that occurs after "at least 6 months have passed between the traumatic event and the onset of the symptoms" (425).

139. Richard J. McNally, *Remembering Trauma* (Cambridge, MA: Harvard University Press, 2003), 79.

140. For undermining the much-embattled concept of recovered memory syndrome, McNally's book received rave reviews by Frederick J. Crews, an emeritus professor of English at the University of California at Berkeley, writing in *The New York Review of Books*, and by Sally Satel, a psychiatrist and lecturer at Yale University School of Medicine, writing in *The New Republic*. Both authors describe McNally's book as "measured" (Satel) and without "polemic" or "sermon" (Crews), but they overtly demonstrate their own hostility toward recovered memory syndrome by celebrating the demise of what Satel dubs "the Church of Traumatology" and "the trauma industry." Crews argues that McNally has cleared "away a heap of junk theory," theories that Satel considers "concocted by the repression enthusiasts." Satel further charges "overzealous therapists" with having "tragically misled [patients] about the source of their unhappiness," and with "successfully implant[ing] dramatic childhood memories" in their patients. In a particularly callous comment, Satel states that those with multiple personalities have "latch[ed] onto an attractive illness narrative and transformed [their] distress into a recognized mental disorder." Identifying Robert Jay Lifton as the "spearhead" of "a band of self-described antiwar psychiatrists," Satel then dismisses his widely admired work out of hand, just as she does that of feminist Judith Lewis Herman. In a manner that suggests that their perspectives may be informed by their political conservatism, both Satel and Crews cite McNally's attention to Lifton's and Herman's left and feminist politics. See Frederick C. Crews, "The Trauma Trap," *New York Review of Books* 51, no. 4 (March 11, 2003). Accessed at http://www.psychiatrie-und-ethik.de/infc/en/Trauma-Trap.htm. See also Sally Satel, MD, "The Trauma Society," *New Republic*, May 19, 2003. Accessed at http://www.aei.org/article/17181.

For a particularly unsavory commentary that exhibits extreme aggression against recovered memory syndrome, see Mick Hartley, "Remembering Trauma" (February 25, 2004), in Hartley's blog *Politics and Culture*. Accessed at http://mickhartley.typepad.com/blog/2004/02/.

141. Ian Hacking, *Rewriting the Soul: Multiple Personality and the Sciences of Memory* (Princeton, NJ: Princeton University Press, 1995).

142. See, for example, Susan Roth and Matthew J. Friedman, *Childhood Trauma Remembered: A Report on the Current Scientific Knowledge Base and Its Applications* (North-

brook, IL: International Society for Traumatic Stress Studies, 1998), and Linda J. Koenig, Lynda S. Doll, and Ann O'Leary, eds., *From Child Sexual Abuse to Adult Sexual Risk* (Washington: American Psychological Association, 2004).

143. It is unclear who first used the term that is often attributed to the British artist Tracey Emin's work.

144. This movement attests to Julia Kristeva's very influential book *Powers of Horror: An Essay on Abjection*, translated by Leon S. Roudiez (New York: Columbia University Press, 1982, 1980). See Craig Hauser, Jack Ben Levi, Leslie C. Jones, and Simon Taylor, eds., *Abject Art Repulsion and Desire in American Art* (New York: Whitney Museum of American Art, 1993). Artists often associated with abjection include Louise Bourgeois, Helen Chadwick, Paul McCarthy, Gilbert and George, Robert Gober, Cindy Sherman, Kiki Smith, and Jake and Dinos Chapman.

145. Jill Bennett, *Empathic Visions: Affect, Trauma, and Contemporary Art* (Stanford, CA: Stanford University Press, 2005).

146. Mark Selzer, "Wound Culture: Trauma in the Pathological Public Sphere," *October* 80 (Spring 1997): 3–26.

147. Arlene Croce, "Discussing the Undiscussable," *New Yorker*, December 26, 1994 / January 2, 1995), 54–60. Croce coined the term to criticize choreographer and dancer Bill T. Jones' performance "Still/Here," describing Jones' use of HIV-positive dancers and video testimony by AIDS patients as a "traveling medicine show [of] victim art." Among many who criticized Croce was Susan Sontag, who lambasted her for feeling entitled to write about "Still/Here" even though she had refused to actually attend the performance. See Susan Sontag, letter to the editor, *New York Times*, February 26, 1995.

148. Respecting how art mediates between the public and an individual life does not mean elevating victims to morally superior positions, as Ghassan Hage has cautioned, referring especially to such tendencies in postcolonial studies. See Ghassan Hage, "Multi-Cultural Ethics," presented at the symposium "Postcolonial + Art: Where Now?" Artspace, Sydney, October 28, 2000; quoted in Bennett, *Empathic Vision*, 5.

149. Bennett, *Empathic Vision*, 149–53. See also Harold Rosenberg, *The Tradition of the New* (New York: Horizon Press, 1960).

150. Kristine Stiles, "Corpora Vilia: Valie Export's Body," in *Valie Export's Visual Syntagmatics* (Philadelphia: Goldie Paley Gallery, 2000), 16–33.

151. Kristine Stiles, "Thresholds of Control: Destruction Art and Terminal Culture," in *Out of Control* (Linz, Austria: Ars Electronica & Landesverlag, 1992, 29–50); reprinted in Timothy Druckrey, ed. *Ars Electronica: Facing the Future (A Survey of Two Decades)* (Cambridge, MA: MIT Press, 2000); www.aec.at/en/archiv_files/19911/E1991_029.pdf.

152. The online catalogue may be accessed at http://shuffle.rauschenbergfoundation.org/exhibitions/nasher/.

153. Kristine Stiles, *Questions* (San Francisco: KronOscope Press, 1982).

154. Alain Badiou, *The Century*, translated, with a commentary and notes, by Alberto Toscano (Cambridge: Polity Press, 2007; originally published in Paris by Editions du Seuil as *Le Sìecle*, 2005).

155. Giorgio Agamben, "What Is the Contemporary?" in Giorgio Agamben, *Nudities* (Stanford, CA: Stanford University Press, 2011), 13.

156. Ibid., 12.

157. Georges Bataille, "The Sacred," first published in *Cahiers d'art* 14, nos. 1–4 (1939): 47–50; reprinted in Bataille's *Visions of Excess: Selected Writings 1927–1939*, edited and with an introduction by Allan Stoekl, translated by Allan Stoekl with Cark R. Lovitt and Donald M. Leslie, Jr. (Minneapolis: University of Minnesota Press, 1985), 242.

158. Georges Bataille, "Concerning the Accounts Given by the Residents of Hiro-

shima," originally appeared in *Critique* 8–9 (1947); it was reprinted in Cathy Caruth, ed., *Trauma: Explorations in Memory* (Baltimore and London: Johns Hopkins University Press, 1995), 232.

159. Ibid.

160. ORLAN, "Manifesto of Carnal Art," on ORLAN's official website: http://www.orlan.net/texts/.

161. Badiou, 9.

162. Ibid.

163. Ibid.

164. Kristine Stiles, "Never Enough Is Something Else: Feminist Performance Art, Probity, and the Avant-Garde," in James M. Harding, ed., *Contours of the Theatrical Avant-Garde: Performance and Textuality* (Madison: University of Wisconsin–Madison, 2000), 239–89.

165. Agamben, 14.

166. Louis MacAdams, "Sex with the Dead," *Wet* 30 (March-April 1981): 60.

167. John Duncan, unpublished statement sent in a letter dated September 28, 1997, to Susan L. Jenkins, research associate at the Museum of Contemporary Art, Los Angeles. For a close examination of Duncan's work, see Karen Gonzalez Rice's unpublished dissertation "Enduring Faith: Performance, Trauma, Religion," Duke University, 2010.

168. Kristine Stiles, "Uncorrupted Joy: International Art Actions," in Paul Schimmel, ed., *Out of Actions: Between Performance and the Object 1949–1979* (Los Angeles: Museum of Contemporary Art, 1998), 241–42.

169. Ibid.

170. All quotes from this installation come from John Duncan's "If Only We Could Tell You . . . ," *High Performance* 3, no. 3/4 (Fall–Winter 1980), unpaginated.

## SURVIVAL ETHOS AND DESTRUCTION ART

1. This essay first appeared in *Discourse: Journal for Theoretical Studies in Media and Culture* 14, no. 2 (Spring 1992), 74–102; excerpts appeared in *Out of Control* (Linz: Ars Electronica, 1991), 29–50, and in Tracy Warr, ed., *The Artists' Body* (London: Phaidon Press, 2000), 227–29.

2. Robert Jay Lifton and Eric Markusen, *The Genocidal Mentality: Nazi Holocaust and Nuclear Threat* (New York: Basic Books, 1990), 253.

3. Ibid., 3.

4. Ibid., 193.

5. Ibid.

6. Robert Jay Lifton, *The Future of Immortality and Other Essays for a Nuclear Age* (New York: Basic, 1987), 238.

7. Gottfried Hattinger in *Out of Control*, 2.

8. See Hans Moravec's *Mind Children: The Future of Robot and Human Intelligence*. Cambridge, MA: Harvard University Press, 1988.

9. Günter Brus, *Bild-Dichtungen* (London: Whitechapel Art Gallery, 1980), 61.

10. Lifton, *The Future of Immortality and Other Essays for a Nuclear Age*, 235.

11. Ibid., 31.

12. Ibid., 236–40.

13. Ibid., 245.

14. Jean-François Lyotard, *Heidegger and "the jews"*, trans. Andreas Michel and Mark S. Roberts (Minneapolis: University of Minnesota Press, 1990), 3.

15. Ibid., 43.

16. Ibid., 3.

17. Friedrich Nietzsche, "Preface (November 1887–March 1888)" to *The Will to Power*, trans. Walter Kaufmann (New York: Vintage, 1967), 3.

18. See Metzger's *Auto-Destructive Art Metzger at AA*. The text contains all of Metzger's manifestos.

19. Paul Virilio and Sylvére Lotringer, *Pure War* (New York: Semiotext(e), 1983), 137.

20. Ibid., 21.

21. Gustav Metzger "Manifesto Auto-Destructive Art," March 10, 1961.

22. Carol Cohn, "Sex and Death in the Rational World of Defense Intellectuals," *Signs: Journal of Women in Culture and Society* 12, no. 4 (1987), 688–89.

23. Lifton, *The Future of Immortality and Other Essays for a Nuclear Age*, 240.

24. See Jacques Derrida, *De la grammatologie* (Paris: Minuit, 1967).

25. Jonathan Culler, *On Deconstruction: Theory and Criticism after Structuralism* (Ithaca, NY: Cornell University Press, 1982), 156.

26. Berke went to Kingsley Hall in 1965. There he worked with Mary Barnes, a nurse in her forties who had been diagnosed as a severe schizophrenic, and whom Laing and Berke brought through what they described as an "emotional death and rebirth experience" as a radical means to heal her. Once at Kingsley Hall, she was encouraged to "regress," to re-experience the trauma of birth as a means through which to reconstruct her present life experience. Berke gave a talk at DIAS on the "unbecoming and self-destruction" of the individual. Excerpts from his talk were later published in Joseph Berke, "DIAS: Excerpts from Selected Papers Delivered at the 1966 Destruction in Art Symposium," *Studio International* 172, no. 884 (December 1966), 283. When I reached Berke by telephone in 1982, he denied participation in DIAS and refused to talk with me; in recent years (the 2000s) he now acknowledges his part in DIAS. On Berke, see "'Anti-Psychiatry': An Interview with Joseph Berke," in *The Radical Therapist* (Harmondsworth, UK: Penguin, 1974). See also Joseph Berke, *Butterfly Man: Madness, Degradation and Redemption* (London: Hutchinson, 1974), and Joseph Berke, ed., *Counter Culture* (London: Peter Owen, 1969). See also Mary Barnes and Joseph Berke, *Mary Barnes: Two Accounts of a Journey through Madness* (New York: Harcourt, 1971).

27. During DIAS a number of discussions took place about staging further DIAS events in New York City and in Tokyo. When Ortiz returned to New York, he began to organize DIAS/USA with the assistance of artist Jon Hendricks. Ortiz and Hendricks eventually canceled the event after the murder of Martin Luther King. But a "DIAS Preview" took place in 1968 featuring works by Hermann Nitsch, Charlotte Moorman, Bici Hendricks, Ortiz, and others. Ortiz was an advisor for the exhibition *Destruction Art*, organized by Elaine Varian at Finch College Museum in New York, 1968. Hendricks and Ortiz also collaborated in "12 Evenings of Manipulations" at the Judson Church, New York, 1967, an event in which destructive processes were included in many actions. Nam June Paik performed *Cutting My Arm*, an action in which Paik cut long X-shaped or cross-shaped marks into his arms with a razor blade. See photographs in John G. Hanhardt, *Nam June Paik* (New York: Whitney Museum of American Art), 40. Carolee Schneemann also took part in "12 Evenings of Manipulations," staging Allan Kaprow's *Push Pull for Hans Hofmann*. As Schneemann was connected to all these events, so too was Jon Hendricks. Together Hendricks, Jean Toche, Poppy Johnson, and Ortiz also formed a brief alliance that led to the formation of GAAG, the Guerrilla Art Action Group. Toche had participated in DIAS; the formation of GAAG owes as much a debt to DIAS and Ortiz as it was a reaction to the destruction actions staged by Ortiz in New York from 1967 on. See *GAAG: The Guerrilla Art Action Group 1969–1976, a Selection* (New York: Printed Matter, 1978).

28. Based on notes taken by the journalist Sheldon Williams during the DIAS trial, I reconstructed the trial in my dissertation. The official transcripts of this trial have all been destroyed. See also David Cooper, *To Free a Generation: The Dialectics of Liberation* (New York: Collier, 1969).

29. Michel Foucault, "The Discourse on Language," in Foucault's *The Archaeology of Knowledge and the Discourse on Language* (New York: Harper, 1972), 219.

30. Kristine Stiles, *Rafael Montañez Ortiz: Years of the Warrior 1960–Years of the Psyche, 1988*. (New York: El Museo de Barrio, 1988), 52. This catalogue also contains my annotated bibliography.

31. In the original publication of this essay, I wrote: "Vostell, also a Jew, spent his youth in nomadic terror fleeing the Gestapo." Subsequent dissertation research on Vostell by both Benjamin Lima and Erin Hanas has shown that Vostell may have had distant Jewish relations on his mother's side; that while the family moved to the former Czechoslovakia, it is impossible to say that they lived a nomadic life "fleeing the Gestapo," as I had written. My original sentence reflects the stories Vostell told me about his youth, stories that other scholars have now corrected. See Benjamin Lima's dissertation *Wolf Vostell's Decollage and the Forms of Destruction* (Yale University, 2009); and Erin Hanas's dissertation *Re-Routing History: Wolf Vostell's* Fluxus Zug, *1969–1981* (2012, Duke University).

32. There are many performances by men that also concentrate on such self-reconstructions. Some of those I particularly value include Ortiz's *Self-Destruction* (1966); Brus's *Zerreißprobe* (1970); early works of Vito Acconci, Chris Burden, and Stuart Brisley; and Sherman Fleming's *Something Akin to Living* (1980).

33. R. D. Laing, "Preface to the Pelican Edition," in *The Divided Self: An Existential Study in Sanity and Madness* (Baltimore: Penguin, 1970), 12.

34. Karen Finley, "I Was not Expected to Be Talented," in Finley's *Shock Treatment* (San Francisco: City Lights, 1990), 108–9.

35. Yoko Ono, "Statement," *Village Voice* 7 (October 1971): 20.

36. Valie Export, *Valie Export: Austria Biennale di Venezia 1980* (Vienna: Galerie in der Staatsoper and the Austrian Federal Ministry of Education and Art, 1980), 14. This text accompanies Export's *Eros/ion*, a body-material interaction performed at the Electric Cinema, Amsterdam, 1971.

37. When I published this article in the spring of 1992, I could not have known that Hershman would continue *The Electric Diary* until 1994. See also Lynn Hershman, "The Electronic Diary: An Ongoing Diary," in *Whitewalls* 25 (Spring 1990): 71–79.

38. Elaine Scarry, *The Body in Pain: The Making and the Unmaking of the World* (Oxford, UK: Oxford University Press, 1985), 162.

39. Ibid., 4.

40. Ibid., 6.

41. Yoko Ono, *Grapefruit*, 2nd Edition (New York: Simon and Schuster, 1970), unpaginated.

42. Tut Schlemmer, ed., *The Letters and Diaries of Oskar Schlemmer*, trans. Krishna Winston (Middletown, CT: Wesleyan University Press, 1972), 50.

43. Ibid., 17.

44. Oskar Schlemmer, "Man and Art Figure," in Walter Groupius, ed., *Theater of Bauhaus*, trans. Arthur S. Wesinger (Middletown, CT: Wesleyan University Press, 1961), 22.

45. Schlemmer sets forth these terms in "Man in the Sphere of ldeas" (1928), his drawing reproduced in the exhibition catalogue *Oskar Schlemmer, Man and the Sphere of Ideas* (Baltimore: Baltimore Museum of Art, 1986). Marcel Duchamp is another artist whose work fundamentally translates painting and sculpture into corporeal discourse. Both

Schlemmer and Duchamp identified the human body as the site of visual knowledge. Duchamp's preoccupation with the body is legendary, beginning with his figurative paintings and ending in *Étant donnés: 1° la chute d'eau, 2° le gaz d'éclairage)* (1946–66).

46. Oskar Schlemmer, "Theater," in Walter Gropius, ed., *The Theater of the Bauhaus*, 92.

47. Yves Klein, "Truth Becomes Reality," in *Yves Klein* (Houston: Institute for the Arts, Rice University, 1982), 230.

48. Caroline Tisdall, "'Materia': The Context of *Arte Povera,"* in Emily Brau, ed., *Italian Art in the Twentieth Century: Painting and Sculpture 1900–1988* (Munich: Prestel, 1989), 366.

49. Anthony Cox, "Instructive Auto-Destruction," *Art and Artists* 1, no. 5 (1966): 17.

50. Herbert Blau, *The Impossible Theater: A Manifesto* (New York: Macmillian, 1964), 126.

51. Serge Guilbaut, *How New York Stole the Idea of Modern Art: Abstract Expressionism, Freedom, and the Cold War*, trans. Arthur Goldhammer (Chicago: University of Chicago Press, 1983), 108.

52. John Hersey, *Hiroshima* (New York: Bantam, 1968), 59.

53. Guilbaut, 108.

54. Ibid., 113.

55. When I began research and writing on these artists in the late 1970s, they were relatively unknown and marginalized. Today this is no longer the case.

56. This view countered Benjamin H. D. Buchloh's comments in "Figures of Authority, Ciphers of Regression: Notes on the Return of Representation in European Painting," in Benjamin H. D. Buchloh, Serge Guilbaut, and David Solkin, eds., *Modernism and Modernity: The Vancouver Conference Papers* (Halifax, Nova Scotia: Press of the Nova Scotia College of Art and Design, 1983), 81–115. Buchloh charged that neoexpressionism of the late 1970s and early 1980s represented a return to figuration similar to that which occurred with the modernist avant-garde after 1915. Buchloh further argued that "the masters of modernism . . . were in fact the servants of an audience craving for the restoration of the visual codes of recognizability for the reinstatement of figuration" (81). For a perceptive critique of Buchloh's article, see Andy Patton, "Buchloh's History," in *C [Toronto]* 5 (Spring 1985): 29–33.

57. Ernesto Laclau and Chantal Mouffe, *Hegemony and Socialist Strategy: Towards a Radical Democratic Politics*, trans. Winston Moore and Paul Cammack (London: Thetford, 1985), 43.

58. Michel Foucault, *The Care of the Self. Volume 3: The History of Sexuality*, tTrans. Robert Hurley (New York: Pantheon, 1986), 50, 60–66.

59. Herbert L. Dreyfus and Paul Rabinow, *Michel Foucault: Beyond Structuralism and Hermeneutics* (Chicago: University of Chicago Press, 1983), 243–45.

60. Lifton, *The Future of Immortality and Other Essays for a Nuclear Age*, 245.

## SHAVED HEADS AND MARKED BODIES: REPRESENTATIONS FROM CULTURES OF TRAUMA

1. I gave the first version of this essay at an international conference on "War and Gender" organized by miriam cooke and Alex Roland at the Bellagio Center, Bellagio, Italy, in August of 1993. It was first published in *Strategie II: Peuples Méditerranéens* 64–65 (July–December 1993): 95–117; reprinted in *Lusitania* 6 (1994): 23–39; reprinted in *Dan Perjovschi: Anthroprogramming* (New York: Franklin Furnace, 1996); reprinted in German in *kur-*

*siv* 2–3 (1995): 19–25, reprinted in Romanian in many Romanian publications; reprinted with a new afterword in Jean O'Barr, Nancy Hewitt, and Nancy Rosebaugh, eds., *Talking Gender: Public Images, Personal Journeys, and Political Critiques* (Chapel Hill: University of North Carolina Press, 1996), 36–64; and reprinted in Bruce Lawrence and Aisha Karim, eds., *The Chain of Violence: An Anthology* (Durham, NC: Duke University Press, 2007).

2. In addition to my formulation of "cultures of trauma," critics have mentioned such terms as "shame culture" and "guilt culture," among many others. See Bernard Knox's review of Bernard Williams' *Shame and Necessity* (1992) and Ruth Benedict's *The Chrysanthemum and the Sword* (1946); and Knox, "The Greek Way," in *The New York Review of Books* (18 November 1993): 42.

3. Michael R.Trimble, "Post-Traumatic Stress Disorder: History of a Concept," in Charles R. Figley, ed., *Trauma and Its Wake: The Study and Treatment of Post-Traumatic Stress Disorder* (New York: Brunner/Mazel, 1985), 13.

4. Figley, introduction to *Trauma and Its Wake*, xviii–xix.

5. Trimble reports that Charles Dickens was unable to recover from having witnessed a horrifying railway accident in 1865, and Samuel Pepys became suicidal after a fire in his home. Trimble, "Post-Traumatic Stress Disorder," in *Trauma and Its Wake*, 7. See also R. J. Daly, "Samuel Pepys and Post-Traumatic Stress Disorder," *British Journal of Psychiatry* 143 (1983): 64–68; and J. Forster, *The Life of Charles Dickens*, 2nd vol. (London: J. M. Dent and Sons, 1969).

6. Raymond M. Scurfield, "Post-Trauma Reactions and Symptoms," in *Trauma and Its Wake*, 233. See also Judith Lewis Herman, "Complex Post-Traumatic Stress Disorder," in *Trauma and Recovery*, 121.

7. I wrote this essay twenty years before Jodi Rudoren's article "Proudly Bearing Elders' Scars: Their Skin Says 'Never Forget,'" published in *The New York Times*, October 6, 2012: http://www.nytimes.com/2012/10/01/world/middleeast/with-tattoos-young-israelis-bear-holocaust-scars-of-relatives.html?pagewanted=all.

8. I am indebted to Judit Katona-Apte of the United Nations World Food Programme for her paper "Refugee Women: An International Existential Anomaly?" presented at the 1992 Bellagio Conference on War and Gender. See also Diane Weathers, "Impact of Refugee Camps," *WFP and the Environment* (Rome: World Food Programme, 1990), 9–10. In 2016, massive refugee camps exist nearly worldwide.

9. On the subject of nuclear proliferation, see Frank Barnaby, ed., *Plutonium and Security: The Military Aspects of the Plutonium Economy* (London: MacMillan, 1992). I consider this subject in my essay, "Irreparable Damage: James Lerager's Documentary Photography and Social Activism in the Nuclear Age," in Kristine Stiles, *Tales from the Nuclear Age* (Raleigh, NC: City Gallery of Contemporary Art, 1995).

10. See Frank Capa, *Robert Capa, Photographs* (New York: Alfred A. Knopf, 1985), 162–65; Carl Mydans, *Carl Mydans, Photojournalist* (New York: Harry H. Abrams, 1985), 104. Ophuls's film includes extensive interviews with Pierre Mendes-France, Albert Speer, Sir Anthony Eden, Claude Levy, and others, but no comments from the women with shaved heads! See also Alain Brossat's *Les Tondues: Un Carnaval Moche* (Mesnil sur Estrée: Éditions Manya, 1993).

11. Susan Sontag was one of the first to theorize about the sexual aggression (akin to rape) of the photograph in *On Photography* (New York: Farrar, Strauss & Giroux, 1973). See also Bill Jay's "The Photographer as Aggressor," in David Featherstone, ed., *Observations: Essays on Documentary Photography* (Carmel, CA: Friends of Photography, 1984), 7–23.

12. In the fifth century BCE, Herodotus accounted for the importance of women in the Persian Wars when he pointed out that, "as for the carrying off of women, it is the

deed, they say, of a rogue; but to make a stir about such as are carried off, argues a man a fool. . . . The Asiatics, when the Greeks ran off with their women, never troubled themselves about the matter; but the Greeks, for the sake of a single Lacedaemonian girl, collected a vast armament, invaded Asia, and destroyed the kingdom of Prima, hence they ever looked upon the Greeks as their open enemies." Herodotus, *The Persian Wars*, trans. George Rawlinson (New York: Random House, 1942), 3; quoted by Barbara Harlow in her introduction to Malek Alloula's *The Colonial Harem*, trans. Myrna Godzich and Wlad Godzich (Minneapolis: University of Minnesota Press, 1966), xiv–xv. See also Sara Ruddic, "Maternal Thinking and Peace Politics," in Sara Ruddic, ed., *Maternal Thinking: Toward a Politics of Peace* (New York: Ballantine Books, 1989).

13. For discussion of the term "phallocratic," see Luce Irigaray, *This Sex Which Is Not One*, trans. Catherine Porter and C. Burke (Ithaca, NY: Cornell University Press, 1985), and Jacques Lacan's "The Signification of the Phallus" in *Écrits: A Selection*, trans. Alan Sheridan (New York: W. W. Norton, 1977), 281–91.

14. James M. Glass, *Shattered Selves: Multiple Personality in a Postmodern World* (Ithaca, NY, and London: Cornell University Press, 1993), 127.

15. On the subject of comfort women, I am indebted to Kazuko Watanabe's unpublished paper "Militarism, Colonialism and the Trafficking in Women: Military Comfort Women Forced by the Japanese Imperial Army," presented at the Bellagio Conference on War and Gender, 1993. See also Iryumiyon Kim, *Emperor's Army and Korean Comfort Women* (Tokyo: Sanichi Shobo, 1976). On Bosnian rape, see Catherine A. MacKinnon, "Turning Rape into Pornography: Postmodern Genocide," *Ms.* 4, no. 1 (July/August 1993):, 24–30.

16. Helene Cixous and Catherine Clement, *The Newly Born Woman*, trans. Betsy Wing (Minneapolis: University of Minnesota Press, 1986), 65.

17. Bertolt Brecht, "Ballade von der 'Judenhure' Marie Sanders," in *Bertolt Brecht Gedichte: Ausgewahlt von Autoren Mit einem Geleitwort von Ernst Bloch* (Frankfurt am Main: Suhrkamp Verlag, 1977), 132–33.

18. Ishmael Reed, *Reckless Eyeballing* (New York: St. Martin's Press, 1986), 55.

19. Frantz Fanon, *A Dying Colonialism*, trans. Haakon Chevalier (New York: Grove Press, 1967), 39. I am grateful to Bruce B. Lawrence for his comments on Fanon during the Bellagio Conference on War and Gender. See also Spivak, quoted by Barbara Harlow in her introduction to Malek Alloula*'s The Colonial Harem*, xviii. Harlow also points out that the French in Algeria and the British in India and Africa attempted "to collaborate with the women under the pretext of liberating them from oppression by their own men," and that this "would happen later in Iran during the Khomeini-led revolution against the Shah's dictatorship" (xviii–xix).

20. Reed, 55.

21. Judit Katona-Apte and Mahadev Apte brought this film to my attention.

22. James Ridgeway, *Blood in the Face: The Ku Klux Klan, Aryan Nations, Nazi Skin-Heads, and the Rise of a New White Culture* (New York: Thunder's Mouth Press, 1990), 164.

23. Dick Hebdige, *Subculture: The Meaning of Style* (London: Meuthen, 1979), quoted in Ridgeway, 164.

24. Very different groups rapidly assimilated the style, or fashion, of skinheads, groups ranging from punks to neo-hippie ecological skins who do not identify with white supremacism. Sinead O'Connor's shaved head, for example, represents popular cultural icons of protest, while the shaved and tattooed head of a current Parisian fashion model demonstrates how quickly style transforms ideology.

25. See Julia Kristeva, *Powers of Horror: An Essay on Abjection* (New York: Columbia University Press, 1982).

26. Toni Morrison, *Playing in the Dark: Whiteness and the Literary Imagination* (Cambridge, MA, and London: Harvard University Press, 1992), xiii.

27. Ibid., 51–52.

28. When performance artist John Duncan purchased a female corpse in Tijuana in the early 1980s for the purpose of having sex with it, his act was a desperate exhibition of this excruciating lack. Duncan's pain is palpable, however contemptible.

29. Cixous and Clement, 64–65.

30. Katherine Verdery and Gail Kligman explain that many Romanians now believe that the December 1989 revolution was a coup which may have been plotted for up to two decades, that it may have been supported by the former Soviet Union, and that it was carried out by the National Salvation Front—reformed communists, many of whom are still in control of the government and the Romanian Securitate. See Verdery and Kligman's "Romania after Ceausescu: Post-Communist Communism?" in Ivo Banac, ed., *Eastern Europe in Revolution* (Ithaca, NY, and London: Cornell University Press, 1992), 119.

31. The Romanian Securitate, unlike the German Stasi or the Russian KGB, has yet to be purged. This is still true as this book goes to press in 2015. Katherine Verdery notes that in Romania "merely required people to acknowledge past collaboration after which their political careers might continue." See Verdery's public lecture, "Purity and Danger in Romania's 'Transnational Justice': Purging Enemies through Securitate Files," at the University of Michigan on November 11, 2009: https://www.youtube.com/watch?v=0uVRayVPHho.

32. Auschwitz survivor Primo Levi and philosopher Walter Benjamin both believed that the concentration camp was a microcosm of the external world. See Levi, *Survival in Auschwitz and The Reawakening: Two Memoirs* (*Se questo e un uomo* [1958] and *La tregua* [1963]) (New York: Summit Books, 1986); and Levi, *The Drowned and the Saved*, trans. Raymond Rosenthal (*Sommersi e i salvati* [1986]) (New York: Vintage International, 1989). See also Pietro Fransisca, *Primo Levi as Witness: Proceedings of a Symposium Held at Princeton University* (Florence: Casalini Libri, 1990); and Hans Sahl, *Walter Benjamin: Im Lager* (Frankfurt: Suhrkamp, 1972).

33. Katherine Verdery, *National Ideology under Socialism: Identity and Cultural Politics in Ceauşescu's Romania* (Berkeley: University of California Press), 101. This history involves claims made by Romanian intellectuals for the priority of Romanian cultural inventions as well as the cultural and political history of Europe. Verdery charts "protochronism" (temporal priority) in several chapters.

34. Ibid., 122.

35. Ibid., 107.

36. Ralph Earle, "On the Virtues of Distrust: An Interview with Andrei Codrescu," *The Sun* 143 (October 1987): 8.

37. Unpublished comments from Katherine Verdery's talk "Nationalism and the 'Transition' in Romania," Duke University, February 23, 1993.

38. Ion Bitzan, unpublished interview with the author, October 1992. All further quotes from Bitzan come from this discussion.

39. Alexandra Cornilescu, "Transitional Patterns: Symptoms of the Erosion of Fear in Romanian Political Discourse," unpublished talk at the Modern Language Association annual meeting, New York, 1992. All further quotes by Cornilescu come from this article.

40. Andrei Codrescu, *Monsieur Teste in America and Other Instances of Realism* (Minneapolis: Coffee House Press, 1987), 14.

41. Herman, 83.

42. Henry Krystal, "Trauma and Affects," *Psychoanalytic Study of the Child* 33 (1978): 81–116, quoted in Herman, 84.

43. On the "conspiracy of silence," see Yael Danieli, "The Treatment and Prevention of Long-Term Effects and Intergenerational Transmission of Victimization: A Lesson from Holocaust Survivors and Their Children," in Figley's *Trauma and Its Wake*, 298–99, 307–8, 311; and Milton E. Jucovy, "Therapeutic Work with Survivors and Their Children: Recurrent Themes and Problems," in Paul Marcus and Alan Rosenberg, eds., *Healing Their Wounds: Psychotherapy with Holocaust Survivors and Their Families* (New York: Praeger 1989), 51–66.

44. Herman, 9.

45. Ion Grigorescu shed new light on this work in a letter to me of February 28, 2015. As a result, I have updated the meaning of this work from my original discussion of it in 1993. All subsequent quotes by Grigorescu on this work of art come from this letter.

46. Verdery and Kligman, 143.

47. Elaine Scarry, *The Body in Pain: The Making and Unmaking of the World* (Oxford: University of Oxford Press, 1985), 4.

48. Sanda Agalidi, "Notes on 'Vox,'" *Oversight* [Los Angeles] 2 (1990): 23.

49. See Mikhail Bakhtin, *The Dialogical Imagination* (Austin: University of Texas Press, 1981), quoted in Verdery, 122.

50. See Gilles Deleuze and Felix Guattarti, *Anti-Oedipus: Capitalism and Schizophrenia*, preface by Michel Foucault, trans. Robert Hurley, Mark Seem, and Helen R. Lane (Minneapolis: University of Minnesota Press, 1975); originally published as *L'Anti-Oedipe* (Paris: Les Editions de Minuit, 1972). See also Jean Baudrillard, *The Ecstasy of Communication* (New York: Semiotext[e], 1987).

51. Glass, 158.

52. Scarry, 6.

53. Stiles, "Synopsis of the Destruction in Art Symposium and Its Theoretical Significance," *The Act* 1 (Spring 1987): 22–31, 28–29.

54. Helene Cixous, *Inside*, trans. C. Barko (New York: Schocken, 1986), 97.

55. Herman, 9.

56. V. Vale and Andrea Juno, introduction to "Modern Primitives," a special issue of *RE/Search* 12 (1989): 4.

57. Marianna Torgovnick, *Gone Primitive: Savage Intellects, Modern Lives* (Chicago and London: University of Chicago Press, 1990), 245.

58. My student, Duc Phong Nguyen, recounted a story her mother told after hearing about my essay "Shaved Heads." There is a custom in some Vietnam villages, she explained, in which an adulterous woman is taken from her home, her head is shaved, her body is covered with lime, and she is tied to a boat and set adrift to die on the river. I have been unable to substantiate this story, but it parallels Western practices. See also Ruth Mellinkoff, *Outcasts: Signs of Otherness in Northern European Art of the Late Middle Ages* (Berkeley: University of California Press, 1993), which includes a chapter (chapter 9) entitled "Hair and Heads: Close-Cropped, Balding, Hairless, and Shaved." Claudia Koonz recommended several articles on how tattoos and shaved heads in Ireland and Russia signified traumatic conditions. "Since the collapse of communism and the decay of Russia's old social welfare system, statistics show that teen criminals are becoming even more violent and aggressive," Jennifer Gould has written. "One of the most harrowing teenage crimes this year involved a group of boys who raped a 16-year-old girl and burned her to death in southern Russia. . . . Some (of these) teens also amuse themselves by getting tat-

toos, although getting caught often means serving in solitary." See Gould, "Inside Russia's Gulag for Teenage Criminals," *Toronto Star*, May 30, 1993, F2.

59. Paglia's oratory is seductive in that she summons myths of women and states of being (i.e., primitivism) that are familiar in a time of great change and challenges to dominant patriarchal paradigms. Writing on Elizabeth Taylor's performance in the film *Suddenly Last Summer* (1959), Paglia stated: "It is an astonishingly rich picture, full of the paradoxes of concealment and exhibitionism that make woman so elusive and so dominant." On Madonna's video, "Open Your Heart," Paglia opined: "Responding to the spiritual tensions within Italian Catholicism, Madonna discovered the buried paganism within the church." Paglia concluded: "The old-guard establishment feminists who still loathe Madonna have a sexual ideology problem." The mysticism of interiority, paradox, concealment, and exhibitionism associated with women conforms precisely to the phallocratic universe about which I have been writing; summoning the "pagan" in the Church is calling forth the "primitive." See Paglia's *Sex, Art, and American Culture* (New York: Vintage Books, 1992), 17, 11.

60. See Madonna, *Sex*, edited by Glenn O'Brien and photographed by Stephen Meisel, with artistic direction by Fabien Baron (New York: Warner Books, 1992).

61. See Susan McClary, "Living to Tell: Madonna's Resurrection of the Fleshly," in *Feminine Endings: Music, Gender, and Sexuality* (Minneapolis: University of Minnesota Press, 1991), 148–66; or Lisa Lewis, *Gender Politics and MTV: Voicing the Difference* (Philadelphia: Temple University Press, 1990), especially "Female Address Video (1980–1986)," 109–48. Thanks to Victoria C. Vandenberg's unpublished senior distinction thesis paper "Bodies, Gender, and Rock-n-Roll: Making Music Dance on MTV," Duke University, 1990.

62. Angela Carter offers an excellent critique of the claim that women may appropriate signs of negativity as representations or practices of self-construction and self-empowerment. See Carter, *The Sadeian Woman and the Ideology of Pornography* (New York: Pantheon Books, 1978).

## REMEMBERING INVISIBILITY: DOCUMENTARY PHOTOGRAPHY OF THE NUCLEAR AGE

1. I would like to thank Simon Anderson for the invitation to give this essay as the Norma U. Lifton Lecture at the School of the Art Institute of Chicago in 1998. I would also like to thank James Lerager, Robert del Tredici, and Arjan Makhijani for helping to educate me to the topic; Richard J. Powell, Richard Shiff, Martin Jay, and Jock Reynolds for their belief in and support of my research on this subject; and Adam Starr and Rebecca Katz for their invaluable research assistance. My work on the nuclear age began in 1992 when I contacted Lerager about his work in Kazakhstan. This led to an exhibition of James Lerager's photographs at the now defunct City Gallery of Contemporary Art in Raleigh, North Carolina, for which we produced a catalogue on his photographs as well as my essay "Irreparable Damage: Meditation on James Lerager's *Tales from the Nuclear Age*," in *James Lerager: Tales from the Nuclear Age* (Raleigh: City Gallery Contemporary Art, 1993): 3–7. The US Department of Education, through the Center for Documentary Studies at Duke University, then under the direction of Josefina Tiryakian, awarded me a global studies undergraduate curriculum development grant for research on this exhibition and the development of my course "Documentary Photography and Social Activism in the Nuclear Age," which I regularly taught from 1992 to 2009. I curated a second exhibition of Lerager's work at the former Duke Museum of Art in 1993. That show was titled *Kazakhhstan in the Nuclear Age*, and was accompanied by a symposium entitled

Documentary Photography and Social Activism in the Nuclear Age. The Department of Art and Art History, Comparative Area Studies, the University Art Museum, and the Institute for the Arts funded these events. Thanks to Michael Mezzatesta, then director of the now defunct Duke Museum of Art, and to Jill Meredith. The Institute for Energy and Environmental Research (IEER) in Takoma Park, Maryland, under the direction of Dr. Arjun Makhijani, is an invaluable archive and resource for working on issues of the nuclear age.

2. Paul W. Tibbets Jr. with Clair Stebbins and Harry Franken, "My God, What Have We Done?" in *The Tibbets Story* (New York: Stein and Day, 1978), 221.

3. Japan Peace Museum/Japan Confederation of A- and H-Bomb Sufferers Organizations, *The Nuclear Century: Voices of the Hibakusha of the World* (Tokyo: Heiwa no Atorie, 1997), 331. An anonymous US military photographer took the photograph on November 20, 1945.

4. Testimony of Yoshito Matsushige, http://www.konradh.net/jp/history/hibakusha/yoshito.html.

5. Robert J. Lifton and Eric Markusen, *The Genocidal Mentality: Nazi Holocaust and Nuclear Threat* (New York: Basic Books, 1992).

6. Paul Virilio in Sylvère Lotringer and Paul Virilio, *Pure War* (New York: Semiotext[e], 1983), 2.

7. Ibid., 6

8. Ibid., 16.

9. Ibid., 170.

10. Ibid.

11. Ibid., 170–71.

12. See, for example, Rex Applegate, *Riot Control: Materiel and Techniques* (Harrisburg, PA: Stackpole Books, 1969); Rex Applegate, "Nonlethal Police Weapons," *Ordnance* (July–August 1971): 62–66; Joseph F. Coates, "Non-Lethal Police Weapons," *Technology Review* (June 1972): 49–56; Stockholm International Peace Research Institute (SIPRI), *The Problem of Chemical and Biological Warfare. Volume II: CB Weapons Today* (Stockholm: Almqvist & Wiksell, 1973); Malvern Lumsden, "Electric, Acoustic and Electromagnetic-Wave Weapons,." in Malvern Lumsden, *Anti-Personnel Weapons* (London: Taylor and Francis, 1978), 203; Gerry Northam, *Shooting in the Dark: Riot Police in Britain* (London: Faber and Faber, 1988).

13. A draft of Eisenhower's speech contained the phrase "military-industrial-congressional complex," which was excised in order not to embarrass the Congress and its unfaltering role in support of the military industry. See Geoffrey Perret's biography, *Eisenhower* (New York: Random House, 1999).

14. Virilio, 27.

15. Ibid., 137.

16. Ibid., 20.

17. Ibid., 37.

18. Ibid., 47.

19. As of this writing, among the members of the Atomic Photographer's Guild are Berlyn Brixner, James Crnkovich, Blake Fitzpatrick, Harris Fogel, Carole Gallagher, Kenji Higuchi, James Lerager, Yoshito Matsushige, David McMillan, Patrick Nagatani, Mark Ruwedel, Paul Shambroom, and Hiromi Tsuchida.

20. Robert Del Tredici, *At Work in the Fields of the Bomb*, introduction by Jonathan Schell (New York: Harper & Row, 1987), plate 39.

21. "Plutonium belongs to the class of elements called transuranic, . . . whose atomic number is higher than 92, the atomic number of uranium. Isotopes of plutonium were first prepared and studied by the American chemist Glenn T. Seaborg and his associates at

the University of California at Berkeley in 1941. All isotopes of plutonium are radioactive, but they have widely varying half-lives. The half-life is the time it takes for half the atoms of an element to decay. The various isotopes also have different principal decay modes. The most important isotope of plutonium is Pu-239. It's virtually nonexistent in nature. It is produced by bombarding uranium-238 with slow neutrons. This forms neptunium-239, which in turn emits a beta particle and forms plutonium-239. Plutonium-239's principal mode of decay is alpha decay. Various sources give slightly different figures for the half-life. The values found include 24,360, 24,400, 24,110, and 24,000 years. None of these measurements agree." See Janice Ching, "Plutonium-239," *The Physics Hypertextbook*, http://hypertextbook.com/facts/JaniceChing.shtml.

22. Del Tredici, plate 56.

23. Del Tredici, plate 90.

24. Del Tredici, plate 105.

25. Ibid. Del Tredici explains, "Of the 95,000 reindeer taken for human consumption during the first year after the accident, 75,000 had to be thrown away" (page 192).

26. Tilman Ruff, "Bomb Tests Attack the Food Chain," *Bulletin of the Atomic Scientists* 46:2 (March 1990). "Although it is rarely fatal, ciguatera poisoning causes a wide variety of debilitating symptoms, including vomiting, diarrhea, abdominal pain, trembling, and paralysis. Symptoms may vary widely, even if individuals have eaten the same fish. The effects of the disease may last for weeks, months, or years, with persistent chronic symptoms: tingling pain, deranged sensations (particularly with cold objects producing acute pain), itching, and loss of balance and muscular coordination. There exists no known cure, nor a proven effective and safe treatment. . . . In the 1950s, Marshall Islanders attributed an increase in ciguatera poisoning to the U.S. nuclear testing program at Eniwetok and Bikini. The disease was not reported on Eniwetok itself, but nearby atolls had severe outbreaks. 7 Hospital records show that overall clinic visits increased by 60 percent, but visits for gastrointestinal illness (much of which may have been ciguatera) increased 200/300 percent. Before resettling the native population, the U.S. Energy Department's predecessor agency, ERDA, conducted a survey of fish toxicity at Bikini and Eniwetok between 1974 and 1978. Although the study's author discounted the problem, the survey revealed that 37 percent of the fish sampled at Eniwetok were toxic to some degree, and 16.2 percent were considered toxic enough to cause the disease. At Bikini 19.7 percent of the fish were toxic, 1.4 percent at a level likely to cause the illness." http://www.bullatomsci.org/issues/1990/mar90/mar90ruff.html.

27. Del Tredici, plate 86.

28. W. J. T. Mitchell, "Ekphrasis and the Other," *Picture Theory: Essays on Verbal and Visual Representation* (Chicago and London: The University of Chicago Press, 1994), 151–81.

29. All quotes from Warehime come from James Lerager, *In the Shadow of the Cloud: Photographs & Histories of America's Atomic Veterans* (Golden, CO: Flucrum, 1988), 88.

30. Roland Barthes, *Camera Lucida: Reflections on Photography*, translated by Richard Howard (New York: Hill & Wang, 1981), 53.

31. John Whittier Treat, *Writing Ground Zero: Japanese Literature and the Atomic Bomb* (Chicago: University of Chicago Press, 1995), 362.

32. Treat, 439n2.

33. See, Derrida's "No Apocalypse, Not Now," *Diacritics* 14, no. 2 (Summer 1984): 21.

34. Ibid.: 23. Derrida wrote: "American bombs in 1945 ended a 'classical,' conventional war; it did not set off a nuclear war." Jacques Derrida, quoted in Treat, 353–54.

35. Karl Popper, *Quantum Theory and the Schism in Physics* (Totowa, N.J: Rowman and Littlefield, 1982), 2, as quoted in Treat, 361.

36. Treat, xii.

37. Del Tredici, plate 51.

38. See Cohn, "Emasculating America's Linguistic Deterrent," in Adrienne Harris and Ynestra King, eds., *Rocking the Ship of State: Toward a Feminist Peace Politics* (Boulder, San Francisco, London: Westview Press, 1989), 164.

39. See Cohn, "Sex and Death in the Rational World of Defense Intellectuals," *Signs: Journal of Women in Culture and Society* 12,no. 4 (Summer 1987): 687–718.

40. Carole Gallagher, *American Ground Zero: The Secret Nuclear War* (Cambridge, MA: Random House, 1994), xxiii.

41. Del Tredici, 169.

42. Lerager, 12.

43. Benjamin A. Goldman with Kate Millpointer, *Deadly Deceit: Low-Level Radiation High Level Cover-Up* (New York: Four Walls Eight Windows, 1990), 165, 135–41.

44. Alexander Wilson, "On the Frontiers of Capital: Nuclear Plants and Other Environmental Architectures," in *The Culture of Nature: North American Landscape from Disney to the Exxon Valdez* (Cambridge, MA: Blackwell, 1992), 280. On medical issues related to health risks, see H. Jack Geiger, *Dead Reckoning: A Critical Review of the Department of Energy's Epidemiologic Research* (Washington: Physicians for Social Responsibility, 1992).

45. See, for example, *Wise News Communiqué* 386 (12 February 1993): 7; or Craig Whitney, "Illicit Atom-Material Trade Worries Germans," *New York Times International* (Tuesday, October 20, 1992).

46. Robert L. Gallucci, "Nuclear Proliferation and the National Security," Duke University, October 22, 1998.

47. See quotes in news clippings in the Institute for Energy and Environmental Research archive files, including an Associated Press story reported December 3, 1992.

48. See Taryn Toro, "Radiation Sickness Caesium Smugglers," *New Scientist* 17 (October 1992): 8.

49. Gallucci, "Nuclear Proliferation and the National Security."

50. The event occurred when workers in a missile tracking station in northern Russia saw a troubling blip on their screens. It indicated that a rocket had been launched from somewhere in Norway, and within minutes Boris Yeltsin was advised. This was "the first time ever, that [the] 'nuclear briefcase' was activated for emergency use. The unidentified object turned out to be a US scientific probe sent up to investigate the northern lights. Weeks earlier the Norwegians had duly informed Russian authorities of the planned launch from the offshore island of Andoya but somehow word of the high-altitude experiment had not reached the right ears." Bruce G. Blair, Harold A. Feiveson, and Frank N. von Hippel, "Taking Nuclear Weapons off Hair-Trigger Alert," *Scientific American* 277, no. 5 (November 1997): 75–77.

51. Siegfried Kracauer, "Photography," *Critical Inquiry* 19 (Spring 1993): 429. This originally appeared as "Die Photographie" in *Frankfurter Zeitung*, October 28, 1927.

52. See Thierry de Duve, "Time Exposure and Snapshot: The Photograph as Paradox," *October* 5 (Summer 1978): 113. See also Barthes, "The Photographic Message," "The Rhetoric of the Image," and "The Third Meaning," in Stephen Heath, ed., *Image-Music-Text* (New York: Fontana/Collins, 1977).

53. John Tagg, *The Burden of Representation: Essays on Photographies and Histories* (Amherst: University of Massachusetts Press, 1988), 1.

54. Gallagher, 65.

55. Ibid., 66.

56. Ibid.

THE IDEAL GIFTS AND *THE TRINITY SESSION* OF ISTVAN KANTOR

1. This essay first appeared in Linda Feesey and Mireille Bourgeois, eds., *Permanent Revolution: Istvan Kantor* (Toronto: Kantor Collective, 2014. Thanks to Istvan Kantor for identifying stupidity and having the consistent courage to show that the emperor has no clothes. Thanks also to Jasmina Tumbas for reading and commenting on this text, to Linda Feesey for editorial suggestions and questions that initiated this essay, and to Mireille Bourgeois for final edits.

2. Robert Musil, *The Man Without Qualities*, Books I and II (Oakville, ON: Capricorn Books, 1965), 160–61.

3. Unpublished text by Cassandra Sung-Hyan [aka Istvan Kantor] in Kantor's self-produced unique "scrap book," assembled as a gift to the author in 2001. Hereafter footnoted as Kantor's unpublished "Scrap Book" (2001) in Stiles' Papers, Special Collections of the Rubenstein Library, Duke University.

4. Istvan Kantor e-mail to Kristine Stiles, March 18, 2013.

5. Kantor arrived at this conclusion a decade before the more celebrated work of the artist group Neue Slowenische Kunst (NSK) of the former Yugoslavia, now Slovenia.

6. Istvan Kantor, "Introduction to My Childhood." Stiles' Papers, Special Collections of the Rubenstein Library, Duke University.

7. Kantor, "Scrap Book."

8. Ibid.

9. Homi K. Bhabha, book endorsement for Martin Jay and Sumathi Ramaswamy, eds., *Empires of Vision: A Reader* (Durham, NC: Duke University Press, 2013).

10. Musil, Book II, 205.

11. Ibid., 218–19.

12. Ibid.

13. Kantor, "Scrap Book."

14. Ibid.

15. Ibid.

16. Musil, Book I, 63–64.

17. Musil, *The Man Without Qualities: Into the Millennium (The Criminals)*, Book III (London: Picador, 1979), 414.

18. Following Kantor, the act of supreme sacrifice—the draining of one's blood—has also been undertaken by artists like Uri Katzenstein, Ron Athey, and Fanco B, to name the most prominent artists using this method of self-representation.

19. See "Shaved Heads and Marked Bodies: Representations from Cultures of Trauma," in this volume.

20. Musil, Book II, 63.

21. Kantor, "Scrap Book."

22. Ibid.

23. Victor Sebestyen, *Twelve Days: The Story of the 1956 Hungarian Revolution* (New York: Vintage, 2006), xxv.

24. Sebestyen, xxiii.

25. Kantor, "Scrap Book."

26. Istvan Kantor, e-mail to the author, March 18, 2013.

27. Kantor, "Scrap Book."

28. On this critical aspect of trauma, and why trauma studies pose a vital challenge to historical narrative, see Dori Laub's essay "An Event Without a Witness: Truth, Testimony and Survival" in Shoshana Felman and Dori Laub, *Testimony: Crises of Witnessing in Literature, Psychoanalysis and History* (London and New York: Routledge, 1992), 75-92.

29. "I Am Monty Cantsin! The Beauty of Vandalism and the Spectacle of Noise," in *Revolutionary Art is of Necessity*, in Kantor, "Scrap Book."

30. Kantor has also written, in "Accumulation: Puppet Government 1999 Toronto," that "in a decaying world the only real thing is the moment of death. Death, just like bird-shit, is essential to increase the production of accumulation. . . . It's always six o'clock. . . . Accumulation is the result of the production of everyday life. It is life itself without the measuring force and authority of time. It is a mass of confusion composed of information, history, objects and people. Accumulation is a continuous and ongoing process that will never be interrupted by any means of culture, economy or politics, in other words, the spectacle of noise. In fact the spectacle is buried under the accumulated noise that makes up this multi-layered mass that is all. . . . The products of my life . . . are just as much alienated from me as I am alienated from the whole society. Therefore, I'm standing alone without any belongs and without belonging to anywhere." Kantor, "Scrap Book."

31. Kantor, "Scrap Book."

32. Gregory Bateson, Don D. Jackson, Jay Haley, and John Weakland, "Towards a Theory of Schizophrenia," *Behavioral Science* 1 (1956): 251–64.

33. Kantor, "Introduction to My Childhood."

34. For an excellent, scholarly, and artistic discussion of the conditions of institutions in Canada where Istvan Kantor makes his home, see Clive Robertson, *Policy Matters: Administrations of Art and Culture* (Toronto: YYZBOOKS, 2006).

35. Kantor, "Scrap Book."

36. Kantor has performed this "gift" at other museums, like the Museum of Modern Art in New York, where he splashed blood between two Picasso paintings in 1988. In a letter to the museum relating to the action, he wrote under the pseudonym Monty Cantsin: "I'm very happy to donate to the Museum of Modern Art a very expensive and extremely beautiful blood painting, entitled 'GIFT.' It is one of the most sincere and most important works of art history. Shall it become the proper pride of your museum? Your immortal friend MONTY CANTSIN."

37. Musil, Book III, 361.

38. Monty Cantsin, "The Poetical Plunderground of Neosism?!" in Kantor, "Scrap Book."

39. Musil, Book III, 417.

40. Musil, Book II, 65.

41. The part of the essay was first published in *Future Species: Hybrids, Exoskel, Cybor Living Makeover Madness* (Toronto: Museum of Contemporary Canadian Art, 2009), 35–38.

42. Terry Eagleton's *Sweet Violence: The Idea of the Tragic* (Oxford: Blackwell, 2003), 241.

43. Karl Kraus, quoted by Walter Benjamin in "Karl Kraus," in *Reflections: Essays, Aphorisms, Autobiographical Writings* (New York: Schocken, 1986), 243.

44. Klaus Theweleit analyzed such states of mind in his two-volume study of the German nationalist, quasi-mercenary, paramilitary group the Freikorps. See Theweleit, *Male Fantasies. Volume 1: Women, Floods, Bodies, History* (1977), trans. Stephen Conway with Erica Carter and Chris Turner, and *Volume 2: Male Bodies: Psychoanalyzing the White Terror* (1978), trans.d by Erica Carter and Chris Turner (Minneapolis: University of Minnesota Press, 1987, 1989).

45. See Istvan Kantor's website: www.ccca.ca/mikidot/istvansite/dex.html.

46. Quotes are from an e-mail by Kantor to the author, December 23, 2004.

47. Georges Bataille, *Eroticism: Death & Sensuality* (San Francisco: City Lights Books, 1986), 256. First published as *L'Erotisme* (Paris: Les Editions de Minuit, 1957).

48. Ibid., 140.

49. Kantor is heir to Viennese Actionism, especially the psychophysical extremes of Otto Mühl's AA Commune's *selbstdarstellung* (self-realization actions), and Hermann Nitsch's "Orgies Mysteries Theater," which condenses Dionysian orgiastic celebration, Greek tragedy (especially Sophocles' *Oedipus Rex* and Euripides' *Bacchae*), and Christian notions of guilt and redemption with destructive aspects of Western ontology, epistemology, and technology.

50. Kantor's work developed in parallel with the technorobotic performances of destruction created by Survival Research Laboratories in San Francisco in the late 1970s and early 1980s. Kantor's blood actions anticipate the performances of Uri Katzenstein, Franko B, Bálint Szombathy, and Ron Athey.

51. The highly celebrated group Laibach established itself in Trbovlje, an industrial and coal mining town in what is now Slovenia, not far from Budapest. In 1984, Laibach founded the aesthetic movement Neue Slowenische Kunst (NSK), which, like Kantor, emphasized the ambiguity of visual signifiers.

52. Istvan Kantor, e-mail to the author, December 21, 2008.

53. Eagleton, 250.

54. Kantor, e-mail to the author, December 21, 2008.

55. Eagleton, ix. Eagleton's reference here is to the English translation of Milan Kundera's political novel *The Unbearable Lightness of Being* (New York: Harper & Row, 1984).

## FRANZ WEST'S DIALOGIC *PASSSTÜCKE*

1. This essay was first published in the exhibition catalogue *Franz West* (London: Whitechapel Gallery, 2003), 104–21.

2. Ian Hacking, *Rewriting the Soul: Multiple Personality and the Sciences of Memory* (Princeton, NJ: Princeton University Press, 1998), 18, 19, 110–11.

3. Achim Hochdörfer, "Allegorizing Actionism: West's Doubts," in *Inside Franz West* (London: Gogosian Gallery, 2001), 8.

4. Franz West, "From a Talk over Lunch between Franz West, Marianne Brouwer, and Peter Pakesch," in *Franz West: Proforma*, Museum Moderner Kunst Stifftung Ludwig (Vienna: Oktagon, 1996), 285.

5. See Robert C. Carson, James N. Butcher, and Susan Mineka, *Abnormal Psychology and Modern Life, Tenth Edition* (New York: Harper Collins, 1995), 157. See also *Diagnostic and Statistical Manual of Mental Disorders DSM-IV-TR* (Washington: American Psychiatric Association, 2000).

6. Hochdörfer, 8.

7. Paul Ricoeur, *Oneself As Another*, trans. Kathleen Blamey (Chicago and London: University of Chicago Press, 1992), 9.

8. Ibid.

9. René Descartes, "Third Meditation," from *Meditations on First Philosophy*, trans. Donald A. Cress (Indianapolis: Hackett, 1979), 30.

10. Ricoeur, 9.

11. Ibid., 12.

12. Friedrich Nietzsche, *Will to Power*, trans. Anthony M. Ludovici (Edinburgh: T. N. Fowlis, 1910), p. 7; quoted in Ricoeur, 14.

13. Ricoeur, 15.

14. See W. J. T. Mitchell, “Ekphrasis and the Other,” in *Picture Theory* (Chicago: University of Chicago Press, 1995), 151–81.

15. Lucy Lippard, “Eccentric Abstraction,” *Art International* 10, no. 9 (November 1966): 284.

16. Robert Fleck, “Sex and the Modern Sculptor,” in Robert Fleck, Bice Curiger, and Neal Benezra, *Franz West* (London: Phaidon, 1999), 39.

17. Hochdörfer, 3.

18. Hubert Klocker, “Gesture and the Object, Liberation as Action: A European Component of Performative Art,” in Paul Schimmel, ed., *Out of Actions: Between Performance and the Object 1949–1979* (Los Angeles: Los Angeles Museum of Contemporary Art), 172.

19. Fleck, 48.

20. Louis Lavelle, *The Dilemma of Narcissus*, trans. W. T. Gairdner (London and New York: George Allen & Unwin, and Humanities Press, 1973), reprinted from *L'Erreur de Narcisse* (Paris: Editions Bernard Grasset, 1939).

### 1.1.78–2.2.78: LYNN HERSHMAN'S *ROBERTA BREITMORE*

1. This essay first appeared in *Roberta Breitmore Is Not Lynn Hershman* (San Francisco: De Young Memorial Museum, 1978), 5–14.

2. From an unidentified psychology textbook that I read over the shoulder of a passenger on a bus.

3. Sigmund Freud, “The Uncanny,” *The Standard Edition of the Complete Psychological Works of Sigmund Freud* (London: Hogarth Press, 1953), 245.

4. Christian Metz, “The Imaginary Signifier,” *Screen* 15, no. 2 (1977): 59–60.

5. Christian Metz, “History/Discourse: Note on Two Voyeurisms,” *Edinburg Magazine* 1, no. 1 (1976): 24.

6. Rolfe Bari, *Behind the Mask* (San Francisco: Persona Products, 1977), 10.

7. Definitions of the metaphorical metonymical processes of condensation and displacement come from Serge Leclaire, *Psychoanalyser: Un essai sur l'ordre de l'inconscient et la pratique de la lettre* (Paris: Edition du Seuil, 1975), 149–50. See also Roman Jakobson, “Linguistic Types of Aphasia” in Roman Jakobson and Morris Halle, *Fundamentals of Language* (The Hague: Mouton, 1956) and Jacques Lacan, *The Language of the Self: The Function of Language in Psychoanalysis* (Baltimore: Johns Hopkins University Press, 1968).

8. Roland Barthes, *Mythologies*, trans. Annette Lavers (New York: Hill and Wang, 1972), 110.

9. Marshall Sahlins, “Colors and Culture,” *Semiotica* 6, no. 1 (1976): 5.

10. All quotations are taken from Roberta Breitmore's journal-diaries.

11. See Otto Rank, *The Double: A Psychoanalytic Study*, trans. and ed. by Harry Tucker Jr., Chapel Hill: University of North Carolina Press, 1971.

12. R. D. Laing, *The Divided Self: An Existential Study in Sanity and Madness* (Baltimore: Penguin Books, 1965), 143.

13. Friedrich Nietzsche, quoted in Rank, *The Double*, 49.

14. Roland Barthes, “Rhetoric of the Image,” *Working Papers In Cultural Studies* 1, no. 1 (1971): 45.

15. Taken from Roberta Breitmore's journal-diaries.

16. Umberto Eco, “Semiotics of Theatrical Performance,” *Drama Review* 21, no. 1 (March 1977): 42.

17. Richard Sennett, “Narcissism and Modern Culture,” *October* 1, no. 4 (Fall 1977): 73.

18. William K. Stevens, "The Cult of 'I' Reaches Adulthood," *San Francisco Chronicle*, December 18, 1977, 1.

19. Lynn Hershman, "Roberta Breitmore: An Alchemical Portrait Begun in 1975," *Art Contemporary La Mamelle* 2, no. 5 (1976): 24.

20. Sennett, 75.

21. Ibid.

22. Roman Jakobson, *Shifters, Verbal Categories and the Russian Verb* (Cambridge, MA: Harvard University Press, 1957), 3.

23. Ibid., 2.

### LARRY MILLER'S *MOM-ME*

1. Parts of this essay first appeared in "Anomaly, Sky, Sex, and Psi in Fluxus," in the exhibition catalogue edited by Geoffrey Hendricks, *Critical Mass: Happenings, Fluxus, Performance, Intermedia, and Rutgers University, 1958–1972* (New Brunswick, NJ: Rutgers University Press, 2003), 60–88. I gave versions of this paper at the Ottawa Art Gallery, Ottawa, Canada, in 2000; at the WRO International Media Biennale, WRO Center for Media Art, Wroclaw, Poland, 2000; and at the Annual College Art Association, on a panel devoted to the topic "Consciousness in the New Millennium," where the title of my talk was "To See Knowing: Dissociative Consciousness, Parapsychology, and Art." Other parts of the paper were presented at the symposium for the fortieth anniversary of Fluxus, *4T Fluxus*, at the École Nationale Supérieure des Télécommunication, Paris, 2002; the symposium and performance festival *Zone 4*, Timisoara, Romania, in 2002; and the Rhine Research Center in Durham, North Carolina, in 2003.

2. Larry Miller, in discussion with the author, New York City, October 16, 2000; hereafter Miller/Stiles.

3. Ibid.

4. On the impact of pornography on children, see Susan Roth and Ronald Batson, *Naming the Shadows: A New Approach to Individual and Group Psychotherapy for Adult Survivors of Childhood Incest* (New York: Free Press, 1997), 64–70.

5. Larry Miller, e-mail to the author, May 10, 2001.

6. Ronald Batson, conversation with the author, summer 1992.

7. A substantial literature on nightmares and sexual abuse exists. See especially Angela Browne and David Finkelhor, "Impact of Child Sexual Abuse: A Review of the Research," *Psychological Bulletin* 99, no. 1 (January 1986): 66–77.

8. See, for example, Kenneth Ring, *Heading Toward Omega: In Search of the Meaning of the Near-Death Experience* (New York: W. Morrow, 1984).

9. Larry Miller, e-mail to the author, July 21, 2002. These experiences led Miller to study C. G. Jung's *Memories, Dreams, Reflections* (New York: Pantheon Books, 1963).

10. Larry Miller, telephone conversation with the author, August 13, 2002.

11. Miller discovered Lao Tzu in high school and was struck by one of the most beautiful of the Lao Tzu texts: "Thirty spokes unite in one hub; / It is precisely where there is nothing that we find the usefulness of the wheel. / We fire clay and make vessels; / It is precisely where there's no substance that we find the usefulness of clay pots. / We chisel out doors and windows; / It is precisely in these empty spaces that we find the usefulness of the room. / Therefore, we regard having something as beneficial; / But having nothing as useful." Lao-Tzu, *Te-Tao Ching*, trans. by Robert G. Henricks (New York: Ballantine Books, 1989), 63.

12. Larry Miller, unpublished transcripts of psychometric readings of "Stone," and

"Lines to Grow." One of the psychics asked if Miller's rock came from the moon, perhaps telepathically reading Miller's inspiration for the project while looking at rocks from the moon in the Smithsonian museum.

13. Larry Miller, e-mail to the author, July 21, 2002.

14. Ibid.

15. As Miller points out in the video, an Airedale held the record for "thinking animals" (animals that can count, spell, and do other cognitive acts involving memory and knowledge) before Jim's feats.

16. There are many public records of the feats of Jim, and the Jim the Wonder Dog Memorial Park was unveiled on May 1, 1999, on the spot where his home, the Hotel Ruff, had once stood on the downtown square of Marshall, Missouri. Among other writings, see Larry Mueller, "Jim, The Wonder Dog," *Outdoor Life* (August 1985), 53, 9–102; and Henry N. Ferguson, "Jim the Wonder Dog," http://www.ruralmissouri.org/10pages/10MarchJim WonderDog.html; and see, also www.roadsideamerica.com/pet/jim.html.

17. For more detailed research on psychic animals, see Robert L. Morris, "Psi and Animal Behavior: A Survey," *Journal of the American Society for Psychical Research* 64, no. 3 (July 1970): 242–60; Rupert Sheldrake, *Seven Experiments that Could Change the World: A Do-It-Yourself Guide to Revolutionary Science* (New York: Riverhead Books, 1995); Rupert Sheldrake, *Dogs That Know When Their Owners Are Coming Home and other Unexplained Powers of Animals* (New York: Crown Publishers, 1999); and J. Moussaieff Masson and Susan McCarthy, *When Elephants Weep: The Emotional Lives Of Animals* (London: Cape, 1994).

18. Larry Miller, unpublished "Notation on Two Photo-document Panels of *Mom-Me*," 1973.

19. Larry Miller, e-mail to the author, July 21, 2002.

20. Larry Miller, *Mom's Feet: My Hands* (1972–74), in *As if the Universe Were an Object: Larry Miller, Selected Works: 1969–1985* (Richmond, VA: Anderson Gallery, Virginia Commonwealth University, 1986), 20.

21. Ibid.

22. Henri Bergson, *Matter and Memory* (1896), trans. by Nancy Margaret Paul and W. Scott Palmer (New York: Zone Books, 1988).

23. Such paradoxical behaviors of mind also parallel the operations of matter, a point I discussed in a paper entitled "To See Knowing: Dissociative Consciousness, Parapsychology, and Art," at the Annual College Art Association meeting in New York, 2000. For example, David Albert, a professor of theoretical physics at Columbia University, and Bryan Loewer, a philosopher from Rutgers University, have discussed conditions of nonlocality in "the micro-world of sub-atomic particles." Describing the behavior of electrons in "super-position," they state that an "electron is located somewhere, but it is not located in any particular place," a behavior that is "paradoxical and strange." They note that if the properties of an electron in super-position can be thought of metaphorically as a question of color, then to say that those properties are either blue or green would be false. Electrons in super-position require an entirely different mode of thinking, a model that would identity them as "nor both nor neither." Albert and Loewer add: "What is going on here is that we are being forced to confront odd (and metaphysically odd) claims about the structure of the world by the mathematical structure of our best scientific theory of how the world operates." See D. Albert and B. Loewer, "Physics and Philosophy with Wayne Pond on Soundings, National Public Radio," 1989. Similarly, the Princeton Engineering Anomalies Research (PEAR) Laboratory program calls for a "generously expanded model of reality . . . one that regards many of the concepts of observational quantum mechanics, most importantly the principles of complementarity and wave mechanical

resonance, as fundamental characteristics of consciousness, rather than as intrinsic features of an objective physical environment." See the statement by Princeton Engineering Anomalies Research, "Scientific Study of Consciousness-Related Physical Phenomena," http://www.princeton.edu/~pear/.

24. Jacques Lacan, "Of the Gaze as Object Petit à," in Jacques-Alain Miller, ed., *The Four Fundamental Concepts of Psychoanalysis: The Seminar of Jacques Lacan.* trans. by Alan Sheridan (New York: W.W. Norton, 1988), 67–122.

25. D. Spiegel, introduction to D. Spiegel, ed., *Dissociation*, ix.

26. M. H. Erdelyi, "Dissociation, Defense, and the Unconscious," in D. Spiegel, ed., *Dissociation*, 3. See also B. G. Braun, "Multiple Personality Disorder and Posttraumatic Stress Disorder: Similarities and Differences," in J. P.Wilson and B. Raphael, eds. *The International Handbook of Traumatic Stress Syndromes* (New York and London: Plenum Press, 1993), 35–36, 583.

27. D. J. Bem, and C. Honorton, "Does Psi Exist? Replicable Evidence for an Anomalous Process of Information Transfer," in *Psychological Bulletin* 115, no.1 (1994): 4–18.

28. See Kristine Stiles, "*Corpora Vilia*: Valie Export's Body," in *Valie Export's Visual Syntagmatics* (Goldie Paley Gallery, Moore College of Art and Design, Philadelphia, 2000), 16–33. See also "Shaved Heads and Marked Bodies: Representations from Cultures of Trauma," in this volume.

29. Michel de Certeau, *The Writing of History*, trans. by Tom Conley (New York: Columbia University Press, 1988), 257.

30. C.A. Ross, "Dissociation and Physical Illness," in D. Spiegel, ed., *Dissociation: Culture, Mind, and Body* (Washington and London: American Psychiatric Press, 1994), 173.

31. Jim Schnabel, *Remote Viewers: The Secret History of America's Psychic Spies* (New York: Dell, 1997), 15.

32. Many performance artists are interested in, or state that they possess, various forms of nonlocal consciousness traditionally associated with psychic phenomena. A short list includes Marina Abramovic, Joseph Beuys, John Duncan, Michel Journiac, Paul McCarthy, Linda Montano, Raphael Montanez Ortiz, Ulricke Rosenbach, and Carolee Schneemann.

33. Jean Sellem has researched the relationship between Fluxus and the Kabalistic numerical system. See Jean Sellem, ed., "Fluxus Research," *Lund Art Press* 2, no. 2 (1991): 53–63.

34. Ibid.

35. Larry Miller, telephone conversation with the author, August 13, 2002.

36. Louise Bourgeois, "Select Diary Notes 1960–1979," in *Louise Bourgeois: Destruction of the Father / Reconstruction of the Father: Writings and Interviews 1923–1997*, ed. by Marie-Laure Bernadac and Hans-Ulrich Obrist (Cambridge, MA: MIT Press, 1998), 72.

37. See Lucy Lippard, "Louise Bourgeois: From the Inside Out," *Artforum* 13 (March 1975): 26–33.

38. Louise Bourgeois, "Child Abuse (Portfolio)," *Artforum* 21 (December 1982): 40–47.

39. I do not think that this is an exaggeration of the importance of Miller's *Mom-Me*, as Bourgeois clearly maintained a keen interest in Fluxus in general, and even attended Maciunas' *Fluxwedding*, as well as his memorial service at the crematorium, all in 1978.

40. Larry Miller, e-mail to the author, May 10, 2001.

41. Ibid.

42. Henri Bergson, *Matter and Memory*, 14.

43. For writings by artists on this subject, see the special issue on "Art and Healing" that I edited for *WhiteWalls: A Magazine of Writings by Artists* 25 (Spring 1990).

44. Robert G. Jahn and Brenda J. Dunne, "Science of the Subjective," *Journal of Scien-*

*tific Exploration* 11, no. 2 (1997): 201–24, also available at http://www.princeton.edu /~pear/sos.pdf.

45. Yoko Ono, e-mail to the author, July 3, 2002.

46. I have had numerous conversations with Schneemann about the paranormal foundations of her art in which the artist expressed apprehension about being considered "nuts" for exposing that aspect of her inspiration and knowledge.

47. Rupert Sheldrake, Terence McKenna, and Ralph Abraham, *Chaos, Creativity, and Cosmic Consciousness* (Rochester, VT: Park Street Press, 1992, 2001).

## UNBOSOMING LENNON: THE POLITICS OF YOKO ONO'S EXPERIENCE

1. I dedicate this essay to Sherman Fleming, whose collaborations with me in performance art and whose unconditional personal support provided the emotional foundation upon which I gained intellectual insight into the depths of LENONO. I presented the first version of this essay at a symposium on "Feminisms, Performance and Postmoderism," organized by Kathy O'Dell and David Joselit at the Institute of Contemporary Art, Boston, on April 8, 1990. The essay was published in *Art Criticism* 7, no. 2 (Spring 1992): 21–54. See also my essay "Being Undyed: The Meeting of Mind and Matter in Yoko Ono's Events," in Alexandra Monroe, ed., *Yes Yoko Ono* (New York: Japan Society, 2000), 145–49.

2. John Lennon and Yoko Ono, *Double Fantasy*, Lenono Music (BMI) (Los Angeles: Geffen Records, 1980). All quotes from songs in this essay come from this album unless otherwise noted.

3. Jonathan Cott and Christine Doudna, eds., *The Ballad of John and Yoko* (Garden City, NY: Rolling Stone Press, 1982), xviii.

4. LENONO is an important but unrecognized antecedent for the significant holistic aesthetic practices of such artist couples as Helen and Newton Harrison, Kate Erickson and Mel Ziegler, Jean-Claude and Christo, John Latham and Barbara Steveni, and others.

5. Vaclav Havel, *Letters to Olga: June 1979–September 1982*, trans. by Paul Wilson (New York: Henry Hold and Company, 1989), 158. Originally published by Rowohlt Taschenbuch Verlag Gmbll, Reinbek bei Hamburg, 1983.

6. Susan R. Bordo, "The Body and the Reproduction of Femininity: A Feminist Appropriation of Foucault," in Alison M. Jagger and Susan R. Bordo, eds., *Gender/Body/Knowledge, Feminist Reconstructions of Being and Knowing* (New Brunswick, NJ, and London: Rutgers University Press, 1989), 13.

7. Muriel Dimen, "Power, Sexuality, and Intimacy," 48.

8. Pete Hamill, "Long Night's Journey into Day," in *The Ballad of John and Yoko*, 147.

9. Ibid.

10. Barbara Graustark, "The Real John Lennon," *Newsweek* (September 29, 1980): 44.

11. Yoko Ono, Melody Sumner, Kathleen Burch, and Michael Sumner, eds., *The Guests Go in to Supper: John Cage, Robert Ashely, Yoko Ono, Laurie Anderson, Charles Amirkhanian, Michael Peppe, K. Atchley* (Oakland and San Francisco: Burning Books, 1986), 178.

12. George Maciunas demonstrated an example of how Ono's work was perceived sometimes to be opportunistic when he wrote "A Footnote," published in *Film Culture* 48–49 (Winter/Spring 1970): 33. Maciunas explained: "'No. 5' film of Yoko is exact copy of first half of Chieko Shiomi's 'Disappearing Music for Face' which she (that is, Yoko) herself performed in winter 1965. Shiomi's film was shot at 2000 frames per second (which makes sense for transition but not for just smile). 'No. 5' by Yoko, made in 1967, also uses 2000 frames per second. Ben Vautier has a 'smile piece of 1961.'" Jon Hendricks insists that "Smile was Yoko Ono's idea." Jon Hendricks, conversation with the author, May 1991.

13. Yoko Ono, "To the Wesleyan People (Who Attended the Meeting)," January 23, 1966, reprinted in Yoko Ono's *Grapefruit*, 2nd edition (New York: Simon and Schuster, 1972). *Grapefruit* was originally printed in Tokyo and Bellport, NY, in 1964 by Wunternaum Press.

14. Jerry Hopkins, *Yoko Ono* (New York and London: Macmillan and Collier Macmillan, 1986), 29. A cautionary word is in order concerning Hopkin's quotes, as no sources are cited. During the period when I wrote this essay, I attempted to contact Ono, who never returned my calls or letters, and I was therefore unable to substantiate Hopkins's claims about her performance with peas: "Ono came out with a bag of peas and threw them at the audience, while at the same time whirling her head so that her long black mass of hair hissed in the loft air. She said the movement of her hair was providing the musical accompaniment to her pea throwing" (p. 25). It is of note that Ono's name does not appear on the "official" record of the performances that took place at her loft between December 18, 1960, and June 7, 1961. Only the following artists' names appear on the programs: Toshi Ichiyanagi, Joseph Byrd, Jackson Mac Low, Richard Maxfield, La Monte Young, Simone [Forti] Morris, and Bob Morris. In an unpublished taped interview, however, Maciunas states, "This series of La Monte Young at Yoko Ono's loft got in touch with serious composers such as Yoko Ono, Toshi Ichiyanagi, Henry Flynt . . . . In this series I met with such composers as Dick Higgins, Walter De Maria, Ray Johnson and Ayo. This whole series gave me an idea to imitate it and make an even more extensive series at our new gallery." That Maciunas mentioned Ono's name suggests that while the Hopkins description of the pea/hair performance may not be precise, Ono was performing, and perhaps performed something similar. In addition, immediately following the end of these performances in June, Maciunas invited Ono to exhibit at his nearly bankrupt AG Gallery in late July 1961. He recalled that her two-week show of paintings and drawings included "Do It Yourself Paintings," paintings "that looked like cleaning rags hung on the wall . . . [a] painting with holes in it that you could look through," and other items that he deemed "Very successful [although] we didn't sell anything." See George Maciunas, unpublished taped discussion on the AG Gallery, in the Jean Brown Fluxus Archive, now housed in the J. Paul Getty Center for the History of Art and the Humanities.

15. Willoughby Sharp, "Body Works," *Avalanche* 1 (Fall 1970): 14–17.

16. Luce Irigaray, *Ce Sexe qui n en pas un* (Paris: Editions de Minuit, 1977), trans. in *New French Feminism*, eds. Elaine Marks and Isabelle de Courtivron (Amherst: University of Massachusetts Press, 1980), 103.

17. Barbara Moore has explained: "*The Stone* was a collaboration between Ono, Anthony Cox, Michael Mason, and Jeff Perkins that was organized by Jon Hendricks during his tenure as directory of the Judson Gallery, New York, March 1966. Somewhat inspired by Ono's earlier *Bag Piece* (in which two people get into a bag, take off their clothes, take a nap, put their clothes back on, and get out), Cox built a sound, light, and film environment in which visitors enclosed themselves in Ono's bags ("Bagwear" was also available for sale at the time of the show), appearing as stones to an outside observer." In addition, Ono created "a large rectangular bag of crinkled cotton, open at one end," that had been "washed and somewhat faded, particularly on one side." See *Catalogue C* (New York: Backworks, ca. 1978).

18. Cox met Ono in 1961, and she divorced Ichinagi in 1962. Cox and Ono's child, Kyoko, was born in 1963, and Cox helped Ono to recover from a nervous breakdown in Japan in 1964. They lived in London beginning in 1966, and divorced in 1969. Cox then disappeared with then eight-year-old Kyoko in 1971, and only in 1994 did Kyoko and Yoko Ono begin to reestablish their relationship.

19. Hopkins, *Yoko Ono*, 52. Ono told me that she never had sex on the stage in the bag.

20. Ono later commented on the subject of surrender when, on January 24, 1983, she took out an advertisement in *The New York Times* to publish her essay "Surrender to Peace," reprinted in Jon Wiener, "Give Peace a Chance: An Anthem for the Anti-War Movement," in Marianne Philbin, ed., *Give Peace a Chance* (Chicago: Chicago Review Press, 1983), 29. In this article, Ono remembered: "In the summer of '72 in New York City, John and I invited the press to announce the founding of a conceptual country called Nutopia. Anybody could be a citizen in this country. Citizens were automatically the country's ambassadors. The country's body was the airfield of our joint thoughts. Its flag was the white flag of surrender: a surrender to peace. . . . A radical friend of ours expressed that he . . . disliked the term [surrender]. 'Surrender sounds like defeat,' he said. 'Well, don't you surrender to love, for instance?' I looked at him. 'No.' . . . I thought 'Are women the only people whom know the pride and joy or surrender?' . . . 'It's a waste of time to explain to a macho radical, didn't I tell you?' said John, a man who surrendered to the world, life, and finally to the universe."

21. See, for example, Ono in *The Guests Go in to Supper*, 171–84; see also Donald Kirk, "In Tokyo," in *The Ballad of John and Yoko*, and Jerry Hopkins, *Yoko Ono*.

22. René A. Spitz, "Hospitalism: An Inquiry into the Genesis of Psychiatric Conditions in Early Childhood," *The Psychoanalytic Study of the Child* (New York) 1 (1945): 53–74. This essay is reprinted in René A. Spitz, *Dialogues from Infancy: Selected Papers*, ed. by Robert N. Emde (New York: International Universities Press, 1983). Spitz wrote: "The term 'hospitalism' designates a vitiated condition of the body due to long confinement in a hospital, or the morbid condition of the atmosphere of a hospital. . . . At the beginning of our century one of the great foundling homes in Germany had a mortality rate of 71.5 percent in infants in the first year of life" (p. 5). While those conditions had "greatly changed" after the war, Spitz still could write: "The Children in Foundling Home showed all the manifestations of hospitalism, both physical and mental. In spite of the fact that hygiene and precautions against contagion were impeccable, the children showed, from the third month on, extreme susceptibility to infection and illness of any kind" (p. 10). I would like to thank Angela O'Rand, professor of sociology at Duke University, for her assistance on this section of the text.

23. For a historical account of the conditions that resembled those in which Lennon matured, see Alan Sinfield's *Literature, Politics, and Culture in Postwar Britain* (Berkeley and Los Angeles: University of California Press, 1989).

24. Yoko Ono, "Yoko Ono on Yoko Ono," *Film Culture* 48–49 (Winter/Spring 1970): 32.

25. John Hanhardt, *Yoko Ono* (New York: Whitney Museum of American Art, 1989), 8.

26. Ibid., 1–2.

27. Yoko Ono, letter to Ivan Karp, June 4, 1965, in *Grapefruit*, n.p.

28. For more on the subject of the word "nigger," see Sherman Fleming, "Nigger as Antibody," in a special edition on art and healing edited by Kristine Stiles for *Whitewalls* 25 (Spring 1990).

29. John Lennon & Plastic Ono Band, *Shaved Fish* (Los Angeles: Capitol Records, 1975).

30. Mae G. Henderson, "Toni Morrison's *Beloved*: Re-Membering the Body as Historical Texts," in Horilinar Speelers, ed., *Comparative American Identities* (New York: Routledge, 1991), 63–64.

31. Dimen, "Power, Sexuality, and Intimacy," 37.

32. Hanhardt, *Yoko Ono*, 9–10.

33. Dimen, "Power, Sexuality, and Intimacy," 39.

34. Susan Gubar, "'The Blank Page' and the Issues of Female Creativity," in Elaine Showalter, ed., *The New Feminist Criticism: Essays on Women, Literature, and Theory* (New York: Pantheon Books, 1985), 295, 299.

35. Mary Field Belenky, Blythe McVicker Clinchy, Nancy Rule Goldberger, and Jill Mattuck Tarule, eds., *Women's Ways of Knowing: The Development of Self, Voice, and Mind* (New York: Basic Books, 1986), 18.

36. Ibid.

37. Ibid.

38. Emily Wasserman, "This Is Not Here: Yoko Ono at Syracuse," *Artforum* 10, no. 6 (January 1972): 73.

39. See Ono's "Statement" in the *Village Voice* (October 7, 1971), 20. Ono has consistently de-emphasized her participation in DIAS. Furthermore, this critical biographical event is frequently absent from accounts of her art and is not mentioned in either of the two prominent critical articles on her work. See, for example, Carlo McCormick's "Yoko Ono Solo," *Artforum* 27, no. 6 (February 1989): 116–21, and Wasserman, "This Is Not Here."

40. Ono in *The Guests Go in to Supper*, 174.

41. Carolee Schneemann, *More Than Meat Joy: Complete Performance Works & Selected Writings*, ed. by Bruce McPherson (New Paltz: Documentext, 1979), 196.

42. Barry Miles (b. 1943), British writer associated with the international counterculture in the 1960s.

43. Wouters Buikhuisen, a Dutch sociologist, coined the term PROVOS in his doctoral dissertation, presented January 22, 1965, at the State University of Utrecht. Derived from the two syllables of the word "provocateur," Buikhuisen used the word PROVO to draw a distinction between the Black Shirts of an earlier generation and the aims, behavior, and social composition of discontented urban youth of the late 1950s and early 1960s, such as beatniks, mods, rockers, and the Dutch nozzems. A loosely knit movement of initially no more than fifty activists in Amsterdam, the PROVOS adopted the term to describe their members who were often artists, poets, and bilingual students (usually Dutch, French, English, and German) in the social sciences, mostly between the ages of eighteen and thirty. These poets and artists admired the COBRA group and were influenced by the International Situationists. PROVO leader Bernhard de Vries was in 1966 a twenty-five-year-old poet, artist, and student of Dutch literature who won a seat in Amsterdam government in a municipal election that reflected the momentary political power exercised by the PROVOS in 1965–66. De Vries and Irene Donner van der Weetering arrived in London on June 22, 1966, for a press conference to kick off DIAS. Their action included riding about London on white bicycles, the symbol for the PROVOS' urban platform of reform, which was called the "White Plans." For more information on the PROVOS, see Bernhard de Vries, "Provo vu de l'interirut," in F. E. Frenkel, ed., *Provo Lanttekemngen bij een deelverschijnsel* (Amsterdam: Polak and Gennep, 1967); Hans Tuyman, *Full-Time PROVO* (Amsterdam: Uitgeverij de Bezige Bij, 1966); Duco can Weerlee, *Wat De Provo's Willen* (Amsterdam: Uitgeverij de Bezige Bij, 1966); C. Vassart and A. Racine, *Provos et Provotariat: Un an de recherche participante en milieu Provo* (Brussels: Centre d'etude de la Delinquance Juvenile, 1968); Brenda Jordan, "Some Facts about the Provos," *Socialist Leader* (London), July 23, 1966; and "On the Poverty of Student Life: Considered in its Economic, Political, Psychological, Sexual, and Especially Intellectual Aspects, with a Modest Proposal for its Remedy" (1967) reprinted in *Situationist Anthology* (Berkeley, CA: Bureau of Public Secrets, 1981), esp. 323–24.

44. See Paul Overy, "London," *Artcanada Supplement* 24 (June–July 1967): 10–11. See also the *Evening Standard* (London), April 12, 1967, which features a photograph of Ono in a picket protest outside the offices of the British Board of Film Censors.

45. Jean-Jacques Lebel, *Happenings, interventions et actions diverses (1962–1982)* (Paris: Cahiers Loques et Polyphonix, 1982), n.p.

46. Ritchie Yorke, "Boosting Peace: John and Yoko in Canada, February 7, 1969," in *The Ballad of John and Yoko*, 57. See also John Papworth, "An Open Letter to John and Yoko," *Resurgence* (London) 2 (Spring 1970): 2–4.

47. On Nam June Paik, see *Art for 25 Million People: Bon Jour, Monseiur Orwell: Kunst und Satelliten in der Zukunft* (Berlin: Daadgalerie, 1984).

48. "Briefly," *Art and Artists* 2 (August 1967): 4.

49. John Bushnell, *Moscow Graffiti: Language and Subculture* (Boston: Unwin Hyman, 1990), 125–26.

50. Ibid., 133, 120.

51. Raphael Montañez Ortiz, in an unpublished interview with the author, February 27, 1982, Piscataway, New Jersey. A fascinating paradox is that while Ono publicly deplored Ortiz's art, his development in destruction art was the impulse for the social psychologist Arthur Janov's development of "primal scream" therapy, which Ono and Lennon later undertook under Janov's direction (as did the Viennese action artist Otto Mühl). In the introduction to his book *The Primal Scream*, Janov credits Ortiz as the source for his development of primal scream therapy. See Janov's *The Primal Scream, Primal Therapy: The Cure for Neurosis* (New York: Delta, 1970), 9–10. See also my own *Raphael Montañez Ortiz: Years of the Warrior 1960–Years of the Psyche 1988* (New York: Museo del Barrio, 1988).

52. George Maciunas, "A Footnote," *Film Culture*, 33.

53. Yoko Ono in Wasserman, "This Is Not Here," 69.

54. See "Action No. 39" in *GAGG: The Guerrilla Art Action Group 1969–1976, A Selection* (New York: Printed Matter, 1978), n.p.

55. See Ralph J. Gleason, "Fair Play for John and Yoko," June 22, 1972; Joel Siegel, "Back in the U.S.S.A." October 10, 1974; and Chet Filippo, "Imagine: John Lennon Legal," September 9, 1976, all in *The Ballad Of John and Yoko*, 135–41.

56. Yoko Ono in *The Guests Go in to Supper*, 175.

57. Barbara Haskell, *Yoko Ono*, 3.

58. Jasia Reichardt, "Art Is Bit, Round and Good," *Studio International* 174 (September 1967): 80.

59. For an analysis of Asian women's perception, see Amy Ling, "Chinamerican Women Writers: Four Forerunners of Maxine Hong Kingston," in *Gender/Body/Knowledge*, 309–23.

60. Ono, "To the Wesleyan People," n.p. Many critics misunderstand Ono's astute strategy and understanding of the differences between art and life. Most recently, see Carlo McCormick, "Yoko Ono Solo," 120. While McCormick seekd to explicate Ono's art, his glib commentary works at cross-purposes to his intent and diminishes the cultural significance and political import of artworks like *Bed-In*.

61. Emily Wasserman, "This Is Not Here," 72.

62. See R. D. Laing, *The Politics of Experience* (New York: Penguin Books, 1967). It is noteworthy that Laing had been involved in DIAS and was powerfully influenced by some of the artists who later participated in it, especially Jeff Nuttall, John Latham, and Gustav Metzger.

## BURDEN OF LIGHT: CHRIS BURDEN

1. This essay first appeared in Fred Hoffman, John Berger, Kristine Stiles, and Paul Schimmel, *Chris Burden* (Newcastle, UK: Merrell and Locus Plus, 2007), 22–37.

I am indebted to Rachel Leah Baum and Laurel Fredrickson for their exhaustive close readings and editorial suggestions on this manuscript, as well as to Susan Jarosi and Jay Bloom for their thoughtful commentary on the content and structure of my essay. Thanks to Katy Lucas for all her cheerful assistance in working in Burden's archive. My sincere appreciation goes to Nancy Rubins and Chris Burden for their hospitality, and to Burden for his willingness to engage in days of discussions; his openness, good will, and humor; and his fundamental insight into the nature of art, which has changed my concept of art and life over the past thirty years.

2. Cathryn Vasseleu, *Textures of Light: Vision and Touch in Irigaray, Levinas and Merleau-Ponty* (London and New York: Routledge, 1998), 129. Between 1971 and 1980, Burden staged his own disappearance in the following performances: *Five Day Locker Piece* (April 26–30, 1971), *You'll Never See My Face in Kansas City* (November 6, 1971), *Disappearing* (December 22–24, 1971), *Bed Piece* (February 18–March 10, 1972), *Jaizu* (June 10–11, 1972), *Deadman* (November 12, 1972), *B.C. Mexico* (May 25–June 10, 1973), *Oh, Dracula* (October 7, 1974), *Dreamy Nights* (October 15, 1974), *The Visitation* (November 9, 1974), *White Light/White Heat* (February 8–March 1, 1975), *Oracle* (May 14, 1975), *The Citadel* (August 8–12, 1976), *Warning! Relax, or You Will Be Nuked Again* (September 13, 1980), and *Hercules* (March 27, 1982). After 1980, Burden made a number of installations, sculptures, and visionary unrealized works that used light or its absence, including but not limited to *A Tale of Two Cities* (1981), *Scale Model of the Solar System* (1983), *The Speed of Light Machine* (1983), *The Fist of Light* (1993), *The Hidden Force* (1995), and *Urban Light* (2005).

3. James Collins, "Reviews," *Artforum* 11, no. 9 (May 1973): 72.

4. In 1972, Robert Hughes authored an article that has had an enduringly negative impact on the reception of performance art and on the understanding of its cultural meaning and social purpose. Hughes wrote that Schwarzkogler "proceeded inch by inch to amputate his own penis, while a photographer recorded the act as an art event. . . . Successive acts of self-amputation finally did Schwarzkogler in." See Robert Hughes, "The Decline and Fall of the Avant-Garde," *Time* (December 18, 1972): 111.

5. Mäns Wrange, "A Conversation with Chris Burden," in *Chris Burden* (Stockholm: Magasin 3 Stockholm Konsthall, 1999), n.p.

6. Howard Singerman, "Chris Burden's Pragmatism," in *Chris Burden: A Twenty-Year Survey* (Newport Beach, CA: Newport Harbor Art Museum, 1988), 22.

7. Robert Horvitz quoted in Singerman, 22. See also Horvitz's "Chris Burden," *Artforum* 14, no. 9 (May 1976): 27.

8. Donald Kuspit, "Man For and Against Machine," in Peter Noever, ed., *Chris Burden: Beyond the Limits* (Vienna and Ostfildern, Austria: MAK and Cantz Verlag, 1996), 83.

9. Kathy O'Dell, *Contract with the Skin: Masochism Performance Art and the 1970s* (Minneapolis: University of Minnesota Press, 1998). O'Dell's book is an insightful psychoanalytic, sexual, and political theory of the masochistic artist, a study that moves from Jacques Lacan's Law of the Father and the laws of the state to the failure of the social contract in the Vietnam War and the social and the politics of the sadomasochistic exchange. O'Dell describes Burden as a masochistic artist in the context of Rousseau. Lebel's enactment of situations of danger and pain do, however, summon consideration of what I have called the "social contract" between performance artists and their publics. I developed this concept in relation to performance practices during the seminar I taught at Berkeley in 1979, a class that O'Dell took as a graduate student. O'Dell later formulated a much deeper, richer, and broader concept of the "social contract" for her doctoral dissertation, which became the basis for her book *Contract with the Skin*. My own notion of the "social contract" in 1979 was limited to the role that interpersonal responsibility plays in the work of Burden and other performance artists. At my invitation Burden, Tom

Marioni, Linda Montano, and Laurie Anderson all came to my seminar to discuss their work in 1979.

10. See Kenneth Evett, "Death Wish," *New Republic* (May 17, 1975):, 31.

11. The lyrics of the song include the following phrases: "White light, white light goin' messin' up my mind / White light, and don't you know its gonna make me go blind." See the Velvet Underground, "White Light/White Heat" (New York: Scepter Studios, 1967).

12. All of the documentation on *White Light/White Heat* neglects to mention that Burden drank this juice each day. Burden revealed this critical aspect of the work in our extended, unpublished conversations of September 11–14, 2003, at his Topanga Canyon studio in California. Hereafter this interview is cited as Burden/Stiles.

13. Moreover, by removing himself from view, Burden strategically refused to accede to what Frank Perrin has called "the egotistical desires of artists and American society in general." See Frank Perrin, "An Administration of Extreme Urgency," in *Chris Burden: Un Livre de Survie* (Paris: Blocnotes Éditions, 1995), 149.

14. Johannes Lothar Schröder, "Science, Heat and Time," in Peter Noever, ed., *Chris Burden: Beyond the Limits*, 203.

15. See Paul Grobstein's commentary on October 16, 2005, in Kristine Stiles and Paul Grobstein, "The Art Historian and the Neurobiologist: A Conversation About Proprioception, the 'I-function,' Body Art, and Story Telling?" in *Serendip*, Bryn Mawr College: http://serendip.brynmawr.edu/bb/artneuro/.

16. Ibid.

17. Alain Berthoz, *The Brain's Sense of Movement* (Cambridge, MA: Harvard University Press, 2000), 25.

18. See Grobstein's student Shannon Lee's "Proprioception: How and Why?" http://serendip.brynmawr.edu/bb/neuro/neuro02/web2/slee.html (accessed June 5, 2005). See also Nana Dawson-Andoh, "Phantom Limbs, Phantom Pain, and the 'I-Function,'" http://serendip.brynmawr.edu/bb/neuro/neuro01/web1/Dawsonandoh.html (accessed June 5, 2005). For more on phantom limbs, see Rupert Sheldrake, "Extended Mind," in *Seven Experiments That Could Change the World: A Do-It-Yourself Guide To Revolutionary Science* (London: Fourth Estate, 1995).

19. Robert Horvitz, "Chris Burden," *Artforum* 14, no. 9 (1976): 24.

20. Grobstein also uses the phrase "story teller" for the "I-function" in order to give increased emphasis to the point that there is an arbitrariness, and potentially a creative/discretionary element, inherent in the process that produces what we are aware of. Grobstein writes: "In addition, it has become clear to me that not all awarenesses are centered around 'I' . . . but can also be about communities or other less individualized, egocentric actors. Thirdly, the original I-function concept seemed to make the process equivalent to verbal report/language usage, and it is clearly not. It is a process on which language depends but one that exists prior to language." Paul Grobstein, e-mail to the author, October 22, 2005.

21. Berthoz, 28.

22. While this is not the place to expand on the central importance of proprioception to performance art and its viewers, it is a heretofore unexplored foundational aspect of art that uses the body as its primary material. Moreover, it is no accident that such art should emerge in an historical period in which the body is under great threat from revolution, terrorism, wars, nuclear holocaust, environmental warming, disease and pandemics (such as HIV-AIDS and avian flu), as well as genetic engineering and the posthuman or postbiological age. I further explored my theory of proprioception in Burden's work in a lecture entitled "The 'I-Function' and Proprioception in Chris Burden's Performances and

Installations" at the nineteenth annual meeting of the Society for Literature, Science, and the Arts (SLSA) in Chicago, 2005.

23. Noel Frackman, "Chris Burden," *Arts* 49, no. 8 (April 1975): 9.

24. Porn star Linda Lovelace was pictured on the cover of the issue. A photograph of Burden dazed and bandaged, taken immediately following *Shoot*, appeared on a two-page spread next to a picture of L. Patrick Gray III, J. Edgar Hoover's replacement as director of the FBI. Other individuals featured in the issue included the flamboyant preacher Reverend Ike (Frederick J. Eikerenkoetter II); a card shark named Amarillo Slim, a novelist and former policewoman named Dorothy Uhnak, and the basketball legend Julius Erving. See *Esquire* 79, no. 5 (May 1973): 159.

25. Ibid.

26. Claes Oldenberg, "I Am for an Art . . . ," *Environments, Situations, Spaces* (New York: Martha Jackson Gallery, 1961). See also Claes Oldenburg and Emmett Williams, eds., *Store Days: Documents from The Store (1961) and Ray Gun Theater (1962)* (New York: Something Else Press, 1967), 39–42; reprinted in Kristine Stiles and Peter Selz, eds., *Theories and Documents of Contemporary Art: A Sourcebook of Artists' Writings* (Berkeley: University of California Press, 1996), 336.

27. Frank Perrin, "An Administration of Extreme Urgency," 149.

28. Burden/Stiles.

29. Chris Burden quoted in Corina Ferrari, "Interview with Chris Burden," *Domus* 549 (August 1975): 50.

30. Burden remembers the incident this way: "During one of the last days, a young lady came in and she said she wanted to take pictures. People weren't allowed to take pictures. [She pulled] the old art student: 'Oh I'm just taking pictures for my art report.' All of a sudden she has this super long monopod and I am staring right at the lens of this camera. So the gallery people catch her. Ron [Feldman] and her tussle on the floor; he opens her camera and pulls the film out. She's screaming: 'You manhandled me, I'm calling the cops. Give us back the film.' There is this whole brouhaha. About two or three years later, she was going around Soho trying to sell these photos. She tricked them. She got to keep her real film and gave them a faux film. She outfoxed them. She was doing that, I'm convinced, because she was sure that nobody was up there [on the platform], and she was going to show the world with photographic proof that it was a fraud. She was surprised to see me there." Burden/Stiles.

31. Larry Grobel, "Chris Burden: Picasso Used Canvas, Michelangelo Used Marble. Chris Burden Uses His Body," *Playgirl* (April 1978): 48–51, 64–66.

32. Performance artist Marina Abramovic has questioned the truth of Burden's twenty-two day feat of endurance in *White Light/White Heat* while assuring the public of the veracity of her own perseverance in *The House with the Ocean View* (November 15–26, 2002), a twelve-day action in which she lived on three platforms in the Sean Kelly Gallery in New York without eating or speaking. Rather than being invisible like Burden, she exposed all of her activities, living without privacy in rooms open to spectators who could also observe her in close-up with a high-powered telescope. Moreover, based on her questioning of its authenticity, Abramovic proposed to remake *White Light/White Heat* for a series of reenacted performances based on the work of artists of the 1970s at the Guggenheim Museum in New York, October 2005. Burden does not remake his works, and denied her permission to do so.

33. It has often been rumored that Beuys left the gallery each night to enjoy an evening meal and a good night's rest after gallery hours, and this fact is confirmed by Uwe M. Schneede in *Joseph Beuys Die Aktionen*, the most authoritative and comprehensive study

of Beuys's performances. Schneede wrote: "An den drei Tagen dauerte die Aktion jeweils von 10 bis 18 Uhr" (On the three days, the action lasted from 10 to 6 p.m.). See Uwe M. Schneede, *Joseph Beuys Die Aktionen: Kommentiertes Werkverzeichnis mit fotografischen Dokumentationen* (Ostfildern-Ruit bei Stuttgart: Verlag Gerd Hatje, 1994), 331.

34. Peter Clothier, "Chris Burden: The Artist as Hero," *Flash Art* 94/95 (January/February 1980): 49.

35. Johannes Lothar Schröder, "Science, Heat and Time," 207.

36. Burden/Stiles.

37. Howard Singerman, "Chris Burden's Pragmatism," 22.

38. Burden remembered: "After being up there three weeks, I really didn't want to come down. *White Light, White Heat* became really spooky for me because it became a microcosm for life, for one's life itself. It seems infinite when you start, and as you get through it, "Whoa, it's almost over: Jesus Christ!" Burden/Stiles.

39. Robin White, "Interview with Chris Burden," *View* 1, no. 8 (January 1978): 7.

40. Burden/Stiles.

41. Kathy O'Dell, *Contract with the Skin*, 66. O'Dell categorized the following performances as "bed pieces": *Bed Piece*, *Oh, Dracula*, *White Light/White Heat*, *Doomed*, and *Oracle*. O'Dell deftly raised the psychological dimension of Burden's repetitive focus on the bed, referring to a bedroom oedipal drama. Again, she was correct: Burden spent his childhood in the midst of parental conflict.

42. In 1955, Edward Steichen organized the exhibition *The Family of Man* at the Museum of Modern Art in New York. It included Margaret Bourke-White, Matthew Brady, Robert Capa, Henri Cartier-Bresson, Jack Delano, Alfred Eisenstaedt, Dorothea Lange, Carl Mydans, Ben Shahn, and Edward Weston, among others. See Edward Steichen, *The Family of Man: The Greatest Photographic Exhibition of All Time—503 Pictures from 68 Countries* (New York: Museum of Modern Art and Maco Magazine Corp., 1955).

43. Burden felt isolated even before the accident, as he "was going to do correspondence school, this Quaker thing," and had not enrolled in public school. Burden/Stiles.

44. Ibid.

45. Ibid.

46. See Chris Burden's comments in Peter Noever, ed., *Chris Burden: Beyond the Limits*, 183.

47. Robin White, "Interview with Chris Burden."

48. For a discussion of dualisms related to light, see P. F. M. Fontaine, *The Light and The Dark: A Cultural History of Dualism*, Vols. I, II, and III (Amsterdam: J. C. Gieben, 1986).

49. Discussing the necessity to feed himself and provide for his physical needs during *Bed Piece*, Burden noted that he "was trying to confront Josh Young, who was the guy who ran [the gallery], that I was both an object and a human being. This was a special art show. He couldn't just lock the doors and go home. The object had problems. If I had to get up and pee, I had to pee behind the desk on the floor or in the wastebasket or something. He had a problem on his hands, and he had to deal with it." Burden/Stiles.

50. Kristine Stiles, "Chris Burden's Free Physics," in *Chris Burden* (New York: Zwirner & Wirth Gallery, 2004), 4.

51. See also the following projects: The Reason for the Neutron Bomb (1979), Pearl Harbor (1979), Atomic Alphabet (1979), Warning! Relax, or You Will Be Nuked Again (1980), and A Tale of Two Cities (1982).

52. Burden/Stiles.

53. Ibid.

54. Chris Burden in Frances Morris, *Chris Burden: When Robots Rule: The Two-Minute Airplane Factory* (London: Tate Gallery Publishing, 1999), 43.

55. Plato, *Republic*. Translated by G. M. A. Grube, revised by C. D. C. Reeve (Indianapolis and Cambridge: Hackett, 1992), 287.

56. Burden/Stiles. With regard to the impact of Fascism on Burden's imagination, his sculpture/installation *Pizza City* (1996) bears a striking resemblance to the aerial view of Nuremberg in the opening sequence of Leni Riefenstahl's film *The Triumph of the Will* (1935), in which Hitler's plane flies over the city, with its steeples and half-timber houses.

57. Paul Schimmel, "Just the Facts," in *Chris Burden*, 16.

58. Burden/Stiles. On January 4, 1979, the state of Ohio agreed to pay $675,000 to families of the dead and injured victims of the Kent State University shootings.

59. Chris Burden quoted in Susan Freudenheim, "The Artist as Canyon Jumper," *Los Angeles Times Magazine* (July 13, 2003): 23.

60. Burden/Stiles.

61. Burden/Stiles.

62. From an unpublished letter by Chris Burden, dated November 19, 1971, and addressed to Willoughby Sharp and Liza Bear; currently in Chris Burden's personal archive, Topanga, California. This terse statement parallels the infamous action, which took place in a fraction of a second when an assistant fired a .22 rifle and hit the artist in the arm. A photograph captures the image, recalling the relationship between photography and guns in the development of the history of photography, from Etienne Jules-Marey's revolver-gun camera (*fusil photographique*) to the Austrian philosopher Ernst Mach's collaboration in 1886 with the Austrian photographer Peter Salcher to photograph bullets in flight. Schlieren photography is a technique that requires casting a light source onto a knife edge so that changes in the density of a transparent medium (such as glass or air) between the light source and the knife edge alter the refractive index more or less, thereby diverting the light and causing light or dark areas in the picture.

63. Don DeLillo's novel *The Body Artist* (2001), which portrays a performance artist in the most arcane and unrealistic way, comes to mind, as does *Legal Eagles* (1986), the Hollywood film comedy staring Daryl Hannah as a "crazy performance artist." Moreover, in the December 11, 2005, issue of *The New York Times Book Review*, Barry Gewen, its editor, opened his essay "State of the Art" with a comment meant to undermine contemporary art with a description of a work by Burden, presented without comment or context: "In 1974, Chris Burden had himself crucified on the roof of a Volkswagen" (p. 28). Precisely such sensationalized representations of Burden's work, and of performance art in general, detract from a rich and deep understanding of this medium of art, and fail to account for its appearance as a dominant global practice in the wake of the Holocaust and the atomic bomb, when the body and survival of the planet itself became an abiding dilemma for humanity. Burden's performances, installations, and sculptures are resounding testimonies to the question of survival in the twentieth and twenty-first centuries.

64. Burden/Stiles.

65. Ibid.

66. R. J. Zwi Werblowsky, "Light and Darkness," in *The Encyclopedia of Religion* (New York: MacMillan, 1987), 549.

67. Burden's documentation of this performance uses the sentence "Screaming for me, the engine was run at full speed for two minutes." Any publication on this work contains these words. See, for example, Peter Noever, ed., *Chris Burden: Beyond the Limits*, 69.

68. Burden/Stiles.

69. Gerald Lucas, "Tarkovsky's Solaris." http://litmuse.maconstate.edu/~glucas/archives/000359.shtml (accessed May 30, 2005).

70. Burden in Chris Burden: Un Livre de Survie, 141–42.

71. Robin White, "Interview with Chris Burden."

72. Burden in Peter Noever, ed., *Chris Burden: Beyond the Limits*, 174.

73. Thanks to Karen Gonzales Rice for discussions on this formulation.

74. By igniting gasoline on six-foot sheets of glass resting on his own shoulders, Burden created wings of flame in *Icarus*. By referring to the mythic boy intoxicated with flight, who plunged to his death in the sea when he got too near the sun and his wax wings melted, *Icarus* raises more oedipal questions related to Kathy O'Dell's study of Burden. Icarus's father, Daedalus, who was an architect, sculptor, and inventor, had constructed the wings. This parallels the relation of Burden and his father, who was a diplomat and engineer, and therefore suggests an intertwining between the violence and destruction in Burden's art and his relationship with his father.

Georges Bataille compared Icarus to Prometheus and the Mithraic bull as examples of those who challenged the mythical alliance between the eagle and the sun, thus challenging "the unconstrained development of individual authoritarian power." Bataille also notes: "The myth of Icrarus is particularly expressive from this point of view: it clearly splits the sun in two—the one that was shining at the moment of Icarus's elevation, and the one that melted the wax, causing failure and screaming fall when Icarus got too close. This human tendency to distinguish two suns owes its particular importance . . . to the fact that the psychological movements described are not ones that have been diverted, nor their urges attenuated, by secondary elements." Georges Bataille, "The 'Old Mole' and the Prefix *Sur*," in *Visions of Excess: Selected Writings, 1927–1939*, ed. and trans. by Allan Stoekly with Carl R. Lovitt and Donald M. Leslie Jr. (Minneapolis: University of Minnesota Press, 1985), 34, 58.

75. *Fire By Friction* (1982), *From Neanderthal to the 20th Century* (1983), and *The Frictionless Sled* (1983) all call for fire or friction, the prelude to fire.

76. Gaston Bachelard, *The Psychoanalysis of Fire*, trans. by Alan C. M. Ross (Boston: Beacon Press, 1964; published first in Paris by Gallimard, 1938).

77. Steve Mumford, in a review of *The Fist of Light* (1993), associated Burden's work with "boys' toys" and described his strength as an artist in inane terms, as a "mean streak of adolescent megalomania." See Mumford's "Art and Adolescent Megalomania: Boy Toys and Other Cool Stuff" (1997), in *Plexus Reviews*, http://www.plexus.org/review/mumford/boytoys.html#MUMFORD (accessed May 22, 2005).

78. Paul Schimmel, "Just the Facts," 15.

79. Donald Kuspit, "Man for and against Machine": 79. In *Poem for L.A.* (1975), Burden stated, "SCIENCE HAS FAILED." Nevertheless, Burden often consults scientific and technological manuals, subscribing to more than fifty magazines ranging in subject matter from news, science, nature, and culture to popular mechanics.

80. Howard Singerman, "Chris Burden's Pragmatism," 20.

81. Kristine Stiles, "Chris Burden's Free Physics," 1.

82. Meg Cranston and John Baldessari, *100 Artists See God* (London: Institute of Contemporary Arts, 2004), n.p.

83. Arthur Zajonc, *Catching the Light: The Entwined History of Light and Mind* (New York: Bantam Books, 1993), 2.

84. Ibid., 341.

### *TEACHING A DEAD HAND TO DRAW*: KIM JONES, WAR, AND ART

1. This text was first published in *Mudman: The Odyssey of Kim Jones* (Cambridge, MA: MIT Press, 2007), 45–84. I would like to thank Kim Jones, for his honesty and the audacious beauty of his art; Sandra Firmin, for including my text in this important and worthy

project; Kathy O'Dell and Karen Gonzalez Rice, with whom I discussed this essay; and Julie Joyce and Jane Hyun, for their review of the text.

2. Edward Tick, *War and the Soul: Healing Our Nation's Veterans from Post-Traumatic Stress Disorder* (Wheaton, IL: Quest Books, Theosophical Publishing House, 2005), 86.

3. Kim Jones, *Teaching a Dead Hand to Draw*, video by David Schmidlapp and Steve Staso, 2001.

4. Kim Jones, quoted in Susan Swenson, "Conversation with Kim Jones: April 25, 2005. New York City," in *Kim Jones: War Paint* (Brooklyn, NY: Perogi, 2005), 4.

5. Ibid.

6. William Hescox, quoted in "Preliminary Investigation Report by the Los Angeles Police Department for Cruelty to Animals Charge," February 18, 1976, reprinted in Jones's *Rat Piece: Feb. 17, 1976* (New York: Kim Jones, 1990), 94. The self-published book was made possible by a grant to the artist by the John Simon Guggenheim Memorial Foundation.

7. Jones, in a telephone conversation with the author, September 2, 2006. I also spoke with the artist by telephone on August 19, 2006. Unless otherwise noted, all quotes from Jones come from these two phone conversations. Hereafter, I shall refer to both conversations simply as Jones/Stiles.

8. Jones would represent these "others" in more concrete form some twenty-five years later in *Dressing Room* (2003), for which he lined up a group of chairs and covered the back of each with a T-shirt printed with the kind of battle drawing as in *Khaki Marine Shirt*. The "chair-beings" appear to be in training, and they face a wall covered with more battle drawings.

9. Damian Sharp, untitled text (1976), reprinted in Jones, *Rat Piece*, 63.

10. Hescox, "Preliminary Investigation Report," 94.

11. Psychologist Larry Gonzalez reported that when he was an undergraduate at Louisiana State University in the early 1970s, a crowd of anti–Vietnam War protesters burned a rat alive. Gonzalez, in conversation with daughter Karen Gonzalez Rice, a graduate student and my advisee at Duke University, October 20, 2006. I do not know how common this kind of action was during the period, but it demonstrates that Jones's performance was not an isolated incident.

12. Antecedents for the destruction of animals in art exist, from Hermann Nitsch and Raphael Montañez Ortiz in the 1960s to Tom Otterness's *Shot Dog Piece*, in which Otterness adopted a dog and then filmed it being shot to death in the 1980s. While Joseph Beuys used dead hares in his work, he did not kill the animals in the making of his art. Antecedents for "walking sculpture" reside in assemblage and in sculptures worn by artists such as Lygia Clark, Franz Erhard Walther, and Franz West. All of these artists, among others, explored sculpture as something useful in the exploration of psychological relationships. In addition, Jones acknowledges Bruce Conner's use of silk stockings as a precedent for his own art. This material, especially in a torn condition, evokes violence, decay, eroticism, and death.

13. Jones, untitled text, in *Rat Piece*, 7.

14. For the role of sex in the Vietnam War, see psychiatrist Jonathan Shay, who worked for decades with Vietnam veterans, and his chapter devoted to this subject in *Odysseus in America: Combat Trauma and the Trials of Homecoming* (New York: Scribner's, 2002).

15. Raymond Monsour Scurfield, "Posttraumatic Stress Disorder in Vietnam Veterans," in John P. Wilson and Beverley Raphael, eds., *International Handbook of Traumatic Stress Syndromes* (New York: Plenum Press, 1993), 191. This article summarizes the unprecedented study of trauma and Vietnam veterans in R. Kulka, W. Schlenger, J. Fairbank,

R. Hough, B. K. Jordan, C. Marmar, and D. Weiss, *National Vietnam Veterans Readjustment Study (NCCRS): Description, Current Status and Initial PTSD Prevalence Estimates* (Research Triangle Park, NC: Research Triangle Institute, 1988).

16. Robert Jay Lifton, "From Hiroshima to the Nazi Doctors: The Evolution of Psychoformative Approaches to Understanding Traumatic Stress Syndromes," in *International Handbook of Traumatic Stress Syndromes*, 14–15.

17. Jones in Swenson, "Conversation with Kim Jones," 12. A skeleton can also be someone (or something) reduced to its minimal form, as well as a secret, something hidden, as in the expression "the skeleton in the closet." But finally it is, in actuality, the internal support structure that gives a body or artifact its shape.

18. Shay writes in *Odysseus in America* about the common "hostility and habitual disrespect toward women of psychologically injured Vietnam combat veterans," which brought home a "painful and destructive legacy . . . [of a] visceral sense that women are dangerous" (pp. 67–68). This hostility was initiated by the "context of prostitution," brothels that provided "steam bath, massage, and ejaculation," and the common experience of "rape and rape-murder" that contributed to "fear, anger, and violence . . . as the groundwork for postwar sexual life" (70).

19. Scurfield, "Posttraumatic Stress Disorder," 288.

20. Judith Lewis Herman has observed:

> Fight or flight doesn't work in conditions of terror and helplessness. Under those conditions, it appears that some kind of biological rewiring seems to happen in people and in animals as well. So that even after the danger is over, the person continues to respond to reminders, to both specific reminders and to generally threatening situations, as though this terrifying event were still occurring in the present. So you have the activation of the fear system, hyper-arousal. You have a kind of re-experiencing of the trauma that takes the form of flashbacks, nightmares, and so forth. And then you have this other more poorly understood part of the traumatic syndrome that has to do with a shutting down of responsiveness. Numbing, a sense that things aren't real. There may be amnesia for some, more, or all of the event. A sense in the aftermath that one is just not really oneself. One is going through the motions. There's a loss of connection of things that are or previously of interest. And these are called the numbing or withdrawal or symptoms of PTSD. So hyper-arousal, re-experiencing, numbing is the triad. It's a descriptive formulation.

See Harry Kreisler, "The Case of Trauma and Recovery: Conversation with Judith Herman, M.D., Psychiatrist and Author," September 21, 2000, for the Institute of International Studies series *Conversations with History, University of California, Berkeley*, http://globetrotter.berkeley.edu/people/Herman/herman-con0.html.

21. My understanding of Jones's work as a kind of Möbius strip is indebted to discussions with the Romanian artist Lia Perjovschi, who described the "costumes" she made in 1989 (titled *Maps of Impressions*) as "Moebius strips, able to exhibit the continuity between my inner and outer worlds." Perjovschi, in conversation with the author, October 8, 2006, Bucharest, Romania. Two artists—separated by gender, age, experience, and nationality, but whose work comes out of traumatic circumstances—compellingly created similar constructions, each without the benefit of knowledge of the other.

22. Scurfield, "Posttraumatic Stress Disorder," 291.

23. Ibid.

24. Jones, "Statement about 'Rat Piece'," in Reese Williams, ed., *Unwinding the Vietnam War: From War into Peace* (Seattle: Real Comet Press, 1987), 114.

25. On rats and the Black Plague, see Norman F. Cantor, *In the Wake of the Plague: The Black Plague and the World it Made* (New York: Free Press, 2001).

26. Statistics provided in *Unwinding the Vietnam War*, 7–8.

27. In 1993, before the United States lifted the embargo against Vietnam, I had the opportunity with other scholars and teachers to visit Vietnam with several US Vietnam veterans. We went both to Hanoi and Saigon (now Ho Chi Minh City), where we met Vietnamese combatants who had fought against the US soldiers. For the US veterans, this trip was a draining and highly emotional confrontation with the past, but their Vietnamese counterparts did not share such emotions. When asked why the Vietnamese soldiers did not have the same painful re-encounter, the answer was always the same: Vietnam as a nation recognized that it had won the war on national and moral grounds, and it had also collectively mourned, while the United States as a nation had never examined either its collective experience or the individual experiences of its veterans.

28. Max Kozloff, letter to James Woods, president of the Studio Watts Endowment Fund, April 5, 1976, published in *Rat Piece*, 67.

29. The play *US* was by Peter Brook, not Peter Hall, and was produced by the Royal Shakespeare Company in London in 1966.

30. Robert Hughes, letter to David B. Riles, California State University, n.d., published in *Rat Piece*, 65.

31. "Prayer to St. Jude," published in *Rat Piece*, 117.

32. See the "Pray to St. Jude" page on the National Shrine of St. Jude website: http://shrineofstjude.claretians.org/site/PageServer?pagename=ssj_share_pray&gclid=CMvPoaT7j4gCFQlTVAodwiPaOw.

33. James G. Souden, letter to Jones, May 5, 1972, published in *Rat Piece*, 118.

34. Among the list of experiences that are sources of rage for Vietnam veterans "peculiar to the Vietnam War and its aftermath back in the United States" are the following: (1) the nature of guerrilla warfare, in which there are hit-and-run ambush tactics, the involvement of all segments of the population, and the promotion of terror; (2) the view of the body count, rather than terrain objectives, as a measure of progress in the war; (3) the conflict between political and military decision-making; (4) the one-year tour of duty in a maximally stressful environment; (5) the veterans' rejection and betrayal or nonresponse by society upon their return to the United States; (6) the absence of knowledgeable healthcare programs for war-related PTSD and other veteran-specific mental health concerns; (7) the absence of counseling programs for veterans and their families; (8) the abandonment of the Vietnamese people and armies to be overrun by Communist forces; (9) the difficulties in securing employment and educational opportunities after the war; and (10) the uncertainties of herbicidal exposure (e.g., Agent Orange), and the denial or minimization of any responsibility on the part of government and private industry. Scurfield, "Posttraumatic Stress Disorder," 291–92.

35. Kathy O'Dell, *Contract with the Skin: Masochism, Performance Art and the 1970s* (Minneapolis and London: University of Minnesota Press, 1998), 11.

36. Jones, in Unwinding the Vietnam War, 120.

37. Ho Chi Minh, *Prison Diary*, 5th Edition (Hanoi: Foreign Languages Publishing House, 1972), 123.

38. When I visited the History Museum in Hanoi together with US Vietnam veterans in 1993, we were shown a bronze jar from the Dong Son civilization (seventh to second centuries BCE) in Vietnam. After being told that the bronze was nearly three thousand years old, one veteran turned to me and asked, "He means three hundred years old?" I responded that, no, the history of Vietnamese civilization was very ancient and very accomplished. The veteran broke into tears and stated: "They never told us."

39. The National Front for the Liberation of South Vietnam People's Liberation Armed Forces (PLAF or Viet Cong), together with North Vietnam's People's Army of Vietnam (PAVN), fought against South Vietnam's Army of the Republic of Vietnam (ARVN), the US military, and other ARVN-allied forces.

40. Albert Auster and Leonard Quart, *How the War was Remembered: Hollywood and Vietnam* (New York: Praeger, 1988), 132.

41. The DMZ was established after Vietnam ousted the French in 1954. It was to be the neutral area between the communist Democratic Republic of Vietnam (in North Vietnam), led by Ho, and South Vietnam, under the puppet regime of Ngo Dinh Diem, who in 1955 (with the encouragement of the United States) claimed to have won a referendum, declaring himself president of the Republic of Vietnam (in Saigon he had received a third more votes than there were registered voters).

42. As Robert Jay Lifton has noted,

> Vietnam veterans . . . were patriotic. And they had a kind of macho feeling that war was a kind of testing ground for manhood. And also, the idea that in many cases they'd literally sat on their father's knee, he'd been a veteran of World War II and told them about the glorious victory, and they wanted their moment, with war glorified sometimes in that way. But when they experienced their first deads . . . [and] were in some way involved in a death encounter, their comfort in all of this was shattered. And in many cases they simply could no longer justify their being there. And they felt everything there seemed strange and bizarre and, for many of them, wrong. There was something wrong or dirty about that war.

See Harry Kreisler, "Evil, the Self, and Survival: Conversation with Robert Jay Lifton, M.D., Psychiatrist and Author," in *Conversations with History: Institute of International Studies, University of California at Berkeley* (November 2, 1999), http://globetrotter.berkeley.edu/people/Lifton/lifton-con0.html.

43. Khe Sanh housed the strategic Marine Corps base located a few miles from the borders of North Vietnam and Laos. This Marine base was built in 1965, and was heavily fortified in late 1967 by General William Westmoreland. It was designed as a site from which to stage attacks on troop movements down the Ho Chi Minh Trail. During the US buildup, North Vietnamese forces also developed excellent defensive positions on nearby hills that were impervious to ground and tactical air attacks.

44. Hill fights were staged in the Khe Sanh area in April and May 1967 between US Marines and North Vietnamese troops on Hills 861, 881 North, and 881 South during the period of Jones's tour of duty. The North Vietnamese launched these attacks in preparation for the Tet Offensive, strategically hoping that significant numbers of US troops would be drawn off into the countryside.

45. Jones/Stiles.

46. Ibid.

47. Jones explained that he was deemed a "fuck-up" for such actions as "getting really drunk." He continued: "One night I drank a bottle of Jack Daniels. We gave this Vietnamese guy a K-bar [knife]. We were giving weapons to the enemy, but we didn't care. I think we had several of them. I spent the whole night drinking with these guys and passed out and pissed in my pants, and went outside the door of the hooch to piss. I was so screwed up and I was supposed to go on a convoy, and I remember leaning on the back of a truck and I forgot my rifle and passed out on the way to Camp Carroll. That explains the 'fuck-up.'" When I asked if most soldiers were like that, Jones replied: "Yeah, but it depends on the situation. I remember some guys saying that every time they heard that

there was information that Viet Cong were in one area they would go in the opposite direction." Ibid.

48. Ibid.

49. Ibid.

50. John Ketwig, "... And a Hard Rain Fell," in *Unwinding the Vietnam War*, 13.

51. Jones/Stiles.

52. Ibid.

53. Ibid. My emphasis.

54. Ibid.

55. Interesting parallels exist between Jones's battle drawings and the drawings by Adolf Wolfli, the renowned schizophrenic artist identified with "outsider" art. See, for example, Edward M. Gomez, *Adolf Wölfli: Master of his Universe* (Saint Louis: Envision, 2003).

56. Jones/Stiles.

57. Ibid. Born in Uzbekistan (then part of the Soviet Union), Mirit Cohen (1945–90) spent her early years in displaced-person camps before immigrating to Israel. She moved to New York, where she did her most productive art in the mid-1970s before committing suicide in 1990.

58. Jones/Stiles.

59. See PIKE Military Research website, www.militaryunits.com/VNammaps.htm.

60. Jones, e-mail to the author, November 2, 2006.

61. Jones/Stiles.

62. Jones, "Valley of Death," in *A Life of Secrets* (New York: AC Project Room, 1994), 10. In this text, Jones wrote: "I'm alone in the Santa Monica Mountains. It's the month of May. I don't belong here. I prepare myself for the journey back to the city of Los Angeles. I need to live with rats. I take a bottle of rat shit and blood out of my bag. This is a gift from another time. The shit and blood are mixed with mud and rubbed all over my body."

63. Jones has never been interested in drugs or a regular user of them. Jones/Stiles.

64. Scurfield, "Posttraumatic Stress Disorder," 288.

65. Jones/Stiles.

66. Ibid.

67. Kim Jones, *Spit*, an illustrated story, edition of 200, published by the artist in 1981.

68. Jones/Stiles.

69. Jones, *A Life of Secrets*, 7.

70. Ibid.

71. Tick, *War and the Soul*, 99.

72. Roméo Dallaire, *Shake Hands with the Devil: The Failure of Humanity in Rwanda* (Toronto: Random House Canada, 2003).

73. Scurfield, "Posttraumatic Stress Disorder," 285.

74. Ibid.

75. Ibid., 287.

76. Ibid.

77. In Mary Crowley's overview of "Psychobiology of Post-Traumatic Stress Disorder, A Decade of Progress," psychiatrist Rachel Yehuda (director of the traumatic stress studies division at Mount Sinai School of Medicine and Bronx Veterans Affairs Medical Center), noted that "PTSD research is 'on the threshold of a paradigm shift.' The condition is understood as not merely a response to an external event, but a response linked to a specific phenotype that has an inability to incorporate stress. Noting that most people do not develop PTSD in response to trauma, she describes this phenotype as an abnormal one in the sense of the difference between talking about how badly you felt in response

to some stressful event versus re-experiencing the event again and again. Identifying this phenotype provides opportunities for both prevention and treatment." Yehuda, quoted in the New York Academy of Sciences' *Academy Briefings*, posted February 24, 2006. This article also contains a very useful list of the various current studies on the psychobiology of traumatic response: http://www.nyas.org/Publications/Ebriefings/Detail.aspx?cid=b856385b-a328-40ea-924d-044db0ac8a84.

78. Harry A. Wilmer, "The Healing Nightmare: A Study of the War Dreams of Vietnam Combat Veterans," in *Unwinding the Vietnam War*, 68.

79. Scurfield, "Posttraumatic Stress Disorder," 287.

80. Phillip Roth, *The Human Stain* (Boston: Houghton Mifflin, 2000), 72.

81. Ibid., 74.

82. I address this topic in my manuscript for a book entitled *Props for the Memory: Joseph Beuys and the Legacy of Fascism.*

83. O'Dell, *Contract with the Skin*, 15. See also Didier Anzier, *The Skin Ego: A Psychoanalytic Approach to the Self*, trans. Chris Turner (New Haven: Yale University Press, 1989).

84. Ibid.

85. Lifton, quoted in Kreisler, "Evil, the Self, and Survival."

## JEAN TOCHE: *IMPRESSIONS FROM THE ROGUE BUSH IMPERIAL PRESIDENCY*

1. This essay was first published as the exhibition catalogue for *Jean Toche: Impressions From The Rogue Bush Imperial Presidency* (Durham, NC: John Hope Franklin Center for Interdisciplinary and International Studies, 2009). I wish to thank Jean Toche for his inspiring art and for his friendship; Rob Sikorski for initiating this exhibition and catalogue; Kathy Hudson, Jane Christy, and Molly Renda for helping me to realize both; and Kathy O'Dell for commenting on this text.

2. Graham Clarke, *The Photograph* (Oxford and New York: Oxford University Press, 1997), 145.

3. Ibid., 147.

4. The exhibition *Impressions from the Rogue Bush Imperial Presidency*, curated by Kristine Stiles, took place at the Franklin Center Gallery, John Hope Franklin Center for Interdisciplinary and International Studies, Duke University, September 17 to November 20, 2009. This was the catalog essay for that show.

5. Jean Toche, December 17, 2004.

6. Jean Toche, "Crimes against Humanity," September 29, 2001, in Jean Toche, *Waiter! There Is a Terrorist in My Soup!* (Stuttgart: Edition Hundertmark, 2002), n.p.

7. Toche produced twelve issues of *Of Piss @N' Pus*, all postmarked in 2002. Nevertheless, on the back of a number of the issues, as well as on the bottom of some of the letters contained therein, the date is 2003. When I spoke to Toche about this discrepancy on August 5, 2009, he could not explain the oddity, except that he was "very busy during this period" and may have confused the date.

8. Toche puts a copyright symbol on the front of his works so that, as he says on the back, those who appropriate his works respect the integrity of his art.

9. Toche, in conversation with the author, September 2008; hereafter cited as Toche/Stiles.

10. See Jennifer Blessing, *Rrose is a Rrose is a Rrose: Gender Performance in Photography* (New York: Guggenheim Museum, 1997).

11. Toche/Stiles.

12. Toche's reference to the German word for "culture" is addressed in another aspect of his manifesto, in which the artist recalled: "Twenty-five years ago, when the Nazis fled from Belgium, my native country, after four years of military occupation, I saw people burning in the streets all over the country whatever had been German: books, magazines, records, films. . . . Buildings which had been occupied, or built, by the Germans were dynamited. The Belgians wanted to erase forever whatever had been part of that Deutschland Kultuur." In this memory, Toche linked the response of those who destroyed the artist's work on Ward Island to the Belgians' response to the imposition of German culture and force.

13. Jean Toche, "AGGRESSION ART," October 9, 1969, reprinted in Guerrilla Art Action Group, *GAAG, the Guerrilla Art Action Group, 1969–1976* (New York: Printed Matter, 1978), n.p.

14. See Nicolas Bourriaud. *Relational Aesthetics* (Paris: Presses du réel, 2002). See also Claire Bishop's response to Bourriaud, "Antagonism and Relational Aesthetics," *October* 110 (2004): 51–79.

15. See Claire Bishop, "The Social Turn: Collaboration and Its Discontents," *Artforum* 44, no. 6 (February 2006): 179–85, and the many responses to this article in subsequent issues of the magazine.

16. Michael Fried, following Jean-François Chevrier, has also pointed out that "starting in the late 1970s and 1980s, art photographs began to be made not only at large scale but also . . . for the wall," and that such images brought viewers to stand before photographs "as they had never previously" done. See Fried, *Why Photography Matters as Art as Never Before* (New Haven and London: Yale University Press, 2008), 2, 13.

17. Barthes distinguished between the *studium* (the overall effect of the image) and the *punctum* (its point of disturbance), noting that all photographs have a *studium* but not all "prick" the imagination of the viewer, which is the function of the *punctum*. See Roland Barthes, *Camera Lucida: Reflections on Photography*, translated by Richard Howard (New York: Hill & Wang, 1981), 59.

18. John Dewey, *Art as Experience* [1934] (New York: Capricorn Books, 1959), 133.

19. Toche/Stiles.

20. Ibid.

21. On September 29, 2002, Toche left a message for me with the art historian Edward A. Shanken, who recorded the conversation in a letter that he placed in issue no. 9:

> On the day this issue of Of Piss @N' Pus (No. 09) arrived, I spoke with Jean Toche. He had left a message for Kristine (who was in Romania) to call him back about an urgent matter. He explained to me over the phone that he had recently been subject to an experience that left him frightened for his life and well being. On a trip to the local post office, a postal employee called the police, and told them to arrest Toche. The police did not see any reason to do so, and declared the situation a false alarm. Nonetheless, postal workers who had in [the] past treated him cordially (as a result of his art practice he makes routine, if not daily, visits) now treated him coldly and with suspicion. The accuser later bumped into him, an incident that Toche is certain was meant as an intentional act of aggression. Toche suspects that a copy of his journal [Of Piss @N' Pus] was damaged in transit and that his accuser felt the content (which was exposed when the envelope broke) was un-American and suspicious. Toche fears no reprisals from the police, but is afraid of vigilante aggression from individuals like his accuser in the very conservative community of Staten Island, in which he has lived since 1979.

Shanken's letter is in issue 9 of Toche's journal *Of Piss @N' Pus*, in "Stiles Papers," Toche boxes, Special Collections, Duke University Library.

22. Ibid.

23. Toche/Stiles. V1 bombs were the first guided missiles carrying high-explosive warheads. Manufactured by the Third Reich, they were called the "Buzz Bomb" for the sound they made.

24. All quotes come from *July 31, 2004*, in which Toche also added: "She was a ballerina with the De Basil Ballet Russes. She was a part of the Hawthorne Concert Dance Group. She was a Broadway performer (Oklahoma, By Jupiter, Billion Dollar Baby, Allegro, Sadie Thompson, Hazel Flagg, Wonderful Town . . .). She danced at The Folies Bergère and at Las Vegas' Flamingo (June Taylor Group). She performed on the Ed Sullivan TV Show and the Milton Berle TV Show. She was Miss Cincinnati 1948. She was a member of the Guerilla Art Action Group."

25. When asked if his performance *I ACCUSE* (1968), was influenced by Émile Zola's "J'accuse" (1898)—the letter Zola published in the Paris newspaper *L'Aurore*, in which he argued that "the conviction of Alfred Dreyfus was based on false accusations of espionage and was a misrepresentation of justice"—Toche explained that he "was very influenced by Zola when I was young, but *I ACCUSE* was, of course, about quite different matter and was a performance." Toche's use of letters as a format for making art nevertheless may have been rooted in such epistolary forms for political action; this is a subject for further research on his work. Toche, in a telephone conversation with the author, August 5, 2009.

26. See Sally Banes, *Democracy's Body: Judson Dance Theater, 1962–1964* (Durham, NC: Duke University Press, 1993); and Sally Banes, *Greenwich Village, 1963: Avant-Garde Performance and the Effervescent Body* (Durham, NC: Duke University Press, 1993).

27. Lil Picard, *East Village Other* 3, no. 24 (17 May 1968): 7. "LIGHT" referred to Toche's use of high-intensity spotlights to assault viewers visually; "SIT-IN" situated his action in the context of organized political demonstrations in which protestors seated themselves in strategic places and refused to move.

28. Jean Toche, *I ACCUSE* (Brussels: Galerie Le Zodiaque, 1968).

29. Guerrilla Art Action Group, *GAAG*, n.p.

30. Silvianna [aka Silvianna Goldsmith], feminist filmmaker.

31. Toche/Stiles. All subsequent quotations of Toche come from this discussion.

32. Ibid. See Commission of Inquiry for the International War Crimes Tribunal, "International War Crimes Tribunal United States War Crimes against Iraq: Initial Complaint Charging George Bush, J. Danforth Quayle, James Baker, Richard Cheney, William Webster, Colin Powell, Norman Schwarzkopf and Others to Be Named with Crimes against Peace, War Crimes, Crimes against Humanity and Other Criminal Acts and High Crimes in Violation of the Charter of the United Nations, International Law, the Constitution of the United States and Laws Made in Pursuance Thereof," available at http://deoxy.org/wc/warcrim2.htm.

33. Will Bunch, "Obama Would Ask His AG to 'Immediately Review' Potential of Crimes in Bush White House," *Philadelphia Daily News*, April 14, 2008, http://www.philly.com/philly/blogs/attytood/Barack_on_torture.html.

34. Ibid.

35. Siobhan Gorman, "CIA Had Secret Al Qaeda Plan: Initiative at Heart of Spat with Congress Examined Ways to Seize, Kill Terror Chiefs," *Wall Street Journal*, July 13, 2009; http://online.wsj.com/article/SB124736381913627661.html.

36. Max Kozloff, "The Awning That Flapped in the Breeze and the Bodies That Littered the Field: 'Painting and the Invention of Photography,'" in *The Privileged Eye: Essays on Photography* (Albuquerque: University of New Mexico Press, 1987), 251.

37. Ibid., 254.

38. Ibid.

39. Ibid., 267.

40. Ibid., 253.

41. Art & Language, the influential group of conceptual artists, was founded in the United Kingdom in 1967, and it published the journal *Art-Language* (1969–78). The remaining members still working together in 2009 include artists Michael Baldwin and Mel Ramsden.

42. Michael Corris, e-mail to the author, July 13, 2009.

## CLOUD WITH ITS SHADOW: MARINA ABRAMOVIĆ

1. I would like to thank Craig Garrett of Phaidon Press for commissioning this essay; Melissa Larner for her editorial assistance; and Marina Abramović for her art, which is rooted in history, condenses life into exquisite works, and is startlingly honest in a period when truth and responsibility for one's actions are under crushing pressure. This essay first appeared in *Marina Abramović* (London: Phaidon, 2008), 33–94.

2. Pierre Coulibeuf, *Balkan Baroque* (1999), UbuWeb Film: http://www.ubu.com/film/coulibeuf.html.

3. Abramović spoke this phrase at the end of *The House with the Ocean View*, and in several interviews.

4. The artist Neša Paripović, Abramović's first husband, whom she married in 1970.

5. "Knez Mihailova" is Prince Mihailo Street, the main pedestrian and shopping street in Belgrade, with buildings dating from the end of the 1870s, including the Renaissance-style villa that in 1937 became the Academy of Fine Arts where Abramović studied.

6. Martin Suter, "Whirlwind in New York," *Swiss Magazine* 2 (February 2006): 35.

7. Aaron Moulton, "Marina Abramović: Re: Performance," *Flash Art* 38, no. 244 (October 2005): 87.

8. See Willoughby Sharp's important early essay "Body Works," *Avalanche* 1 (Fall 1970): 14–17.

9. Marina Abramović and Velimir Abramović, "Time-Space-Energy or Talking about Asystemic Thinking," in *Marina Abramović: Artist Body: Performances 1969–1998* (Milan: Charta, 1997), 415.

10. Bette Denich, "Dismembering Yugoslavia: National Ideologies and the Symbolic Revival of Genocide," *American Ethnologist* 21, no. 2 (May 1994):378. Thanks to Jasmina Tumbas for alerting me to this article.

11. Evel Gasparini, "Studies in Old Slavic Religion: *UBRUS*," *History of Religions: An International Journal for Comparative Studies* 2, no. 1 (Summer 1962): 133–34.

12. Ibid., 113–14.

13. Ibid.

14. Paul Barber, *Vampires, Burial, and Death: Folklore and Reality* (New Haven: Yale University Press, 1988), 59.

15. Marina Abramović, *Artist Body*, 336.

16. Sigmund Freud, *Beyond the Pleasure Principle* (1920), trans. by C. J. M. Hubback (London: Hogarth Press, 1948).

17. This scene recalls the performance that Abramović realized with Ulay in 1978, entitled *Installation 'One,'* part of which included Ulay lying naked on the floor with an erection, looking at the ceiling, while Abramović sat naked on the floor, looking at the wall.

18. Fredrik Carlström and Marina Abramović, "A Conversation on 'Balkan Erotic Epic,'" in *Marina Abramović, Balkan Epic* (Milan: Skira, 2006), 66.

19. Alison Behnke, *Serbia and Montenegro in Pictures* (Minneapolis: Lerner Publisher Group, 2007), 49.

20. Michael Sells, *The Bridge Betrayed: Religion and Genocide in Bosnia* (Berkeley: University of California Press, 1996), 15.

21. Anonymous editors of the preface to Patriarch Varvana of Serbia, "I Love the Russian People" (on the 75th anniversary of his enthronement), June 9, 1930, in the *Russian Orthodox Church outside Russia* (Snyod of Bishops of the Russian Orthodox Church outside of Russia, 2002): http://www.russianorthodoxchurch.ws/01newstucture/pagesen/articles/arbvarnava.html.

22. Abramović narrates this story in *The Biography*.

23. See also Bojana Pejić, "Balkan for Beginners," *New Moment* (Belgrade) 7 (Spring 1997); reprinted in Laura Hoptman, Tomas Pospiszyl, Majlena Braun, and Clay Tarica, eds., *Primary Documents: A Sourcebook for Eastern and Central European Art Since the 1950s* (New York and Cambridge, MA: Museum of Modern Art and MIT Press, 2002), 325–39.

24. Philip Cohen, *Serbia's Secret War: Propaganda and the Deceit of History* (College Station: Texas A&M University Press, 1996), 72.

25. Ibid.

26. Bojana Pejić, "Im-Körper-Sein: Über das Geistige in Marina Abramovićs Kunst," in *Marina Abramović* (Ostfildern: Hatje Edition Cantz, 1993), 32. Thanks also to Eržebet Tumbas for his thoughts on this subject.

27. Ibid.

28. Abramović, in conversation with Phyllis Rosenzweig, April 20, 2001, in *Marina Abramović: Balkan Epic*, 40.

29. Abramović, e-mail to the author, November 26, 2007.

30. Abramović, *The Biography*.

31. Marina Abramović: *Artist Body*, 240.

32. D. C., "Marina Abramović: Balkan Erotic Epic," *Modern Painters* (March 2006): 118.

33. Marina Abramović and Velimir Abramović, "Time-Space-Energy," 402.

34. Jacques Derrida, *The Gift of Death*, trans. David Wills (Chicago: University of Chicago Press, 1995), 109, 113.

35. Marina Abramović: *Artist Body*, 355.

36. Ibid, 366.

37. The film *Izbavitelj* (Rat Savior, the Zero) by Yugoslavian filmmaker Krsto Papić, premiered in Yugoslavia in 1976 and was widely discussed. Thanks to Petar Tumbas for this citation.

38. Abramovic in conversation with the author, April 17, 2007, New York City; hereafter cited as Abramović/Stiles.

39. In her book *Marina Abramović: Artist Body*, Abramović included a photograph of her mother "giving a speech" in 1965.

40. Bojana Pejić, "Balkan Baroque, Balkan Mind," in *Marina Abramović: Balkan Epic*, 28.

41. Abramović/Stiles.

42. Rosenzweig, 40.

43. Later Abramović would add to the installation of *The Hero* the contents of a leather bag, the only article her father left her. It contained photographs and small objects, the most salient of which for Abramović was a pencil sharpener, an object whose function might suggest a range of psychological implications.

44. This piece took place during a body art festival at de Appel Gallery, a pioneering alternative space for body art and installation founded in Amsterdam in 1975.

45. Anna Novakov, "Point of Access: Marina Abramović's 1975 Performance *Role Exchange*," *Women's Art Journal* 24, no. 2 (Fall 2003/Winter 2004), 31.

46. Ibid., p. 32; quoted from Anna Novakov, "Role Exchange: Desire, Beauty and the Public," in Anna Novakov, ed., *Veiled Histories: The Body, Place and Public Art* (New York: Critical Press, 1997), 27.

47. Judith Lewis Herman with Lisa Hirschman, *Father-Daughter Incest* (Cambridge, MA: Harvard University Press, 1981), 115. An incestuous environment is one in which actual sexual relations between child and parent may never occur but the atmosphere of the home is sexualized and the child's response is similar to that of those who have been molested.

48. Abramović cites two unrealized works—*Come to Wash with Me* (1969) and *Untitled* (1970)—as her first performances. Her first realized action was *Rhythm 10*, performed in Edinburgh in 1973.

49. Marina Abramović: *Artist Body*, 54.

50. Ibid., 55.

51. Abramović, in Coulibeuf.

52. Abramović/Stiles.

53. Ibid.

54. Ibid.

55. Marina Abramović: *Artist Body*, 356.

56. Abramović/Stiles.

57. Marina Abramović: *Artist Body*, 356.

58. Jean-Paul Sartre, *The Words*, trans. Bernard Frechtman (New York: Fawcett Crest, 1964), 159.

59. Antonin Artaud, "The Theater of Cruelty," in Susan Sontag, ed., *Antonin Artaud's Selected Writings* (New York: Farrar, Straus and Giroux, 1976), 242.

60. Martin Heidegger, "The Origin of the Work of Art," from *Sein und Zeit* (Halle, Germany: M. Niemeyer, 1929); trans. as *Being and Time* (London: SCM Press, 1962), and reprinted in Preziosi, *The Art of Art History A Critical Anthology* (Oxford and New York: Oxford University Press, 1998): 413–26.

61. Bojana Pejić believes that "nearly all Abramović's body works are ritual in character," and that the artist "did not use the body as a vehicle of socialization." See Pejić's "Yugoslavia," in Zdenka Badovinac, ed., *Body and the East: From the 1960s to the Present* (Ljubljana: Museum of Modern Art, Ljubljana, 1998), 78.

62. Kristine Stiles, "Between Water and Stone: Fluxus Performance, A Metaphysics of Acts," in Elizabeth Armstrong and Joan Rothfuss, eds., *In The Spirit of Fluxus* (Minneapolis: Walker Art Center, 1993), 93.

63. Bosnia and Herzegovina, Croatia, Macedonia, Montenegro, Serbia (including Kosovo and Vojvodina), and Slovenia.

64. Pejić, "Im-Körper-Sein," 30.

65. This performance has also been called *Communist Body/Capitalist Body*. See Marina Abramović/Ulay, *Relation Work and Detour* (Amsterdam: Idea Books, 1980), 164.

66. Kathy O'Dell, *Contract with the Skin* (Minneapolis: University of Minnesota Press, 1998), 63–64. While O'Dell wrote that Abramović presented her "1962 student identification" in *Communist Body/Capitalist Body*, as shown in Ulay/Abramović's 1980 book *Relation Work and Detour*, Abramović wrote in *Marina Abramovic: Artist Body* that she displayed her birth certificate (p. 216).

67. Pejić, "Im-Körper-Sein," 31.

68. Significations of the pentagram vary from Greek associations with light and

knowledge to Pythagorean mathematical perfection, and from the five wounds of Christ to European Satanism and witchcraft.

69. Abramović/Stiles.

70. Milovan Djilas, *Tito: The Story from Inside*, trans. by Vasilije Kojic and Richard Hayes (New York and London: Harcourt Brace Jovanovich, 1980), 119.

71. Marina Abramović: *Balkan Epic*, 45.

72. These included *Rhythm 5*, *Rhythm 2*, *Rhythm 0*, and *Thomas Lips*. See "Marina Abramović," *Vision* 2 (January 1976): 27–30.

73. Laura J. Hoptman, *Beyond Belief: Contemporary Art from East Central Europe* (Chicago: Museum of Contemporary Art, 1995); and Nena Dimitrijević's text in the exhibition catalogue *In Another Moment* (Belgrade: Gallery SKC, 1971).

74. On Yugoslavian avant-gardes, see Endre Bojitar, "The Avant-Garde in Central and Eastern European Literature," *Art Journal* 49, no. 1 (Spring 1990): 56–62; Steven A. Mansbach, *Modern Art in Eastern Europe: From the Baltic to the Balkans, ca. 1890–1939* (Cambridge and New York: Cambridge University Press, 1999); and Milanka Todić, *The Impossible: Surrealist Art, Homage to Marko Ristić*, http://www.serbiansurrealism.com/. For the histories of the New Tendencies movement, see Jack Burnham, *Beyond Modern Sculpture: The Effects of Science and Technology on the Sculpture of This Century* (New York: George Brazilliers,1968); Jonathan Benthall, *Science and Technology in Art Today* (New York: Praeger, 1972); Valerie L. Hillings, "Concrete Territory: Geometric Art, Group Formation, and Self-Definition," in *Beyond Geometry: Experiments in Form, 1940s–70s* (Los Angeles and Cambridge: Los Angeles Country Museum of Art and MIT Press, 2004), 49–75; Katherine Carl, "The Relay of Art and Democracy in 1960s and 1970s Yugoslavia," *Centropia* 8, no. 1 (January 2008): 49–61.

75. Abramović remembered: "Dunja was not just anyone. She was an art historian, extremely bright, and rich. She was a Croatian and her father was the minister of culture of Croatia. . . . So it was incredibly important because whatever she was doing there, she had the background and the protection of the party. We [the SKC] became the island of the freedom of experiment in art in the middle of the old things. It was really like a miracle." Dunja Blazević also traveled extensively and showed Abramović the important *Documenta V* exhibition catalogue in 1972, the first major international exhibition of body art, video, and installation. Abramović/Stiles.

76. Ibid.

77. Ibid.

78. Marina Abramović: *Artist Body*, 302.

79. Marina Abramović, e-mail to the author, March 3, 2008.

80. Stanley Milgram, "The Perils of Obedience," *Harper's Magazine* (December 1973): 62–77.

81. Marina Abramović/Ulay, *Relation Work and Detour*, 152.

82. Doris Krystof, "City of Angels: Marina Abramović/Ulay," in *40 Yearsvideoart.De—Part I. Digital Heritage: Video Art in Germany from 1963 to the Present* (Ostfildern: Hatje Cantz Verlag, 2006), 196–97.

83. Marina Abramović: *Artist Body*, 299.

84. Tina Ballantine, "To and Fro in Shadow: Not I," in *The Modern Word*'s special issue on "Beckett: Apmonia,": accessed at http://www.themodernword.com/beckett/paper_ballantine.html.

85. Abramović, in Coulibeuf.

86. Abramović, quoted in Johan Pijnappel, *Art Meets Science and Spirituality in a Changing Economy* (Amsterdam: SDL, 1990), 301; quoted in Pejić, "Im-Körper-Sein," 29.

87. Ibid., 98; *Marina Abramović: Artist Body*, 370. Flagellation has been traced from the cults of Isis in Egypt and Dionysus in Greece to many religious movements, but was condemned by the Catholic Church as a means of piety and self-discipline.

88. Abramović quoted in Pijnappel, quoted in Pejić, "Im-Körper-Sein," 29. While Pejić argues that the European tradition is "anti-corporeal" and based in "cartesian cogito" (p. 29), a long history of bodily-centered philosophies belong to European intellectual traditions.

89. Pejić, "Im-Körper-Sein," 30.

90. Marina Abramović: *Artist Body*, 56.

91. Marina Abramović and Velimir Abramović, "Time-Space-Energy," 401–2.

92. The literature on trauma and self-harming has burgeoned since the late 1980s. A few salient works include Barent W. Walsh and Paul M. Rosen, *Self-Mutilation: Theory, Research, and Treatment* (New York: Guilford, 1988); Judith Lewis Herman, *Trauma and Recovery: The Aftermath of Violence—From Domestic Abuse to Political Terror* (New York: Basic Books, 1992); J. P. Wilson and Beverley Raphael, eds., *International Handbook of Traumatic Stress Syndromes* (New York: Plenum Press, 1993); Sarah Hodgson, "Cutting Through the Silence: A Sociological Construction of Self-Injury," *Sociological Inquiry* 74, no. 2 (1994): 162–79; Jennifer Egan, "The Thin Red Line," *New York Times Magazine* (July 27, 1997): 20–25; and Steven Levenkron, *Cutting: Understanding and Overcoming Self-Mutilation* (New York: W. W. Norton, 1998).

93. For the body in pain bereft of language, see Elaine Scarry, *The Body in Pain: The Making and Unmaking of the World* (New York: Oxford University Press, 1985).

94. Abramović/Stiles.

95. Marina Abramović, interviewed by Chris Thompson and Katarina Weslien, "PURE RAW: Performance, Pedagogy, and (Re) Presentation," *Performance Art Journal* 82 (2006): 43.

96. *Marina Abramović: Student Body* (Milan: Charta, 2003), 49.

97. Marina Abramović, interviewed by Chris Thompson and Katarina Weslien, "PURE RAW," 35.

98. Kristine Stiles, "Never Enough Is Something Else: Feminist Performance Art, Probity, and the Avant-Garde," in James M. Harding, ed., *Contours of the Theatrical Avant-Garde: Performance and Textuality* (Madison: University of Wisconsin-Madison, 2000), 239–89.

99. James Westcott identifies intimate details of the performance that other writers neglected, such as that from time to time Abramović sang Slavic songs, that she once crawled under her bed to avoid viewers' gazes, and that she often cried. See Westcott, "Marina Abramović's *The House with the Ocean View*: The View of the House from Some Drops in the Ocean," *Drama Review* 47, no. 3 (Fall 2003): 129–36.

100. *The House with the Ocean View* was also a response to, and an artistic dialogue with, Chris Burden's *White Light/White Heat* (1975), in which Burden lived for twenty-two days on an elevated platform in the Ronald Feldman Gallery in New York; he neither saw nor spoke to anyone, never came down from the platform, drank only a glass of celery juice daily, and remained invisible throughout the duration of his action. It could also be said that the telescope in *The House with the Ocean View* recalled Marcel Duchamp's *Etant donné* (1946–66), which required viewers to peep through holes in a door in order to complete the work revealed inside.

101. Marina Abramović: *Public Body: Installations and Objects 1965–2001* (Milan: Charta, 2001), 294.

102. Ibid.

103. Kristine Stiles, '"Uncorrupted Joy: International Art Actions," in Paul Schimmel, ed., *Out of Actions: Between Performance and the Object 1949–1979* (Los Angeles: Museum of Contemporary Art, 1998), 233.

104. Maurice Merleau-Ponty, *The Visible and the Invisible* (Evanston, IL: Northwestern University Press, 1968); first published as *Le visible et l'invisible: Suivi de notes de travail* (Paris: Gallimard, 1964).

105. Amelia Jones, *Body Art: Performing the Subject* (Minneapolis: University of Minnesota Press, 1998), 140.

106. Kathy O'Dell, "Toward a Theory of Performance Art: An Investigation of Its Sites" (PhD dissertation, City University of New York, 1992), 204.

107. Attention to sound in this piece, as in others, reflects Abramović's early interest in sound, manifest in sound installations at the Student Cultural Center in Belgrade from 1970 to 1973.

108. Abramović, in conversation with Bojana Pejić, January 1, 1993; quoted in Pejic, "Im-Körper-Sein," 26.

109. Pejić describes Abramović and Ulay's performances as a "metaphysics of presence" in "Im-Körper-Sein," 25.

110. Abramović/Ulay, *Relation Work and Detour*, 188–89.

111. Pejić, "Im-Körper-Sein," 26.

112. Abramovi/Ulay, quoted in Thomas McEvilley, "Marina Abramović/Ulay," *Artforum* 22, no. 1 (September 1983): 54.

113. Abramović/Ulay, quoted in *Marina Abramović: Artist Body*, 258.

114. Each performance included "serious design objects . . . created with shamanic attention to materials, numerological relationships, and so forth." McEvilley, 54.

115. Kathy O'Dell, e-mail to the author, January 18, 2006.

116. McEvilley, 52–53.

117. Ibid., 53.

118. The ancient system of numerology ascribes symbolic meaning to numbers: three, seven, twelve, and forty, for example, are often considered sacred. The number three signifies the divine in many religions. The Kabbalah associated it with "Binah," or understanding. Astrology is made up of three signs belonging to the same element, and so on.

119. *Three Houses* (1984), a series of photographs made after three different performances as part of the larger work *Anima Mundi*, included the colors red, black and white, and showed the artists in three positions: sleeping in a spooning position, poised in the dance position of the tango, and Abramović holding Ulay in the position of Michelangelo's *Pietà*. In each piece, the artists also wore one of the three colors.

120. Marina Abramović and Ulay, in a 1978 conversation with Heidi Grundmann in *Sur la Voie* (Paris: Centre Georges Pompidou, 1990), 68; quoted in Pejić, "Im-Körper-Sein," 33.

121. Marina Abramović, interviewed by Chris Thompson and Katarina Weslien, 'PURE RAW, 46.

122. Marina Abramović, in conversation with Jörg Heiserr, "Do it Again," *Frieze* 94 (October 2005): 176–83.

123. Moulton, 87, 89.

124. Abramović, interviewed by Thompson and Weslien, 'PURE RAW, 38.

125. See Robert Blackson, "Once More . . . with Feeling: Reenactment in Contemporary Art and Culture," *Art Journal* 66, no. 1 (Spring 2007): 39; quoted in Mark Cameron Boyd, "Performance Simulacra: Reenactment as (Re)Authoring," in Mark Cameron Boyd, *Theory Now: An Ongoing Discursive Site about the Relevance of Contemporary Art*

*Theory*, accessed on May 31, 2007, at http://theorynow.blogspot.com/2007/05/performance-simulacra-reenactment-as.html.

126. Mark Cameron Boyd, "Performance Simulacra," Theorynow.blogspot.com.

127. Pil and Galia Kolletiv, "Retro/Necro: From Beyond the Grave of the Politics of Re-Enactment," *Art Papers* 31, no. 6 (November/December 2007): 45.

128. Philip Auslander, "Liveness," in Elin Diamond, ed., *Performance and Cultural Politics* (London: Routledge, 1996),198; quoted in Pil and Galia Kolletiv, 46.

129. Guy Debord, *La Société du spectacle* [1967] (Paris: Gallimard, 1992), 151; quoted in Sven Lütticken, "Planet of the Remakes," *New Left Review* 25 (January–February, 2004): 119.

130. Gilles Deleuze, *Différence et répétition* (Paris: Presses Universitaires de France, 1968): 92, 123–25, 383–84; quoted in Lütticken.

131. Friedrich Nietzsche, *The Gay Science: With a Prelude in Rhymes and an Appendix of Songs*, trans. by Walter Kaufmann(New York: Random House, 1974).

132. Lütticken, 119.

133. Abramović, interviewed by Thompson and Weslien, "PURE RAW," 46.

134. Joseph Roach, "History, Memory, Necrophilia," in Peggy Phelan and Jill Lane, eds., *The Ends of Performance* (New York: New York University Press, 1998): 29; quoted in Pil and Galia Kolletiv, 51.

135. Abramović, quoted in Moulton, 87.

136. Ibid. Abramović permitted the Belgian director and choreographer Michael Laub to direct *The Biography Remix* (2004), a version of *The Biography* that ceded Laub full control over the production, including permission to eliminate what Abramović described as the "strong Balkan element" in her work.

137. Abramović, interviewed by Thompson and Weslien, "PURE RAW", 39.

138. Letter from Marina Abramović, in Brazil, to her brother Velimir Abramović, April 1991, in *Marina Abramović: Artist Body*, 416.

139. A link exists between these works and Abramović's interest in the study of magnetic fields and electricity by the Serbian inventor, physicist, mechanical engineer, and electrical engineer Nicola Tesla (1856–1943). This is a potentially productive area of further research on Abramović.

140. Marina Abramović: *Public Body*, 88.

141. Ibid., 118.

142. Marina Abramović and Velimir Abramović, "Time-Space-Energy," 406.

## *THUNDERBIRD IMMOLATION*: WILLIAM POPE.L AND BURNING RACISM

1. This essay first appeared in Mark Bessire, ed., *William Pope L: Eracism* (Cambridge, MA, and Portland, ME: MIT Press and the Institute of Contemporary Art at Maine College of Art, 2002), 36–42.

2. Laura Lee, *The Name's Familiar: Mr. Leotard, Barbie, and Chef Boyardee* (Gretna, LA: Pelican, 1999), cited in http://www.uselessknowledge.com/ll/gallo.shtml.

3. Ellen Hawkes, *Blood and Wine: The Unauthorized Story of the Gallo Wine Empire* New York: Simon & Schuster, 1993; reported in "Ernest Gallo," PBS and WGBH/*Frontline*, 1998: http://www.pbs.org/wgbh/pages/frontline/president/players/gallo.html.

4. William Pope.L, e-mail to Mark H. C. Bessire, December 17, 2001; hereafter Pope.L/Bessire.

5. Ibid.

6. William Pope.L, fax to the author, June 23, 2000.

7. The artist has acknowledged Piper's performances for the ways in which they opened a space for a new kind of "readability and legibility in a way that no other artist was doing at that time." Pope.L/Bessire.

8. William Pope.L, e-mail to the author, January 17, 2002.

9. Kobena Mercer, "Engendered Species: Danny Tisdale and Keith Piper," *Artforum* 30, no. 10 (Summer 1992): 75.

10. Pope.L/Bessire.

11. Ibid.

12. LeRoi Jones, *Blues People: The Negro Experience in White America and the Music That Developed from It* (New York: William Morrow, 1963), 83.

13. Graham Hodges, foreword to John A, Williams, *The Man Who Cried I Am*, second edition (New York and Chicago: Thunder's Mouth Press, 1967, 1985), unpaginated.

14. William Pope.L, fax to the author, June 23, 2000.

15. Thelma Golden, "My Brother," in *Black Male: Representations of Masculinity in Contemporary American Art*, (New York: Whitney Museum of American Art, 1994), 22.

16. Manning Marable, in "Racism, Prisons and the Future of Black America," has written, "The rate of incarceration of black Americans in 1989 had even surpassed that experienced by blacks who still lived under the apartheid regime of South Africa." http://www.zmag.org/racismandblam.htm.

17. Greg Tate, "Cult-Nats Meet Freaky-Deke," in *Flyboy in the Buttermilk: Essays on Contmporary America* (New York: Simon & Shuster, 1992), 200.

18. William Pope.L, fax to the author, June 23, 2000.

19. Ibid. All of the following discussion of "Singing" comes from this fax to the author.

20. Richard Powell, *Black Art and Culture in the 20th Century* (London: Thames and Hudson, 1997), 13.

21. Ibid., 15.

### BARBARA TURNER SMITH'S HAUNTING

1. This essay first appeared in *The 21st Century Odyssey Part II: The Performances of Barbara T. Smith* (Pomona, CA: Pomona College Museum of Art, 2005), 37–50.

2. Barbara Turner Smith, telephone conversation with the author, September 4, 2004. Smith and I exchanged numerous e-mails related to questions and drafts of this essay. Rather than litter the text with footnotes, I note here that all subsequent quotations of the artist come from these e-mails.

3. Smith was interested enough in McLuhan's work to make *Scan I* (1974), a work addressed to his ideas.

4. Edward A. Shanken has written a history of the photocopy machine in art:

> Starting in 1962, the New York School of Correspondence Art, founded by Ray Johnson, used photocopiers as a tool for propagating Mail Art. . . . Bruno Munari's "Machine Art Manifesto" of 1938 anticipated his series Xerographie Originale begun in 1964. Taking a more conceptual approach, German artist Timm Ulrichs's *Die Photokopie der Photokopie der Photokopie* (1967) . . . photocop[ied] an encyclopedia entry about photocopying, then copying the copy through ninety-nine successive generations, revealing the intrinsic qualities of the process as the image degraded. Sonia Landy Sheridan started using copy machines in the late 60s and was artist-in-residence at 3M, where she used their first color copier in 1969.

Edward Shanken, e-mail to the author, October 27, 2004.

5. Jackson Pollock, Georges Mathieu, Yves Klein, Piero Manzoni, Günter Brus, Otto Mühl, Rudolf Schwarzkogler, Robert Morris, and Carolee Schneemann created actions for the camera in the 1950s and early 1960s. Marcel Duchamp's "Rrose Selavy" was also a persona created for the photograph in 1921.

6. Judy Chicago would install her notorious *Dinner Party*, featuring dinner plates with explicit vaginal imagery, only thirteen years later, in 1979. Carolee Schneemann's *Eye Body* (1963) was not created for the purpose of displaying vaginal imagery (although her clitoris is visible in one photograph). In 1965, Schneemann began to make her erotic film *Fuses*, which contains explicit genital imagery and depicts Schneemann and her husband, composer James Tenney, making love. Schneemann did not finish *Fuses* until 1967.

7. Smith is "embarrassed" by some of these Xerox book images and wants to remind readers that "the Sixties" were a very different period in American and world history. In this regard, that cultural period was one of much greater tolerance and exploration than is the current conservative era.

8. One had a red triangular shape about the size of a hand span right on the edge of the right vertical side. Another had a very thin (maybe one and-a-half inches at the base) triangle that rose to a point in light yellow Codit paint (maybe two and-a-half to three feet high in the center of the field). . . . Another had a thin yellow line that matched the shape of the painting itself about four inches in from all sides.

9. Jacques Lacan's "Of the Gaze as Object Petit a," in Jacques-Alain Miller, ed., *Four Fundamental Concepts of Psycho-analysis*, trans. by Alan Sheridan (New York: W. W. Norton, 1977), 72.

10. Speaking about her relationship to her father's profession, Smith remembered: "It was really scary. We didn't understand what he did as a funeral director. He was a compassionate, fun person who wanted to help people who experienced loss. People would be grieving and I felt that I was able to help them also. Part of my psyche is a very haunted place that is about some of that [grieving and death]."

11. Judith Lewis Herman, *Father-Daughter Incest* (Cambridge, MA, and London: Harvard University Press, 1981), 109.

12. M. H. Erdelyi, "Dissociation, Defense, and the Unconscious," in D. Spiegel, ed., *Dissociation: Culture, Mind, and Body* (Washington and London: American Psychiatric Press, 1994), 3. See also J. P. Wilson and B. Raphael, eds., *The International Handbook of Traumatic Stress Syndromes* (New York and London: Plenum Press, 1993).

13. Jacques Derrida's theory of deconstructive writing as "haunted" resembles such traumatic structures of mind by drawing attention to the fact that a writer's intellectual inheritances, which comprise and inform the very project of writing, are often absent from the text and from the memory of the writer. See Derrida's *Specters of Marx: The State of the Debt, the Work of Mourning, and the New International* (New York and London: Routledge, 1994).

14. Ulrich Baer, *Spectral Evidence: The Photography of Trauma* (Cambridge and London: MIT Press, 2002), 8.

15. Herman, *Father-Daughter Incest*, 110.

16. I am thinking of such performances as *Ritual Meal* (1969), *Mass Meal* (1969), *Celebration of the Holy Squash* (1971), *The Longest Day of Night* (1973), *Liebestod* (with Cheri Gaulke; 1977), *Light Wait* (1980), *Council* (1984), *The Cauldron* (1986), and *Pageant of the Holy Squash* (1988).

17. During this period, Smith performed *Pure Food* (1973), a private piece in which she "received food from the air, nature, and cosmos."

18. *Feed Me* is the most frequently discussed work in Smith's oeuvre, and often the

only work mentioned by critics and art historians. See, for example, Amelia Jones, "Survey," in Tracey Warr, ed., *The Artist's Body* (London: Phaidon, 2000), 29.

19. Ernest Becker, *The Birth and Death of Meaning: An Interdisciplinary Perspective on the Problem of Man*, Second Edition (New York: Free Press, 1971).

20. Ruth Leys, *Trauma: A Genealogy* (Chicago: University of Chicago Press, 2000), 289–99.

21. Trauma requires a witness, someone who listens and empathizes, in order for healing to take place. Performance as a medium provides that witness. For the role of witness in the healing of trauma, see Dori Laub, "Bearing Witness, or the Vicissitudes of Listening" and "An Event without a Witness: Truth, Testimony and Survival," in Shoshana Felman and Dori Laub, *Testimony: Crises of Witnessing in Literature, Psychoanalysis and History* (New York: Routledge, 1991), 57–74, 75–92.

22. Barbara Turner Smith, *Barbara Turner Smith* (Santa Monica: New Gallery of the 18th Street Arts Complex, 1994), 2.

23. Marina Abramovic/Ulay, Ron Athey, Jerzy Bereś, Joseph Beuys, Günter Brus, John Duncan, Sherman Fleming, Terry Fox, Ion Grigorescu, Tibor Hajas, FX Harsoni, Lynn Hershman, Tehching Hsieh, Zhang Huan, Istvan Kantor, Mike Kelley, Milan Knížák, Elke Krystufek, Oleg Kulik, Laibach, James Luna, Paul McCarthy, Linda Montano, Otto Mühl, Yoko Ono, ORLAN, Raphael Montañez Ortiz, Dan and Lia Perjovschi, William Pope L., Petr Stembera, Raša Todosjević, Wolf Vostell, and the list goes on. Chris Burden, whose many troubling experiences as a child may also contribute to his durational work, presents a special case. See Kristine Stiles, *Chris Burden's Free Physics* (New York: Zwirner and Wirth Gallery, 2004).

24. See Kristine Stiles, "Thoughts on Destruction Art," *Impakt 1997* (Utrecht: Impakt Festival, 1997), 2–5.

25. The Christian Eucharist evolved from the Chaburah, in which a group of male friends met for conversation and a formal supper, often held on the eve of holy days. Blessings were given, and on important occasions a cup of wine, "the cup of blessing," was passed to each guest. The Last Supper is the best-known example of the Chaburah in the New Testament.

26. Thomas McEvilley, "Art in the Dark," *Artforum* 21, no. 10 (Summer 1983): 62–71, reprinted in Tracey Warr, ed., *The Artist's Body* (London: Phaidon, 2000), 225.

27. There are "complex relationships among hypnosis, dissociation, absorption, fantasy-proneness, somatization, and paranormal experiences" in both artists and traumatized people. See D. S. Weiss, "Structured Clinical Interview Techniques," *International Handbook of Traumatic Stress Syndromes* (New York: Springer, 1993), 183.

28. In conversation with the author, Smith has noted that as a child, she was "more afraid of my mother" than of her father. Such a response is consistent with the etiology of incest and incestuous environments, where children frequently blame the nonabusing parent unconsciously for not protecting them from the abusing parent.

29. See, for example, Susan Roth and Ronald Batson, *Naming the Shadows: A New Approach to Individual and Group Psychotherapy for Adult Survivors of Childhood Incest* (New York and London: Free Press, 1997), 156–57.

30. See Judith Butler, *Bodies that Matter: On the Discursive Limits of "Sex"* (New York: Routledge, 1993); and Amelia Jones, *Body Art: Performing the Subject* (Minneapolis and London: University of Minnesota Press, 1998). Michael Hardt and Antonio Negri, in their otherwise sober reading of late capitalism and the future of Marxism, suggest that playing with identity and sexuality may operate as a form of "resistance" to empire. See Hardt and Negri, *Empire* (Cambridge and London: Harvard University Press, 2000). Butler has admitted the limits of performativity as a means to destabilize political conditions in Judith

Butler, Ernesto Laclau, and Slavoj Žižek, *Contingency, Hegemony, Universality: Contemporary Dialogues on the Left* (London: Verso, 2000); and Judith Butler, John Guillory, and Kendall Thomas, eds., *What's Left of Theory? New Work on the Politics of Literary Theory* (New York: Routledge, 2000).

31. Jodey Castricano, for example, has theorized Derrida-like phantoms as a model of subjectivity, suggesting that "to be" may mean to be troubled by a specter at the very core of being itself. Similarly, but in a different context, Ruth Leys has identified a "*post-originary* [her emphasis] model of subjectivity wherein the ego splits in the very process of subject formation." Castricano and Leys believe that subjectivity itself is split. See Jodey Castricano, *Cryptomimesis: The Gothic and Jacques Derrida's Ghost Writing* (Montreal and Kingston: McGill-Queen's University Press, 2003), and Leys, *Trauma*.

32. This is not to say that directed role-playing under supervised therapeutic conditions is not helpful to recovery; it is, as many such programs have shown.

33. The Electronic Café International (cofounded by artists Sherrie Rabinowitz and Kit Galloway in Santa Monica, California), which supplied simultaneous three-way interactive hookups for Smith on her travels.

34. Biosphere 2 is "located in the foothills of Arizona's Santa Catalina Mountains about thirty miles north of Tucson. . . . Built in the late 1980s with $150 million in funding from Texas oil magnate Edward Bass, Biosphere 2 was designed as an airtight replica of Earth's environment (Biosphere 1). This 7,200,000-cubic-foot sealed glass and space-frame structure contains 5 biomes, including a 900,000-gallon ocean, a rain forest, a desert, agricultural areas and a human habitat." Accessed at www.desertusa.com/mag99/apr/stories/bios2.html.

35. Circe orchestrated this event after Odysseus and his crew arrived on her island of Aeaea, where she turned the crew into wolves, swine, asses, and lions. Threatened with death, Circe restored the crew and helped Odysseus find the way to Hades, where he was instructed by Tiresias about his return to home (Ithaca) and his future fate.

36. Tragically, Walford's service in Biosphere 2 compromised his health, and he emerged continually struggling: "He had carpel tunnel syndrome; he had to have root canals; he had back problems and . . . back surgery . . . then he was diagnosed with Parkinson's disease, but it was Lou Gehrig's disease," Smith reported. Walford died in April 2004. Smith's longing for Walford, however, was predetermined to fail, as the pair ceased being lovers when Walford entered Biosphere 2 and Smith embarked on her odyssey.

37. See Franz Alexander, "The Principle of Corrective Emotional Experience," in Franz Alexander et al., *Psychoanalytic Therapy: Principles and Application* (New York: Ronald Press, 1946), 66–70.

38. Max Horkheimer and Theodor Adorno, *Dialectic of Enlightenment*, trans. by John Cumming (New York: Continuum, 1987), 14.

39. Ibid., 43.

40. Ibid., 78.

41. Ibid., 50–51, 78.

42. On November 21, 2004, Smith wrote to the author: "There are three things I have recalled which will just confirm all you have written [in this essay]: a) I was freaked out when in the 80's or so I looked back on my work and it appeared I had annihilated myself. The work was a sort of self-annihilation. I could not understand it nor why it had this effect on me; b) I have in some piece, I can't recall which, remarked "I am haunted!"; c) I have announced lately as I talk to friends and work on pieces, "I am a professional mourner."

43. Jacques Derrida, *The Gift of Death* (Chicago: University of Chicago Press, 1996), 44.

44. Ibid., 43–44.

### THE AESTHETICS OF THE MISFIT: THE CASE OF HENRY FLYNT AND DAVID TUDOR

1. I gave the first version of this essay, entitled "Creep and Brend: Henry Flynt's Utopian Proposals for Subjective Authenticity," at the Annual College Art Association meeting in New York in 1990; I presented a second version, entitled "David Tudor: Alive, Free, and Without Need of Culture," at the symposium "The Art of David Tudor: Indeterminacy and Performance in Postwar Culture," held at the Getty Research Institute, May 17–19, 2001. A version of this text entitled "David Tudor: Alive, Free, and Without Need of Culture," was first published in the special issue "Composers inside Electronics: Music after David Tudor," in *Leonardo Music Journal* 14 (2004): 62–63. Accessed at www.getty.edu/research/conducting_research/digitized_collections/davidtudor/symposium.html.

2. Teddy Hultberg, "I Smile When the Sound Is Singing through the Space," an Interview with David Tudor by Teddy Hultberg, Düsseldorf (May 17, 18, 1988), 5. Accessed at www.emf.org/tudor/Articles/hultberg.html.

3. Larry Austin, "David Tudor and Larry Austin: A Conversation," Denton, Texas (April 3, 1989), 2. Accessed at www.emf.org/tudor/Articles/austin.html.

4. Hultberg.

5. Austin.

6. Alison Knowles, e-mail to the author, February 4, 2001.

7. Schneemann in a telephone conversation with the author March 29, 2001; hereafter Schneemann/Stiles.

8. John Cage, *Silence: Lectures and Writings by John Cage* (Middletown, CT: Wesleyan University Press, 1961), 108.

9. Ibid., 265.

10. Ibid., 269.

11. Hultberg, 6.

12. Ibid.

13. Flynt rejects the idea that he belonged to Fluxus and what he deems its "aesthetic of crappiness." Henry Flynt, interview with the author, September 22, 1989; hereafter Flynt/Stiles.

14. For a broader discussion of the role that Flynt's politics played in Fluxus until mid-1963, see Kristine Stiles, "Between Water and Stone: Fluxus Performance, a Metaphysics of Acts," in Elizabeth Armstrong and Joan Rothfuss, eds., *In The Spirit of Fluxus* (Minneapolis: Walker Art Center, 1993), 62–99.

15. Henry Flynt, "The Important Significance of the Creep Personality," unpublished audio recording of Flynt's May 15, 1962 lecture at Harvard University. The original lecture appears with a shortened title, "Creep," in Henry Flynt, *Blueprint for a Higher Civilization* (Milano: Multhipla Edizioni, 1975).

16. Flynt/Stiles.

17. Flynt's critique of "serious culture" recalls Matthew Arnold's argument against high culture in *Culture and Anarchy*, in which he accused popular instruction in countries like the United States of bringing about intellectual mediocrity and vulgarity of manners. See Matthew Arnold, *Culture and Anarchy* (New York: Macmillan, 1924; reprinted from the original 1869 publication).

18. While Flynt's 1962 Harvard lecture represented "a plea to extend tolerance to the creep," by the 1980s a culture lacking in heroes extended more than tolerance to its misfits and celebrated their extravagances. Flynt anticipated the transformation of the "creep" and "geek" into what has become the popular cultural hero of the "nerd." Alfred E. Neuman of *Mad* magazine was the prototypical creep of the 1950s, as was Andy

Warhol, who successfully exploited that identity. With the advent of the computer age, the creep became a nerd or a dork, celebrated in the film *Revenge of the Nerds* (1984) and its sequels, followed by *Back to the Future* (1985), in which a mad scientist lives alone in a garage tinkering with future technologies, and the father of the adolescent hero in the film (Michael J. Fox) is a skinny, awkward, ill-kept, cowardly, shy, and sexually naïve man. Three otherwise androgynous nerdlike figures—Paul Reubens (aka Pee Wee Herman), Michael Jackson, and Woody Allen—all came to public attention in the 1990s, ironically for their sexual transgressions: Reubens was arrested for masturbating at a XXX porn theater; Jackson was accused of child abuse; and Allen had sexual relations with Soon-Yi Previn, the teenage daughter whom his common-law wife, actress Mia Farrow, had adopted with her former husband, André Previn, and whomAllen eventually married. Talking Heads lead singer David Byrne eroticized the "dork." The "geek—or nerd, dork, spaz, freak, misfit, outcast, outsider" has continued to be an "inspiring American hero," according to Craig D. Lindsey, "Glorifying the Geek," *News & Observer* (August 2, 2004): 1C. Even young male movie and television stars became the erotic carriers of semi-nerd identities: Edward Norton, Tobey Maguire, Ryan Gosling, Steve Carell, and many others. In high-tech circles of the 2000s, Steve Jobs and Bill Gates also come to mind.

19. Flynt formulated the creep hypothesis during a period in which he successfully obtained a psychiatrist's letter declaring him unfit for military service. His resistance to the military is linked to his analysis of the extension of childhood in "creep, a cognitive culture." Flynt/Stiles.

20. See also Henry Flynt, "Down with Art," in *Blueprint*, 64–66. In "Instructions for the Flyntian Modality" (also in *Blueprint*), Flynt urged: "STOP ALL 'GROSS BELIEVING.' His rejection of codified social modes of knowing and behaving would enable one to "walk through walls (if you can find them)" (p. 25). Although Flynt's extreme leftist politics have no affinity with the extreme right, his antagonism to "serious culture" recalls the German playwright and Nazi poet laureate Hanns Johst's famous line—"Wenn ich Kultur höre . . . entsichere ich meinen Browning!" (Whenever I hear of culture . . . I release the safety catch of my Browning!)—from act 1, scene 1 of his play *Schlageter*, performed on Hitler's forty-fourth birthday, April 20, 1933. Hermann Göring, misquoting the line, became responsible for the famous slogan, "When I hear the word 'culture,' I reach for my revolver." Such a comment epitomizes what was long considered the uncultured reaction to the authority of culture.

21. Much work still needs to be done on Robert Morris's writings of the late 1960s. For letters to Flynt from composers, poets, and artists, see *Blueprint*, 67–71.

22. Flynt/Stiles.

23. George Maciunas, letter to Wolf Vostell, November 3, 1964, in Adriani Götz, Winfried Konnertz, and Karin Thomas, eds., *Joseph Beuys: Life and Works* (Woodbury, NY: Barron's, 1979), 85.

24. Many key artists associated with Fluxus, not the least of whom included Dick Higgins, Alison Knowles, and George Brecht, strongly disagreed with Flynt and Maciunas's principles; Maciunas eventually distanced himself from Flynt's ideas in order to appease these artists, especially Brecht.

25. Tamara Levitz, "David Tudor's Corporeal Imagination," paper delivered May 18, 2001, at the Getty Research Institute symposium "The Art of David Tudor: Indeterminacy and Performance in Postwar Culture."

26. Wolff described it to Flynt, and Flynt related this to me in a letter of January 31, 2001.

27. Many artists associated with Fluxus might be categorized as misfits, rejecting cultural and sexual norms. On George Maciunas's sexual orientation and practices, see

Susan L. Jarosi, "Selections from an Interview with Billie Maciunas," in *The Fluxus Reader*, ed. by Ken Friedman (Academy Editions, 1998), 199–211; and Kristine Stiles, "Foreword; or, Unbuckling the Belt of Fluxus through Billie Maciunas' Experiences," in Billie Maciunas, *The Eve of Fluxus* (Winter Park, FL: Arbiter Press, 2010), ix–xvi.

28. See Henry Flynt, "Brend," in *"From 'Culture' to Brend,"* in *AGAINST "PARTICIPATION": A Total Critique of Culture* (1994). Accessed at http://www.henryflynt.org/aesthetics/brend.html Flynt has written several different versions of this passage. The original version that appeared in *Blueprint for a Higher Civilization*, pp. 64–65, reads: "Consider all of your doings, what you already do. Exclude the gratifying of physiological needs, physically harmful activities, and competitive activities. Concentrate on spontaneous self-amusement or play. That is, concentrate on everything you do just because you like it, because you just like it as you do it. Actually, these doings should be referred to as your just-likings. . . . These just-likings are your 'brend.'"

29. Robert Filliou and Daniel Spoerri organized the *Festival of Misfits* in London at Victor Musgrave's Gallery One (October 23–November 8, 1962). The handbill to the exhibition described the participants as follows: Addi Koepcke, "German professional revolutionist"; Benjamin Patterson, "captured alive Negro"; Emmett Williams, "Pole with the elephant memory"; Daniel Spoerri, "Romanian adventurer"; Ben Vautier, "God's broker"; Robert Filliou, "one-eyed good-for-nothing Huguenot"; Per Olof Ultvedt, "red-faced strongman from Sweden"; Gustav Metzger, "escaped Jew"; and Robin Page, "Yukon lumberjack." Neither Flynt nor Tudor participated, but they would have been in comfortable company with this body of artists.

## NOTES ON RUDOLF SCHWARZKOGLER'S IMAGES OF HEALING, A BIOGRAPHICAL SKETCH

1. A different version of this essay first appeared in a special issue I edited entitled "Art & Healing," *WhiteWalls* 25 (Spring 1990): 13–26. It was reprinted in Scott Watson and Kristine Stiles, *Rudolf Schwarzkogler* (Vancouver: University of British Columbia Fine Arts Gallery, 1993), 29–39.

2. Dieter Schwarz and Veit Loers, eds., *Von der Aktionsmalerei zum Aktionismus Wien 1960–65: Günter Brus, Adolf Frohner, Otto Mühl, Hermann Nitsch, Alfons Schilling, Rudolf Schwarzkogler*, Vol. 1 (Klagenfurt, Austria: Ritter Verlag, 1988), 304.

3. Edith Adam, unpublished correspondence with the author dating from July 1978 until 1990.

4. Ibid., 340.

5. Hubert Klocker, ed., *Wiener Aktionismus 1960–1971: The Shattered Mirror, Günter Brus, Otto Mühl, Hermann Nitsch, Rudolf Schwarzkogler*, Vol. 2 (Klagenfurt, Austria: Ritter Verlag, 1989), 380–81.

6. Schwarz and Loers, *Von der Aktionsmalerei zum Aktionismus Wien 1960–65*, 293.

7. Hermann Nitsch, *Das Orgien Mysterien Theater: Die Partituren Aller Aufgenführten Aktionen 1960–1979*, Vol. I (Naples: Studio Morra, 1979), 92.

8. Ibid. Schwarzkogler served as a passive actor in the following actions by Nitsch: #8, January 22, 1965; #9, June 12, 1965; #10, June 24, 1965; #11, June 30, 1965.

9. Klocker, *Wiener Aktionismus*, 379.

10. See Kristine Stiles's papers, 1900–2012, Special Collections in the David M. Rubenstein Rare Books and Manuscript Library, Duke University.

11. Klocker, *Wiener Aktionismus*, 380–81.

12. Nitsch employed Cibulka as the principal model in his 12 Action (September 6, 1965).

13. See Malcolm Green in *Viennese Actionism: Günter Brus, Otto Muehl, Hermann Nitsch, Rudolf Schwarzkogler* (Seville: Junta de Andalucía, Consejería de Cultura 2008), 437.

14. Hermann Nitsch, "Rudolf Schwarzkogler," in Valie Export and Peter Weibel, eds., *Wien. Bildkompendium Wiener Aktionismus und Film* (Frankfurt: Kohlkunstverlag 1970), 281–82.

15. See Robert Hughes, "The Decline and Fall of the Avant-Garde," *Time* (December 18, 1972): 111. In 1990 I published two articles: "Notes on Rudolf Schwarzkogler's Images of Healing," *WhiteWalls* 25 (Spring 1990): 13–26; and "Readings: Performance and Its Objects," *Arts* 65, no. 3 (November 1990): 35–47. These essays refuted the Schwarzkogler myth on the basis of my intensive archival research in Schwarzkogler's own library and extensive interviews, conducted over a period of twelve years, with Schwarzkogler's common-law wife Edith Adam, all the artists associated with Viennese action art, and Austrian art historians and art dealers like Hubert Klocker and Ursula Krinzinger. In 1996, Hughes responded to the debunking of his story in a short commentary, "The Talk of the Town: Schwarzkogler's Ear," *New Yorker* (November 11, 1996): 36. Hughes wrote: "This is one of these pieces of art-world folklore and it was in circulation before I got to it. . . . I was wrong [and I] will . . . sprinkle ashes upon my head while kneeling on a piece of sackcloth and apologize to the offended shade of Rudy Schwarzkogler." No one called Schwarzkogler "Rudy."

16. Schwarzkogler is never the figure in his performances or in the photographs taken of them, except in *Hochzeit*, photographed by Michael Epp, and in his last *6. Aktion* (1966).

17. Umberto Eco, "Semiotics of Theatrical Performance," *Drama Review* 21, no. 1 (March 1977): 115.

18. Edith Adam, in conversation with the author, April 1978.

19. Jacques Lacan, "The Signification of the Phallus," in *Ecrits* (New York and London: W. W. Norton, 1977), 281.

20. Dr. Franz Xavier Mayr, *Die Darmtragheit: Stuhlverstopfung* (Vienna: Verlag Neues Leben, 1912, 1953), 273.

21. Wiener Actionismus, 380.

22. In a letter to the author, July 7, 1978, Edith Adam provided a full list of the books that Schwarzkogler read. Among them are Dr. Detlef Schultz, *Heilkraft des Gesanges* (The Healing Power of Song, 1953); Dr. Franz X. Mayr, *Darmtragheit und Stuhlverstopfung* (Intestinal Sluggishness and Constipation, 1953) and *Schonheit und Verdauung* (Beauty and Digestion, 1954); Charles Waldmar, *Magie des Sexus* (Sexual Magic, 1958); Dr. Alfred Hasterlik, *Von Reiz u. Rauschmittein* (From Stimulus to Intoxication, 1918); and Dr. Karl Schmeidecker, *Untrugliche Zeichen der Gesundheit* (Infallible Signs of Health, 1955). Schwarzkogloer also read Joyce, Nietzsche, Heidegger, Trakl, Kafka, Celine, Wittgenstein, Shakespeare, Levi-Strauss, Foucault, and others.

23. Heinrich Däath, *Medizinische Astrologie* (London: L. N. Fowler, 1914); reprinted in German in Berlin by Becker, 1926.

24. Ibid., 9.

25. Ibid., 30.

26. Herbert Klocker, "The Dramaturgy of the Organic," in Klocker, *Wiener Aktionismus*, 49.

27. Mabel Lang, *Cure and Cult in Ancient Corinth: A Guide to the Asklepio* (Princeton, NJ: American School of Classical Studies at Athens, 1977), 175.

28. Ibid., 15.

29. Ibid., 23.

30. Ibid.

31. Ibid., 28.
32. Klocker, *Wiener Aktionismus*, 378.
33. Robert Graves, *The Greek Myths* (Garden City, NY: Doubleday, 1981), 176.
34. Ibid.
35. Mircia Eliade, *Myth and Reality* (New York: Harper Colophon, 1963), 45.
36. Ibid., 51–52.
37. Jacques Derrida, "The Theater of Cruelty and the Closure of Representation," in *Writing and Difference* (Chicago: University of Chicago Press, 1978), 232.
38. Ibid., 234.
39. Ibid.
40. Ibid., 242.

### RAUSCHENBERG'S "GAP"

1. A longer version of this essay, entitled "Rauschenberg, Looking Long and Thinking Hard," first appeared as the introduction to the catalog for the exhibition *Rauschenberg: Collecting & Connecting*, which I curated at the Nasher Museum of Art at Duke University. The Robert Rauschenberg Foundation in New York published the online catalog in 2014: http://shuffle.rauschenbergfoundation.org/exhibitions/nasher/essays/Stiles_introduction/.

I am grateful to Kathy O'Dell, Stephen R. Dolan, Julie Tetel Andresen, Bruce B. Lawrence, and Simon Deakin for conversations on topics related to this essay.

2. Robert Rauschenberg, "Statement," in Dorothy C. Miller, ed., *Sixteen Americans* (New York: Museum of Modern Art, 1959), 58. Diamondstein mistakenly introduced Rauschenberg's text as a "casual comment" made to Alan Soloman, curator of his first retrospective at the Jewish Museum in 1963.

3. In his famous discussion of Rauschenberg's horizontal (or "flatbed") approach to painting, Leo Steinberg has already identified his art with "post-Modernist painting [that] has made the course of art once again non-linear and unpredictable. . . . a shakeup which contaminates all purified categories. . . . deepening inroads of art into non-art." See Leo Steinberg, *Other Criteria: Confrontations with Twentieth-Century Art* (Oxford, UK: Oxford University Press, 1972), 91.

4. Nicolas Bourriaud, *Traffic* (Bordeau, France: CAPC musée d'art contemporain de Bordeau, 1996), followed by Bourriaud, *Esthétique relationnelle* (Dijon, France: Les presses du réel, 1998), published in English in 2002 as *Relational Aesthetics*.

5. Robert Rauschenberg in Barbaralee Diamonstein, ed. *Inside New York's Art World: Robert Rauschenberg and Leo Castelli*. Video by Dick Cook; edited by Brian Connell in cooperation with the New School for Social Research, New York, 1977.

6. Parts of this interview are quoted in Kristine Stiles, "Material Culture and Everyday Live," in Kristine Stiles and Peter Selz, eds., *Theories and Documents of Contemporary Art: A Sourcebook of Artists' Writings*. 2nd Edition (Berkeley: University of California Press, 2012), 374–75.

7. Integrity is an issue that emerges in Rauschenberg's reflections on the *Rauschenberg Overseas Cultural Interchange (ROCI)*: "I think our failures in making ROCI run smoothly gave it a lot more honor and integrity. With the exception of contributions from personal friends, we never took a dime from anyone. That protected one side of us from criticism. . . . The whole world is very suspicious, still, even after ROCI. Somehow ROCI maintained its integrity by my being able to say, 'I did, through my work or selling my collection of my favorite things.' Continuing ROCI was definitely worth it and this was a decision I had to re-make every time I parted with something that I loved so much" (156–57). In order to

finance ROCI, Rauschenberg "sold [his] big 1951 black and white Cy Twombly that he had done in my studio on Fulton Street. And [he] sold the first cartoon, *Alley Oop*, the first non-monocolored Jasper Johns. That had a kind of family history because he lived above me and came down one Sunday morning and said, 'I can't paint in more than one color at a time.' And that's serious; that's a serious problem" (156–57). Rauschenberg, "A Conversation about Art and ROCI: Robert Rauschenberg and Donald Saff," in ROCI: *Rauschenberg Overseas Culture Interchange* (Washington: National Gallery of Art, 1991), 156.

8. In 1948, Rauschenberg met Weil in Paris at the Académie Julian, where they studied art together; he married her in 1950. The following year their son Christopher was born. They divorced in 1952, remaining friends for the rest of their lives.

9. Rauschenberg met Pearman in California, and she encouraged him to study at the Kansas City Art Institute, where in 1947 he discovered his vocation as an artist.

10. The photographs accompanied Robert Goodnough's article, "Pollock Paints a Picture," which inspired Harold Rosenberg's "The American Action Painters," *Art News* 51, no. 8 (December 1952): 22–23, 48–50.

11. Denys Riout, *Yves Klein L'Aventure monochrome* (Paris: Découvertes Gallimard Arts, 2006), 67. The first public performance of what Klein called *Anthropométrie de l'Époque bleue* took place in concert with his "Monotone Symphony," March 9, 1960, at the Galerie internationale d'art contemporain in Paris.

12. On action painting, see Harold Rosenberg, "The American Action Painters," *Art News* 51, no. 8 (December 1952).

13. Rauschenberg would engage in performances associated with theater, especially throughout the 1960s, and he explained: "I don't call my theatre pieces Happenings. Because of my involvement in theatre through dance, I think I'd refer to them as dance theatre or maybe just theatre or anything else, because my understanding of Happenings is that they came out of a desire painters had who were working with objects, or objects were their content, their subject, a desire to animate those materials. I think mine comes out of really quite a traditional response to dance." Rauschenberg quoted in Dorothy Seckler, "Oral History Interview with Robert Rauschenberg," December 21, 1965, Archives of American Art, Smithsonian Institute (1965), pp. 35–36. See also Nancy Spector, "Rauschenberg and Performance, 1963–67: A 'Poetry of Infinite Possibilities,'" in Walter Hopps and Susan Davidson, *Robert Rauschenberg* (New York: Solomon R. Guggenheim Museum, 1997), 227, note 82. Spector appropriately identifies "the performative sensibility of Rauschenberg's art" and his "theatrical sensibility," as products of his intense interest in "temporality, collaboration, and the elemental presence of a viewer."

14. Martin Duberman, *Black Mountain: An Exploration in Community* (New York: Anchor Books, 1973), 379.

15. Ibid.

16. Ibid.

17. Brandon W. Joseph reads Rauschenberg interest in "multiplicity" through Michael Hardt and Antonio Negri's *Empire* (2000) in order to argue for how Rauschenberg "critique[d] the transcendent and dialectical structure of modern sovereign or disciplinary power," and for how he "open[ed] . . . the appropriated, commercial realm to subrepresentational forces of multiplicity and temporal difference." My interest in the "gap" is directed to the phenomenology of Rauschenberg's approach rather than its political or economic effect. See Brandon W. Joseph, *Random Order: Robert Rauschenberg and the Neo-Avant Garde* (Cambridge, MA: MIT Press, 2003), 17–18.

18. See Joseph's excellent discussion of the antecedent role of Antonin Artaud in Cage's work as "representation's larger expropriation of life" in *Random Order*, 255–58.

19. Robert Rauschenberg, quoted in André Parinaud, "Un misfit de la peinture newyorkaise se confesse," *Les Arts et Spectat Arts* 821 (May 10, 1961): 18.

20. Ibid. I would like to thank Molly Renda for observations in this part of the text.

21. Robert Rauschenberg quoted in Sam Hunter, "Robert Rauschenberg: Art and Life," in *Robert Rauschenberg: Works, Writings and Interviews* (Barcelona: Ediciones Poliígrafa, 2006), 37.

22. Rauschenberg first appropriated an engraving of da Vinci's famous painting in 1952 for his small collage, *Untitled [Mona Lisa]*, comprised of fabric, foil paper, Arabic texts, and several unrelated engravings, one of classical columns, another of cupids, and a third sporting jellyfish-like forms.

23. Hunter, "Robert Rauschenberg: Art and Life," in *Robert Rauschenberg: Works, Writings and Interviews*, 109.

24. Robert Rauschenberg, "Note on Painting" (October 31–November 2, 1963), reproduced in Hunter, *Robert Rauschenberg: Works, Writings and Interviews*, 123.

25. Richard Kostelanetz, "A Conversation with Robert Rauschenberg," *Partisan Review* 35, no. 1 (Winter 1968): 92–106; reprinted as "'I Never Thought of It as Much of an Ability': An Interview by Richard Kostelanetz," in Hunter, *Robert Rauschenberg: Works, Writings and Interviews*, 134.

26. The critic Irit Rogoff commented in 2012: "I genuinely have no idea what anyone means when they say 'art.' This was not a rhetorical gesture. I genuinely have no idea what anyone means when they say art. I think that the sort of knock on impact of a lot of what I see is the fact that this kind of evacuation of a set of originary meanings within our field has had a kind of knock on affect in evacuating a whole set of meanings. But not just as a kind of epistemological lesson—'Well, if they don't know what art is, we don't know what art is,' and everything is destabilized—but by kind of cross-collaboration between, sort of between practices." "Discussion with Ruth Sonderegger and Irit Rogoff," in "3rd Former West Research Congress: Beyond What Was Contemporary Art, Part I (April 19–20, 2012), Academy of Fine Arts Vienna and Secession," between 8:52 and 9:48 minutes into the discussion: http://vimeo.com/41625855.

27. A comment a number of prominent scholars, as well as graduate students—the latter born in the 1970s—have made to me.

28. Michael Archer, "The Moral Gap between Art and Everyday Life," in *Political, Minimal* (Nürnberg: Verlag für moderne Kunst, 2009), 175.

29. Robert Rauschenberg, fax to Monsignor Mario Codognato, August 20, 1999, in the Robert Rauschenberg Foundation archive box "Padre Pio," New York City.

30. Archer, "The Moral Gap," 175.

31. Hunter, "Robert Rauschenberg: Art and Life," in *Robert Rauschenberg: Works, Writings and Interviews*, 24.

32. Rauschenberg to Walter Hopps, quoted in Lynn Wainwright, "Robert Rauschenberg's Fabrics: Reconstructing Domestic Space," in Christopher Reed, ed., *Not at Home: The Suppression of Domesticity in Modern Art and Architecture* (London: Thames and Hudson, 1996), 200.

33. Ibid.

34. Rauschenberg's answer to Barbara Lee Diamonstein, Inside New York's Art World: Robert Rauschenberg and Leo Castelli.

35. Rauschenberg in Barbara Rose, *Rauschenberg* (New York: Vintage, 1987), 10.

36. Ibid., 18.

37. Mary L. Kotz, *Rauschenberg: Art and Life* (New York: Harry N. Abrams, 2004), 56.

38. Robert Rauschenberg, in Rose, *Rauschenberg*, 14–15.

39. For example, in his well-known 1970 *Artforum* essay, "Some Notes on the Phenomenology of Making," Robert Morris did not cite Rauschenberg together with those artists Morris identified as demonstrating a "commitment to the means of production. . . . Duchamp, Cage, Pollock, Johns, and Stella." The oversight is especially odd as Morris worked closely with Rauschenberg in Judson Dance Theater and in his Surplus Dance Theater. Perhaps the answer to the absence of Rauschenberg as an example of one devoted to the "phenomenology of making" lies in a comment by Yvonne Rainer: "The truth of the matter," she explained, was that during this period younger artists such as herself, "Carolee Schneemann, Alex Hay, and Bob Morris . . . were simply not in [Rauschenberg's] league as far as previous accomplishment went." See Morris's "Some Notes on the Phenomenology of Making: The Search for the Motivated," *Artforum* 8, no. 8 (April 1970): 62–66. See also Yvonne Rainer, *Feelings Are Facts: A Life* (Cambridge, MA, and London: MIT Press, 2006), 240. On minimal and process art as they relate to Rauschenberg and Morris's writings, see Sarah Roberts, "White Painting [Three Panel]" in *SFMOMA on the Go* (July 2013): http://www.sfmoma.org/explore/collection/artwork/25855/essay/white_painting.

40. Hunter, "Robert Rauschenberg: Art and Life," in *Robert Rauschenberg: Works, Writings and Interviews*, 25.

41. Kotz, *Rauschenberg: Art and Life*, 98.

42. Robert Rauschenberg, quoted in Alain Jouffroy, "Barge," *Quadrum* 15 (1963): 182.

43. Walter Hopps, *Robert Rauschenberg: The Early 1950s* (Houston: Menil Collection and Houston Fine Art Press, 1991), 65.

44. Robert Rauschenberg, "L'OBELISCO" statement (March 3–10, 1953), reprinted in Hopps, *Robert Rauschenberg: The Early 1950s*, 232.

45. Robert Rauschenberg, quoted in "The Emperor's Combine," *Time* 75, no.16 (April 18, 1960): 92.

46. The images on this side of the canvas are derived from Rauschenberg's gelatin silver print *Fort Meyers, Florida* (1980).

47. Robert Rauschenberg, quoted in James Schuyler, "Is Today's Artist with or Against the Past?" *Art News* 57, no. 4 (Summer 1958): 46.

48. Rose, Robert Rauschenberg, 114.

49. Richard Kostelanetz, "A Conversation with Robert Rauschenberg," 134.

50. See René Magritte, "To Michel Foucault," May 23, 1966, printed in Michel Foucault, *This Is Not a Pipe*, trans. and ed. by James Harkness (Berkeley: University of California Press, 1982), 57.

51. Ibid.

52. Ibid.

53. James Harkness, "Introduction" to Foucault's *This Is Not a Pipe*, 5–6.

54. Michel Foucault, *The Order of Things* (New York: Pantheon, 1970), 48.

55. The archive of Rauschenberg's correspondence demonstrates that he took special care with spelling, making multiple drafts and correcting spelling errors. Dave Hickey noted that when he visited the artist at one point, Rauschenberg had "a large dictionary on a stand." Dave Hickey, "Apogamy Pods: Rauschenberg Erases Rauschenberg," in *Rauschenberg Apogamy Pods* (New York: PaceWildenstein, 2000), 6.

56. Hickey explained that Rauschenberg has often been taken to be "un-intellectual," but that the artist "invested a lifetime of tactical and strategic understanding into the creation of a rational support system that facilitates his ongoing, instantaneous visual decision-making [which displays] his deep understanding of the position of intellect in the art-making process." Hickey, "Apogamy Pods," 7.

57. I am indebted to a discussion with Julie Tetel Andresen on the point of the missing "a" as Rauschenberg's intentional aim to resonate with the missing "r."

58. Magritte, "To Michel Foucault," 57.

59. John Arnen, "Robert Rauschenberg: An Audience of One," *Art News* 76, no. 2 (February 1977): 48; quoted in Hunter, "Robert Rauschenberg: Art and Life," in *Robert Rauschenberg: Works, Writings and Interviews*, 28.

60. In these broader considerations of diffraction as related to history, memory, and society, and more, Donna J. Haraway and Thyrza Nichols Goodeve informed my thinking. See the chapter "Diffraction as Critical Consciousness" in Thyrza Nicholas Goodeve, *Like a Leaf: An Interview with Thyrza Nichols Goodeve* (New York and London: Routledge, 2000), 101–9.

61. Rauschenberg in Rose, *Rauschenberg*, 110.

62. Robert Rauschenberg, letter to Betty Parsons, postmarked October 18, 1951, reproduced in Hopps, *Robert Rauschenberg: The Early 1950s*, 230.

63. Rauschenberg often went barefoot, as decades of photographs of him attest in every possible circumstance. One of the earliest of these photographs is the 1951 blueprint described in *Life* magazine as "Underwater Nymph," a picture of Susan Weil that captured his bare foot in the image while he was making an exposure of her with light on the blueprint paper.

64. The cereus cactus blooms only once a year, in the dark. It was particularly popular in the South during the Great Depression, as well as in the period when Rauschenberg studied at Black Mountain. Eudora Welty named a group of her literary friends the "Night-Blooming Cereus Club," and when a cereus plant she owned began to show buds each year, she held parties at her home in Jackson, Mississippi, to watch the flower unfurl and die. Describing the plant as "a naked, luminous, complicated flower" in one of the short stories in her book *The Golden Apples* (1949), Welty also concluded that when it died, the beauty of the night-blooming cereus ended up resembling "a wrung chicken's neck."

65. The phrase "the pulse and movement the truth of the lies in our pecul[i]ar preoccupation," is the most inscrutable section of the letter. One can only speculate on its meaning. But Rauschenberg's emphasis on "pulse and movement," or time, might relate to *This is the First Half of a Print Designed to Exist in Passing Time*, the series of fourteen woodcuts he created at Black Mountain sometime during the year 1948–49. It might also be that he was thinking about movement in dance, as in the fall of 1948 he illustrated Joel Oppenheimer's poem "The Dancer," which commemorated a performance by Black Mountain College dance instructor Katherine Litz.

66. Rauschenberg amplifies his zealous comparison of his paintings to the one white (light) of one God by describing his experience of "dealing with the suspense, excitement, and body of an organic silence, the restriction and freedom of absence, the plastic fullness of nothing, the point a circle begins and ends."

67. Rauschenberg, fax to Monsignor Mario Codognato.

68. Hopps, *Robert Rauschenberg: The Early 1950s*, 29.

69. Ibid., 29–30.

70. Ibid., 230.

71. Susan Davidson, "Early Work: 1949–1954," in Hopps and Davidson, *Robert Rauschenberg*, 44.

72. Ibid.

73. Hunter, "Robert Rauschenberg: Art and Life," in *Robert Rauschenberg: Works, Writings and Interviews*, 14.

74. Barbara Rose, "Rauschenberg: On and Off the Wall," in Gilbert Perlein, Susan

Davidson, and David White, *Robert Rauschenberg: On and Off the Wall: Works from the 80s and the 90s* (Nice: Musée d'Art moderne et d'Art contemporain, 2005), 69.

75. Ibid., 72.

76. Joseph quotes "Rauschenberg from notes of an interview with Walter Hopps at Captiva Island, Fla., 18–20 January 1991, in the Rauschenberg archives in New York." See Joseph, *Random Order*, 26. I have not been able to locate these notes.

77. Ibid. See also 295, note 4.

78. Ibid., 29.

79. Ibid.

80. Joseph corrects the sentence by leaving out the repetition of "the," adding a comma after movement, and correcting the spelling of "peculiar."

81. Ibid., 30.

82. See John Cage quoted in Richard Kostelanetz, *Conversing with Cage* (New York: Limelight Editions, 1994), 67.

83. Cage's handout was quoted in its entirety in Emily Genauer, "Art and Artists: Musings on Miscellany," *New York Herald Tribune* (December 27, 1953), sec. 4, p. 6. The text was also published under the title "[Robert Rauschenberg] *John Cage*," in Richard Kostelanetz, ed., *John Cage: An Anthology* (New York: Da Capo, 1970), 111–12. See the text reprinted in a different form in Joan Young and Susan Davidson, "Chronology," in *Robert Rauschenberg*, ed, Walter Hopps and Susan Davidson, 553.

84. Cage seems to have been competitive with Rauschenberg right from the beginning of their friendship, in the summer of 1952, as I have noted regarding his comment about "lagging" behind Rauschenberg. Regarding their collaboration on *Automobile Tire Print* (1953) in his 1961 essay on Rauschenberg, Cage made little of Rauschenberg's originating concept and strategy for executing the print, and much of his own role in the work, writing: "I know he put the paint on the tires. And he unrolled the paper on the city street. But which one of us drove the car?" See John Cage, "On Robert Rauschenberg, Artist, and His Work," in *Silence* (Middletown, CT: Wesleyan University Press, 1961), 98. There are so many snide remarks in Cage's essay that it deserves careful reading and analysis. This is also the essay in which Cage preempts Rauschenberg's unique attention to the register of shadows on his *White Paintings*, writing, "The white paintings were airports for the lights, shadows, and particles" (p. 102). Cage's comment is the one most often cited, rather than Rauschenberg's more sophisticated understanding of how his paintings functioned. But it was in 1964, when Rauschenberg won the grand prize at the Venice Biennial and commented in an interview that he "regarded the Merce Cunningham Dance Company as [my] biggest canvas," that Cage's enmity surfaced. As Alastair Macaulay has written, the comment offended "John Cage, who seems to have felt it sounded too proprietorial." But, as Macaulay adds, Rauschenberg's comment "was completely justified, [as] at that time there was no better place to see the range of Mr. Rauschenberg's inventiveness than the Cunningham repertory." Hiroki Ikegami also discusses this comment, as well as Rauschenberg's resignation from the Cunningham Dance Company at the end of the tour in 1964, when he was hurt by Cunningham and Cage's late appearance and early departure from his public performance at the Sogetsu Art Center, Tokyo, during which he painted the Combine *Gold Standard*. See Alastair Macaulay, "Rauschenberg and Dance, Partners for Life," *New York Times*, Dance section (May 14, 2008): http://www.nytimes.com/2008/05/14/arts/dance/14coll.html. See also Hiroki Ikegami, *The Great Migrator: Robert Rauschenberg and the Global Rise of American Art* (Cambridge, MA: MIT Press, 2010).

85. Cage, *Silence*, 105–6.

86. Robert Rauschenberg, quoted in Barbara Rose, "Rauschenberg: On and Off the

Wall," in Gilbert Perlein, Susan Davidson, and David White, *Robert Rauschenberg: On and Off the Wall* (Nice: Musée d'Art moderne et d'Art contemporain, 2005), 54.

87. It is worth recounting Reinhardt's twelve points, which are very close to those of Cage, although many were followed by Reinhardt's textual amplification, not cited here: "1. No texture; 2. No brushwork or calligraphy; 3. No sketching or drawing; 4. No forms; 5. No design; 6. No colors; 7. No light; 8. No space; 9. No time; 10. No size or scale; 11. No movement; 12. No object, no subject, no matter. No symbols, images, or signs. Neither pleasure nor paint. No mindless working or mindless non-working. No chess-playing." See Ad Reinhardt, "Twelve Rules for a New Academy," *Art News* 56, no. 3 (May 1957): 37–38, 56.

88. For example, in the publishing of Reinhardt's text in Stiles and Selz's *Theories and Documents of Contemporary Art*, the copyright owned by Anna Reinhardt required the date of 1953 to follow the title of the work. Thus, Reinhardt's text is listed in this volume as "Twelve Rules for a New Academy" (1953) in *Art News* 56, no. 3 (May 1937): 37–38, 56; reprinted in Barbara Rose, ed., *Art as Art: The Selected Writings of Ad Reinhardt* (1975) (Berkeley: University of California Press, 1991), 203–7.

89. "Ad Reinhardt draft chronology, circa 1966," Smithsonian Archives of American Art: http://www.aaa.si.edu/collections/viewer/ad-reinhardt-draft-chronology-15181/43621.

90. "Ad Reinhardt draft chronology, circa 1965," Smithsonian Archives of American Art: http://www.aaa.si.edu/collections/viewer/artists-chronology-10289/26793.

91. "Ad Reinhardt draft chronology, circa 1966," Smithsonian Archives of American Art: http://www.aaa.si.edu/collections/viewer/ad-reinhardt-draft-chronology-15181/43622.

92. See Emily Genauer, "Art and Artists: Musings on Miscellany," *New York Herald Tribune* (December 27, 1953), sec. 4, p. 6., cited in Joan Young and Susan Davidson, "Chronology," in Walter Hopps and Susan Davidson, *Robert Rauschenberg*, 553.

93. Lippard, 77.

94. Ibid.

95. Ibid.

96. Harlan Phillips, "Oral History Interview with Ad Reinhardt, ca. 1964," *Archives of American Art*. Accessed at: http://www.aaa.si.edu/collections/interviews/oral-history-interview-ad-reinhardt-12891.

97. Rauschenberg, *Rauschenberg Overseas Culture Interchange*, 177.

98. Rauschenberg used blindness in a number of works, as in *Map Room II*, when he had nineteen performers blindfolded onstage while they made "nonsensical sentences by switching places and flipping through sign cards painted with words." See Nancy Spector, "Rauschenberg and Performance, 1963–67: A 'Poetry of Infinite Possibilities," in Hopps and Davidson, *Robert Rauschenberg*, 329.

99. Rauschenberg, "A Conversation about Art and ROCI," 178.

100. Robert S. Mattison, *Robert Rauschenberg: Breaking Boundaries* (New Haven and London: Yale University Press, 2003), 14.

101. Ibid., 18.

102. Kotz, Rauschenberg: Art and Life, 153.

103. Robert Rauschenberg, in John Richardson, "Epic Vision," *Vanity Fair* 1, no. 445 (September 1997): 281.

104. Robert Rauschenberg, in Mattison, *Robert Rauschenberg: Breaking Boundaries*, 10.

105. Kotz, *Rauschenberg: Art and Life*, 37.

106. Robert Rauschenberg, in André Parinaud, "Un 'misfit' de la peinture newyorkaise se confesse": 18.

107. Dave Hickey, "Open Charms," *Artforum* 36, no.1 (September 1997): 152.

108. Rauschenberg, in "A Conversation about Art and ROCI," 161.

109. Ibid.

110. Drawing on Harold Rosenberg's famous reference to the action painter's "encounter" in the act of painting, Cage would write in 1961: "There is in Rauschenberg, between him and what he picks up to use, the quality of an encounter." John Cage, "On Robert Rauschenberg, Artist, and His Work," 103.

111. Stephen Rogers Dolan, in a telephone conversation with the author, May 22, 2014.

112. Rauschenberg, "Photographs," in *Robert Rauschenberg Photographs* (New York: Pantheon, 1981), unpaginated.

113. Robert Rauschenberg, "The Tabago Statement" (October 22, 1984) in Jack Cowart, *Rauschenberg Overseas Culture Interchange* (Washington: National Gallery of Art, 1991), 154.

## WARHOL'S "WHAT?"

1. This essay has a long genealogy, beginning in a talk I gave at the now defunct Duke University Museum in 1993, and in a second public lecture, "Ever So Far at Close Shooting Range: Warhol's Spectral Polaroids," at the Nasher Museum of Art at Duke University, 2009. I gave another version as the Robert and Avis Burke Lecture at Indiana University, 2010.

2. Several speakers at the 1962 symposium on Pop Art at the Museum of Modern Art in New York, organized by Peter Selz, then curator of painting and sculpture at MoMA, discussed Warhol in these terms—especially Selz and the critics Dore Ashton and Hilton Kramer (then writing for *The Nation*). Henry Geldzahler, then the assistant curator of American painting and sculpture at the Metropolitan Museum, participated in the symposium but was a staunch supporter of Warhol and Pop art. Other panelists included Leo Steinberg, then associate professor of Aat history at Hunter College, and the Pulitzer prize–winning poet Stanley Kunitz.

3. Carolee Thea, "Interview with Carolyn Christov-Bakargiev," in *On Curating: Interviews with Ten International Curators* (New York: Distributed Art Publishers, 2009), 70.

4. Rainer Crone, *Andy Warhol* (New York: Praeger, 1970), 10. Forty years later, in an article for the *New York Review of Books*, Crone would still praise Warhol's "production methods" and the "conceptual properties" of his art:

> Warhol and I had a debate over two weeks on the merits and importance of his early hand-painted works on canvas (1960 to 1962), which the artist had hidden away in his attic and nobody had seen before I discovered a tiny photograph of one of them in a fashion magazine. Finally, one day, Warhol came with Polaroid photographs that he had taken of these paintings in his attic and handed them over to me for publication in my catalogue raisonné. Warhol expressed his wish to have these photographs of his so-called "early works" published in my book, to contrast with the later, more mechanically produced, silk-screened works he created after 1962. No photographic documentation existed of the "early" paintings until I published them, with Warhol's authorization. All such details, included in the catalog at his request, were significant to Warhol, since he intended to clarify the evolution of his artistic position and his avant-garde concept of questioning the six-hundred-year-old tradition (since Giotto) of the imperative notion of authorship.

See Rainer Crone, "What Andy Warhol Really Did," *New York Review of Books* (February 25, 2010): www.nybooks.com/articles/archives/2010/feb/25/what-andy-warhol-really-did/.

5. For individual citations, see Crone, 61, notes 9–13.

6. Andy Warhol, "What is Pop Art?" interview by Gene Swensen, *Art News* (November 1963).

7. Stephen Koch, *Stargazer: Andy Warhol's World and His Films* (New York and Washington: Praeger, 1973), 120.

8. Koch, 38–39.

9. Ibid., 41.

10. Ibid.

11. Ibid., 32.

12. Sigmund Freud, "Screen Memories," in Peter Gay, ed., *The Freud Reader* (New York and London: W. W. Norton, 1985): 117–26.

13. Ibid., 126.

14. *The Shadow* debuted on July 31, 1930. James LaCurto first played the role of the Shadow, followed by radio veteran Frank Readick, Jr., who endowed the character with what writer Anthony Tollin described as a voice with "a hauntingly sibilant quality that thrilled radio listeners." After the show's enormous success, magician and writer Walter B. Gibson developed the character into the star of the magazine *The Shadow*, which *Detective* magazine published. Its first issue, "The Living Shadow," appeared on April 1, 1931. Gibson wrote under the pen name of Maxwell Grant, a character who claimed that his stories had come directly from "the Shadow's private annals as told to" him.

15. Andy Warhol, *The Philosophy of Andy Warhol (From A to B and Back Again)* (San Diego, New York, and London: Harcourt Brace Jovanovich, 1975), 21.

16. Jennifer Doyle, Jonathan Flatley, and José Esteban Muñoz, eds., *Pop Out: Queer Warhol* (Durham, NC: Duke University Press, 1996).

17. Warhol, *The Philosophy of Andy Warhol*, 123.

18. Ibid.

19. Ibid., 36, 38.

20. Ibid., 41.

21. Ibid.

22. Ibid.

23. Ibid., 42.

24. Ibid.

25. Ibid.

26. Ibid., 46.

27. Ibid.

28. Ibid., 46.

29. Foster's expansive essay covers "a traumatic notion of the real, a contemporary version of the optical unconscious, a historical confusion between private fantasy and public reality, a hysterical relay between mass subject and mass object, [and] a forging of a psychic nation through mass-mediated disaster and death" (p. 58).

30. Koch, 117.

31. Arthur Danto, "The Philosopher as Andy Warhol," in *Philosophizing Art: Selected Essays* (Berkeley: University of California Press, 1999), 62.

32. Warhol, *The Philosophy of Andy Warhol*, 229.

33. Ibid.

34. Ibid.

35. Ibid., 238.

36. Ibid., 240.

37. Ibid., 241.

38. Frances Gerety coined the slogan in 1947 for the South African diamond company De Beers. Ian Fleming adapted the phrase for the title of his novel *Diamonds are Forever* (1956), which premiered as a James Bond film in 1971, four years before the publication of *The Philosophy of Andy Warhol*. The phrase was very much in circulation when Warhol asked the question: "Forever what?"

39. Crone, 21–22.

40. See also "Warhol's Activities in Off-Off Broadway Theater," in Rainer Crone, *Andy Warhol: A Picture Show by the Artist* (New York: Rizzoli, 1987), 73–76.

41. Ibid., 21–22.

42. Ibid., 32.

43. Julian Schnabel, introduction to *Andy Warhol Shadow Paintings November 1989* (New York: Gagosian Gallery, 1989), 4.

44. Wayne Koestenbaum, *Andy Warhol* (New York: Lipper/Viking, 2001), 172.

45. Ibid., 172–74.

46. In "What Wittgenstein and Warhol Had in Common," the clinical psychologist Patricia Howlin compares Warhol to Asperger, Wittgenstein, and Einstein as someone who might have been autistic and suffered Asperger's syndrome. See Howlin's review of Valerie Paradiyz, *Elijah's Cup: A Family's Journey into the Community and Culture of High-Functioning Autism and Asperger's Syndrome* (2003) in *The Times: Higher Education* (March 28, 2003): http://www.timeshighereducation.co.uk/175632.article.

47. In this way, Warhol's approach to art and life also corresponded with Wittgenstein's "picture theory of language" (derived from Propositions 1, 2, and 3 in the *Tractatus*). Wittgenstein argued that language is a representational system, as well as the means by which we "make to ourselves pictures of facts" (2.1). Wittgenstein also asserted that propositions are both facts and pictures, and that statements are meaningful if they can be defined or pictured in the real world. He relegated this picture theory to a metaphor for human psychology in *Philosophical Investigations* (1953).

48. Bob Colacello, *Holy Terror: Andy Warhol Close Up* (New York: HarperCollins, 1990), 338–39.

49. Other paradoxes of Warhol's life included being a millionaire and appearing to be in need of money; being stingy about spending money and yet generous to his family; creating "an image of himself as being trendy and liberal, but . . . surprisingly conservative . . . a devout Catholic who went to Mass every Sunday"; and so on. See Paul Alexander, *Death and Disaster: The Rise of the Warhol Empire and the Race for Andy's Millions* (New York: Villard, 1994), 17.

50. David Freedberg, *The Power of Images: Studies in the History and Theory of Response* (Chicago and London: University of Chicago Press, 1989), 432.

51. Koch, 49.

52. Schnabel, 6–7.

53. Colacello, 341.

54. Ibid.

55. Steve Cox, "Andy Warhol: Killing Papa." Accessed at http://www.stevecox.com.au/ANDY-WARHOL-KILLING-PAPA.

56. Victor Bockris, *The Life and Death of Andy Warhol* (New York: Bantam, 1989), 67.

57. Warhol, *The Philosophy of Andy Warhol*, 10.

58. Andy Warhol and Pat Hackett, *POPism: The Warhol Sixties* (New York: Harcourt Brace Jovanovich, 1980), 199–200.

59. Michal's photograph, *Andy Warhol's Hand* (1973), is reproduced in *Andy Warhol Photography* (Pittsburgh and Hamburg: Andy Warhol Museum and Hamburg Hunsthalle,

Edition Stemmle, 1999), 304. See also Roland Barthes's discussion of this photograph and Warhol's hands in *Camera Lucida* (New York: Hill and Wang, 1981), 45. See, too, Nicholas de Villiers, *Opacity and the Closet: Queer Tactics in Foucault, Barthes, and Warhol* (Minneapolis:University of Minnesota Press), 2012.

60. Art historian John Richardson's description of Warhol to Bob Colacello following Warhol's funeral, as quoted in Colacello's *Holy Terror*, 500.

61. Foster, 36.

62. Eleanor Heartney, "The Warhol of Our Minds," *Art in America* 97, no. 9 (October 2009): http://www.artinamericamagazine.com/books/the-warhol-of-our-minds/.

63. John Richardson quoted in David Bourdon, *Warhol* (New York: Harry N. Abrams, 1989), 414.

64. Simon Watney, "Queer Andy," quoted in Jennifer Doyle, "Tricks of the Trade: Pop Art/Pop Sex," in Doyle, Flatley, and Muñoz, eds., *Pop Out*, 23.

65. Dave Hickey quoted in David Wallace-Wells, "Andy Warhol: Factory Man," *Newsweek* (December 2, 2009): 66. http://www.thedailybeast.com/newsweek/2009/12/02/andy-warhol-factory-man.html.

66. Dave Hickey, "Andy and the Dreams That Stuff Is Made Of," in *Andy Warhol: GIANT Size* (London: Phaidon, 2006), 7.

67. David Bourdon writes:

> The public Warhol differed considerably from the private one. Though constantly in the public eye, he remained something of an enigma, aloof despite his accessibility. His "official" persona was to a large extent a deliberate fabrication. Many reporters made the mistake of portraying him as a simpleton who talked in a childlike, "gee-whiz" manner that called for cartoon balloons. But Warhol was not as simple as some writers wanted to believe. He clammed up around interviewers, manipulating the session in such a way that he could answer every question with a simple "yes" or "no." . . . No matter how inaccurate the reportage, he made no effort to clarify. It was as if he realized all along that legends are based on a cloud of rumors . . . .

See Bourdon, *Warhol*, 10.

68. Brian Wallis, "Absolute Warhol," *Art in America* 7, no. 3 (March 1989): 31. Warhol packed up his overt party persona to become all business "in the summer of 1974," Pat Hackett reports, when "the Factory moved from 33 Union Square to the third floor of 860 Broadway . . . [and] Andy instructed the receptionists to stop answering the phone with 'Factory'—Factory had become 'too corny,' he said—and the place became simply 'the office.'" Hackett, *The Andy Warhol Diaries*, xii.

69. Geldzahler, "Andy Warhol," in Crone, *Andy Warhol*, 35.

70. Bockris, 81.

71. Koestenbaum, 8–9.

72. Ibid., 7.

73. Barthes does not see the hands as the punctum of this photograph, but rather Warhol's "spatulate nails." (p. 45).

74. Michael Moon, "Screen Memories," in Doyle, Flatley and Muñoz, eds., *Pop Out*, 86.

75. Duane Michals, "Duane Michals: Asking Questions without Answers," in a 1994 interview with Karl-Peter Gottschalk: http://easyweb.easynet.co.uk/˜karlpeter/zeugma/inters/michals.htm.

76. Ibid.

77. Alan R. Pratt, *The Critical Response to Andy Warhol* (Westport, CT, and London: Greenwood Press, 1996), xxv.

78. Colacello, 62.

79. Ibid.

80. Pat Hackett worked closely with Warhol on three books, beginning with *The Philosophy of Andy Warhol*. She apparently was not as involved with chapter 15, "Underwear Power," as with other chapters, as Hackett explains: "I did eight separate interviews with Andy on the basis of which I wrote chapters 1 through 8 and chapter 10. Then, using material from conversations Andy had taped between himself and Bob Colacello and Brigid Berlin, I wrote the introductory chapter and chapters 9, 11, 12, 13 and 14. . . . He asked me to co-author the second book with him—his memoirs of the sixties, which we decided to call *Popism*." Hackett in Andy Warhol, *The Andy Warhol Diaries*, ed. by Pat Hackett (New York: Warner Books, 1989), xiii. Thus, I quote and interpret Warhol's "thoughts" in his published writings as his own, while acknowledging Hackett for having provided special access to Warhol's ideas. In fact, Warhol dedicated his *Philosophy* in part to Hackett, writing, "To Pat Hackett, for extracting and redacting my thoughts so intelligently." I suspect that the word "redacting" was a Hackett intervention.

81. Paul Alexander, *Andy Warhol: Death and Disaster* (Houston: Menil Collection and Houston Fine Art Press, 1988), 43.

82. Crone, 12.

83. For an account of how strapped Warhol was for money even in 1965, see Richard Dorment, "How Andy Warhol's Red Self-Portraits Were Made," *New York Review of Books* (August 18, 2011): http://www.nybooks.com/articles/archives/2011/aug/18/how-andy-warhols-red-self-portraits-were-made/#fn-3.

84. Quoted from Gretchen Berg, "Andy Warhol," *Los Angeles Free Press* (March 17, 1967), in Crone, 12.

85. Ibid.

86. Benjamin Buchloh, "Anniversary Notes for Andy Warhol," in *Andy Warhol: Shadows and Other Signs of Life* (Cologne: Verlag der Buchhandlung Walther König and Galerie Chantal Crousel, 2007), 77.

87. Warhol, *The Philosophy of Andy Warhol*, 229.

88. Ibid., 32. With regard to *The Andy Warhol Diaries*, Hackett has explained that she took notes on Warhol's daily phone conversations with her, transcribed her notes, corrected grammar, filled in names, and, for readability and to eliminate redundancy, also eliminated many names that Warhol cited. She remarked, "To Andy, putting things in a format that made sense was enough of a compromise. He'd get exasperated when I'd occasionally make him repeat or rephrase something until I understood it." The word "redacting" was probably Hackett's addition to his dedication of the book to her, but her uncanny ability to translate Warhol's "thoughts so intelligently" and accurately is what matters. Hackett in Andy Warhol, *The Andy Warhol Diaries*, xix.

89. Warhol in *The Andy Warhol Diaries*, 3. This entry is dated Sunday, November 28, 1976.

90. Ibid., 9. This entry is dated Tuesday, December 14, 1976.

91. Paula Cooper, in conversation with the author, April 14, 2012.

92. Warhol, *The Andy Warhol Diaries*, 9.

93. Koch, 26.

94. Warhol, *The Andy Warhol Diaries*, 11. Dated Saturday, December 25, 1976.

95. Warhol died following gall bladder surgery, preceded by more than a decade of pain and health complications caused by having been shot repeatedly in the chest by the writer Valerie Solanas on June 3, 1968.

96. Bockris, 325.

97. Jason Rubell, in conversation with the author, April 14, 2012.

98. Helen Molesworth, "This Will Have Been: Art, Love & Politics in the 1980s," in *This Will Have Been: Art, Love & Politics in the 1980s* (New Haven and London: Museum of Contemporary Art Chicago in association with Yale University Press, 2012), 38.

99. Ibid.

100. Paula Cooper, in conversation with the author, April 14, 2012.

101. This is a one of the few texts written by Warhol that Pat Hackett, the editor of three of Warhol's books, did not edit.

102. Faiyaz Kara, "Pop Prose: The Critical Response to Warhol Literature," in Pratt, 269.

103. Some of these people include Cheryl Tiegs, Jane Fonda, Pee-Wee Herman, Michael Jackson, Tony Bennett, Madonna, Boy George, Liberace, John Sex, Liza Minnelli, Diana Ross, Mick Jagger, Sean Lennon, Grace Jones, Laurie Anderson, David Byrne, Keith Haring, Bryan Ferry, Francesco Clemente, Julian and Jacqueline Schnabel, Jean-Michel Basquiat, Jed Garet, Kenny Scharf, Michael Heizer, Eric Fischl, Robert Rauschenberg, Georgia O'Keeffe, Philip Johnson, Edward Albee, Louise Nevelson, Robert Wilson, Christopher Knowles, David Hockney, Maureen Stapleton, Elizabeth Taylor, Lillian Hellman, Gloria Swanson, Lillian Gish, Christopher Reeve, John Travolta, Mel Gibson, Farrah Fawcett, Ryan O'Neal, Alexander Godunov, Jacqueline Bisset, Bette Davis, Joan Bennett, Lance Loud, Linda Evans, John Forsythe, Lloyd Bridges, John McEnroe, Ronald and Nancy Reagan, Jerry Hall, Niki de Saint Phalle, Paloma Picasso, Calvin Klein, Gloria Vanderbilt, Norman Mailer, William Burroughs, and Truman Capote.

104. Andy Warhol, *America* (New York: Harper & Row, 1985), 194.

105. Ibid., 212.

106. Ibid., 214.

107. Ibid., 223.

108. Ibid.

109. Warhol, *America*, 186.

110. Marjorie Miller, "American," *Library Journal* 11 (February 15, 1986): 176.

111. Tom Crow, "Saturday Disasters: Trace and Reference in Early Warhol," first published in *Art in America* 75, no. 5 (May 1987), and quoted by Foster in "Death in America," 70.

112. Colacello, 11.

113. Elaine Rusinko, *We Are All Warhol's Children: Andy and the Rusyns* (Pittsburgh: University of Pittsburgh Press, forthcoming). Thanks to Elaine Rusinko for generously sharing her research, and to Kathy O'Dell for introducing me to Rusinko's work.

114. Rusinko notes that Paul Robert Magocsi's *The People from Nowhere* (2006) offers a history of Carpatho-Rusyns, that Raymond Herbenick hypothesizes in *Warhol's Religious and Ethnic Roots* (1997), that many forms of Warhol's work are traceable to Rusyn *pysanký* (Easter egg decoration) and sacred church art, and that Rudo Prekop and Michal Cihlář consider the links between the Warhola family and Czechoslovakia in *Andy Warhol a Československo* (2011).

115. Emile de Antonio, in a conversation with Warhol on the reason why Jasper Johns and Robert Rauschenburg shunned him; quoted in Andy Warhol and Pat Hackett, *POPism: The Warhol Sixties* (New York: Harcourt Brace Jovanovich, 1980) 11–12.

116. By the mid-1960s, as a 1966 lead article in *Time* magazine would announce, "on Broadway, it would be difficult to find a production without homosexuals playing important parts, either onstage or off. And in Hollywood, says Broadway Producer David Merrick, 'you have to scrape them off the ceiling.' The notion that the arts are dominated by a kind of homosexual mafia—or 'Homintern,' as it has been called—is sometimes exaggerated, particularly by spiteful failures looking for scapegoats. But in the theater, dance and music world, deviates are so widespread that they sometimes seem to be running a

kind of closed shop." Even the art critic Harold Rosenberg is reported to have described "homosexual painters and their nonpainting auxiliaries" as "banding together. . . . Homosexual ethics and esthetics are staging a vengeful, derisive counterattack on what deviates call the 'straight' world. This is evident in 'pop,' which insists on reducing art to the trivial, and in the 'camp' movement, which pretends that the ugly and banal are fun." See "Essay: The Homosexual in America," *Time* (January 21, 1966): http://www.drjudithreisman.com/archives/2011/06/time_essay_the.html.

117. Jonathan D Katz, "John Cage's Queer Silence," in David W. Bernstein and Christopher Hatch, eds., *Writings Through John Cage's Music, Poetry and Art* (Chicago: University of Chicago Press, 2001), 49; quoted in Cox: http://www.stevecox.com.au/ANDY-WARHOL-KILLING-PAPA.

118. Cox, http://www.stevecox.com.au/ANDY-WARHOL-KILLING-PAPA.

119. Ibid.

120. Watney, 23.

121. Marianne Hancock, "Soup's On," *Arts Magazine* 39 (May/June 1965): 16–18.

122. Susan Sontag, "Notes on Camp," *Partisan Review* 31 (Fall 1964): 515–30.

123. Watney, 22. I have been unable to find a reference to Warhol "wearing" his mother's clothes, but Bockris describes how he liked picking out clothes *for* his mother to wear.

124. Ann Cvetkovich, *An Archive of Feelings: Trauma, Sexuality, and Lesbian Public Cultures* (Durham, NC: Duke University Press, 2003),

125. Alice Lum, "The J. A. Murray House—No. 57 E. 66th Street," in Daytonian in Manhattan (January 31, 2013): http://daytoninmanhattan.blogspot.com/2013/01/the-j-murray-house-no-57-e-66th-street.html. See also Edward Hayes and Susan Lehman, *Mouthpiece: A Life in—and Sometimes Just Outside—the Law* (New York: Broadway Books, 2006).

126. John W. Smith, quoted in Mary Thomas, "Warhol's House of Stuff," *Post-Gazette.com* (March 1, 2002): http://old.post-gazette.com/ae/20020301warhol1.asp.

127. Ibid.

128. Following John W. Smith's interpretation of Warhol's collecting habits as part of his "aesthetic and artistic endeavors," it is worth conjecturing that Fiestaware (founded in 1936 and discontinued in 1972) may have influenced the artist's riotous combinations of complementary colors, especially in his silkscreen portraits.

129. Joseph D. Ketner II, "Image Machine: Andy Warhol & Photography," in *Image Machine Andy Warhol & Photography* (Cincinnati, Nürnberg, and New York: Contemporary Arts Center, Verlag für Moderne Kunst, and Andy Warhol Foundation, 2012), 41.

130. Tom Miller, "The J. A. Murray House—No. 57 E. 66th Street," (Thursday, January 31, 2013). Accessed at http://daytoninmanhattan.blogspot.com/2013/01/the-j-murray-house-no-57-e-66th-street.html.

131. Bockris, 295.

132. Jed Johnson, quoted in Bockris, 295.

133. Many of these characteristics today are associated with the schizotypal personality. In addition to the biographers quoted in this essay, such as Bockris, Bourdon, Alexander, and Koestenbaur, see Fred Lawrence Guiles, *Loner at the Ball: The Life of Andy Warhol* (London: Bantam Press, 1989); Tony Scherman and David Dalton, *POP: The Genius of Andy Warhol* (New York: HarperCollins, 2009); and Gary Indiana, *Andy Warhol and The Can that Sold the World* (New York: Basic Books, 2010), among others.

134. Bockris, 294–95.

135. William V. Ganis, *Andy Warhol's Serial Photography* (Cambridge: Cambridge University Press, 2004), 21.

136. Hackett, *The Andy Warhol Diaries*, xv.

137. Erin Byrne, "Time Capsule: Blog," *The Andy Warhol Museum* (January 17, 2012). Accessed at http://blog.warhol.org/time-capsules/back-into-the-trunk/.

138. Colacello, 348.

139. Ibid.

140. Capote, quoted in Alexander, 16.

141. Ibid., 17.

142. Foster, 42.

143. Susan Jarosi, "Art & Trauma Since 1950: A Holographic Model" (unpublished PhD dissertation, Duke University, 2005) contains a chapter on Warhol.

144. Quoted in Michelle Bogre, "Q&A: Andy Warhol, the Art World's Most Famous Voyeur, Looks at America with a Camera," *American Photographer* 15, no. 4 (October 1985): 80.

145. Warhol, *The Philosophy of Andy Warhol*, 91.

146. Ketner, 55, note 46.

147. Ibid., 55.

148. Bockris, 271.

149. Ibid.

150. Ibid., 271.

151. Gregory Bateson et al., "Towards a Theory of Schizophrenia," *Behavioral Science* 1 (1956): 251–64. See also Howard Berenbaum, Eve M. Valera, and John G. Kerns, "Psychological Trauma and Schizotypal Symptoms," *Oxford Journals, Medicine, Schizophrenia Bulletin* 29, no. 1 (2003): 143–52.

152. Koch, 117.

153. Ibid., 20.

154. Ibid., 41.

155. Ibid.

156. John Richardson, "Warhol at Home," in *Sacred Monsters, Sacred Masters* (London: Pimlico, 2001), 247–48.

157. Asked about the book years later, Warhol quipped: "Stephen Koch's book was interesting because he was able to write a whole book about it." Paul Taylor, "Andy Warhol's Final Interview," *Flash Art* 133 (April 1987): 96–97.

158. Warhol, *The Philosophy of Andy Warhol*, 7.

159. Ibid.

160. Ibid, 11.

161. After being released on bail, Solanas "called the Factory and Andy answered the phone. She wished him a Merry Christmas and threatened to shoot him again if he didn't meet her demands which include her appearance on the Johnny Carson show, publication of the *SCUM Manifesto* in the *Daily News* and $25,000 in cash." Ultra Violet, *Famous for 15 Minutes: My Years with Andy Warhol* (New York: Harcourt Brace Jovanovich, 1988), 187; cited in Gary Comenas, *Warholstars.com:* http://www.warholstars.org/chron/1968.html.

162. Ibid., 11.

163. Ibid., 26.

164. Warhol, *The Philosophy of Andy Warhol*, 21.

165. Sometimes the disease begins as "a species of convulsions . . . being first exhibited in a kind of lameness, or instability in one of the legs, which the patient drags about." See S. E. Swedo et al., "High Prevalence of Obsessive-Compulsive Symptoms in Patients with Sydenham's Chorea," *American Journal of Psychiatry* 146 (1989): 246–49.

166. J. Gerstley et al., "Chorea: Is It a Manifestation of Rheumatic Fever?" *Journal of Pediatrics* 6, no. 1 (January 1935): 42–50.

167. Joseph Collins, MD, "The Etiology of Sydenham's Chorea: An Analysis of 100 Consecutive Cases," *Philadelphia Medical Journal* 5 (February 24, 1900): 456.

168. A. H. Chapman, Loraine Pilkey, and Mary Jane Gibbons, "A Psychosomatic Study of Eight Children with Sydenham's Chorea," *Pediatrics* 21, no. 4 (April 1, 1958): 582–95. See also John M. Freeman et al., "The Emotional Correlates of Sydenham's Chorea," *Pediatrics* 35, no. 1 (January 1, 1965): 42–49.

169. Fernando R. Asbahr et al., "Obsessive-Compulsive Symptoms among Patients with Sydenham Chorea," *Biological Psychiatry* 57 (2005): 1073–76.

170. See J. J. McGrath and R. M. Murray, "The Secondary Schizophrenias," in Steven R. Hirsch and Daniel Roy Weinberger, eds., *Schizophrenia* (Malden, MA: Blackwell Science, 2003), 187–202.

171. Bockris, 18. This incident is cited in many biographies, but I refer here only to Bockris for his extensive interviews with Warhol's family and childhood friends.

172. Bockris, 15.

173. Ibid. Warhol's childhood friend Lillian Lanchester recalled: "He was particularly neat and very clean, all the time. With me he talked a lot, but he was very shy with other people. When a picture was taken of him he would have his head down and he would look up at you as though he was afraid he didn't trust you" (p. 18).

174. Ibid., 19. Moreover, Brockris explains: "In times of sickness, Julia always [gave] her boys enemas," and "at the height of his career as a filmmaker, Andy insisted on shooting a number of his performers being given enemas. The footage was never used in a movie."

175. Ibid.

176. Ibid.

177. Ibid., 17.

178. Ibid.

179. Warhol, *The Philosophy of Andy Warhol*, 229. Warhol, the immigrants' son, knew only too well the social implications of underwear, as it is called to testify for character in such well-known phrases as "Don't wash your dirty underwear in public," "Don't air your dirty laundry/linen in public," and "Always wear clean underwear in case of an accident." Such colloquialisms refer to the cultural importance attributed to discretion, privacy, and cleanliness, themselves standard measures of the propriety and inner virtues of a person—values Warhol alluded to in the opening lines of his chapter "Underwear Power," when he remarked that "buying underwear is the most personal thing you can do."

180. Ibid., 109. Italics here indicate Freud's emphasis throughout. The nineteenth-century term "hysteria" became the twentieth-century concept of trauma, and these passages from Freud's text remain foundational in trauma studies and clinical psychology, and in some psychiatric practices specializing in trauma today.

181. Andy Warhol, "Love (Puberty)," in *The Philosophy of Andy Warhol*, 21.

182. Warhol's fascination with celebrity emerged in these years. He would later pose in the same stance that Greta Garbo had struck in one of her promotional photographs, and in another position that mimicked Truman Capote's posture on a book jacket cover.

183. Bockris, 21.

184. Koestenbaum, 210–11.

185. Kirsten Hope Bigelow, "Warhol's Weegee," *New Art Examiner* 22 (October 1994): 21–25.

186. Ibid. Bigelow was the first scholar to identify Weegee as an influence on Warhol and to track down the fact that Weegee's *Naked City* was in Warhol's library when Sotheby's sold it in auction lot 1593. Although Judith Keller does not quote Bigelow's 1994

essay, Keller writes much the same in *Weegee: Photographs from the J. Paul Getty Museum* (Los Angeles: Getty Publications, 2005).

187. Ibid.

188. Ibid

189. Ibid., 21.

190. Ibid.

191. Lynne Cooke, "Andy Warhol: Introduction," to the Dia Art Foundation's exhibition *Andy Warhol* (May 3, 2003–March 31, 2014). Accessed at http://www.diaart.org/exhibitions/introduction/98. Cooke cites a telephone conversation with Ronnie Cutrone on November 26, 1998. She also states: "Mark Francis cites a slightly different account by Cutrone, suggesting that the images were produced by children's small building blocks." See Mark Francis, "No There There or Horror Vacui: Andy Warhol's Installations," in *Andy Warhol: Paintings 1960–1986* (Lucerne: Kunstmuseum, 1995), 72.

192. Cooke gives an excellent account of the choices Warhol made in making the paintings, and of how they are installed:

> Purchased as a single entity by Lone Star Foundation (now the Dia Art Foundation), this cycle of paintings was first exhibited in January 1979, at 393 West Broadway in New York City. Its current presentation in Dia:Beacon mimics that debut, for it, too, incorporates as many canvases, hung edge to edge and close to the floor, as will fit the space, but it sequences the works by acquisition number—an equally random order. Warhol left decisions regarding the initial order of the paintings to Cutrone and his assistants. In adhering to no system, they conformed to Warhol's own practice when he chose the colors for the grounds, or selected prints from contact sheets to be made into screens. Yet his method was far from completely arbitrary: restricting the vocabulary of the group to two compositional formats, confining the total number of hues to seventeen, and limiting each canvas to a single color, Warhol filtered a controlled and circumscribed serendipity through the proclivities of taste to create an environmental ensemble that pertains as much to decor as it does to high art. In fact, in typically disarming fashion, Warhol referred to Shadows not as art but as "disco decor." Soon after the exhibition, he employed it as a backdrop in a fashion shoot for the April 1979 edition of his magazine Interview.

Ibid.

193. Colacello, 429.

194. Danto, 132.

195. He even once asked whether Howdy Doody had a penis. Ibid., 128.

196. "Shadows and Andy Warhol" (March 1, 2012) in *This is Now, Making Art Happen* http://makingarthappen.com/2012/01/03/shadows-andy-warhol/.

197. Sigmund Freud, "Beyond the Pleasure Principle," in Peter Gay, ed. *The Freud Reader*, 602.

198. See Jeffrey Moussaieff Masson, *The Assault on Truth: Freud's Suppression of the Seduction Theory* (New York: Simon and Schuster, 1984).

199. Robert Jay Lifton, "From Hiroshima to the Nazi Doctors: The Evolution of Psychoformative Approaches to Understanding Traumatic Stress Syndromes," in *International Handbook of Traumatic Stress Syndromes* in *International Handbook of Traumatic Stress Syndromes* (New York: Plenum Press, 1993), 17–18.

200. Ibid., 16.

201. Ibid., 21.

202. See. Sigmund Freud, 'The Uncanny', in *The Standard Edition of the Complete Psychological Works of Sigmund Freud*, Vol. 17, ed. and trans. by James Strachey, (London: Hogarth, 1953), 252.

203. Victor I. Stoichita, *A Short History of the Shadow* (London: Reaktion Books, 1997), 15.

204. Ibid., 17.

205. Erwin Rohde, *Psyche: The Cult of Souls and Belief in Immortality among the Greeks*. London: Routledge & Kegan Paul, 1925. See also Jan M. Bremmer, *The Early Greek Concept of Soul* (Princeton, NJ: Princeton University Press, 1983), 78–79.

206. Stoichita, 23.

207. Ibid., 24–25. Particularly focusing on Warhol's *Shadow* (1979) paintings, Stoichita notes a debt to Giorgio De Chirico, with whom Gianfranco Gorgoni photographed Warhol in New York in about 1974, some five years before the *Shadow* paintings, but at the time when, as noted above, Warhol began to insert shadows in several series.

## 7:47 A.M. (THE TRAUMATIC VISUAL VOCABULARY OF MAURICE BENAYOUN'S *SO.SO.SO. SOMEBODY, SOMEWHERE, SOME TIME*)

1. This essay was first published in French as, "7h 47 du matin (Le vocabulaire visuel traumatique de So.So.So Somebody Somewhere Some Time de Maurice Benayoun)," in *Maurice Benayoun/MoBen OPEN ART* (Paris: CDA d'Enghien and Les Nouvelles éditions Scala, 2011), 83–85.

2. Maurice Benayoun, website statement about *So.So.So*. Unless otherwise cited, all quotations from the artist come from this site: http://www.benayoun.com/projet.php?id=25.

3. Rungis is a Parisian suburb known for having one the largest wholesale food markets in the world.

4. Praslin is the second largest of the Seychelles islands, a place for lovers and tourists with its white sands, tropical forests, and exotic birds and for its vanilla orchids, which are used in the commercial production of vanilla.

5. Maurice Beayoun, http://www.benayoun.com/sososotxteng.htm.

6. Maurice Benayoun, e-mail to the author, March 6, 2011.

7. Marianne Hirsch, *Family Frames: Photography, Narrative, and Postmemory* (Cambridge, MA: Harvard University Press, 1997).

8. Kristine Stiles, "Thresholds of Control: Destruction Art and Terminal Culture," in Gottfried Hattinger and Peter Weibel, eds., *Out of Control* (Linz, Austria: Arts Electronica, 1991), 29–50.

9. Siegfried Kracauer, "Photography," *Critical Inquiry* 19 (Spring 1993): 431, 425. Originally published as "Die Photographie" in *Frankfurter Zeitung* 28 (October 1927).

10. Roland Barthes, *Camera Lucida: Reflections on Photography*, trans. by Richard Howard (New York: Hill & Wang, 1981), 64. Originally published as *La Chambre Claire* (Paris: Editions du Seuil, 1980).

11. "The emotional hurt is *so* painful."

12. "They were happy, and we anticipate that they will remain *so*."

13. "Look at the magazines *so* [in this way]."

14. "She was *so* tired that the bride fell asleep."

15. "And *so* home and to bed."

16. "It is late, and *so* we must go."

17. "He did *so* do it!"

1. This essay first appeared in *Wangechi Mutu: A Fantastic Journey* (Durham, NC: Nasher Museum of Art at Duke University, 2013), 51–79. I would like to thank Wangechi Mutu for sharing her time and work with me so generously, Trevor Schoonmaker for offering me the opportunity to write about Mutu, Alexandra Giniger and Virginia Wagner for working closely with me on images to accompany this essay, and Alexa Dilworth for superbly sensitive editing.

2. Binyavanga Wainaina, "Wangechi Mutu: The Extent of Your Citizenry," in Marion Arnold, ed., *Art in Eastern Africa* (Dar es Salaam: Mkuki na Nyota Publishers, 2008), 179.

3. Wangechi Mutu, quoted in Lauri Firstenberg, "Perverse Anthropology: The Photomontage of Wangechi Mutu: A Conversation with the Artist," in Laurie Ann Farrell, ed., *Looking Both Ways: Art of the Contemporary African Diaspora*. (New York and Ghent: Museum for African Art, Snoeck Publishers, 2003); reprinted in *Wangechi Mutu: My Dirty Little Heaven* (Ostifildern, Germany: Hatje Cantz Verlag, 2010), 42. Hereafter cited as Mutu/Firstenberg; all quotes are from p. 42.

4. Mutu/Firstenberg.

5. Mary Louise Pratt, "Arts of the Contact Zone," *Profession* 91 (1991): 33. See also Tanya L. Shields, "Critical Connection: Method, Power, and Knowledge," *Enculturation* 6, no. 1 (2008): http://enculturation.gmu.edu/6.1/shields#_edn1.

6. *English Roses* and *African Kings* are two from among a wide assortment of visual reference books in Mutu's studio library that she uses as sources for her work.

7. Wangechi Mutu, in conversation with the author in Brooklyn, New York, on July 23, 2012. Cited hereafter as Mutu/Stiles.

8. H. G. Wells, quoted in Nikos Papastergiadis, *Cosmopolitanism and Culture* (Cambridge: Polity, 2012), 81.

9. Peter Hitchcock, "The Impossibly Intersubjective and the Logic of the Both," in Silke Horstkotte and Esther Peeren, eds., *The Shock of the Other: Situating Alterities* (Amsterdam and New York: Editions Rodopi B.V., 2007), 27.

10. Gayatri Chakravorty Spivak, *Death of a Discipline* (New York: Columbia University Press, 2003), 98.

11. Jean-Luc Nancy, *Being Singular Plural*, trans. by Robert D. Richardson and Anne E. O'Byrne (Stanford, CA: Stanford University Press, 2000); and Hitchcock, "The Impossibly Intersubjective and the Logic of the Both."

12. Ernesto Leclau and Chantal Mouffe have already mapped this goal of fluid political forms in their pivotal book *Hegemony and Socialist Strategy: Towards a Radical Democratic Politics* (London: Verso, 1985).

13. Okwui Enwezor, "Between Worlds: Postmodernism and African Artists in the Western Metropolis," in Olu Oguibe and Okwui Enwezor, eds., *Reading the Contemporary: African Art from Theory to the Marketplace* (Cambridge, MA: MIT Press, 1999), 244–75. For further discussion of the question of authenticity in African art, see Shannon Fitzgerald and Tumelo Mosaka, eds., *A Fiction of Authenticity: Contemporary Africa Abroad* (Saint Louis: Contemporary Art Museum St. Louis, 2003); and Jean-Hubert Martin, ed., *Magiciens de la terre* (Paris: Editions du Centre Georges Pompidou, 1989).

14. Olu Oguibe, "Art, Identity, Boundaries: Postmodernism and Contemporary African Art," in Oguibe and Enwezor, eds., *Reading the Contemporary*, 28.

15. Mutu/Firstenberg.

16. Simon Njami, "Chaos and Metapmorphosis," in Simon Njami, ed., *Africa Remix: Contemporary Art of a Continent* (Ostfildern, Germany: Hatje Cantz Verlag, 2005), 13.

17. Ibid., 14.

18. Olu Oguibe, "In the Heart of Darkness," in Oguibe and Enwezor, eds., *Reading the Contemporary*, 323.

19. Alain Badiou, *The Century* (New York: Polity, 2007), 7; originally published as *Le Siècle* (Paris: Editions Gallimard, 2005).

20. Ibid. This is the title of the thirteenth and final chapter of *The Century*.

21. Ibid., 3.

22. Wangechi Mutu, quoted in Friedhelm Hütte, "On the Exhibition," in *My Dirty Little Heaven: Wangechi Mutu: Artist of the Year 2010* (Frankfurt am Main: Deutsche Bank AG, 2010), 18.

23. The full title of the book is *El cuerpo del hombre; ó, La anatomia y la fisiologia humanas puestas al alcance de todas las clases de la sociedad: Con un gran número de láminas litografiadas* (San Sebastian, Spain: Ignacio Ramon Baroja, 1843).

24. Wangechi Mutu, "My Dirty Little Heaven," for the Penny W. Stamps Distinguished Speaker Series at the University of Michigan, School of Art and Design (November 18, 2010): www.youtube.com/watch?v=SNBjxPM6JDM.

25. Mutu appropriated this image from *African Ceremonies*, a key visual source in her studio library. This bride received the clay lip plate, on which the black marks of its firing were visible, six months before her marriage. The disk indicated her personal value and the cost a groom would have to pay in cattle to marry her. See Carol Beckwith and Angela Fisher, *African Ceremonies* (New York: Harry N. Abrams, 2002), 194. Lip disks are not limited to gender, but are common among Mursi women of Ethiopia, who fashion their own lip plates within a discourse of female strength and self-esteem. Shauna LaTosky, "Reflections on the Lip-Plates of Mursi Women as a Source of Stigma and Self-Esteem," in Ivo Strecker and Jean Lydall, eds., *Perils of Face: Essays on Cultural Contact, Respect and Self-Esteem in Southern Ethiopia* (Berlin: Lit Verlag, 2006), 382–97.

26. Additional titles that I discovered in Mutu's studio include *African Ceremonies*, *Africa: The Art of a Continent*, *Cabinet of Natural Curiosities*, and *African Safari*.

27. Jean-Luc Nancy, *Being Singular Plural*, xiii.

28. After "the initiate has healed sufficiently to be able to walk," he hunts small birds, "eviscerates the carcasses and stuffs them with ashes and dried grass," before tying "them to a circular frame, which he wears as a ceremonial crown." Each guest also "wears a headdress of colorful stuffed birds." Beckwith and Fisher, *African Ceremonies*, 57.

29. One of the ancestor kings of the people of Burkina Faso, a landlocked country in west Africa, Mogho Naba Baongho carries on the line of a king who "preferred to die in exile in Ghana rather than to shake hands with a white man" even though during "the colonial era, the governments had maintained the Mossi emperors, whom they considered to be people of high stature." Daniel Lainé, *African Kings* (Berkeley and Toronto: Ten Speed Press, 2000), 157.

30. For example, see Walter Mignolo's *The Darker Side of Western Modernity: Global Futures, Decolonial Options* (Durham, NC: Duke University Press, 2011).

31. Gilles Deleuze and Félix Guattari, defining the rhizome, write, "Literature is an assemblage" (p. 4) that "has to do with surveying, mapping" (p. 5) and follows the "cut-up method" (p. 6). Such practices, which are derived from the visual arts (though Deleuze and Guattari do not cite collage or the aesthetic geneology of either the collage or cut-up method) depart from the "fascicular system" to become a new model, "a rhizome" (p. 6). See Deleuze and Guattari, *A Thousand Plateaus*, trans. by Brian Massumi (Minneapolis: University of Minnesota Press, 1987), 4–6.

32. See, for example, Ronald Jeffrey, *Queer Words, Queer Images: Communication and*

*the Construction of Homosexuality* (New York: New York University Press, 1994); Aaron Betsky, *Queer Space: Architecture and Same-Sex Desire* (New York: William Morrow, 1997).

33. Wangechi Mutu, "Bio," on EIL Escapeintolife (no date): www.escapeintolife.com/artist-watch/wangechi-mutu.

34. Many authors writing on Mutu string together descriptions of her subject in a manner akin to her collage techniques. A particularly evocative example is that of Michael E. Veal, who, in referring to how Mutu's work encompasses feminism and feminist theory, describes one of her figures as "lover, giver, and receptacle . . . predator and merciless avenger," a woman enmeshed in "colonial tropes of Africa as site of sex, mysticism, and unbridled nature . . . diseased, blood-stained horror," and as a "hybrid . . . primitivist and post-human [being in an] oasis of erotic beckoning carved out of dystopic, Double-XX African science fiction [with] curvaceous, maimed . . . mutants . . . visages of half-human, half-animal . . . leggy, leopard-hunter . . . ape-maidens . . . fabricated from the rotting remains of open sewers, garbage heaps, or toxic waste [with bodily] punctures and ruptures, alternately alluring or disconcerting." See Veal, "Enter Cautiously," in *A Shady Promise*, 9–10.

35. African Ceremonies, 321.

36. Wangechi Mutu, "Magnificent Monkey Ass Lies," in Kristine Stiles and Peter Selz, eds., *Theories and Documents of Contemporary Art*, 2nd ed. (Berkeley: University of California Press, 2012), 320.

37. Simon Njami, "Mozart and Me," in *Looking Both Ways*, 15.

38. E. A. T. Dutton, *Kenya Mountain* (London: Jonathan Cape, 1929), 1–2.

39. Okwui Enwezor, "Cut & Paste: Interview with Wangechi Mutu," *Arise* 11 (2011): www.ariselive.com/articles/cut-paste/87416. Cited hereafter as Mutu/Enwezor.

40. Okwui Enwezor, "Weird Beauty: Ritual Violence and Archaeology of Mass Media in Wangechi Mutu's Work," in *Wangechi Mutu: My Dirty Little Heaven*, 32.

41. Linda Stupart, "'Distant Relatives / Relative Distance' at Michael Stevenson Contemporary," *Artthrob* 107 (July 2006): www.artthrob.co.za/06july/reviews/stevenson.html.

42. Ibid. Commenting on a draft of this essay, art historian Karen Gonzalez Rice noted, "Presidio is very near to Marfa, Texas. For me Mutu's performance is a serious critique of Donald Judd's colonization of this part of the world and art historical attempts (by art historian David Raskin, namely, but also others) to locate Judd's work in radical politics, which is particularly untenable in comparison to Mutu's work." Gonzalez Rice refers here to the Chinati Foundation's administration of the museum founded by Judd in Marfa where his work and installations can be seen, as well as to the art of artists related to minimalism.

43. Friedhelm Hütte, "My Dirty Little Heaven: Wangechi Mutu at the Deutsche Guggenheim," *Deutsche Bank ArtMag* 60 (April 2010): db-artmag.com/en/60/on-view/wangechi-mutu-at-deutsche-guggenheim.

44. Mary Douglas, *Purity and Danger: An Analysis of Concepts of Pollution and Taboo* (London: Routledge and Kegan Paul, 1966), 35.

45. Mutu/Enwezor.

46. Enwezor, "Weird Beauty," 26.

47. Wangechi Mutu, quoted in Isolde Breilmaier and Wangechi Mutu, "Interview, Part III: Figure Symbiotic," in *A Shady Promise*, 83.

48. Mutu/Firstenberg.

49. Wangechi Mutu, quoted in Isolde Breilmaier and Wangechi Mutu, "Interview, Part II: Watercolor Femme Noir," in *A Shady Promise*, 53.

50. Ibid.

51. Michael Hardt and Antonio Negri, *Empire* (Cambridge, MA, and London: Harvard University Press, 2000), xii, xv.

52. Ibid., 16. See Ernst Bloch, *L'Esprit de l'utopie* (Paris: Gallimard, 1977).

53. Mutu/Firstenberg.

54. Wangechi Mutu, quoted in Isolde Breilmaier and Wangechi Mutu, "Interview, Part IV: Space Wander," in *A Shady Promise*, 117.

55. Ibid.

56. Mutu/Enwezor.

57. John S. Mbiti, *African Religions and Philosophy*, 3rd ed. (London: Heinemann, 1990).

58. Mutu/Enwezor.

59. Ibid.

60. Enwezor, "Cut & Paste."

61. See Colette Dowling, *The Cinderella Complex: Women's Hidden Fear of Independence* (New York: Simon & Schuster, 1981).

62. Yael Samuel, *Reclaiming Women's Bodies: Wangechi Mutu and the Aesthetics of Violence* (February 2011): ospace.otis.edu/ysamuel/Wangetchi_Mutu/published/?sh_7086372=7&moduleinstid=7086372&page_mode=published.

63. Wangechi Mutu, quoted on http://www.tumblr.com/tagged/wangechi-mutu?before=1328342393.

64. Ibid.

65. Mutu/Stiles.

66. Mutu/Enwezor. The school was St. Kizito Vocational Training Institute in Akithii, Kenya.

67. Ibid.

68. Ibid.

69. For a more detailed account of this extraordinary event, see Angella Nazarian, "Pioneer of the Possible: The Story of Kenyan Nobel Peace Prize Laureate Wangari Maathai," in *The Mindful Word* (August 17, 2012): www.themindfulword.org/2012/pioneer-of-the-possible-the-story-of-kenyan-nobel-peace-prize-laureate-wangari-maathai.

70. Wangechi Mutu, commenting on the Sudan civil war in her talk, "My Dirty Little Heaven," for the Penny W. Stamps Distinguished Speaker Series at the University of Michigan, School of Art and Design (November 18, 2010): vimeo.com/18012538.

71. Wangechi Mutu, quoted in Merrily Kerr, "Wangechi Mutu's Extreme Makeovers," *Art on Paper* 8, no. 6 (July/August 2004): newyorkarttours.com/blog/?=291.

72. Statistics have shown that since the 1990s, most female sex workers have been physically or sexually abused as children. Melissa Farley and Howard Barkan have written: "Fifty-seven percent reported a history of childhood sexual abuse, by an average of three perpetrators. Forty-nine percent of those who responded reported that as children, they had been hit or beaten by a caregiver until they had bruises or were injured in some way. . . . Many seemed profoundly uncertain as to just what 'abuse' is. When asked why she answered 'no' to the question regarding childhood sexual abuse, one woman whose history was known to one of the interviewers said: 'Because there was no force, and, besides, I didn't even know what it was then—I didn't know it was sex.'" See Melissa Farley and Howard Barkan,'s "Prostitution, Violence against Women, and Posttraumatic Stress Disorder," *Women & Health* 27, no. 3 (1998): 37–49. The statistics for sexual abuse in childhood for male sex workers resemble those of women in sex work.

73. Wangechi Mutu, artist's statement for the exhibition *Creatures by Wangechi Mutu*, Jamaica Center for Arts and Learning, New York, 2003; quoted in Barbara Thompson, ed.,

*Black Womanhood: Images, Icons, and Ideologies of the African Body* (Hanover, NH: Hood Museum of Art, Dartmouth College; Seattle, WA: In association with University of Washington Press, 2008), 280.

74. Mutu/Stiles.

75. Bettina Stumm, "Testifying to the Infinity of the Other: The Scared and Ethical Dimensions of Secondary Witnessing in Anne Karpf's *The War After*," in Holly Faith Nelson, Lynn R. Szabo, and Jens Zimmermann, eds., *Through a Glass Darkly: Suffering, the Sacred, and the Sublime in Literature and Theory* (Waterloo, ON: Wilfrid Laurier University Press, 2010), 350.

76. Allan J. Hamilton, MD, *Zen Mind, Zen Horse: The Science and Spirituality of Working with Horses* (North Adams, MA: Storey Publishing, 2011), 42.

77. Wangechi Mutu, quoted in Aimée Reed, "Interview with Wangechi Mutu," accessed at dailyserving.com/2010/04/interview-with-wangechi-mutu.

78. Stumm, "Testifying to the Infinity of the Other," 353.

79. For a provocative interpretation of "the new black portraiture," see chapter 4 of Richard J. Powell's *Cutting a Figure: Fashioning Black Portraiture* (Chicago: University of Chicago Press, 2008), 171–209.

80. Merrily Kerr, "Wangechi Mutu's Extreme Makeovers," *Art on Paper* 8, no. 6 (July/August 2004): 28–29; excerpted on Saatchi Online, where Mutu is quoted about *Forensic Forms*: www.saatchi-gallery.co.uk/artists/wangechi_mutu_resources.htm. It is difficult to tell whether this comment comes from Kerr's original essay.

81. Mutu/Enwezor.

82. Mutu/Firstenberg.

83. Ibid.

84. See Miriam Schapiro and Melissa Meyer, "Waste Not Want Not: An Inquiry into What Women Saved and Assembled—FEMMAGE," in Stiles and Selz, eds., *Theories and Documents of Contemporary Art*, 173–76.

85. On the grotesque, see Sara Cohen Shabot, "The Grotesque Body: Fleshing Out the Subject," in Silke Horstkotte and Esther Peeren, eds., *The Shock of the Other*, 57–67.

86. Mutu/Stiles.

87. Ibid.

88. Ibid.

89. Aimé Césaire, quoted in René Depestre, "An Interview with Aimé Césaire" (1967), in Aimé Césaire, *Discourse on Colonialism* (1955), trans. by Joan Pinkham (New York: Monthly Review Press, 2000), 83–84.

# Index